Better Business

FOURTH EDITION

Better Business

FOURTH EDITION

Michael R. Solomon
Contributing Editor

Mary Anne Poatsy

Kendall Martin

PEARSON

Boston Columbus Indianapolis New York San Francisco
Amsterdam Cape Town Dubai London Madrid Milan Munich Paris Montreal Toronto
Delhi Mexico City São Paulo Sydney Hong Kong Seoul Singapore Taipei Tokyo

Vice President, Business Publishing: Donna Battista
Editor-in-Chief: Stephanie Wall
Acquisitions Editor: Nicole Sam
Development Editor: Amy Ray
Program Manager Team Lead: Ashley Santora
Program Manager: Denise Vaughn
Editorial Assistant: Kaylee Rotella
Vice President, Product Marketing: Maggie Moylan
Director of Marketing, Digital Services and Products:
Jeanette Koskinas
Executive Product Marketing Manager: Anne Fahlgren
Field Marketing Manager: Lenny Ann Raper
Senior Strategic Marketing Manager: Erin Gardner
Project Manager Team Lead: Judy Leale
Project Manager: Ilene Kahn
Operations Specialist: Diane Peirano
Creative Director: Blair Brown
Senior Art Director: Janet Slowik

Interior Designer: Wee Design Group
Cover Designer: Wee Design Group
Cover Image: Eric Gregory Powell/Photonica/Getty Images
VP, Director of Digital Strategy & Assessment:
Paul Gentile
Manager of Learning Applications: Paul Deluca
Digital Editor: Brian Surette
Digital Studio Manager: Diane Lombardo
Digital Studio Project Manager: Robin Lazrus
Digital Studio Project Manager: Alana Coles
Digital Studio Project Manager: Monique Lawrence
Digital Studio Project Manager: Regina DaSilva
Full-Service Project Management: S4Carlisle Publishing
Services/Cindy Sweeny
Composition: S4Carlisle Publishing Services
Printer/Binder: Manufactured in the United States
by RR Donnelley
Text Font: 10/12, Palatino

Library of Congress Cataloging-in-Publication Data
Solomon, Michael R.
  Better business / Michael R. Solomon, contributing editor; Mary Anne Poatsy,
Kendall Martin. — Fourth edition.
    pages cm
Includes bibliographical references and index.
ISBN 978-0-13-392058-1 — ISBN 0-13-392058-5 1. Business. 2. Entrepreneurship.
  3. Commerce. I. Poatsy, Mary Anne. II. Martin, Kendall. III. Title.
  HD31.P555 2016
  658—dc23

                                                    2014032205

V011
10 9 8 7 6 5 4

ISBN 10:   0-13-392058-5
ISBN 13: 978-0-13-392058-1

Dedication

To Rose
—Michael R. Solomon

For my husband, Ted, who unselfishly continues to take on more than his fair share to support me throughout this process; and for my children, Laura, Carolyn, and Teddy, whose encouragement and love have been inspiring.
—Mary Anne Poatsy

For all the teachers, mentors, and gurus who have popped in and out of my life.
—Kendall Martin

Brief Contents

Contents

About the Authors

Michael R. Solomon, PhD, *Contributing Editor*

Michael R. Solomon is professor of marketing and director of the Center for Consumer Research in the Haub School of Business at Saint Joseph's University in Philadelphia. He also is professor of consumer behaviour at the Manchester School of Business, University of Manchester, United Kingdom. Michael's primary research and consulting interests include consumer behavior, branding, and marketing applications of virtual worlds. He has written several textbooks and trade books; his *Consumer Behavior* text is the most widely used in the world. Michael often speaks to business groups about new trends in consumer behavior and marketing strategy.

Mary Anne Poatsy, MBA, CFP

mpoatsy@mc3.edu

Mary Anne Poatsy is a senior adjunct faculty member at Montgomery County Community College, teaching various business, management, and computer application and concepts courses in face-to-face and online environments. She holds a BA in psychology and education from Mount Holyoke College and an MBA in finance from Northwestern University's J. L. Kellogg Graduate School of Management.

Mary Anne has been teaching since 1995 at a variety of elementary and secondary institutions, including Gwynedd Mercy College, Montgomery County Community College, Muhlenberg College, and Bucks County Community College, as well as training in the professional environment and presenting at several conferences. Before teaching, she was a vice president at Shearson Lehman Hutton in the Municipal Bond Investment Banking Department.

Kendall Martin, PhD

kmartin@mc3.edu

Kendall Martin has been teaching since 1988 at a number of institutions, including Villanova University, DeSales University, Arcadia University, Ursinus College, County College of Morris, and Montgomery County Community College, at both the undergraduate and the graduate level.

Kendall's education includes a BS in electrical engineering from the University of Rochester and an MS and a PhD in engineering from the University of Pennsylvania. She has industrial experience in research and development environments (AT&T Bell Laboratories) as well as experience with several start-up technology firms.

As a professor at Montgomery County Community College, she presents nationally on topics of entrepreneurship, student engagement, and technology in the classroom.

Acknowledgments

Like any good business, this project could not have been completed without the dedicated efforts of a talented group of people to whom we are eternally grateful. The authors would like to take this time to thank the many colleagues, friends, and students who have contributed toward our vision of an introductory textbook that excites and challenges students.

From the very conception of *Better Business* and into this latest edition, a remarkable board of reviewers at schools across the nation has guided us with wise counsel. Our joy in working with such talented and student-centered faculty is deep. We extend our sincerest gratitude to our reviewers.

The division of Business Publishing at Pearson has been incredible in devoting time and resources to the creation of the *Better Business*, 4th edition learning system. We are indebted to Jodi McPherson, our former executive editor, who had the vision for a new introduction to business textbook system that engages and excites students, and Stephanie Wall, our editor in chief, whose guidance provided the foundation for this edition. We also welcome our new acquisitions editor, Nicole Sam, who despite her most recent arrival has already positively impacted our work. Without their vision, passion, dedication, and drive, this textbook would not exist. Our thanks also extend to our project manager, Ilene Kahn, who diligently kept us on track with only gentle threats when we went astray! Ilene's fine management skills enabled this complex project to be completed on time—a feat not easily accomplished. We also benefited greatly from the thoughtful contributions of Amy Ray, developmental editor. Amy's diligent and enthusiastic efforts ensures that this edition's content is compatible with or exceeds user needs. Maggie Moylan, director of marketing, has been very instrumental in shaping the message of the book. We are so appreciative of her ardent attention to all the marketing details that are so important. We're also appreciative for the dedication of the media team of Robin Lazrus and Alana Coles, who were instrumental in the development of all the multimedia products that make up MyBizLab, and for their efforts to ensure that it works seamlessly with the textbook. Additionally, we would like to thank Janet Slowik and Judy Leale for their efforts in the design and production of *Better Business*, 4th edition. Finally, our thanks to Paul Corey, president of business publishing, and Stephanie Wall, editor in chief, who have backed this project with the necessary financial and human resources to make our vision a reality.

We would be completely negligent if we did not acknowledge all the incredibly talented and devoted designers, permissions researchers, and others who contributed to the project and to whom we extend our sincerest thanks.

Additionally, we would like to thank the many supplement authors for this edition: Kate Demarest, Linda Hoffman, and Maureen Steddin.

Everything we do is inspired by the experiences we have in the classroom. We want to thank and encourage our students, whose experiences, struggles, victories, and honesty have shaped this project turn by turn. We strive for *Better Business*, 4th edition, to serve our students as a stepping-stone to meaningful careers and lives.

Last but not least, close to home, our families have sacrificed much to let us focus on the project. We appreciate their patience and support throughout the writing process.

Reviewers

Wendi Achey, *Northampton Community College*

Mustafa Akcadogan, *Pikes Peak Community College*

Joni Anderson, *Buena Vista University*

Lydia Anderson, *Fresno City College*

Natalie Andrews, *Sinclair Community College*

Sally Andrews, *Linn Benton Community College*

Roanne Angiello, *Bergen Community College*

Brenda Anthony, *Tallahassee Community College*

Maria Aria, *Camden County College*

Corinne Asher, *Henry Ford Community College*

Susan Athey, *Colorado State University*

Michael Aubry, *Grossmont College*

David Bader, *Columbus State Community College*

Mazen Badra, *Webster University*

Michael Baran, *South Puget Sound Community College*

Ruby Barker, *Tarleton State University*

William Barrett, *University of Wisconsin*

Denise Barton, *Wake Technical Community College*

Dick Barton, *El Camino College*

Crystal Bass, *Trinity Valley Community College*

Jeffrey Bauer, *University of Cincinnati*

Christine Bauer-Ramazani, *Saint Michael's College*

Leslie Beau, *Orange Coast College*

Gayona Beckford-Barclay, *Community College of Baltimore County*

Robert Bennett, *Delaware County Community College*

George Bernard, *Seminole Community College*

Patricia Bernson, *County College of Morris*

Rick Bialac, *Georgia College and State University*

Danielle Blesi, *Hudson Valley Community College*

Chuck Bowles, *Pikes Peak Community College*

Malcolm Bowyer, *Montgomery Community College*

Steven Bradley, *Austin Community College*

Charles Braun, *Marshall University*

Edwin Breazeale, *Midlands Technical College*

Sharon Breeding, *Bluegrass Community Technical College*

Richard Brennan, *North Virginia Community College*

Robert Bricker, *Pikes Peak Community College*

Lisa Briggs, *Columbus State Community College*

T. L. Brink, *Crafton Hills College*

Dennis Brode, *Sinclair Community College*

Katherine Broneck, *Pima Community College*

Harvey Bronstein, *Oakland Community College*

Deborah Brown, *North Carolina State University*

Sylvia Brown, *Midland College*

Janet Brown-Sederberg, *Massasoit Community College*

Lesley Buehler, *Ohlone College*

Barry Bunn, *Valencia Community College*

Carroll Burrell, *San Jacinto College*

Marian Canada, *Ivy Technical Community College*

Diana Carmel, *Golden West College*

John Carpenter, *Lake Land College*

Deborah Carter, *Coahoma Community College*

Tiffany Champagne, *Houston Community College*

Glen Chapuis, *St. Charles Community College*

Bonnie Chavez, *Santa Barbara City College*

Sudhir Chawla, *Angelo State University*

Lisa Cherivtch-Zingaro, *Oakton Community College*

Desmond Chun, *Chabot College*

John Cicero, *Shasta College*

Michael Cicero, *Highline Community College*

Subasree Cidambi, *Mount San Antonio College*

Joseph Cilia, *Delaware Technical & Community College*

Mark Clark, *Collin County Community College*

William Clark, *Leeward Community College*

Paul Coakley, *Community College of Baltimore County*

Ken Combs, *Del Mar College*

Jamie Commissaris, *Davenport University*

Rachna Condos, *American River College*

Charlie Cook, *University of West Alabama*

Solveg Cooper, *Cuesta College*

Douglas Copeland, *Johnson County Community College*

Julie Couturier, *Grand Rapids Community College*

Brad Cox, *Midlands Technical College*

Diane Coyle, *Montgomery County Community College*

Chad Creevy, *Davenport University*

Geoff Crosslin, *Kalamazoo Valley Community College*

Ebony Crump, *Kennedy-King College*

H. Perry Curtis, *Collin County Community College*

Dana D'Angelo, *Drexel University*

Mark Dannenberg, *Shasta College*

Jamey Darnell, *Durham Tech*

Amlan Datta, *Cisco College*

Shirley Davenport, *Prairie State College*

Helen Davis, *Jefferson Community Technical College*

Peter Dawson, *Collin County Community College*

David Dearman, *University of Arkansas*

Sherry Decuba, *Indian River Community College*

Andrew Delaney, *Truckee Meadows Community College*

Kate Demarest, *Carroll Community College*

Donna Devault, *Fayetteville Tech*

Susan Dik, *Kapiolani Community College*

Michael DiVecchio, *Central Pennsylvania College*

Gerard Dobson, *Waukesha County Technical College*

Kathleen Dominick, *Bucks County Community College and University of Phoenix Online*

Ron Dougherty, *Ivy Technical Community College*

Karen Drage, *Eastern Illinois University*

Nelson Driver, *University of Arkansas*

Allison Duesing, *Northeast Lakeview College*

Timothy Durfield, *Citrus College*

David Dusseau, *University of Oregon*

Dana Dye, *Gulf Coast Community College*

C. Russell Edwards, *Valencia Community College*

Karen Edwards, *Chemeketa Community College*

Stephen Edwards, *University of North Dakota*

Stewart Edwards, *North Virginia Community College*

Susan Ehrfurth, *Aims Community College*

Patrick Ellsberg, *Lower Columbia College*

Susan Emens, *Kent State University*

Karen Emerson, *Southeast Community College*

Theodore Emmanuel, *State University of New York Oswego*

Kellie Emrich, *Cuyahoga Community College*

Vince Enslein, *Clinton Community College*

Steven Ernest, *Baton Rouge Community College*

Mary Ewanechko, *Monroe County Community College*

Marie Farber-Lapidus, *Oakton Community College*

Geralyn Farley, *Purdue University*

Janice Feldbauer, *Schoolcraft College and Austin Community College*

Mary Felton-Kolstad, *Chippewa Valley Technical College*

Louis Ferracane, *University of Phoenix*

David Fitoussi, *University of California*

Joseph Flack, *Washtenaw Community College*

Jacalyn Flom, *University of Toledo*

Carla Flores, *Ball State University*

Carol Flowers, *Orange Coast College*

Jake Flyzik, *Lehigh Carbon Community College*

Thomas Foley, *Kent State University*

Craig Fontaine, *Northeastern University*

Joseph Fox, *Asheville-Buncombe Technical Community College*

Mark Fox, *Indiana University–South Bend*

Victoria Fox, *College of DuPage*

Charla Fraley, *Columbus State Community College*

John Frank, *Columbus State Community College*

Leatrice Freer, *Pitt Community College*

Paula Freston, *Merced College*

Fred Fry, *Bradley University*

Albert Fundaburk, *Bloomsburg University*

William Furrell, *Moorpark College*

Michael Gagnon, *Kellogg Community College*

Wayne Gawlik, *Joliet Junior College*

George Generas, *University of Hartford*

Vanessa Germeroth, *Ozarks Technical Community College*

Gerald GeRue, *Rock Valley College*

John Geubtner, *Tacoma Community College*

Katie Ghahramani, *Johnson County Community College*

David Gilliss, *San Jose State University*

Eric Glohr, *Lansing Community College*
Robert Goldberg, *Northeastern University*
Constance Golden, *Lakeland Community College*
Gayle Goldstone, *Santa Rosa Junior College*
Alfredo Gomez, *Broward Community College*
Phillip Gonsher, *Johnson County Community College*
Robert Googins, *Shasta College*
Karen Gore, *Ivy Technical Community College–Southwest*
Carol Gottuso, *Metropolitan Community College*
Gretchen Graham, *Community College of Allegheny County (Boyce campus)*
Selina Griswold, *University of Toledo*
John Guess, *Delgado Community College*
Kevin Gwinner, *Kansas State University*
Peggy Hager, *Winthrop University*
Lawrence Hahn, *Palomar College*
Semere Haile, *Grambling State University*
Lynn Halkowicz, *Bloomsburg University*
Clark Hallpike, *Elgin Community College*
Paula Hansen, *Des Moines Area Community College*
Frank Harber, *Indian River Community College*
LaShon Harley, *Durham Technical Community College*
Jeri Harper, *Western Illinois University*
Deborah Haseltine, *Southwest Tennessee Community College*
Carol Heeter, *Ivy Tech Community College*
Linda Hefferin, *Elgin Community College*
Debra Heimberger, *Columbus State Community College*
Dennis Heiner, *College of Southern Idaho*
Cheryl Heitz, *Lincoln Land Community College*
Charlane Held, *Onondaga Community College*
Rebecca Helms, *Ivy Tech Community College*
Heith Hennel, *Valencia Community College*
Dorothy Hetmer-Hinds, *Trinity Valley Community College*
Linda Hoffman, *Ivy Technical Community College–Fort Wayne*
Merrily Hoffman, *San Jacinto College*
Gene Holand, *Columbia Basin College*
Phillip Holleran, *Mitchell Community College*
Robert Hood, *Chattanooga State Technical Community College*
Sheila Hostetler, *Orange Coast College*
Larry Hottot, *North Virginia Community College*
William Huisking, *Bergen Community College*
Lynn Hunsaker, *Mission College*
Steven Huntley, *Florida Community College at Jacksonville*
Johnny Hurley, *Iowa Lakes Community College*
Kimberly Hurns, *Washtenaw Community College*
Holly Hutchins, *Central Oregon Community College*
Linda Isenhour, *Eastern Michigan University*
Katie Jackson, *Columbus State Community College*
Linda Jaeger, *Southeast Community College*
Dolores James, *University of Maryland University College*
Pam Janson, *Stark State College of Technology*
Larry Jarrell, *Louisiana Technical University*
Earlene Jefferson, *Kennedy-King College*
Joe Jenkins, *Tarrant County College*
Brandy Johnson, *Columbus State Community College*

Dennis Johnson, *Delaware County Community College*
Floyd Johnson, *Davenport University*
M. Gwen Johnson, *Black Hawk College*
Carroll Jones, *Tulsa Community College*
Jeffrey Jones, *The College of Southern Nevada*
Kenneth Jones, *Ivy Technical Community College–Central Indiana*
Gayla Jurevich, *Fresno City College*
Alex Kajstura, *Daytona Beach College*
Dmitriy Kalyagin, *Chabot College*
Radhika Kaula, *Missouri State University*
John Kavouras, *Ohio College of Massage Therapy*
Dan Keating, *Fox Valley Technical College*
Albert Keller, *Dixie State College of Utah*
Ann Kelly, *Georgia Southern University*
Jeffrey Kennedy, *Broward Community College*
Jeffrey Kennedy, *Palm Beach Atlantic University*
Daniel Kipley, *Azusa Pacific University*
William Kline, *Bucks County Community College*
Susan Kochenrath, *Ivy Technical Community College*
Linda Koffel, *Houston Community College Central*
Todd Korol, *Monroe County Community College*
Jack Kraettli, *Oklahoma City Community College*
Jim Kress, *Central Oregon Community College*
John Kurnik, *St. Petersburg College*
Paul Laesecke, *University of Denver*
Martha Laham, *Diablo Valley College*
Mary LaPann, *Adirondack Community College*
Deborah Lapointe, *Central New Mexico Community College*
Rob Leadbeater, *Mission College*
David Leapard, *Eastern Michigan University*
Denise Lefort, *Clemson University*
Ron Lennon, *Barry University*
Angela Leverett, *Georgia Southern University*
Sue Lewis, *Tarleton State University*
Kathleen Lorencz, *Oakland Community College*
Mark Lowenstein, *College of St. Joseph*
John Luke, *Delaware County Community College*
John Mago, *Anoka-Ramsey Community College*
Jan Mangos, *Valencia Community College*
Christine Marchese, *Nassau Community College*
James Marco, *Wake Technical Community College*
Suzanne Markow, *Des Moines Area Community College*
Gary Marrer, *Glendale Community College*
Calvin Martin, *Davenport University*
James Martin, *Washburn University*
Kathleen Martinez, *Red Rocks Community College*
Thomas Mason, *Brookdale Community College*
Marian Matthews, *Central New Mexico Community College*
Kelli Mayes-Denker, *Carl Sandburg College*
Kevin McCarthy, *Baker University*
Gina McConoughey, *Illinois Central College*
Lisa McCormick, *Community College of Allegheny*
Patrick L. McCormick, *Ivy Tech Community College*
Pamela McElligott, *Meramec Community College*
Edward McGee, *Rochester Institute of Technology*
Donna McGill-Cameron, *Yuba College*
Vince McGinnis, *Bucks County Community College*

Allison McGullion, *West Kentucky Community & Technical College*
Lorraine McKnight, *Eastern Michigan University*
Bruce McLaren, *Indiana State University*
Juan Meraz, *Missouri State University*
James Meyers, *Pikes Peak Community College*
Miriam Michael, *American River College*
Jeanette Milius, *Iowa Western Community College*
Carol Millard, *Scottsdale Community College*
John Miller, *Pima Community College*
Linda Miller, *Northeast Community College*
Pat Miller, *Grossmont College*
Morgan Milner, *Eastern Michigan University*
Diane Minger, *Cedar Valley College*
Susan Mitchell, *Des Moines Area Community College*
Theresa Mitchell, *Alabama A&M University*
Joseph Molina, *MiraCosta College*
Carol Moore, *California State University*
Wayne Moore, *Indiana University of Pennsylvania*
Richard Morris, *Northeastern State University*
Jennifer Morton, *Ivy Tech Community College of Indiana*
David Murphy, *Madisonville Community College*
Gary Murray, *Rose State College*
John Muzzo, *Harold Washington College*
Mark Nagel, *Normandale Community College*
Conrad Nankin, *Pace University*
Kristi Newton, *Chemeketa Community College*
Steven Nichols, *Metropolitan Community College*
Simon Nwaigwe, *Baltimore City Community College*
Mark Nygren, *Brigham Young University*
Asmelash Ogbasion, *Southwest Tennessee Community College*
Cynthia L. Olivarez Rooker, *Lansing Community College*
David Olson, *California State University*
Anthony O'Malley, *Baruch College*
Lori Oriatti, *College of Lake County*
Robert O'Toole, *Crafton Hills College*
Mary Padula, *Borough of Manhattan Community College*
Esther Page-Wood, *Western Michigan University*
Lauren Paisley, *Genesee Community College*
Dyan Pease, *Sacramento City College*
Jeffrey Pepper, *Chippewa Valley Technical College*
Clifford Perry, *Florida International University*
Melinda Phillabaum, *Indiana University–Purdue University*
Rose Pollard, *Southeast Community College*
Jackie (J. Robinson) Porter, *Eastfield College*
Kathleen Powers, *Henry Ford Community College*
Dan Powroznik, *Chesapeake College*
Sally Proffitt, *Tarrant County College*
Joe Puglisi, *Butler County Community College*
James Pullins, *Columbus State Community College*
Kathy Pullins, *Columbus State Community College*
Bobby Puryear, *North Carolina State University*
Martha Racine Taylor, *College of the Redwoods*
Anthony Racka, *Oakland Community College*
Robert Reck, *Western Michigan University*

Philip Regier, *Arizona State University*

Delores Reha, *Fullerton College*

David Reiman, *Monroe County Community College*

Robert Reinke, *University of South Dakota*

Gloria Rembert, *Mitchell Community College*

Reina Reynolds, *Valencia Community College*

John Ribezzo, *Community College of Rhode Island*

Cheri Rice, *Stark State College of Technology*

Carla Rich, *Pensacola Junior College*

Gayle Richardson, *Bakersfield College*

Dwight Riley, *Richland College*

Renee Ritts, *Cuyahoga Community College*

Susan Roach, *Georgia Southern University*

John Robertson, *Amarillo College*

Robert Robicheaux, *University of Alabama*

Tim Rogers, *Ozarks Technical Community College*

June Roux, *Delaware Technical & Community College*

Carol Rowey, *Community College of Rhode Island*

Mark Ryan, *Hawkeye Community College*

Ray Saenz, *Del Mar College*

Joanne Salas, *Olympic College*

Andy Saucedo, *New Mexico State University*

Jacqueline Scerbinski, *Kingsborough Community College*

David Schaefer, *Sacramento City College*

Elisabeth Scherff, *Alabama A&M University*

Glen M. Schmidt, *University of Utah*

Tobias Schoenherr, *Eastern Michigan University*

Marcianne Schusler, *Prairie State College*

James Scott, *Central Michigan University*

Carolyn Seefer, *Diablo Valley College*

Eugene Seeley, *Utah Valley State College*

Gary Selk, *University of Alaska*

Pat Setlik, *William Rainey Harper College*

Phyllis Shafer, *Brookdale Community College*

Dennis Shannon, *Southwestern Illinois College*

Richard Sherer, *Los Angeles Trade Technical College*

Lynette Shishido, *Santa Monica College*

Lance Shoemaker, *West Valley College*

Carole Shook, *University of Arkansas*

Dwight Shook, *Catawba Valley Community College*

Susan Sieloff, *Northeastern University*

William Silver, *University of Denver*

Denise Simmons, *North Virginia Community College*

Lakshmy Sivaratnam, *Johnson County Community College*

Steven Skaggs, *Waubonsee Community College*

Jacqueline Slifkin, *Monroe County Community College*

Kimberly Smith, *County College of Morris*

Anne Snell, *Pikes Peak Community College/ Tulane University*

Fred Sole, *Youngstown State University*

Sandra Sousa, *Bristol Community College*

Ed Southeard, *Chattanooga State Technical Community College*

Ray Sparks, *Pima Community College*

Rieann Spence-Gale, *North Virginia Community College*

Cheryl Stansfield, *North Hennepin Community College*

Keith Starcher, *Indiana Wesleyan University*

Carol Steinhaus, *Northern Michigan University*

Jim Stemach, *College of the Redwoods*

John Stern, *Davenport University*

Richard Stewart, *Gulf Coast Community College*

Jack Stone, *Linn Benton Community College*

Connie Strain, *Arapahoe Community College*

John Striebich, *Monroe County Community College*

Chelakara Subbaraman, *Central Michigan University*

Dottie Sutherland, *Pima College*

Deanna Teel, *Houston Community College*

Rodney Thirion, *Pikes Peak Community College*

Carol Thole, *Hartnell College*

Michael Thomas, *Henry Ford Community College*

Alexis Thurman, *County College of Morris*

Frank Titlow, *St. Petersburg College*

Kathy Toler, *Asheville-Buncombe Technical Community College*

Edward Tolle, *Ivy Tech Community College*

Terry Tolliver, *Indiana University–Purdue University*

Francis Douglas Tuggle, *Chapman University*

Fran Ucci, *College of DuPage*

Shafi Ullah, *Broward Community College*

Dorothy Umans, *Montgomery College*

Robert Urell, *Irvine Valley College*

Richard Vaughan, *Durham Tech*

Sal Veas, *Santa Monica College*

Kam Vento, *Lassen Community College*

Victor Villarreal, *Austin Community College*

Richard Vobroucek, *State University of New York–Rockland*

Carol Vollmer-Pope, *Alverno College*

Randall Wade, *Rogue Community College*

Leatha Ware, *Waubonsee Community College*

Richard Warner, *Lehigh Carbon Community College*

Michael Washington, *Eastfield College*

Louis Watanabe, *Bellevue Community College*

Bill Waters, *Clackamas Community College*

Tom Watkins, *Solano Community College*

Barbara Joann Wayman, *Columbia College*

Sally Wells, *Columbia College*

Susan Wheeler, *Folsom Lake College*

Donald Wilke, *Okaloosa-Walton College*

Alta L. Williams, City Colleges of Chicago -Richard J. Daley

Fred Williams, *University of Michigan*

George Williams, *Bergen Community College*

H. Brock Williams, *Metropolitan Community College*

Doug Wilson, *University of Oregon*

Marcus Wilson, *Fullerton College*

Mildred Wilson, *Georgia Southern University*

Colette Wolfson, *Ivy Technical Community College*

John Womble, *Cedar Valley College*

Dan Wubbena, *Western Iowa Technical Community College*

Merrill Yancey, *Ivy Technical Community College*

Sandra Yates, *University of District of Columbia*

Bernard Zannini, *Northern Essex Community College*

Charles Zellerbach, *Orange Coast College*

Preface

New to the Fourth Edition

We have invested a great deal of work creating the fourth edition of *Better Business* to give students and instructors a powerful learning and teaching tool that captures the evolving issues and opportunities of business. Enhancements for the fourth edition follow:

- One of the most significant shifts in the business environment since the first edition of *Better Business* is the explosive growth of social media in all parts of business. The fourth edition of *Better Business* continues to feature social media strategies and technologies in over 85 percent of its chapters as well as significant updates to the technology chapter.

- Better Business continues to have superior coverage of cutting-edge topics. In addition to social and mobile media, the fourth edition includes coverage on big data, crowdsourcing and crowdfunding, the Affordable Care Act, search engine optimization and pay-per-click advertising, augmented reality and 3D printing.

- All of the end-of-chapter materials have been reviewed, and we have modified up to 25 percent of these materials to include the most recent events and trends in the business environment. The fourth edition of *Better Business* provides instructors with wide-ranging choices for discussion topics, assessment questions, and group activities that cover the most current and timely topics in the business community, such as major economic shifts, changes in technologies, and ever-increasing globalization.

- All of the time-sensitive material has been updated. Stories and examples from the previous editions that have continued to evolve have been updated and placed in the most current context. Timely examples have replaced older material, continuing to give *Better Business* an up-to-date feel that resonates with students.

- Feedback from the previous editions of *Better Business* indicated that the "The List" feature in each chapter not only interested students but also pushed them to go more deeply into the body of the text. For the fourth edition, we updated these lists, adding new ones where appropriate that reflect current market trends, with a focus on selecting topics that appeal to students.

- The fourth edition also includes new boxed features in many chapters with topics such as Keurig's monopolistic market presence, Patagonia's corporate responsibility, Augmented Reality, Hard Lessons on Social Media, Dove's Real Beauty advertising campaign, and Advertising and child obesity.

Instructor Resources

At the Instructor Resource Center, www.pearsonhighered.com/irc, instructors can easily register to gain access to a variety of instructor resources available with this text in downloadable format. If assistance is needed, our dedicated technical support team is ready to help with the media supplements that accompany this text. Visit http://247.pearsoned.com for answers to frequently asked questions and toll-free user support phone numbers.

The following supplements are available with this text:

- Instructor's Resource Manual
- Test Bank
- TestGen® Computerized Test Bank
- PowerPoint Presentation

Letter from the Authors

When we set out on this project, we had several goals in mind—and one guiding philosophy. We wanted to have a conversation with our students, not merely to write a book that we hoped they would read. We wanted to change the expectation that students will come to class unprepared. Why can't they come ready for class, with a desire to know about business? Why can't we have a little fun with the course while teaching students about the lighter side of business? We think we can.

To that end, we worked tirelessly on selecting our topics and our resources to help you, the student. We incorporated a question-and-answer format throughout to get you to want to know the answer and see more—and not simply because it will be on the test. We paid more attention to the details because that is where the course often comes together for you.

In each chapter, the "On Target" and "Off the Mark" features illustrate positive and negative outcomes of business ventures related to the chapter material. These features, along with "The List" found in each chapter, can fuel in-class dialogue.

Mini chapters are five special sections in the book that give you additional information on key topics in business: Business Law, Constructing an Effective Business Plan, Business Communications, Finding a Job, and Personal Finance.

Better Business, 4th edition, offers the content you need for a solid overview of business—but in a *better* way. By presenting the material in a stimulating way, *Better Business* encourages you to come to class prepared to have better conversations and a truly engaging classroom experience.

Prologue

The **10 Easy Steps** for **Better Business** Success

Step 1: It's all up to you

You've heard that before, right? You've bought textbooks and read some of the materials, but maybe still haven't ended up with the grade you wanted. So the key to success is not just buying the book or simply reading it. Instead, your success depends on three skills:

- Finding
- Understanding
- Applying the information found within this textbook and all of its resources

The following steps will help you succeed in this course, and if you apply some of these steps outside the classroom, you may also succeed in business and in life.

Step 2: Go to class with intent

How do your classes go for you? Are you generally able to follow what the instructor and your classmates are saying in lecture and class discussions? Are you able to actively participate in a group discussion, or do you simply observe other group members? Your attitude and the plan you have for using class time can change the entire experience for you. Try these quick tips to make sure your classroom experience is as rich and fulfilling as possible:

66 *You should know the material so well you can explain it to others so that they understand it—even your mom.* 99

—Brett Neslen, *student*

Review the Syllabus

If you have trouble speaking up in class, try this strategy. The syllabus is one of the most important documents in the course. It acts as a binding contract between you and the professor. Read the syllabus in detail as soon as it comes out. Then, in the next class, ask at least one question about it. It will show the professor you're serious about meeting your responsibilities in class—and will get you in the habit of speaking up in class.

Show Up!

As Woody Allen says, "Eighty percent of success is showing up." It's basic advice, but many students lose sight of how important it is to come to class. You should be punctual, if not early; be attentive; and be noticed. Sit near the front and ask good questions so that the professor gets to know your face and name. It's just as important that the professor knows you as it is that you know your professor (see Step 3).

Preface

New to the Fourth Edition

We have invested a great deal of work creating the fourth edition of *Better Business* to give students and instructors a powerful learning and teaching tool that captures the evolving issues and opportunities of business. Enhancements for the fourth edition follow:

- One of the most significant shifts in the business environment since the first edition of *Better Business* is the explosive growth of social media in all parts of business. The fourth edition of *Better Business* continues to feature social media strategies and technologies in over 85 percent of its chapters as well as significant updates to the technology chapter.

- Better Business continues to have superior coverage of cutting-edge topics. In addition to social and mobile media, the fourth edition includes coverage on big data, crowdsourcing and crowdfunding, the Affordable Care Act, search engine optimization and pay-per-click advertising, augmented reality and 3D printing.

- All of the end-of-chapter materials have been reviewed, and we have modified up to 25 percent of these materials to include the most recent events and trends in the business environment. The fourth edition of *Better Business* provides instructors with wide-ranging choices for discussion topics, assessment questions, and group activities that cover the most current and timely topics in the business community, such as major economic shifts, changes in technologies, and ever-increasing globalization.

- All of the time-sensitive material has been updated. Stories and examples from the previous editions that have continued to evolve have been updated and placed in the most current context. Timely examples have replaced older material, continuing to give *Better Business* an up-to-date feel that resonates with students.

- Feedback from the previous editions of *Better Business* indicated that the "The List" feature in each chapter not only interested students but also pushed them to go more deeply into the body of the text. For the fourth edition, we updated these lists, adding new ones where appropriate that reflect current market trends, with a focus on selecting topics that appeal to students.

- The fourth edition also includes new boxed features in many chapters with topics such as Keurig's monopolistic market presence, Patagonia's corporate responsibility, Augmented Reality, Hard Lessons on Social Media, Dove's Real Beauty advertising campaign, and Advertising and child obesity.

Instructor Resources

At the Instructor Resource Center, www.pearsonhighered.com/irc, instructors can easily register to gain access to a variety of instructor resources available with this text in downloadable format. If assistance is needed, our dedicated technical support team is ready to help with the media supplements that accompany this text. Visit http://247.pearsoned.com for answers to frequently asked questions and toll-free user support phone numbers.

The following supplements are available with this text:

- Instructor's Resource Manual
- Test Bank
- TestGen® Computerized Test Bank
- PowerPoint Presentation

Philip Regier, *Arizona State University*

Delores Reha, *Fullerton College*

David Reiman, *Monroe County Community College*

Robert Reinke, *University of South Dakota*

Gloria Rembert, *Mitchell Community College*

Reina Reynolds, *Valencia Community College*

John Ribezzo, *Community College of Rhode Island*

Cheri Rice, *Stark State College of Technology*

Carla Rich, *Pensacola Junior College*

Gayle Richardson, *Bakersfield College*

Dwight Riley, *Richland College*

Renee Ritts, *Cuyahoga Community College*

Susan Roach, *Georgia Southern University*

John Robertson, *Amarillo College*

Robert Robicheaux, *University of Alabama*

Tim Rogers, *Ozarks Technical Community College*

June Roux, *Delaware Technical & Community College*

Carol Rowey, *Community College of Rhode Island*

Mark Ryan, *Hawkeye Community College*

Ray Saenz, *Del Mar College*

Joanne Salas, *Olympic College*

Andy Saucedo, *New Mexico State University*

Jacqueline Scerbinski, *Kingsborough Community College*

David Schaefer, *Sacramento City College*

Elisabeth Scherff, *Alabama A&M University*

Glen M. Schmidt, *University of Utah*

Tobias Schoenherr, *Eastern Michigan University*

Marcianne Schusler, *Prairie State College*

James Scott, *Central Michigan University*

Carolyn Seefer, *Diablo Valley College*

Eugene Seeley, *Utah Valley State College*

Gary Selk, *University of Alaska*

Pat Setlik, *William Rainey Harper College*

Phyllis Shafer, *Brookdale Community College*

Dennis Shannon, *Southwestern Illinois College*

Richard Sherer, *Los Angeles Trade Technical College*

Lynette Shishido, *Santa Monica College*

Lance Shoemaker, *West Valley College*

Carole Shook, *University of Arkansas*

Dwight Shook, *Catawba Valley Community College*

Susan Sieloff, *Northeastern University*

William Silver, *University of Denver*

Denise Simmons, *North Virginia Community College*

Lakshmy Sivaratnam, *Johnson County Community College*

Steven Skaggs, *Waubonsee Community College*

Jacqueline Slifkin, *Monroe County Community College*

Kimberly Smith, *County College of Morris*

Anne Snell, *Pikes Peak Community College/ Tulane University*

Fred Sole, *Youngstown State University*

Sandra Sousa, *Bristol Community College*

Ed Southeard, *Chattanooga State Technical Community College*

Ray Sparks, *Pima Community College*

Rieann Spence-Gale, *North Virginia Community College*

Cheryl Stansfield, *North Hennepin Community College*

Keith Starcher, *Indiana Wesleyan University*

Carol Steinhaus, *Northern Michigan University*

Jim Stemach, *College of the Redwoods*

John Stern, *Davenport University*

Richard Stewart, *Gulf Coast Community College*

Jack Stone, *Linn Benton Community College*

Connie Strain, *Arapahoe Community College*

John Striebich, *Monroe County Community College*

Chelakara Subbaraman, *Central Michigan University*

Dottie Sutherland, *Pima College*

Deanna Teel, *Houston Community College*

Rodney Thirion, *Pikes Peak Community College*

Carol Thole, *Hartnell College*

Michael Thomas, *Henry Ford Community College*

Alexis Thurman, *County College of Morris*

Frank Titlow, *St. Petersburg College*

Kathy Toler, *Asheville-Buncombe Technical Community College*

Edward Tolle, *Ivy Tech Community College*

Terry Tolliver, *Indiana University–Purdue University*

Francis Douglas Tuggle, *Chapman University*

Fran Ucci, *College of DuPage*

Shafi Ullah, *Broward Community College*

Dorothy Umans, *Montgomery College*

Robert Urell, *Irvine Valley College*

Richard Vaughan, *Durham Tech*

Sal Veas, *Santa Monica College*

Kam Vento, *Lassen Community College*

Victor Villarreal, *Austin Community College*

Richard Vobroucek, *State University of New York–Rockland*

Carol Vollmer-Pope, *Alverno College*

Randall Wade, *Rogue Community College*

Leatha Ware, *Waubonsee Community College*

Richard Warner, *Lehigh Carbon Community College*

Michael Washington, *Eastfield College*

Louis Watanabe, *Bellevue Community College*

Bill Waters, *Clackamas Community College*

Tom Watkins, *Solano Community College*

Barbara Joann Wayman, *Columbia College*

Sally Wells, *Columbia College*

Susan Wheeler, *Folsom Lake College*

Donald Wilke, *Okaloosa-Walton College*

Alta L. Williams, *City Colleges of Chicago -Richard J. Daley*

Fred Williams, *University of Michigan*

George Williams, *Bergen Community College*

H. Brock Williams, *Metropolitan Community College*

Doug Wilson, *University of Oregon*

Marcus Wilson, *Fullerton College*

Mildred Wilson, *Georgia Southern University*

Colette Wolfson, *Ivy Technical Community College*

John Womble, *Cedar Valley College*

Dan Wubbena, *Western Iowa Technical Community College*

Merrill Yancey, *Ivy Technical Community College*

Sandra Yates, *University of District of Columbia*

Bernard Zannini, *Northern Essex Community College*

Charles Zellerbach, *Orange Coast College*

(Trust us: It's much better to have a buddy give you the information you missed than to ask the instructor, "Did I miss anything important?")

Use the People around You

Do you know students who already took this class? Spend some time with them and ask the right questions. What sections of the course will demand more time out of your schedule? What tools in the library helped them out with their projects?

Be sure to look around the class for older students. Many colleges are seeing a large influx of people returning to college after successful careers. These people have that precious thing you may lack: real-world experience. Buy someone a cup of coffee and ask him or her for advice that helps you in the course or in finding a job.

Use All the Resources the School Provides

The faculty and staff at your school want you to succeed—we all take pride in our students' accomplishments! So be sure to investigate all the resources available to you at your school. Talk to your adviser about services such as the following:

Writing Support

Many schools provide special clinics that can help you with your writing. Some also provide writing labs where you can get assistance in editing and proofreading your work.

Support Services

Look for support services that offer help with note-taking techniques, strategies to combat stress in test taking, and workshops on helping you organize and manage your time. If you discover that you have a pattern of specific struggles (e.g., you always underperform on tests), see if free screening for learning disabilities is offered. You may need specific testing accommodations (such as additional time or larger-print exams), or you may be eligible for help with an in-class note taker. The key is to become your own best advocate. Be informed—know how your mind works and what conditions make you perform your best.

Step 4: Explore the world of business in real time

While this textbook intends to apply business concepts to current situations, the examples cannot be as current as those that are exposed in the business press. Until now, you may not have been interested in picking up the *Wall Street Journal*, *Financial Times*, *BusinessWeek*, or *The Economist* because you did not have the necessary background or interest. Try the following technique. Every day, go online and read the lead story in the *Wall Street Journal*. Keep a log that notes the theme of the article (e.g., the economic situation in the United States or some other part of the world, a government action that impacts business, an acquisition by a major company, trends in the workplace, the stock market, a new technology, and so on). Also, rate how easy it was for you to understand the article, with "1" being the easiest and "10" being the most difficult. Similarly, rate how interesting the article was, with "1" being absolutely fascinating and "10" being massively boring. Note any questions about the article and how it relates to material being covered in class or note from the syllabus or table of contents where it might apply to future class content. As the end of your course approaches, review your log. You should see that the articles are becoming easier to understand and perhaps more interesting. In addition, you will also have created an informal study of the current business landscape, including the hottest business trends. For example, if you see that a

Ask Questions

If you're confused during class, ask a question right then. Don't think, "I'll look really dumb if I ask this" or "I'll probably understand it after I read the text" or "I'll wait to ask someone else, or go to office hours tomorrow." Asking now will save you time and effort and will probably help other students in the room. You'll learn so much more if you ask questions in class. If you do need to contact your instructor after class to clarify a point, stop by during office hours rather than asking the question electronically or over the phone. Keep in mind, face-to-face visits trump e-mail or voice mail. Now, aren't you glad you invested some time earlier to get to know your instructor (Step 3)? After all, it's easier to ask for help from someone with whom you already feel comfortable.

Write a One-Minute Review

Immediately at the end of class, take one minute and write all that you can recall from today's lecture. Try to identify what the main takeaway points are by highlighting key ideas. Forcing yourself to be quick and brief helps you to capture the main ideas without the smaller details providing distraction.

Write Down Your "Muddiest" Point

When class is finished, also take a quick moment to write down two sentences that describe the most confusing part of today's lecture. Keep this in one specific part of your notebook—it's a great thing to bring along to your study group or to office hours. It will also work well in creating your own personalized study guide for the next exam.

Step 3: Connect with people

Business is all about people. Right now, your business is getting a great grade in this class. As in any business, there are many people available to provide help: instructors, fellow students, and school staff. Look around for these people—and then enlist their help.

Get to Know Your Instructor: Go to Office Hours

Your teachers can be your most helpful contacts on campus. Not only can they become mentors, but as you near graduation, they can write job recommendations or references. They can't do that unless you get to know them beyond the focus of the course. So plan to make a couple of trips to office hours—even if you know everything.

Create or Join a Study Group

Find study buddies early. In the first few days of class, try to get acquainted with at least two classmates in every course. Watch the people in your class to figure out who seems to know what's going on, who seems dependable, and who you could work well with. Approach those people and ask if they wouldn't mind forming a study group. You don't need to meet all the time—the group can be available on an "as-needed" basis. But it's good to have a group of connected students who can help you prep for exams, confirm or clarify points made during class, and exchange notes if you miss a class.

66 *When studying for a test, I've found that it's very helpful to use a partner and a study guide. I like to come up with a study guide full of questions relating to every important topic that I think will be on the test and write the answers directly below them. Then, my partner and I go through the study guide and quiz each other. This way we can read aloud all of the main ideas and begin to remember key concepts. After we have gone through the study guide a couple times, we quiz each other from memory. Once we've memorized small concepts, it's easier to understand the bigger picture.* **99**

—**Mallory Hensel,** *student*

significant percentage of the articles are about government actions, it is fair to assume that governments are taking a more active role in business and the economy for some reason. But, above all, this exercise will demonstrate that business—once you really understand it—is far more fascinating than you ever imagined, and it will also help you develop the exceedingly valuable habit of reading the business press regularly, a habit that will serve you well in both life and business.

Step 5: Experience business

Business is about people. If you want to be a business success, leave your house and find someone who runs a small business (a restaurant, a print shop, a car wash, and so on) where you are a regular customer because you value the quality of their products. It doesn't matter if you don't have aspirations to work in this line of business, as you are just trying to understand the foundations of any small business that seems successful to you. Ask the owner or manager if you can interview him (or her). Ask him how he spends his time, what is most important to the success of his business, and what his most troublesome problems are. Perhaps you can even volunteer a few hours per week to do odd chores for him so that you can observe firsthand how he manages the business and continue to ask questions. It may start with meaningless errands, but one day you'll appreciate the foundation when a real opportunity arrives. Until that day, you'll be learning by watching a successful businessperson run a company.

Step 6: Know your learning style

Determining what kind of learner you are will help you apply the most appropriate resources to create a successful learning program. Knowing your learning style can help you select and use the study strategies that best fit the way you learn. ■ **TABLE 1** will help you figure out whether you learn best by seeing (visual), hearing (auditory), or touching/doing (tactile and kinesthetic). Read the word in the far left column of the chart and then place a check mark next to the statement in one of the successive three columns to the right that best describes how you respond to each situation. Count the number of check marks in each column, placing the total at the bottom of the table. Your answers may fall into all three columns, but one column will likely contain the most answers, which indicates your primary learning style. If one of the remaining columns nears in the number of check marks to your primary learning style, that can be considered your secondary learning style.

After you've determined your primary—and perhaps secondary—learning style, you can best match up the textbook, system, and resources from your instructor to help you achieve a better grade. And, if you can figure out how to succeed in this course, you can apply the same study strategies to succeed in other courses.

Note that your instructor also has a specific style of learning and teaching with which he or she is most comfortable. Watching how your instructor works can be a great clue to helping you succeed in the course. For example, does he or she talk without ever drawing a picture? Or does he or she use visuals to illustrate points? Figure out your instructor's learning style and use it to predict what kinds of interactions he or she wants in the classroom and on your assignments.

Step 7a: Read this book

What is the best investment you can make in yourself right now? If there were something that could promise you an A in this course and that would help you to succeed in college in general, it would be worth paying for, right? There is: this book, plus

TABLE 1 What's Your Learning Style?

When you . . .	Visual	Auditory	Kinesthetic and Tactile
Spell	☐ You try to see the word.	☐ You sound out the word or use a phonetic approach.	☐ You write the word down to find if it looks right.
Listen	☐ You get easily distracted when asked to listen for a long time.	☐ You grasp the information quickly and easily.	☐ You find yourself doodling as you listen.
Talk	☐ You favor words such as *see*, *picture*, and *imagine*.	☐ You use words such as hear, tune, and think.	☐ You gesture and use expressive movements. You use words such as feel, touch, and hold.
Concentrate	☐ You become distracted by untidiness or movement.	☐ You become distracted by sounds or noises.	☐ You become distracted by activity around you.
Meet someone again	☐ You forget names but remember faces or remember where you met.	☐ You forget faces but remember names or remember what you talked about.	☐ You remember best what you did together.
Contact people for class or business	☐ You prefer direct, face-to-face, personal meetings.	☐ You prefer talking on the phone.	☐ You prefer talking with people while walking or participating in an activity.
Read	☐ You like descriptive scenes or pause to imagine the actions.	☐ You enjoy dialogue and conversation or imagine the characters talking.	☐ You prefer action stories or are not a keen reader.
Do something new at school or work	☐ You like to see demonstrations, diagrams, slides, or posters.	☐ You prefer verbal instructions or talking about it with someone else.	☐ You prefer to jump right in and try it.
Put something together	☐ You look at the directions and the pictures.	☐ You prefer verbal instructions or talking about it with someone else.	☐ You ignore the directions and figure it out as you go along.
Need help with a computer application	☐ You seek out pictures or diagrams.	☐ You call the help desk, ask a neighbor, or growl at the computer.	☐ You keep trying to do it or try it on another computer.
Total			

Source: Based on Colin Rose's Accelerated Learning (1987).

your time. Really, all you need to succeed in this course is this book and its resources, plus some investment of your own time and energy. Doing well in this course is a good start at getting As in follow-up business courses that you might take in the future. That leads to a great job after graduation, followed by huge wealth, fame, and fortune! (Well, maybe not those last three, but you get the picture.)

Step 7b: Use the system, not just the textbook

Most likely, when you shelled out the cash to buy your textbook, you thought you were just getting a book, right? As it turns out, you actually bought a "system."

TABLE 2	**Better Business Resource Guide**		
Resource	**Where Is It?**	**When Does It Help Me?**
BizSkills (interactive simulations that let you try out your skills in many common business situations)	On mybizlab.com	For test prep concept reinforcement
PowerPoint presentations	On mybizlab.com	Before the chapter starts For test prep
End-of-chapter exercises	On mybizlab.com At the end of each chapter	When you're on the go For test prep concept reinforcement

Determining what kind of learner you are will help you apply the most appropriate resources to create a successful learning program. Knowing your learning style can help you select and use the study strategies that best fit the way you learn. ■ **TABLE 2** walks you through everything that comes with the purchase of this book. Remembering your learning style, consider how each of these resources can help you study and learn!

Step 8: Take awesome notes

Even if you're a strong auditory learner, you'll benefit from taking notes. Awesome notes are the key when you review and prepare for papers and exams. Take advantage of learning about different types of note-taking strategies. One will certainly work better for your learning style than another. Experiment and see which one best meets your needs. Three popular strategies are outlining, mind mapping, and the Cornell System.

Outlining

You might already use an outlining system. The main points are written down, and any supporting or additional points are indented and listed below the relevant main point. Outlining is a great system for taking notes from a book or PowerPoint presentation because the material has already been organized for you. However, this system may not be as effective to record the points made in a lecture or class discussion because the hierarchy structure of an outline is not very flexible, and this makes it hard to insert points that are made later on in a discussion but relate to something mentioned earlier.

Mind Mapping

A mind map is a graphic representation of the content of a lecture or reading. It is a flexible system, and many visual learners find mind mapping beneficial because it organizes a lecture graphically. ■ **FIGURE 1** shows one example.

Mind maps capture main and supporting ideas similar to an outline, but instead of a fixed hierarchy, the structure of a mind map is more fluid. The main points are captured in a box or circle in the middle of a page. Supporting points, or subtopics, are then drawn as smaller boxes or circles that radiate from the main circle. If later on another subtopic needs to be added, then a new branch can be drawn. If there is anything off topic that should be noted, it can be recorded in a cloud or circle that is not connected to anything and that sits outside the main concept area.

Later, when reviewing, add colors to connect ideas or concepts that aren't necessarily connected by branches but do share the same theme (such as those topics that your instructor pointed out will be on the test, that were from a PowerPoint presentation, or that should be further explored). As you review for a test or while

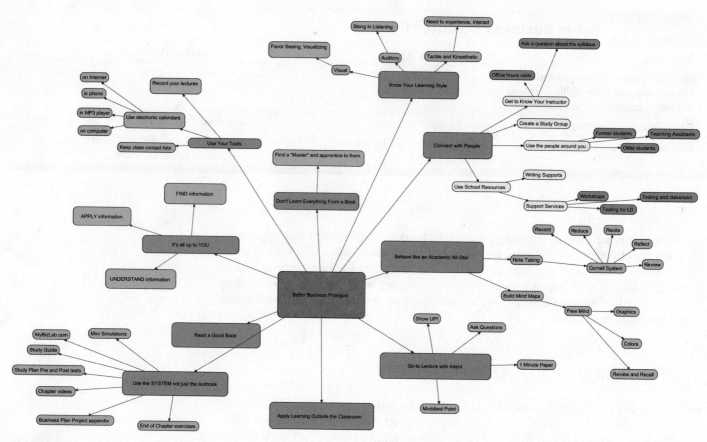

■ FIGURE 1
An Example of a Mind Map of This Prologue

preparing for a paper, you can use the boxes and colors to help you connect the main ideas of several lectures. Consider creating a *progressive mind map* (separate from individual lecture mind maps) that will express how specific topics relate to the course overall. Many free online resources, including software and templates, can help you begin to use mind maps. One such free product is FreeMind from SourceForge. Even if you just have paper and pencil, you can build useful mind maps.

> ❝*I use a mind map to arrange the material before writing a paper. It helps me get all of my ideas on paper and makes the information easier to organize logically.*❞
>
> —Laura Poatsy, *student*

The Cornell System

The Cornell System is a simple and powerful system that, if used correctly, can help with recall and increase the usefulness of your notes. When using the Cornell System, you don't need to rewrite or retype your notes. Instead, you use a specific setup to define your notes. Begin by setting up your 8½- by 11-inch notepaper as shown in **■ FIGURE 2**. Draw a vertical line 2½ inches from the left side of the page. Next, draw a horizontal line about an inch or so from the bottom of the page for a summary. You can also use a product such as Microsoft One Note, which comes preloaded with a Cornell Note System template (see Figure 2).

In the largest and main section of the paper, capture the main ideas of the lecture. You can use an outline or mind mapping system, whichever suites you best. Then, as soon as possible after the lecture, jot down in the skinny column ideas or key words that will define the main idea of the lecture. Finally, in the bottom section of the page, summarize the key points in your own words. This forces you to process the information in a new way.

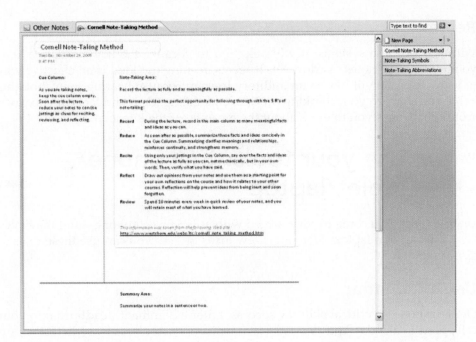

■ FIGURE 2
The One Note Template for the Cornell Note-Taking System

THE LIST

Extra Tips for the Online Learner

Taking this class online? Here are some additional tips for success:

1. Purchase your textbook and any other course materials before class begins. If you're buying online, allow for delivery time.

2. Check your technology needs. Make sure your computer, software, and Internet connection are sufficient for the requirements of the course before the class starts. Faulty technology is not a good excuse for missing assignments in an online course. Have a backup computer you can use, just in case.

3. Establish a regular study time. Without specific classroom meeting times, it's easy to forget about the class. Time passes quickly, and before you know it, your "other life" has taken precedent and you're playing catch-up to meet the requirements of the course. Set a regular study time—one that works with your schedule—when you can log into the class and do whatever work may be required.

4. Be proactive asking questions about assignments. If you have questions on an assignment, remember that sometimes getting answers is not immediate. You should always count on things taking more time than in a classroom.

5. Participate in discussions and ask questions. Your online instructor should provide a way for you to interact with other students and ask questions. Active participation will enable you to grasp the material better—and to know your classmates better.

6. Exchange contact information. Although it's harder to meet and interact with others in an online class, try to get contact information for at least one or two people with whom you can share information and questions.

7. Make sure the instructor knows who you are. Take the time in the first week or so to introduce yourself to the instructor via e-mail or through the class chat room. It's harder for an instructor to get to know you in an online course than in a traditional face-to-face class.

8. Know how to work your class website and course management software. Especially know how you can get and submit your assignments, check your grades, and communicate with your instructor as well as with your classmates.

9. Be organized and don't procrastinate. Especially if the class is self-paced, make sure you know when the big assignments and tests are due. As soon as you get your syllabus, record all assignment due dates on your own personal calendar.

10. Become comfortable expressing your ideas in writing. You'll need to communicate in a professional way about both course content and your future career.

Review

With any of these systems, it will help you to vocalize the key points made as you review your notes. As dorky as it seems, reciting out loud is an effective way to learn, especially if you're an auditory learner, because hearing your thoughts helps you sharpen your thinking process, and stating ideas and facts in your own words challenges you to think about the meaning of the information.

Step 9: Use your tools: Cell phone/ tablet/laptop

Undoubtedly, you come to class armed with at least a cell phone—and may even have a tablet or a laptop. Here are a few ideas of how you can use these tools to get you to that A.

Use a Calendar

Organization is a critical skill for success. Enter assignment deadlines into your cell phone's calendar. You also can use organizational tools such as Microsoft Outlook or Google Calendar to track key due dates and access them from your laptop.

Keep a Class Contact List

Collect the contact information for at least three classmates and for your professor in your cell phone or laptop contact list. Be sure to have it all—home phone, cell phone, IM identity, and e-mail address. This way, you'll have the information at your fingertips when you really need it and don't have your notebook with you. This habit will create all kinds of opportunities for you later in the real world. Successful folks call it networking!

Record Audio or Video of the Class

Smart phones and tablets are equipped to record audio, which can help in class. Note-taking applications allow you to write notes as the audio is being recorded. Then simply tapping on a note you jotted down takes you to that point of the audio recording.

Any cell phone that has a built-in camera can record video. Although the video may be low resolution, it will still be a useful review of what was said back on Tuesday. By adding a larger memory card, you can record back-to-back lectures with no storage problems.

66 *Take breaks during a study session—just be sure to come back to the work!* **99**

—**Devin Kownurko, student**

Laptops equipped with a camera can do the best job of video recording. Cameras such as the Logitech QuickCam Pro 5000 plug right into a USB port and actually track the voice of the lecturer, moving to keep him or her in focus even if he or she walks around the room while lecturing.

Many instructors are now beginning to create their own audio and video recordings of lectures and deliver them as podcasts to the class. If your instructor is not, ask for permission to record him or her and explain that you are happy to make the files available to him or her or willing to post them to the other students.

Step 10: Apply these rules outside the classroom

All of these classroom tips also can apply to your career. For example, Step 7 suggests that you find, understand, and apply the information from this textbook system to meet the demands of your instructor. In your working life, you'll need to find out what your boss or client wants and figure out the best way to meet his or her needs. Likewise, Step 6 encourages you to understand how you best learn. Revisit Table 1—many of the actions apply to a business context as well. Knowing your learning style will help you be successful in business as well as in the classroom.

Because business is all about people, think about how you can apply the strategies in Step 3 to your job. If you can, get to know your boss or supervisor. They, too, can become your mentors and be instrumental in recommending you for advancement within the company. Bosses don't have office hours, but you can stop by their offices periodically to just say hello or ask to meet them for lunch or coffee every month or so. Get to know the people you work with and develop a contact list. You never know when you may need to contact someone in the office when you're not there or vice versa. So get a coworker's e-mail, home or cell phone number, and maybe even his or her IM address. Again, it's much better to have someone in the office to ask, "What did I miss?" or "Can you help me?" than running to your boss (or not having anyone at all) to ask the same questions. Also, don't ignore the other people outside your immediate office. Get to know the cleaning staff, the elevator attendants, and the security guards in your building. They can help you in a pinch and are more willing to do so if they know your face and name.

To get ahead, follow Step 2 and come to work with intent! Don't be afraid to ask questions; good questions indicate that you're thinking about the situation at work and trying to apply it to what you already know. If things don't make sense or you don't understand something, ask for clarification.

Do you think you won't ever take notes again once you're out of the classroom? Think again. The workday includes attending lots of meetings, even when they occur over the phone. Use your college career and Step 8 to perfect note taking so when you get to the business world, you'll have that skill down pat. And although you might occasionally get lucky with an instructor who ignores your absences in the classroom, such luck most likely will not follow you into the office. We also suggested ways you can use your cell phone, MP3 player, and laptop in the classroom in Step 9. These tools can also be used in the office as well. Again, you need to make sure people know about and agree to your taping/recording them, but having good records of meetings and discussions can be helpful to you and to your colleagues. And because many people are afraid of technology, establishing yourself as someone who is comfortable and innovative with technology can also be a good thing.

Don't stop learning and reading! In Step 7 we encouraged you to read this book. When you find a career you're interested in pursuing, seek out books for advice and insight about that career. There is no end to learning—it's a lifetime activity, so embrace it. And by following the advice in Step 4, you should already have developed a love for reading real-time press. Knowing what is happening in the world around you helps anytime.

Finally, in Step 5, we encouraged you to interview a manager or owner of a business, or perhaps even volunteer some of your time. Becoming involved in a business and learning it from the ground up puts you in the position of better understanding any business in which you are involved. After all—as we say in Step 1: It's all up to you!

We hope you have found these steps to Better Business success helpful and hope you will be able to apply them to your academic and professional careers. Good luck in whatever endeavors you pursue!Better Business

Better Business

Chapter 1
Business Basics

▶ The Business Landscape

The business landscape in the United States is vast and varied. Ben Silberman launched the successful website Pinterest. Meanwhile, the Chang family opened a small Chinese restaurant. What do these seemingly unrelated businesses have in common?

▶ Common Business Challenges and Opportunities

Leroy Washington is the owner of a local deli in Florida. When a Subway franchise moved in across the street, Washington had to think creatively to deal with the new competition. How did he manage to keep his small deli in business despite the major franchise nearby?

▶ Types of Businesses

Wawa convenience stores are located in the mid-Atlantic region of the United States. Although the chain has over 500 stores, it is still considered a small, regional business. What would Wawa have to do to expand its business and become a national franchise?

▶ Taking Business Personally

Do you run your life like a business? Managing a business requires many of the same financial and personal skills you use in your daily life. Understanding how you use business concepts and methods in your life can help you understand how they are used in business.

OBJECTIVES

1 What is profit, and what is the difference between a good and a service? (pp. 3–4)

2 How do for-profit businesses and not-for-profit organizations compare? (p. 4)

3 What are the factors of production? (pp. 4–5)

4 How do competition, the social environment, globalization, and technological changes challenge and provide opportunities to business owners? (pp. 5–13)

5 What are the four types of businesses? (pp. 14–17)

6 How do life skills translate to the business environment? (pp. 17–18)

MyBizLab®

⭐ **Improve Your Grade!**

Over 10 million students improved their results using the Pearson MyLabs.
Visit **mybizlab.com** for simulations, tutorials, and end-of-chapter problems.

The Business Landscape pp. 3–5

Ben Silberman had a hobby when he was a kid in Des Moines, Iowa: He collected bugs. As a twenty-something now out of college and working, Silberman watched social networking sites take off. He thought there should be a better way to trade information about their hobbies with their friends. After his girlfriend heard him complain about wanting to leave his job and start a company one time too many, he did just that. He and a couple of friends, Evan Sharp and Paul Sciarra, began working on a Web app that would help people pick up new hobbies.1 They named it Pinterest.

Source: Nhvabe/Getty Images, Inc.

   Meanwhile, in a small town in Pennsylvania, members of the Chang family, who emigrated from Hong Kong three decades ago, fulfilled a lifelong dream of opening a Chinese restaurant. Although opening the new business was challenging, the Changs built a reputation for treating people like family and developed a loyal customer base. ■

What do a billion-dollar software company with hundreds of millions of users and a small-town family restaurant have in common? These organizations represent the varied spectrum of *business* in the United States. In this chapter, you'll learn about the basic skills it takes to run a successful business.

Business Defined

What exactly is a business? Both Pinterest and the Changs' Chinese restaurant are **businesses**—entities that offer products to their customers to earn a profit. A **profit** is earned when a company's **revenue** (the money it brings in) is greater than its **expenses** (the money it pays out). When expenses exceed revenue, the company posts a *loss*.

What kinds of products do businesses offer? A product can be either a *good* or a *service*. **Goods** are physical products a business sells. A roast beef sandwich at Arby's, a 42-inch television at Best Buy, and a Honda Fit at your local car dealership are all considered goods because they are tangible items. Conveyer belts, pumps, and parts sold to other businesses are also goods, even though they are not sold directly to consumers.

   A **service** is an intangible product that is bought or sold. Services include haircuts, health care, car insurance, and theatrical productions. Unlike a polo shirt on a rack at Hollister Co., services cannot be physically handled.

   Some companies offer products that are both goods *and* services. Take, for example, restaurant franchises like T.G.I. Fridays. When you order a sirloin steak at T.G.I. Fridays, you're paying for the good (a fire-grilled sirloin) as well as the service of preparing, cooking, and serving the steak.

   Countries change over time in whether goods or services dominate their economic system. Historically, the United States was primarily agricultural based

Many not-for-profit organizations, such as Amnesty International, operate like a business but do not pursue profits. Instead, they seek to service their community through social, educational, and political means.
Source: NetPhotos/Alamy.

but then moved to a strong manufacturing base that centered on producing goods. Today, that has diminished, and the service sector dominates. Other countries are following different trajectories; for example, in China, the manufacturing of goods is now the dominant business model.

What do businesses do with their profits? More often than not, profits are the driving force behind a business's growth. As more profits are generated, a company can reward its employees, increase its productivity, or expand its business into new areas.

The proprietor of a business is not the only one who benefits from the profits it generates. A successful business benefits society by providing the goods and the services consumers need and want. Businesses also provide employment opportunities for members of the community. Because they offer desired goods and services, provide employment, and generate income and spending in the economy, successful businesses contribute to the quality of people's lives by creating higher standards of living for society.

What about not-for-profits? Not-for-profit organizations do not go into business to pursue profits for their owners. Instead, a not-for-profit organization seeks to service its community through social, educational, or political means. Organizations such as universities, hospitals, environmental groups, and charities are examples of not-for-profit organizations. Any profits they generate are used to further the organizations' causes by expanding the services they provide.

The Factors of Production

What do businesses use to create the products they sell? To fully understand how a business operates, you have to consider its **factors of production**, or the resources it uses to produce goods and services. For years, businesses focused on the traditional factors of production: labor, natural resources, capital, entrepreneurial talent, intellectual property, and technology:

- **Labor.** Needless to say, businesses need people to produce goods and provide services. **Labor** is a human resource that refers to any *physical* work or *intellectual* work (ideas and knowledge) people contribute to a business's production.

- **Natural resources.** **Natural resources** are the raw materials provided by nature that are used to produce goods and services. Soil used in agricultural production; trees used for lumber to build houses; and coal, oil, and natural gas used to create energy are all examples of natural resources.

- **Capital.** There are two types of capital: *real capital* and *financial capital*. **Real capital** refers to the physical facilities used to produce goods and services, such as office buildings and factories. **Financial capital** refers to money used to facilitate a business enterprise. Financial capital can be acquired via business loans, from investors, through other forms of fund-raising, or by tapping into one's personal savings.

- **Entrepreneurial talent.** An **entrepreneur** is someone who assumes the risk of creating, organizing, and operating a business and directs all of a business's resources. Entrepreneurs are a human resource, just like labor, but what sets them apart from labor is not only their willingness to bear risks but also their ability to effectively manage businesses. For successfully doing so, entrepreneurs are rewarded with profits from the businesses.

- **Intellectual property.** Intellectual property consists of privately owned, intangible assets developed as a result of people's intellect and creativity. Drug patents held by pharmaceutical companies, copyrights to songs, and trademarks for products such as Coca-Cola are examples. Holding a patent on a drug, for example, means that no other company can compete with your product while the patent is in force.

- **Technology.** In our twenty-first-century economy, an additional factor of production has become increasingly important: technology. **Technology** refers to goods and services such as computers, smart phones, software, and digital broadcasting that make businesses more efficient and productive. Successful companies are able to keep pace with technological progress and harness new knowledge, information, and strategies. Unsuccessful companies often fail because they have not kept pace with the latest technology.

You will learn more about labor (Chapter 9), capital (Chapter 15), entrepreneurs (Chapter 5), and technology and knowledge factors (Chapter 10) as you continue reading this text.

Recall the examples of Pinterest and the Changs' Chinese restaurant. Pinterest provides a service to its users: the ability to instantly communicate their interests, hobbies, and projects to other people. The Changs provide goods to their customers in the form of the food they sell. They also provide a service in the form of the preparation and delivery of that food. Although the business models and products offered by these businesses vary considerably, the two businesses are similar because both were started by creative entrepreneurs determined to make a profit. Pinterest is now worth billions of dollars. For the Chang family, the profits are much more modest. The members are making a solid living but are far from seeing a 10-figure profit. Although these two enterprises differ greatly in many ways, both the Changs and the founders of Pinterest have realized their dreams by starting successful new businesses.

Common Business Challenges and Opportunities pp. 5–13

In 2008, Leroy Washington inherited his family's deli. The deli had a loyal clientele with a regular lunch crowd. Then a new Subway store moved into a building directly across the street. Because Subway is a national franchise that advertises heavily, the new store has great name recognition. The store also occupies a larger space, has more workers and ovens, and has a more extensive menu.

Leroy found his lunch crowd dwindling as people switched to the national chain with its faster service and greater variety of sandwiches. To better compete with Subway, Leroy had to get creative. So, instead of just offering traditional deli choices, he expanded the restaurant's menu to include Cuban pressed sandwiches and an "early bird special" consisting of light fare on the dinner menu. Leroy hoped that the changes would appeal to the large number of Cuban immigrants and senior citizens populating the area. ■

Dealing with competition is just one of the many challenges business owners such as Leroy face. However, as Leroy found, confronting these challenges can sometimes lead to opportunities for growth as well. Next we'll discuss how competition, the social environment, globalization, and technological change create both business challenges and opportunities like they have for Leo.

THE LIST

Ten Tech Entrepreneurs— Under 30. Very Successful.²

1. Ben Silberman: Pinterest valued at $4 billion
2. Mark Zuckerberg: Facebook tops $100 billion
3. Arash Ferdowsi and Drew Houston: Dropbox valued at $4 billion
4. Daniel Ek: Spotify $1 billion in revenue
5. Naveen Selvadurai: Foursquare $600 million in revenue
6. Kevin Systrom and Mike Krieger: Instagram sold for $1 billion
7. Jennifer Hyman and Jenny Fleiss: Rent the Runway $105 million
8. Ben Lerer: Thrilllist $150 million projected revenue
9. Kim Kardashian: Shoedazzle merging with JustFab will bring over $400 million revenue
10. Danile Kafie and Josh Kushner: Vostu largest social gaming company in South America

Source: Rui Dias-aidos/Thinkstock,/Getty Images, Inc.

Competition

How does competition influence business? In a market-based economy, such as that in the United States, there is an emphasis on individual economic freedom and a limit on governmental intervention. In this type of market, competition is a fundamental force. **Competition** arises when two or more businesses vie with one another to attract customers and gain an advantage. The private enterprise system in the United States is predicated on the fact that competition benefits consumers because it motivates businesses to produce a wider variety of better and cheaper goods and services.

Competition in Today's Marketplace

A competitive environment is where a free market economy thrives. Competition forces companies to improve their product offerings, lower their prices, aggressively promote their brands, and focus on customer satisfaction. Having to compete for a finite number of consumers usually weeds out less efficient companies and less desirable products from the marketplace. To win at the competitive game of business, today's companies need to deliver customer satisfaction and understand the power of social networking and are finding they need to empower their employees.

CUSTOMER SATISFACTION AND BEYOND To understand how successful businesses provide products that are either better or less expensive than those of their competitors, consider the market for home video: As more manufacturers and retailers jumped into the high-definition television (HDTV) market a number of years ago, the prices for HDTV sets fell sharply. This created a market of people hungry for Blu-ray players so they could watch high-definition programs on the new sets. As a result, the sales of Blu-ray players—once the sole dominion of high-end retailers and manufacturers—rose dramatically as the players became a staple in people's home entertainment systems. The prices of Blu-ray players dropped too. Customers could find moderately priced ones at a variety of retailers, such as Amazon.com, Costco, and Best Buy. These companies are able to turn over merchandise quickly and in high volumes, which allows them to lower the prices they pay for products as well as what their customers pay for them.

Later as the market continued to evolved, streaming media became an option through companies like Comcast and Verizon as well as via Netflix and Google Play. Disc sales plummeted, as did the sales of disc players. Other companies like Amazon and Pandora began offering streaming media services as well, and

Nantucket Nectars: Tom and Tom's Partnership

Tom First and Tom Scott were college buddies who did not want to climb the traditional corporate ladder. After graduating from Brown University, the friends moved to Nantucket, Massachusetts, where they started a floating convenience store called Allserve in a red boat in Nantucket Harbor. The store provided delivery service of almost any item, from newspapers to laundry, to neighboring boats.

While Allserve proved to be a modest success, "Tom and Tom" soon had another idea. They decided to sell their own natural juice blend, and Nantucket Nectars was born. The popularity of the juice spread quickly in Nantucket. Allserve then purchased a distribution company to expand the reach of its products, which many national chains now carry. The two entrepreneurs maintained their local roots by subsequently starting the Juice Guys Juice Bar in Nantucket.[3] This partnership is an example of how a successful business can be started by two eager and driven people. Tom and Tom have come a long way since their days as floating delivery boys in Nantucket Harbor, and they are now running a nationally recognized corporation.

television manufacturers began integrating streaming players for Netflix, Amazon .com, and Pandora into their television sets. Competition is what made this all happen.

SOCIAL NETWORKING Websites like Pinterest, Facebook, Twitter, and many others are examples of social networking sites. **Social networking sites** are websites that make it easier for people to connect with one another online for the purposes of building and supporting social relationships. With over 1.3 billion users, Facebook is probably the best-known social networking site. Twitter is another popular social networking site.

What do social media have to do with business competition? Today more than ever, customers are connected to each other through a great variety of media— e-mail, texting, blogs, and social networking sites. Companies are therefore increasingly using social networking to connect to their customers. Through these sites, they can promote their products, offer discounts, and build relationships with people interested in their companies.

Individuals can use social networking sites to quickly spread the word about very good (or very bad) services or products. If a customer is dissatisfied, word can spread at the speed of light. As discussed later in this book, a happy customer base can be a powerful marketing tool for a company.

Other social networking sites are specialized for the needs of businesses. LinkedIn, for example, has more than 270 million users. LinkedIn users exchange résumés and build networking contacts by connecting with old acquaintances, former employers, and coworkers. Companies also use the site to find job candidates and get them interested in their firms.

EMPLOYEE EMPOWERMENT In a competitive environment, it is essential for a company to empower workers to feel free to deal with customer needs. This means employers seek workers who have interpersonal, communication, and decision-making skills. Companies today need to be more reactive to customers' needs to retain their competitive advantage. Therefore, more companies are giving employees greater decision-making responsibilities rather than having decisions trickle down through layers of management. This also leads to greater satisfaction and more career advancement opportunities for employees.

Apple: Taking a Bite Out of Microsoft?

In an effort to dominate the personal computer (PC) market, Apple and Microsoft have had a long and bitter rivalry. Originally, the main point of contention between the two companies was the graphical user interface (GUI), which is the user interface for the main program that runs PCs. Apple released the first GUI, which included folders and long file names, in 1983. When Microsoft released Windows 2.0 in 1988, Apple took Microsoft to court, complaining that the "look and feel" of the Windows interface was stolen from the Apple interface. This suit continued until 1992, when Apple finally lost.

Microsoft led the competition in the early 1990s. It became an industry standard to have Windows operating systems pre-installed on most PCs, which were dominating the computer market at the time. The 10-year battle finally ended when Apple announced an official alliance with Microsoft in 1997. Microsoft

and Apple agreed to a five-year deal in which Microsoft would continue to develop Office software for Apple computers and Apple agreed to bundle Microsoft's Internet Explorer in all its operating systems.[4]

So competition can create new partnerships—strange ones at times. Today, Microsoft is actively wooing Apple in an effort to have promote and sell their products to Apple users. If you own an Apple iPhone and use the company's digital personal assistant "Siri" to conduct a Web search, she will use Microsoft's Bing browser instead of Google to search the Web. What's in this for Apple? Google has become one of Apple's main competitors in the mobile phone market with its Android phone platform. The element of competition between these rival high-tech companies drives them all to keep innovating and producing higher-quality products than if no one challenged them.

Social Environment

How does the social environment affect businesses? A social environment is an interconnected system of different demographic factors, such as the race, ethnicity, gender, age, income distribution, sexual orientation, and other characteristics of a population. Social, economic, and political movements and trends are constantly changing the social environment of the United States and other countries. An influx of immigrants can change the racial demographic, or an economic slump can change the income distribution demographic. These changes affect where we live, what we buy, and how we choose to spend our money. To best serve their employees, customers, and the community, businesses must consider the shifts and changes in the social environment when making decisions. Let's discuss three specific issues surrounding the social environment that present potential challenges and opportunities for today's businesses.

AN AGING POPULATION   Not only are older Americans living longer, healthier lives, but they are also better educated, are wealthier, and have achieved higher living standards than previous generations. *Baby boomers*, the generation born between 1946 and 1964, make up the majority of the aging population in the United States. Not only do the 78 million baby boomers make up one of the largest population groups in the United States, but they are also the wealthiest. Baby boomers, who in 2014 were between the ages of 50 and 68, have an estimated spending power of over $2 trillion per year. This makes baby boomers a large and lucrative target for businesses. For example, the cosmetics company Garnier is eager to make a profit from the aging population with its anti-aging beauty line called UltraLift, which is aimed at baby-boomer women. Garnier released the line in an effort to keep its product offerings aligned with the shift in demographics.

Although an aging population presents many opportunities for businesses, it also presents challenges for the U.S. economy. Many analysts have warned that the nation will be faced with difficult choices as baby boomers continue to reach retirement age. Some potential problems include the government having to raise taxes to fund entitlement programs such as Social Security and Medicare, reduce the benefits of these programs, or face higher federal budget deficits.

Why does this matter to businesses? As shown in ■ **FIGURE 1.1**, in 2050, there will be over 80 million Americans age 65 or older. Today, almost 40 percent of the total personal income for senior citizens comes from Social Security payments. Together these trends imply that there will be a decrease in the number of workers and an increase in the demand for social services. Longevity is another aspect of this demographic shift; in 2010, there were over 53,000 centenarians (people age 100 or older) in the United States.[5] Projections place that number at 580,000 by 2040. The health care programs and services required to care for this population will need to be in place.

Along with these challenges, as we noted, caring for the needs of an older population will present businesses with opportunities for growth, especially retirement centers, health care and pharmaceutical companies, and the travel industry. A bigger population translates to a larger market for these goods and services.

INCREASING WORKFORCE DIVERSITY   In business, there is no one-size-fits-all way to manage employees and appeal to customers because every person is different. As the United States becomes more diverse, it is important for businesses to mirror that diversity in their workforce. Firms that don't

■ **FIGURE 1.1**

U.S. Population Age 65 and Over: 1990–2050

Source: Data from U.S. Census Bureau.

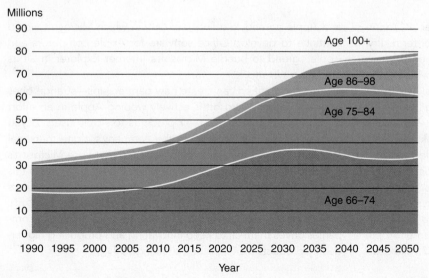

Millions

Age 100+

Age 86–98

Age 75–84

Age 66–74

Year

are at risk for losing touch with their new, more diverse customer base. According to the latest data available, the U.S. Census Bureau reports that the minority population in the United States is about 35 percent, making one in three residents a minority. In some companies, minorities account for the majority of the workforce. At the hotel chain Four Seasons, for example, minorities represent 64 percent of the company's 12,400 employees.[6]

However, in today's business climate, increasing and managing a company's diversity involves more than just employing an ethnically diverse workforce. Companies must also develop a diversity initiative that outlines their goals and objectives for managing, retaining, and promoting a diverse workforce. A diversity initiative might include a nondiscrimination policy, a minority network, or diversity education. To increase diversity within a business, the company must treat it as a business-critical goal.

Although the inclusion and advancement of racial minorities in the workplace is an important step in establishing a diverse workforce, it is only part of the process. Today, the term *minority* applies to more than just people of different ethnicities. Minority groups might represent a person's gender, culture, religion, sexual orientation, or disability. Companies must include these minority groups in their diversity initiative to ensure that all minority employees are treated fairly by their managers and coworkers.

THE GREEN MOVEMENT The public's increasing anxieties about global warming and climate change have motivated businesses to become involved in a **green economy**—one that factors ecological concerns into business decisions. Because their customers are concerned about the environment, businesses that manufacture products that contribute to higher emissions of carbon dioxide and consume inordinate amounts of fossil fuels must adapt to this new environmental awareness to remain competitive.

In the automotive industry, for example, hybrid vehicles, which run on a combination of electricity and gasoline, have not only become hot sellers but also are critical to meeting national objectives. New fuel economy standards[7] in the United States will require cars to get almost 55 miles per gallon by 2025. Almost every major car manufacturer—including Toyota, Honda, and BMW—now offers hybrid models. Vehicles that run on other types of energy sources are appearing as well, such as the Tesla Model S and the Nissan Leaf, which are all-electric vehicles. The Leaf has a range of almost 100 miles on a single charge—and not a tailpipe to be seen.

Nissan Leaf electric cars are an example of how the automobile manufacturers are responding to changes in the social environment.
Source: YASUYOSHI CHIBA/AFP/ GettyImages.

A focus on environmental issues also opens up a brand-new market that will be increasingly important in the future. The demand for more green products presents new opportunities for entrepreneurs to meet those needs. These "green-collar" jobs can revitalize large swaths of the U.S. manufacturing economy that have been decimated. Creating wind energy turbines, installing solar panels, and landscaping designs that make your microclimate (the climate immediately surrounding your home) energy efficient will be necessary businesses of the twenty-first century.

THE SOCIAL ENVIRONMENT AND YOU   As a prospective employee, any one of these social issues will probably affect the company for which you end up working. Because workers are increasingly retiring at later ages, the competition for certain jobs and career advancement might be fiercer than in years past. On the other hand, the culture of business is constantly shifting to meet the ever-evolving needs of U.S. demographics. This means more opportunity for employees who can navigate a diverse environment. In addition, jobs aimed at responding to the needs of the growing green economy will also likely present new opportunities for job seekers. Entrepreneurial possibilities always exist for those who have the vision and desire to succeed and are willing to take risks.

Globalization

How has globalization affected businesses? You're familiar with multinational companies such as Nike, McDonald's, and Coca-Cola. **Multinational enterprises—**companies that have operations in more than one country—are among the leaders of a movement called globalization. **Globalization** is a movement toward a more interconnected and interdependent world economy. This means that economies around the world are merging as technology, goods and services, labor, and capital move back and forth more easily across international borders. For example, FedEx, the world's largest express transportation company, conducts business in more than 220 countries and territories around the world.[8]

The effects of globalization on the business world vary widely, from the economic transformation of China to the shutting down of major manufacturing plants in the United States. The Internet and modern technological advances are making it possible for a company of any size from anywhere in the world to compete globally. Lower tariffs and other trade restrictions give U.S. companies the option to export or import goods to and from other countries or conduct their business overseas. Instead of building their products in plants at home, a growing number of companies are relocating their production facilities overseas or subcontracting at least some of the components of their products to foreign companies around the world to achieve lower manufacturing costs. This is called **offshoring**. The low labor costs in countries such as China and India make these countries ideal locations for multinational companies seeking technology services and manufactured products at a low cost.

Although the concept of globalization is essential for many companies, it is still a highly controversial subject for many. Globalization presents both benefits and risks to the U.S. economy. For example, lowered production costs allow firms to lower the cost of products for consumers like you. Yet people remain concerned about workers in the United States who lose their jobs to workers overseas. Globalization poses other risks for U.S. companies, including the following:

- Increased competition from international companies
- Fluctuations in the value of the U.S. dollar
- Security and patent protection concerns
- Unstable political climates in foreign countries

Globalization has therefore sparked fierce debates among politicians, businesspeople, and the general public for the past few decades. We'll discuss the controversies surrounding globalization in greater depth in Chapter 4.

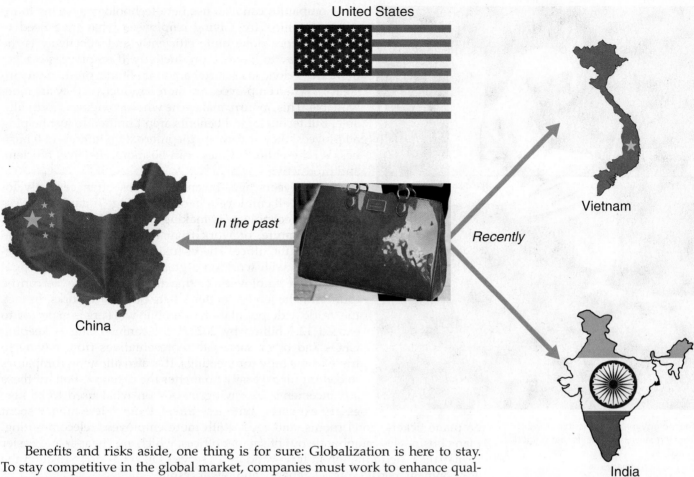

Global outsourcing is always changing. Coach, the American handbag manufacturer, has outsourced production to China in the past but now is moving to lower-wage countries, such as India and Vietnam.
Source: China: daboost/Fotolia; US flag: daboost/Fotolia; Coach bag: Kirstin Sinclair/ Getty Images, Inc.; Vietnam: Yahia Loukkal/ Fotolia; India: daboost/Fotolia.

Benefits and risks aside, one thing is for sure: Globalization is here to stay. To stay competitive in the global market, companies must work to enhance quality and develop and implement innovative strategies for the long term. The increasingly global nature of business increases the demand for workers who can communicate with international business partners, have up-to-date technological talents, can demonstrate excellent communication and creative problem-solving skills, and possess leadership skills.

Technological Changes

Why does the pace of technological change present challenges to businesses today? Over the past 20 years, advancements in information technology (IT) have been revolutionary. In today's business world, companies must stay on the cutting edge of technology to remain competitive. No matter the business, technology can be used to keep a company flexible, organized, and well connected—with either customers or employees. There is no question that keeping up with the pace of technology is an expensive and time-consuming operation. The rapid pace of technological innovation means that computers are often outdated after three years and obsolete after five.[9] Add to that the cost of applicable software, training, and infrastructure, and it is no wonder that IT is often the single-largest expense for many companies.[10] But IT costs aren't the only challenge. In the same way that robotics completely revolutionized the automotive industry, advancements in computer and telecommunication technology are completely changing the foundation and focus of how many businesses are run.

What benefits does technology provide to business? Technology, when used and implemented effectively, can help streamline businesses and cut costs. Technology products such as Twitter and Facebook can promote better communications with customers. Companies now can place specialized ads inside of music recognition software like Shazam or use location-aware software to send ads to your mobile device or even your car's media center as you approach the store.

Technology makes it possible to work from virtually anywhere. Is that a good thing?
Source: Getty Images, Inc.

Companies can also use new technology systems to increase productivity. Giving employees what they need to get their work done more efficiently and effectively is the simplest way to increase productivity. If employees can get more work done in a shorter amount of time, productivity increases. When employees are more productive, they are more valuable. This, in turn, makes the whole company more valuable. But technological benefits aren't limited to just helping employees; they streamline the internal operations of a business so the entire business can be more effective, efficient, and productive.

Thirty years ago, businesses were often centrally located, with all employees in one building. Today, this is less common. Technology is making it possible for employees to **telecommute**, or work from home or another location away from the office. The virtual global workforce, or telecommuters who work on a global scale, expands the pool of potential employees so that the right employee can be found for the job no matter where he or she works. In fact, the worldwide population of mobile workers is expected to exceed 12.4 billion by 2020.[11] Teleconferencing is keeping CEOs and other corporate representatives from having to travel constantly for meetings. It is also allowing companies to communicate easily no matter the distance. Both of these advancements are saving money on what used to be necessary expenses. With less travel, there is less money spent on plane tickets, hotel rooms, and food. With more employees telecommuting, many businesses can operate out of smaller offices, which are cheaper and easier to manage. The reduction in travel and other services also has an impact on the environment, consuming less energy and fewer resources.

What role does the Internet play in technological growth? If IT is the tool that is changing the functions of business, the Internet is the tool that is changing the scope of business. Although IT by itself would be extremely influential for the business world, the Internet makes it truly revolutionary. In 1995, the Internet was just starting to proliferate. Many people were intrigued by this new technology, but initially there weren't high hopes for companies that operated solely on the Internet. But this changed in 1995 when both eBay and Amazon.com launched. These companies showed that such an endeavor was not only possible but also potentially lucrative. Their high-profile success paved the way for the general acceptance of public e-commerce. As **FIGURE 1.2** shows, people now are buying every type of product online. We'll discuss online business and technology in more detail in Chapter 10.

■ **FIGURE 1.2**
What Are People Buying Online?
Source: Laptop: Ruslanchik/Shutterstock; bags: urfin/Shutterstock.

E-COMMERCE **E-commerce** consists of three different kinds of business trade: *business to consumer (B2C)*, *business to business (B2B)*, and *consumer to consumer (C2C)*. B2C interactions are the ones you're probably most familiar with, such as buying books at Amazon.com or songs or movies from iTunes. B2C interactions take place between a business and a consumer. B2B interactions involve the sale of goods and services, such as personalized or proprietary software, from one business to another. Although both are fairly similar in many ways, the ways in which they differ are significant. B2B e-commerce often involves large transactions to few customers and customized products and pricing, with numerous managers from both businesses making sure that the transaction is beneficial to both parties. This process is obviously more involved than typical B2C transactions, such as downloading a new ring tone for your cell phone or buying an item from Amazon. C2C transactions have become possible through consumer-driven storefronts like Etsy.com, where individuals can offer their handmade crafts directly for sale to customers.

Every year, e-commerce becomes a more significant element of the overall economy. E-commerce has been growing rapidly since the new millennium, forcing many businesses to either adapt or be left in the dust. For example, the CEO of Procter & Gamble (P&G) Bob MacDonald, has announced plans to expand electronic sales of its products from $500 million to $4 billion annually, using Amazon.com and the firm's own websites.[12] P&G even allowed Amazon to set up shop in P&G's warehouses so that they could fill orders for Pampers and other P&G products more quickly. As ■ **FIGURE 1.3** shows, almost 75 percent of all U.S. Internet users have made online purchases. So far, this trend shows no sign of stopping. As it becomes easier for consumers to find even the most obscure items at competitive prices, e-commerce will continue to be a driving force in our economy.

It is important to note that the commercialization of the Internet has been around only less than two decades. The Internet, as a medium for sales, has yet to reach its full potential. As the Internet and its influence continue to grow, so will its economic importance and necessity for businesses. This growth will also affect the dangers and concerns associated with the Internet.

ONLINE SECURITY   The widespread access to information that the Internet affords affects businesses in a variety of ways. Personal information, such as Social Security numbers, credit card numbers, addresses, and passwords, are all accessible online. This sensitive information, even when it is secured, can be vulnerable to hackers. Because businesses often store this and other types of personal information, the responsibility is on them to take measures to protect the online security of all their customers. It's no coincidence that as the number of people and businesses who trade and store personal information online rises, so does the number of people who are victims of **identity theft**—the illegal gain and use of personal information. In 2012, over 16 million people had their identity information misused.[13] New forms of identity theft are emerging as well, such as taking someone's identity for the purpose of getting medical care.[14] In 2013, online hackers infiltrated a number of businesses, including Target, and stole tens of millions of customers' credit card information. The need for more awareness of personal online security and better tools to ensure corporate online security is clear.

PRIVACY   Privacy is another important issue for businesses. E-mails, internal documents, and chat transcripts all contain private information that is not intended for public viewing. Nevertheless, many of these documents can be accessed online because online storage in the "cloud" has become so convenient. With all this universal access, it is increasingly difficult to ensure that information remains private. Cloud-based storage and services offer many benefits to business. Yet privacy and security concerns cannot be overlooked. Over time, technology will continue to introduce challenges.

Remember our opening story about Leroy Washington? When competition from a national franchise threatened his business, Leroy confronted the challenge head-on. To capitalize on the diversity of the area—particularly the sizable populations of both Latinos and seniors—Leroy expanded his menu. His strategy was a success. The Cuban pressed sandwiches became a local favorite. Moreover, the deli was soon packed every day from 3:30 to 5:30 P.M., when the "early bird special" fare—consisting of sandwiches, soups, and salads at reasonable prices—was offered. As Leroy Washington demonstrated, challenges and opportunities abound and overlap in the business world.

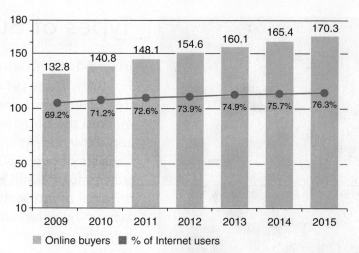

■ **FIGURE 1.3**
Online Buyers among Internet Users
Source: Data taken from U.S. Online Buyers and Penetration, 2009–2015. http://www.emarketer.com

Source: Andre Jenny/Alamy.

Types of Businesses pp. 14–17

In 1964, Grahame Wood opened a convenience store in Folsom, Pennsylvania. The business's focus was on providing fresh dairy products and produce and a full-service delicatessen. This marked the beginning of the Wawa chain of convenience stores, which serve the mid-Atlantic region of the United States. The chain now consists of over 630 stores in five states.15 Although Wawa is certainly successful, it's still a regional company that does not currently serve a national or international market. Regional businesses, such as Wawa, face unique challenges that don't affect larger businesses, especially involving access to adequate funding and insurance. Wawa continues to expand in the mid-Atlantic region and may one day move into the category of a national business. Is that the best move for this regional chain? ■

What's the difference between a small business and a large corporation? What about everything in between? A small business has different goals and challenges than a large corporation. Small businesses, such as a local dry cleaner, often provide limited goods or services to a small population. A large multinational corporation, such as Johnson & Johnson, supplies a wide range of goods or services to many customers worldwide. A local or regional business will have very different needs and concerns. In this section, we'll look at the different types of businesses and what constitutes each.

Local and Regional Businesses

What defines local or regional businesses? Take a walk around your town or city, and you'll see a variety of local and regional businesses. Used bookstores, bakeries, shoe repair shops, boutiques, restaurants, and specialty shops are often local businesses. A **local business** is usually one of a kind, and it relies on local consumers to generate business. A company is local if it serves a limited surrounding area. A local catering company in Baltimore, for example, might have one kitchen and cater events in Baltimore and its surrounding suburbs. Local companies generally have small numbers of employees and are associated with the towns or cities in which they are located. **Regional businesses** serve a wider area although, like local companies, they do not serve a national or international market. Wawa convenience store chain is an example of a regional business.

What special challenges do local and regional businesses face? The most common challenge for local and regional businesses is managing their money. Poor financial planning, as well as unfavorable economic conditions, can lead to bankruptcy. **Undercapitalization** occurs when a business owner cannot gain access to adequate funding. When a business can no longer afford to produce goods or provide services, it goes out of business. The owner must anticipate the cost of doing business and estimate the revenue that the business will generate. To avoid going into debt, the owner should have enough projected revenue to cover expenses for at least the first year. So if the owner of a local catering company has $100,000 in expenses and expects to generate $75,000 in the first year of business, then the owner should have at least $25,000 to fund the company. Even with adequate funding, there is always a chance that the economy will not support the business. Many small businesses fail when the economy slows down because consumers are less likely to spend extra money.

Business owners also have to take taxes and insurance costs into consideration, such as health insurance plans to cover their employees. They also need liability insurance to protect their companies if property is stolen or damaged or if employees are injured on the job. If a local jewelry store is broken into and jewelry is stolen, liability insurance will cover the cost of the broken window and the stolen property. If the jewelry store is not insured, the business could go bankrupt if the owner can't afford to cover the loss and damages.

National Businesses

What defines national businesses in the United States? If you drive from New York to Los Angeles, you'll encounter many CVS/pharmacies along the way. CVS/pharmacy has over 7,000 locations and can be found in every part of the United States.[16] All CVS/pharmacy locations essentially look alike and carry similar merchandise—all within a similar price range. With companies such as this, the customer knows what to expect. A **national business** serves the country, but it does not serve an international market. It provides goods or services to virtually all U.S. residents, no matter where in the country they live. A car insurance company, such as Allstate, is another example of a national business. It has offices in 49 states and serves the entire country. National companies have become standard symbols of U.S. business.

What special challenges do national companies face? Like local and regional companies, national companies also have to worry about their budgets and managing their finances. But they have other concerns that local businesses don't have. Because laws vary from state to state, national companies must be aware of state laws in every state in which they do business. For example, each state has its own tax laws. In most states, retail businesses are required to apply for a state sales tax permit to be able to collect sales tax from their customers. Every state imposes a corporate income tax, but the rate varies across states. And some states, such as New Jersey and Rhode Island, require businesses to pay for temporary disability insurance for their employees.[17] These laws can be difficult to keep up with and prevent companies from having standardized operating policies.

Another challenge that national companies face is longer, more complex supply chains. A **supply chain** refers to the flow by which a product, information, and money move between a supplier and a consumer (see ■ **FIGURE 1.4**). In the case of a manufactured good, raw materials flow from their suppliers to a manufacturer, which makes them into a product, which then flows to wholesalers, to retailers, and finally to the consumer. If the product is returned, it flows from the consumer back to the retailer and then potentially further back through the supply chain. Information flow includes the status of orders and their delivery. Financial flow includes manufacturing costs, payments, credit terms, and profits.

Let's look at an example of a supply chain. When you go to Target to buy a bottle of Tide detergent, you are a part of the supply chain, as is the Target store itself. Target's stock of Tide was supplied by a distributor, whose supply of detergent came from its supplier, P&G. P&G has its own set of suppliers that provide the chemicals and packaging materials required to manufacture the detergent.

The bigger a business is, the longer and more complicated its supply chain becomes. If not managed properly, long supply chains can be inefficient because products and materials have to pass through more warehouses and sustain more shipments. Products may get backed up in long supply chains, which can result in delayed shipments and late payments. A lack of communication among companies in the chain can cause mix-ups and delays, especially if there is a sudden change in the process. A national company must therefore rely on the cooperation of all members of the supply chain to keep the business running smoothly.

Businesses like CVS/pharmacy are national businesses in that they have locations throughout the United States but do not serve an international market.
Source: Kristoffer Tripplaar/Alamy.

Supplier   Manufacturer   Wholesaler   Retailer   Consumer

■ **FIGURE 1.4**
The Supply Chain
Source: Left to right: Anita/Shutterstock;
Uwe Bumann/Shutterstock; Nat Ulrich/
Shutterstock; Supertrooper/Shutterstock;
Tyler Olson/Fotolia.

Multinational (International) Businesses

What categorizes a company as multinational (or international)? As we discussed earlier, *multinational businesses* make and/or sell products in several countries. They are businesses that have expanded to provide goods or services to international consumers or serve only one country but have suppliers or production facilities in other countries. For example, you can now find a McDonald's restaurant in more than 119 countries, all serving distinctly U.S. food.[18] However, not every McDonald's restaurant is exactly the same. They have all been adapted to fit the cultures of the countries in which they are located. For example, if you enter a McDonald's restaurant in some parts of Canada, you'll see a McLobster on the menu. The McAloo Tikki Burger is a vegetarian sandwich made with potatoes, peas, and spices served in McDonald's restaurants in India. Because of the large Hindu population in India, beef is not used in any of their menu items.[19] This is the nature of multinational businesses.

What special challenges do multinational corporations face? Multinational corporations must be familiar and comply with the laws of the countries in which they operate. Laws concerning the import and export of goods vary greatly from one country to another. Things can get particularly complicated if a product is shipped to one country for assembly, another for packaging, and then yet another country for distribution. Often, several countries are involved in the manufacturing of one product, in which case the laws and regulations of all those countries must be adhered to. It might be necessary for a U.S. company to work with the governments of foreign countries if there are strict importing restrictions or a multitude of taxes. Safety regulations and quality control, copyright, and patent laws are some of the other laws multinational corporations must comply with when doing business in foreign countries.

Cultural differences related to business practices have as much impact as legal differences on international business. Some of these issues, which we'll discuss further in Chapter 4, include the following:

- Language barriers present challenges to businesses trying to establish themselves in foreign countries.
- Countries may have different business hours or workweek schedules. For example, in Spain, workers tend to take lunch from 1:30 to 3:30 P.M.
- Values and customs relating to business etiquette may vary. For example, timeliness is highly valued in Germany, but it is less important in Italy.
- Violating local taboos can be a concern, such as the preference for group harmony in many Asian countries.
- Multinational companies may have difficulty determining wages for foreign workers and pricing for international markets.

Multinational companies also must contend with many important economic differences among countries, such as the different levels of economic development, interest rates, and inflation rates that make international business more complicated than purely domestic business.

The move from being a regional business to a national or even a multinational business is an exciting one, but it also brings a new set of challenges. With operations in five states—New Jersey, Maryland, Pennsylvania, Delaware, and

Virginia—Wawa currently deals with issues that impact a regional company. However, recent attempts to expand into nearby states, such as Connecticut, have proved challenging. Wawa has had difficulty finding the right locations for its stores and duplicating its successful customer service and teamwork outside its regional base.[20] Instead of expanding toward being a national chain, Wawa has begun moving into gas retailing, creating superstores that combine the traditional Wawa convenience center with a gas station. Clearly, businesses must proceed carefully when making such decisions.

Taking Business Personally pp. 17–18

Taylor Evans is a very organized and orderly person. He prides himself on being efficient and meticulous with his schoolwork, finances, and social life. His friends joke with him about this and tell him that he runs his life like a business. But Taylor doesn't take offense; why shouldn't he run his life like a business? His life is just as complicated. He has revenue, expenses, and assets. He participates in commerce. Taylor even likes to keep up with the latest technology to make sure he runs his life most efficiently. He is always looking for cost-effective ways to operate his life, and any profits (or money he has left over after paying his bills) are set aside for future purchases. In many ways, his life *is* a business. Do you maintain your life like a well-run business? ■

Source: Rubberball/Getty Images, Inc.

Each of you probably has a different level of familiarity with the basics of business. Some of you may have witnessed the operations of a business firsthand while employed at a part-time job. For others, your business knowledge may be limited to what you've read in books or seen on television or in the movies. Regardless of your prior work experience and business knowledge, you all have experience running a business, and that business is your life. Similar to a small company, your life requires careful planning, precise record keeping, and openness to change. To help you understand some of the business concepts discussed in this book, let's look at how you run your "business."

How do you receive funding? Regardless of whether you have a job or not, you're receiving money from somewhere. It could be from work, a family member, a student loan, or your own savings. You need these funds to secure the necessities of your life. Similarly, all businesses need funds to operate. Ideally, a business would produce revenue right away. However, until they get established, many businesses operate on funds received from a bank loan, investors, or their owners' capital.

What are your expenses? Rent, clothing, food, tuition—these are expenses whether they are paid for with cash, credit, or a loan. Ultimately, you will want to generate enough revenue, or income, to cover your expenses and have leftover cash. The lives of some students operate a bit like a start-up business; you may have to pay for expenses with loans until you have enough experience to generate a profit.

How does the social environment affect your life? The social environment probably presents similar opportunities and challenges to you as it does to businesses. How do you deal with these opportunities and challenges? Are you open to learn from people who are different from you? Do you embrace diversity? How do you relate to people from an older generation? What about the green movement? Are you finding ways to make your lifestyle more eco-friendly? It is important to address these issues so you can live a more harmonious life and prepare yourself for the modern work environment.

How does globalization affect your life? Not only is the world getting smaller for businesses, but the world is also getting smaller for you. Your favorite music group may be a band from Germany. You might like to chat online about movies

Most e-commerce requires credit cards to complete transactions. How do you keep your online transactions secure? *Source:* LDProd/Thinkstock/Getty image.

with a friend from Japan. Just as businesses now have the opportunity to work with other firms from all over the world, you have the ability to make friends or connections on any continent. You purchase items that are designed and/or manufactured in other countries. As the forces of globalization continue, the chances of you working in a foreign country for part of your career continue to climb.

How do you keep up with new technology? Whether or not you consider yourself to be tech-savvy, chances are you still use some sort of technology to run your life. Perhaps you deposit your checks using the camera on your phone or settle a bet by paying your friend using Google Wallet. Similar to a business, if you don't keep up with new technology, you may find yourself in trouble.

What sort of e-commerce do you use? E-commerce is a popular form of purchasing goods. What sort of things do you buy online? There are many online clothing stores that let you design the products yourself, like the Sole Brother Custom Sneakers online store. Perhaps you even sell things over the Internet. Posting old clothing or other unwanted items on eBay might be your way of making a few extra dollars and gaining more room in your closet.

How do you keep your business secure? As businesses work to keep personal information secure, so also should customers. You can help keep your information secure by changing your online passwords on a regular basis, making sure your wireless connections are secure, switching to paperless mail, and removing personal information, such as phone numbers or addresses, from your Facebook account or other social networking sites. Keeping your personal information secure can help you avoid identity theft or other dangerous blows to your financial health.

What types of financial goals do you have? The goals of a business typically revolve around achieving financial success. You, too, might have certain financial goals that you would like to achieve in your life. To reach these goals, you'll need to make informed decisions about how you spend and save your money. Mini Chapter 5 (see p. 508) can help you manage your personal finances and plan for the future.

So when Taylor's friends say he runs his life like a business, maybe that is a compliment! Many of the same concepts and strategies used to run a business can be used to monitor your day-to-day activities. As you learn new business concepts in upcoming chapters, you may find them easier to understand by applying them to your own life. However, not everything in the business world parallels your own life. The business world has its own unique issues and strategies that may not work for your personal life. Think about the material presented in this course carefully both as a consumer of business goods and services and as a future business leader.

Summary

1 What is profit, and what is the difference between a good and a service? (pp. 3–4)

- **Profits** (p. 3) are earned when a company's **revenue** (p. 3) exceeds its **expenses** (p. 3).
- **Goods** (p. 3) are the physical products offered by a business. **Services** (p. 3) are intangible products, such as a haircut, health care, or car insurance.

2 How do for-profit businesses and not-for-profit organizations compare? (pp. 3–4)

- A **business** (p. 3) is an entity that offers goods and services to its customers to earn a profit. A **not-for-profit organization** (p. 4) is an organization that does not pursue profits but instead seeks to service its community through social, educational, or political means.

3 What are the factors of production? (pp. 4–5)

- The **factors of production** (p. 4) are the resources used to create goods and services. The factors of production include **labor** (p. 4), **natural resources** (p. 4), **capital** (p. 4), **intellectual property** (p. 5), **entrepreneurial talent** (p. 5), and **technology** (p. 5).

4 How do competition, the social environment, globalization, and technological changes challenge and provide opportunities to business owners? (pp. 6–13)

- **Competition** (p. 6) arises when two or more businesses vie to attract customers and gain an advantage over one another. Competition forces companies to improve their product offerings, lower their prices, aggressively promote their brand, and focus on customer satisfaction.
- **Social environment** (p. 8) encompasses demographic factors, such as race, ethnicity, gender, age, income distribution, sexual orientation, and other characteristics. An aging population, increasing diversity, and the green movement both challenge and pose opportunities to business owners.

- **Globalization** (p. 10) involves the merging of economies around the world as technology, goods and services, labor, and capital move back and forth across international borders. Although globalization provides profitable opportunities, such as increased markets and offshoring, it also leads to greater competition for U.S. businesses and workers.
- **Technology** (p. 11) items and services such as smart phones, computer software, and the Internet make businesses more efficient and productive. E-commerce is well established and still growing, offering even small firms a chance to sell to a global market. At the same time, keeping up with the pace of technology is an expensive and time-consuming operation for many businesses.

5 What are the four types of businesses? (pp. 14–17)

- A **local business** (p. 14) relies on local consumers to generate business.
- **Regional businesses** (p. 14) are companies that serve a wider area than local businesses but do not serve national or international markets.
- A **national business** (p. 15) has several outlets throughout the country, but it does not serve an international market. It provides goods or services to all U.S. residents, no matter where in the country they live.
- **Multinational enterprises** (p. 16), also known as multinational companies or corporations, multinational businesses, or international businesses, are companies that have operations in more than one country. They are among the leaders of a movement called globalization.

6 How do life skills translate to the business environment? (pp. 17–18)

- You have income, expenses, and profits.
- You are affected by globalization and technology.
- You have concerns with security.

Key Terms

businesses (p. 3)
competition (p. 6)
e-commerce (p. 12)
entrepreneur (p. 4)
expenses (p. 3)

factors of production (p. 4)
financial capital (p. 4)
globalization (p. 10)
goods (p. 3)
green economy (p. 9)

identity theft (p. 13)
intellectual property (p. 5)
labor (p. 4)
local business (p. 14)
multinational enterprise (p. 10)

Key Terms *(continued)*

national business (p. 15)

natural resources (p. 4)

not-for-profit organization (p. 4)

offshoring (p. 10)

profit (p. 3)

real capital (p. 4)

regional business (p. 14)

revenue (p. 3)

service (p. 3)

social environment (p. 8)

social networking sites (p. 7)

supply chain (p. 15)

technology (p. 5)

telecommute (p. 12)

undercapitalization (p. 14)

MyBizLab

Go to **mybizlab.com** to complete the problems marked with this icon .

Self Test

Multiple Choice *You can find the answers on the last page of this book.*

1-1 **Which of the following are the factors of production?**

a. Labor, natural resources, capital, entrepreneurs, technology, and intellectual property

b. Labor, capital, entrepreneurs, motivation, and good ideas

c. Natural resources, entrepreneurs, profits, and creativity

d. Labor, profits, natural resources, technology, and motivation

1-2 **Goods are products a business sells like**

a. haircuts.

b. conveyer belts.

c. car insurance.

d. health care.

1-3 **Which of the following is a current sociocultural trend?**

a. A decrease in the overall U.S. population

b. An increase in the population of Americans ages 30 to 45 years old

c. A decrease in the U.S. minority population

d. An increase in the population of Americans ages 65 and over

1-4 **Social networking makes it possible for**

a. companies to better manage their employees.

b. customers to spread the word about great products.

c. companies to keep network information secure.

d. social gatherings to be monitored.

1-5 **If a firm decides to shift the production of goods or services to an overseas company, this firm is**

a. diversifying.

b. offshoring.

c. telecommuting.

d. forming a partnership.

1-6 **The four types of businesses are**

a. foreign and domestic, large and small.

b. local, regional, national, and multinational.

c. private, public, government, and medical.

d. employee owned, government owned, foreign owned, and bank owned.

1-7 **B2B and B2C interactions are**

a. common now because of the explosive growth of e-commerce.

b. important only for businesses, not consumers.

c. two different names for the same thing.

d. dominated by sole proprietorships.

1-8 **To avoid debt, a new business owner should have enough projected revenue to cover expenses for the first**

a. six months.

b. year.

c. two years.

d. five years.

1-9 **Which of the following is NOT a common challenge facing most national companies?**

a. Undercapitalization

b. A complex supply chain

c. Complying with each state's different tax rates

d. Differences in state laws

1-10 **You are managing your own life like a business when you**

a. consider how your expenses, the social environment, and globalization impact your life.

b. create an online avatar.

c. post revealing photos on your Facebook page.

d. None of the above

True/False *You can find the answers on the last page of this book.*

1-11 Businesses are entities that offer goods and services to earn a profit.
☐ True or ☐ False

1-12 Identity theft is mainly a problem for senior citizens.
☐ True or ☐ False

1-13 The supply chain is the process by which products, information, and money move between a supplier and the consumer.
☐ True or ☐ False

1-14 Globalization poses risks to the U.S. economy because of security and patent protection concerns.
☐ True or ☐ False

1-15 A not-for-profit organization uses any revenue to reward the management team.
☐ True or ☐ False

Critical Thinking Questions

✪1-16 Consider all the factors of production: labor, natural resources, capital, entrepreneurs, technology, and knowledge. Is each resource a vital part of the school you attend or the company for which you work? Which factors do you believe are most important to the goods and services provided by your organization?

✪1-17 It is increasingly important for businesses to have green practices—reducing their carbon footprint, offering green options for consumers, and so on. What examples can you think of where a company's marketing campaign has highlighted its concern for the environment? What might the costs to a company be for going green? What consequences might a company face if it does not?

✪1-18 Many businesses now both maintain an online presence and have physical stores. Select a few specific companies and research the options for delivering product to customers. In what way does the online store compete with the physical store? How do the two storefronts support each other?

Team Time

THE COMPETITIVE EDGE

You now know that competition arises when two or more businesses contend to attract consumers and gain an advantage over one another. Divide into three groups: Company A, Company B, and Consumers.

Process

Step 1. **Companies A and B.** Collectively decide what type of business you want to represent, for example, sports apparel companies, beauty salons, or pet care agencies. Then choose a product or service applicable to that type of business. (Both groups should choose the same type of business and product or service.)

Step 2. **Companies A and B.** Decide how you will present your product to your customers. Focus on the following factors:

- Packaging/presentation
- Price/budget
- Quality

Consumers. Compile a list of what is important to you when choosing this product or service.

Step 3. **Companies A and B.** Provide a brief presentation to your competition and consumers.

Consumers. Provide in-depth feedback to both companies as to how they could improve; consider your initial list.

Team Time (continued)

Step 4.   **Companies A and B.** Use the consumer feedback to alter your product or service to gain advantage over your competition.

Consumers. Discuss how the two companies compare to real-life companies offering similar products or services. Would you consider purchasing from either of these two companies? Why or why not?

Step 5.   **Companies A and B.** Present your product again. Explain why your product or service surpasses that of your competition.

Consumers. Discuss the changes made by both companies and consider how they accommodated your needs. Did each company effectively incorporate your feedback into its revised presentation? Choose one company that you think gained the competitive advantage.

Entire Class. Openly discuss the factors real companies must face in competition. Were these factors considered in the challenge?

Ethics and Corporate Social Responsibility

CULTURAL AWARENESS: UNWRITTEN LAWS

There are many challenges facing multinational companies. Complete the following exercise to experience one challenge.

Process

Step 1.   Divide into six groups, each representing one of the following countries: Hong Kong, France, Egypt, Japan, Mexico, and the United States. Examine the cultural practices, customs, and values of the country you will represent. This may be done in class, if you have Internet access, or as homework.

Step 2.   Each group should pair together with a second group as follows: United States with Japan, Mexico with Egypt, and Hong Kong with France.

Step 3.   Each group should produce one scenario of a business transaction that would be affected by cultural differences found in your research. Fabricate specific companies, characters, interactions, and resolutions.

Step 4.   Answer these questions and discuss with the class:

- What were some challenges encountered in your business scenario, and how did you overcome them?
- Why is it important for multinational companies to research a foreign country with which they intend to conduct business?

Web Exercises

1-19   Are You Savvy to Society?
Imagine you are starting a new business. To what demographic area would you market? Think about the following factors: the race, ethnicity, gender, age, income, and sexual orientation of the population. Visit www.census.gov to locate reports on the demographic area you are interested in. Do you believe your business can thrive in this area? If not, what area would be conducive to your future customers?

1-20   The Languages of the Global Marketplace
As globalization increases and the world markets become more intertwined, language barriers become important. Investigate online resources for automated translation tools. How could you add a website translator gadget to your Web page? What happens if you want to read a web page posted by a German firm? Can you make online purchases from a company based in Asia? What resources are there for translating telephone

conversations in real time? Investigate Babelfish.com and personal interpreter services like LanguageLine .com.

1-21 Business Technology On-the-Go
Mobile devices are evolving quickly and are setting the style of advertising and marketing. From www.exacttarget.com, select Resources then Downloads. Find the current Mobile Behavior report.

1-22 Nonprofit Business Is Still Business
What tools are available to help evaluate the performance of a nonprofit business? Visit CharityNavigator .org. Examine three different nonprofit organizations and compare their performance, suggesting specific issues that concern you or that impress you.

1-23 Comparing Companies
Consider two national companies discussed in this chapter—Allstate and CVS/pharmacy. In what states is each based? Go to www.sba.gov to research the laws applicable in the states in which these companies are based. How do the workers' compensation and tax laws differ for each company? Which company do you think was more difficult to establish based on state laws?

MyBizLab

Go to **mybizlab.com** for Auto-graded writing questions as well as the following Assisted-graded writing questions:

1-24 Most business owners agree that keeping up with the pace of technological change is a challenging task. Imagine you are the owner of a new business and must decide what technology would best suit your needs. From what types of technology would this business benefit? Consider the factors of production, organization, and communication in your decision.

1-25 Select a regional or local business in your area. Do you think the company would be successful in a national setting? As a multinational? Are there barriers keeping the company confined to a specific region?

References

1. Pinterest, 2013, https://about.pinterest.com/press.
2. D. Fenn, "Meet the 30 under 30, Class of 2013," May 28, 2013, www.inc.com/ss/donna-fenn/30-under-30-meet-the-winners-2013.
3. Nantucket Allserve, Inc., "Nantucket Nectars from the Beginning," www.nantucketnectars.com/fullstory.php? PHPSESSID=996c6c936ce6351082022525b73e9fce.
4. Joe Wilcox, "Microsoft, Apple Alliance at Key Juncture," February 22, 2002, http://news.cnet.com/2100-1040-843145.html.
5. J. Meyer, U.S. Department of Commerce, U.S. Census Bureau, *Centenarians: 2010 Census Special Report* (C2010SR-03), 2012, www.census.gov/prod/cen2010/reports/c2010sr-03.pdf.
6. Four Seasons Hotels, 2014, http://money.cnn.com/magazines/fortune/best-companies/2014/snapshots/91.html.
7. "Obama Administration Finalizes Historic 54.5 MPG Fuel Efficiency Standards," August 28, 2012, www.whitehouse .gov/the-press-office/2012/08/28/obama-administration-finalizes-historic-545-mpg-fuel-efficiency-standard.
8. FedEx, "About Us," http://about.fedex.designcdt.com/our_company/company_information.
9. "Client Question: How Long Is My Computer Technology Really Supposed to Last?," July 19, 2013, www.intechit.net/client-question-how-long-is-my-computer-technology-really-supposed-to-last.
10. R. van der Meulen, "Gartner Says Organizations Must Focus on Continuous IT Cost Optimization," August 20, 2013, www.gartner.com/newsroom/id/2576517.
11. J. Rizzo, "Navigant Research Predicts That by 2020 We Will See Twice as Many Global Utility Mobile Workers," January 6, 2014, www.mobilitytechzone.com/topics/4g-wirelessevolution/articles/2014/01/06/365518-navigant-research-predicts-that-2020-we-will-see.htm.
12. Jack Neff, "Beyond Online Ads: P&G Sets $4 Bil E-Commerce Goal," *Advertising Age* 80, no. 29: 3–25.
13. E. Harrell and L. Langton, U.S. Department of Justice, Bureau of Justice Statistics, *Victims of Identity Theft, 2012* (NCJ 243779), 2013, www.bjs.gov/content/pub/pdf/vit12.pdf.
14. Pamela Lewis Dolan, "Amednews: Medical Identity Theft a Growing Problem," *American Medical News*, October 17, 2011, www.ama-assn.org/amednews/2011/10/17/bisa1017.htm.
15. "The Wawa Facts," March 7, 2014, http://s3.amazonaws .com/Wawa.com/WawaFactSheet.pdf.
16. CVS Caremark, "History," http://info.cvscaremark.com/our-company/history.
17. Rhode Island Department of Labor and Training, "Temporary Disability Insurance," www.dlt.ri.gov/tdi.
18. McDonald's, "About Us," www.mcdonalds.ca/en/aboutus/faq.aspx.
19. J. Wood, "8 Strange Foods Served at McDonalds around the World," November 21, 2013, www.huffingtonpost.com/conde-nast-traveler/8-strange-foods-served-at_b_4316314.html.
20. Robert Wolcott, Kellogg School of Management, "Building a Business within Wawa," http://hbr.org/product/wawa-building-a-new-business-within-an-established/an/KEL240-PDF-ENG.

Chapter 2
Economics and Banking

▶ The Basics of Economics

Why does water cost less than diamonds? It's a matter of supply and demand—a problem that Bryan Weirmoyer faces every day as a sales executive for a real estate development company. How can businesses use basic economic concepts to their advantage?

▶ Determining Price: Supply and Demand

For many business owners, weathering shifts in supply and demand is like playing tug of war. The levels of supply and demand for a given good or service shift constantly, each influenced by a variety of factors. Consider the example of a kiosk owner selling coffee on a college campus. Ideally, the owner wants to sell the coffee at a price most students are willing to pay without anyone wanting more, or without any being left over. What factors play into this decision?

▶ Degrees of Competition

Perhaps you've played the board game Monopoly. Once you own all the property of the same color in the game, you have a monopoly and control all that happens on that property. Although that's the goal of the board game, large monopolies are rarely allowed in the United States. What is a monopoly? Why are there laws against it? And how does it differ from an oligopoly, monopolistic competition, and perfect competition?

▶ Economic Indicators

Greg Johnson is managing the inventory of a large automobile dealership. Before the Great Recession, ordering inventory was simple because the demand for new cars seemed relatively constant. These days, Greg's not sure about his company's direction. The economy seems to be improving, but is it really? Are there economic measurements he can use to help him make his decision?

▶ Government and the Economy

Nick and Jacinta Robertson are looking to buy their first home. What information do they need before getting a mortgage? Can government actions have an effect on what Nick and Jacinta do?

OBJECTIVES

1 What is economics, and what are the different types of economic systems? (pp. 25–28)

2 What are the principles of supply and demand and the factors that affect each principle? (pp. 28–35)

3 What are the various degrees of competition? (pp. 35–38)

4 How do economic indicators—particularly the gross domestic product (GDP), price indices, the unemployment rate, and productivity—reflect the health of an economy? (pp. 38–42)

5 What are the four stages of the business cycle? (pp. 42–43)

6 How does the government use both fiscal policy and monetary policy to control swings in the business cycle? (pp. 43–47)

MyBizLab®

⭐ Improve Your Grade!

Over 10 million students improved their results using the Pearson MyLabs.
Visit **mybizlab.com** for simulations, tutorials, and end-of-chapter problems.

The Basics of Economics pp. 25–28

It was the third phone call this week, and Bryan Weirmoyer knew it wouldn't be the last. Bryan is the sales executive for a residential and commercial real estate developer in Oregon. A couple of years ago, he enjoyed taking phone calls that generally ended by closing contracts for the construction of new homes. But now, the phone doesn't ring much, and when it does, it's generally a call to cancel contracts Bryan had worked hard to negotiate. Why were there so many sales a couple years ago and so few now? ■

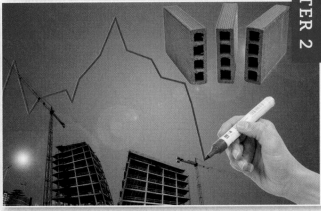

Source: Sergio Martínez/Fotolia.

Bryan's dilemma of diminishing sales is due to the economic concept of supply and demand. Have you ever wondered why water, a basic commodity that is critical to life, is priced so low, and diamonds, which aren't necessities, are expensive? This paradoxical situation illustrates a fundamental concept of economics—*supply and demand*. Supply and demand determine how goods are priced and how much of them are exchanged. The exchange of products and services between people, companies, and even countries is the very root of economics. In this chapter, we'll examine the laws of supply and demand, discuss economic indicators, and look at how government actions affect the economy. First, let's begin with a discussion of some basic economics concepts.

Economics Defined

So what is economics? **Economics** is the study of how individuals and businesses make decisions to best satisfy wants, needs, and desires with limited resources. It is about businesses making *goods* (such as books, pizza, or computers) or supplying *services* (such as giving haircuts, painting houses, or installing home entertainment centers) that we want or need to buy.

Because businesses don't have enough tools, money, or products to provide *all* the books, pizza, or haircuts that we want, they must decide what and how much to make. Likewise, not everyone will be able to have what he or she wants because people's resources are limited. Therefore, economists look at how resources are distributed in the marketplace and how equitably and efficiently those resources are disbursed. There are two basic studies of economics: *microeconomics* and *macroeconomics*.

MICROECONOMICS **Microeconomics** is the study of how individual businesses, households, and consumers make decisions to allocate their limited resources in the exchange of goods and services. When Bryan Weirmoyer tries to determine how a change in prices may help generate sales or analyzes the number of existing houses that are already for sale in the local market, he is using the microeconomic principles of supply and demand.

MACROECONOMICS Macroeconomics looks at the bigger picture. **Macroeconomics** is the study of the behavior of the overall economy. Economy-wide occurrences, such as changes in unemployment, interest rates, inflation, and price levels, are all part of the study of macroeconomics. Macroeconomists, for example, look at how changes in interest rates affect the demand for housing or how changes in the housing market affect the overall economy. The government and individuals in a society also affect how resources are allocated and the type of economic system the society utilizes.

Economic Systems

What are the types of economic systems? An **economy** is a system that tries to balance the available resources of a country, such as land, capital, and labor, against the wants and needs of consumers. An economy is defined by (1) what is produced, (2) how it is produced, and (3) who gets the finished product. The world's various economies can be classified into three basic economic systems:

- Planned (or controlled) economies
- Free market economies
- Mixed economies

■ **TABLE 2.1** explains the differences between these basic types of economic systems. Planned and free market economies lie at opposite ends of the spectrum in terms of government control. Keep in mind that no economy is purely "free market" and that no economy is purely "planned;" that economies exhibit elements of both. In other words, they are mixed economies.

Planned Economic Systems

In a **planned economic system**, the government plays a significant role in determining the goods and services produced and distributed. Communism and socialism are examples of planned economic systems.

Communism is an economic system in which a state's government makes all economic decisions and controls all the social services as well as many of the major resources required for the production of goods and services. Karl Marx, the originator of communist principles, envisioned in his landmark book *The Communist Manifesto* that workers themselves would eventually take over the government's responsibilities to provide services. No country operating in a communist system

TABLE 2.1	Types of Economic Systems around the World		
Type	**What to Produce**	**How to Produce**	**For Whom to Produce**
Planned (Controlled): • Communism • Socialism	The government or other centralized group completely or partially determines what to produce.	The government or other centralized group completely or partially determines and controls the resources and means of production.	The government or other centralized group completely or partially determines wages and sets prices. Resources and products are distributed to the common group.
Market: • Capitalism	Individuals and businesses make decisions based on consumer needs and wants.	Individuals and businesses determine the production methods. The focus is on efficiency and profitability.	Individual income ultimately controls purchasing decisions.
Mixed	A blend of planned and market economies. Individuals and businesses determine what to produce, along with some level of government involvement.	Individuals, businesses, and the government control resources and determine production methods.	The government distributes some goods and services through selected social programs. Individual income determines purchasing decisions for other goods and services.

has achieved this level of Marx's vision. Existing communist states, including North Korea and Cuba, are failing economically. This is a result of problems that have arisen with communist systems, such as shortages of goods and services. In fact, in the later years of the twentieth century, most former Soviet republic states and Eastern European countries turned from communism-based economies to market economies to combat these problems.

Socialism is a system whereby the government owns or controls many basic businesses and services and the profits from them are distributed evenly among the people. In socialist economic systems, governments traditionally run some of the social services, such as education, health care, retirement, and unemployment, as well as other necessary businesses, such as utility companies (telephone, electric, water, and sewer companies). The government charges high tax rates to pay for the services it provides. For example, the economies of the Scandinavian countries of Norway, Sweden, Finland, and Denmark are more characterized by socialism than the United States is. Scandinavian countries have some of the highest tax rates in the world: Average tax rates are between 52 and 58 percent. By contrast, in the United States, the average tax rate is 15.3 percent.[1]

Although Scandinavians pay higher tax rates, they benefit from social programs that the taxes fund. For example, education at even the best universities in Denmark is free. Not surprisingly, Denmark has an 84 percent literacy rate as a result.[2] Although paying high taxes may seem unappealing, recent studies have indicated that Scandinavians rank among the most satisfied people in the world.[3]

Although government-controlled and -supplied social services likes those associated with communism and socialism can lead to resources being equitably distributed among a nation's citizens, these economic systems have a downside: They tend to reduce people's motivation to work as hard as they might otherwise. Why work harder when you will receive as many goods and services as your neighbor who doesn't? Or why work a lot of overtime if you have to give half of your overtime pay to the government in the form of taxes? Therefore, it is difficult to find purely socialist economies. For this reason, numerous formerly socialist and communist countries have changed their economies into free market economies through the practice of **privatization**—the conversion of government-owned production and services to privately owned, profit-seeking enterprises.

Market Economies

In a **market economy** like we have in the United States, individuals are more able to make their own economic decisions. For example, there may be several pizza parlors in your town, and each one may sell slices of pizza at different prices. No one is restricting the number of pizza parlors, and no one is controlling what prices they can charge. Similarly, you are free to buy any pizza you'd like. This freedom of choice for both the buyer and the seller defines a free market economy.

Capitalism is an economic system that allows freedom of choice and encourages private ownership of the resources required to make and provide the goods and the services we enjoy. Capitalism has become a major influence in the Western world's economic systems. In a capitalist economy, the production and pricing of goods and services is determined through the operation of a **market**—the mechanism by which buyers and sellers exchange goods and services.

Mixed Economies

As we have explained, today, most economic systems are **mixed economies**— a blend of market and planned economies. One way to think about the various economies and how they relate to each other is to place them on a continuum, as shown in ■ **FIGURE 2.1**.

■ **FIGURE 2.1**
Continuum of Economic Systems:
Degree of Government Control

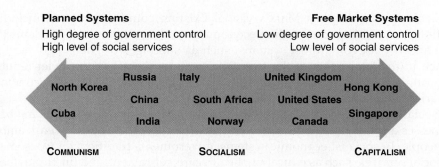

Planned Systems	Free Market Systems
High degree of government control	Low degree of government control
High level of social services	Low level of social services

North Korea, Russia, Italy, United Kingdom, Hong Kong, China, South Africa, United States, Cuba, India, Norway, Canada, Singapore

COMMUNISM — SOCIALISM — CAPITALISM

Most Western European countries, for example, operate with a mixed economy of privately owned businesses and government control of selected social programs, such as health care. The United States has been more of a capitalist economy than its European counterparts, but recently with the passage of the Affordable Care Act, a U.S. health care law passed in early 2010, the United States economic system has shifted.

Business and Economics

Why do business managers need to be concerned with economics? Business managers and owners need to understand the principles of economics because the very nature of business is to provide items or services for purchase in exchange for something, generally money. Businesses need to know how much of their goods to produce or services to offer as well as how much to charge for these goods and services. Additionally, business managers need to be aware of the potential impact that government decisions (such as changing interest rates) and the decisions of collective businesses (such as the general level of unemployment) can have on their individual business or industry. We will discuss how economics impacts business throughout this chapter.

One dilemma Bryan Weirmoyer faces as the need for new housing dwindles is whether he'll have customers to build houses for. His decisions affect other areas of the business, such as land acquisitions, inventory purchases, and staffing. Bryan watches the movement of interest rates carefully because he knows that even the smallest change in interest rates will affect whether homebuyers are more or less inclined to take out mortgages, which will affect Bryan's sales.

Source: revelpix/Fotolia.

Determining Price: Supply and Demand pp. 28–35

Eddie Walker finally received the approvals he needed to open a coffee kiosk on his college's campus. He knew there would be demand, as he had seen how coffee stores on other campuses seemed to make a killing—how hard could this be? He wasn't sure how much to charge for a cup of coffee but felt that the need was so great that students would be willing to buy coffee at almost any price! Was Eddie right? Would students buy coffee at any price? What is the relationship between supply, demand, and prices? ■

In the days of bartering, when people traded goods or services without an exchange of money, the price of something was determined by the needs of each person in the bartering exchange and what they were willing to trade. For example, suppose you wanted milk but had no cow. Instead, you had chickens, and you were willing to exchange eggs for milk. Then you would look for someone who wanted to trade his or her milk for your eggs. At the end of the trade, everyone was happy because you received the milk you needed and the other person received the eggs he or she needed.

However, there are problems with this exchange system. Bartering can be inefficient and inconsistent. What if the person who had the cow didn't need eggs, or what if the cow owner thought his milk was worth a chicken but the egg owner thought it was worth only a dozen eggs? To offset some of the difficulties of bartering, the concept of currency, or money, was developed. **Currency**, a unit of exchange for the transfer of goods and services, provides a consistent standard. Initially, the value of the standard was based on an underlying commodity, such as gold. Today, the U.S. currency isn't based on gold but rather on a perceived value of its worth.

Currency developed as a means to make the exchange of goods and services more consistent and equitable. *Source:* Brad Pict/Fotolia.

In a system using currency, items such as milk, eggs, cows, and chickens are assigned a price, or a value, based on how much the item was worth. Although we do have currency, ultimately the price for a good or service is determined by two fundamental concepts of economics: supply and demand.

Supply and demand is actually a very complicated process because many factors are involved, such as income levels and tastes, as well as the amount of competition in the market. However, to simplify things, economists ignore those factors for the moment (they call it "all else held constant") and examine the fundamentals only. When just the fundamentals are examined, we find that the **market price** for a good or a service is the price at which everyone who wants the item can get it—without wanting more or without any of the items being left over. When the need and availability for an item are in balance, the price is in equilibrium. The need or want for an item is *demand*, and the availability of that item is *supply*.

The closest real-world example of determining a market price that is based on pure supply and demand is the auction process, like that found on eBay. In an auction process, bidders state the price they are willing to pay for a particular item. The price increases depending on the demand: The greater the demand, the higher the price the bidders are willing to pay. Supply also affects price: If similar or identical items are available for auction, the supply of those items increases, and so the price for them overall is lower. By contrast, when a unique item is auctioned, prices tend to be higher because demand is higher and supply is lower. Eventually, the winning bid establishes the market price.

Supply

What is supply? **Supply** refers to how much of a good or a service is available for purchase at any given time. Supply is dependent on the resources that are required to produce the good or offer the service, such as land, labor, and capital (buildings and machinery), and the quantity of similar products that can easily be substituted for the product and that are competing for a customer's attention. However, if all these factors are ignored or held constant, then supply is directly affected by price.

Supply is derived from a producer's desire to maximize profits. The more money a business can get for its good or service, the more of its product it is willing to supply. In economic terms, the amount supplied will increase as the price increases; also, if the price is lower, less of the product will be supplied. This is known as the **law of supply**.

Let's look at an example. Eddie opens a coffee kiosk in the middle of his college campus. He will want to supply more cups of coffee at $2.00 per cup than at $0.50 per cup. The reason for this is obvious: Eddie has a greater incentive to supply more cups of coffee if he can sell them at $2.00 each rather than at $0.50 each

TABLE 2.2

The Relationship between Price and Supply

Price ($)	Coffee Supplied (cups)
0.50	10
0.75	30
1.00	50
1.25	70
1.50	85
1.75	100
2.00	115

TABLE 2.3

The Relationship between Price and Demand

Price ($)	Coffee Demand (cups)
0.50	120
0.75	95
1.00	72
1.25	55
1.50	38
1.75	23
2.00	12

because he'll generate more profit at the higher price. Notice in ■ **TABLE 2.2** that Eddie wants to supply only 10 cups of coffee at $0.50 per cup. However, if Eddie can charge $1.25, Eddie will supply 70 cups of coffee because he has a greater incentive to supply more cups than at the lower price. Finally, at the price of $2.00, Eddie's incentive to supply coffee is at its greatest. At that highest price, Eddie wants to supply 115 cups. We can illustrate this relationship between supply and price in a graph that economists call a **supply curve**, like the one shown in ■ **FIGURE 2.2**. You can see that Eddie's desire to supply, or sell, more cups of coffee is affected by price. The more he can charge, the more he wants to supply. However, as you can imagine, the demand for coffee has a very different reaction to price.

Demand

What is demand? Demand refers to how much of a good or a service people want to buy at any given time. People are willing to buy as much as they need, but they have limited resources (money). Therefore, people will buy more of an item at a lower price than at a higher price. In our coffee example, as shown in ■ **TABLE 2.3**, students buy only 12 cups of coffee when Eddie charges $2.00 a cup. When he reduces the price to $1.25, there is more demand with 55 cups being purchased. But the most demand is generated when the price is lowered to $0.50 a cup, and 120 cups are sold. In other words, as price decreases, demand increases. Again, economists illustrate the relationship between demand and price with a graph that they call a **demand curve**, as shown in ■ **FIGURE 2.3**.

Factors That Determine Price

What factors determine price? As you've seen with Eddie's coffee kiosk, there is an obvious conflict when setting a market price. Notice that Eddie wanted to supply coffee at a higher price but that he didn't attract many customers by doing so. Customers were more willing to pay for coffee as the price dropped. As the price of a product increases, more of it is likely to be supplied. As the price of the product decreases, more of it is likely to be demanded by customers. Because these two concepts of pricing are at odds with each other, what determines the final price? Holding all other factors constant, prices are set at a point where supply equals demand.

The supply-and-demand relationship is one of the fundamental concepts of economics. At Eddie's coffee kiosk, for example, at some point, supply and demand balance each other out. Although Eddie would love to sell coffee at $2.00 a cup (or even more), he realizes that not too many students are willing to buy coffee at that price. At $2.00 a cup, Eddie would not completely use up his entire supply, and he would end up with unsold product left over, creating a **surplus**. As Eddie begins to lower his price, he finds that more students are willing to buy his coffee. However, if Eddie lowers his price too much, to $0.50 a cup, for example, then the demand would be so great that Eddie would run out before he was able to satisfy all the students who wanted coffee, creating a **shortage**.

Ideally, Eddie would strive to determine a price at which he is willing to supply the coffee and at which students are willing to buy (demand) the coffee without anyone wanting more or without any coffee being left over. A surplus usually means that suppliers will lower prices to clear out inventory, while a shortage means suppliers will raise prices to take advantage of the higher demand. In both cases, the price will converge toward the *market price*, which, as noted earlier, is the price at which supply equals demand. The market price (or **equilibrium price**) is illustrated in a supply-and-demand curve, as shown in ■ **FIGURE 2.4**. In this case, 60 cups of coffee is equally demanded and supplied at a price of $1.15.

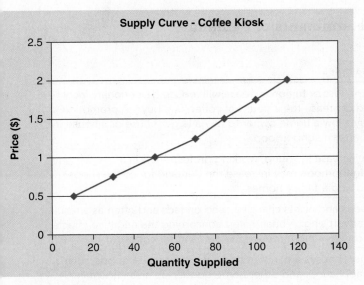

■ FIGURE 2.2
The Supply Curve
The supply curve illustrates the incentive to supply more of an item as prices increase.

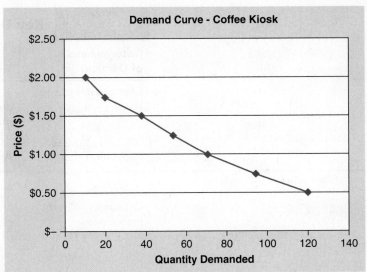

■ FIGURE 2.3
The Demand Curve
The demand curve illustrates that demand increases as prices decrease.

In a perfect world, this is how pricing for products would be set. But we don't live in a perfect world. Other factors that make us want more or less of a product outside of price can affect demand. There are also factors that affect our willingness or ability to provide a product, which can affect supply. We'll look at those factors next.

Factors That Affect Demand

What other factors besides price affect demand? Not too long after Eddie figured out the "perfect price" for a cup of coffee, he receives news that the college's bookstore will begin to offer coffee, too. In addition, the college announces a tuition increase. How do these events affect the student's willingness to buy coffee from Eddie? Will the new competition and higher student costs decrease demand for Eddie's coffee?

There are many factors that affect the demand for a product besides its price. These factors, known as the **determinants of demand**, are as follows:

- Changes in income levels
- Population changes
- Consumer preferences
- Complementary goods
- Substitute goods

A positive change in any of these determinants of demand shifts the demand curve to the right, and negative changes shift the demand curve to the left. **■ TABLE 2.4** summarizes the key determinants of demand. Let's look at each in more detail.

CHANGES IN INCOME LEVELS When income levels increase, people are able to buy more products. Conversely, when income levels decrease, most people

■ FIGURE 2.4
The Market Price
The market price is determined at the point where supply equals demand.

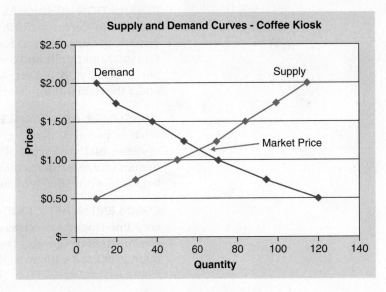

TABLE 2.4	Key Determinants of Demand
Determinants of Demand	**Examples**
Changes in income levels	A job loss or tuition increase will reduce discretionary income and decrease the amount of coffee one buys. A promotion may allow a home owner to buy a larger house or a house in a better neighborhood.
Population changes	An increase in young, working professionals in a neighborhood may increase the demand for coffee shops and single-family homes.
Consumer preferences	Needs and wants change based on fads and often as a result of advertising. A health alert concerning the negative effects of caffeine might reduce the demand for coffee.
Complementary goods	If new houses are in demand, complementary goods, such as appliances and other home goods, are also in demand. A reduction in new housing would negatively affect these complementary industries. If donuts or other food products are offered along with the coffee, the demand for coffee may increase.
Substitute goods	Products or services that can be used in place of another. A purchase of a treadmill may substitute for a gym membership, or you could use Google Chrome as a Web browser instead of Internet Explorer or Firefox. The bookstore offering coffee could shift the demand curve for Eddie's coffee to the left.

cut back on spending and buy fewer products. Therefore, as we'll discuss later in this chapter, when the economy enters a recession and people begin to lose their jobs, the demand for some goods and services decreases. An improving economy will bring an increase in spending as more people find jobs and create an increase in demand for some goods and services. A change in income levels is one factor that affects the housing market, for example. With an increase in income, people can afford to buy a home for the first time or can afford to upgrade to a bigger, more expensive home if they already own a home. On the other hand, if people begin to lose their jobs, they may need to downsize into a smaller home and sell their more expensive home.

POPULATION CHANGES Businesses in resort communities experience an increase in demand during the "in" or "high" season. Increases in population create a greater demand for utilities (such as telephone, electric, sewer, and water services) and public and consumer services (such as restaurants, banks, drugstores, and grocery stores). Demographic changes, such as the aging baby boomers, also affect the demand for certain goods and services.

CONSUMER PREFERENCES The demand for a product can change based on what is popular at any given moment. Tickle Me Elmo dolls, Xbox One game systems, and the Apple iPad are all products that had high initial demand. As demand for these items increases, the demand curve shifts to the right. As demand begins to wane, the demand curve shifts to the left.

COMPLEMENTARY GOODS Products or services that go with each other and are consumed together, such as the iPhone and the apps associated with it, are considered **complementary goods**. The demand for apps is great as long as consumers are buying and using iPhones. When the Android-based phones emerged on the market, the demand for iPhones and apps in the Apple store decreased, shifting the demand curve for iPhone apps to the left. When the new iPad came out, the demand to download content from iTunes and the Apple store increased, shifting the demand curve for the online site to the right.

SUBSTITUTE GOODS Goods that can be used in place of other goods, such as Coke for Pepsi or McDonald's Quarter Pounder for Burger King's Whopper, are **substitute goods**. Suppose, for example, someone reported getting violently ill after eating a McDonald's Quarter Pounder. The demand for the McDonald's Quarter Pounder will decrease, shifting that demand curve to the left, while the demand for the Burger King Whopper might increase, shifting the Whopper's demand curve to the right.

In our example, a tuition increase may mean that students have less money to spend on items such as coffee, so Eddie may see his demand decrease. Additionally, the bookstore offering coffee might also decrease Eddie's demand, as ■ **FIGURE 2.5** shows. Eddie should also expect a temporary decrease in demand during the summer and holidays when fewer students are on campus. However, if Eddie begins to offer complementary items, such as breakfast and lunch foods, he may see an increase in demand.

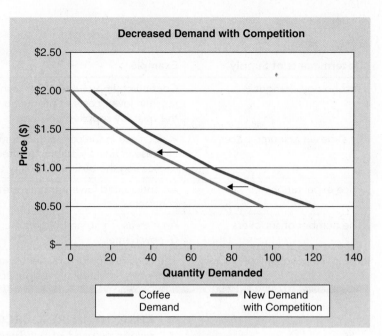

■ **FIGURE 2.5**
Demand and Competition
Increased competition negatively changes coffee demand and moves the demand curve to the left.

Factors That Shift Supply

What makes supply change? Eddie started his business with a used industrial-sized coffeemaker. It makes good coffee, but Eddie is now thinking that he might need to buy a newer coffeemaker that would make coffee faster. In addition, he has heard that the price of the type of coffee beans he uses is going up. He could switch to a lower-quality bean, but he doesn't want to reduce his standards. How could these new costs affect Eddie's business? Both could if he consequently needed to raise prices to cover the added expenses. There are many factors that can create a change in supply. These factors, known as the **determinants of supply**, are as follows:

- Technology changes
- Changes in resource prices
- Price expectations
- The number of suppliers
- The price of substitute goods

Changes in any of these factors that help to create a good or a service can affect its supply and shift the supply curve to the left (have a negative impact on supply) or to the right (have a positive impact on supply). ■ **TABLE 2.5** summarizes the key determinants of supply and how they might affect business. Let's look at each in more detail.

TECHNOLOGY CHANGES Improvements in technology enable suppliers to produce their goods or services more efficiently and with fewer costs, thus increasing their ability to supply more. For example, if a bakery purchases a new modern oven, it would be able to make more fresh desserts in less time. Similarly, in other industries, a sales force that uses software on their smart phones to connect immediately to inventory when placing orders will be more efficient than the sales force having to process paper orders.

TABLE 2.5	Key Determinants of Supply
Determinants of Supply	**Example**
Technology changes	Continuing improvements in technology, such as a better coffeemaker or software program, result in lower costs of production and create a higher level of productivity, which increases the quantity supplied and lowers the price.
Changes in resource prices	A decrease in the cost of lumber may increase the number of new homes built, or an increase in union wages may affect the number of workers a business can afford to employ, decreasing the business's ability to generate a product.
Price expectations	An anticipated lowering of interest rates may indicate a future increase in new housing contracts.
The number of suppliers	An increase in home builders increases the supply of new homes and decreases the cost of new homes.
The price of substitute goods	The construction of cheaper townhouses in an area could lead to less building of more expensive single-family residences.

CHANGES IN RESOURCE PRICES Increases and decreases in the price of the resources used to produce a good or a service affect the cost of their production. An increase in resource prices increases the cost of production and reduces profits, thus lowering the incentive to supply a product. For example, an increase in the minimum wage will increase the cost of labor, thus potentially affecting how many workers a small business could employ. Not having enough workers could limit a company's ability to supply the necessary quantities of a product, shifting the supply curve to the left. Likewise, a decrease in the price of gasoline could reduce the costs of shipping services and shift the supply curve to the right.

PRICE EXPECTATIONS The expected future price of a product will affect how much producers are willing to supply of it. For example, if the price of crude oil is expected to increase, companies like ExxonMobil will ramp up their production to supply more oil at the higher price. However, sometimes if prices are expected to increase significantly in the future, a supplier might stockpile the product and supply more at a later time when prices are higher. Similarly, if prices are expected to significantly decrease in the future, the supplier might make every attempt to sell its supply of the product while prices are high.

From a buyer's perspective, the reverse can be true as well. For example, if Eddie is anticipating an increase in the price of coffee because a cold snap adversely affected the supply of coffee beans, he may want to buy more coffee beans than he needs to now at a lower price to continue to keep his prices low. Or he will need to consider raising his prices to compensate for the future increase in his costs.

NUMBER OF SUPPLIERS The supply of a good or a service increases as the number of competitors increases. It makes sense that the number of suppliers often increases in more profitable industries. Think about what Starbucks has done to the coffee business. Although Starbucks remains the leader in the retail coffee market, there are many companies, such as Dunkin' Donuts and McDonald's, supplying beverages to coffee drinkers, thus increasing the availability of good coffee. Similarly, as an industry becomes less popular due to a change in technology or other cause, the number of suppliers decreases. For example, when the digital camera became popular, the number of suppliers of film cameras decreased drastically.

PRICE OF SUBSTITUTE GOODS The price of comparable substitute goods also affects the supply of a product. If there are equally comparable goods available at a lower price, the supply of the more expensive goods will be affected. For example, if cable Internet access, a substitute for DSL Internet access, is priced lower than DSL, then consumers switching from DSL to cable may affect the supply of cable (which will increase) and the supply of DSL (which will decrease).

Degrees of Competition pp. 35–38

In 1996, Microsoft developed its own Web browser, Internet Explorer, and tried to pressure computer manufacturers and Internet service providers to carry it exclusively. As a result, the U.S. Department of Justice began investigating the corporation for attempting to establish a monopoly over the market. In 1999, a U.S. district court found Microsoft to be in violation of the Sherman Antitrust Act and ordered the company to break up. In 2001, an appeals court overturned this order but maintained that Microsoft was illegally monopolizing the market for Web browsers. What exactly is a monopoly? And why doesn't the government allow large monopolies to exist in the United States? ■

Source: FJstudio/Fotolia.

Some products or services have no substitutes, whereas others share the market with many similar products. The number of substitutes for a certain good or service determines the *level of competition*. Various degrees of competition exist, from monopolies to perfect competition, as shown in ■ **FIGURE 2.6**.

Keep in mind that these degrees of competition are points on a continuum, not absolute measures. For example, many industries fall somewhere between a monopolistic competition and an oligopoly.

Monopolies

What is a monopoly? A **monopoly** occurs when a provider of a service or a good has control of all or nearly all of its market. If one company were the sole provider of automobile tires and no other tire manufacturers were available to the automobile industry, that would be considered a monopoly. Monopolies can also happen in a local or a regional market. For example, if Eddie's coffee kiosk is the only place students can buy coffee on campus, then Eddie has a monopoly on campus coffee sales. In the United States, as well as in other countries, large monopolies are rarely allowed.

Why aren't there many monopolies? Without competition, a firm that has a monopoly can charge a higher price and may be less responsive to consumer needs. Monopolies can occur when companies that offer the same service or provide the same good merge and thus control the market. The U.S. Federal Trade Commission and the Department of Justice must review mergers between large competitors to determine whether the combined firm would result in a monopoly that would thwart competition. For example, in 2011, the Department of Justice blocked the proposed merger between AT&T and T-Mobile on the grounds that the deal was anticompetitive. When US Airways and American Airlines recently merged, the Department

■ **FIGURE 2.6**
Degrees of Business Competition

MONOPOLY
• One company dominates an entire industry; no substitutes exist

DUOPOLY
• Only two suppliers exist in an industry or have dominant control

OLIGOPOLY
• Only a few sellers exist, and each seller has a fairly large share of the market

MONOPOLISTIC COMPETITION
• Many buyers and sellers and little differentiation exists between the products, but there is a perceived difference among consumers

PERFECT COMPETITION
• Many buyers and sellers of virtually identical products; no barriers to market entry

Keurig's Monopoly

In 1998, Keurig Green Mountain Inc. began shipping its first single-cup coffee-brewing machines to customers, starting a revolution in how coffee is prepared. Today, Keurig machines are in nearly 16 million U.S. households, with little threat of competition. In the single-cup coffee machine industry, because of patent protection, Keurig holds a monopoly.

In addition to the machines, Keurig sells more than 200 different flavors of coffee packets, or "pods," used in the machines. Like the machines, Keurig's $2.4 billion coffee-pod business also faces little competition.[4] However, this situation is beginning to change. In 2012, Keurig's patent on the coffee pods expired. Since then, generic brands of pods have been creeping into the marketplace. In 2013, they had captured 11 percent of Keurig's market share.

To protect the company's market dominance and the source of much of its revenue, Keurig announced it was making a new coffee-brewing machine, the Keurig 2.0, which will be compatible only with pods that Keurig produces—not generic coffee pods. The Keurig 2.0 has spurred several complaints and lawsuits from competitors claiming the new machine will help Keurig maintain its monopoly.[5]

of Justice required the companies to sell the gates they own in certain airports to other airlines in order to enhance competition in the airline industry postmerger.[6]

In the United States, natural monopolies are an exception. Utility companies, such as those that sell natural gas or water to consumers, may be permitted to hold monopolies in an effort to conserve natural resources. However, the government regulates the prices for these goods and services, thus preventing the utility companies from overcharging for their products.

Duopolies and Oligopolies

What happens when one or two other companies enter a monopolistic market? To answer this question, let's look again at Eddie and his coffee kiosk from the previous section. At first, Eddie's coffee kiosk was the only place on campus to buy coffee; Eddie had a monopoly. But after the bookstore on campus opened a café and started to sell coffee, students now had a choice to buy coffee at two places—either at the bookstore or at Eddie's coffee kiosk. The situation changed from a monopoly to a **duopoly**. A true duopoly is where only two suppliers exist, although in reality the definition is generally used to describe situations where only two firms dominate a market. Examples of duopolies include PepsiCo and Coca-Cola in the soft-drink market and Intel and AMD in the computer processor market.

However, if the campus cafeteria also begins to sell coffee, then an oligopoly is created. An **oligopoly** is a form of competition in which only a few sellers exist, each with a fairly large share of the market. For example, the cellular phone market in the United States is controlled by an oligopoly of four companies: Verizon, AT&T, Sprint, and T-Mobile. Typically, oligopolies (and duopolies) occur in industries in which a high investment of capital must be made to enter the market.

Because there is little differentiation between products, competition is strong in a duopoly and an oligopoly, and prices differ only slightly, if at all, between the few suppliers. If one company cuts prices, its action is usually matched quickly by the competition. Therefore, firms that compete as duopolies and oligopolies more often compete by differentiating their products from one another (making one product stand out from another) rather than competing on their prices.

Monopolistic Competition

What happens when there isn't much differentiation between products? Let's assume that the coffee the cafeteria begins to offer is perceived among

Verizon, AT&T, Sprint, and T-Mobile together control the majority of the U.S. cellular phone market, forming an oligopoly.
Source: Newscom.

Is Sirius XM Radio a Monopoly?

In 1992, satellite radio service hit the U.S. airwaves after the U.S. Federal Communications Commission awarded licenses to American Mobile Radio and CD Radio to use the newly created frequencies. American Mobile Radio spun off XM Satellite Radio, which launched its first radio service officially in September 2001. CD Radio changed its name to Sirius Satellite Radio and went live nine months later. Since then, there have been no further entries into the satellite radio market. Satellite radio offers a wide variety of programs to large geographic regions with no or little advertisements. A subscription service is required to enjoy satellite radio.

XM Radio and Sirius Satellite Radio competed fiercely with each other to grow their market share, causing each company to operate unprofitably because of accumulated heavy debt burdens. It became apparent that to survive, the two companies would need to merge. A merger would combine the exclusive contracts each service offered. A potential subscriber who wanted to listen to Howard Stern (offered by Sirius) but who also wanted to receive play-by-play delivery of Major League Baseball games (offered by XM Radio) would not need to choose between the two subscription services or pay for subscriptions for both services.

The merger clearly created a monopoly, yet in 2008, the U.S. Justice Department approved the merger. Why was the merger allowed to go through? Broadcasters and consumer groups predicted the price of satellite radio in the United States would increase, new programming options would decrease, and subscribers would get poorer service from the merged company. The Justice Department's antitrust division believed otherwise. The Justice Department also claimed that although the merged firm would create a monopoly, consumers had other music source options, such as HD Radio and MP3 players, they could connect to in their cars and homes. Meanwhile, the Federal Communications Commission was worried that without the merger, the two competing companies would drive each other into bankruptcy, thus eliminating satellite radio in the United States altogether.

Since the combined company, Sirius XM Radio, was established, the prices the firm has charged its listeners have gone up. Although there has been some improvement in the service the merged company provides, it has begun to drop stations, and critics say its playlists are smaller and more repetitive. What are your thoughts on satellite radio? Did the Justice Department make the right decision?

---

students to be superior to Eddie's and the bookstore's coffee. The added choice of a perceived superior product creates monopolistic competition. **Monopolistic competition** occurs when there are many buyers and sellers and the products are similar but not identical (coffee versus coffee). Often there is a *perceived* difference among consumers who thereby favor one product offering over another so that the products are not perfectly substitutable products.

Monopolistic competition is everywhere. Think of the traditional strip mall or local shopping center in your neighborhood where most likely there is a pizza parlor, a dry cleaner, a hair or nail salon, a bank, and a dollar store. These mom-and-pop stores are traditional, monopolistic competitive businesses because there are many buyers and sellers and the products are similar but not identical. Often, the real distinction between these products is price.

Perfect Competition

What happens when products are almost identical? Perfect competition occurs when there are many buyers and sellers of products that are virtually identical and any seller can easily enter and exit the market. When these conditions exist, no single supplier can influence the price. In reality, there are very few, if any, examples of perfect competition. However, agricultural products, such as grains, fruits, and vegetables, come close. Many of these products appear to be identical, and, because there are many sellers in the market, no single seller can set the prices for these products.

Competition encourages businesses to make creative decisions and gives customers options. Because of this need for competition, U.S. businesses face stiff penalties if they are found holding illegal monopolies. By keeping a close watch on monopolies, the U.S. government tries to ensure that no single seller drastically influences the price of a certain service or good.

Source: Happy Alex/Fotolia.

Economic Indicators pp. 38–42

Greg Johnson needs to decide how much inventory to purchase for his large automobile dealership. A few years ago, the recession resulted in fewer new car purchases but improved the sales of used cars on his lot. His company's service department also did better because customers were choosing to fix their cars rather than trade them in. As a result, Greg found he needed to stock more auto parts.

Now, however, Greg is beginning to see the demand for new cars rise. He knows his staffing needs and inventory supply will mostly likely be affected—but how quickly? Does he continue to retain the same number of service-repair personnel and increase the number of salespeople he hires? How many new cars should he be buying for the upcoming sales season? Not knowing exactly by how much demand will increase, how is Greg to decide how much inventory to hold or what staff to retain or hire? ■

The economy plays a big part in business. Which aspects of the economy should Greg watch to help him make his business decisions? How can he tell how well or how poorly the economy is doing?

Business managers need to be aware of certain statistics about economic activities, called **economic indicators**. (*Leading indicators* are statistics that can be used to help predict how the economy will do in the near future. *Coincident indicators* are statistics that reflect how the economy is currently doing. *Lagging indicators* are statistics that change only after the economy as a whole changes.) The following three economic indicators are closely watched by businesspeople:

- Gross domestic product
- Consumer and producer price indices
- The unemployment rate

▶ THE **LIST**

Countries by GDP, 2012

Country	GDP (Billions of U.S. Dollars)
United States	16.245
China	8.227
Japan	5.960
Germany	3.428
France	2.613
United Kingdom	2.472
Brazil	2.253
Russian Federation	2.015
Italy	2.015
India	1.842

Source: Central Intelligence Agency, "The World Factbook: Country Comparison: GDP (Purchasing Power Parity)," https://www.cia.gov.

Gross Domestic Product

How do we determine the health of an economy? The broadest measure of the health of any country's economy is its **gross domestic product** (GDP), which measures how productive a nation is, that is, the overall market value of final goods and services produced in a country in a year. It is important to note that only those goods that are actually *produced* in the country are counted in the country's GDP (hence the term *domestic* in *gross domestic product*). For example, Toshiba Corporation, a Tokyo-based high-tech company, has a plant in Lebanon, Tennessee, that manufactures color television sets. The value of all television sets produced in the Tennessee plant is counted in the U.S. GDP, not in Japan's GDP.

How does the GDP act as an economic indicator? GDP is the most widely used indicator of economic growth by countries worldwide. It is a coincident indicator and moves at the same time the economy does. A rising GDP indicates that more goods and services are being produced and that businesses are doing well. A downward-moving GDP indicates that fewer goods are being produced, fewer services are being sold, and businesses are not doing as well. Business owners such as Greg use GDP data to forecast sales and adjust production and their investment in inventory.

A nation's GDP is often viewed in tandem with the country's debt level. A low debt-to-GDP ratio indicates an economy that is healthy, whereas a high debt-to-GDP ratio indicates a country that is spending beyond its means. The debt-to-GDP ratio is calculated by dividing either the amount of government debt or total

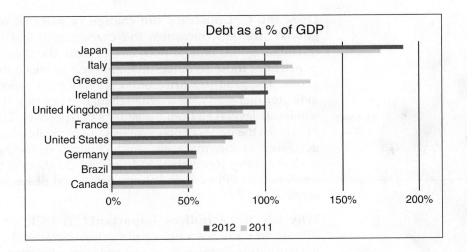

national debt by the country's GDP. As ■ **FIGURE 2.7** shows, in 2012, Japan's debt-to-GDP ratio was the largest, nearing 200 percent; that of the United States was nearly 80 percent.

Consumer and Producer Price Indices

What else is used to gauge the health of an economy? There are two price indices used as economic indicators: the consumer price index and the producer price index. You may not hear about these indicators often, but you've probably heard of inflation and deflation. A consistent increase in either indicator indicates inflation. **Inflation** is a rise in the general level of prices over time. A decrease in the rate of inflation is **disinflation**, and a continuous decrease in prices over time is **deflation**.

How are changes in the price of consumer products measured? The **consumer price index** (CPI) is a benchmark used to track changes in the price of goods and services that consumers purchase over a period of time. It is a lagging indicator, so it shifts after the economy changes. The CPI measures price changes by creating a "market basket" of a specified set of goods and services that represent the average buying pattern of urban households. The value of this market basket is determined by the combined prices of these goods and services and is compared to its value in a prior period (generally a month). The change in the overall price of these goods is then noted.

What goods and services are included in the CPI? The basket of goods and services is evaluated by the U.S. Bureau of Labor Statistics to ensure that it reflects current consumer buying habits. The market basket as of December 2013 was determined by tracking the spending habits of about 7,000 families during 2009 and 2010.[7] The goods and services are classified into 200 categories, which are further arranged into eight major groups[8] (see ■ **FIGURE 2.8**):

- Apparel
- Education and communication
- Food and beverages
- Housing
- Medical care
- Recreation
- Transportation
- Other goods and services (such as tobacco and smoking products, haircuts and other personal services, and funeral services)

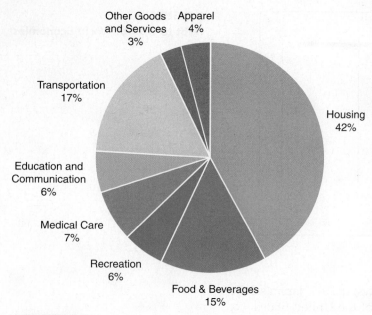

■ FIGURE 2.8
CPI Components
Source: Bureau of Labor Statistics.

Does the CPI measure the change in price of all goods? The CPI measures the change in prices of consumer goods only. It does not measure the change in prices of those resources that are used to create the goods. The **producer price index** (PPI) is a coincident indicator that tracks the average change in prices at the wholesale level (i.e., from the seller's perspective). The PPI tracks the prices of goods sellers use to create products, such as raw materials, product components that require further processing, and finished goods sold to retailers. The PPI excludes energy prices and prices for services.

Why are price indices important? The CPI and PPI are important economic indicators because they measure purchasing power and consequently trigger some business decisions. During periods of increasing prices as reflected by the CPI, the purchasing power of a dollar decreases—meaning that less is bought with a dollar today than could have been purchased with the same dollar yesterday. As a result, wages eventually need to be increased to compensate employees for the higher cost of living (see the Biz Chat in this section). Businesses in turn must eventually increase the prices of their products to offset the higher cost of labor. Similarly, if the price of intermediary products used to produce final goods or services sold to consumers increases (as measured by the PPI), businesses may need to pass on those cost increases in the form of higher prices, again decreasing the consumer's purchasing power. Therefore, business leaders watch the CPI and the PPI to determine the rate at which consumer and wholesale prices, respectively, change.

The Unemployment Rate

What other indicators are used to measure the economy? The **unemployment rate** is a lagging indicator that measures the number of workers who are at least 16 years old who are not working but have tried to find jobs within the past four weeks. Because there are different reasons why people are not working, there are several different measurements of unemployment:

- **Frictional unemployment** is temporary unemployment that results when workers move between jobs, careers, and locations. Frictional employment occurs because it simply takes a certain amount of time for workers to find the right jobs and employers to find the right workers.

How Much Money Do You Need to Get By?

The cost of living is the average monetary costs of the goods and services required to maintain a particular standard of living. It is closely related to the CPI. In fact, to keep up with inflation, the Social Security Administration calculates automatic cost-of-living adjustments to the Social Security benefits retirees receive. The adjustments are based on annual percentage increases in the CPI. As you can imagine, the cost of living varies greatly by state and city. The cost of living in New York City or San Francisco is much higher than in Topeka, Kansas, or Little Rock, Arkansas. Why do you think these differences exist? What factors account for the differences?

- **Structural unemployment** is permanent unemployment that occurs when an industry changes in such a way that those jobs are terminated completely. Many steelworkers and miners lost their jobs when there was a decline in those industries. Likewise, robots have replaced many automobile workers, and computers have replaced many newspaper typesetters. Workers displaced by these types of circumstances can hopefully learn new skills or receive additional training in an effort to keep their jobs or find new ones.

- **Cyclical unemployment** is unemployment that occurs when firms must cut back their workforces when there is a downturn in the business cycle. Once the demand for goods and services increases, companies begin to hire again.

- **Seasonal unemployment** occurs when workers get laid off during the off-season, such as those in snow- or beach-related industries or agriculture or after the holiday shopping season ends.

The unemployment rate is an economic measure that businesses and the government watch carefully.
Source: Zimmytws/Fotolia.

Unlike other economic recoveries, unemployment in the United States has remained at historically high levels since the end of the Great Recession. There is still no consensus as to what's causing the high unemployment rate. The debate centers around whether it's due to reduced demand as a direct result of the recession (cyclical unemployment) or whether the lost jobs are never coming back due to changes in business and technology (structural unemployment).[9]

Why is unemployment an important economic measure? Businesses, as well as government policymakers, pay close attention to unemployment rates. High unemployment results in an increase in unemployment benefits and government spending on social programs, such as Social Security, welfare (now called Temporary Assistance for Needy Families), and Medicare. High unemployment can also result in increases in mental stresses and physical illnesses and can bring on increases in crime. It is costly for businesses to lay off workers and then, as the economy improves, hire and train new employees. In a declining economy, businesses prefer to reduce their workforces through retirement and natural attrition, which takes planning.

Ironically, if the unemployment rate drops too low, meaning the workforce is nearly fully staffed, policymakers in the government become concerned that the economy is overheating: More workers have increased buying power and spend more, which ultimately causes prices to increase, resulting in increasing inflation. The challenge for policymakers is to keep both inflation and unemployment low—a difficult task because the two seem to have an inverse relationship to each other.

Productivity of Firms

How is the productivity of a firm's workforce measured? In its broadest terms, **productivity** measures the quantity of goods and services that a firm's human and physical resources can produce in a given time period. It can be calculated as a physical measure or as a monetary measure. For example, an automobile assembly plant might measure its productivity in terms of the total *number* of cars it produced in a given period of time (week, month, or year) per worker-hours needed to produce them. Or the plant might measure its productivity as the total dollar *value* of cars produced in a given period per worker-hours needed to produce the cars. As you might expect, the calculation of productivity in the service sector may be slightly different, but it generally focuses on revenues generated per employee for a certain time period.

Why is measuring productivity important to businesses? No matter how it is measured, productivity is an indicator of a business's health. An increase in productivity indicates that workers are producing more goods or services in the same amount of time. Therefore, higher productivity numbers often result in lower costs and lower prices. Increasing productivity means that the existing resources are producing more, which generates more income and more profitability. Companies can reinvest the economic benefits of productivity growth by increasing wages and improving working conditions, by reducing prices for customers, by increasing shareholder value, and by increasing tax revenue to the government, thus improving the GDP. In aggregate, overall productivity is an important economic indicator of an economy's health.

So how do all these indicators help Greg and his inventory and staffing decisions? After ensuring there is inventory to fill current needs, Greg keeps a close eye on all economic indicators, especially the CPI and the unemployment rate, to help guide his future buying decisions. He knows that movements in the CPI determine the trend of current prices. Such trends can help Greg determine whether it is better to stock up on inventory and hire new employees now or wait until later.

Equally important is the unemployment rate. A continued improvement in the economy will decrease the unemployment rate, an indicator for Greg that his new car inventory might move more quickly because more people are working and have money to spend. Although none of the indicators can guide Greg's decisions precisely, watching the indicators over time allows Greg to get a feel for future expectations and helps him make better business decisions.

Source: Andy Dean/Fotolia.

Government and the Economy pp. 42–47

Nick and Jacinta Robertson have been saving for years to buy their first house. Over the past several years, the interest rates banks charge for home loans have been at historically low levels. Recently, however, all Nick and Jacinta hear about is news of the rapid changes in the stock market, reports from the chairman of the Federal Reserve Board about changes in interest rates, and debates on how the government might change its tax policies to control the economy. Nick and Jacinta aren't sure what effects all of this will have on their ability to be approved for a mortgage loan and buy a home. Is now the best time to buy a house? ■

If you or someone you know has tried to buy a house or if you know a small business owner who needs to make a big investment, you may have realized that the state of the economy can have a big impact on that decision. What makes the economy change? How does the government help control the economy? What do you need to be aware of when deciding whether to make a large investment?

Economic Policies

Why does the state of the economy change? In 1980, the rate of inflation was at its highest level—nearly 15 percent.[10] Only eight years before and six years after that high inflationary period (1972 and 1986), inflation was hovering around 2 percent.[11] Over time, the economy naturally goes through periodic increases and decreases in inflation. Economists refer to these increases and decreases as the **business cycle**.

There are four stages of the business cycle, as illustrated in ■ **FIGURE 2.9**:

- **Peak.** The peak occurs when an economic expansion is at its most robust point.
- **Recession.** By definition, a **recession** is a decline in the GDP for two or more successive quarters of a year. In recessionary times, corporate profits decline, unemployment increases, and the stock market reacts with large selling sessions that result in decreasing stock prices. The U.S. economy has experienced seven recessions over the past 40 years; the most recent recession began in late 2007 and ended in the fall of 2009. This was the country's worst and longest

recession since the Great Depression. A very severe or long recession is a **depression**. Depressions are usually associated with falling prices (deflation). After the onset of the Great Depression in 1929, the government used policies to control the economy to avoid another such depression.

- **Trough.** A trough occurs when the recession hits bottom and the economy begins to expand again.
- **Expansion or recovery.** After a recession or a depression, the economy hits a trough and begins to grow again and therefore enters into an expansionary or recovery phase. Eventually, the recovery will hit a peak, and the cycle begins again.

How does the government control swings in the business cycle? Ideally, the economy should stay near its peak all the time. But left to its own forces and in reaction to external actions on the economic system, such as wars and variations in the weather, it is inevitable that the economy cycles through recessions and recoveries. To smooth out the swings in the business cycle, lawmakers use **fiscal policy** to determine the appropriate level of taxes and government spending.

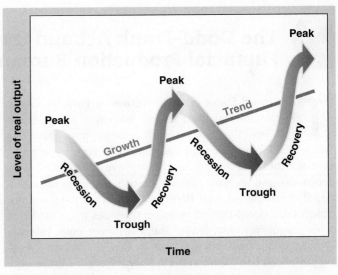

■ **FIGURE 2.9**
The Business Cycle

Fiscal Policy

Why does the government increase taxes to influence the economy? Threats of increasing taxes are a concern to Nick and Jacinta. They feel they pay too much already and need as much of their paychecks as possible to make their anticipated mortgage payments. However, they are told that an increase in taxes is necessary to offset rising inflation. Higher taxes translate into consumers spending less money, which in turn slows the growth of businesses and consequently slows down the economy by reducing the amount of money in the system. This, in turn, lowers inflation.

Decreasing taxes does not have quite the opposite effect on the economy as increasing taxes. It would seem that if increasing taxes would slow down an economy, a tax cut would help stimulate the economy. Although that is partially true, the amount of money entering into the system depends on how much of the reduction in taxes consumers spend and how much of it they save. Money put into savings does not help stimulate the economy immediately. To stimulate the economy more quickly, the government uses another form of fiscal policy: government spending.

How does government spending help stimulate the economy? The government spends money on a wide variety of projects, such as infrastructure improvements and projects that benefit the military, education, and health care. Because the money gets spent immediately and not saved, government spending increases the cash flow in the economy faster than decreasing taxes does. Often, government spending creates additional jobs, which also helps stimulate the economy. The American Recovery and Reinvestment Act was a huge stimulus plan introduced in 2009 to help jump-start the failing economy. It included government spending for infrastructure, education, and health care improvements. During periods of high economic growth, the government may decrease its spending. But reducing government spending is more easily said than done. There always seem to be government programs that are essential and cannot be cut regardless of the state of the economy. This is always a debate around election time, and there really isn't one right answer to this issue. Overall, fiscal policy has its critics. Some economists think government spending has a mixed record when it comes to jump-starting the economy. That was the case with the last stimulus. Other economists believe the impact of the spending would have been greater if the stimulus had been larger. This issue is still being debated.

The Dodd-Frank Act and the Consumer Financial Production Bureau

The United States is slowly recovering from the Great Recession—the most serious economic plunge since the Great Depression, which persisted throughout the 1930s. The Great Recession was caused, in part, by large financial institutions making risky, highly leveraged "bets" with depositors' money that ultimately didn't pay off. Huge and steadfast companies filed bankruptcy and even permanently closed their doors due to receding revenues that could not cover staggering debt levels. The investment bank Lehman Brothers closed its doors with over $600 billion of debt, creating the largest bankruptcy in U.S. history.[12] General Motors filed the fourth-largest bankruptcy proceedings with over $170 billion of debt,[13] and Chrysler followed suit shortly thereafter with a much smaller but nonetheless significant bankruptcy.

The recession hit individuals with similarly severe results. Prior to the recession, consumers were carrying significant levels of personal debt in the form of mortgages, auto loans, home equity loans, and credit card debt. The amount of accumulated personal debt became unmanageable as wage increases began to slow down and layoffs began to rise. Personal bankruptcies rose sharply.[14]

In 2010, the government passed the Dodd-Frank Act in an effort to prevent another collapse of a major financial institution like Lehman Brothers as well as protect consumers from being taken advantage of by aggressive lending and mortgage practices by banks. As part of the Dodd-Frank Act, the Consumer Financial Protection Bureau (CFPB) was created. The bureau's purpose is to crack down on unfair deceptive acts and financial practices that can affect consumers, including transactions related to all types of consumer banking products, such as mortgages, private student loans, and other consumer bank products and services. The CFPB also requires financial information about mortgages to be presented in "plain English" to customers along with their credit scores.

Monetary Policy

What else can be done to control the economy? The second tool used to manage the economy is **monetary policy**. Monetary policy is not exercised by the government. Instead, it is exercised by the **Federal Reserve System** (the Fed). The Fed is the central banking system of the United States. Created by Congress as an independent governmental entity, it includes 12 regional Federal Reserve Banks (see ■ **FIGURE 2.10**) and a Board of Governors based in Washington, D.C. The Federal Reserve Banks carry out most of the activities of the Fed. The Fed also includes the **Federal Open Market Committee**, which sets the policies of the Fed, including its monetary policies. Through its monetary policy, the Federal Reserve affects the nation's money supply and helps shape the direction of the economy.

What is the money supply? It is natural to think that just all the coins and bills held by people, businesses, and banks make up the country's money supply. However,

■ **FIGURE 2.10**
The 12 Federal Reserve Districts
Source: Federal Reserve.

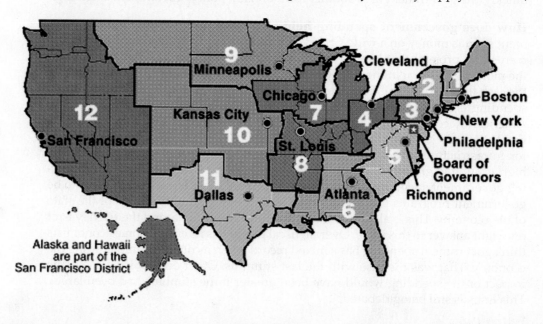

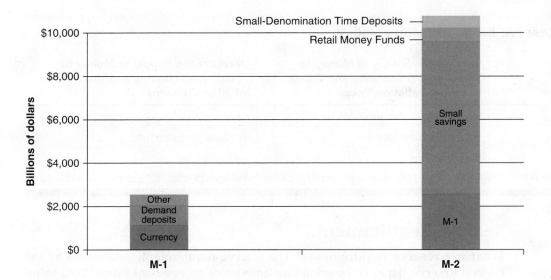

■ **FIGURE 2.11**
**Money Supply Measures
for M-1 and M-2**
Surprisingly, currency is not the
biggest component of the U.S.
money supply. Savings and other
deposits represent the largest
components of the money supply.

that would represent only a portion of the country's money. The **money supply** is the combined amount of money available within an economy, and it includes not only currency (coins and bills) but also personal savings and checking accounts as well as the deposit accounts from large institutions. In particular, the money supply consists of the following different "layers" of funds (see ■ **FIGURE 2.11**):

- **M-1.** Coins and bills (currency), traveler's checks, and checking accounts constitute the narrowest measure of our money supply, which is referred to as **M-1**. M-1 assets are the most liquid in that they are already in the form of cash or are the easiest to convert to cash.

- **M-2.** Another part of the money supply is that which is available for banks to lend out, such as savings deposits, money market accounts, and certificates of deposit (CDs) less than $100,000. This layer of the money supply, in addition to the M-1 layer, constitutes **M-2**.

- **M-3.** The third layer of the money supply is **M-3**. M-1 and M-2, plus less liquid funds, such as larger CDs (greater than $100,000), money market accounts held by large banks and corporations, and deposits of Eurodollars (U.S. dollars deposited in banks outside the United States), make up M-3. The Federal Reserve Board of Governors has stopped publishing M-3 data.

Why is the money supply important? Money has a direct effect on the economy: The more money we have, the more we tend to spend. When we as consumers spend more, businesses do better. The demand increases for resources, labor, and capital due to the stimulated business activity, and, in general, the economy improves. However, too much money in the economy can be too much of a good thing. When the money supply continues to expand, eventually there may not be enough goods and services to satisfy demand, and, as was previously discussed, when demand is high, prices will rise, resulting in inflation. (Remember the demand curve? It shifts to the right.) Economists carefully watch the CPI to monitor inflation, because they don't want inflation to go too high.

An opposite effect can happen when the supply of money becomes limited following a decrease in economic activity. When the economy begins to slow down due to decreased spending, either disinflation (reduced inflation) or deflation (falling prices) results. To help manage the economy from being in the extreme economic states of inflation or deflation, the Fed uses three tools to affect money supply (see ■ **TABLE 2.6**):

- Reserve requirements
- Short-term interest rates
- Open market operations

TABLE 2.6	Federal Reserve Bank Monetary Policy

Federal Reserve System Action	Increase the Supply of Money to Stimulate the Economy and Offset Potential Deflation/Recession	Decrease the Supply of Money to "Cool" the Economy and Tame Inflation Concerns
Reserve requirements	Lower reserve requirement	Increase reserve requirement
Short-term interest rates	Lower discount rate	Increase discount rate
Open market operations	Buy securities	Sell securities

Source: Based on data from Federal Reserve Bank of New York, "Historical Changes of the Target Federal Funds and Discount Rates 1971–Present," www.ny.frb.org.

Reserve Requirements

What are reserve requirements? The **reserve requirement**, determined by the Federal Reserve Bank, is the minimum amount of money banks must hold in reserve to give to their depositors who want to withdraw it. When you deposit money in a bank, the money does not sit in a vault waiting for you to withdraw it later. Instead, banks use deposits to make loans to others: people, small businesses, corporations, and other banks. Banks make money by the interest charged on those loans; however, a bank must be able to give you back your money when you demand it. If a bank doesn't have enough money to cover what its customers want to withdraw on a given day, they might get nervous and try to withdraw all of their funds. This is referred to as a *bank run*. Bank runs that occurred in 1929 helped spark the Great Depression. At that time, people were so nervous about banks not being able to cover their deposits that the massive withdrawals forced many banks to close.

Banks do not lend out the entire balance of their deposits. The Fed mandates banks retain a certain reserve requirement sufficient to cover the demands of their customers for on any given day. This includes trips to automatic teller machines, the use of debit cards, requests for loans, and the payment of checks that you write. The Fed can ease or tighten the money supply by increasing or decreasing the reserve requirement. For example, if the Fed increases the reserve requirement, it forces banks to hold on to more money rather than lending it out. This slows down economic activity. However, the Fed rarely uses the reserve requirement as a means of monetary policy, as these actions would be very disruptive to the banking industry.

Short-Term Interest Rates

What is the discount rate? The Federal Reserve Bank serves as the bank to other banks. Occasionally, commercial banks have unexpected draws on their funds that might put them near their reserve requirements. In those instances, banks may turn to the Federal Reserve Bank for short-term loans. For this reason, the Fed is sometimes referred to as the "lender of last resort."

When banks borrow emergency funds from the Fed, they are charged an interest rate, called the **discount rate**. The Federal Reserve has the power to increase or decrease the discount rate in its efforts to control monetary supply. When the Fed lowers the discount rate, commercial banks are encouraged to obtain additional reserves by borrowing funds from the Fed. Commercial banks then lend out the reserves to businesses, thereby stimulating the economy by injecting funds into the economic system. However, if the economy is too robust, the Fed can increase the discount rate, which discourages banks from borrowing additional reserves. Businesses are then discouraged from borrowing because of the higher interest rates that the banks charge on their loans.

Is the discount rate the same as the federal funds rate? The federal funds rate is not the same as the discount rate. It is often reported in the news that the Fed intends to change the federal funds rate in its efforts to stabilize the economy. The **federal funds rate** is the interest rate banks charge other banks when they borrow funds overnight from one another. (As mentioned above, the Fed requires banks to have so much money on reserve, depending on the deposits in the bank and the other assets and liabilities held by each bank. Banks avoid dipping below their required reserves by borrowing from each other before they have to borrow from the Fed at the discount rate.) Despite news reports, the Fed does not control the federal funds rate directly. Instead, the federal funds rate is the equilibrium price created through the Fed's open market operations and the exchange of securities.

The excess reserves that are available to lend between banks come from securities that the Fed buys and sells through its open market operations. If there are excess reserves on hand, banks have adequate funds to lend to other banks. On the other hand, if excess reserves are not as plentiful, banks lend funds to one another more sparingly. To increase the federal funds rate, the Fed sells bonds in the open market. Banks buy the securities, thus reducing their excess reserves available for loans. The decrease in excess reserves increases the federal funds rate.

The opposite holds true as well. To decrease the federal funds rate, the Fed will buy bonds in the open market. Buying securities from banks increases the banks' excess reserves, making money more available, which decreases the federal funds rate and helps stimulate the economy. ■ **FIGURE 2.12** shows the trend of federal funds rates over the past several decades. As you can see, the federal funds rate has been at a historically low of .25 percent for many years.

Open Market Operations

What are open market operations? The primary tool the Fed uses in its monetary policy is **open market operations**, buying and selling U.S. Treasury and federal agency bonds on the "open market." The Fed does not place transactions with any particular security dealer; rather, securities dealers compete for federal transactions in an open market. When the Fed buys or sells U.S. securities, it is changing the level of monetary reserves in the banking system by adding or taking away money from the system. When the Fed sells securities, reserves are reduced to pay for the securities (money is said to be "tight"), and interest rates rise. However, when the Fed buys securities, it adds reserves to the system (money is said to be "easy"), and interest rates drop. Lower interest rates help stimulate the economy by decreasing people's desire to save and increasing their demand for loans, such as home mortgages. Using open market operations is probably the most influential tool the Fed has to alter money supply.

To make their decision about whether to buy a home, Nick and Jacinta would benefit by paying attention to the Fed's monetary policies. If the Fed buys securities, it's likely that interest rates for mortgage loans will fall. Additionally, Nick and Jacinta can look to the discount rate and the federal funds rate. News about the lowering of the discount rate will signal that banks might have funds available to lend out at potentially lower rates. Although the federal funds rate does not have a direct impact on mortgage rates, it does have an indirect effect because interest rates respond to economic growth and inflation. Reports on the news that the Fed is striving to change the federal funds rate will indicate to Nick and Jacinta whether it's likely that interest rates will increase or decrease in the near future. This in turn can help them determine the best time to buy a home.

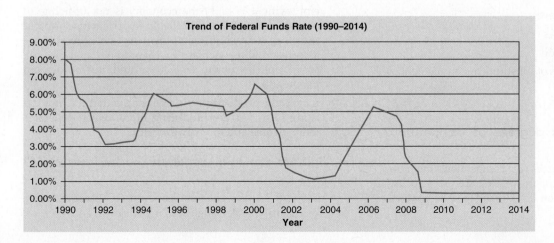

■ FIGURE 2.12
Trend of Federal Funds Rate (1990–2014)
Source: "Historical Changes of the Target Federal Funds and Discount Rates 1971– present," Federal Reserve Bank of New York. http://www.ny.frb.org/.

Chapter 2

Summary

1 What is economics, and what are the different types of economic systems? (pp. 25–28)

- **Economics** (p. 25) is the study of how individuals and businesses make decisions to best satisfy wants, needs, and desires with limited resources and how efficiently and equitably resources are allocated.

- There are different types of economic systems.

- A **planned economic system** (p. 26) is a type of economy in which the government has more control over what is produced, the resources to produce the goods and services, and the distribution of the goods and services. **Communism** (p. 26) and **socialism** (p. 27) are planned economic systems.

- In **market economies** (p. 27), which are characterized by **capitalism** (p. 27), individuals and private firms make the decisions about what to produce and how goods and services are distributed.

- Most modern economies in the Western world are **mixed economies** (p. 27), which are a blend of market and planned economies.

2 What are the principles of supply and demand and the factors that affect each principle? (pp. 28–35)

- **Supply** (p. 29) refers to how much of a good or service is available. The amount of it supplied will increase as its price increases. Supply is affected by five factors:
  - Technology changes
  - Changes in resource prices
  - Price expectations
  - The price of substitute goods
  - The number of suppliers

- **Demand** (p. 30) refers to how much people want to buy of a product at any given time. The amount demanded increases as a product's price declines. Demand is affected by five factors:
  - Changes in income levels
  - Consumer preferences
  - Changes in population
  - Changes in the prices of substitute or complementary goods
  - Changes in expectations

3 What are the various degrees of competition? (pp. 35–38)

- There are several degrees of competition, including **monopoly** (p. 35), **oligopoly** (p. 36), **duopoly** (p. 36), **monopolistic competition** (p. 37), and **perfect competition** (p. 38).

- In a monopoly, where only one seller supplies a good or service, supply may be limited. The supplies may increase with a duopoly, or an oligopoly, in which two or a few sellers exist, respectively. Monopolistic competition is characterized by many sellers that sell slightly different products at slightly different prices. This increases the supply of the products and choices for consumers. Similarly, there are many sellers in perfect competition, which also increases the supply of a good or service. In a perfectly competitive market, the product being sold is virtually identical across suppliers and sells for the same price. No single producer is able to affect the price at which the product is sold.

4 How do economic indicators—particularly the gross domestic product, price indices, the unemployment rate, and productivity—reflect economic health? (pp. 38–42)

- The **gross domestic product (GDP)** (p. 38) measures the overall market value of final goods and services produced in a country in a year. GDP is an important economic indicator of an economy's productivity and health. When a nation's GDP goes up, the country's economy is moving in a positive direction.

- The **consumer price index (CPI)** and **producer price index (PPI)** (p. 40) are indicators of **inflation** (p. 39) or **deflation** (p. 39).

- The CPI tracks changes in prices over time by measuring changes in the prices of goods and services that represent the average buying pattern of urban households.

- The PPI tracks the average change in prices of those goods sellers use to create products, such as raw materials and product components that require further processing, and finished goods sold to retailers.

- **The unemployment rate** (p. 40) is watched as an indicator of how well the economy is performing. If unemployment is high, the economy is not utilizing all of its resources and is probably experiencing a downturn. An increasing unemployment rate generally has a corresponding increase in government spending on social policies (such as welfare and unemployment payments).

- Increasing **productivity** (p. 41) means that a firm's existing resources are producing more, which generates more income and more profitability.

5 What are the four stages of the business cycle? (pp. 42–43)

- The four stages of the **business cycle** (p. 42) are the peak, **recession** (p. 42), trough, and expansion or recovery.

6 How does the government use both fiscal policy and monetary policy to control swings in the business cycle? (pp. 43–47)

- The government's **fiscal policy** (p. 43) determines the appropriate level of taxes and government spending. An increase in taxes translates into lower consumer spending and helps contain an economy that is growing too quickly. Lowering taxes will stimulate spending and help boost a sluggish economy.

- **Monetary policy** (p. 44) is the means by which the **Federal Reserve** (p. 44) manages to control inflation by changing interest rates, buying and selling government securities, and/or trading in foreign exchange markets.

- The **Federal Reserve System** (p. 44) is responsible for the **monetary policy** (p. 44) of the United States. The Fed keeps the economy from experiencing severe negative or positive swings by controlling the **money supply** (p. 45) through **open market operations** (p. 47) and by making changes in banks' **reserve requirements** (p. 46) and changes in the **discount rate** (p. 46).

Key Terms

business cycle (p. 42)

capitalism (p. 27)

communism (p. 26)

complementary goods (p. 32)

consumer price index (p. 39)

currency (p. 29)

cyclical unemployment (p. 41)

deflation (p. 39)

demand (p. 30)

demand curve (p. 30)

depression (p. 43)

determinants of demand (p. 31)

determinants of supply (p. 33)

discount rate (p. 46)

disinflation (p. 39)

duopoly (p. 36)

economic indicators (p. 38)

economics (p. 25)

economy (p. 26)

equilibrium price (p. 30)

federal funds rate (p. 46)

Federal Open Market Committee (p. 44)

Federal Reserve System (p. 44)

fiscal policy (p. 43)

frictional unemployment (p. 40)

gross domestic product (p. 38)

inflation (p. 39)

law of supply (p. 29)

M-1 (p. 45)

M-2 (p. 45)

M-3 (p. 45)

macroeconomics (p. 25)

market (p. 27)

market economy (p. 27)

market price (p. 29)

microeconomics (p. 25)

mixed economy (p. 27)

monetary policy (p. 44)

money supply (p. 45)

monopolistic competition (p. 37)

monopoly (p. 35)

oligopoly (p. 36)

open market operations (p. 47)

perfect competition (p. 37)

planned economic system (p. 26)

privatization (p. 27)

producer price index (p. 40)

productivity (p. 41)

recession (p. 42)

reserve requirement (p. 46)

seasonal unemployment (p. 41)

shortage (p. 30)

socialism (p. 27)

structural unemployment (p. 41)

substitute goods (p. 33)

supply (p. 29)

supply curve (p. 30)

surplus (p. 30)

unemployment rate (p. 40)

MyBizLab

Go to **mybizlab.com** to complete the problems marked with this icon .

Self Test

Multiple Choice *You can find the answers on the last page of this book.*

2-1 **Which of the following is a good example of microeconomics?**

    a. How a specific company would maximize its production and capacity so it could better compete in its industry

    b. How an increase in the unemployment rate would affect a country's GDP

    c. How a decrease in taxation affects consumer spending

    d. All of the above

2-2 **There are four coffee shops in your town. All of them claim to have the "freshest tasting coffee." Each shop advertises the unique benefits of its coffee and prices. This is an example of**

    a. pure monopoly.

    b. monopolistic competition.

    c. a regulated monopoly.

    d. an oligopoly.

Self Test (continued)

2-3 Jeannette has a successful organic spa business in which she gives massages, facials, and organic body treatments. Last summer, another organic spa opened up in town. The supply curve for Jeanette's business would shift in which direction?

    a. To the right

    b. To the left

    c. No change would occur.

    d. There is a shift along the demand curve only.

2-4 Which of the following is a determinant of demand?

    a. Technology changes

    b. Changes in income levels

    c. Price of substitute goods

    d. Price expectations

2-5 Racerback Swimwear, an Australian company, opens a factory near Tallahassee, Florida. The value of the swimsuits produced in the new Florida factory is included in which country's GDP?

    a. Australia

    b. United States

    c. Both Australia and the United States

    d. It is not included in the GDP at all.

2-6 Which of the following tracks the prices of goods and resources sellers use to create their products?

    a. GDP   b. CPI   c. PPI   d. GNP

2-7 Jackson Paulson works as a waterskiing instructor at Migis Lodge on Sebago Lake. He claims unemployment from October through April. Jackson experiences which type of unemployment?

    a. Frictional   c. Cyclical

    b. Seasonal   d. Structural

2-8 Which of the following is an example of the government's fiscal policy to stimulate an economy?

    a. Increased government spending

    b. Increased taxes

    c. Decreases in the discount rate

    d. Selling government securities in open markets

2-9 What results when there is an increase in overall prices?

    a. Inflation   c. Expansion

    b. Deflation   d. Recession

2-10 At which point in the business cycle is the economy when GDP declines for two or more successive quarters?

    a. Peak   c. Trough

    b. Recession   d. Expansion or recovery

True/False *You can find the answers on the last page of this book.*

2-11 Microeconomics is the study of the behavior of the overall economy.

    ☐ True or ☐ False

2-12 The discount rate is what is charged when banks borrow emergency funds from each other.

    ☐ True or ☐ False

2-13 Sweden, with its high taxes and widespread government programs, is a good example of a market economy.

    ☐ True or ☐ False

2-14 To celebrate the first day of summer, an ice cream shop dropped the price of its cones to 10 cents and sold out of them within two hours. This created a shortage of ice cream cones.

    ☐ True or ☐ False

2-15 The M-1 money supply measure consists of currency, traveler's checks, and checking accounts.

    ☐ True or ☐ False

Critical Thinking Questions

2-16 To smooth out swings in the business cycle, the government influences the economy through its fiscal and monetary policies. Compare and contrast the monetary and fiscal policies of the United States.

✪ 2-17 The U.S. Postal Service and Amtrak are examples of large organizations operated by the federal government. Discuss the pros and cons of privatizing these businesses.

✪ **2-18** The text defines GDP as a measurement of economic activity. Think about other things that may "help" the GDP that are really not good for our society in general, such as the economic activity required to clean up oil spills or increases in consumer debt to buy more goods. In addition, there are other situations that may "hurt" the GDP by limiting expenditures on items but help the overall good of society, such as reusing plastic bags or installing solar water heaters (thus limiting spending on oil, gas, or electricity). Does the definition of GDP need to be revised?

Team Time

THE GREAT DEBATE

Your instructor will divide the class into three groups and assign each group one of the following debate topics. Once in your group, divide the group into two smaller groups to prepare stances on your assigned debate issues.

Debate Topics

2-19 In 2009, the government bailed out several large banks and automotive and insurance firms in an effort to thwart a huge financial crisis. Were the government's actions successful?

2-20 Minimum-wage laws were introduced in the 1930s to protect workers after the Great Depression. Whether to increase the minimum wage continues to be an animated topic of discussion. What impact does increasing the minimum wage have on small business owners? Does increasing the minimum wage benefit the worker, or does it ultimately result in higher unemployment?

2-21 Taxation and tax cuts are fodder for volatile debate among political leaders. Many of them claim that tax cuts help strengthen the economy by freeing up money to increase spending. Others claim that past tax cuts have not had a positive effect on the economy, have caused greater stress on the government's budget, and have reduced the government's ability to spend on important public needs. Do tax cuts benefit the economy?

Process

Step 1. After dividing your group into two debate sides, meet separately to discuss the issues of the debate.

Step 2. Group members should then individually prepare their responses to their side of the debate issue.

Step 3. Gather your smaller groups and discuss the responses provided by each group member. Develop a single list of responses.

Step 4. Determine who will be the group's primary spokesperson for the debate.

Step 5. Each group will be given five minutes to present its side of the issue. After each group has presented its argument, each team will be given five minutes to prepare a rebuttal and then three minutes to present the rebuttal.

Step 6. Repeat this process with the other groups.

Ethics and Corporate Social Responsibility

ECONOMIC INEQUALITY

Economic inequality refers to the differences of assets and income among groups. It has long been the subject for great discussion and can refer to the inequality among individuals, city/rural areas, countries, or economic structures.

Questions for Discussion

2-22 How do you define economic equality? For example, is economic equality simply making sure everyone has equal income, or is it enough to provide all equal opportunity to earn income?

2-23 Is economic equality feasible? Would other problems result from economic equality?

2-24 One method used to measure differences in national income equality around the world is the national Gini coefficient. Research the Gini coefficient. Which countries have the most equality? Which have greater inequality?

2-25 What other methods could be used to measure economic equality?

Web Exercises

2-26 **Getting Acquainted with Your Local Federal Reserve Bank**
What Federal Reserve Bank branch is nearest your home or school? Go to the website of your local Federal Reserve Bank and outline its latest policies. What kind of information does the website give you?

2-27 **AT&T and Antitrust Regulations**
Watch the video "AT&T History" by Stephen Colbert, which is posted on YouTube. Then look at a more complete diagram of the outcomes of the forced breakup of AT&T in 1984 on the Quest Communications page on Wikinvest. Briefly describe the government's rationale for forcing the breakup of AT&T in 1984 and then comment on the subsequent corporate actions by AT&T and the "Baby Bells." How have these corporate actions impacted the communications industry?

2-28 **Learning More about Supply and Demand**
Find the Supply and Demand Game on Shmoop.com and play a round or two. Using information you learned from this chapter, discuss your experience. How did you

do? What are the important variables? How does this game illustrate the effects of supply and demand?

2-29 **Pro Sports and the Economy**
How do professional sports and the economy interact? Play Peanuts and Crackerjacks on the Boston Federal Reserve Bank's website (under Education Resources: Games and Online Learning) and test your knowledge of basic economic principles in the context of professional sports. Write a brief summary of your experience. What did you learn from playing the game?

2-30 **Monetary Policy: You're in Control**
How would it feel to be in control of the monetary policy for a country? Go to the Federal Reserve Bank of San Francisco website and under Student Activities find the Fed Chairman Game. In this game, you act out the role of a fictitious central bank by implementing monetary policy in a simple virtual economy so you can get a feel for the options and limitations of monetary policy. Write a brief summary of your experience. What did you learn from playing the game?

MyBizLab

Go to **mybizlab.com** for Auto-graded writing questions as well as the following Assisted-graded writing questions:

⊘ **2-31** How have the Kindle and the iPad affected the supply and demand for newspapers and other printed material (such as textbooks)? Discuss the impact of technology on those industries that produce printed information.

⊘ **2-32** The text discusses the unemployment rate as a measure of economic performance. While the U.S. unemployment rate has reached historically high levels, ranging between 8.5 and 10.2 percent in 2009–2011, consider the dire unemployment situation in Spain, where the jobless rate has reached over 20 percent. What happened in that European country to provoke such drastic employment consequences? What actions might be taken to begin to increase jobs in Spain?

References

1. Average tax rate is defined as total tax revenue divided by gross domestic product. See "Taxes and Other Revenues," in *CIA World Factbook*, www.cia.gov/library/publications/the-world-factbook/rankorder/2221rank.html (Country Comparisons: Taxes and Other Revenues n.d.).

2. *CIA World Fact Book*, www.cia.gov/library/publications/the-world-factbook/geos/da.html#People

3. Ruut Veenhoven, "World Database of Happiness," http://worlddatabaseofhappiness.eur.nl.

4. Vanessa Wong, "Rival K-Cup Makers Are Climbing Green Mountain," *Bloomberg Businessweek*, August 9, 2013, www.businessweek.com/articles/2013-08-09/rival-k-cup-makers-are-climbing-green-mountain (accessed March 23, 2014).

5. Vanessa Wong "With Keurig 2.0, Green Mountain Wants Its Monopoly Back," *Bloomberg Businessweek*, March 11, 2014, www.businessweek.com/articles/2014-03-11/green-mountain-releases-keurig-2-dot-0-to-help-restore-its-monopoly (accessed March 23, 2014).

6. U.S. Department of Justice, "Justice Department Requires US Airways and American Airlines to Divest Facilities at Seven Key Airports to Enhance System-Wide Competition and Settle Merger Challenge," November 12, 2013, http://www.justice.gov/opa/pr/2013/November/13-at-1202.html (accessed March 23, 2014).

7. Bureau of Labor Statistics, "Frequently Asked Questions, Question 6," www.bls.gov/cpi/cpifaq.htm#Question_6.

8. Bureau of Labor Statistics, "Table 1: Relative Importance of Components in the Consumer Price Indexes: U.S. City Average," December 2010, www.bls.gov/cpi/cpiri2010.pdf.

9. Allison Schrager, "The Great Debate," Reuters, August 28, 2013, http://blogs.reuters.com/great-debate/2013/08/28/five-years-after-recession-we-still-cant-agree-on-what-causes-joblessness.

10. "Historical Inflation," www.inflationdata.com/Inflation/Inflation_Rate/HistoricalInflation.aspx.

11. "The U.S. Inflation Rate—1948–2007," www.miseryindex.us/irbyyear.asp.

12. Sam Mamudi, "Lehman Folds with Record $613 Billion Debt—MarketWatch," *Wall Street Journal*, September 15, 2008, www.marketwatch.com/story/lehman-folds-with-record-613-billion-debt?siteid=rss.

13. "Humbled GM Files for Bankruptcy Protection Business Autos Msnbc.com," June 1, 2009, www.msnbc.msn.com/id/31030038/ns/business-autos/t/humbled-gm-files-bankruptcy-protection.

14. Teresa Sullivan, "Bankruptcy Statistics 1980–2010," www.bankruptcyaction.com/USbankstats.htm.

Chapter 3
Ethics in Business

▶ Ethics: The Basics

Ethics and business—many people consider these terms to be unrelated. How can you maintain your own personal integrity while still fulfilling your business responsibilities? Examining your own personal ethical code is the first step in successfully navigating this potentially tricky terrain.

▶ Personal Ethics Meets Business Ethics

Randy Marks had a recipe for success with his pottery business, but it went against his personal beliefs. What do you do if your own ethics conflict with your business success?

▶ Corporate Social Responsibility

Although the primary focus in business seems to be on making money, many businesses also make meaningful contributions to the social, environmental, and economic development of the world. CEO Howard Schulz runs Starbucks with a mission to be a company with values and guiding principles that his employees could be proud of. How can such a lofty goal lead to amazing profits and growth?

▶ Dangers of a Weak Ethical Focus

Of course, DVDs are copyrighted, but with a big trade show coming up, Lana's project team needed to rip some videos to hard drives for testing. Who would it hurt, after all? Sometimes it seems that if you break ethical standards just a bit, you'll come out ahead. But does it really pay in business to ignore ethics? Or do good guys come out ahead?

▶ Business Opportunities Created by Ethical Needs

Richard Stephenson saw a need—more compassionate medical care that was still state of the art in terms of its quality. By creating new markets based on ethical needs, many companies like Stephenson's reap financial rewards, improve employee morale, and make valuable contributions to the world.

▶ How Businesses Develop an Ethical Environment

Unbelievable. There they were—the once-frozen test tubes of samples, leaking all over the back delivery dock. Rashid Divecha's heart sank. He needed to manage his client—and his bosses—in an ethical way. But what did that mean exactly?

OBJECTIVES

1 What are ethics and different ethical systems? (pp. 55–58)

2 How does someone create a personal code of ethics? (pp. 56–58)

3 How might personal ethics play a role in the workplace? (pp. 58–60)

4 How can you evaluate a company's ethical code using available resources, such as a mission statement? (pp. 60–61)

5 How do a company's policies and decisions affect its achievement of corporate social responsibility? (pp. 61–69)

6 What challenges does a company face in balancing the demands of social responsibility with successful business practices? (pp. 64–67)

7 What is legal compliance, and how does it affect ethical conduct? (pp. 69–72)

8 What strategies can a company use to recover from ethical lapses? (pp. 71–72)

9 How can companies apply ethical standards to create new business opportunities? (pp. 72–74)

10 What approaches can a company use to develop and maintain an ethical environment? (pp. 75–76)

Ethics: The Basics pp. 55–58

When Tracy Bingham gets up each morning, he turns on SiriusXM Radio to listen to the Howard Stern broadcast, laughing along with the quips and jokes about stereotypes. Next, Tracy grabs his keys and heads out the door to school. As he leaves the line in the school cafeteria, he realizes that he received $20 in change instead of $1 and just keeps on walking. He then heads into the photocopy room to duplicate his homework but discovers that the answer key to his next exam was left on the machine. He shoves the answer key into his backpack, not sure what, if anything, he'll do with it. Before the end of class, the professor compliments him in front of everyone for outstanding writing on his last paper. Tracy knows the writing came from a friend in class but just nods in thanks. That night, he thinks over the day, reviewing the choices he made along the way as he drifts off to sleep. What would you have done if you were in Tracy's shoes? ■

Source: Ivelin Radkov/Fotolia.

Like Tracy, we all make ethical decisions every day. We decide how we will act, which thoughts we will feed, and which we will dispel. We make these decisions based on a set of beliefs about how the world works and what kinds of behaviors are rewarded. These beliefs can be classified as our set of values. In this chapter, we'll see that businesses are similar in that they also have a set of values that guide their actions. Let's examine how values and beliefs about how the world operates influence our personal and business lives.

Ethics Defined

What exactly is ethics? Ethics is the study of the general nature of morals and the specific moral principles that govern a person's behavior.[1] In effect, ethics represents the guidelines you use to make decisions every day. But not all people share the same ethics. Many systems of ethical conduct exist. Some are based on religious systems, some are cultural or national, and some have been passed from generation to generation within a specific ethnic group.

MyBizLab®

⭐ Improve Your Grade!

Over 10 million students improved their results using the Pearson MyLabs. Visit **mybizlab.com** for simulations, tutorials, and end-of-chapter problems.

Systems of Ethical Conduct

What are the different systems of ethical conduct? One ethical system is **moral relativism**, a perspective that holds that there is no universal moral truth; instead, there are only people's individual beliefs, perspectives, and values. This means that there is no single view that is more valid than any other. Thus, no single standard exists to assess ethical truth. According to moral relativists, each person has his or her own ideas of right and wrong, so no one should judge anyone else. Imagine trying to organize any group of people—a family, a company, or a country—according to this ethical system.

Another ethical system is **situational ethics** whereby people make decisions based on a specific situation instead of universal laws. Joseph Fletcher, a Harvard Divinity School professor, developed the concept of situational ethics because he believed that applying the Golden Rule—treating others as you would like to be treated—was more important when it comes to making ethical decisions than applying complex sets of moral rules. Because it challenged the idea that universal rules exist and can be applied to every situation, Fletcher's ethical system was considered very controversial.

Many other ethical systems exist, some of which are defined by religious traditions. For example, **Judeo-Christian ethics** refers to the common set of basic values shared across both Jewish and Christian religious traditions. These include respecting property and relationships, respecting one's parents, and being kind to others.

Of course, people sometimes act in a manner that violates the beliefs they hold or the beliefs of the ethical system they say they follow. **Unethical behavior** is defined as behavior that does not conform to a set of approved standards of social or professional behavior. This is different from **amoral behavior**, in which a person has no sense of right and wrong and no interest in the moral consequences of his or her actions.

Personal Ethics

What are personal ethics? Every day, you have thoughts that lead you to say and do certain things. As you choose your words and actions, you're following a set of **personal ethics**, the principles that guide the decisions you make in your life. Sometimes, people have a very clear, well-defined set of principles that they follow. Other times, a person's ethics are inconsistent or are not applied the same way in every situation. Still other times, people have not taken the time to clarify what they value most.

Sometimes, it seems clear that making an unethical decision will produce an immediate benefit. This is when it is hardest to adhere to your own ethical system. Consider this example: When applying for a dream job, a college senior exaggerates a bit on her résumé about her experiences and responsibilities during an internship to seem more qualified. Is this lying, or is it justified behavior?

Now consider how you treat property. Say you bring home a few pads of paper, some pens, and a stack of blank DVDs from the supply closet at work. Is this stealing? What if it were just one piece of paper you brought home? Some people would say it depends on whether you use the material to do work at home. What if you used some of it on work projects and some of it on personal projects? What if it wasn't you who was taking office supplies but someone else with whom you work? It's often easy to have one view when you're taking the supplies and another when it's the person you like least in the office taking the supplies.

How can I clarify what my personal ethics are? Taking the time to examine your personal ethical code is of great value. If you have a clear idea of which values are most important to you, it will be easier to handle situations in your personal and professional life that require you to make complex ethical decisions. ■ **TABLE 3.1** outlines one way to analyze your own ethical system. Let's look at each step in the process:

1. Write down what kind of person you are. What is your *character*? Would a friend describe you as honest and kind? Ambitious and self-serving? Interested in others' well-being? Be honest in your assessment of yourself.

TABLE 3.1	**Determining Your Code of Personal Ethics**	
	Questions	**Examples**
Base character	What characteristics would others use to describe you?	Honest, reliable, kind, self-centered, aggressive, courageous
Beliefs	What are the most important beliefs you hold and use to make decisions in your life?	"Nice guys finish last." "Hard work always pays off." "We must stand for right against wrong."
Belief origins	Where did your beliefs and your view of your character come from?	Family, religion, movies, personal experiences, people you admire
Behavior	How do your relationships reflect your character and beliefs?	"I have mostly shallow relationships because I tend not to follow through on my commitments." "I have many deep, long-lasting friendships because I value friendship and work to take care of my friends."

2. List the *beliefs* that influence your decision making. For example, would you feel comfortable working in a lab that uses animal testing for medical research purposes? Do you think it is okay to lie? If so, which kinds of lies are acceptable to you, and which kinds are not acceptable? Are your answers inflexible—that is, are you committed to adhering strictly to your ethical positions?

3. Now that you have your beliefs written down, think about *how you came to believe them*. What we experience during our lives offers all of us opportunities to develop our personal ethics. We also are taught about ethical behavior by our families, places of worship, first-grade teachers, and so on. Sometimes, our experiences lead us to abandon some ethical rules and adopt others. And for some of us, our ethical rules are modified depending on what is at stake. Have you accepted your ethical beliefs without investigation, or do they stand up to the test of real-world experiences in your life?

4. Consider your *behavior* with regard to the places you work, study, and live and how you relate to people around you. Would you like to change anything about your behavior? For example, do you ever find yourself gossiping or speaking in a way that creates a more divisive atmosphere? You may feel justified in the comments you're making, but is your ethical position on gossiping creating the kind of environment you ultimately want to live in?

How can an ethical life get me ahead? Sometimes, ethics feels like an abstract ideal—ideas that would be nice in a utopian world but have no real impact on your life in the here and now. Yet there are some clear benefits from living ethically.

First, society has established its own set of rules of conduct as *laws*. Of course, ignoring laws can have an immediate negative impact on your life. But because we live in a society of many different cultures, religions, and ethical systems, the laws do not always reflect our personal ethics. Acts of civil disobedience occur when people choose to nonviolently follow their own beliefs even when they go counter to current laws. Whether it is complying with a law about the way you run your business or following laws that affect your personal life, deciding how your own ethics align with a society's laws is critical.

Living ethically may even be good for your health. When your day-to-day decisions are in conflict with the values you consider most important, you often feel stressed and angry. In situations where constant conflict exists between what you value and what actions you take, a variety of types of mental and physical damage may follow. Renate Schulster* is an example. Schulster, a vice president for the human resources department at a financial services firm, was asked to investigate an employee's allegation that the company's CEO's had engaged in sexual harassment.[2] Schulster's investigation led her to believe that the CEO of

Can Living Ethically Make You Happy?

Research suggests that happiness itself is a result of living ethically. Psychology has established this as a new focus with the emergence of an area of psychology known as *positive psychology*. Dr. Martin Seligman of the University of Pennsylvania's Positive Psychology Center pioneered this field.[3] Seligman and his colleagues have worked to discover the causes of happiness instead of addressing the treatment of mental dysfunctions. His research has shown that by identifying your personal strengths and virtues (things like having empathy or a sense of justice) and aligning your life so you can apply your personal strengths and values every day, you will see an increase in happiness (and a decrease in depression) equivalent to the effects of antidepressant medication and therapy. Finding a way to identify and then apply your ethics and virtues to your daily life does indeed have an impact on your happiness.

the corporation *was* guilty of the offense. Her personal ethics dictated following through with the employee's claim, which put her at odds with the company. As pressure from the conflict between her own values and those of the CEO grew, she sought psychological counseling for the emotional impact of the stress she was experiencing. Schulster was eventually able to recover her medical and legal expenses from her employer and left the company. Although she held on to her integrity, the battle was not an easy one.

Personal ethics are a large part of how people define themselves, their roles in society, and their business conduct. Remember Tracy? Like all of us, Tracy will continue to face ethical decisions throughout his lifetime. By truly thinking about his thoughts and actions—that is, by developing a code of personal ethics—he will be in a better position to see what his options are in complex and challenging situations.

Source: imagesbykenny/Fotolia.

Personal Ethics Meets Business Ethics pp. 58–61

"It was a beautiful glaze," Randy Marks says with a sigh. His small pottery shop depends on orders from individuals and small architecture firms looking for authentic, custom pieces of tile to adorn their kitchens, floors, or fountains. "I used copper and a special firing method to give the glaze a stunning crimson color," Randy explains. "It was our best-selling item." An architect in New York City quickly contracted with Randy's shop to produce a much larger number of tiles for his clients. This meant Randy had to work more hours and hire more employees to handle the extra business. However, part of the production process entailed the introduction of additional copper during firing, producing a thick black smoke laced with toxic copper. As the orders increased, more often than not, the kiln in the back of the workshop spewed this smoke into the air, in contrast to the clean white smoke produced by normal glazes.

Randy had been part of environmental groups in his community for years, so he knew how detrimental to the environment this process was. How could he find a way to stay true to his ethical standards and still be mindful of his responsibilities to his employees and customers? ■

We often find ourselves torn between several choices, and finding a path that works for both you and the company you work for can be challenging. In some settings, the line between right and wrong is difficult to see. Other times, your own personal values just won't align with the company's, and you may wish you had better understood the company's sense of ethical culture early in your career—before you invested your time and effort. Let's review some examples, resources, and techniques to help you navigate ethical conflict in the workplace.

You as a Person and as an Employee

What role do personal ethics have in a business environment? Our personal ideas of right and wrong influence our actions, words, and thoughts. But how does that carry over into the work environment? After all, our employer is purchasing our time and energy. As employees, we feel a responsibility to follow the ethics that the owner or director has established for the business. However, a business owner has no control over or even input into your conduct outside the office.

But is this really true? Perhaps at one time this model applied to life in the United States, but the modern workplace is more complex. Today, off-the-job behavior, integrity, and honesty relate to on-the-job performance. For example, in the modern workplace, workers telecommute, working from home using technologies to connect electronically to office documents and meetings. In this newly expanded workplace, an employer may indeed care if an employee drinks at home during the workday or experiments with drugs recreationally. Corporate boards of directors may keep a close eye on the decisions their CEOs make in using social media. Tech CEO Greg Gopman posted a scathing rant on Facebook about the homeless population of San Francisco, painting an image of an elite, uncaring tech industry. The business environment is a changing landscape, and the lines of privacy laws are becoming blurred. Do employers really have a say over an employee's behavior outside the office if that behavior may affect the company for which the person works?

Likewise, stockholders (people who own stock in a company) and employees sometimes have a say over the behavior of management outside the office. A classic example is seen when Boeing was recovering from a set of scandals involving how it obtained military contracts.[4] The aerospace leader fired its current CEO and hired a former Boeing employee, Harry C. Stonecipher, to lead the company back to stability. Fifteen months later, Stonecipher, who was married, was discovered having an affair with a female employee. The very same code of ethical conduct that Stonecipher had created and pointed to as a sign of the return of ethical conduct at Boeing was used to force his resignation. There were no charges of sexual harassment, and the woman did not work directly for Stonecipher. He never showed her any favored treatment within Boeing. But there still was a conflict between his personal ethics and his role in the business. It took a great toll on him personally as well as the company he was working to restore.

What if you are asked to do something that conflicts with your understanding of ethical behavior? It can be challenging to decide whose ethics to follow, yours or your company's, and each path has legal and moral consequences. For example, Andrea Malone* was ordered by the president of her company to fire an employee who had a brain tumor because the tumor had lowered the employee's productivity.[5] Andrea knew that the Americans with Disabilities Act (ADA) covered such situations

Boeing fired its CEO, Harry Stonecipher, for unethical conduct. Ironically, Stonecipher had been hired to lead Boeing back to stability after a number of scandals had rocked the aerospace company.
Source: PIERRE VERDY/Getty Images, Inc.

ADM was at the center of an international price-fixing scandal, meeting with its own competitors to set the price and amount of product it sold. ADM employee Mark Whitacre became an FBI informant for three years to expose the scandal. He was portrayed by Matt Damon in *The Informant*, a dark comedy about these events.
Source: TIMOTHY A. CLARY/Getty Images, Inc.

and that it was a violation of federal law to fire the employee under these conditions. However, her company insisted she fire the employee and say that it was for other reasons, not the tumor. Andrea chose to leave the company rather than fire the person unfairly, but she has since had difficulty finding another job. Andrea held to her personal ethics but was not properly prepared for the short-term consequences.

What if you find you are taking part in unethical activity without realizing that you were doing so? Before Bruce Forest* accepted a job offer as a human resources director, he asked the firm about rumors that they hired undocumented immigrants. He was assured that was no longer the case. However, soon after Bruce started to work for the company, he began receiving information that the illegal hiring was still going on at the company. Bruce's boss ordered him not to investigate the situation, saying that the company would prefer the risk of being fined by U.S. Citizenship and Immigration Services. According to his boss, the fine would be "an acceptable business expense."[6] So now Bruce was complicit in an illegal activity and had to make some tough decisions. Should he quit his job? Doing so might mean he would have to move his family, take a pay cut, and lose a bonus his company had promised him.

Mark Whitacre faced a situation similar to Bruce's. Whitacre was a senior executive with the agricultural giant Archer Daniels Midland (ADM). For years, ADM was involved in a multinational price-fixing scheme. **Price fixing** occurs when a group of companies agree among themselves to set a product's price artificially high so customers have to pay more than they should for the product. Whitacre was a participant in the illegal activities and was set to rise to the very top of the organization. His wife, however, became increasingly conflicted with what was happening at ADM and with her own ethical values. She finally threatened to divorce Whitacre unless he found a way to end his involvement. Whitacre then went to the FBI and became the highest-level corporate executive in U.S. history to become a whistle-blower. He agreed to record secret meetings at ADM, ultimately capturing incriminating audiotape and videotape for the FBI over a three-year period.[7] Whitacre himself ended up spending almost nine years in prison. He is now the chief operating officer of a biotech firm in California. The story is so compelling that it was made into a film starring Matt Damon—*The Informant*.

To stumble unknowingly into unethical and even illegal activity like Whitacre did puts people in a difficult situation, especially when their jobs are on the line. Although some people decide they will "be flexible" with their own ethical standards in the workplace, it can often take a toll on their mental state, relationships, and physical health.

Identifying a Company's Ethics

How do I examine a company's ethics? Some companies may have a written **code of ethics**, or a statement of their commitment to certain ethical practices. Also called a *code of conduct*, it is meant to give employees guidance on how to handle themselves in challenging ethical situations. Additionally, many companies have a public **mission statement** that defines the core purpose of the organization—why it exists. The mission statement describes the company's values, goals, and aspirations. Consider the following mission statement of Fetzer Vineyards:

Working in harmony with nature and with the utmost respect for the human spirit, we are committed to the continuous growth and development of our people, the quality of our wines, and the care of our planet.[8]

This mission statement has led to 100 percent organic wine production for Fetzer, awards for its conservation of energy, and a company-wide English as a Second Language training program offered as part of its education package for its employees.

How can I find out the best and worst aspects of a company's ethical conduct? In addition to a company's code of ethics and mission statement, other resources allow you to evaluate the acts of a company and legal violations it may have committed. For example, you can check the legal compliance of a corporation by researching actual charges that have been filed or cases that have been adjudicated against a company. Websites such as **lawcrawler.findlaw.com** help you find relevant case law generated by lawsuits filed by or against many corporations.

There are also organizations, such as the Boston College Center for Corporate Citizenship, that work with corporations to help them define, plan, and institute their corporate citizenship. This center also highlights companies that act in positive ways by publicizing responsible corporate activities and listing on its website reports in the general media of ethical issues in business. By doing so, the center works with companies to "leverage their assets to ensure both the company's success and a more just and sustainable world."[9] We'll discuss other ways you can assess a company's ethics and sense of corporate responsibility in the next section.

What did Randy Marks decide to do when his personal and business ethics collided with the production of the special pottery glaze? No one was "watching"; there was no censure from any environmental authority, and no laws were being broken. But the conflict for Randy was too much. "I had campaigned against factory emissions of air pollution for years," Randy said. "The ethical conflict was too great; I had to stop making the glaze." Randy's decision led to difficult times for the shop. The New York architect canceled his order—the glaze had been the winning factor for his business. The workers in the shop were also frustrated. They loved producing interesting, beautiful pieces, and the new orders meant extra hours and extra earnings. Their shop was so small, they argued, how could a little smoke possibly matter in the big scheme of things?

Although Randy's pottery shop does not have a formal written mission statement, his behavior and willingness to discuss his decision behind discontinuing the popular glaze let each employee see clearly the priorities Randy held for the business. Randy had to be firm, repeatedly explaining that his personal ethics had to be consistent with his workplace ethics and that he was sure that, in the long run, the shop would benefit from his decision. Even though Randy's employees did not easily accept his decision, they felt the larger mission of the business was well defined and respected.

Corporate Social Responsibility pp. 61–69

With a lofty mission of becoming a national company with values and guiding principles his employees could be proud of, in 1987, Howard Schulz purchased Starbucks, a Seattle storefront that sold fresh-roasted whole-bean coffee. Since then, Starbucks has become an entrepreneurial dream business, with over 19,000 stores in over 60 countries. How are the goals of helping communities, protecting the environment, and inspiring employees related to the bottom line of business—profit and growth? ■

Source: eongJoon Cho/Bloomberg/Getty Images.

Corporate decisions reflect a company's desire to fulfill a sense of corporate social responsibility. Every day, large companies like Gap,

Disney, and Shell, as well as medium-size firms and small local businesses, must make decisions that reflect their corporate social responsibility. Let's look at what corporate social responsibility means, who it affects, and how companies can achieve it.

The Five Pillars of Corporate Social Responsibility

What is corporate social responsibility? Corporate social responsibility (CSR) is defined as a company's obligation to conduct its activities with the aim of achieving social, environmental, and economic development. Being socially responsible requires a company to make good decisions in the following five major areas (see ■ **FIGURE 3.1**):

1. Human rights and employment standards in the workplace
2. Ethical sourcing and procurement
3. Marketing and consumer issues
4. Environmental, health, and safety concerns
5. Community and good-neighbor policies

Let's look at each of these areas.

Human Rights and Employment Standards in the Workplace CSR concerns affect the world outside the office in both local and global communities. For example, employment standards—how a company respects and cares for its employees—are reflected locally in the policies a company sets and the impact

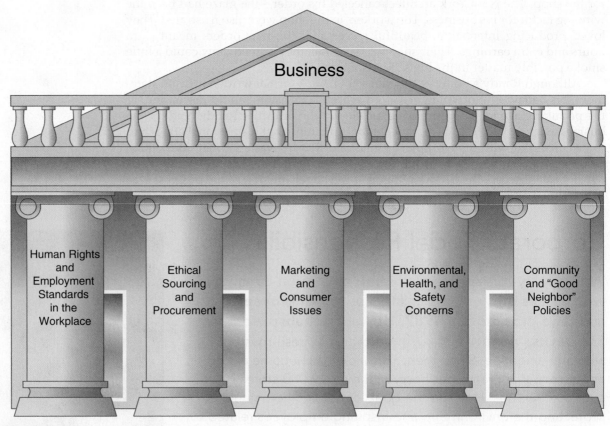

■ **FIGURE 3.1**
The Five Pillars of Corporate Social Responsibility
Corporate social responsibility is the collection of policies covering five major areas and can be the foundation of a business.
Source: Pearson Education, Inc.

Marketing Campaign Meets Ethics

The new marketing campaign had just begun for Cathay Pacific airlines. The catchy new slogan that emphasized the company's willingness to do "a little extra" to make their passengers' flight experience special was ready to go.

But then a photograph made its way onto the Internet showing a Cathay pilot and a flight attendant on board a plane in a compromising position. Knowing the rate at which the image could go viral over social networking, Cathay's CEO pulled the campaign.

Could Cathay Pacific airlines have dealt with the problem differently?

---

a company has on the community. As a business interacts more with the global marketplace, a company will have to make decisions about ethical standards on tough issues, such as child labor, pollution, fair wages, and human rights. Consider the case of the Vadanta Resources, a mining and aluminum-refining company based in the United Kingdom. When Vadanta came into the Indian community of Orissa, it promised great gains in the quality of life for its employees and the entire region. Such gains have not appeared, however, and, because of the refining company's practices, the air is hard to breathe. Meanwhile, the river that runs through the community and that is the main source of drinking water is so polluted that bathing in it causes rashes and blisters.[10] What responsibility does Vadanta have to its employees, the people of the area, and company stockholders?

Ethical Sourcing and Procurement Finding a source for raw materials and making agreements with suppliers is an aspect of many businesses. In today's global marketplace, many companies find themselves working with international suppliers. Once a business considers purchasing materials from a supplier in a different country or even a different region of their home country, the company is tied to environmental and social concerns in that area. Consider a company that has an assembly plant in a different country. That company is now tied to the social conditions there. To keep its supplier operating or keep an assembly plant running smoothly, the company has a vested interest in the quality of the schools in that area so that the local workforce is educated.

The banana supplier Chiquita, for example, has a vested interest in the parts of the world where it gets its produce. Chiquita had a decades-long reputation of allowing its farmworkers to toil in dangerous conditions, contaminating water and clear-cutting tropical forests. Because workers' rights and environmental issues were endangering its brand name, Chiquita began to improve conditions. It constructed housing for its workers and schools for their children. Now the environmental group Rainforest Alliance certifies all of Chiquita's farms, ensuring they meet specific standards regarding the use of pesticides, workers' health issues, and related topics.[11] A commitment to CSR means that companies must be aware of the ethical impact of their actions—both at home and in communities far from their shores.

Many people have purchased the Apple iPhone, but until a few years ago, few of these buyers were aware of the working conditions at the plants of Apple's suppliers. An audit of suppliers' factories in China revealed the use of underage workers, environmental violations, and unsafe worker conditions sometimes so severe that there were suicide attempts by workers. Apple disclosed the results of this audit publicly in a supplier responsibility progress report it issues periodically. Over the next year, Apple increased the number of supply chain audits and trained workers on their rights.[12] By some measures, things improved, but the company continues to address juvenile worker protection with its suppliers.

Marketing and Consumer Issues Marketing can often present ethical challenges. In addition to issues regarding truth in advertising, marketers must consider messages that may be manipulative even if they contain no outright lies. For example, several major fashion labels, such as Prada, Versace, and Armani, have agreed to ban size-zero models from their fashion shows. As more medical authorities have linked the viewing of these images with an increase in eating disorders among women, the fashion industry is faced with a decision. There are many marketing and consumer issues that companies must consider if they are to behave in a socially responsible way. What do you think? Is the use of size-zero professional models socially irresponsible? What about retouching photos for advertisements so that the models look perfect? Is that okay? How do we judge when responsible behavior turns into irresponsible behavior?

Environmental, Health, and Safety Concerns Many industries, even small companies, make decisions every day that affect the environment and the safety of their workers or neighbors. From multinational manufacturing giants to local auto body shops, any industry involved with processes that produce toxic waste must make decisions that directly affect the environment. Meanwhile, the production of toxic materials is moving at a far faster pace than the growth of proper storage and disposal facilities and techniques, so disposing of the materials becomes more and more expensive.

> ### THE **LIST**
>
> **Nine Causes Americans Think Charities Should Focus On**
>
> 1. Education
> 2. Youth and families
> 3. Medical research
> 4. Human rights
> 5. Environment
> 6. Disaster relief
> 7. Global health
> 8. Animal rights
> 9. Arts

One of the most infamous cases was documented in the award-winning book *A Civil Action* (Vintage, 1996). A high incidence leukemia among the children in a small Massachusetts town led to the case. Ultimately, it was discovered that the town's water supply had been poisoned by trichloroethylene dumped by two local businesses. What are the short- and long-term costs of ignoring these concerns? Companies that have a CSR focus work to recognize the social impact of their decisions.

Community and Good-Neighbor Policies Finally, CSR relates to how a company affects the communities in which it does business, particularly the surrounding neighborhoods. This issue has been a challenge for Walmart for years. In the documentary *Wal-Mart: The High Cost of Low Price*, film director Robert Greenwald argues that Walmart pays its associates so little that the arrival of a Walmart outlet in a community actually costs the community.[13] Some stores have held holiday food drives for their own employees. Because workers are paid poorly and are not offered medical benefits to cover their children, Medicaid expenditures for the communities increase, which the public must pay with their taxes. In addition, Greenwald argues that many local and smaller businesses cannot compete with the giant and are forced to close. Adding insult to injury, often a community has given Walmart subsidies to attract the company to the area. Finding a way to be a good corporate neighbor is important to avoid the tensions and bad publicity that Walmart has struggled against.

Walmart's impact on local communities is hotly debated. Detractors argue that the company's employees are paid so little that they often need social services in combination with their Walmart jobs just to survive.
Source: Bill O'Leary/The Washington Post/Getty Images.

The Conflict of CSR in the Business Environment

Can a corporation really be socially responsible? The Nobel Prize–winning economist Milton Friedman said, "Asking a corporation to be socially responsible makes no more sense than asking a building to be."[14] He argued that an abstract idea, like a corporation, cannot perform human functions, such as meeting responsibilities. There has long been debate around these ideas. The Citizen United decision of the U.S. Supreme Court in 2010 ruled that corporations have the same constitutional rights as people to choose elected officials—and therefore have the ability to make unlimited political contributions.

A company has a unique responsibility to its stockholders: to deliver a profit at the end of the year. It is difficult to measure how that responsibility interacts with a long-term responsibility to the community or the planet. There can be a conflict between a company's need to produce profit for its shareholders and the demands of CSR. Are the demands worth it? Although a business reaps benefits by being socially responsible, managers at very high strategic levels must have a common vision of how the interests of the business can be supported by an effective CSR policy.

The Benefits of CSR

What are the benefits of CSR? Having a strong and clear ethical policy helps a business in a number of ways:

- A company develops a positive reputation in the marketplace with consumers as well as with its suppliers and vendors.
- A company is able to recruit and retain the best available talent.
- Efficiency increases when companies use materials resourcefully and minimize waste.
- Sales increase through new product innovations and environmentally and ethically conscious labeling.

Measuring CSR

Is it possible to measure a company's CSR level? It may seem impossible to measure something as complex as CSR, but there are ways to get a picture of the overall strength of a company's CSR effort.

Social Audits

A **social audit** is a study of how well a company is meeting its social responsibilities. It is an internal and systematic examination that measures and monitors what goals a company has set, what progress it has made, and how resources, such as funding and labor, have been applied to the CSR goals.

Ratings and Rankings

In addition to social audits, organizations like the Boston College Center for Corporate Citizenship assess corporate responsibility and publish their findings. And companies like the Calvert Investment Company provide corporate responsibility

Corporations as People

In the famed Citizen United case, the U.S. Supreme Court ruled that corporations, which are made up of individuals, have the same constitutional rights as people to choose elected officials and so can make unlimited contributions to political campaigns. It opened the door to a discussion of the state of democracy in America. Does this decision allow corporations and a small collection of the ultrarich to overpower the voice of the individual in American politics?

Should a corporation have all the same rights as an individual? Could a company plead the Fifth Amendment and avoid self-incrimination in criminal proceedings? In what sense do we want corporations to be legal entities with rights and responsibilities? Should corporations be measured to the same standard of ethical conduct and compassion that we hold for the people we admire?

ratings and reports to consumers. The Calvert Investment Company assigns companies a score based on their performance in the categories of environment, workplace, business practices, human rights, and community relations. Investors can use the "Know What You Own®" tool to investigate a fund and check the environmental and social performance of the companies in the fund.

In addition to social audits and the Calvert ratings, various magazines, such as *Fortune*, publish lists of admired companies each year. Other organizations award businesses for superior CSR. For example, as a recipient of the WorldBlu Most Democratic Workplaces Award, Chroma Technology Corp., a manufacturer of optical filters, has many innovative practices.[15] In this global company, employees hold all the seats on the board of directors. In addition, the company's salary structure heavily rewards loyalty. Each employee makes a base salary that depends on his or her specialty in the organization that then increases on the basis of seniority.[16]

Another often-cited CSR award winner is Clif Bar, Inc., a manufacturer of organic energy bars. Gary Erickson started the company in his kitchen with $1,000. After 10 years of consistent growth, Erickson was about to accept an offer of $120 million for the company. At the last minute, he learned that the purchasers were planning to move Clif Bar out of state and lay off all the firm's current employees. He felt his integrity and vision were at stake, so he canceled the deal and took over the company again.

Self-Reporting

The practice of companies self-reporting their own efforts when it comes to addressing ethically complex issues and issues of social responsibility is also becoming more prevalent. Every year, the entertainment company Time Warner presents to its stockholders a CSR report that discusses its advances in corporate citizenship, including its focus on journalistic integrity, socially responsible programming (including issues such as the depiction of smoking in films), content accessibility, consumer privacy, content diversity, and child protection.[17]

Corporate Philanthropy

Many companies participate in **corporate philanthropy**, which is the practice of donating some of their profits or resources to charitable organizations. Often, companies view philanthropic activities as a marketing investment designed to build stronger relationships with the communities in which they do business, their own employees, and consumers in general. Target, for example, donates 5 percent of its pretax profits to charity, which is about $3 million a week.[18] This is more than twice the average of other American corporations.

Another example is the Bill and Melinda Gates Foundation, started by Microsoft chairman Bill Gates. With an endowment of $40 billion, the Gates Foundation has tackled issues like global infant survival rates, began an initiative for a malaria vaccine, and is working to support innovation in education. Even though the foundation is not directly associated with Microsoft, it has had a positive impact on the public's perception of the company.

CSR and Social Networking

What does social networking have to do with CSR? As is the case with many aspects of business, social networking is changing the face of CSR. At one point, the hamburger chain Wendy's used Twitter to raise money for its founder's foundation, the Dave Thomas Foundation for Adoption.

The Bill and Melinda Gates Foundation commits more than $1.5 billion a year in grants to global health and development projects, such as vaccination campaigns against polio in India.
Source: Jeff Christensen/Liaison/Getty Images, Inc.

Each time the message #TreatItFwd was retweeted, Wendy's contributed 50 cents to help kids in foster care. The Father's Day promotion raised $1.8 million.[19]

The banking conglomerate Chase has moved into crowdsourced philanthropy with its Chase Community Giving Program. Since 2009, Chase has used a Facebook page to let visitors to the site decide to which nonprofits the company makes donations.

What does Chase get in return? Perhaps a more positive reputation and increased engagement by its customers.

The Challenges of CSR

What challenges does CSR pose? It's clear that the many conflicting demands facing businesses today pose numerous ethical challenges. Consider the dilemma facing companies that produce unique products, such as pharmaceutical companies that develop medications to treat AIDS. What is their exact moral and ethical obligation with regard to the AIDS pandemic in sub-Saharan Africa? Over 23 million people are living with HIV in Africa.[20] One-third of them are also infected with tuberculosis. Another 1 million or more people in Africa die from malaria each year, mostly children.[21] Meanwhile, 70 percent of Africans exist on less than $2 a day and are unable to pay for the medications that would reimburse pharmaceutical companies for their research investment to develop them. It is a challenge for modern business leaders to balance their need to respond to investors and produce a profit with their desire to alleviate human suffering. There is no fixed training that prepares and equips business decision makers to navigate such difficult decisions.

Nonetheless, some corporations manage to consistently balance the demands of social responsibility and successful business practices. Intel scores high as an industry leader in terms of its commitment to strong CSR practices.[22] Environmentally, it has decreased the emissions from its operations over the past four years, mitigating its impact on global warming. It has shown a strong commitment to its employees by providing benefits for domestic partners as well as carefully monitoring workers for exposure to hazardous chemicals. The company also has human rights policies in place in each country in which it operates. In addition, it donates computer equipment to many organizations, supports many charitable organizations through monetary donations, and is responsive to community needs.

The Effects of CSR on Society

How does CSR affect society as a whole? Businesses do not operate separately from society as a whole, so CSR affects us all in many ways.

Environmental Effects

Environmentally, how businesses operate has both local and global effects. For example, people living in the Silicon Valley area near San Francisco rely on groundwater for their main supply of water. This leaves the entire Silicon Valley area dependent on proper industry practices by the many semiconductor manufacturers in the area. If these companies allow chemical contaminants to enter the groundwater system, the entire region suffers.

Businesses raise troubling environmental questions on a global scale as well. Some say that allowing free trade—in which countries produce and sell products anywhere in the world—is exporting pollution to less developed countries. Are companies moving "dirty industries"—those that have a high risk of pollution, danger to workers, or toxic damage of the environment—to countries where environmental regulations are lacking? It is increasingly important for industry leaders to have some structured ethical system to make such complex, long-reaching decisions.

Economic Effects

As an individual, CSR affects you as well. Financially, the long-term consequences of businesses implementing a strong CSR plan have an impact on the prices you pay for products, the products that are available to you, and the quality of those products. Industries that act in ways that jeopardize their own long-term sustainability can create economic ripples that affect the bottom line of individual consumers.

Effects on Employee Morale

Think of your own career. Your potential for advancement, day-to-day work environment, and overall sense of purpose are affected by the degree to which the company you work for is socially responsible. The ethical culture of a company and its leadership has effects on its workers every day. Sometimes, this effect is a positive one. Consider the Publicis Kaplan Thaler advertising agency, the fastest-growing advertising firm in the country, started by Linda Kaplan Thaler and Robin Koval. The billion-dollar company, which began as a one-client startup, prides itself on creating unique ad campaigns, such as the Aflac duck campaign, that grab viewers' attention.

Yet for all of its success, the core philosophy of the company, as Thaler and Koval describe in their book *The Power of Nice*, is that being nice *pays*. After spending years at high-powered, high-pressure firms where "those who eat their young get raises," Thaler and Koval instead founded a firm dedicated to the principles of being empathetic.[23] They assume that the people you work with are there to help you, and remember that emotionally, well-adjusted people earn higher incomes, live longer, and have more satisfying lives.[24] The company founders' beliefs affect the employees at the firm each and every day.

Even from the initial interview, aspects of a company's CSR plan may be apparent. For example, it's becoming increasingly common for companies that practice CSR to try to attract job candidates and hire employees who match their own corporate values. Doing so results in a workforce that's more dedicated and performs better, firms are finding. Human resources management professionals refer to this practice as *value-based* recruiting and hiring.

The Effects of Individuals on CSR

How can I affect how businesses operate ethically? There are many ways that individuals can work toward a more ethical world filled with more ethical businesses. In addition to contributing by means of your own personal conduct, both at the workplace and outside of it, your choices about where and on what to spend your money greatly influence corporate behavior. Companies survive only because consumers buy their products or use their services. If you don't believe in a company's ethics, you can take your business elsewhere.

Meanwhile, if you choose to invest money in mutual funds and the stock market, you have another opportunity to make a statement about corporate ethics. **Socially responsible investing** (SRI) is the practice of investing only in companies that have met a certain standard of CSR. Investment-fund managers who practice SRI look at the social and environmental behavior of companies to decide which of them to include and exclude from their investment portfolios. As a shareholder, you can also use your voice to encourage a company to improve or maintain a high standard of ethics.

Finally, when you choose an employer, you're making a clear statement on ethical conduct by offering the company your valuable time and energy. By agreeing to work for a company, you're saying that you agree with its mission and ethics.

As a boy, Starbucks founder Howard Schulz watched his father grow ill and his family lose their home and be driven into public housing as a result. Schulz was determined that any company he ran would never let such a thing happen to an employee. When he bought Starbucks in 1987, he immediately extended a company-subsidized health care package to all full- and part-time employees and their dependents. The deductibles, copays, and benefits are the same for all employees. The incredible success of Starbucks could be an accident that happened in spite of the company's commitment to ethics and social responsibility, but Howard Schulz would tell you something different.

Dangers of a Weak Ethical Focus pp. 69–72

"To me, it was stealing, and, bottom line, stealing is wrong."
The software firm Lana Phillips worked for had finished developing
a program to deliver movie content on demand to people's mobile
devices. Before the company could break into the market, however, it
needed to test its product and make appearances at big electronics
trade shows. To test the program, the company needed movies. But
movies are copyrighted, and DVDs of them are encrypted so they cannot
be copied onto a computer hard drive. As the testing phase approached,
word came down from management: purchase some DVDs, break the
encryption, and rip them to hard drives to use as testing. After all, the
managers reasoned, the company was not going to make money from
violating DVD copyrights; it was just using it to test its software. And if
it worked well, it would then run demos for clients and at trade shows
using those DVDs. What was the harm?

Source: alexskopje/Fotolia.

The company consulted its attorneys, and half felt the use of the DVDs
might be illegal and half felt it could be defended. Lana suggested
some other solutions: The company could use Hollywood films that
were older and not covered by copyright protection or public domain
documentaries, which were freely available for public use. Company
managers worried what the impact on business would be. Would a
product shown running a 30-year-old movie or an unknown documentary
grab the attention of buyers at a busy Las Vegas trade show? The
danger on the other side was that a successful product launch by the
company might not save it from facing future legal action for copyright
infringement. How could Lana and her boss resolve the issue when it
wasn't even clear what the correct legal path was? ■

**Depending on the industry, there may be significant legal consequences to
business behavior that ignores agreed-on ethical standards.** Companies are responsible for following complex sets of laws, and if they violate them, even unknowingly, their businesses may be in jeopardy. Next we'll examine some of the
business dangers of ignoring ethical conduct.

Legal Regulations and Legal Compliance

How is a company regulated legally? **Legal regulations** are the specific laws
governing the products or processes of a specific industry. When enough people
feel that a particular ethical standard is important, it eventually becomes law. For
example, in 1962, the Consumer Bill of Rights was passed in Congress. This bill
made the following ethical standards legal rights: the right to safety, the consumer's right to choose, their right to information, and their right to be heard.[25]

Another example is the Organic Seal of the U.S. Department of Agriculture
(USDA), which assures consumers of the quality and integrity of organic products. To certify a product as organic, a company must meet stringent conditions
set by the USDA, including annual and random inspections to check on standards.

Legal compliance refers to conducting a business within the boundaries
of all the legal regulations of an industry. Various government agencies, such
as the Equal Employment Opportunity Commission (EEOC) and the Securities
and Exchange Commission (SEC), provide guidance to companies to help them
maintain legal compliance. The EEOC monitors their compliance by investigating complaints about discrimination, sexual harassment, or violations of the ADA
in the workplace. The ADA of 1990 requires companies to make a reasonable

accommodation to the known disabilities of an applicant or employee, as long as it doesn't require undue hardship for the employer. The SEC governs the securities industry to ensure that all investors are treated fairly and have the same access to information about companies.

Violations of federal laws can severely damage a company. We mentioned earlier how ADM, the agriculture giant, was involved in a large price-fixing scheme in which it bilked its own customers out of millions of dollars. The company was later fined $100 million for its role in the price fixing. Likewise, in 2010, British Petroleum agreed to establish a fund of $20 billion to begin to meet claims of damage resulting from the Deepwater Horizon oil spill.[26]

Don't companies often break the law and still make money? There are plenty of cases in which companies have broken the law and seemed to benefit—for a time. Take the case of Enron. With 21,000 staff members in more than 40 countries, Enron had grown to become the seventh-largest company in the United States. The company was lauded by *Fortune* magazine as the Most Innovative Company in America many times and was in the top 25 of *Fortune*'s 100 Best Companies to Work For. Enron had published its social and environmental positions, noting that the company made decisions based on three values:[27]

- **Respect.** Mutual respect with communities and stakeholders affected by the company's operations
- **Integrity.** Examining the impacts, positive and negative, of the business on the environment and society and integrating human health, social, and environmental considerations into the company's management and value system
- **Excellence.** Continuing to improve performance and encouraging business partners and suppliers to adhere to the same standards

However, by 2001, it was discovered that Enron's success had been based largely on fraudulent activities. The company had hidden debts totaling more than $1 billion to inflate its own stock price; manipulated the Texas and California power markets, causing enormous hardship; and bribed foreign governments to win contracts abroad. A few months later, the company filed bankruptcy, and founder Kenneth Lay was convicted on 10 counts of fraud and conspiracy. He later died while awaiting sentencing. CEO Jeffrey Skilling was convicted of 18 counts of fraud and is now serving a 14-year prison sentence.

The global accounting firm that Enron had hired, Arthur Andersen, was convicted of obstruction of justice for destroying thousands of documents relating to its work with Enron and its knowledge of the fraud. The fraud ultimately led to the internal collapse of both companies. Thousands of employees who did not know their managers were participating in illegal activities lost their jobs and pensions as a result.

To avoid future occurrences such as these, the Sarbanes-Oxley Act of 2002 was enacted. Under this act, CEOs are required to verify their companies' financial statements and vouch for their accuracy with the SEC. The act didn't put an end to financial fraud though. In 2008, one of the largest financial scandals of all time was exposed: a massive Ponzi scheme led by New York financier Bernie Madoff. A Ponzi scheme is a swindle whereby investors believe their money is being invested and earning returns for them but is instead being siphoned off by the schemer. A Ponzi scheme works as long as there are not as many investors wanting to withdraw their money from the investment fund. When too many of them do, there is not enough to pay them all, and the scheme is exposed. For decades, Madoff had been collecting billions of dollars in funds from his many prestigious clients, including celebrities, pension funds, and not-for-profit charities. But then it was revealed that over $65 billion was missing from his clients' accounts.[28] He was ultimately convicted and is serving a 150-year prison sentence.

Recovering from Weak Ethical Conduct

What if your company is breaking the law and you want it to stop? Some people risk their positions and future careers to stop corporate abuse when they see it in the workplace. A **whistle-blower** is an employee who reports misconduct, most often to an authority outside the firm. Famous examples include Jeffrey Wigand, a vice president of a tobacco company who, in 1996, revealed on the television show *60 Minutes* that his company was deliberately upping the nicotine in its cigarettes to make them more addictive. Another example is Sergeant Joseph Darby, who sent to the U.S. Army Criminal Investigation Command an anonymous note and photos of prisoners being abused at the U.S. prison Abu Ghraib in Iraq. The information sparked an investigation that eventually revealed to the public the abuses at the prison. Darby later received a John F. Kennedy Profile in Courage Award, but he and his wife were forced to live in protective custody in an undisclosed location because of threats made against them.

Legal protection for whistle-blowers varies from state to state and industry to industry. For the people who take such a step, the pressure of the conflict between what they see and their own ethical standards forces them to make tremendous sacrifices.

Can a company really recover from an ethical lapse? Companies that try to recover from highly publicized ethical lapses often face a long road. Recovering from a scandal almost certainly requires pervasive change. Usually, employees who were not involved in the wrongdoing work to forge a new image. If the corruption is bad enough, sometimes a company goes so far as "clean house"—that is, terminate all of its current managers and maybe even its employees to try "save face" with the public. That's what happened at Tyco International when it was discovered in 2003 that the firm's president and chief financial officer had ripped off the company by hundreds of millions of dollars. The money was siphoned off via illegal corporate loans and by manipulating the company's stock price. Both men were convicted of fraud and later sentenced to up to 25 years in prison. Within a few months of being hired, Tyco's new CEO replaced all of the members of the company's board of directors as well all of the firm's 290 employees.

Companies that are attempting to recover from scandal often follow some common strategies:

- They work to find a leader who will set an example of the new ethical image of the company.

- They restructure their internal operations to empower all employees to consider the ethical implications of their decisions and feel free to speak up when they spot a concern.

- They redesign internal rewards, for example, restructuring their incentive packages for sales employees so that they are financially rewarded for building ongoing relationships with their clients rather than just closing one-time sales.

By using creative thinking and adhering to clearly stated ethical principles, a company can actually turn a scandal into something good. For example, in 2004, many shoppers boycotted Target because the chain had a policy of not allowing solicitors to collect money outside its doors, including volunteers collecting for the Salvation Army. The Salvation Army reported the ban cost the charity more than $9 million in possible donations. Target could have responded with a defensive attack on the Salvation Army or by pointing out that the retailer has been investing 5 percent of its profit in local communities since 1946. Instead, the company chose to work with the Salvation Army, first donating the lost $9 million directly and then creating an online "wish list" shoppers could use to donate toys, clothes, and household items to needy families during the holiday season. By acting together with the Salvation Army in new ways, Target was able to turn a negative situation into something beneficial for both itself and the community.

Now think back to Lana Phillips's company copying movies from DVDs. Even though the firm wasn't committing fraud on the scale of the Enron scandal, many of the same principles are at play. The temptation to ignore existing laws to make a profit—or even the chance for profit—lies at the heart of both stories. Enron's misdeeds devastated thousands, if not millions, of people. At Lana's firm, future penalties could cripple the company, but simply knowingly violating her own personal code of ethics was the driving force for Lana. She was forced to decide whether she would refuse to work on the project and potentially lose her job, knowing that her manager would assign the work to another employee who would then be breaking the law. Lana decided to urge her company to not use the copyrighted DVDs. Ultimately, executives agreed with her. They felt that the risk of future copyright infringement lawsuits was too great. Lana's persistence paid off, and she was able to maintain both her job security and a personal code of ethics.

Business Opportunities Created by Ethical Needs pp. 72–74

Source: Fuse/Thinkstock/Getty Images, Inc.

In the early 1980s, Mary Stephenson lost her battle with cancer. After her death, her son, Richard Stephenson, tried to explore what options the family might have pursued that would have made his mother's final days with her family of higher quality. He found facilities that were equipped to provide top-notch technical care but none that provided compassion and nurturing for the whole person who was ill as well as for his or her entire family. How could he give his mother's death meaning and positively affect the lives of others? Was there a way that the business of health care could be both successful and compassionate? ■

So far, we've addressed the extra work and the difficult decisions that have to be made to conduct business ethically. But there are also opportunities and potential for gains for doing so. Like Richard Stephenson, some companies focus on creating new markets with an ethical focus. Others redesign their businesses so that they no longer have a negative impact on the environment. Still others use ethical challenges as a tool to unite and empower employees.

Creating New Markets with an Ethical Focus

How can firms create business by acting ethically? By examining the world with an eye toward social responsibility, many firms have created opportunities with new types of products and services. Let's examine a few.

Offering Clean Fuel

Topia Energy, an energy company in Canada, has launched a chain of alternative fuel stations named GreenStop. At GreenStop stations, only renewable fuel blends, such as gasoline combined with corn ethanol, are sold. The fuel blends can be used in regular cars, and the stations themselves are constructed from renewable, chemical-free products. Inside you won't see the same lineup of cigarettes and candy, but you will have your choice of organic veggie wraps and coffee roasted using solar energy.[29]

Creating Medical Vaccines

Other companies have created business opportunities by addressing the world's most serious medical needs. Malaria kills up to 3 million people a year, mostly children, and is the leading cause of death in children worldwide, mostly in Africa. The disease is transmitted very easily, whereas the drugs currently used to treat it are becoming increasingly ineffective.

Many businesses haven't found a way to balance the tremendous research costs associated with creating a malaria vaccine with the anticipated meager profits from it. Enter Sanaria, a new pharmaceutical company founded by Dr. Stephen Hoffman, whose mission is to create a malaria vaccine. Hoffman remarks, "I haven't spent 25 years working on diseases of the most disadvantaged and neglected people in the world to start a company that's just here to make money."[30] Already the company has secured government grants and a $29.3 million Gates Foundation grant. The malaria vaccine the company has developed has completed its first phase of clinical trials. If all goes well, the vaccine may get approved by the U.S. Food and Drug Administration (FDA) in a few more years.[31]

Mosquito nets work to reduce the risk of malaria, but the discovery of a malaria vaccine would benefit millions.
Source: ROBERTO SCHMIDT/AFP/Getty Images.

Fighting Censorship

Still other companies are creating business opportunities by fighting censorship. The Chinese government maintains a tight rein on the flow of information to its citizens, including controlling the accessibility of certain Internet sites. This policy of censorship garnered the attention of the international business community when, in 2010, after four years of complying with China's system of censorship so that search results were edited before being presented to users, Google did an about-face and announced it would no longer censor search results for China.[32] Google's announcement was met by an announcement from Microsoft that its Bing search engine would continue to abide by Chinese censorship laws. The Bing search engine has even been charged with censoring information for Chinese language users in the United States in the same way.[33]

This censorship left the founder of Dynamic Internet Technology (DIT), Bill Xia, with a very skewed view of the world when he arrived in the United States from China. ("I was a believer of the propaganda," says Xia, a native of China.[34]) DIT and similar companies provide a paid service that counteracts the impact of censorship. When a site is placed on the list of censored sites by the Chinese government, DIT quickly creates a new, uncensored Web address that points users to the same material. A list of the new accessible sites is then e-mailed to Web surfers who want full Internet access. Chinese censors often stamp out the new site within a few days, at which point DIT starts the process again, determined to override China's censorship. DIT and other companies are showing there are ways to fight censorship and profit from it. The service DIT provides may continue to be important because other countries, including India, are now asking Google to restrict content their governments feel are "antisocial" or "antireligious."[35]

Businesses Going Green

How can businesses benefit by going green? Increasingly, companies are attempting to reduce the impact they have on the environment. Take Interface, Inc., the world's largest commercial carpet manufacturer. The company was careful to follow all laws and regulations related to its industry in its first 21 years of business, but it made no special commitment to stewardship of the environment beyond that. Then CEO Ray Anderson read *The Ecology of Commerce*.[36] Anderson was so inspired by the book's message that he began reorganizing his $1.4 billion company around the principles of sustainability. **Sustainability** is the practice of improving the quality of people's lives in ways that simultaneously protect and enhance the earth's life support systems.[37] Interface has

Starbucks discounts coffee if customers bring their own recyclable tumblers. Customers bring in tumblers over 35 million times a year.
Source: SeongJoon Cho/Bloomberg/Getty Images.

a mission statement, nicknamed Mission Zero, that reads, "Our promise is to eliminate any negative impact Interface has on the environment by 2020."[38]

Interface is rethinking all aspects of its business in an effort to meet its sustainability goal. It is eliminating waste and toxic substances from its products, using renewable energy, and finding how to route its trucks along more efficient transportation routes.[39]

Cool Carpet is one product that demonstrates how Interface now operates. The "cool" part of Cool Carpet is that Interface makes sure that all carbon dioxide emissions over the full life cycle of Cool Carpet—from its manufacture through its delivery—are offset so as to minimize global warming. Actions like purchasing energy from wind farms and choosing suppliers that are ecologically friendly balance out the necessary carbon dioxide produced in other stages of carpet production. Anderson recognized the choices Interface makes today will ultimately affect future generations and hoped his customers would see the value in these choices and go green themselves.

Another large international company that has worked for over a decade to reduce its environmental footprint is Starbucks. Its "Shared Planet" progress plan sets clear objectives for the company in terms of its recycling, energy and water usage, building, and efforts to reduce climate change.[40] Starbucks also held a summit with local governments, cup manufacturers, and recyclers to identify the steps required to make its cups recyclable. Stores are being designed with recycling bins in the front, and customers are given $0.10 off each cup of coffee served in a reusable tumbler. Today, more than 35 million Starbucks customers bring their personal tumblers to the firm's stores to have them refilled.

Richard Stephenson responded to his mother's death by founding a network of hospitals called the Cancer Treatment Centers of America (CTCA). At CTCA, providers are guided to treat patients with the "Mother Standard of care," the level of compassion and support that you would want for your own family members. CTCA treats patients with the latest conventional therapies but also provides a full range of complementary treatment options and access to multidisciplinary team support. Hospital staff members are available for nutritional consultations, spiritual support, mind–body counseling, and the latest treatments in chemotherapy, radiation, and surgery. The hospital policies are centered on a model called "Patient Empowerment Medicine,"[41] in which both the patient and caregivers play an active role in treatment options. From the pain of his mother's illness and the lack of compassionate, integrated care available for her, Richard Stephenson recognized the opportunity for a more ethical and humane medical system.

How Businesses Develop an Ethical Environment pp. 74–76

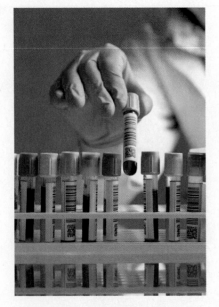

Rashid Divecha has seen it all as a project manager for a major clinical laboratory: samples left on the dock over the Fourth of July weekend (thawed beyond repair), tests done with old chemicals, and reports delivered late and incomplete. But Divecha knew he'd really be in hot water with a client when a lab technician walked in on Friday and announced that three key samples from the testing for a major client were missing. The results for those samples were critical to the report that was being delivered to the client on Monday—but now there was no proof for the FDA that the samples and the data they contained had ever really existed. As Rashid pondered how to handle the situation, his e-mail in-box was filling up with demands from his supervisors not to say anything to the client until a complete "story" had been developed that would make the lab appear blameless. Some even suggested covering up the whole episode with false data. What would Rashid do? ■

Almost every business wants to promote an ethical environment, but sometimes managers find it difficult to know how to implement this successfully. Let's look at some different ways this can be accomplished.

Ethical Focus from the Start

How can a business improve its own culture of ethical and responsible conduct? There are steps that businesses can take to make sure employees get off to an ethical start:

- Managers can make sure a strict code of ethics and a meaningful and current mission statement are in place and that both are clearly communicated to employees when they start working at an organization. The code of ethics and mission statement should be posted throughout the workplace.

- A company can offer orientation programs to new employees to inform them of the ethical standards in place and the conduct expected of them from the beginning of their careers at a company.

Companies should set the right tone at the beginning—show how serious they are about ethics and act with the highest regard to ethical behavior.

Ethical Focus Every Day

How can a business maintain its policy of ethical conduct in the workplace? When employees are faced with unethical situations on a daily basis, adhering to a company's code of ethics can be very difficult. Business leaders must take steps to make sure that all employees are making ethical decisions. This becomes even more of a challenge during tough economic times.[42]

Companies often report trying many things to promote ethical conduct within their organizations. These efforts include having managers talk regularly with employees about acceptable and unacceptable business practices and check to determine that the code of ethics is being followed. Good managers focus on ethics themselves, setting clear examples for the behavior expected at all levels

---

Playing the Ethics Game

A unique approach to ethics training is emerging in the corporate world: games. For example, Cadbury Schweppes, an international confectionery and beverage company, has created a board game called "Ethical Risk" its employees play to help bridge the gap between the values the company wants to achieve and the day-to-day decision making and practices of its managers.[43] Lockheed Martin uses a computer game called "Gray Matters," which presents a series of ethical dilemmas. Group discussion with a facilitator leads to a better understanding of how to resolve complex ethical issues.[44] A school in Norway is even using the video game "The Walking Dead" to teach ethics because the characters in the zombie-filled postapocalyptic world depicted in the game often find themselves faced with ethical decisions.[45] Many other companies offer self-paced online training in ethics awareness issues. The use of multimedia and a gaming environment promotes a stronger dialogue and builds insight into the practical ways to address the complex issues of corporate ethics and social responsibility.

of the organization. Often, companies create a hotline for employees to anonymously report violations of the ethics code and make sure the allegations are followed up.

Companies also employ ongoing **ethics training programs** designed to boost the awareness of their employees about ethics issues. Such training occurs at all levels of the organization. From top management that makes strategic and far-reaching decisions, to frontline managers who use their decision-making skills to put out fires, to salespeople who work with vendors and must navigate ethics questions, to lower-level employees who make decisions regarding whether to follow the advice of their leaders, all levels of employees are involved in ethics training.

Of course, private-sector businesses are not alone in wanting ethics training programs for their employees. State and government organizations face similar challenges. Many law enforcement agencies—including local police, state police, and the FBI—have ethics training programs to help officers deal with cases in which there may be no clear ethical response.[46] For example, when an officer responds to a domestic disturbance call but decides no crime has been committed, does he or she have a responsibility to try to prevent a potential escalation into a future criminal incident? By discussing, role-playing, and writing about these scenarios, the officers are more prepared for the ethical dilemmas facing them on the job.

Developing an ethical environment involves implementing several components and often requires a concentrated investment of time and resources. However, it remains a priority for most businesses. Think back at Rashid's story. What did he decide to do? Although he was pressured by his supervisors not to say anything to the client until a complete "story" had been developed, Rashid knew how he would want to be treated and was willing to live up to his personal ethical beliefs even in this crisis. In doing so, he set an example for his own employees to emulate.

Next, he went looking for the company's stated procedure for the ethical handling of a corrective action like this. It turned out there was no such document at his facility, but the company's Salt Lake City lab had a corrective procedures document, so Rashid obtained a copy of it. He then began a series of interviews with all the employees involved, not as a hunt to place blame but with a clear message of improving lab performance. Some practices were identified that needed to be changed—for example, scientists often just walked into the lab and took samples they wanted for their own research. It also became clear there was one employee who had been involved in several instances of sample mishandling. It was never proven whether this was due to incompetence or unethical conduct, but the employee was given a performance-improvement plan to help train him and monitor and improve the situation. As these results were communicated to the client, its trust in the lab began to grow again. Rashid's supervisors saw the value of being of honest and up front with the client, and the firm's policies were modified formally.

Summary

1 What are ethics and different ethical systems? (pp. 55–58)

- **Ethics** (p. 55) are the moral choices people make.
- Ethical systems include the following:
  - **Moral relativism** (p. 56), a perspective that holds that there is no universal moral truth but instead only individuals' beliefs, perspectives, and values
  - **Situational ethics** (p. 56), which encourages people to make ethical decisions based on the circumstances of a particular situation, not on fixed laws
  - Systems defined by religious traditions, such as **Judeo-Christian ethics** (p. 56), which refers to the common set of basic values shared across both Jewish and Christian religious traditions

2 How does someone create a personal code of ethics? (pp. 56–58)

- Determine your base character.
- List all the beliefs that influence your decision making.
- Think about how your behavior reflects these beliefs.
- Now think about where your beliefs and view of your character come from. Why do you hold these beliefs?

3 How might personal ethics play a role in the workplace? (pp. 58–60)

- Having a strong ethical foundation can help you achieve success in business and greater happiness in life.
- In the modern workplace, there is less distinction made between how you conduct yourself inside and outside the office. Telecommuting is one instance when a person's employer may influence how an employee behaves at home. Conduct on social media sites can also influence a person's workplace, even though it happens outside of work.
- Conflicts can emerge when your **personal ethics** (p. 56) are different from those of your company.

4 How can you evaluate a company's ethical code using available resources, such as a mission statement? (pp. 60–61)

- Some companies may have a written **code of ethics** (p. 60), or a statement of their commitment to certain ethical practices.
- Many companies have a public **mission statement** (p. 60) that defines the core purpose of the organization and often describes its values, goals, and aspirations.

5 How do a company's policies and decisions affect its achievement of corporate social responsibility (CSR)? (pp. 61–69)

- **Corporate social responsibility** (**CSR**) (p. 62) consists of five major areas: employment standards, ethical sourcing, marketing issues, environmental concerns, and community policies.
- A strong CSR plan allows a company to serve its local and global communities well. It also benefits a corporation in direct and indirect ways.

6 What challenges does a company face in balancing the demands of social responsibility with successful business practices? (pp. 64–67)

- Companies must balance their moral and ethical obligations to consumers with their need to respond to investors and produce a profit.
- It's also important for companies to show a strong commitment to their employees (by ensuring workplace safety), the local community (by responding to community needs), and all the countries in which they operate (by upholding human rights policies). At times, it can be difficult to balance these commitments with the need to ensure that the business remains financially successful.

7 What is legal compliance, and how does it affect ethical conduct? (pp. 69–72)

- **Legal compliance** (p. 69) refers to conducting a business within the boundaries of all the legal regulations of that industry.
- Companies that establish and adhere to high ethical standards are more likely to maintain legal compliance.

8 What strategies can a company use to recover from ethical lapses? (pp. 71–72)

- A company can work to find a leader who will set an example of the new ethical image of the company.
- A company can restructure its internal operations to empower all employees to consider the ethical implications of decisions and feel free to speak up when they have concerns.
- A company can redesign its internal rewards.

9 How can companies apply ethical standards to create new business opportunities? (pp. 72–74)

- While some businesses are tackling ethical issues and offering consumers more ethical choices through their businesses, others are attempting to reduce the impact they have on the environment.

10 What approaches can a company use to develop and maintain an ethical environment? (pp. 75–76)

- Managers can make sure a mission statement is in place and set clear examples for the standards of behavior expected at all levels of the organization.

- Companies can offer orientation programs to new employees to inform them of the ethical standards in place.
- **Ethics training programs** (p. 76) can boost the awareness of employees about ethics issues.

Key Terms

amoral behavior (p. 56)

code of ethics (p. 60)

corporate philanthropy (p. 66)

corporate social responsibility (p. 62)

ethics (p. 55)

ethics training program (p. 76)

Judeo-Christian ethics (p. 56)

legal compliance (p. 69)

legal regulations (p. 69)

mission statement (p. 60)

moral relativism (p. 56)

personal ethics (p. 56)

price fixing (p. 60)

situational ethics (p. 56)

social audit (p. 65)

socially responsible investing (p. 68)

sustainability (p. 73)

unethical behavior (p. 56)

whistle-blower (p. 71)

MyBizLab

Go to **mybizlab.com** to complete the problems marked with this icon .

Self Test

Multiple Choice *You can find the answers on the last page of this book.*

3-1 Ethics are based on

a. the current popular culture.

b. religious, cultural, or ethnic systems.

c. society's legal system.

d. each situation and the moral consequences of an action.

3-2 A corporation can behave in a socially responsible way by

a. having strong policies in place to help the community.

b. acting to reduce the negative impact a company has on the environment.

c. being truthful with consumers in its market.

d. All of the above

3-3 Employees can be sure their behavior out of the office

a. has no impact on stockholders.

b. cannot impact their career if they blog under a fake name.

c. matters to employers only during the hours they are officially telecommuting.

d. None of the above

3-4 CSR can be measured by

a. a company's rate of growth.

b. organizations that monitor and rank performance on social issues.

c. the happiness level of employees in a company.

d. businesses that have high profit margins and gross sales.

3-5 A business is in legal compliance if

a. it follows all the laws of which it is aware.

b. it cannot be proven guilty of violating any laws.

c. it meets all local, state, and federal regulations.

d. it hires only employees who do not have criminal records.

3-6 A company's ethics can be examined by

a. following its stock price.

b. interviewing employees.

c. checking documents filed when it was incorporated.

d. reviewing its code of ethics and mission statement.

3-7 Socially responsible investing (SRI) means that you are investing in

   a. companies making the largest gains in profit for the past three years.

   b. only companies that meet a certain standard of CSR.

   c. only nonprofit companies.

   d. companies that sponsor food banks.

3-8 Ethical sourcing means that

   a. people should make ethical decisions based on a particular situation.

   b. there is one accepted source for guiding ethical decision making.

   c. a company follows accepted conduct when acquiring raw materials from suppliers.

   d. companies will not work with international suppliers.

3-9 Which of the following strategies is *not* designed to help a company recover from an ethical lapse?

   a. Ensuring whistle-blowers face legal consequences

   b. Working to find a leader who will set an example of the new ethical image of the company

   c. Restructuring internal operations to empower all employees to consider ethical implications of decisions and allowing them to feel free to speak up when they have ethical concerns

   d. Redesigning a firm's internal rewards—for example, restructuring the incentive package for sales employees so there's a financial reward for building relationships with clients rather than just closing a sale

3-10 The practice of corporate philanthropy

   a. is only a marketing strategy.

   b. can build stronger relationships with employees and the community at large.

   c. states that success can be found by competing fiercely to provide the lowest price.

   d. is a strategy that works only in certain segments of industry where there is a lot of media attention.

True/False *You can find the answers on the last page of this book.*

3-11 A mission statement details the plans of how a company will achieve profitability.

☐ True or ☐ False

3-12 Minimizing a company's carbon footprint is part of a plan to increase corporate philanthropy.

☐ True or ☐ False

3-13 Ethics is the study of the general nature of morals and the specific moral choices a person makes.

☐ True or ☐ False

3-14 When a company follows a strong CSR program, it will restrict opportunities for growth.

☐ True or ☐ False

3-15 A weak ethical focus in a company allows it to compete more aggressively.

☐ True or ☐ False

Critical Thinking Questions

✪**3-16** Do you believe being ethical will lead to a better quality of life for you? Do cheaters win in the real world, or does ethical conduct lead to a more satisfying outcome? Are there times you would be willing to compromise your ethics for business gain?

3-17 Which of the five pillars of CSR seems the most important to you? How do the five areas relate to each other?

✪**3-18** How should the online companies Google and Facebook react to requests for censorship? Does a government have the right to exercise a filtering of the information available if they feel it protects and increases the safety of its citizens?

Team Time

ONE ISSUE, THREE SIDES

Divide into three teams, one to represent each of the following:

a. Pharmaceutical company executives

b. People with a catastrophic but treatable illness

c. People identified as having "unique" DNA

Scenario

Are there some things that can't be owned? Leukemia patient John Moore would answer yes. After Moore had his cancerous spleen removed at the University of California, Los Angeles, the university kept the spleen and was eventually granted a patent for DNA removed from the organ. The value of the DNA was estimated to be more than $1 billion. When Moore demanded his cells from his spleen be returned, the California Supreme Court ruled against him, saying that he had no right to his own cells after they had been removed from his body. Pharmaceutical researchers, like those at the University of California, often hope to later license the DNA patterns or sell them to other companies so they may use them to develop drugs or tests for the presence of disease. In 2010, a Maryland state judge ruled that patents on two other genes, BCRA1 and BCRA2, breast cancer markers claimed by the University of Maryland and Myriad Genetics, were invalid. However, the judge chose not to rule on the larger issue of whether people own the genetic information their cells carry.[47]

Does a person or a group of people who have that specific, perhaps unique gene have ownership? Do they deserve payment? Do they have a right to a voice in the use of their genetic material? Or are their interests trumped by the value of such discoveries to the greater good?

Process

Step 1. Record your ideas and opinions about the issue presented in this scenario. Be sure to consider the issue from your assigned perspective.

Step 2. Meet as a team and review the issue from multiple perspectives. Discuss together what one best policy could be developed to address the concerns of all three groups.

Ethics and Corporate Social Responsibility

PERSONAL AND BUSINESS ETHICS

As you've learned, sometimes a person's personal code of ethics does not fall within the code of ethics used in his or her profession. What is your personal code of ethics? What profession do you hope to have in the future? How does your personal code of ethics match the code of ethics used in that profession? Would you be willing to ignore your personal ethical code for business?

Process

Step 1. Draft your personal code of ethics. Use the steps for analyzing one's own ethical system outlined at the beginning of this chapter.

Step 2. Think about a profession you'd like to have in the future. Visit a website describing the code of ethics employed in this profession.

Step 3. Compare your personal code of ethics to the profession's code of ethics. Then write a paragraph explaining how the two codes compare.

Web Exercises

3-19 Government's Role in Happiness
The country of Bhutan is the only country that measures its progress by the level of happiness of its citizens, a metric named the gross national happiness (GNH). Examine www.grossnationalhappiness.com and see if you think the idea of a GNH measurement can be incorporated into organizational decision making.

3-20 Identifying Your Strengths
Visit the website of Martin Seligman, a psychologist who promotes the field of positive psychology, at www.authentichappiness.sas.upenn.edu/Default.aspx. Complete the VIA Survey of Character Strengths. Consider how you can use your strengths each day in the work schedule you have right now.

3-21 Socially Conscious: How Do Your Investments Measure Up?
When you invest in mutual funds, you can make decisions in different ways. You may want to just put money into funds that had the greatest gain last year, or you may want to invest in funds that are collections of socially responsible companies. Find several socially conscious mutual funds. What restrictions do they make on the companies they include? What is their average rate of return?

3-22 Whistle-Blower or Traitor?
Worldwide repercussions were felt when Edward Snowden released thousands of classified documents showing that the National Security Agency was running an international surveillance program. Snowden was charged with espionage and theft and fled the country. Find supporting evidence for both points of view—that Snowden committed espionage and endangered the country and that his actions were in the interest of the citizens of the United States. Does whistle-blowing include illegal behavior? Should he be convicted or pardoned?

3-23 Corporate Social Responsibility with Your Prescription
CVS Pharmacy has made the decision to stop selling cigarettes and other tobacco products, even though they earn an estimated $2 billion a year from these products. Visit the CVS Caremark website and examine their Code of Conduct and statements on corporate responsibility. Discuss how this decision could be presented to customers, to stockholders, and to employees. How should a pharmacy balance the health needs of its customers with the business demands of its stockholders? Do you think these policies attract more customers to the store?

MyBizLab

Go to **mybizlab.com** for Auto-graded writing questions as well as the following Assisted-graded writing questions:

3-24 How can a person determine his or her personal ethical code? What is your personal ethical code? What forces have helped build your personal code of ethics?

3-25 How does a corporation's responsibility to shareholders to produce a profit interact with its social responsibility? Name several areas of possible conflict and analyze them from both a short-term view and a long-term view.

References

1. "Ethics," *The Oxford Dictionary* (Oxford: Oxford University Press, 2014), www.oxforddictionaries.com/us/definition/american_english/ethics.

2. Ann Pomeroy, "The Ethics Squeeze," *HR Magazine*, March 2006, 53.

3. University of Pennsylvania Positive Psychology Center, "Authentic Happiness,", www.authentichappiness.sas.upenn.edu/Default.aspx.

4. Renae Merle, "Boeing CEO Resigns over Affair with Subordinate," *Washington Post*, March 8, 2005, www.washingtonpost.com/wp-dyn/articles/A13173-2005Mar7.html?nav=rss_topnews.

5. From Pomeroy, "The Ethics Squeeze," 53.

6. From Pomeroy, "The Ethics Squeeze," 53.

7. "Once a Whistleblower," March 11, 2014, www.wcpo.com/news/local-news/once-a-whistleblower-embezzler-the-man-who-inspired-the-informant-talks-redemption-in-cincy.

8. Fetzer Vineyards, "Fetzer Vineyards Philosophy," March 11, 2014, www.fetzer.com/Philosophy, reprinted with permission of Fetzer Vineyards.

9. Boston College Center for Corporate Citizenship, March 11, 2014.

10. Amnesty International, "Indian Government Must Stop Refinery Expansion until Human Rights Are Addressed," www.amnesty.org/en/news-and-updates/report/vedanta.

11. T. Webb, "Case Study: Chiquita," May 23, 2013, www.slideshare.net/Tobiaswebb/chiquita-case-study-from-octopus-to-csr-pioneer.

12. D. Reisinger, "Apple Touts Better Working Conditions as Factory Audits Jump," February 13, 2014, www.cnet.com/news/apple-touts-better-working-conditions-as-factory-audits-jump.

13. Brave New Films, "Citations of Statistics Used in the Film," www.walmartmovie.com/facts.php.

14. The Corporation, "Who's Who," www.thecorporation.com.

15. Chroma Technology Group, "Chroma Wins Worldwide Award for Democracy in the Workplace," www.chroma.com/newsevents/articles/chroma-wins-worldwide-award-democracy-workplace.

16. Chroma Technology Group, "Being Their Own Bosses," www.chroma.com/newsevents/articles/being-their-own-bosses.

17. Time Warner, "Citizenship," www.timewarner.com/corp/citizenship/index.html.

18. Target, "Community Outreach," http://sites.target.com/site/en/company/page.jsp?contentId=WCMP04-031700&ref=sr_shorturl_community.

19. Suzanne Vranica, "Twitter Crowns Wendy's Promo as 'Most Retweeted,'" *Wall Street Journal*, December 8, 2011, http://blogs.wsj.com/digits/2011/12/08/twitter-crowns-wendys-promo-as-most-retweeted.

20. World Health Organization, "Global Health Observatory," January 2014, www.who.int/gho/hiv/epidemic_status/deaths_text/en.

21. World Health Organization, "World Malaria Report 2013," www.afro.who.int/en/clusters-a-programmes/dpc/malaria/features/3998-world-malaria-report-2013.html.

22. Intel, "Corporate Responsibility Report," www.intel.com/intel/corpresponsibility/awards.htm.

23. Linda Kaplan and Robin Koval, *The Power of Nice: How to Conquer the World with Kindness* (Crows Nest: Allen & Unwin, 2007).

24. Kaplan and Koval, *The Power of Nice*.

25. Val Lush, "Consumer Bill of Rights," www.bookrags.com/research/consumer-bill-of-rights-ebf-01.

26. British Petroleum, "BP Establishes $20 Billion Claims Fund for Deepwater Horizon Spill and Outlines Dividend Decisions," June 16, 2010, www.bp.com/genericarticle.do?categoryId=2012968&contentId=7062966.

27. Data from Enron's *Corporate Responsibility Annual Report*, 2000, www.corporateregister.com/a10723/enr00-cr-usa.pdf.

28. "Ponzi Scheme," www.merriam-webster.com/dictionary/ponzi%20scheme.

29. Topia Energy, "GreenStop," www.topiagreenstop.com.

30. "Malaria Prevention," *The Medical News*, © 2007, 2012 *Interface Inc.* All rights reserved. Used with permission.

31. B. Flook, "With the World Watching, Sanaria Maps Out Its Future," August 30, 2013, www.bizjournals.com/washington/blog/techflash/2013/08/with-the-world-watching-sanaria-maps.html?page=all.

32. Steven Musil, "Week in Review: Google Slams China Censorship," http://news.cnet.com/8301-1001_3-10435702-92.html.

33. D. Rushe, "Bing Censoring Chinese Language Search Results for Users in the U.S.," February 11, 2014, www.theguardian.com/technology/2014/feb/11/bing-censors-chinese-language-search-results.

34. Bill Xia, quoted in Ben Elgin and Bruce Einhorn, "Outrunning China's Web Cops," *BusinessWeek*, February 20, 2006, www.businessweek.com.

35. K. Subramanian, "India Requests for Web Censorship Increase," April 27, 2013, www.thehindu.com/sci-tech/technology/internet/indias-requests-for-web-censorship-increase/article4658617.ece.

36. Interface, Inc., "Our Progress," www.interfaceglobal.com/Sustainability/Sustainability-in-Action.aspx.

37. Interface, Inc., "What Is Sustainability?," www
.interfacesustainability.com/whatis.html.

38. Interface, Inc., "Interface's Values Are Our Guiding Principles," © 2007, 2012 Interface Inc. All rights reserved. Used
with permission.

39. Interface, Inc., "Groups," http://missionzero.org/groups.

40. Starbucks, "Being a Responsible Company," www
.starbucks.com/responsibility.

41. Cancer Treatment Centers of America, "CTCA Quality
Story," www.cancercenter.com.

42. "Employers Find Maintaining an Ethical Workplace Is
Paramount, Especially in Tough Ethical Times," April 6,
2010, www.businesswire.com/portal/site/home/
permalink/?ndmViewId=news_view&newsId=
20100406005609&newsLang=en.

43. Mark Young, "HR as the Guardian of Corporate Values
at Cadbury Schweppes," *Strategic HR Review* 5, issue 2
(2006),: 10–11.

44. "Lockheed Martin Gray Matters Ethics Game," www
.e-businessethics.com/Game.htm.

45. K. Akash, "Walking Dead Video Game Used in Norway
to Teach Ethics and Morality," January 18, 2014, www
.ibtimes.co.uk/walking-dead-video-game-used-by-
norwegian-school-teach-students-ethics-morality-1432832.

46. International Association of Chiefs of Police, "Ethics
Training in Law Enforcement,"www.theiacp.org/
PoliceServices/ExecutiveServices/ProfessionalAssistance/
Ethics/ReportsResources/EthicsTrainingin
LawEnforcement/tabid/194/Default.aspx.

47. Megan Carpenter, "Judge Overturns Corporate
Patent on Human DNA," *Washington Independent*, http://washingtonindependent.com/80919/
judge-overturns-corporate-patent-on-human-dna.

Chapter 4
Business in a Global Economy

▶ What Is Globalization?
Devin Kay always "buys American"—but what does that mean in the new global marketplace?

▶ International Trade
As foreign companies begin to compete in U.S. markets, there is more competition and more pressure on U.S. businesses. What are the benefits of international trade? What are the costs?

▶ Free Trade and Protectionism
Trying to compete in the world marketplace means using every means available. So when the members of the family who operate the Miller farm found that genetically modified organisms (GMOs) helped boost the farm's crop output, they were thrilled. Now, however, they have discovered they can't sell their crops in 28 countries because they used GMOs. How do free trade agreements affect businesses and members of a community?

▶ Conducting Business Internationally
When you're conducting business internationally, many factors come into play. What are the strategies of international business? How can you enter a foreign market? Which entry mode is best? Hachimo Isu needs some answers before he expands his business.

▶ International Business: Economic Factors and Challenges
Economic factors affect what products get imported and exported. Exchange rates both encourage and deter countries from trading with one another and therefore have a big impact on imports and exports. Business owners like Rachel Gao, who sells jewelry, want to import goods from countries with favorable exchange rates. How do exchange rates affect the bottom line of Rachel's business, and how do they affect a nation's economy overall?

▶ Creating Successful International Businesses
How would you feel if a potential client from Venezuela wouldn't sign a contract with you because you didn't pat him on the shoulder when you first met? Joe Stein lost one account that way. He now thinks he may lose another by accepting and opening a gift from a client in India. What challenges does Joe face there? Is there a problem accepting and opening a gift when it's received? Knowing the answers to such questions is vital to running a successful global business.

OBJECTIVES

1. What are the implications of the globalization of markets and the globalization of production? (pp. 85–87)

2. Why has globalization accelerated so rapidly? (pp. 87–88)

3. What are the costs and benefits of international trade? (pp. 89–91)

4. What are the different types of trade barriers? (pp. 91–97)

5. What are the three basic strategies of international business? (pp. 97–98)

6. How can international firms successfully enter foreign markets? (pp. 98–101)

7. What are exchange rates, and how do they affect international business? (pp. 101–104)

8. What economic factors and challenges play a role in conducting business on a global scale? (p. 104)

9. What are the sociocultural, political, legal, and ethical challenges to conducting business in a global marketplace? (pp. 105–108)

What Is Globalization? pp. 85–88

Devin Kay is a worldly guy who has traveled globally. But he is very loyal to U.S. products and tries to buy American whenever he can. For example, Devin wouldn't dream of buying a car like an Italian Maserati. "Italian car? Never! I'd rather buy a good ol' American Jeep," he says. When he vacations, he chooses to take a weekend getaway in Manhattan rather than spending money to vacation abroad. He believes high tariffs on foreign products sold in the United States are a good idea because they make products more expensive relative to American products, which then sell better. "The world is a tough place, and we should do whatever we can to give American companies an edge," he tells his friends. ■

Source: vege/Fotolia.

Former President Bill Clinton once said, "Globalization is not something we can hold off or turn off . . . it is the economic equivalent of a force of nature—like wind or water."[1] In recent years, the rise of globalization has made a dramatic impact on the lives of people around the world. The United States and other nations are increasingly **importing**, or buying products from other countries, and **exporting**, or selling domestically produced products to other countries. People from the United States to Taiwan to Argentina are interconnected and dependent on one another for a variety of goods and services.

Many products we own were made in countries other than the United States. If you inspect the items you buy, such as laptop computers, clothes, and cars, you will see that many of them and their parts are manufactured in other countries. ■ **FIGURE 4.1** shows how Ford cars, which many people think are made in America, are comprised of components manufactured in other countries or are assembled outside the United States. Even relatively small companies are marketing their products to the United States and vice versa.

What can people do to enhance their country's ability to compete in the global economy? What can a country do to provide good-paying jobs for its citizens? How can U.S. companies increase their profitability in the face of foreign competition at home or enhance their market share overseas? When the U.S. dollar is stronger or weaker than the currencies of other countries, how does it affect business in the United States? After studying this chapter, you'll be able to answer these questions.

> **THE LIST**

Powerful People to Know

Do you know every name on this list?

1. Hu Jintao
2. Angela Merkel
3. Jim Yong Kim
4. Sergey Brin and Larry Page
5. Carlos Slim Helu
6. Dilma Rousseff
7. Abdullah bin Abdu Aziz al Saud
8. Tenzin Gyatso
9. Narendra Modi
10. Christine Lagarde

MyBizLab®

⭐ **Improve Your Grade!**

Over 10 million students improved their results using the Pearson MyLabs. Visit **mybizlab.com** for simulations, tutorials, and end-of-chapter problems.

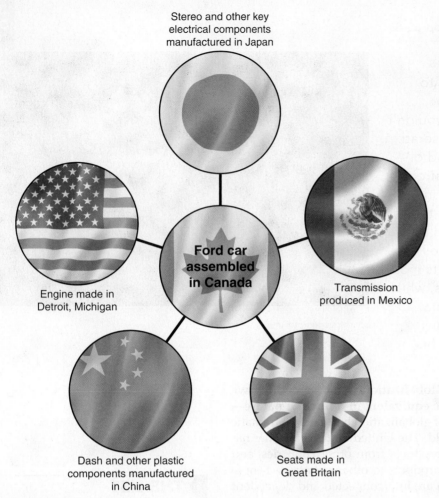

Stereo and other key electrical components manufactured in Japan

Engine made in Detroit, Michigan

Ford car assembled in Canada

Transmission produced in Mexico

Dash and other plastic components manufactured in China

Seats made in Great Britain

■ **FIGURE 4.1**
Made in the USA?
Many brand-name products are composites of components manufactured around the world. For example, most people think that Ford cars are made in the United States. But is it really "made in the USA" if most of its components are manufactured in other countries or it is assembled outside the United States?

The Effects of Globalization

How does globalization affect the United States? The old saying "No man is an island" can be used to describe globalization. **Globalization**, the movement toward a more interconnected and interdependent world economy, may be one of the most profound factors affecting people in the United States and around the globe. Why is this? Whatever happens today in the U.S. economy—the world's largest economy—will have a significant impact on people not only in the Unites States but also worldwide. Meanwhile, economic conditions in other countries also affect the U.S. economy, producing changes and challenges for U.S. consumers, businesses, and workers.

One example of this can be seen in the booming economies of India and China. Their growth is a major reason for the increasing global demand for energy. Increased energy demand is a major cause of the world's rising oil prices, which have created higher prices at the gas pump for people around the world. As a result, people have less money to spend on other things, such as eating out. Local restaurants and businesses feel the pinch, so their sales fall, and they must curtail their production and lay off employees. Higher energy prices can also drive up production costs, which, in turn, drive up the prices businesses must charge for products.

How does globalization offer more marketing opportunities to businesses?
Globalization has two main components:

- The globalization of markets
- The globalization of production

The **globalization of markets** refers to the movement away from thinking of the market for your products as being local or national and the entire world instead. This offers incredible new opportunities for businesses. Companies such as General Electric (GE), Dell, and Toyota are not just selling to customers in Dallas or Atlanta, California or Vermont, or Japan or Europe; they're selling to customers all over the globe. Figure 4.2 shows why all auto manufacturers are looking to sell their vehicles in China. Why China? Because more than 1.3 billion consumers live there. That's more than quadruple the number of consumers who live in the United States. In 2013, people in China purchased over 21 million cars. By comparison, only 15 million were purchased in the United States.[2]

When it comes to doing business abroad, most marketing experts advise firms to "think globally and act locally." In other words, companies should adjust their products or marketing campaigns to suit the unique tastes and preferences of their local customers, wherever they may be. For example, Coca-Cola often must tweak its recipes to appeal to the tastes of consumers in different parts of the world. In India, Coca-Cola adapted its Minute Maid orange soda recipe to suit the tastes of people there, most of whom prefer a sweeter version of the drink than the version sold in the United States.[3] Similarly, many foreign-owned companies advertise or adapt their products for sale in the United States to attract consumers here.

How does globalization make it easier to manufacture products? The **globalization of production** refers to the trend of moving a firm's production to different locations around the globe to take advantage of lower costs or enhance the quality of products. *Outsourcing* is often part of the globalization of production. **Outsourcing** is the assignment of certain tasks, such as production or accounting, to an outside company or organization. Currently, much outsourcing is **offshore outsourcing** (or **offshoring**), which involves moving production from a domestic site to a foreign location. In addition, companies may decide to relocate at least some of their own production facilities to other countries where production costs are lower.

Reasons for the Rise in Globalization

Why has globalization accelerated so rapidly? Two main factors underlie the trend toward greater globalization:

- **A dramatic decline in trade and investment barriers.** Trade and investment barriers are government restrictions that prevent the flow of goods, services, and financial capital across countries. Lowering trade barriers makes global business cheaper and easier to conduct and allows a firm to move its different production activities to the lowest-cost locations. For example, a firm might design its product in one country, produce parts for it in two or three other countries, assemble the product in yet another country, and then export it around the world.

- **Technological innovations.** Advances in technology, communications, and transportation have made it possible to better manage the global production and marketing of products. Using Web conferencing tools, a business manager in New York can meet with contacts at a firm's European and Asian operations centers without ever leaving the office. This has significantly reduced the cost of doing business. Technological advancements are a great equalizer for small companies, enabling them to inexpensively access customers worldwide through their websites and effectively compete with huge global corporations.

The globalization of production has resulted in some international firms becoming so large that they actually generate more revenue than the gross domestic product of many nations. As you can see in ■ **FIGURE 4.2**, several American companies rank above many countries in the world in terms of the total revenue they generate.

Global Business Trends

Where will trends in global business take us? Some noteworthy global business trends likely to continue are as follows:

1. **A growing role for developing nations.** Over the last several decades, developing countries, including China, India, and Brazil, have been expanding rapidly. This trend is expected to continue as countries such as these increase their presence on the world economic stage.

2. **A rise in non-U.S. foreign direct investment.** Previously, the United States was the world's leader in terms of **foreign direct investment**, which is the purchasing of property and businesses in foreign nations. Now many other countries are investing in businesses abroad, including businesses and property located in the United States. You might think of Budweiser as an American company, but did you realize that not too long ago it was purchased

■ **FIGURE 4.2**

**Company Revenue Versus
National Incomes**

Today some international businesses are
larger than entire countries in terms of
the revenue they generate.

Source: Business Insider.

Source (photos): epa european pressphoto
agency b.v./Alamy; Patti McConville/
Alamy; Alistair Laming/Alamy; Horizons
WWP/Alamy.

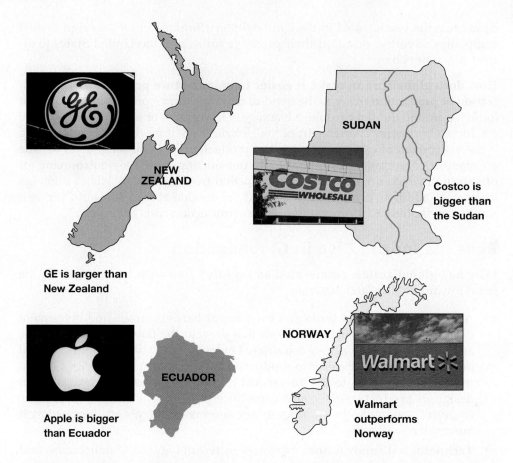

GE is larger than
New Zealand

Costco is
bigger than
the Sudan

Apple is bigger
than Ecuador

Walmart
outperforms
Norway

by the Dutch firm In-Bev? Not only is more foreign direct investment flowing
into the United States than ever before, but more and more foreign direct investment is flowing into developing nations.

3. **A rise in multinational enterprises.** Over the last several decades, there
   has been a rise in the importance of **multinational enterprises**, businesses
   that manufacture and market products in two or more countries. Moreover,
   mini-multinationals (small and medium-size multinational enterprises) have
   become prominent on the world stage. Consider Transferwise, a company that
   allows people to electronically transfer money between accounts in different
   countries quickly and at much lower rates than what banks offer. By using
   technology to change how international banking is done, Transferwise has
   been able to expand its services abroad rapidly.

4. **Increasing democratization.** With the movement toward democratization and the adoption of free market economies around the globe, many
   more nations are becoming involved in the global economy. If this trend
   continues, the opportunities for international business will be enormous
   as the global marketplace expands and more locations open as potential
   production sites.

Remember Devin? Due to globalization, he is probably finding it difficult to buy
"only American" products. Today, the Maserati he would never buy is owned by
the Italian carmaker Fiat, which owns 20 percent of the Chrysler Group, which produces American Jeeps. And his vacation in New York City? More than one-tenth of
all the goods and services produced in New York and 1 in 20 jobs are supplied by
companies controlled by foreign investors.[4] And although Devin argues that tariffs
will protect U.S. products, most economists today believe that tariffs reduce a nation's trade and hamper its economy, which can lead to the loss of domestic jobs.

> **THE LIST**
>
> **Countries in Which It Is Easy
> to Start a Business, 2013**
>
> 1. New Zealand
> 2. Australia
> 3. Canada
> 4. Singapore
> 5. Macedonia
> 6. Hong Kong
> 7. Georgia
> 8. Rwanda
> 9. Belarus
> 10. Ireland

International Trade pp. 89–91

Thom McGovern runs a successful textile manufacturing firm.
The business was started by his father and has grown every year since
Thom took over. The firm creates high-quality clothing products sold
to retail stores. Thom's company is a dependable supplier with many
satisfied customers. Over the past several years, though, high-quality
foreign clothing has been showing up in the U.S. market in greater
numbers and selling at prices far below anything Thom can match.
Slowly, his customers are switching to other suppliers. Thom could drop
prices to his customers and increase his company's profits if he offshored
his production. But that would mean he would have to lay off his
employees. What should he do? ■

Source: wavebreakpremium/Fotolia.

Economists argue that international trade flourishes because it is in the best
interest of the country as a whole. However, competition in the international market often puts new pressures on domestic businesses like Thom McGovern's firm
unless they find ways to keep up with the high-quality and low-cost products that
international trade provides. Let's take a closer look at why countries participate
in international trade, how trade affects a firm's competitiveness, and what costs
and benefits are associated with international trade.

International Competition

What is the theory of comparative advantage? Many theories apply to
international trade. The most popular theory is the **theory of comparative
advantage**, which states that specialization and trade between countries benefit
all who are involved. If this method is practiced, each nation will have a greater
quantity and variety of higher-quality products to consume at lower prices.

For this mutually beneficial system to work, each country must specialize in
the production of those products for which it possesses a **comparative advantage**—
that is, produce the goods and services it can produce relatively more efficiently
compared to other countries. A comparative advantage should not be confused
with an **absolute advantage**, which is the ability to produce *more* of a good or a
service than any other country. Just because a large country can produce more of
a good than a small country can doesn't necessarily mean it is relatively more efficient at producing that good. What matters is relative efficiency, or comparative
advantage—not absolute advantage.

When all countries focus on producing products for which they have a
comparative advantage, collectively they all have more production to share.
This, in turn, creates higher standards of living for these countries. As you've
probably guessed, countries export products for which they have a comparative advantage and import products for which they do not have a comparative
advantage.

Fostering Competitiveness

What can a country do to have an edge in world markets? Governments often
focus on improving their nations' competitiveness by improving their resources—
natural resources, labor, capital (plant, equipment, and infrastructure), technology,
innovation, and entrepreneurialism. A nation can only do so much to improve its
natural resources, however; it has to work with the natural resources with which it is
endowed. Nations with abundant natural resources will likely have a comparative
advantage in the production of goods that require these raw materials. For example,

big-leaf mahogany trees are found in only a few countries, including Mexico and Belize. So, these countries have a comparative advantage in the production of mahogany furniture and musical instruments made from mahogany.

However, governments can and do invest in health, education, and training designed to increase the productivity of their labor forces. All international businesses are constantly looking for good workers, and each country wants to attract businesses to enhance the employment opportunities for its citizens. Officials in Queensland, Australia, have recently budgeted a massive $9.5 billion in education and training, including vocational training and apprenticeships, in the hopes of building a strong employment force for the country.[5]

Many governments try to create incentives to attract the investments made by private companies, such as investments in plant and equipment. One way to do this is for a government to try to keep interest rates low so that private companies will invest in the latest state-of-the-art equipment, thereby giving them an edge over foreign competition. Governments also invest in *public capital*, which is sometimes called *infrastructure*. Infrastructure includes roads, bridges, dams, electric grid lines, and telecommunication satellites that enhance productivity.

Governments also try to promote technological advances to give their nations a competitive edge. This can include investments in basic and applied research at state-funded higher-educational institutions. Finally, governments also promote innovation and entrepreneurialism. In countries like Korea, France, and Norway, there are few women entrepreneurs.[6] To close the gap in Norway, the government there created an action plan to increase grant accessibility for female entrepreneurs. The objective is to have women own at least 40 percent of entrepreneurial businesses.[7] On the flip side, sometimes governments use trade restrictions and added tariffs on goods from other countries to create an artificial competitive advantage. We'll discuss these practices later in the chapter.

What can businesses do to be more competitive? To be competitive, businesses must grapple with many of the same issues nations trying to be more competitive do. That is, successful companies try to gain access to cheap raw materials, invest in their workers' training and productivity, and purchase state-of-the-art plants and equipment that will give them an edge. Successful companies also invest in cutting-edge technology in their research-and-development departments. Finally, they promote innovativeness throughout their organizations.

Conversely, if a company, an entire industry, or even a nation has lost its **competitive advantage**, then it probably failed in one or more of these areas. For example, at one time, the U.S. steel and textile industries had a competitive advantage in the world. Today, however, those industries have fallen behind their international competitors. It is the joint job of government and private businesses to determine the ways to improve to compete more effectively.

The Benefits and Costs of International Trade

What are the benefits and costs of international trade? The theory of comparative advantage indicates that countries that participate in international trade will experience higher standards of living because of the greater quantity and variety of higher-quality products offered at lower prices. These results stem from the increased competition associated with more open trade. But these benefits are not without their costs.

The costs of international trade are borne by those businesses and their workers whose livelihoods are threatened by foreign competition. Some domestic businesses may lose market share to foreign companies, stunting their profitability and ability to create jobs. Other firms may face so much foreign competition that they're driven out of business entirely.

Do the benefits of international trade outweigh the costs? This is a difficult question to answer. The costs of increased international trade—including lost jobs to foreign competitors—are often easy to identify. The benefits are not always easily seen, however, as they are spread out among millions of consumers. One measure used to quantify a country's international trade is the **balance of payments** (BOP). The BOP summarizes all of the transactions—payments, financial aid, and gifts—that take place between residents of a country and the external world.

However, one number does not express the complexities of international trade. For example, a greater quantity and variety of higher-quality products to purchase may not be easily traced to increased international trade because these benefits are often slow and subtle. Price reductions may save people only a nickel here and a dime there. But the sum of these lower prices for the public as a whole can be dramatic—especially over time. As we'll see in the next section, governments play a large role in determining how much international trade they will support, for example, by choosing to impose restrictions on the quantity and types of goods that can cross their nations' borders.

When foreign imports arrive in the United States, they increase the supply of a product, pushing its price down. Consumers welcome competition and lower prices, but domestic competitors aren't pleased.
Source: Universal Images Group/Getty Images, Inc.

We started this section by discussing Thom McGovern's textile business, which was struggling to compete against foreign competition. Did Thom just close up shop, or did he adapt to the pressures and take advantage of the opportunities of globalization? As company president, Thom chose to invest in new equipment and training for his workers to try to gain a competitive advantage. He also began acquiring lower-cost raw materials from foreign suppliers, a process the Internet has made easier to coordinate. Finally, he investigated new markets for his specialty products and is expanding into countries like India and China. Thom is not sure what his company will look like in five years, but he is sure that the globalization of the world marketplace will result in both challenges and opportunities.

Free Trade and Protectionism pp. 91–97

Farming has changed, and the Miller farm has always changed with the times. A few years ago, the Millers began using genetically modified organisms (GMOs) to grow crops that are more resistant to frost and improve their farm's output. But recently, the European Union (EU)—a major group of European countries—issued a new health directive: To be eligible for sale in the EU, any product meant for human consumption could not contain any GMOs. The Millers worry that the manufacturers they sell to in these countries will no longer do business with them. ■

Source: Savcoco/Fotolia.

Countries implement trade barriers for a variety of reasons. Sometimes, trade barriers are implemented to protect consumers. Other times, trade barriers are established to protect domestic businesses from international competition. Many people believe that such protectionist trade barriers are the best way to defend a nation's economy; others are in favor of free trade. **Free trade** refers to the unencumbered flow of goods and services across national borders. That is, free trade is free from government intervention or other impediments that can block the flow of goods across borders. The vast majority of economists recognize that the benefits of free trade far outweigh the costs for a nation. However, some people—especially those who feel their livelihoods are threatened by free trade—are not convinced. In this section, we'll examine both sides of this debate.

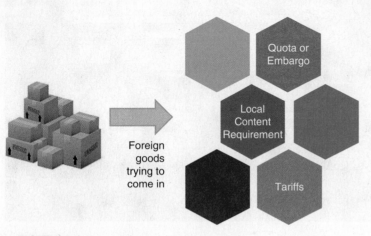

■ FIGURE 4.3
Trade Barriers
Countries use these strategies to make it more difficult for foreign firms to sell their products competitively.

Types of Trade Barriers

What trade barriers can governments put in place? As **■ FIGURE 4.3** shows, there are three types of trade barriers:

- **Tariffs and subsidies.** The most common trade barrier is a **tariff**, a tax imposed on an imported good or service, such as a U.S. tariff on imported French wine. Governments prefer to impose tariffs because they raise tax revenues. The opposite of a tariff is a **subsidy**, in which a government makes payments to *domestic* producers. In the United States, subsidies are provided to a wide variety of businesses, including many agricultural businesses. A subsidy can take many forms. It can be a direct cash grant or a tax concession or a low-interest loan.

- **Quotas and embargoes.** A **quota** is a limitation on the amount of an import allowed to enter a country. For example, a U.S.-imposed quota on French wine might limit the quantity of it that can be imported to 10,000 cases per day. The most heavy-handed government trade barrier is an **embargo**, a total restriction on an import (or an export). For example, the United States has imposed an embargo on most goods traded with Cuba. Embargoes are usually tools designed to achieve a political goal. In the case of Cuba, the U.S. embargo began in the 1960s when Fidel Castro adopted a one-party communist system. The embargo has been used as a tool to pressure Cuba to adopt a more democratic system of government.[8]

- **Administrative trade barriers.** Several other types of trade barriers can be lumped under the heading of *administrative trade barriers*—government rules designed to limit imports. One example is a **local content requirement**, which is a requirement that some portion of a good be produced domestically. This usually drives up the cost of an import. Administrative trade barriers might also require an import to meet some technical standard or bureaucratic rule, effectively shutting out the import from a domestic market. For example, the EU has banned the importation of all animal meats in which steroids were used to stimulate growth. This decision has heavily impacted the U.S. beef and dairy industries. Although administrative trade barriers can be legitimate, they may be designed purely to protect domestic producers from international competition.

Trade Barriers: Winners and Losers

Who benefits and who suffers from trade barriers? Without a doubt, trade barriers benefit domestic producers and their workers but hurt domestic consumers. Trade barriers increase costs to foreign companies or restrict the supply of imports, driving up prices and reducing sales in the domestic market. As a result, higher-priced imports increase the demand for domestically produced substitute goods or services. This higher demand also increases the domestically produced product's price, although it simultaneously increases domestic sales.

Because domestic firms are selling more at higher prices, they are more profitable. This profitability also creates more job security for their employees. The undesirable outcome, however, is that both imports and domestically produced substitute products are now more expensive. Domestic consumers lose, while domestic producers and their workers gain. Trade barriers also hurt consumers because the overall quantity, variety, and quality of products are lower as a result of curtailing foreign competition.

What are common arguments in favor of protectionist trade barriers? Four main arguments for and against trade barriers are as follows:

- **National security.** The *national security argument* states that certain industries critical to national security should be protected from foreign competition. For example, the United States wouldn't want to become dependent on another nation for a component critical to the nation's defense. Critics of this argument point to the fact that very few industries seeking protection fall into this category.

- **Infant industry.** The *infant industry argument* states that an undeveloped domestic industry needs time to grow and develop to compete in the global economy. Once the industry has grown and is more competitive, protection from foreign competition will no longer be necessary. Opponents of this view argue that, in practice, it can be very difficult to determine whether an industry legitimately holds the promise of becoming competitive. In addition, these people argue that rarely do infant industries ever "grow up." Instead, governments continue to protect them at the expense of consumers.

- **Cheap foreign labor.** The *cheap foreign labor argument* centers on lower wages paid to workers of foreign companies. This issue has become a growing concern. How can domestic companies compete with these low wages? Critics of protecting a nation's workers against cheap labor argue that a company's costs of production can be lower even when it pays its workers twice as much if the productivity of the workers is at least twice as high. If a country wants to maintain high wages in a global marketplace, it needs to find a way to increase the productivity of its labor force, not impose trade barriers.

- **Threat of retaliation.** The *threat of retaliation* (or the *bargaining chip*) *argument* says that if a trading partner increases its trade barriers on your exports or fails to reduce trade barriers when you reduce yours, then an uneven playing field is created. For example, domestic companies are often adversely affected if a foreign firm is dumping its product. **Dumping** refers to selling a product at a price below its cost in a foreign country to drive competitors there out of business so you can take over the market. Dumping can be difficult to prove, however, and even harder to stop. One way to stop it is for a government to threaten to impose higher trade barriers on the imported product being dumped—in other words, to use trade barriers as a bargaining chip. The problem with this tactic, critics argue, is that it can result in a trade war if the exporting country raises its trade barriers in response. A trade war is likely to harm the economies of both countries.

How do economists feel about protectionist trade barriers? Most economists believe that the best way to address the concerns of those industries and their workers whose livelihoods are threatened by foreign competition is *not* to impose protectionist trade barriers. Instead, these displaced individuals need to be equipped with the education, training, and skills necessary to smooth their transition into a line of business or work in which the nation has a comparative advantage and demand is rising. Although all governments have protectionist trade barriers in place, they have been working to reduce them because they believe the economic benefits of doing so generally outweigh the costs. This helps explain the recent trend toward freer trade and greater globalization. ■ **TABLE 4.1** summarizes the economic benefits and costs of free trade and protectionism for a nation.

International Organizations Promoting Free Trade

What groups are working to promote free trade? Countries realize that unilaterally reducing their trade barriers puts their businesses at an unfair disadvantage. The key for realizing the mutual benefits of international trade is to

TABLE 4.1	Economic Benefits and Costs of Free Trade and Protectionism for a Nation	
	Free Trade	**Protectionism**
Economic benefits	A *greater quantity* and variety of *higher-quality* products at *lower prices*	*Increased sales* at *higher prices* improves the profitability of protected domestic companies, creating *greater job security* for their workers
Economic costs	*Reduced sales* and *lower prices* for domestic firms that find it difficult to compete internationally, which *reduces their profitability* and *lowers job security* for their workers	A *lower quantity* and variety of *lower-quality* products at *higher prices*

get all countries to lower their trade barriers simultaneously, which was the reason for creating organizations such as the General Agreement on Tariffs and Trade and the World Trade Organization.

The **General Agreement on Tariffs and Trade** (GATT) was created in 1948 with 23 member nations and grew to 123 member nations by 1994. Although GATT was not an organization with any real enforcement powers, its eight rounds of negotiated agreements or treaties successfully reduced tariffs and other obstacles to the free trade of goods. Thereafter, the amount of global trade increased dramatically, as did world economic growth.[9] However, GATT was not as successful in terms of reducing trade barriers on services, protecting intellectual property rights, or enforcing agreements among member nations. As a result, the **World Trade Organization** (WTO) replaced GATT in 1995.

The WTO has strengthened the world trading system by extending GATT rules to services and increasing the protection for intellectual property rights. But, perhaps most significantly, the WTO has taken on the responsibility for arbitrating trade disputes and monitoring the trade policies of member countries.[10] The WTO operates as GATT did—on the basis of consensus—when settling disputes. However, unlike GATT, the WTO doesn't allow losing parties to ignore the arbitration reports of the WTO. The WTO has the power to enforce its decisions. ■ **FIGURE 4.4** shows which countries are members of the WTO.

Can more be done to promote free trade? Advocates of free trade argue that much more can be done to reduce trade barriers. The first round of WTO meetings took place in Seattle, Washington, in 1999 but were derailed by antiglobalization protestors. The meetings were relaunched in 2001 in Doha, Qatar, with the goal of curtailing dumping, reducing trade barriers, protecting intellectual property rights, and reducing government barriers on foreign direct investment.[11] The Doha Round was slated to last three years but had not yet concluded as of the publication of this text. It has been far more difficult than anyone imagined to reach concrete results.

What problems can result from free trade? WTO protests reflect an ongoing concern that free trade encourages firms to shift their production to countries with low wages and lax labor standards and that the exploitation of workers in low-wage countries contributes to the gap between the rich and the poor. Environmentalists are also concerned that free trade encourages companies to move their production to countries that allow the firms to pollute the environment and emit unlimited amounts of greenhouse gases that contribute to global warming. Environmentalists highlight the fact that the *economic* benefits and costs of free

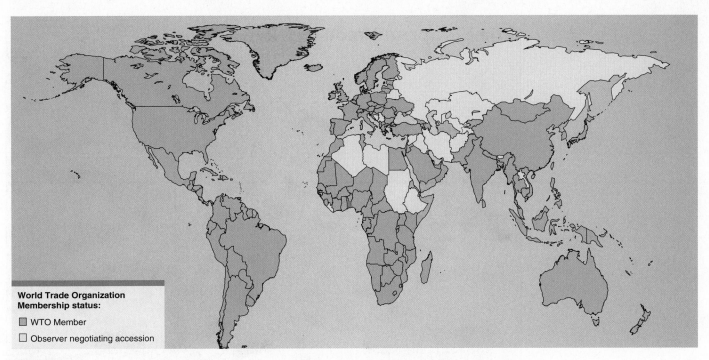

■ FIGURE 4.4
Countries in the WTO

trade are not the only costs and benefits it results in. Important social, ethical, political, and environmental concerns also need to be considered.

Regional Free Trade Agreements

What are regional free trade agreements? Many nations have been so eager to achieve the higher standards of living associated with free trade that they have struck out on their own by creating their own **regional free trade agreements**. Let's look at some of the most powerful regional free trade agreements.

The European Union

The oldest and largest free trade area in the world is the European Union (EU). The EU can trace its roots to 1957 with the creation of the European Economic Community (or Common Market), which consisted of six founding countries. Although many obstacles had to be overcome, such as the concern over the potential loss of national sovereignty, the EU now includes 28 countries, as shown in **■ FIGURE 4.5**. Its success is due in large part to its demonstrated commitment to the free flow of goods, services, capital, and people across borders in Europe.

The EU accounts for approximately one-third of the world's total production. It is the largest exporter in the world and the second-largest importer.[12] In 1999, the EU also surpassed all other free trade areas with respect to economic integration by adopting a common currency—the euro. The euro is currently used by 18 of the 28 countries in the EU and has become a major currency in global financial markets.[13] The EU is likely to continue to grow as other countries, particularly those in Eastern Europe, apply to join the organization.

The EU's economic power and political clout has a huge influence on international businesses worldwide. For example, some international businesses have been motivated to invest in production facilities within the EU to hedge against any potential trade barriers. The EU has also established many legal, regulatory, and technical standards for imports to the EU market. In addition, the EU's antitrust rulings have significantly affected U.S. businesses.

■ FIGURE 4.5
The European Union
As of 2014, the EU has 28 member countries. It is the most economically integrated free trade area in the world.

The North American Free Trade Agreement

The **North American Free Trade Agreement** (NAFTA) is an ongoing agreement to move the United States, Mexico, and Canada closer to true free trade. NAFTA was established in 1994 after a considerable amount of political opposition. Over 20 years after the agreement, NAFTA has quadrupled the trade between the three countries. None of the worst fears about NAFTA have come to pass—there has been no huge loss of jobs to Mexico, nor has there been an enormous increase in immigration rates from Mexico. It has successfully created a regional market of over $19 million in trade. The United States participates in other free trade agreements as well, such as the Dominican Republic–Central American Free Trade Area (DR-CAFTA) as well as agreements with Israel, Korea, and Australia.

Other Free Trade Areas

Many other free trade areas exist in the world. The following are some of the more noteworthy examples:

- *MERCOSUR* is a regional coalition of South American countries including Brazil, Argentina, Paraguay, Uruguay, and Venezuela.
- The *Association of Southeast Asian Nations (ASEAN)* includes Indonesia, Malaysia, the Philippines, Singapore, Thailand, Brunei, Vietnam, Laos, Myanmar, and Cambodia. ASEAN has negotiated free trade agreements with many countries and is working to create a free trade agreement with the EU.

- The *Asia-Pacific Economic Cooperation (APEC)* currently has 21 member countries, including economic powerhouses such as the United States, Japan, and China.

Most free trade areas haven't had the kind of success that the EU and NAFTA have had in reducing their trade barriers. However, it is clear that most countries are eager to come together to reduce trade barriers in an attempt to realize the economic benefits of greater free trade.

We started this section with a story about the Miller farm and its struggles to determine what to do in light of an EU decision to disallow GMO products in its member countries. Regional free trade agreements create powerful negotiating bodies, and, as the Millers have found, the EU can make decisions that ripple through many levels of government, all the way to impacting the Miller's farm management.

Now that you have reviewed both sides of the issues concerning protectionism and free trade, what is your opinion? Can a balance be struck between protecting domestic businesses and consumers and opening markets up to more free trade?

Conducting Business Internationally pp. 97–101

Hachimo Isu worked as a professional translator for many years before opening his own successful translation business in the United States. Over the years, Hachimo has hired additional translators, and his company has grown. Now he thinks it would grow more if he were to open some offices in other countries. To which countries should he expand and how? ■

Source: Thanapol Marattana/ Getty Images, Inc.

All business operations are undertaken within economic, sociocultural, political, and legal environments that change over time. Even the savviest managers can have trouble keeping up with the changes. Managing an international business is even more complex because a firm has to stay abreast of changes occurring in multiple countries.

The rest of this chapter will explore some of the numerous important economic, sociocultural, political, and legal differences among nations. An understanding of these differences is critical for successfully conducting global business. First we'll discuss the strategies of international businesses and how firms enter foreign markets.

International Business Strategies

What types of strategies can an international business pursue? There are different types of strategies companies can use to expand abroad. Let's look at them.

- **Global strategy.** Companies that pursue a **global strategy** sell a standardized (or homogeneous) product across the globe. Standardized products are basic products that meet universal needs. Examples of standardized products include agricultural products, oil, and raw material commodities. These goods are essentially the same from company to company and have the same appeal to consumers across many cultures. When selling standardized products, firms compete aggressively on the basis of price. The company with the lowest price usually captures the most market share.

- **Multidomestic strategy.** Companies that pursue a **multidomestic strategy** customize or differentiate their products to meet unique local needs, tastes, or preferences. For example, in Asian countries, McDonald's offers seaweed-flavored fries. Firms pursuing a multidomestic strategy face relatively low pressures for cost reduction because price is often of secondary concern to buyers. Instead, what is important to customers is whether a product meets their needs or is distinct from a competitor's product.

- **Transnational strategy.** Companies that pursue a **transnational strategy** offer a product globally, to many countries, working simultaneously to sell it at the lowest possible price. An example of the pursuit of this type of strategy is a product like Coca-Cola soda or a computer model from Dell. While the language on the packaging will be changed country to country, the product is the same.

Entering Foreign Markets

How do firms enter foreign markets? In addition to determining a business strategy, businesses must determine how they will serve foreign customers. Companies may undertake one of six strategies:

- Export their products
- Implement turnkey projects
- Sell franchises
- Enter into licensing agreements, joint ventures, or strategic alliances
- Engage in contract manufacturing
- Establish wholly owned subsidiaries

Let's look briefly at each strategy.

Exporting

Many firms initially enter foreign markets by exporting their products. Exporting is relatively easy and inexpensive compared with establishing a physical presence in a foreign market. In addition, exporting may help a firm realize lower costs because companies can move production to an inexpensive location and then export its product from that location around the world. Exporting also has a few disadvantages. It is not economical for heavy or bulky products with high transportation costs. Exporting may also become uneconomical if foreign trade barriers are unexpectedly imposed.

Turnkey Projects

When firms export their technological know-how in exchange for a fee, they have implemented a **turnkey project**. Turnkey projects are common in the production of sophisticated and complex manufacturing facilities, such as those involved in petroleum refining, steel, and hydroelectric energy production. Once a facility is up and running and the locals are trained, the keys are turned over to the new foreign owners. For example, the largest traffic control system in China is the Wuhan Urban traffic control system, delivered by the German electronics firm Siemens.[14] Turnkey projects allow firms with specialized know-how, like Siemens, to earn higher profits from their technical expertise. The drawback is that a firm may create a viable competitor if their technological expertise is easily accessible.

Franchising

Franchising involves selling a well-known brand name or a proven method of doing business to an investor in exchange for a fee and a percentage of sales or profits. The seller is the *franchisor*, and the buyer is the *franchisee*. Franchising is popular both domestically and internationally. Examples of franchising abound. McDonald's and Kentucky Fried Chicken (KFC) restaurants are now found all over the world.[15] In India, the Walt Disney Company has sold more than 100 franchises for its stores.[16] Undoubtedly, all of these franchises must be careful to adapt their goods and services to appeal to their different global customers.

The main advantage of franchising is that the franchisor shifts to the franchisee the costs and risks of opening a foreign market. The disadvantages include enforcing franchise contracts that ensure quality control over distant franchisees and ensuring that the franchised product is properly adapted to appeal to customers abroad.

Licensing

Licensing is an agreement in which the licensor's *intangible property*—patents, trademarks, service marks, copyrights, trade secrets, or other intellectual property—may be sold or made available to a licensee in exchange for a royalty fee. The *licensor* holds the original patent or copyright, and the *licensee* is paying a fee to be allowed to use that property. The advantage of licensing is the speed with which the licensor can enter a foreign market and the assumption of risks and costs by the licensee. The disadvantage is the loss of technological expertise to the licensee and the creation of a potential competitor. SRI International is a company that holds patents in the areas of biosciences, computing, and chemistry-related materials.[17] They license their vast array of intellectual property around the world.

Joint Ventures

Joint ventures are formed when two firms team up to better take advantage of a business opportunity than either one of them could alone. Frequently, a company wishing to expand abroad will partner with a local firm that has knowledge of how business is done in the foreign country. The two companies will then share the costs and risks of developing and selling the product the joint venture has to offer.

Sometimes the only way a company can enter a market is via joint venture. With 1.2 billion people, the market for consumer goods, such as soap, detergent, and shampoos, in India is huge. However, to protect small Indian businesses, the country restricts the entry of foreign businesses. So, Walmart has had to enter India through a joint venture with the Indian company Bharti Enterprises, an expansion that has proved to be difficult due to the cultural and other differences between the firms.[18]

Entering into a joint venture, like entering into a marriage, requires considerable thought in the selection of a complementary partner. The disadvantage of joint ventures is losing control over a company because compromise with the partner is inevitable. The risk of losing proprietary technology in the event of dissolution or divorce of the joint venture is also a major drawback

Strategic Alliances

Strategic alliances are cooperative arrangements between actual or potential competitors. Unlike a joint venture, in a strategic alliance each partner retains its business independence. Typically, strategic alliances are agreements for a specific

Because of international franchising, you can eat at Kentucky Fried Chicken in India, China, and Egypt, among other countries.
Source: Dhiraj Singh/Bloomberg/Getty Images; STEPHEN SHAVER/AFP/Getty Images; Dana Smillie/Bloomberg/Getty Images.

period of time or the duration of a particular project. The advantages of strategic alliances include the pooling of unique talents and expertise and the sharing of the costs and risks of a project for mutual benefit. The disadvantages include a loss of technology and initial difficulty in finding a compatible partner.

Microsoft has a strategic alliance with Japanese mobile phone manufacturer Nokia. The companies work together to optimize the mobile phone experience for Microsoft's Windows software and Nokia's phone hardware. Together they joined their workforces of talented engineers and their financial clout; now they have the power to compete more effectively.[19]

Contract Manufacturing

Contract manufacturing occurs when a firm subcontracts part or all of its goods to an outside firm as an alternative to owning and operating its own production facility. When doing international business, the subcontractor is a foreign firm. Therefore, contract manufacturing is really a form of offshore outsourcing.

Dell, Apple, and Hewlett Packard all use contract manufacturing to produce their computer products. Although the design for Apple computers is done in the United States, for example, many are shipped directly from Asian manufacturers to customers.[20] Contract manufacturing allows business to enter a foreign market by placing its label on the good and selling it in the foreign market where it was produced. Contract manufacturing also enables a firm to test-market its product in a foreign market with very little expense compared with the high start-up costs of building its own facility on foreign shores.

The disadvantage centers on the lack of quality control over the subcontractor. For example, when the toy maker Mattel used a contract manufacturer in China to produce Hot Wheels cars and Barbie dolls, Mattel ended up recalling the toys and paying millions of dollars in fines imposed by the U.S. Consumer Product Safety Commission. Why? Because the Chinese manufacturer had used lead paint on the toys, a practice that is banned in the United States.[21]

Wholly Owned Subsidiaries

A **wholly owned subsidiary** is a facility owned entirely by the investing firm. For example, Hyundai, a South Korean automotive manufacturer, entered the Russian market by establishing Hyundai Motor Manufacturing Russia, a wholly owned subsidiary.[22] The advantages of this entry choice include total control over foreign operations and technological know-how. The disadvantage is that the parent company must bear all the costs and risks of entering a foreign market.

The Advantages and Disadvantages of Each Entry Mode

Which mode of entering foreign markets is optimal? The optimal entry mode depends on many factors, including a firm's strategy. ■ **TABLE 4.2** summarizes the advantages and disadvantages of the various entry modes.

We started this section with a story about Hachimo Isu, who was considering expanding his business abroad. After spending more time reviewing the idea of going global, he is thinking of two different target countries: Saudi Arabia or Belgium. For each, he needs to consider how he would modify the services he offers to reflect the needs of these countries. For example, Brussels, Belgium, is the headquarters of the EU and has very specific political and legal translation needs. Saudi Arabia is experiencing a construction boom and requires the translation of engineering and legal documents. Hachimo needs to review the different ways these markets can be entered and the pros and cons of each and decide which mode has the most benefits for his company. It is an exciting time, and there are a lot of frequent-flyer miles in his immediate future!

TABLE 4.2	**Advantages and Disadvantages of Foreign Market Entry Modes**	
	Advantages	**Disadvantages**
Exporting	• *Speed* of entry • Production site in *lowest-cost* location	• High *transportation* costs • Threat of trade barriers, such as *tariffs* • Lack of *access* to local information
Turnkey project	• Increased *profits* for high-tech firms	• Loss of technical *know-how* to potential competitors
Franchising	• Costs and *risks* of opening the foreign market fall on the *franchisee*	• Difficulty in maintaining *quality* control over distant franchises
Licensing	• *Speed* of entry	• Licensee may become *competitor* • Loss of *knowledge* to potential competitor
Joint venture	• High potential for *learning* • Benefit of *combined* resources	• *Shared* control of business • Risk of losing *specialized* technology to partner
Strategic alliance	• *Pooled* talents and expertise • *Shared* costs and risks	• Risk of losing *specialized* technology to partner • Difficulty in finding a *compatible* partner
Contract manufacturing	• *Speed* of entry • Low *test-marketing* costs	• Lack of *quality control* over distant subcontractor
Wholly owned subsidiary	• Total *control* over all operations • Preservation of **proprietary** technology	• *Risks* and costs of entering a foreign market

International Business: Economic Factors and Challenges pp. 101–104

Source: Philippe Lopez/Getty Images, Inc.

When Rachel Gao decided to expand her jewelry business to include handbags, she thought importing them would be cheaper than purchasing them from a domestic company. Initially, she thought she would purchase the handbags from a small European designer, but after she saw the exchange rate for the euro, she changed her mind. Because of the high exchange rate of the euro relative to the U.S. dollar, to make a profit, Rachel would have to charge her customers extremely high prices for the bags. She didn't think her customers would pay prices so high. What other options would still allow her to expand into the handbag business? ■

Businesses are impacted by fluctuating exchange rates every day. Transactions between international companies not only have to specify what each side will be paid but also in which curency. In addition, multinational enterprises use foreign currency to pay foreign workers or to invest spare cash in other nations where interest rates may be more attractive. In this seciton, we'll look at exchange rates and how fluctuations in the value of currency affect the global economy. We'll also explore other economic factors and challenges that affect gloabal business.

The Role of Exchange Rates

What are exchange rates? Foreign exchange markets determine **exchange rates**, the rates at which currencies are converted into another country's currency.

A *strong dollar* means that the U.S. dollar exchanges for a relatively large amount of foreign currency. A *weak dollar* does not, and you will get many fewer Mexican pesos for a dollar, for example.

Depending on a firm's perspective, it may prefer a strong dollar or a weak dollar. American exporters prefer a weak dollar because their products will be more affordable to foreigners. However, American importers prefer a strong dollar because the cost of importing foreign goods is cheaper. If goods are imported cheaply, then those savings can be either passed on to the consumer or kept as higher profits.

How do exchange rates affect international business? Changes in exchange rates have a huge impact on firms doing international business. Let's look at the reasons why.

Export and Import Prices

Suppose the value of the dollar rises or gets stronger against the yen (the currency of Japan). What impact will this have on U.S. and Japanese businesses? Goods exported from the United States will become more expensive because people in Japan will now need more yen to purchase each dollar. This means, for example, that the cost of a $40 pair of jeans made in the United States will become more expensive for the Japanese consumer. Japanese consumers will buy fewer U.S. goods, like jeans, and U.S. exports to Japan will fall. Of course, this will hurt U.S. businesses selling their products in Japan.

At the same time, however, the stronger dollar will cause a decline in the relative price of Japanese goods for U.S. consumers because fewer dollars will be needed to purchase each yen. Thus, due to the change in currency exchange rate, the United States will import more Japanese goods, and U.S. businesses will lose market share to Japanese companies.

This example of Japanese and U.S. trade shows how a **currency appreciation**—an increase in the exchange rate of a nation's currency—causes the relative price of imports to fall and the relative price of exports to rise. When currency appreciates, the currency becomes stronger. By contrast, a **currency depreciation**—a decrease in the exchange rate of a nation's currency—has the opposite effect on the relative prices of exports and imports: Exports become cheaper and imports become more expensive. Sometimes the government issuing the currency decides to **devalue** its currency. This deliberate adjustment of the value is different than depreciation, where the change is happening due to outside forces.

Fluctuating exchange rates also affect multinational firms in other ways. Many companies feel pressured to shift their production to countries with weak or low-valued currencies to take advantage of lower costs of production. For example, a weak Chinese currency reduces labor costs in China. If a firm doesn't shift more of its production to China but its competitors do, then its costs will be higher, and the company will lose global market share.[23]

Trade Deficits and Trade Surpluses

Exchange rate changes can also create *trade deficits* and *trade surpluses* for a country. A **trade deficit** exists when the value of a country's imports exceeds the value of its exports. For example, a stronger dollar can create a trade deficit for the United States because it can cause export prices to rise and import prices to fall. A **trade surplus** occurs when the value of a country's exports exceeds the value of its imports. What do countries do when they experience a trade surplus? Often countries that trade in raw materials, such as oil or diamonds, find the commodity price fluctuates a great amount from year to year. So, taking the pool of money that exists in the year of a trade surplus and investing it would be a good strategy. **Sovereign wealth funds** (SWFs) are government investment funds that do just that. They are managed separately from the official currency reserves of a country. In 1953, Kuwait established the first SWF, which is now worth almost $300 billion. Many countries now have SWFs, including Norway, China, Saudi Arabia, and Singapore. The amount held by all SWFs is currently over $6 trillion.[24]

SWFs can invest in anything they want, and sometimes the investments of SWFs stabilize and allow foreign companies to expand. But during the recent credit crisis, many SWFs invested in collapsing banks in Europe and the United

States. In fact, more than $69 billion was invested in a range of struggling banks and financial institutions.[25] The oil-rich emirate of Abu Dhabi made a $7.5 billion investment in the U.S. banking firm Citigroup. The political implications of this level of investment make some uneasy about the rapid growth of SWFs. China's fund has made significant investments in major U.S. financial firms. How might that impact the political tensions between the two countries? What if an Arabian SWF invested in a shipping company, giving it control of U.S. ports?

Fixed and Freely Floating Exchange Rate Systems

Exchange rates can be manipulated or fixed by governments. For example, China has fixed its currency to a rate that is weak compared to the dollar. This means Chinese exports to the United States are cheap and imports from the United States to China are expensive. As a result, the United States faces a huge trade deficit with China. The U.S. government has for years been trying to persuade China to allow its currency to "float," or change in response to changing market conditions. Indeed, most countries operate under a *freely floating* (or *flexible*) *exchange rate system*, a system in which the global supply and demand for currencies determine exchange rates. Many specific factors affect the demand and supply of a nation's currency, such as changing interest rates, tax rates, and inflation rates. Generally, however, changes in exchange rates in a freely floating exchange rate system reflect a country's current economic health and its outlook for growth and investment potential.

The problems with floating exchange rates are that they can create relative price changes outside the control of international businesses and engender risks of losses due to rapid and unexpected changes in exchange rates. For example, in the 1980s, Japan Airlines purchased several 747 airplanes from Boeing and agreed to pay in U.S. dollars. In the interim period between signing the contract and the delivery of the planes for payment, the value of the dollar rose dramatically. The airline company had to pay a lot more money than anticipated for the airplanes, and it almost went bankrupt. This example illustrates that unanticipated exchange rate changes can pose huge risks for international businesses.

Nonconvertible Currency and Countertrade

Governments also reserve the right to restrict the convertibility of their currency. It's not uncommon for a developing country to have a *nonconvertible currency*—currency that can't be exchanged for another currency. For example, the national currency in Morocco is the dirham. It cannot be converted outside Morocco's borders, so visitors want to spend every dirham they have before ending their Moroccan vacations. Governments with nonconvertible currencies often fear that

> **THE LIST**
>
> **Top U.S. Trading Partners, 2014**
>
> | Rank | Country | Percent of Total Trade |
> |------|---------|------------------------|
> | 1. | Canada | 15.8% |
> | 2. | China | 15.6% |
> | 3. | Mexico | 13.2% |
> | 4. | Japan | 5.3% |
> | 5. | Germany | 4.1% |
> | 6. | Korea, South | 2.8% |
> | 7. | United Kingdom | 2.6% |
> | 8. | Saudi Arabia | 2.0% |
> | 9. | France | 1.9% |
> | 10. | Brazil | 1.9% |
> | 11. | Taiwan | 1.7% |
> | 12. | India | 1.7% |
> | 13. | Netherlands | 1.6% |
> | 14. | Hong Kong | 1.5% |
> | 15. | Italy | |
>
> "Foreign Trade," U.S. Top Trading Partners, U.S. Department of Commerce, January 1, 2014, www.census.gov.

Which Is Better—A Strong Dollar or a Weak Dollar?

The answer to this question depends on the type of business a firm undertakes. Companies that do a lot of exporting—such as vehicle manufacturers, chemical manufacturers, and farmers—prefer a weak dollar because it makes the prices of their products lower in the global marketplace, so their sales and profits will be higher. However, companies that import components or finished goods for resale in the domestic market prefer a strong dollar because the relative price of their imports is lower.

From a consumer's perspective, a strong dollar is typically preferred because import prices are lower, which has a tendency to keep domestic competitors' prices low as well. As an employee, if you work for a company that exports much of its product, you would prefer a weak dollar to stimulate sales and ensure your job security.

The benefits of a strong dollar for a nation as a whole are that it results in lower-priced imports. However, a strong dollar can create a trade deficit. A weak dollar, on the other hand, is good for domestic international businesses because it stimulates employment and raises standards of living. The drawback of a weak dollar is that it can lead to higher costs of energy and other imported products. If the costs of these products increase significantly, they can increase a nation's inflation rate. So, which is better—a strong dollar or a weak dollar? Like most real-world issues, the answer depends on your perspective.

allowing convertibility will result in *capital flight*, the transfer of domestic funds into a foreign currency held outside the country. Capital flight would deprive the nation of much-needed funds for investment and development.

Global companies can still do business with countries that have nonconvertible currencies through the use of countertrade. *Countertrade* is a form of international barter, the swapping of goods and services for other goods and services. Currently, countertrade may account for as much as 10 to 15 percent of total world trade. Companies engage in countertrade because of necessity and profitability. Examples of companies that have undertaken countertrade include Goodyear, General Electric (GE), Westinghouse, 3M, General Motors (GM), Ford Motor Company, Coca-Cola, and PepsiCo.[26]

Other Economic Challenges to Conducting International Business

What are some other economic challenges to conducting international business? Changing exchange rates and nonconvertible currencies are not the only economic challenges to conducting international business. Companies must also consider how to adapt their products for sale in developing nations, how certain government policies might affect their business, and how the socioeconomic factors of an area impact the types of products they sell.

Economic Growth and Development

Many developing countries are experiencing more rapid growth than advanced economies are, and they have hundreds of millions of eager new customers ready to put their money into the global market. However, some developing countries still lack the basic infrastructure necessary for the effective transportation of goods and/or lack access to dependable electricity. They may also be lacking in modern communication systems. The implications for companies doing business with these nations are clear. For example, the types of food products offered for sale would have to be altered and packaged differently. The modes of advertising would shift from television to radio, and marketing a product via the Internet wouldn't be effective because few customers would own a computer. Advertising delivered via mobile phones would be critical in these countries. African countries are an example.

Government Economic Policies

International businesses prefer free market economies to state-run or socialized economies because the bureaucratic red tape drives costs up. Other economic factors include the debt load of a nation (the amount of debt a country has), its unemployment and inflation rates, and its fiscal and monetary policies. A country with high unemployment rates and runaway inflation can signal that the nation is unstable and risky to do business in.

Socioeconomic Factors

Several socioeconomic factors also need to be taken into account, such as the demographics of population density and age distribution. The birthrates of many developing countries are high and offer exciting opportunities to toy manufacturers such as Mattel. Other socioeconomic factors that firms must consider include income distribution, ethnicity, and the cultural behaviors of a community.

Remember Rachel Gao? She decided to expand her jewelry business to include handbags and thought importing goods would be cheaper than purchasing them from a domestic company. Although she wanted to buy from a small European designer, she quickly realized that based on the exchange rate for the euro, the goods would be too expensive. After looking at the exchange rates of various countries, she found she would be able to import a variety of handbags from China at inexpensive prices. Not only would her customers appreciate the low prices, she would also be able to make a substantial profit on the sale of the handbags. Do you see any risks related to her decision?

Creating Successful International Businesses pp. 105–108

Source: Fotolia.

International sales is the dream job for Joe Stein. He loves travel and is fluent in several languages. He prides himself on being good with people and loves to negotiate. The part of the job that is the most challenging for him is to understand the unwritten rules that are so different from country to country. In Venezuela, businesspeople want a firm handshake and a pat on the shoulder when they first meet. In Japan, he needs to be sure to immediately read the business cards people hand him and not just put the cards in his pocket. Recently, he traveled to India and was given a gift by an Indian business partner. After opening the gift, Joe thanked him profusely, but he sensed that he had done something wrong. Was this going to cost him the deal? What should he have done differently? ■

When a business expands into an international market and lacks cross-cultural awareness, it is destined to fail. Along with cultural norms, political, legal, and ethical norms vary from country to country. Understanding how the different policies of different governments can affect your business is also critical. And because there is no global court to settle differences and disputes, businesses need to thoroughly study what is acceptable legally and ethically in each country. In this section, we'll review the sociocultural, political, legal, and ethical concerns that can make or break a company working in the global marketplace.

Sociocultural Challenges

How does culture affect business? *Culture* is the complex set of values, behaviors, lifestyles, arts, beliefs, and institutions of a population that are passed on from generation to generation. Culture impacts all aspects of business: management, production, marketing, and more. Most international businesses fail because

---

 # International Business Blunders

OFF THE MARK

Companies must research the cultural norms and languages of the places in which they plan to do business. Not doing so can be disastrous, as the following examples illustrate.[28]

- Translation difficulties can cause a fine slogan to fail miserably in another language. The Pepsi slogan "Come alive with the Pepsi Generation!" was translated into Mandarin Chinese as "Pepsi will bring your ancestors back from the dead!"

- In many Latin American cultures, women do not order their husbands around, and people are not usually very concerned with punctuality. A popular U.S. telephone company didn't know this. When the company showed a commercial in which

a Latino wife tells her husband to call a friend and tell her they would be late for dinner, the commercial bombed.

- P&G could not imagine the backlash it would receive when it ran a popular European television commercial in Japan. The ad showed a man entering a bathroom and touching his wife while she bathed. The Japanese disapproved of this ad because the man's behavior did not adhere to the nation's cultural norms.

- When a manufacturer tried selling its golf balls in packs of four in Japan, the campaign was unsuccessful. Why? Because the pronunciation of the word "four" in Japanese sounds like the word "death" in Japanese, so items packaged in fours are unpopular in the country.

they suffer from a lack of cross-cultural awareness. *Cross-cultural awareness* is an understanding, appreciation, and sensitivity to foreign cultures. **Ethnocentrism**, a belief that one's own culture is superior to all other cultures, makes succeeding in international business very difficult.

Why do aesthetics matter when it comes to international business? *Aesthetics* refers to what is considered beautiful or in good taste. Aesthetics affect a culture's etiquette, customs, and protocols. Few things are more embarrassing than violating a sense of good taste. For example, a company advertised eyeglasses in Thailand by featuring a variety of cute animals wearing glasses. The ad was a poor choice in Thailand because animals are considered a low form of life there, so no self-respecting Thai would wear anything worn by animals. Likewise, former president George H. W. Bush, former Chrysler chairman Lee Iacocca and other U.S. business magnates violated Japanese etiquette in the 1990s when they went to Japan and made direct demands on the country's leaders. The Japanese considered this assertiveness rude and a sign of ignorance or desperation. Japanese businessmen don't "lower themselves" by making direct demands. Some analysts believe this violation of cultural aesthetics doomed the trade agreements the countries were trying negotiate and confirmed to the Japanese that U.S. citizens are barbarians.[27]

What other cultural prejudices must be examined for success in other countries? Attitudes toward time vary considerably across the world. Time is paramount to those in the United States. People are expected to be prompt. Some cultures view this as pushy and impersonal. In addition, the U.S. time horizon differs markedly from, for example, the Japanese perspective. A long-term view to a U.S. citizen might be four to seven years in the future, whereas to a Japanese citizen, the long term is likely to be decades in the future. Attitudes toward work also vary. For example, the Germans argue that people in the United States live to work, whereas Germans work to live. Germans and other Europeans expect four to six weeks of vacation per year. Compare this to the two weeks on average a person in the United States gets, and it is clear which country values vacation time more.

Religion plays a profound role in shaping a culture. International businesses are well advised to educate themselves on varying religious value systems, customs, and practices if they don't wish to offend customers in marketing campaigns. For example, a soft drink was introduced into Arab countries with an attractive label that had stars on it—six-pointed stars. The Arabs interpreted the product as being pro-Israeli and refused to buy it.

Why is knowing the native language not enough? Language, both spoken *and* unspoken, is extremely important. Consider a few more examples of international business blunders due to a lack of cross-cultural awareness. A U.S. oil rig supervisor in Indonesia shouted at an employee to take a boat to shore. Because berating a person in public is abhorred in Indonesia, a mob of outraged workers chased the supervisor with axes.

Unspoken language, or body language, also differs significantly around the world. A U.S. telephone company aired an ad in Saudi Arabia that portrayed an executive talking on the phone with his feet propped up on the desk. The problem? The soles of his shoes were showing—something an Arab would never do. Although the world is getting smaller and a global culture is emerging, significant cultural differences still abound.

Political Challenges

What are the political challenges to conducting international business? International businesses look for nations that have stable governments because political upheaval can severely disrupt commerce and jeopardize the success of their firms. The political differences among nations can also pose a challenge for companies doing business internationally. China, although politically stable, has a questionable record on human rights issues and privacy. When

Google wanted to enter China, the government demanded it abide by the nation's Internet censorship laws. Google complied and became the number-two search engine in the country.

Then Google experienced a cyberattack originating from China that targeted the Gmail accounts of dozens of human rights activists in China. That action, along with an increase in the government blocking of sites such as Facebook, Twitter, and Google Docs, led Google to reverse its decision. It decided to stop censoring results, forcing a standoff with the Chinese government. Ultimately, China did renew Google's license to operate in the country, but this is an example of how the pressure from an international business giant can be at odds with political forces in a foreign country.

Government intervention in the process of determining which goods are undesirable and whether goods should be regulated, taxed, or banned also varies from country to country. Many products that pollute the environment are deemed undesirable and have been regulated in one form or another by most governments around the world. The differences in these regulatory standards can impose big differences in costs of production for global businesses. There are also growing pressures on governments to address global climate change issues that will affect international business.

Legal Challenges

What are the legal challenges to conducting international business? Laws, regulatory standards, and access to unbiased judicial systems differ considerably around the world. No universal laws, regulatory standards, or global courts exist to settle disputes in the global economy. The different laws governing contracts, product safety and liability standards, and property rights are of particular importance when conducting global business. Property rights violations, including violations of patents and copyrights in the software, music, and publishing businesses, have cost businesses billions of dollars a year. Without adequate protection of intellectual property, technological developments would be too expensive and risky for companies to continue to fund.

Different laws also govern the use of bribery throughout the world. The United States passed the Foreign Corrupt Practice Act in the 1970s to prevent U.S. companies from making illegal payments to foreign government officials to secure contracts or other favors. The act was designed to restore public confidence in the business community in the United States. But Congress became concerned that U.S. businesses were being put at a disadvantage by the law. Many foreign companies routinely paid bribes and were even able to deduct the cost of bribes from their taxes as legitimate business expenses. The United States therefore pushed for the creation of the Organization of Economic Cooperation and Development in 1988, which currently consists of 30 member nations committed to combating bribery. In many places in the world, however, bribes are common and may even be necessary for doing business.[29]

Ethical Challenges

What are some ethical challenges faced by international business? Bribery is just one of the many ethical dilemmas global businesses face in different countries. For example, should a firm conform to its home country's environmental, workplace, and product safety standards—even though it's not legally required to do so—while operating in another country? Should a company do business

Should you bow or shake hands when you visit a Japanese client in Japan?
Source: Fotolia.

with a repressive totalitarian regime such as North Korea? When conducting international business, companies must determine whether they are willing to defy ethical codes to enhance their profits.

We started this section by introducing Joe Stein, who works in international sales and must deal with a variety of cultures. Joe has learned a lot about the world and about himself by working in international sales. When his Indian business supplier offered him that gift, he politely said thank you and opened it. But he saw Sheshadri's face wince, and others in the group began to look uncomfortable. Joe quickly apologized and asked Sheshadri privately whether he had done something inappropriate. "In India you should never open a gift before the person has left. It shocked a few of us that you would be so rude." Joe thanked him for the insight and made sure to apologize to the people there. Understanding and respecting the differences in cultures around the world will help Joe succeed in international business.

Chapter 4

Summary

1 What are the implications of the globalization of markets and the globalization of production? (pp. 85–87)

- The **globalization of markets** (p. 86) refers to the movement away from thinking of the market as being local or national to being the entire world. Businesses need to "think globally but act locally," which means that companies must market their products so that they appeal to their local customers.

- The **globalization of production** (p. 87) refers to the trend of individual firms to disperse parts of their production processes to different locations around the world to take advantage of lower costs or enhance the quality of products. The globalization of production often involves **outsourcing** (p. 87), which is contracting with another firm to produce part of a product that formerly was produced in-house. **Offshore outsourcing** (p. 87) has become a significant concern for U.S. workers.

2 Why has globalization accelerated so rapidly? (pp. 87–88)

- The decline in trade and investment barriers, which are government barriers that inhibit the free flow of goods, services, and financial capital across national boundaries, is one factor that has led to increased globalization. This decline has encouraged developing nations to become involved in international trade and allowed companies to base production facilities at the lowest-cost locations.

- Technological changes that have also contributed to the rise in globalization include the following:

  - Teleconferencing, which allows businesspeople to conduct meetings with contacts around the world

  - Information technology, such as the Internet and cable and satellite television systems, which allow companies to advertise and sell products on a global scale

3 What are the costs and benefits of international trade? (pp. 89–91)

- The **theory of comparative advantage** (p. 89) states that specialization and trade between countries benefit all who are involved. This is true because countries that participate in international trade experience higher standards of living due to the greater quantity and variety of higher-quality products sold at lower prices.

- The costs of international trade are borne by those businesses and their workers whose livelihoods are threatened by foreign competition. Businesses may lose market share to foreign companies and have to lay off workers as a result.

4 What are the different types of trade barriers? (pp. 91–97)

- The different types of trade barriers are **tariffs**, **subsidies**, **quotas**, and **administrative trade barriers** (p. 92):

  - Tariffs are taxes imposed on a foreign good or service.

  - Subsidies are government payments to domestic producers in the form of a cash grants, tax concessions, or low-cost loans.

  - Quotas are quantity limitations on the amount of an export allowed to enter a country.

  - Administrative trade barriers are government bureaucratic rules designed to limit imports. One example is a **local content requirement** (p. 92), which is a requirement that some portion of a good be produced domestically.

5 What are the three basic strategies of international business? (pp. 97–98)

- The three basic strategies of international business are the **global strategy**, the **multidomestic strategy**, and the **transnational strategy** (p. 97).

6 How can international firms successfully enter foreign markets? (pp. 98–101)

- There are eight common ways for a company to enter foreign markets, as follows:

  - **Exporting** (p. 85), the sale of domestically produced goods in a foreign market

  - **Turnkey projects** (p. 98), exporting a firm's technological know-how in exchange for a fee

  - **Franchising** (p. 98), selling a well-known brand name or business method in exchange for a fee and percentage of the profits

  - **Licensing** (p. 99), an agreement in which the licensor's intangible property may be sold or made available to a licensee for a fee

  - **Joint ventures** (p. 99), the shared ownership in a subsidiary firm

  - **Strategic alliances** (p. 99), cooperative agreements between competitors

  - **Contract manufacturing** (p. 100), subcontracting part or all of the manufacturing of goods to an outside firm

  - **Wholly owned subsidiary** (p. 100), establishing a foreign facility owned entirely by the investing firm

7 What are exchange rates, and how do they affect international business? (pp. 101–104)

- An **exchange rate** (p. 101) is the rate at which one currency is converted into another.

- **Currency appreciation** (p. 102) is the increase in the exchange rate of a nation's currency, which causes the price of imports to fall and the cost of exports to rise. **Currency depreciation** (p. 102) is the decrease in the exchange rate of a nation's currency and creates the opposite effect.

8 What economic factors and challenges play a role in conducting business on a global scale? (p. 104)

- Economic growth and development present a challenge because some countries lack the infrastructure necessary to transport goods effectively.

9 What are the sociocultural, political, legal, and ethical challenges to conducting business in a global marketplace? (pp. 105–108)

- **Ethnocentrism** (p. 106), the belief that one's own culture is superior to all others, can lead to conflict when conducting business globally. Other sociocultural challenges include differences in aesthetics, religion, and attitudes toward time and work.

- International businesses prefer stable governments. However, many countries do not offer this kind of political and economic environment. Government decisions about taxation, infrastructure investments, and antitrust law enforcement can all affect global business.

- From a legal standpoint, the differences in laws and regulations around the world provide challenges for conducting business. There are no universal laws or policies for governing contracts, product safety and liability standards, or property rights.

- Bribery is an ethical challenge facing international businesses. Decisions about whether to conform to a home country's environmental, workplace, and product-safety standards while operating in a foreign country are other ethical dilemmas.

Key Terms

absolute advantage (p. 89)

balance of payments (p. 91)

comparative advantage (p. 89)

competitive advantage (p. 90)

contract manufacturing (p. 100)

currency appreciation (p. 102)

currency depreciation (p. 102)

devalue (p. 102)

dumping (p. 93)

embargo (p. 92)

ethnocentrism (p. 106)

exchange rate (p. 101)

exporting (p. 85)

foreign direct investment (p. 87)

franchising (p. 98)

free trade (p. 91)

General Agreement on Tariffs and Trade (p. 94)

global strategy (p. 97)

globalization (p. 86)

globalization of markets (p. 86)

globalization of production (p. 87)

importing (p. 85)

joint venture (p. 99)

licensing (p. 99)

local content requirement (p. 92)

multidomestic strategy (p. 97)

multinational enterprises (p. 88)

North American Free Trade Agreement (p. 96)

offshore outsourcing (offshoring) (p. 87)

outsourcing (p. 87)

quota (p. 92)

regional free trade agreement (p. 95)

sovereign wealth funds (p. 102)

strategic alliances (p. 99)

subsidy (p. 92)

tariff (p. 92)

theory of comparative advantage (p. 89)

trade deficit (p. 102)

trade surplus (p. 102)

transnational strategy (p. 98)

turnkey projects (p. 98)

wholly owned subsidiary (p. 100)

World Trade Organization (p. 94)

MyBizLab

Go to **mybizlab.com** to complete the problems marked with this icon .

Self Test

Multiple Choice *You can find the answers on the last page of this book.*

4-1 Governments with nonconvertible currency are

a. often developing countries that are trying to protect themselves from capital flight.

b. countries that have strong economic health and prospects of growth.

c. are planning to move toward a floating exchange rate system.

d. developed countries that are protecting the value of their currency.

4-2 The globalization of markets and the globalization of production means that

  a. people are no longer in control of their own lives.

  b. we are all connected by the Web.

  c. companies can take one product to international markets without having to adapt it.

  d. companies design products for global markets and can produce them offshore.

4-3 The theory that states that specialization and trade are mutually beneficial to all economies involved in trade is called the

  a. theory of comparative advantage.

  b. theory of beneficial trade.

  c. theory of absolute advantage.

  d. theory of relative trade.

4-4 Ethnocentrism is a belief that

  a. ethics are central to doing well in business.

  b. the value of commerce changes in different societies.

  c. all cultures should be respected equally.

  d. can lead to conflict when conducting business globally.

4-5 The theory of comparative advantage indicates that

  a. a country should sell to other countries the products it produces most efficiently and buy from other countries the products that it cannot produce as efficiently.

  b. international trade will force domestic businesses to lose market share to foreign competitors.

  c. countries that participate in international trade will have a higher standard of living.

  d. a limit is placed on the amount of goods and services that can be traded.

4-6 Which of the following international organizations promote free trade?

  a. GATT

  b. The euro

  c. The IMF

  d. All of the above

4-7 A mini-multinational is a company that

  a. is small but still does international sales.

  b. is a large international firm.

  c. is a small local business.

  d. is now illegal because of trade barriers.

4-8 Exchange rates affect international businesses because

  a. nonconvertible currency is worthless.

  b. currency depreciation and appreciation changes the relative price of imports and exports.

  c. U.S. exporters prefer a strong dollar.

  d. exchange rates fluctuate after the G20 meeting each year.

4-9 Which method of entering foreign markets has the advantage of allowing for test-marketing a product in a foreign market at the lowest cost?

  a. Joint ventures

  b. Wholly owned subsidiaries

  c. Exporting

  d. Contract manufacturing

4-10 Doing business in countries with socialist economies that are government controlled

  a. is not legal for businesses headquartered in the United States.

  b. happens often today despite political tension.

  c. almost ensures profit because socialist economies have lower costs of production.

  d. is unprofitable because of embargo sanctions.

True/False *You can find the answers on the last page of this book.*

4-11 A free-floating exchange rate system uses global supply and demand to set exchange rates.
☐ True or ☐ False

4-12 Outsourcing sometimes involves moving the production of a product from a domestic location to a foreign location.
☐ True or ☐ False

4-13 Increasing U.S. dominance of foreign direct investments has helped accelerate globalization.
☐ True or ☐ False

4-14 Entering a foreign market through a joint venture means you will eventually be operating independently in that market.
☐ True or ☐ False

4-15 Trade barriers include tools like embargoes, quotas, and local content requirements.
☐ True or ☐ False

Critical Thinking Questions

⊙ **4-16** Governments invest in education and infrastructure for their citizens, in part to gain a competitive advantage in world markets. Could a government invest too much in education? Could a government invest too heavily in technology? What are the key technologies or services that would give a country more of a competitive advantage in today's markets?

4-17 Review the three basic strategies of international business. Discuss the type of companies that would most likely pursue a global strategy, a multidomestic strategy, and a transnational strategy.

⊙ **4-18** Organizations to promote free trade, like the EU, have had difficulty creating a common currency. Why do you think not all EU countries use the euro? Why do some countries that are not part of the EU choose to use the euro?

Team Time

The Devil's Advocate

Read the following issues and questions. Which side of the issue do you believe is correct? Form a group with other students in the class who share your belief. As a group, play devil's advocate by creating a case for the opposing side of the issue. Now that you've considered both sides, you're ready to debate the opposition.

1. In the recent wave of globalization, developing countries have become the focus for many international businesses. Is this process of globalization the best way to strengthen developing countries and establish a level playing field, or does it keep them under the control of wealthy industries and increase income inequality?

2. Free trade versus protectionism is a heated debate in today's fragile economy. Which is better for the health of the U.S. economy over the next 10 years—free trade or protectionism?

3. Currently, the minimum age for a child to work in Indonesia is 12 years old. The minimum age for a child to work in the United States is 14 years old. If a garment company from the United States decides to outsource production to Indonesia, would it be ethical for the company to hire 12- or 13-year-old workers in the factory?

Process

Step 1. Meet as a group to discuss the issue. Remember that you must build a case for the side you chose. Look for problems with your own personal beliefs to develop a case for your side.

Step 2. Prepare an individual response that supports your side of the issue.

Step 3. Share your response with your group. Think of possible rebuttals for each response. Then alter any responses that can produce a strong rebuttal.

Step 4. Determine who will be the group's primary spokesperson for the debate.

Step 5. Each group will be given five minutes to present its side of the issue. After each group has presented its argument, each team will be given five minutes to prepare a rebuttal and then three minutes to present the rebuttal.

Step 6. Repeat with other groups.

Step 7. After each group has debated, discuss whether anyone's personal views have changed after this assignment.

Ethics and Corporate Social Responsibility

OFFSHORE OUTSOURCING

Workers in the United States often view offshore outsourcing in a negative light. Many people believe that this practice is a way for companies to make more money by eliminating U.S. jobs. However, offshore outsourcing sometimes seems necessary for the survival of a company. Review the following scenario.

Scenario

You are the owner of a company that makes industrial sewing machines. Currently, your company's profits are decreasing because your competitors have lower prices. You cannot lower the price of your machines without losing a significant amount of money. The majority of your costs come from labor. You have 2,000 employees in your factory, and your company is the primary employer in the community. You could sell your product for a third of the price if you outsourced half your production to a foreign country. However, this would eliminate 1,000 jobs and devastate the community. Also, the country that you would be outsourcing to has a reputation for unsafe working conditions and practices. If you don't outsource some of your production, over time your company may be unable to compete, possibly forcing you to shut down your company.

Questions for Discussion

4-19   As a business owner, what are the costs and benefits of moving half your production abroad?

4-20   Do the benefits of offshore outsourcing outweigh the costs? Why or why not?

4-21   Are there any possible alternatives to consider? What other decision could you make so that each side (domestic and international) benefits?

Web Exercises

4-22   **The Complexity of the European Union**
Watch the YouTube video "The European Union Explained." Can you describe the differences between the EU, the Eurozone, and the European Economic Area (EEA)? Why would there be the need for these different agreements? How do these tie to past history of EU member countries?

4-23   **Same Company, Different Products**
Go to the website of the Swedish furniture maker IKEA (www.ikea.com). Under the "select a location" option, choose the United States. Review the site and note the products and the design of the page. Then go back to the home page and choose a different country. Look for differences in the appearance of the website and the products offered. Why do you think these sites are different for each county?

4-24   **Go State!**
Have you ever considered a career with the U.S. State Department? At www.state.gov, under "Youth and Education," select "Student Career Programs." What aspects of these careers appeal to you? Visit the Fulbright

Scholar program. What information in the Fulbright Fellow Orientation Handbook is new to you?

4-25   **Cultural Guidelines**
Knowing how to behave in a variety of countries is critical with increased globalization. Go to www.kwintessential .co.uk to find business etiquette materials on the site. Select three different countries from very different regions of the world. Review the "Doing Business In?" guides for each country. Create a pamphlet for business travelers on the business dos and don'ts for each country.

4-26   **You're the Trader**
Imagine you're in charge of trading goods for a country. Would you focus on building wealth by selling commodities or on developing an industry by purchasing raw materials? Type "IMF trading around the world" into your Internet browser. This should pull up a link to the website of the International Monetary Fund (www.imf.org) where you can play a game in which you become an international trader. Measure your success on the global economics conditions scale.

MyBizLab

Go to **mybizlab.com** for Auto-graded writing questions as well as the following Assisted-graded writing questions:

4-29 Sometimes an international business needs to modify its product to adjust to the specific needs or tastes of the local market. How might a company like Trek modify the design of its line of bicycles for sale in Ghana, China, and England?

4-30 What are the advantages of increased competition in the global market? What are the disadvantages? Is foreign competition *always* good for the consumer? Is foreign competition *always* bad for local businesses?

References

1. President Bill Clinton, "Remarks by the President to Vietnam National University," Embassy of the United States, Hanoi, Vietnam, November 17, 2000.
2. A. Young, "China New Auto Sales 2013: Chinese Consumers Bought over 20 Million Vehicles in 2013 as Foreign Automakers Jockey for Market Share," January 7, 2014, www.ibtimes.com/china-new-auto-sales-2013-chinese-consumers-bought-over-20-million-vehicles-2013-foreign-automakers.
3. Govindkrishna Seshan, "Fruit Punch," *Business Standard*, February 26, 2008, www.business-standard.com/india/storypage.php?autono.
4. Patrick McGeehan, "Foreign Investment in City Is Growing, Report Finds," www.mitchellmoss.com/mentions/NYTimes-27-June-08.pdf.
5. "A Massive Investment in Education to Give Queensland Kids a Flying Start," www.mysunshinecoast.com.au/articles/article-display/a-massive-investment-in-education-to-give-queensland-kids-a-flying-start,17463.
6. Ayala Pines, Miri Lerner, and Dafna Schwartz, "Gender Differences among Social vs. Business Entrepreneurs," http://cdn.intechopen.com/pdfs/31886/InTech-Gender_differences_among_social_vs_business_entrepreneurs.pdf.
7. *Ministry of Trade and Industry*, "Promoting Entrepreneurial-ship," www.regjeringen.no/en/dep/nhd/selected-topics/innovation/promoting-entrepreneurship.html?id=582899.
8. *U.S. Department of State*, "Background Note: Cuba," www.state.gov/r/pa/ei/bgn/2886.htm.
9. *World Trade Organization*, "The GATT Years: From Havana to Marrakesh," www.wto.org/english/thewto_e/whatis_e/tif_e/fact4_e.htm.
10. *World Trade Organization*, "Understanding the WTO," www.wto.org/english/thewto_e/whatis_e/tif_e/tif_e.htm.
11. *World Trade Organization*, "Doha Development Agenda: Negotiations, Implementation, and Development," www.wto.org/english/tratop_e/dda_e/dda_e.htm.
12. Central Intelligence Agency, "Rank Order: Exports," *World Factbook*, www.cia.gov/library/publications/the-world-factbook/rankorder/2078rank.html, and "Rank Order: Imports," *World Factbook*, www.cia.gov/library/publications/the-world-factbook/rankorder/2087rank.
13. Matt Rosenberg, "Euro Countries," http://geography.about.com/od/lists/a/euro.htm.
14. M. Jing, "Siemens Provides the "Brain" for Wuhan's Traffic Control System," October 23, 2013, http://usa.chinadaily.com.cn/epaper/2013-10/23/content_17053310.htm.
15. "Subway Timeline," March 18, 2013, http://www.subway.com/subwayroot/about_us/TimeLine.aspx.
16. *Franchise International*, "Disney Signs India Master," www.franchise-international.net/franchise/Walt-Disney-Company/Disney-signs-India-Master/1554.
17. *SRI International*, "Intellectual Property and Licensing," www.sri.com/rd/hot.html.
18. "FDI in Indian Retail: More Hurdles for Walmart and Others," June 13, 2013, https://knowledge.wharton.upenn.edu/article/fdi-in-indian-retail-more-hurdles-for-walmart-and-others.
19. Rory Cellan-Jones, "Nokia and Microsoft Form Partnership," November 2, 2011, www.bbc.co.uk/news/business-12427680.
20. M. Kan, "Foxconn Mulls Building TVs, Display Panels in Arizona," www.computerworld.com/s/article/9243931/Foxconn_mulls_building_TVs_display_panels_in_Arizona.
21. Parija B. Kavilanz, "Mattel Fined $2.3 Million over Lead in Toys," June 5, 2009, http://money.cnn.com/2009/06/05/news/companies/cpsc.
22. "Hyundai Is First Foreign Automaker to Install a Stamping Shop in Russia," http://news.infibeam.com/blog/news/2010/05/20/hyundai_is_first_foreign_automaker_to_install_a_stamping_shop_in_russia.html.
23. U.S. Department of Commerce, "Foreign Trade," April 1, 2012, www.census.gov/foreign-trade/statistics/highlights/topcurmon.html.

24. K. Armadeo, "Sovereign Wealth Fund," http://useconomy .about.com/od/glossary/g/wealth_fund.htm.

25. Elena Logutenkova, and Yalman Onaran, "Singapore, Abu Dhabi Face Losses on UBS, Citigroup (Update2)," *Business-Week*, March 2, 2010, www.bloomberg.com/apps/news? pid=newsarchive&sid=aeS1DdEYqj_Q.

26. C. G. Alex and Barbara Bowers, "The American Way to Countertrade," *BarterNews* 17 (1988), www.barternews .com/american_way.htm.

27. "Results of Poor Cross Cultural Awareness," www .kwintessential.co.uk/cultural-services/articles/ Results%20of%20Poor%20Cross%20Cultural% 20Awareness.html.

28. Quoted in "Cross Cultural Business Blunders," www .kwintessential.co.uk/cultural-services/articles/ crosscultural-blunders.html.

29. U.S. Department of Justice, "Foreign Corrupt Practices Act," www.justice.gov/criminal/fraud/fcpa.

Chapter 1

Business Law

Every business, whether it is a large multinational corporation, or a small, sole proprietorship, must comply with laws and regulations that govern how businesses operate. Large or complex business entities have lawyers and legal counsel. Small business owners, whether they intend to stay small or plan to grow, generally hire lawyers only on an as-needed basis. Regardless of whether a business is large or small, the people who operate it should have a basic understanding of the laws of the U.S. legal system to be sure they are functioning within the law.

The U.S. Legal System

■ **FIGURE M1.1**
The Legislative System

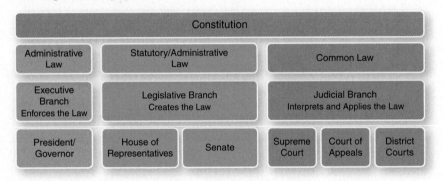

The United States is a federalist system, meaning there is government authority at both national and state levels. The national government has specific powers, and the 50 U.S. states retain substantial autonomy and authority. Both the federal government and state governments are divided into executive, legislative, and judicial branches. Written constitutions, both federal and state, form a system of separated powers, checks, and balances among the branches (see ■ **FIGURE M1.1**).

Sources of Law

There are four sources of law: constitutional law, statutory law, administrative regulations, and common law. **Constitutional law**, the written text in the U.S. Constitution and the Bill of Rights, is the foundation of the laws of the United States. All other laws are subordinate to the laws in these two documents. **Statutory laws** are laws passed by the legislative branches of the government. The executive and legislative branches of the federal or state government also establish regulatory bodies. The Securities and Exchange Commission, the Federal Trade Commission (FTC), and the Food and Drug Administration (FDA) are examples. These regulatory bodies have the power to pass **administrative laws**—rules and regulations within their area of authority. The judicial branches of the government not only apply established constitutional and statutory laws when deciding cases but also create law when their decisions become precedents for future case decisions. This type of unwritten but applied law is referred to as **common law**, or **case law**.

How Laws Affect Businesses

In addition to the laws that govern all citizens of the United States, there are specific laws that pertain more directly to businesses. **Business law** consists of laws that directly affect business activities. Once a legal business structure is determined (see Chapter 6), a wide variety of laws affect how the business is run as well as how it treats its employees and consumers. Finally, there are laws that determine what happens when a business needs to stop operating.

Running a Business—Essential Concepts of Business Law

Even before a business opens its doors, various business laws affect it. There are laws that regulate how the business can be set up and how it interacts with each other businesses, its employees, and its customers. Laws also dictate the consequences when a business acts in a wrongful way. Laws are in place to govern commercial transactions, and laws exist to help protect ideas, inventions, and artistic works as well as designs and images used by businesses. In addition, laws are in place to protect consumers from fraud or deceit and ensure competition between businesses remains vibrant. Finally, laws are in place to ensure that businesses do not threaten the environment. Let's look at these laws in greater detail.

Contract Law

Contracts form the basis for much personal and business interaction. A **contract** is an agreement between two parties. In our personal lives, contracts are used in marriage and divorce, for example. In business, contracts are used when a company hires another company or individual to do work for it, when property is bought or sold, and when services are exchanged (see ■ **FIGURE M1.2**).

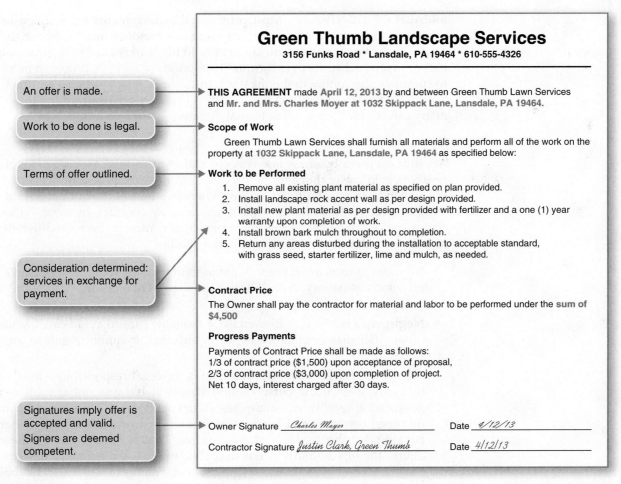

■ **FIGURE M1.2**
A Valid Contract

ELEMENTS OF A CONTRACT   In order for a contract to be valid an offer must be made, the parties must understand and agree on the terms of the contract, consideration must be given, and the offer must be accepted.

- **An offer is made and accepted by competent parties.** The offer (what is given in exchange for goods or services, generally a price) can be spoken or in writing and must be accepted (generally by signing a written contact, oral agreement, or simple handshake). Offers can also be made to the general public in the form of advertisements. For a contract to be valid, all parties entering into it must have the capacity to understand its terms and conditions. Therefore, minors, mentally incompetent individuals, and those who are under the influence of drugs or alcohol do not have the capacity to execute valid contracts. Finally, all parties must enter into the contractual agreement voluntarily without duress, due to fraud, or undue influence.

- **The terms of the offer must be defined and understood and of legal purpose.** Although contracts can be casually created—either verbally or even on a napkin or on the back of an envelope—most are formally drafted. In any contract, however, the terms of the offer must be clearly defined and understood. The underlying purpose of the contract must be legal; otherwise, the contract is void (invalid).

- **Consideration is defined and exchanged.** Something of real value—what lawyers refer to as *consideration*—must be exchanged by both parties to a contract, whether it is entails an exchange of services or goods (trading or bartering) or payment for services or goods.

BREACH OF CONTRACT   Most contractual arrangements are fulfilled to completion, with the terms of the contract being satisfactorily met. However, there are situations in which a party will fail to uphold his or her stated obligation, whether it's because of a dispute over the quality of goods or services provided or a failure to complete the contractual obligation. In these instances when a contract is not fulfilled, a **breach of contract** occurs. Some breaches are resolved in lawsuits, but many can be resolved in a less formal manner.

Tort Law

Another common business law concept is that of torts. A **tort** is a wrongful act, resulting in injury or damages. A tort differs from a breach of contract in that a tort is a violation of a right given by law, whereas a breach of contract occurs when there has been a violation of a right acquired by contract. In some instances, a circumstance can be both a tort and a breach of contract. There are different types of torts: intentional, negligence, and strict liability.

- **Intentional torts** are actions meant to injure another person or person's property, such as battery, assault, fraud, misrepresentation, trespass, slander, and defamation.

- **Negligence** is a failure to exercise reasonable care to avoid causing harm to others. Because negligence is not intentional, it cannot result in an intentional tort.

- **Strict liability (or absolute liability)** is the legal responsibility for damages or injury, even if the person found strictly liable was not at fault or negligent. Strict liability is usually associated with defectively manufactured or designed products and is often referred to as **product liability**. Rather than proving that the producer of the item was somehow negligent, in these situations, the injured party needs to prove only that the item was defective and that the defect caused some type of harm. Failing to warn buyers about the incorrect use of products or their inherent dangers can also result in product liability lawsuits.

A case in which a 79-year-old woman incurred third-degree burns after spilling McDonald's coffee on her lap is a classic example of not only a failure to warn but also a product defect. The woman sued McDonald's for knowingly serving coffee so hot it could cause third-degree burns in two to seven seconds if spilled. Even though McDonald's had a printed warning on its coffee cups that its coffee was hot, the print was small and hard to read. The case went to trial and was settled in the woman's favor. McDonald's subsequently reduced the serving temperature of its coffee and increased the size of the warning on its cups.

No doubt you can think of many other cases in which companies were held liable for damages associated with faulty products. Bridgestone/Firestone recalled nearly 6.5 million Firestone tires after defective products caused death and serious injuries to the owners of Ford Explorers, some of whom filed lawsuits against the company. Mattel settled product liability claims for toys made in China containing high levels of lead paint. And Toyota recalled 10 million automobiles in response to product liability claims of unintended acceleration and braking problems. Sometimes, when product deficiencies affect many individuals, the group will come together and file a **class-action lawsuit**. In these situations, the group of injured individuals (referred to as the class) is jointly represented and acts as one claimant. Class-action lawsuits are usually more powerful than individuals filing separate lawsuits and are often less costly for the individual. If the lawsuit is decided in favor of the class, then the award is split among the group.

Tort reform—proposals to limit tort filings and proceedings and to cap damage awards—is an ongoing source of debate and discussion. The economic effects of the current tort system are the biggest driver of the debate. Manufacturers argue that the cost of litigation and the multi-billion-dollar awards raise the cost of insurance and force companies to increase the prices consumers have to pay for products. Some people feel society has become too litigious and that frivolous lawsuits are out of control. Other people argue that tort reform makes it more difficult for people who are legitimately injured by products to file lawsuits and be fairly compensated. What are your thoughts?

Intellectual Property Laws

Intellectual property laws are put in place to protect **intellectual property**—creations of the mind, such as ideas, inventions, and literary and artistic works as well as symbols, names, images, and designs used in commerce. Intellectual property laws cover patents, trademarks, copyrights, trade secrets, and digital rights. Intellectual property protection encourages innovation by ensuring that authors and inventors are compensated for the costs of developing a product if someone else wants to try to profit from it.

Source: Don Farrall/Getty Images, Inc.

- **Patents.** A patent is a property right granted by the U.S. Patent and Trademark Office (USPTO) on a new and useful invention. A patent grants the patent holder the exclusive right to his or her invention, excluding others from using, making, or selling the same invention for 14 or 20 years, depending on the type of patent issued. There are three types of patents: utility patents, design patents, and plant patents. Utility patents protect inventions for processes, machinery, manufactures, or composites of matter (such as a newly synthesized chemical compound or molecule). Design patents protect the appearance of an object rather than its functionality (which is covered by the utility patent). Plant patents protect new, reproducible plants (organic matter).

  A person who owns a patent can assign, or sell, it for a lump-sum payment to another party. More often, though, the owner *licenses* the patent to a company that markets the invention. The inventor still owns the patent but receives a license fee and royalty payments based on the revenues generated from the invention.

Source: Getty Images, Inc.

- **Trademarks.** A trademark is any word, name, symbol, or device (or any combination of these) used to identify and distinguish a good. A service mark is a similar device but used to identify a service. Trademarks and service marks are often referred to as "brands" or "brand names." Generally, consumers associate products bearing trademarks with certain standards of quality (see ■ **FIGURE M1.3**). What reactions do you have when you see the Nike swoosh, McDonald's golden arches, or Apple's apple? Trademark rights exclude others from using a similar mark, thus protecting the owner of the trademark against any potential fraud. Only those trademarks registered with the USPTO bear the symbol ®, but anyone can use the ™ or ℠ to identify a mark, even though it might not be registered with the USPTO. Trademarks can be licensed, which is generally the case with franchising arrangements.

- **Copyrights.** A copyright is a form of protection provided to creators of original works for a limited period of time. Copyrights protect works such as books, music, photographs, works of art, movies, and computer programs and apply to both published and unpublished works. A copyright makes it illegal for anyone but the creator of a work to reproduce, distribute, or make a derivative of the work (such as a movie from a novel), publicly perform it (such as music or plays), or publicly display it (such as paintings).

- **Trade secrets.** A trade secret is information companies keep undisclosed to give them a competitive advantage. Trade secrets can be any formula, pattern, physical device, idea, process, or compilation of information. Unlike trademarks and patents, trade secrets are not protected under federal statutes; they are protected only under state laws. Another distinction from trademarks and patents is that trade secrets are protected only when the secret is *not* disclosed. Employees of companies who, by the nature of their positions within their firms, have firsthand knowledge of their companies' trade

■ **FIGURE M1.3**
Corporate Logos
Can you identify these corporate logos?

secrets usually are asked to sign a nondisclosure agreement—an agreement not to reveal his or her employer's proprietary information if the employee leaves the company. Violation of such an agreement can lead to imprisonment. For example, two employees of Coca-Cola were sentenced to five- and eight-year federal prison terms for conspiring to steal and sell company trade secrets to Pepsi.

- **Digital rights.** Digital intellectual property is the digital (or electronic) representation of an individual's intellect that holds value on the commercial market. Unlike other intellectual property protected by patents, trademarks, and copyrights, protecting digital intellectual property is much more difficult because it is often easy to electronically copy and distribute quickly and inexpensively to a vast number of individuals. In 1998, the United States passed the Digital Millennium Copyright Act (DMCA) to try to prevent digitized works from being illegally reproduced and distributed, thereby enforcing two 1996 treaties of the World Intellectual Property Organization. The DMCA extends the reach of a copyright by criminalizing the creation and distribution of technology, devices, or services that control access to copyrighted works and tightening the penalties for copyright infringement in the digital environment. Some believe, however, that the DMCA does little to really reduce the confusion that still surrounds the protection of digital works. There are still ongoing debates as to whether the works are indeed protected or whether the current copyright laws, as they apply to digital media, become a detriment to consumers and impair the evolution of the technology.[1]

Sales Law

Many laws govern the sales of goods. The most comprehensive of these laws is the **Uniform Commercial Code** (UCC), a set of model laws that govern businesses selling goods within the United States and its territories. The UCC covers the sale of goods, how they are legally transferred from one owner to another, leases, contracts, securities, and how money can be borrowed. The UCC laws are "model laws" because they first must be adopted by a state—either verbatim or in a modified form. Once adopted, they become state law. All 50 states and territories have adopted some version of the UCC.

■ **TABLE M1.1** outlines the articles and general provisions of each article in the UCC. Everyday business transactions involve provisions in Articles 3, 4, and 5. Article 3 involves negotiable instruments, such as checks, paper money, and commercial paper (short-term debt issued to finance short-term credit needs). The debt for these instruments is unsecured, that is, issued without any form of collateral backing it should the person borrowing the money default on his or her payment. Article 4 pertains to banking matters, and Article 5 applies to letters of credit. A letter of credit is a letter from a bank that guarantees a buyer's payment to a seller will be made, regardless of the buyer's current financial situation.

Antitrust Laws

A healthy economy depends on businesses being able to compete with each other in free and open markets. Competition between sellers benefits consumers by giving them more choices, keeping prices low and the quality of products high, and making products more innovative. **Antitrust laws** are designed to prevent companies from unfairly stifling competition in their markets. The first American antitrust law, the **Sherman Act of 1890**, was created to prevent large, powerful companies from coming together as "trusts" and dominating industries, and the **Clayton Antitrust Act of 1914** added further substance to antitrust legislation, addressing specific practices, such as mergers, that the Sherman Act did not clearly prohibit. Today, the FTC's Bureau of Competition reviews and analyzes potential mergers and other agreements between businesses to prevent anticompetitive conduct and to ensure that competition is maintained.

TABLE M1.1	Description of Articles in the Uniform Commercial Code	
Article	**Title**	**Contents**
1	General Provisions	Principles of interpretation, general definitions
2 and 2A	Sales and Leases	Applies to all contracts for the sale and lease of goods
3	Negotiable Instruments	Checks, banknotes (paper money), and commercial paper
4	Bank Deposits	Bank collections, deposits, and customer relations
4A	Funds Transfers	Corporate to corporate electronic fund transfers and payments such as wire transfers and automated clearinghouse credit transfers
5	Letters of Credit	Laws that address promises by a bank to pay the purchases of a buyer quickly and without reference to the buyer's financial condition
6	Bulk Transfers and Bulk Sales	Imposes an obligation on buyers who order the major part of the inventory for certain types of businesses
7	Warehouse Receipts, Bills of Lading, and Other Documents of Title	Applies generally to trucking companies; includes rules on the relationships between buyers and sellers and any transporters of goods
8	Investment Securities	Rules pertaining to the issuance of stocks, bonds, and other investment securities
9	Secured Transactions	Security interests in real property

- **Mergers.** The FTC monitors mergers to ensure that a combination of two or more businesses will not result in market dominance by the newly formed bigger company. Not all mergers result in monopolies. By combining the operations of firms and getting rid of the duplicate functions in each (two sales departments, two human resources departments, and so on), mergers can create more efficient and competitive organizations. The merger of Office Depot and Office Max in 2013 is an example. However, when Staples tried to buy Office Depot in 1997, the FTC blocked the merger of the two large office supply retail stores. Why? At the time, the FTC reasoned that the merger would reduce the number of competing stores in some parts of the country. By 2013, however, the competitive environment had changed: The FTC concluded that due to the availability of office products through online sites such as Amazon and retailers such as Walmart, the merger of Office Depot and Office Max would not severely limit competition in the office supplies market.[2]

The FTC allowed merger between Office Depot and Office Max, after denying a similar merger between Office Depot and Staples, nearly a decade earlier.

Source: tom carter/Alamy; Justin Sullivan/ Getty Images, Inc.

Antitrust laws are a form of regulation put in place to protect the public against unfair market dominance. In addition, there are many federal and state regulatory agencies, such as the Federal Communications Commission, the FDA, and the Federal Aviation Agency, to name a few, that also are in place to protect the public. However, in the late 1970s and 1980s, many felt some regulated industries were being artificially held back from competition and economic growth, so a trend toward deregulation—breaking up the government regulatory controls on some industries—ensued. Deregulation started with the Railroad Revitalization and Regulatory Reform Act of 1976 and the Staggers Rail Act of 1980. These acts enabled railroads to better compete against the growing trucking and airplane industries. Similarly, the Airline Deregulation Act of 1978 was passed to promote broader competition among air carriers. And the breakup of AT&T in 1984 began deregulation of the telephone industries and was followed by the Telecommunications Act of 1996 to ease the oversight and regulation on cable and Internet communication industries:

- **Price collusion.** The FTC also watches out for companies that collude on price-related matters that then might either make it difficult for competitors to enter a market or artificially inflate the prices consumers pay. For example, the FTC concluded that Apple and five large U.S. publishers had conspired to hike up the prices of electronic books in an effort to keep e-book prices above those of Amazon's significantly discounted prices.[3] The U.S. Justice Department filed suit against Apple and the five companies, and in 2013, they were found guilty. A trial to determine damages is set to occur in mid-2014. In the meantime, a class-action lawsuit has been filed on behalf of e-book customers in 33 states for more than $840 million.

- **Manufacturer/dealer agreements.** Similarly, the FTC monitors any agreements between manufacturers and product dealers. Often these agreements make sense and benefit consumers, such as when a computer manufacturer arranges works with software developer to install certain application on new computers prior to their sale. But the FTC watches for instances when a manufacturer forces an unwanted associated product onto a dealer. This is what happened when Microsoft bundled its Web browser Internet Explorer with its Windows operating system. Doing so gave Microsoft an unfair advantage in the Web browser market, the FTC concluded.

Through such scrutiny of competitive business practices, the FTC strives to ensure that consumers have choices in price, selection, quality, and innovation.

Environmental Laws

The rapid growth of business and industry can have a significant negative impact on the environment. To protect the environment for future generations, in the 1960s and 1970s, U.S. laws were passed to regulate air and water quality, and the Environmental Protection Agency (EPA) was established.[4] The EPA is responsible for maintaining and enforcing national environmental standards as well as conducting research and providing education on environmental issues. Additional regulations have been passed to control the disposal of hazardous waste. More recently, it's been debated whether regulations should be passed to help curb global warming.

The EPA is responsible for maintaining and enforcing environmental standards and controlling air and water pollution, among other things.
Source: Snap Happy/Fotolia.

Laws for Consumers and Employees

Various commerce-related laws are designed protect the employees of firms and their customers. Advertising laws, employee safety laws, and food and drug laws are examples.

Truth-in-advertising laws ensure that advertisements are not deceptive and support the claims they make.
Source: Shutterstock.

Advertising Laws

Consumers are inundated with advertisements that tout product features and benefits. Companies engage in advertising, some of which is very expensive, with the hopes of enticing us to purchase their products. In 2012, advertising accounted for nearly 20 percent of U.S. sales.[5] The FTC regulates all forms of business advertising.

- **Truth-in-advertising** rules help to ensure advertisements are truthful and nondeceptive, that there is sufficient evidence to support the claims they make, and that the advertisements are not unfair (and subsequently cause unavoidable consumer injury that is not outweighed by the benefit).
- **Product labeling** laws include laws that mandate that food products have specific nutritional and product information on their labels, cigarette packages must include warning labels, and any products that might be hazardous to children must contain warnings.

In addition, there are specific product advertisements that the government regulates, including advertisements for cigarettes, alcoholic beverages, automobiles, Internet services, health and fitness products, housing and real estate, and telephone services.

Employment and Labor Law

There are hundreds of laws in place that regulate how companies hire and treat employees. **Employment laws** mandate that companies in their hiring practices do not discriminate against a job applicant or candidate based on his or her disabilities, age, race, religion, sexual orientation, or nationality. These laws include Equal Employment Opportunity laws, the Civil Rights Act, the Americans with Disabilities Act, and the Age Discrimination in Employment Act. See Chapter 9 for more details on employment laws.

Employee laws ensure that all workers and employees are treated fairly with respect to their wages, working conditions, medical care due to a workplace injury, and employee benefits, to name a few. ■ **TABLE M1.2** lists some of the major employee laws.

TABLE M1.2	Examples of Laws That Govern How Businesses Need to Treat Their Employees
Law/Regulation	**Description**
Fair Labor Standards Act	Regulates standards for wages and overtime pay.
Occupational Safety and Health Act (OSHA)	Regulates safety and health conditions for employees.
Workers Compensation	Provides for the compensation and medical care for employees injured on the job or who develop diseases as a result of doing their jobs.
Employee Retirement Income Security Act (ERISA)	Regulates the administration of retirement, pension, and welfare benefits.
Labor-Management Reporting and Disclosure Act	Regulates the fiduciary responsibilities of unions to its members.
Family and Medical Leave Act	Regulates the amount of leave employers must give their employees upon the birth or adoption of a child or for the serious illness of a direct family member.
Lilly Ledbetter Fair Pay Act	Individuals subjected to unlawful pay discrimination are able to seek justice under the federal antidiscrimination laws.
Worker Adjustment and Retraining Notification Act (WARN)	Requires employers to notify all employees 60 days in advance of plant closings or mass layoffs.

Laws That Govern Closing a Business

At some point, businesses close their doors and cease operating. Sometimes, especially with family-owned businesses, sole proprietorships, or partnerships, businesses close because the current leader of the business leaves and there is no further succession in business ownership. Sometimes, through a merger or acquisition, a business is incorporated into another business. In those instances, regulations and processes ensure that all financial obligations (taxes and business debts) have been successfully met, that employees have been notified and paid appropriately, and that all aspects of the business operations, including permits, licenses, and trade names, are canceled. In some instances, businesses are forced to file for bankruptcy because they can no longer meet their financial obligations.

Bankruptcy

Bankruptcy is the legal status of an insolvent person or organization by which their debts are relieved through court action. Bankruptcy can be filed voluntarily or involuntarily; and after all debts have been paid, the debtor is free to begin anew. The source of funds from which creditors can collect is first determined by how the business is structured. For example, when a sole proprietorship files for bankruptcy, the business's assets are first used to pay off its debts. The business owner' personal assets (such as a homes, cars, and bank accounts) can also be used to pay off any remaining debts. Corporations, limited liability companies, and some forms of partnerships protect personal assets, allowing only business assets to be used to pay off debts incurred by the entity.

There are three types of bankruptcy, and they are named for the specific chapter of the U.S. Bankruptcy Code:

- **Chapter 7**. All business (and sometimes personal) assets are liquidated, and outstanding debts are paid off in a Chapter 7 bankruptcy. Any outstanding debts remaining after all assets are used are discharged. The business ceases operation.

- **Chapter 11**. A business applying for Chapter 11 bankruptcy is allowed to continue operating and develops a reorganization plan to pay its creditors over time.

- **Chapter 13**. Chapter 13 is the most common form of bankruptcy for individuals. Chapter 13 allows an individual to use proceeds from the sale of some assets and pay off remaining debts with operating income by following a three- to five-year repayment plan. This enables an individual to keep his or her home and potentially a car and other productive assets.

Although bankruptcy can be a solution to insolvency, it should be only a last resort. Companies and individuals who survive bankruptcy often find it hard reestablish good credit ratings. As a result, banks and other lenders may not extend credit to them or will do so only with high interest rates.

References

1. Michael Rappa, "Managing the Digital Enterprise: Intellectual Property," May 31, 2009, http://digitalenterprise.org/ip/ip.html.
2. David McLaughlin and Matt Townsend, "Office Depot Merger with Office Max Wins U.S. Approval," November 1, 2013, www.bloomberg.com/news/2013-11-01/office-depot-merger-with-officemax-wins-u-s-approval.html.
3. Adi Robertson, "Apple Guilty of Ebook Price Fixing, Rules Federal Court," July 10, 2013, www.theverge.com/2013/7/10/4510338/apple-found-guilty-of-ebook-price-fixing.
4. Environmental Protection Agency, "Our Mission and What We Do," www.epa.gov.
5. IHS Global Insight, Inc., "The Economic Impact of Advertising Expenditures in the United States 2012–2017," January 2014.

Chapter 5
Small Business and the Entrepreneur

▶ Small Business: The Mainstream of the American Economy

Allison Juarez left a secure position in a good company to start her own personal organizing business. For Allison, the financial risks of leaving a set salary and retirement plan were offset by independence and flexibility. What exactly is a small business? And why are they so important to the American economy?

▶ Entrepreneurs and the American Dream

The Wahoo brothers took the concept of a fish taco and created a multi-million-dollar business with several locations. Their success is not based just on their delicious food. What else about these brothers and their business makes them successful entrepreneurs? Do you have what it takes to be an entrepreneur?

▶ Buying Franchises and Existing Businesses

Have you ever thought of owning your own business but didn't know where to start? Aisha Lawrence had always dreamed of running a restaurant. Should she start her own restaurant, buy an established one, or purchase a franchise for a restaurant?

▶ The Risks of Small Businesses and Where to Get Help

There's a good reason why entrepreneurs are known for being risk takers: Starting a small business is risky! Having left a failing company to start his own business, Roger Sherman knew the pressures and risks he was facing as an entrepreneur. After making a good start with his business, Roger needed some assistance. Where could he go to get some short-term financial assistance?

▶ Financing Considerations

All that stands between a would-be entrepreneur and a pot of gold at the end of the rainbow is a way to finance his or her dream business. Although operating a sandwich shop was not Fred DeLuca's dream, it did become his pot of gold, as it turned into one of the world's top franchise opportunities and largest privately held businesses. And it all started with a $1,000 investment from a friend. How do small businesses obtain financing and choose between different types of financing available to them?

OBJECTIVES

1 What is the role and structure of the small business within the U.S. economy? (pp. 127–132)

2 What are the traits of an effective entrepreneur, and what are the different types of entrepreneurs? (pp. 132–138)

3 What are the advantages and disadvantages of franchising? (pp. 139–141)

4 Why is a business plan crucial to small business success, and what factors lead to small business failure? (pp. 144–146)

5 What resources are available to provide assistance and guidance to small business owners? (pp. 146–148)

6 What are the potential benefits and drawbacks of each major source of small business financing? (pp. 148–151)

Small Business: The Mainstream of the American Economy pp. 127–132

After getting job offer a month before graduating and accepting it, Allison Juarez thought she was set for life. She worked for a large, secure company; she received a regular paycheck, had a 401(k) plan, and had already been promoted twice. Still, she felt something was missing. She fantasized about owning her own business, making her own decisions, having some flexibility in her schedule, and hopefully not having someone else set her earning potential. But she never could gather enough courage to leave the stable paycheck.

Finally, when it looked like she could end up being downsized, Allison jumped the corporate ship and started her own professional organizing business. She had helped to organize many garages, closets, and offices for friends and family, but she had never considered charging for her time. It was just fun for her. Now, she was actively seeking clients, marketing her services, and enjoying the results. Business has been steady but not overwhelming. Allison is glad that she has a nest egg to rely on during slow times, but she has not regretted her decision one bit. ■

Source: Bobo/Fotolia.

Like Allison's business, many small businesses are founded to provide innovative solutions to unique problems. Small businesses often fill a niche that large companies do not. As a whole, small businesses in the United States play a major role in the economy.

Small Business and the Economy

What is a small business? The **Small Business Administration** (SBA) is an independent agency of the federal government that was formed to aid, counsel, assist, and protect the interests of small businesses. The SBA defines a **small business** as one that is independently owned and operated and not dominant in its field of operation.[1] To qualify for governmental programs and benefits specifically

MyBizLab®

✪ Improve Your Grade!

Over 10 million students improved their results using the Pearson **MyLabs**.
Visit **mybizlab.com** for simulations, tutorials, and end-of-chapter problems.

■ **FIGURE 5.1**

**U.S. Small Businesses
by Employees**

Source: Data from "Statistics about Small
Business from the Census Bureau." U. S.
Census Bureau. Web. 06 Feb. 2012. http://
www.census.gov.

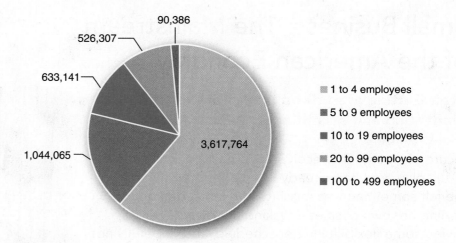

targeted for small businesses, a small business must also meet employee and sales standards established by the SBA. In general, most small businesses must have fewer than 500 employees. However, as ■ **FIGURE 5.1** shows, nearly 90 percent of all small businesses have 20 or fewer employees.[2] The SBA also places restrictions on how much annual revenue a small business can earn to qualify for its programs. The limits on average annual revenue vary significantly by industry. For example, the standard annual revenue is $7 million for one-third of the retail trade industries. A few others industries, such as grocery and department stores and car and electrical appliance dealers, have higher standards, but none exceed $35.5 million.[3]

Why are small businesses important to the economy? Because there are so many small businesses, they are very important to the economy and the job market. Small businesses create about 64 percent of all new jobs in the United Sates and generate nearly one-half of the nation's gross domestic product.[4,5] As ■ **FIGURE 5.2** shows that if U.S. small businesses made up their own economy, it would be one of the world's largest.[6,7] Small businesses also export about one-third of the total goods exported from the United States.[8]

How do small businesses foster innovation? Small companies often introduce new products or procedures that many large businesses do not have the flexibility, the time, the resources, or the inclination to offer. In fact, small businesses create more patents per employee than do large firms.[9] The impact of small business innovations is well known in the computer, information technology, and communications industries. Legendary entrepreneurs include Mark Zuckerberg, who created Facebook from his Harvard dorm room at the age of 19, and two

■ **FIGURE 5.2**

**U.S. Small Businesses versus
World Economies**

Source: Chart based on data from two
sources: World GDP data: http://www.imf
.org/external/data.htm Small Business % of
US Economy: http://www.sbecouncil.org/
about-us/facts-and-data/.

Stanford students, Larry Page and Sergey Brin, who began Google as part of a graduate project. Many years earlier, Michael Dell shook up the computer retail industry by being the first to market computers directly to customers via the Internet rather than through retail stores.

Other industries besides the technology field also have benefited from the innovative contributions of small businesses. For example, in the biotechnology industry, many small businesses have found innovative solutions to medical issues. One such company is the Insulet Corporation, which received an innovation award from the Smaller Business Association of New England for developing the OmniPod. This tiny instrument, weighing a little more than an ounce, sticks to the

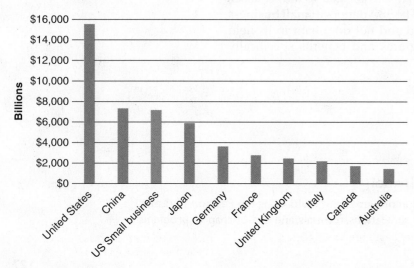

skin and delivers insulin at a constant rate based on a person's insulin needs.[10] The flexibility small businesses such as the Insulet Corporation have allows them to react more quickly than larger companies to changing market trends and needs. As such, small businesses play an important role in maintaining a healthy economy.

The "green industry"—businesses that provide environmentally friendly products and services—are a hotbed for small start-up businesses. Entrants into this new industry seem to be one of two types: Someone either takes an existing product and makes a business out of making it green or has an idea for a green product and creates a business to produce it. Wind turbines, solar panels, recycling, and recycled products have spurred many business initiatives. Giga-Biter is a small business that benefits the environment as well as people's security and privacy by safely grinding old computer equipment into dust that is 100% recyclable.[11] The outdoor clothing and gear maker Patagonia was the first company to use recycled plastic bottles—and later recycled polyester—to create Polartec fleece.[12]

How do small businesses help bigger companies? Small businesses often operate in cooperative relationships with bigger businesses. In the automotive industry, for example, small businesses are important because they make and supply the parts needed to manufacture cars. In fact, many of the parts that go into automobiles, such as seats, engine blocks, and bumpers, are provided by independent suppliers.[13] Small businesses also provide larger companies with new and better product designs. For example, heated seats and intermittent windshield wipers were first developed by small companies and later sold to large car manufacturers.[14]

How do small businesses help consumers? Small businesses directly provide us with many of the specialized products and services we use every day. Service businesses, such as hair salons, landscapers, and dry cleaners, as well as local restaurants, auto repair, and many other mom-and-pop stores, provide the services and goods larger businesses can't or don't want to provide.

Small Business and the Workforce

What kind of workers do small businesses employ? Almost all new businesses are small; therefore, as we have explained, they account for most of the new jobs created in the economy. In addition, small businesses hire a larger proportion of younger workers, older workers, and part-time workers, so they help employ millions of people who do not fit into a traditional corporate structure.[15]

Do small businesses provide opportunities for minorities? Many individuals see owning and operating their own businesses as a means of achieving the American dream. To that end, women, minorities, and immigrants are becoming more important players in the small business arena. According to an SBA report, approximately one-fifth of all U.S. small businesses are owned by minorities. African American–, and Asian American–, and American Indian–owned businesses account for approximately 5 percent each of all U.S. firms, and Hispanic-owned businesses account for 10 percent of all U.S. firms (see ■ **FIGURE 5.3**). Women, who own 5.3 million businesses, make up approximately one-third of all small business owners. The number of minority-owned businesses is increasing. Between 2000 and 2008, the number of Hispanic-owned businesses grew an amazing 80 percent, women-owned businesses increased by nearly 10 percent, and firms owned by Asian Americans and American Indians increased by nearly 50 percent.[16] Unfortunately, the last recession hit small businesses hard. At the peak of the recession, small businesses accounted for nearly 60 percent of job losses. However, hiring has increased as the economy has improved.

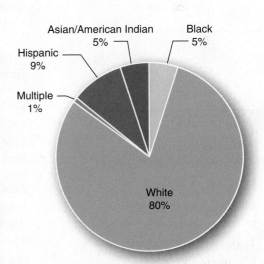

■ **FIGURE 5.3**
Small Business Ethnic Ownership
Source: Created with data from Table A.13 Characteristics of Self-Employed Individuals, 2000–2007. "The Small Business Economy." (2009). U.S. Small Business Economy. http://archive.sba.gov/.

Opportunity & Innovation
New ideas and needs bring new businesses.

Control
More control of business decisions; do not want to work for someone else.

Financial Independence
Owners feel they can make more money operating their own business.

Schedule Flexibility
Looking for a better work/life balance.

Unemployment
Seeking income due to job loss.

■ **FIGURE 5.4**
Reasons to Start a Small Business

Reasons for Starting a Small Business

Why would I want to start my own business? Bill McNeely, a logistics operations manager at a training camp for the Afghan National Police, left his job to start a business so he wouldn't have to be away from his family in Texas. But people start small businesses for many different reasons (see ■ **FIGURE 5.4**):

1. **Opportunity knocks.** An idea for a new company often starts when someone envisions a product or a service that isn't being offered yet. Rajbhog Foods, which provides authentic Indian sweets and snacks, started as a small, family-owned shop that catered to the Indian community in Queens, New York. As the Indian population in the area increased, so did the volume of items made and sold by Rajbhog Foods. The company has expanded its operations to sell to 41 states and Canada, caters large weddings and conventions, and has franchise operations in other East Coast locations. Other people start businesses to overcome obstacles they are personally facing. For example, a father frustrated by watching his autistic child struggle founded the Animated Speech Corporation, which develops software-based conversational language learning systems to help autistic children communicate.[17]

2. **Financial independence.** Many people launch small businesses to achieve financial independence, although this should not be the sole reason you start a business. Why? Because most small businesses don't start out as profitable ventures. Traditionally, it takes three to five years for new businesses to become profitable.

3. **Control.** Being in control and making more business decisions than their current positions allow is another why people start their own businesses. With fewer channels to go through when decisions need to be made, small business owners can often react more quickly to take advantage of immediate opportunities. This can be very rewarding. Other people simply aren't satisfied working for someone else.

4. **Flexibility.** Running their own businesses gives people the flexibility to adjust their work schedules. Many small business owners appreciate the work/life balance owning their own businesses affords.

5. **Unemployment.** It's not uncommon for people to start their own businesses because they have no other employment opportunities. "Life begins when you get fired" was exactly the case for Bruce Freeman, owner of ProLine Communications, Inc. Three months after being fired, he couldn't think of what to do next. Then, encouraged by a friend, Bruce started his own business. His first client was a company he worked with in his previous job. Now, over 10 years later, he's making more money than he ever could have in his old job.[18]

> ▶ **THE LIST**
>
> **Ten Great Industries for Starting a Business**
>
> 1. Healthy fast foods
> 2. Internet marketing
> 3. Elderly home care
> 4. Home fitness trainers
> 5. Green contracting
> 6. Pet care and grooming
> 7. App development
> 8. Home and building services
> 9. Small business services
> 10. Retirement recreation
>
> *Source:* From http://under30ceo.com/ 10-best-industries-to-start-a-business-in-2013.

The Impact of Technology on Small Businesses

How has technology affected small businesses? Technology creates new business opportunities and new ways to conduct business. Entrepreneurial success stories, such as YouTube, Facebook, and Google, have had a big impact on small businesses. Consider entrepreneur Nick Swinmurn. After Swinmurn couldn't find a new pair of his favorite boots while shopping in 1999, he decided to launch an Internet shoe store. The site started small, but after Swinmurn realized the potential for advancement, with the help of CEO Tony Hsieh, he expanded the selection and shipping capacity of the site, and Zappos.com quickly became a billion-dollar success.

Zappos.com quickly became a billion-dollar online shoe merchant when founder Nick Swinmurn created a new solution to buying shoes.
Source: KAREN BLEIER/AFP/Getty Images/Newscom.

Social Media and Mobile Marketing

Small businesses are finding that compared to traditional advertising, social networks, blogs, and mobile devices are more cost effective ways to interact with, market to, and keep abreast of their customers. This is what Sprinkles Cupcakes, a bakery chain based in Beverly Hills, California, does. Each day the company posts a secret word on its Facebook page. Customers who retrieve the word and mention it at any one of the bakery's stores get a free cupcake. The company also uses Facebook to pretest flavor ideas and upcoming promotions in an effort to increase its interaction with its customers. When Sprinkles reached 100,000 Facebook fans, it randomly chose a "BFF" (Best Friend Forever) and gave the person a free to trip to its Hollywood store.

Facebook is not the only social media tool being used by small businesses. Twitter, Yelp, Foursquare, and LinkedIn are also popular ways to connect with customers and prospective employees. Using mobile-device apps such as Foursquare and Gowalla, consumers can access coupons, discounts, and special offers from small businesses. Over the holiday season, to help visitors with their holiday shopping, the Grapevine Mall in Grapevine, Texas, posted signs throughout the mall to remind shoppers how to use their mobile devices to navigate the mall and find deals. Small business owners are also utilizing devices that fit onto smart phones to process credit cards, which is a perfect solution for businesses that do transactions primarily at trade shows, flea markets, and craft shows.

However, social media can also become problematic if not managed well. Creating a fan page on Facebook without monitoring what people are saying about your business can be hazardous to its reputation. Although most consumers report that they use social media to communicate with businesses, only 8 percent are satisfied with businesses' responsiveness on social media. Nearly one-third felt their complaints were ignored, and nearly 9 out of 10 customers felt that if they see their complaint or even another's complaint being ignored, they'd be less likely to buy from that company.[19] Similarly, writing a blog may help get out your message, but if no one reads the blog, it's not effective. A well-thought-out technology plan is an important aspect of any business's overall strategy.

Starting a small business is a sizable challenge, as Allison can attest to. It didn't solve all her problems; in fact, it might have created a few more, but she is glad to be in control of her own situation. It is a challenge to which many entrepreneurs, looking for their piece of the American dream, enthusiastically rise. For Allison, having a flexible schedule, doing what she loves to do, and making money doing it made the risks of starting her home-organizing business worth taking.

Businesses in this Grapevine, Texas, mall use social media and mobile devices to communicate with their customers as they shop.
Source: Joyce Marshall/Newscom.

iSmell

Not all technology-related businesses end up being a successful. One example was the iSmell, a product that plugged into a computer's USB port and promised to enhance a user's Web surfing experience by generating different scents. Using the iSmell, you could smell a new perfume before buying it or conjure up the smell of a ballpark while playing a baseball video game. Unfortunately, iSmell never made it beyond the prototype stage. Its parent company, DigiScents, pulled the plug on it.[20]

Source: Newscom.

Entrepreneurs and the American Dream pp. 132–138

Who would ever have thought that blending Mexican, Brazilian, and Asian cuisines and $30,000 would lead to 50 restaurants in four states 20 years later? Certainly not the Wahoo brothers. If you ask them, it just kind of happened. The Wahoo brothers—Wing, Ed, and Mingo—grew up above their parents' Chinese restaurant. They took the concept of a fish taco—a staple they had grown to love while surfing in Mexico—and enhanced it with their favorite Brazilian and Asian dishes. Combined with a casual, surf-inspired decor, their restaurant concept was well received by the local southern California crowd. The brothers brought in another partner to help manage their second location, and the business quickly took off from there.[21] So, what qualities do the Wahoo brothers have to take their small fish taco eatery and turn it into a multi-million-dollar business? What makes them entrepreneurs? ■

We've all heard of Starbucks, Under Armour, and Amazon.com, but you probably don't associate these big-name companies with small business. At one point, however, each of these companies originated as a small business. They were all started by **entrepreneurs**—people who assume the risk of creating, organizing, and operating a business. Not all small businesses are entrepreneurial. What makes a new venture entrepreneurial is that the idea behind the business is innovative or change oriented. Entrepreneurs most often start a business to satisfy a need in the market that is not being adequately fulfilled. This area of need is called an **opportunity niche**.

Like the Wahoo brothers, Pete Slosberg, founder of Pete's Brewing Company, recognized the rise in popularity of microbreweries and brewpubs around the country and saw an opportunity niche: creating a fantastic-tasting beer, an eye-catching label, and a name that sticks in people's minds. Slosberg wanted to have the name and label encourage folks to try the beer once and the taste of the beer to be good enough that people would continue to buy the beer.[22] In 1998, Pete's Brewing Company had $19 million in sales before being sold to the Gambrinus Company.

The Traits of Successful Entrepreneurs

What are the traits of successful entrepreneurs? Businessman Wayne Huizenga started Waste Management, Inc., a leader in the waste and environmental services industry, by buying a single garbage truck in 1968. He expanded the company by buying other trash collection services, and by 1983 the company had grown into the largest of its kind in the United States. But Huizenga didn't stop there. He also started Blockbuster Video, the video rental company, as well as AutoNation, the behemoth automotive dealer.[23] How can some entrepreneurs like Wayne Huizenga begin successful businesses, whereas others have a difficult time getting their ideas off the ground? How do successful entrepreneurs see an opportunity niche and know exactly what they need to do to seize the opportunity and succeed?

Although luck and timing play a large role in entrepreneurial success, research has also shown that successful entrepreneurs have the following characteristics:

1. Are innovative and have a vision
2. Take risks
3. Are motivated to succeed
4. Are flexible and self-directed
5. Work well with others and possess good leadership skills
6. Are "system thinkers"—view the whole process rather than just its individual pieces

How are entrepreneurs innovative? Successful entrepreneurs see problems to be solved or opportunities that aren't being addressed in the marketplace; they recognize opportunity niches. They also make improvements to existing products or systems, or they introduce something new and make profitable solutions out of problems. Renowned management and business thinker Peter Drucker noted that successful entrepreneurs "exploit change as an opportunity for a different business or a different service."[24] For example, Henry Ford turned his knowledge of engines into the first "horseless carriage," which he later improved to become the Model T.[25] His improvement was not only in creating a new machine but also in developing an assembly-line process by which his company could make multiple automobiles more efficiently. Ford's innovative assembly process became the standard for efficient manufacturing.

Think about other entrepreneurs and the innovation behind their success. Mark Zuckerberg changed how we communicate and network with others by launching Facebook. Steve Jobs, arguably one of the greatest innovators of modern times, helped to bring personal computing to the home with the introduction of the Apple computer and more recently changed how we listen to music with the iPod and iTunes, how we use mobile phones with the iPhone and mobile apps, and how we access media information and entertainment with the iPad. Entrepreneurial doesn't just mean that you start from scratch. Obviously, Jobs had the powerful resources of Apple behind him to launch some of these innovations, but nonetheless his products were innovative and radically changed very traditional processes. ■ **FIGURE 5.5** lists some other important innovations by entrepreneurs in the twentieth century.[26]

How do entrepreneurs take risks? Being an entrepreneur involves risk: the risk of failure, the risk of losing one's career or reputation, and, of course, financial risks. Because entrepreneurs are often creating new and innovative products, the processes they develop often are untried. Successful entrepreneurs are aware of the risks, recognize they can influence events but do not have complete control over them, and know they may fail. Successful entrepreneurs therefore take calculated risks—that is, they consider the likelihood of success before deciding whether to take a particular risk.

What makes entrepreneurs motivated to succeed? Entrepreneurs are motivated by many different factors. Some entrepreneurs are motivated to provide for themselves or their families. These individuals may be driven to pursue multiple ventures before uncovering a successful idea. Other entrepreneurs are motivated to succeed by the personal fulfillment they feel after successfully launching a business.

■ **FIGURE 5.5**
Entrepreneurial Innovations

FM radio	Polaroid camera	Super computer	Portable computer	Digital X-ray	Portable MP3 player	Consumer GPS devices	Apple iPhone	Apple iPad
1933	1947	1958	1981	1983	1998	2000	2007	2010

The keen desire to tackle challenges and achieve success led one entrepreneur, Ted Kennedy (not the former Massachusetts senator), to start a company. Kennedy noticed that many participants in the Ironman Triathlon Challenge were corporate executives. He also noticed that they wanted above-average accommodations and enjoyed meeting and socializing with other CEOs prior to and during their competition. So, Kennedy formed CEO Challenges, a company that puts on sporting competitions specifically for CEOs. Although CEO Challenges initially only offered triathlons, it now offers cycling, hockey, fishing, golf, sailing, tennis, and other competitive adventures to executives and holds challenges in Canada and Europe.

Why do successful entrepreneurs need to be flexible and self-directed? Because new ventures are risky, entrepreneurs need to be able to react quickly to unexpected situations and downturns. Jason Hogg cofounded Revolution Money, an online money-exchange company that's a cross between PayPal and traditional credit cards. The "revolution" was poised to take off when the Great Recession began and Hogg had to make some strategic decisions to keep his fledgling business afloat. He had to quickly reevaluate his business plan and develop new partnerships to continue to grow his business during the recession. He credits his company's success to being "flexible and creative."[27]

An entrepreneur must be able to wear many hats, acting not only as executive but also as sales manager, financial director, secretary, and mailroom person. Entrepreneurs also need to know when to sell or exit a business. In 2009, Hogg decided to sell Revolution Money to American Express.

Why are people skills and leadership skills important to entrepreneurs? They may come up with the initial ideas behind their businesses, but entrepreneurs rarely work by themselves. As much as they have the capacity to wear many hats, at some point most entrepreneurs need other people with complementary skills to join them in their ventures. If their businesses expand, they must hire employees and other managers to help them run it, just as the Wahoo Brothers did when they decided to expand their restaurant business. Leadership and communication skills are therefore important traits of successful entrepreneurs who must motivate others to feel as passionately about the entrepreneurial enterprise as they do.

What does it mean for entrepreneurs to be "system" thinkers? Although entrepreneurs develop companies from an idea, they must focus on the entire process of turning their idea into a business to succeed. Successful entrepreneurs are able to see the whole picture when they establish their businesses. They determine how to resolve a problem or capitalize on an opportunity by developing a solid plan, including producing, financing, marketing, and distributing the service or the product.

Realizing that the hamburger was the best seller in their California restaurant, the McDonald brothers, who started the McDonald's restaurant chain, created an assembly line that allowed them to produce burgers quickly and inexpensively. Business boomed. It expanded even more when businessman and entrepreneur Ray Kroc, who was selling milkshake machines in California, convinced the brothers not only to use his milkshake machines but also to let him open another McDonald's restaurant in Chicago. Seeing the opportunity niche in fast-food franchising, Kroc later bought the McDonald's restaurants from the McDonald brothers. The company now operates over 35,000 restaurants in 117 countries and generates more than $28 billion in revenue annually.[28]

Types of Entrepreneurs

Are there different types of entrepreneurs? Beyond traditional entrepreneurs described in the previous sections, other entrepreneurial categories have begun to crop up:

1. Lifestyle entrepreneurs
2. Micropreneurs

3. Home-based entrepreneurs

4. Internet entrepreneurs

5. Growth entrepreneurs

6. Intrapreneurs

7. Social entrepreneurs and social intrapreneurs

8. Serial entrepreneurs

While each category has its own unique characteristics, they are not exclusive. Entrepreneurs don't necessarily fit into just one of these categories. For example, there are home-based entrepreneurs who are also lifestyle entrepreneurs and Internet entrepreneurs. Let's take a look at each of these types of entrepreneurs.

What are lifestyle entrepreneurs? **Lifestyle entrepreneurs** look for more than profit potential when they begin their businesses. Some lifestyle entrepreneurs are looking for freedom from corporate bureaucracy or the opportunity to work at home or in a location other than an office. Others are looking for more flexibility in work hours or travel schedules. Take Richard Dahl, for example. He is traveling around the country in a travel trailer selling more than 300 items, including his flagship water filter system at trailer parks, campgrounds, and motor home shows.[29] His business, the RV Water Filter Store, allows him to fulfill his passion of traveling around the country with this wife. Gary Veynerchuk started WineLibrary.com, a multi-million-dollar online wine store that married his passion for wine with his entrepreneurial spirit. Gary has since started several other businesses in addition to investing in other start-ups.

What are micropreneurs? **Micropreneurs** start their own businesses but are satisfied with keeping their businesses small in an effort to achieve a balanced lifestyle. For example, a micropreneur might open a new type of restaurant and be satisfied with running only that one restaurant instead of expanding as Ray Kroc did with the McDonald brothers' restaurant. Micropreneurs have no aspirations of growing large and/or hiring hundreds or thousands of employees. Businesses such as dog-walking services, painters, and special-occasion cake bakers would all be considered micropreneurial opportunities.

What are home-based entrepreneurs? As the name suggests, **home-based entrepreneurs** are entrepreneurs who run their businesses out of their homes. Home-based entrepreneurs are often parents who like being able to stay home with their children and run a business. In addition to offering lifestyle advantages, such as being able to stay at home with children, home-based businesses offer several financial advantages. Staying at home eliminates commuting time and costs as well as office rent and other overhead expenses. Also, home-based entrepreneurs can take advantage of deducting from their taxes a part of their rent or mortgage payment, depreciation, property taxes, insurance, utilities, household maintenance, and home repairs and improvements.

P. J. Jonas is a home-based entrepreneur. Jonas launched Goat Milk Stuff on her family's farm after she started making natural soap so she could avoid using chemicals on her children's skin.[30] Jonas, her husband, and all eight of their children work in the business. In 2013, Goat Milk Soap won StartUpNation's "Leading Moms in Business" competition.

What are Internet entrepreneurs? Advances in technology have spawned another type of entrepreneur, the **Internet entrepreneur**, who creates businesses that operate solely online. The early 1990s saw the first group of Internet entrepreneurs, but most did not survive the dot-com bubble and bust. Now, however, with the advent of Web 2.0 technologies (such as blogging and social networking), smart phone apps, contextual Web-based advertising (such as Google Ads) that help to provide revenue, along with faster broadband connections, a greater number of successful online businesses are being established. Some of the most famous Internet entrepreneurs include Mark Zuckerberg (Facebook), Jeff Bezos (Amazon),

Catherine Cook, at the age of 17, co-created the successful website MeetMe with her older brothers Dave and Geoff during spring break. *Source:* Newscom.

Pierre Omidyar and John Donahoe (eBay), Sergey Brin and Larry Page (Google), and Jimmy Wales (Wikipedia).

Youth may have an advantage in this entrepreneurial genre because success requires little investment, some spare time, and a good understanding of what their peers are looking for. For example, David and Catherine Cook and their older brother Geoff started MeetMe (formerly myYearbook.com) over spring break in 2005. The social networking site invites members to meet new people through playing games, chatting, and sending virtual gifts purchased with Lunch Money, the site's virtual currency. Members are also given the opportunity to donate Lunch Money to their favorite charity through their charity application. MeetMe has over 1 billion page views on mobile devices and 1.2 billion page views on the Web each month.[31] In 2013, MeetMe launched two new dating apps, Choosy, which quickly became the top new app in the social category of the Google play store, and Charm, which uses videos rather than photos, like the social networking site Vine does.

A simple homework assignment for a class at Stanford University, now known as the "Facebook Class," spawned many successful companies and ideas. By just asking student teams to create applications for the popular social networking site, the class of 75 students created apps that engaged a total of 16 million users in just 10 weeks.[32] Many of the apps had a short life span, but their creators went on to create other apps for the newly released iPhone or to begin other Internet businesses, such as the social networking site Friend.ly, or have sold their businesses to companies like Zynga. The class, now called Startup Engineering, can be taken for free on Coursera.org.

What are growth entrepreneurs? **Growth entrepreneurs** strive to create fast-growing businesses and look forward to expansion. The companies that these types of entrepreneurs create are known as *gazelles*. Typically, a gazelle business starts with a base revenue of at least $100,000 and experiences at least 20 percent sales growth every year for five years. In other words, over the course of the five years, the firm doubles its revenues.[33] It is hard to recognize a gazelle business during its rapid growth period, though companies such as eBay and Google can clearly be identified in retrospect as having been gazelles in their early years. Gazelle companies also help the economy. Although they only represent approximately 1 percent of all businesses, they have been credited with generating about 10 percent of all new jobs.[34]

What are intrapreneurs? You don't necessarily have to leave your company to have an entrepreneurial experience. Some companies are good at fostering **intrapreneurs**—employees who work in an entrepreneurial way within an organizational environment. Because its success depends on its ability to develop creative solutions to household problems, developing intrapreneurs has been important to the home appliance company Whirlpool. Instead of relying solely on the traditional research-and-development process, Whirlpool taps the creative juices of its employees by encouraging them to generate ideas that will enhance the company's existing products. Although employees are not separately compensated for their ideas, they are pleased that the company asks for their ideas and have responded enthusiastically. By the end of the first year of the program, 60 ideas were in the prototype stage, and 190 were close to entering the marketplace.[35,36]

Technology companies are well known for fostering intrapreneurial creativity. Microsoft encourages employees to work on their own projects in the company's "Garage," a facility with various tools like 3D printers they can tinker with. At Google, employees are encouraged to spend 20 percent of their time working on their pet projects. Gmail and GoogleAds are two products that were developed as a result of this policy. Other examples of products generated from employee innovation include Post-It Notes, the Sony PlayStation, the Java programming language, and ELIXIR guitar strings.[37]

What are social entrepreneurs and social intrapreneurs? Just as a business entrepreneur tries to create innovative solutions that satisfy an unfulfilled corporate or consumer need, the idea can be extended to society at large. **Social entrepreneurs** are entrepreneurs who create innovative solutions designed to solve social problems.[38] For example, Mimi Silbert founded Delancey Street Foundation, a residential education center that teaches substance abusers, former felons, and the homeless the necessary skills to enable them to lead productive lives. The foundation runs on income generated by businesses created by the foundation that act as the training ground for program participants. It has been called the most successful rehabilitation project in the United States.[39]

Similarly, **social intrapreneurs** build and develop ventures within a company that are designed to identify and solve large-scale social problems.[40] In an effort to create a "social corporate enterprise," eBay, for example, gathered 40 employees to discuss ways to make the company more environmentally aware. What resulted was myriad projects, ranging from ride-sharing programs and community gardens to the largest installation of solar-power generators in San Jose, California, at the company's corporate headquarters.[41]

Earlier we mentioned Wayne Huizenga, the entrepreneur who started Waste Management, Blockbuster Video, and Auto Nation. Wayne, like other serial entrepreneurs, seems to like the process of building and growing a business and doing it over and over again. Other successful serial entrepreneurs include Ted Turner (Turner Broadcasting System, CNN, and Ted's Montana Grill), Richard Branson (Virgin Records, Virgin Airways, and Virgin Mobile), and even Oprah Winfrey (*O, The Oprah Magazine*, OWN network, and Harpo Productions). Some might even consider Ben Franklin and Thomas Edison as our earliest serial entrepreneurs. Would you agree?

Entrepreneurial Teams

What if I don't have all the skills to be an entrepreneur? Look at the list of entrepreneurial traits described earlier in this section. In addition to being innovative, motivated, and self-directed, as we have explained, an entrepreneur initially may need to fill the role of executive, sales manager, financial director, secretary, and mailroom person. If you don't possess all of these traits, it doesn't preclude you from starting your own business and becoming a successful entrepreneur. If you have an idea and really want to make it happen, you might want to reach out to others who can do what you can't or don't want to do and assemble an entrepreneurial team.

What is an entrepreneurial team? An **entrepreneurial team** is a group of qualified individuals with varied experiences and skills who come together to form a new venture. The skills of the entrepreneurial team members complement one another so that as a group the team has the necessary skills and traits to manage a successful project. For example, Lin Miao, Andrew Bachman, Lucas Brown, and Lee Brown came together to form Tatto Media, a successful Internet marketing company that changes how advertisers pay for display advertising. After selling Tatto Media, the trio went on to form HasOffers, an advertising performance analytics group.

Entrepreneurial teams are also great for those who want to run their own businesses but perhaps lack the personal experience. For example, college and business school students often form entrepreneurial teams to get their first projects launched. Students from Stanford University have come together to create well-known companies such as Google, HP, Cisco, Imagen, and Yahoo!. Many schools run entrepreneurial challenges, such as the Big Bang competition at the University of California, Davis. During the yearlong competition, students, alumni, staff, and faculty join forces to construct and test their business plans, which serve as the springboards for new companies. A project that developed a new approach to heart valve replacements took the prize in 2013.

Origami Owl

Bella Weems desperately wanted a car for her sixteenth birthday. But her parents had other ideas. They wanted Bella to go to work to so she could buy her *own* car. And that's just what Bella did. At age 14, she started a business with $350 of her own money, an amount her parents matched. Bella ultimately ended up buying herself a white Jeep, but that's only part of the story. The business she created, Origami Owl, uses private home parties to sell Living Lockets, which are mini shadow boxes filled with charms of your choice to tell your own story.

In just two years, the business generated $24 million and has been growing exponentially since. Since Bella is still in school and would like to continue on to college, she has taken intern-like roles in the business so she can learn all aspects from the ground up. In addition to Bella's mother, other family members own and help operate the company. The company's CEO, Robin Crossman, has experience working with companies with strong direct-sales approaches, such as Amway and The Longaberger Company.[42]

Perhaps you're part of an entrepreneurial team or an employee in an intrapreneurial company or prefer to go it alone. Maybe you want to keep your business small or expand it like the Wahoo brothers or McDonald's. Whatever the case, being an entrepreneur is more than just being in business for yourself. Taking advantage of an opportunity niche, riding the bumps along the way, and being a system thinker all describe successful entrepreneurs. Do you have what it takes to be an entrepreneur? Entrepreneurial opportunities exist if you're up to the challenge.

Source: KidStock/Blend Images/Corbis.

Buying Franchises and Existing Businesses pp. 138–143

It was a desired change in lifestyle that prompted Aisha Lawrence to think about starting her own business. She had always dreamed of running her own restaurant, but she didn't have much business background or restaurant experience. What she did have was a lot of tenacity and knowledge of marketing. Additionally, she was a people person—a necessity for restaurant owners. Still, she was unsure of where to begin. Aisha was uncomfortable starting from scratch, as she knew that the risks were way too high to start a restaurant on her own. She felt that she needed the support of someone who had been through the process before. What are her options? Which would be the best route for Aisha to take? ■

For those who want the opportunity of owning their own businesses but, like Aisha, want to avoid the stress of starting them completely from scratch, buying an existing business or purchasing a franchise may be a viable alternative. Franchises are a popular way to enter the world of small business. Alternatively, there are definite advantages to buying an existing business, especially if it has previously enjoyed a good reputation and has an existing customer base. In this section, we'll look at what it means to buy a franchise. We'll also discuss buying an existing business and molding it into your own.

Franchising Basics

What is a franchise? A **franchise** is a method of doing business whereby the business (the **franchisor**) sells its products or services under the company's name to independent third-party operators (the **franchisees**).[43] Franchises have been around for decades if not centuries. In the United States, Singer Sewing Machines, one of the first franchises, started in 1851. Aisha would be a franchisee using a franchisor's marketing methods and trademarked goods under the name of the business. In exchange, she would make monthly payments to the franchise.

What kinds of business opportunities are available as franchises? Franchises play an important role in our economy. There are nearly 760,000 franchised businesses in the United States. They employ approximately 8.3 million people and generate nearly $800 billion annually.[44]

Franchises in the business-services, real-estate, and fast-food industries are expected to experience the greatest growth and have the most employment opportunities in the coming years.[45] But franchise opportunities exist in nearly every industry, and many can be run from your home, which lowers a business owner's start-up costs because there is no need to purchase or rent real estate. Home-based franchises, such as Jan-Pro, Snap-on Tools, and Jazzercise, are among today's top home-based franchises.[46]

If you are thinking of purchasing a franchise, you will need to do your homework. There are several sources of helpful information about franchises that you should study before taking the leap. ■ **TABLE 5.1** lists several helpful Web-based resources that you can begin with.

Pros and Cons of Franchising

What are the advantages of franchising? For many, franchising is an easier, less risky means of starting a business because of the immediate effects of owning a business with an established brand and name. In addition, since the franchisor provides much of the marketing and financial tools needed to run a business, all the franchisee is expected to bring to the table are management and marketing skills, time, and money. There are many other advantages of owning a franchise:

- **It is a proven system of operation.** Instead of wading through the muddy waters of new business ownership by themselves, franchisees benefit from the *collective experience* of the franchising company. It has determined, through trial and error, the best way to open and operate the business. New franchisees can therefore avoid many of the common start-up mistakes made by new business owners because they will be working with standardized products, systems, and financial and accounting systems.

- **There is strength in numbers.** You are not alone when you buy a franchise. Because you belong to a group, you might benefit from economies of scale achieved by purchasing materials, supplies, and services at discounted group rates. In addition, it is often easier to get approved for business loans when

TABLE 5.1	Web-Based Resources for Potential Franchisees

The *SBA* and *FranNet* sponsor a site that features a video that explains what franchising is, how to determine if franchising is right for you, and how to select the right franchise.

The *American Franchisee Association* offers advice on buying a franchise, legal resources, and opportunities to network with other franchisees.

The *Federal Trade Commission* provides consumer information on franchise and business opportunities. The publication *Buying a Franchise: A Consumer Guide* outlines the steps to take before selecting a particular franchise, how to shop at a franchise exhibition, and what you should know before signing the franchisor's disclosure document.

Entrepreneur.com's *Franchise Zone* allows users to search a directory of franchising opportunities and provides tips on buying a franchise. This site also ranks the top franchises in terms of growth, cost, global appeal, and other aspects.

The *International Franchise Association* provides answers to frequently asked questions about franchising and resources for potential and current franchisees. This website also hosts a directory of franchising opportunities in various industries.

Source: SBDCNet.org and *Buying a Franchise* by U.S. Small Business Administration (www.sba.gov).

Franchising

Advantages	Disadvantages
☐ Proven system of operation	☐ Lack of complete control
☐ Strength in numbers	☐ Start-up and ongoing costs can be overwhelming
☐ Training is part of the deal	☐ Work load is no less with a franchise
☐ Marketing support is provided	☐ Competition and cannibalizing can occur within the franchise
☐ Market research is provided	☐ Individual problems can become group problems

■ **FIGURE 5.6**
Pros and Cons of Franchising

■ **FIGURE 5.7**
Franchise Costs and Fees
Source: Scott Eells/Bloomberg via Getty Images; Ulrich Baumgarten via/Getty Images; James M. Thresher/ The Washington Post/Getty Images.

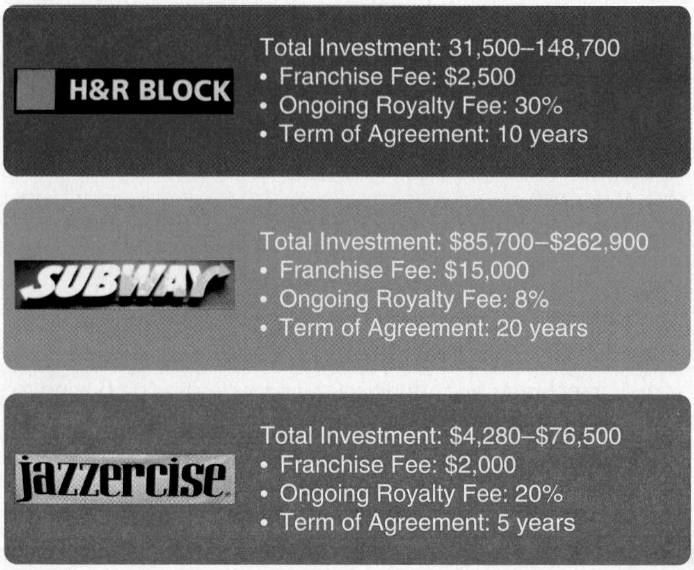

H&R BLOCK
Total Investment: 31,500–148,700
• Franchise Fee: $2,500
• Ongoing Royalty Fee: 30%
• Term of Agreement: 10 years

SUBWAY
Total Investment: $85,700–$262,900
• Franchise Fee: $15,000
• Ongoing Royalty Fee: 8%
• Term of Agreement: 20 years

jazzercise
Total Investment: $4,280–$76,500
• Franchise Fee: $2,000
• Ongoing Royalty Fee: 20%
• Term of Agreement: 5 years

running a franchise, as lending institutions often view that there is less risk associated with franchises.

- **Initial training is part of the deal.** The beauty of franchising is that you're in business *for* yourself but not *by* yourself. The franchisor offers initial training to ensure that you have a successful opening. They might offer ongoing training if new products or services are being incorporated into the franchise line.
- **Marketing support is provided.** As a franchisee, you are often given marketing materials generated at the corporate level and have the benefit of any national advertising programs that are created. Although you are expected to run your own local marketing efforts, you have the support of other franchisees in the area to help you in your efforts.
- **Market research is often provided.** Good franchisors do considerable market research and can generally conclude whether there is demand for the product or service in the area before selling the franchisee a franchise. The franchisor should also help to identify the competition and offer strategies to differentiate the franchise from them.

What are the disadvantages of franchising? Although buying a franchise provides the franchisee with many benefits, there are some disadvantages too (see ■ **FIGURE 5.6**):

- **Lack of control.** There is not much opportunity to contribute creatively to the franchise because the franchisor often controls the look of the store and the product or the service. The franchisee, however, is expected to bring the necessary drive and spirit to make the franchise a success.
- **Start-up and ongoing costs.** Although most franchises require an initial investment (see ■ **FIGURE 5.7**), often one can be purchased for less than $100,000. Franchises such as H&R Block, System4, and CruiseOne can also be purchased with less than $50,000.[47] The franchise fee for a Subway restaurant is $15,000. To purchase a franchise for Jan-Pro, a commercial cleaning company and the fastest-growing franchise in the United States, about $3,000 is required.

Additional start-up costs the franchisee might incur include the cost to rent or purchase real estate or equipment and the cost of the business's initial inventory. In addition, franchisees must pay a monthly royalty fee to the franchisor, which is typically 6 to 10 percent of the business's gross revenues. The royalty fees are due regardless of how the franchisee's business is doing—in other words, whether it is making a profit or not.

- **Workload.** As with any new business, new franchisees shouldn't expect easy hours. Aisha spends a lot more time running her franchise than she thought she would. However, because she can hire employees to run the day-to-day operations, her time is spent more on the business development and management end of the business.
- **Competition.** Some franchises do not restrict the number of their franchise locations. In those instances, franchisees could experience serious competition not only from other companies but also from

other franchisees in the same organization. In addition, some franchises do not offer geographic or demographic studies of the best locations in which to open new stores and instead may expect the franchisee to do a market analysis of the surrounding competition.

- **Share common problems.** If the franchisor or another franchisee is having problems, all franchisees will feel their pain. For example, when a Wendy's restaurant was falsely accused of serving chili with a human thumb mixed in, all of Wendy's restaurants suffered from the fallout.

Franchising Considerations

What are things to watch out for when considering buying a franchise? The most common piece of advice offered to anyone interested in buying a franchise is to do your homework up front. Although much of the start-up process is done for you, you are still buying a business that will require your time and money, and it is not guaranteed to succeed. ■ **TABLE 5.2** shows suggested questions to ask the company that you are buying the franchise from and other people who have bought franchises from the company before you take the plunge.

Buying an Existing Business

Are there other ways to start a business besides starting new or buying a franchise? Another option is to buy an existing business. However, just like

TABLE 5.2	Questions to Ask before Buying a Franchise	
	Questions to Ask the Franchisor	**Questions to Ask Other Franchisees**
Competition	• What is the competitive advantage of the good/service? • What makes the business more attractive to an owner and more attractive to a customer?	• How is your system better than that of competitors? • How does your business match up? • Who are your competitors?
Franchise system	• How time tested and standardized is the franchise system? • What franchise system is used, and how does it work? • How long has the franchise been in business, and what improvements have the franchise company made recently?	• How long have you been in business? • Does your location meet your customers' needs? • Who selected the site?
Support and training	• How much support does the franchisor give the franchisee? • What initial and ongoing training are provided? • Are there toll-free help lines, field support, annual meetings, local meetings, purchasing programs, and marketing promotions?	• How is the relationship with the franchisor? • How were the initial and ongoing training and ongoing support? • How are the marketing, advertising, and promotional programs handled?
Financial strength	• What are the financial strengths of the company and the experience of its managers? • How much revenue comes from franchise fees, and how much revenue comes from royalties? • How has the stock performed?	• Are you pleased with earnings? • Is volume growing?
Franchise relationships	• How important is the franchisee to the franchise? • How can they describe the relationship with the franchisor?	• Have there been lawsuits and/or arbitration? • If so, how have they been resolved? • Do you have second thoughts (would you do this again)? • Would you own more units?

Source: Based on "A Checklist of Questions to Answer before You Buy a Franchise" (PowerHomeBiz.com).

buying a franchise or starting a business from scratch, the decision must be well thought out.

What are the advantages of buying an existing business? Buying an existing business has the following advantages:

- **Ease of start-up.** Like a franchise, it's often simpler to buy an existing business than to start one from scratch. If you are purchasing a business that is operational and doesn't have serious problems, your suppliers, existing staff and management, and equipment and inventory will already be in place to help facilitate the transition.

- **Existing customer base.** An existing business may have a satisfied customer base already in place. If no significant changes are made to drive away current customers, the business can continue to run and provide immediate cash flow.

- **Financing opportunities.** If the business has had a positive track record, it might be easier to obtain financing to purchase it.

What are the disadvantages of buying an existing business? There are also disadvantages to buying an existing business:

- **High purchase price.** Because you may need to buy the owner out of the business, the initial purchase price may be high. The purchase price may be more than the immediate up-front costs associated with starting a business from scratch and in some cases purchasing a franchise. Although you can determine the value of the physical business and its assets, it is more difficult to determine the true value of the previous owner's **goodwill**—the intangible assets represented by a business's name, customer service, employee morale, and other factors—that might be lost with a change in ownership. Often the intangible assets are overvalued, making the business cost more than it is worth.

- **Inheriting the previous owner's mistakes.** In addition, with a preexisting business, you are sometimes stuck with the previous owner's mistakes. This means you might inherit dissatisfied customers, bad debt, and unhappy distributors or purchasing agents. You may need to work to change the minds of people who have had a bad experience with the previous ownership.

- **Unknowns in transition.** There is no guarantee that the firm's existing employees, managers, customers, suppliers, or distributors will continue to do business with you once you own the company. If the staff does stay, you will inherit any problems they may be having that you don't anticipate.

What do I need to do before I buy a business? Existing businesses are sold for many reasons. Before buying an existing business, make sure you perform **due diligence**—which is conducting a reasonable investigation into the business's history, operating and financial records, contracts, and the valuation of the business. You want to avoid buying a company with a dissatisfied customer base or with a large amount of unpaid bills or with unfavorable contracts that cannot be renegotiated. ■ **TABLE 5.3** provides a brief checklist of things you should look into before buying a business.

We started this section with a story about Aisha Lawrence, who had a dream of owning a restaurant. What did she decide? Aisha knew that the risks were way too high to start a restaurant on her own. She considered buying an existing restaurant but still felt that she didn't have enough experience to handle the demands of a full-service restaurant. Instead, she felt that she could run a small, single-product food business, such as a coffee bar or an ice cream shop, to give her the experience she would need to run her own full-service restaurant someday. Ultimately, Aisha decided that she wanted to open an ice cream franchise. There were many to choose from, so she spent months doing product research, visiting and tasting the various frozen treats offered by most of the ice cream franchises. Whether you buy an existing business or franchise or begin a business of your own, you'll be joining a large group of small business owners who make a significant contribution to the U.S. economy.

TABLE 5.3	**Things to Consider before Buying a Business**

Initial Considerations

- Why is the business for sale?
- What do current customers say—in person and via social media?
- Are there opportunities for growth? How much time does the current owner put into the business?
- Who is the competition?

Due Diligence Checklist

- Get an independent valuation of inventory and equipment.
- Have an accountant review the financial statements for the past three years.
- Have a lawyer analyze pertinent business documents—property leases, employment contracts, and so on.
- Talk to suppliers to see if they will continue to supply the business when ownership changes hands.
- Check for lingering or festering hazardous waste problems. They'll become your responsibility as the new owner.

The Risks of Small Businesses and Where to Get Help pp. 143–148

Source: Alphaspirit/Fotolia.

When Roger Sherman heard rumors that the company he was working for was considering filing bankruptcy, he felt he would be better off on his own. Roger took advantage of an early retirement package and, using his life savings, started a business selling energy-efficient, solar-powered scooters and bicycles. But his well-thought-out business was hampered by a massive downturn in the economy. Roger is concerned he might not be able to make payroll or keep all his employees. What should he do? ■

In this section, we'll talk about the risks facing small businesses and where owners can go for help.

Why So Many Small Businesses Fail

What are the risks of owning my own business? Starting a business is a lot of hard work and comes with no guarantee for success. As ■ **FIGURE 5.8** shows, nearly one-fourth of all start-ups fail in the first year, and two-thirds survive only two years. Just over one-half survive after five years of operation.[48]

Some of the common reasons businesses fail are the following:

- Too much accumulation of debt
- Inadequate management
- Poor planning
- Unanticipated personal sacrifices

Let's examine each risk in more detail.

What's in a Name?

Naming a business should be fun, but it can be stressful, especially if you make some of the more common mistakes:

MISTAKE 1 Involving friends, family, employees, or clients in the naming decision. The name should communicate the key elements of your business, not the combined efforts of your friends and family.

MISTAKE 2 Combining description + product + name. Although it might seem catchy at the time, the result of company names that try to marry description with product is forced and often trite. A service franchise named QualiServe or a day spa named TranquiSpa ultimately aren't the right choices.

MISTAKE 3 Using generic names. Gone are the days when ACME Foods works as a corporate name. Similarly, using names such as Joe's Bar or Smith's Hardware is inadequate. In such highly competitive times, when new products or services are fighting for attention, it is best to choose a more unique name.

MISTAKE 4 Making up a name. Although using generic names may not be good, be careful to avoid names that are obscure, hard to pronounce, or hard to spell unless there is solid market research behind it.

MISTAKE 5 Using geographic names. Unless you plan to stay local, including a specific geographic name may imply that you won't go beyond that regional territory.

TIP: You might need to hire a company to create a name for you. Acura, Flixx, and Compaq are all names that were created by experts.

What causes excessive debt accumulation? One reason many new businesses fail is that they accumulate too much debt too soon. Most begin a new business by borrowing funds. Regardless of whether the loan comes from a bank, an outside investor, or a credit card company, if the new business does not generate revenue quickly enough to begin to pay back the loans, the burden of paying the debt balance plus additional interest as well as normal operating expenses can cause an owner to become further entrenched in a potentially unrecoverable situation. The situation might also tempt the owner to take out more loans to keep the business running. What's worse is that some business owners borrow against their personal assets. This puts the owners at risk of not only losing their businesses but also potentially forcing them to file personal bankruptcy as well.

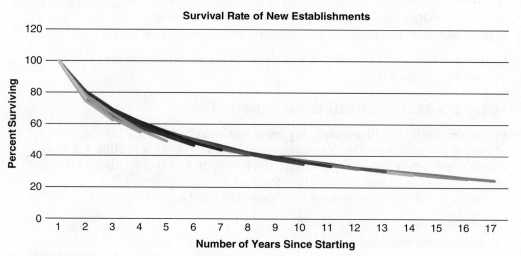

■ **FIGURE 5.8**

Average Survival Rate of Small Business Start-Ups[49]

Source: Data retrieved from Business Employment Dynamics: Entrepreneurship and the U.S. Economy, Bureau of Labor Statistics. http://www.bls.gov/bdm/entrepreneurship/bdm_chart3.htm.

How does poor fiscal management lead to failure? Although entrepreneurs and small business owners are good at coming up with ideas, they may not be great at managing the books. The fact that so many businesses fail due to high levels of debt can be a sign of poor financial and business management. Financial statements and budgets need to be created honestly and adhered to each month, accounts receivable religiously collected, and accounts payable aggressively managed. Take Jodi Gallagher, for example. Jodi owns a business that designs and creates lingerie. In an effort to get her product into as many stores as possible, Jodi was lenient on the collection terms of her accounts receivable. Rather than insisting on immediate payment, she extended stores credit, and, as a result, it took her months to collect. Realizing that her mistake almost cost her business, Jodi no longer extends credit.[50]

What other types of improper management lead to failure? For some new owners, an early surge in sales proves to be overwhelming. This is what happened to many dot-com companies that went bust in the late 1990s. They did not plan for rapid growth and therefore did not have sufficient inventory to fulfill orders when they came in. They also didn't take into consideration the subsequent impact this would have on dealers and retailers who were a part of their distribution channels. Similarly, unexpectedly high demands can lead to overexpanding the business too soon or moving into areas that are less profitable—both of which can cause the business to stray from its original course and set it up for failure.

Many business owners ignore the signs of a business beginning to fail or attribute the failure to the wrong reasons. Good managers stay on top of all aspects of the business, remain objective, and make tough decisions when necessary.

How important is planning to a business's success or failure? Large debt accumulation and poor business management happen after the business is up and running. One of the biggest reasons businesses fail is that there was no formal plan in place to begin with. The old adage "failing to plan is planning to fail" certainly applies to starting a business. Many budding business owners, in the excitement of starting something new, neglect to take the boring and difficult but necessary steps of building an effective business plan. A **business plan** is a formal document that states the goals of the business as well as the plan for reaching those goals.

As **FIGURE 5.9** shows, the plan includes the company's mission statement, history, and the qualifications of the owners and management team and any resources they might have to contribute to the business. It includes a marketing plan, an operational plan, a financial plan, and a risk analysis and identifies the competition and highlights opportunities for success. (You'll learn more about creating successful business plans in Mini Chapter 2.)

Neglecting to consider any of these factors can doom a business from the start. Writing a business plan forces you to think through some of the more difficult aspects of the business up front. Poor planning can lead to unnecessary spending. Equally, a well-written and well-thought-out business plan can lead to greater financing options. Success is a lot more difficult without adequate funding.

New businesses also may fail when their new owners do not adequately anticipate the many personal sacrifices—financial, time, and otherwise—they are forced to make. For example, the cost of health insurance and retirement accounts for the owner and employees falls solely on the shoulders of the new business owner. For businesses with more than 50 employees, providing health care is mandated by the government. For smaller businesses, however, in order to keep the business running, sometimes the expense of health insurance and long-term retirement funding gets postponed. Additionally, the amount of time and effort owners must invest in the business, as well as the necessity to take on multiple responsibilities, makes running your own business not for the faint of heart.

■ **FIGURE 5.9**
A Business Plan Outlines a Company's Goals and Strategies

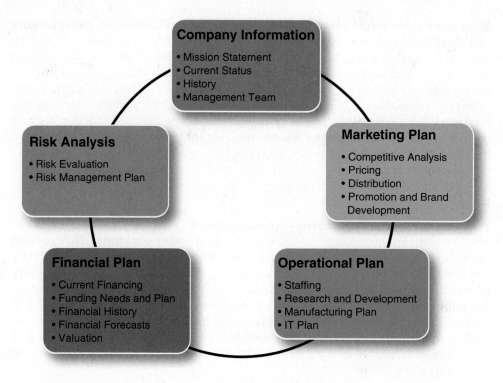

Getting Help

Where do small business owners go for advice? Most new business owners are just that—new. Because they haven't experienced much of what they will encounter, knowing when and where to go for help, a second opinion, or just advice can make all the difference. There are several sources of help and advice that a small business owner can turn to (see ■ **FIGURE 5.10**):

- **The Small Business Administration.** In addition to financial assistance the SBA offers help with the legalities needed to start and operate a business as well as education and training, disaster assistance, and counseling for small business owners. The SBA holds events in major cities in all states, such as workshops in financial analysis, creating a business plan, and launching a business. It also offers free online courses and coordinates links to academic institutions that offer private online training. The SBA also acts as an advocate for small business owners to national and state policymakers. It works to

■ **FIGURE 5.10**
Small Business Support Websites

SBA
- www.sba.org
- Sole purpose is to cater to the needs of small businesses. Provides counseling, workshops, small loans.

SCORE
- www.score.org
- Volunteer organization of retired executives who offer workshops and counseling to small businesses at no cost.

Entrepreneurs Organization
- www.eonetwork.org
- Offers industry-related conferences and seminars, and help to connect business owners with industry experts for individual mentoring.

National Business Incubators Association
- www.nbia.org
- Provides start-ups with information, education, advocacy, and networking resources.

reduce regulatory requirements and maximize benefits that small businesses receive from the government.

- **SCORE.** The nearly 11,000 volunteers who make up the SBA's **Service Corps of Retired Executives** (SCORE) offer workshops and counseling to small businesses at no cost. The volunteers are currently working in or have been in the field and can therefore provide advice to new or existing small business owners. They review business plans, help with tax planning, and offer new ideas and fresh insights. Some SCORE success stories include Vermont Teddy Bear, Vera Bradley Designs, and Jelly Belly Candy.

- **Other mentoring sources.** SCORE is not the only resource new business owners can turn to for mentors. Industry-related conferences or seminars often present new business owners with opportunities to find others who can serve as sounding boards and guides. In addition, other organizations, such as the Entrepreneurs Organization (EO), connect business owners with experts in their industry for individual mentoring. Although the EO is for those who are currently in a viable operation (its requirements are that you must be a founder, cofounder, owner, or controlling shareholder of a business with a minimum of $1 million in annual gross sales and younger than 50 years old), such mentoring services can nonetheless be helpful to small business owners who have already launched their businesses.

What kind of training is appropriate for small business owners? Before jumping into any endeavor, it's always good to have some experience or training. Although many entrepreneurs have advanced degrees in business, that level of formal education is often not necessary. If you are currently in college, look for internship opportunities in your industry of interest. Both large and small companies utilize interns.

Most community colleges offer business classes for credit or noncredit community education classes that are taught by industry professionals. In addition to formal classroom training, you can also obtain hands-on experience by interning or working part-time for a company in a related field; if no opportunities exist in a related field, working for any start-up company can give you experience that can help you run a small company.

Where can small business owners go for support services? One of the biggest overhead costs for many new businesses is the support services required to run the business. **Business incubators** are organizations that support start-up businesses by offering administrative services, technical support, business networking, sources of financing, and more that a group of start-up companies share. Business incubators can be either private organizations or public services. Over the past few decades, many cities, as well as developed and developing countries, have started public business incubators, often in conjunction with universities and research institutions, to promote new business development. For example, the National Science Foundation has created Innovation Corps—a $5 million incubator for student entrepreneurs—and Rensselaer Polytechnic Institute runs one of the oldest incubator programs in the country.

The primary goal of a business incubator is to produce successful businesses that are able to operate independently and become financially viable in the early years when they are most vulnerable to failure. Incubators also create a synergistic environment where companies can act as peer-to-peer mentors, sharing both successes and failures. Incubators also lend legitimacy to a beginning company as well as a more professional atmosphere than someone's home office. Eventually, participants must leave the incubator, but beginning in an incubation program increases the success rate of start-ups by as much as 90 percent.[51]

What other options exist for small business advice and assistance? As noted earlier, starting up a small business requires a business owner to serve many roles. Many owners quickly realize that their strengths lie in only one or a few of these roles and therefore seek assistance from other people. One option is to team up with *partners* who offer the company strengths that the new owner does not possess. The partners in turn share the business's profits and liabilities. Forming an advisory board is another option. An **advisory board** is a group of individuals who offer guidance to the new business owner. It is similar to a board of directors in a publicly held company except it generally does not have the authority to make decisions.

Does where I locate my business make a difference in the type of help I can get? In most cases, new business owners look for a location that is suitable for their business, has good traffic flow, is safe, and so on. However, in an effort to build up and even resuscitate communities throughout the United States, federal and state governments have established **enterprise zones**, geographic areas targeted for economic revitalizing, based on various criteria, such as their population, poverty rates, and amount of economic stress they are experiencing. Businesses receive generous tax benefits for locating and hiring in these enterprise zones. Almost every state has some form of enterprise zone program. In addition, the federal government has enterprise communities and empowerment zones across the United States. The economic benefits companies receive when they locate in an enterprise zone often outweigh the risk of locating in a distressed area.

Remember Roger Sherman? When he found he had troubles with his small business, Roger decided to consult a SCORE volunteer. Many new business owners think they can't afford professional advice, so they rely on their own efforts, advice from friends and family, and trial and error. Often, they find that it takes more than a good idea and hard work to make a business successful. Knowing all the resources available to fledgling businesses can help entrepreneurs avoid making the mistakes that eventually lead to the demise of their businesses. Careful financial decision making, savvy management, meticulous planning, and the willingness to make significant personal sacrifices are all needed to create a successful business. Knowing when, where, and how to ask for help is also a critical factor to success.

Financing Considerations pp. 148–151

Fred DeLuca began his sandwich shop in 1965 when he was 17. He had just graduated from high school and was worried about how he was going to pay for college with his $1.25-per-hour minimum-wage job at a local hardware store. A family friend, Dr. Peter Buck, suggested that Fred open a sandwich shop. All he needed to do was to rent a shop, build a counter, buy some food, and make the sandwiches. Customers would come in and pay. Then Fred could pay his suppliers and still have enough money to pay for college. Dr. Buck was so sure this would work that he gave Fred $1,000 to begin. Four decades later, Subway is one of the largest privately held businesses, with restaurants around the world.[52] ■

Although Fred started with a loan from a family friend, there are other ways for entrepreneurs to finance their new ventures before seeking more formal financing arrangements. In this section, we'll present the many sources of funding available to small business owners, and we'll discuss the pros and cons associated with them.

Cash and Credit

Where can I get the money to start a business? Most new ventures require capital to purchase inventory, secure a physical location, and begin some modest marketing efforts. Often, new business owners must make do with whatever sources of financing are available to them, including their own funds. When entrepreneurs start a business with little capital, they are said to be using **bootstrap financing**. This includes financing using your own money, borrowing funds from family and

Source: Eric Piermont AFP/Getty Images/ Newscom.

friends, and possibly trading services and products with vendors or clients. These informal funding options may be enough to start the business. Friends and family are generally go-to financing options for new business owners because, unlike banks, family and friends often do not require high rates of return on the money they have invested or demand the business turn a quick profit.

However, it is important when borrowing from friends and family that you treat them as professionally as possible. Make sure you give them documents that indicate how you intend to pay them back and outline a contingency plan if things go wrong. In addition, you should inform them up front and during the project of any risks related to the venture. Other means of bootstrap financing include using *trade credit*, *factoring*, and *leasing*. We will discuss these options in Chapter 15.

Is it reasonable to use crowdfunding sites to raise capital? Sites like Kickstarter and Indiegogo have popularized a new type of start-up funding known as *crowdfunding*. Entrepreneurs put together a detailed explanation of their projects or businesses on these sites and ask for funding. People who fund projects on these sites typically donate small amounts of money and are offered free products from the startups they contribute to—perhaps the chance to purchase a product in a special edition or color or meet with the product's designer. People supporting a Kickstarter business do not own any part of the new business and are not guaranteed that it will be successful—they are simply making a donation.

Crowdfunding might sound like a poor way to launch a product, but that's not necessarily the case. The Pebble Watch is an example. The developer of the watch was hoping to raise $100,000 in one month on Kickstarter and ended up raising more than $10 million. Crowdfunding will be discussed in more detail in Chapter 15 as well.

Should I use credit cards to finance my business? Credit cards offer a convenient way to obtain funds quickly, especially with some of the 0 percent financing options available. If used wisely, a credit card can be a convenient way to finance a business's short-term needs but only if you can pay the balance off *completely* every month. If not, the interest charged on the unpaid balances can grow quickly because the interest rates on credit cards are generally extremely high compared to other types of financing. Over time, you're paying interest on any unpaid balances as well as interest on any carryover interest, which quickly can become a huge financial burden.

Small Business Loans and Grants

What if I need more money than what I can provide myself? For larger amounts, new business owners sometimes borrow against their own assets, such as the equity in their homes or against their retirement accounts. However, this is a risky practice since the consequences of the business failing are personally devastating. Bailing out a failing business with your life savings or equity in your home has caused many a person to lose both.

If you're purchasing an existing business or a franchise, banks and savings and loans will often offer loans to help you buy the business, equipment, and machinery and lines of credit (sources of credit that can be drawn on at the borrower's discretion) to help you make your payroll during slower periods. Roughly half of all small businesses use bank loans and lines of credit as part of their financing strategies.

Can I apply for grants to help start my business? Grants are financial awards offered by federal and state governments and some private organizations. Although grants do not need to be repaid, the application process is quite long and includes considerable amounts of paperwork. The biggest hurdle in applying for a grant is writing the proposal. Make sure you understand the grant-writing procedure, as many a good submission has not been funded because of an oversight in the grant application. Depending on the nature of your business, federal grants are usually not available, but state governments typically offer grants to small businesses that are in industries that the states are trying to nurture to expand in their economies. Make sure, however, you read through the entire grant application and understand any requirements that may be expected of a grant recipient. Failure to comply with grant requirements will generally result in the grant proceeds being converted to a loan, with interest.

Angel and Venture Capital Financing

What if I need additional sources of funds through investors? There are other sources of funding if you choose not to finance your business with loans or if loans are not an option. For example, businesses can be financed by outside investors, such as angel investors, venture capital, or small business investment companies:

- **Angel investors. Angel investors** are wealthy individuals who are willing to put up their own money in hopes of a profit return later on. Angel investors fund approximately 30,000 small companies each year, with investments that range between $25,000 and $1 million.[53] Palmer Reynolds, the founder of Phoenix Textile Corp. in St. Louis, Missouri, attributes her success to an angel investor. Out of work with 13 years of experience in the textile business, Reynolds decided to start her own company. Without the angel investor who loaned her $250,000, she would not be running the multi-million-dollar textile company she is today. Angel investors often provide funding in the earlier stages of a business and typically have industry experience in the areas in which they are investing and can provide guidance and advice. Unlike venture capitalists (discussed next), angel investors usually do not seek to manage or control the businesses they are investing in. If you don't personally have any rich friends or connections to rich friends, it's possible to find an angel investor with a simple search on the Internet. The New York Angels (New York), The Old Hand (Chicago), and The Professionals (Palo Alto, California) are regional groups of angel investors. Social networking sites, such as Angel List and Investors' Circle, match entrepreneurs to investors.

- **Venture capitalists. Venture capitalists** are the next step in funding a start-up. Venture capital funding is generally sought when the business is more mature and needs large sources of capital to take the business to the next step. Venture capitalists are corporate entities that use funds from other investors and manage that money by investing it in businesses with prospects for high growth. In return for the investments, venture capitalists get some form of equity— a piece of ownership—in the businesses. Venture capitalists are very picky about the projects in which they invest because they want to minimize the risk of failure. Generally, the financing they offer is available only to businesses that have been operating for several years and have the potential to become larger, publicly owned, regional or national companies. To protect their investments, venture capitalists sometimes demand to play an active role in the management of the company. So, business owners must be open to the idea of relinquishing control when they seek venture capital funding.

Conducting a SWOT Analysis

Recently, you and a fellow engineer friend have been working to boost the performance of hybrid car batteries. As you've learned more about the hybrid car industry, you've discovered a potential unmet need for the service and replacement of these batteries. Some dealerships offer these services, but there may be an opportunity for you to open a specialty shop in your area that focuses solely on these batteries. Can you think of strengths, weaknesses, opportunities and threats for hybrid car battery industry?

Shark Tank, the ABC reality television show, offers a peek into the venture capital arena. The show features high-profile investors who listen to several new business pitches every week. Although many business ideas are turned down, some ended getting funded. For example, Mod Mom Furniture owner, Kiersten Hathcock, received $90,000 for a 33 percent stake in the business and a royalty percentage after sales reached $500,000. The investment allowed her to contract with a local manufacturing company so she could keep up with the demand for eco-friendly toy boxes she had been producing in her garage. Mod Mom Furniture now offers a full line of children's furniture and storage accessories.

- **The small business investment company program.** If venture capital is not available or suitable, an alternative is a **small business investment company (SBIC) program**. SBICs are private venture capital firms licensed by the SBA to make equity capital or long-term loans available to small companies. The size of the financing provided by SBICs is generally in the $250,000 to $5 million range.

As mentioned above, a downside of using outside investors is that, to protect their investments, these investors often are looking for some controlling or managerial role in the business. However, it's the investor's level of business acumen that is often necessary to take a business to the next stage of growth, so generally it's a win/win for both owner and investor.

Funding a business is a task fraught with challenges and difficult decisions, as Fred DeLuca would attest. Beginning with just the money offered by a family friend and his own savings, Fred turned a simple sandwich shop into a global franchise operation. But whether the money comes from your own pocket, a friend, or an outside investor, the stakes—personal, professional, and financial—are quite high. Thorough research and careful planning are essential to navigating these tricky issues. By understanding the available options and being prepared to deal with financial predicaments, business owners give themselves the best chance at success.

Summary

1 What is the role and structure of the small business within the U.S. economy? (pp. 127–132)

- A **small business** (p. 127) is a business that is independently owned and operated, is not dominant in its field, and has fewer than 500 employees. To qualify for government programs from the U.S. **Small Business Administration (SBA)** (p. 127), revenue restrictions are also put in place and vary by industry. Many small businesses are limited to $7 million in annual revenues.

- Small businesses are important to the economy for several reasons. They account for more than one-half of America's economic output, help foster innovation, supply larger companies with products and services that larger companies do not or cannot supply themselves, supply products and services to consumers that large companies cannot or will not provide, and employ approximately 50 percent of the private workforce.

2 What are the traits of an effective entrepreneur, and what are the different types of entrepreneurs? (pp. 132–138)

- An **entrepreneur** (p. 132) is someone who assumes the risk of creating, organizing, and operating a business.

- Entrepreneurs are innovative, risk-taking individuals who are motivated to succeed and who are flexible and self-directed. They work well with people, possess good leadership skills, and are "system thinkers."

- Not all entrepreneurs are the same: **lifestyle entrepreneurs** (p. 135) look for a business that matches their desired lifestyle, **micropreneurs** (p. 135) are satisfied with keeping the business small to achieve a balanced lifestyle, **home-based entrepreneurs** (p. 135) run their businesses out of their homes, and **Internet entrepreneurs** (p. 135) run their businesses strictly online. **Growth entrepreneurs** (p. 136) strive to create fast-growing businesses and look forward to expansion, and **social entrepreneurs** (p. 137) start businesses with a social mission in mind. **Intrapreneurs** (p. 136) are entrepreneurs who work in an entrepreneurial way within organizations owned by other people. Finally, **serial entrepreneurs** (p. 137) create and grow many different businesses over their business career.

3 What are the advantages and disadvantages of franchising? (pp. 139–141)

- A **franchise** (p. 138) is a method of doing business whereby the business sells a company's products or services under the company's name to independent third-party operators.

- The advantages of franchising include that the business is a proven system of operation, franchises benefit from economies of scale, and the franchisor often offers training and marketing support as well as market research.

- The disadvantages of franchising include a lack of control over the look of the store and the product or service being offered, start-up costs and monthly fees that must be paid to the franchisor, and a heavy workload. In addition, franchises will be affected by negative news involving the franchisor or another franchisee of the same company.

4 Why is a business plan crucial to small business success, and what factors lead to small business failure? (pp. 144–146)

- A **business plan** (p. 145) outlines the goals and strategies of a company, including its marketing plans, financial forecasts, a risk analysis, and an operational plan. Neglecting to consider any of these options can doom a business from the start.

- The reasons new businesses fail include accumulating too much debt, inadequate management, poor planning, and unanticipated personal sacrifices.

5 What resources are available to provide assistance and guidance to small business owners? (pp. 146–148)

- The SBA offers assistance in the legalities associated with starting and operating a business as well as education and training, financial assistance, disaster assistance, and counseling.

- **SCORE** (p. 147) volunteers provide free assistance by reviewing business plans, helping with tax planning, and offering new ideas and fresh insights. Other mentoring sources include industry-related conferences and other organizations, such as the EO.

- Business owners can receive formal classroom training at two- and four-year colleges and participate in internships with companies in similar industries for hands-on training.

- **Business incubators** (p. 147) support start-up businesses by offering resources such as administrative services, technical support, business networking, and sources of financing that a group of start-up companies share.

- **Advisory boards** (p. 148) offer guidance to new business owners, but they generally do not have authority to make decisions.

- **Enterprise zones** (p. 148) are geographic areas targeted for economic revitalizing by state and federal governments. Businesses receive generous tax benefits for locating and hiring in these enterprise zones.

6 What are the potential benefits and drawbacks of each major source of small business financing?
(pp. 148–151)

- The benefit of using cash borrowed from friends and family members is that, unlike banks or other lending institutions, these contacts often do not require high rates of return on their investments or demand to see the business turn a quick profit. However, the potential drawback is that these types of personal loans can sometimes be handled unprofessionally.

- The benefit of credit cards is that they are a convenient means of acquiring short-term cash. However, the risk associated with using credit cards for initial business financing is the high rate of interest charged on unpaid balances.

- When more money is needed than credit cards, friends, or family can provide, another source of financing are small business loans from banks and savings-and-loan institutions. Lines of credit or start-up loans are also available and can be used to bridge short-term capital needs. Federal and state **grants** (p. 149) may also be available, depending on the nature of the business.

- **Angel investors** (p. 150) are wealthy individuals who are looking to invest in interesting businesses with good prospects for growth and returns. Generally, angel investors do not seek managerial roles in the businesses they invest in and often have a longer time frame to receive a return on their investment.

- **Venture capitalists** (p. 150) invest in a business in return for some form of equity or ownership in the business. Venture capitalists usually want to play an active role in the management of the companies they invest in. Consequently, this funding option may not be attractive to business owners who aren't open to the idea of relinquishing control of their businesses.

Key Terms

advisory board   (p. 148)

angel investors   (p. 150)

bootstrap financing   (p. 148)

business incubator   (p. 147)

business plan   (p. 145)

due diligence   (p. 142)

enterprise zones   (p. 148)

entrepreneur   (p. 132)

entrepreneurial team   (p. 137)

franchise   (p. 138)

franchisee   (p. 139)

franchisor   (p. 138)

goodwill   (p. 142)

grants   (p. 149)

growth entrepreneur   (p. 136)

home-based entrepreneur   (p. 135)

Internet entrepreneur   (p. 135)

intrapreneur   (p. 136)

lifestyle entrepreneur   (p. 135)

micropreneur   (p. 135)

opportunity niche   (p. 132)

SCORE (Service Corps of Retired Executives)   (p. 147)

Serial enterpreneur   (p. 127)

small business   (p. 127)

Small Business Administration   (p. 127)

small business investment company (SBIC) program   (p. 151)

social entrepreneur   (p. 137)

social intrapreneur   (p. 137)

venture capitalists   (p. 150)

MyBizLab
Go to **mybizlab.com** to complete the problems marked with this icon .

Self-Test

Multiple Choice *You can find the answers on the last page of this book.*

5-1 Which is a key trait of an entrepreneur?
a. Flexibility
b. Risk taking
c. Creative thinking
d. All of the above

5-2 Sally started her new business venture five years ago. The business now operates in three locations, and her sales have increased by 25 percent every year, which is exactly what Sally had in mind. Which type of entrepreneur best describes Sally?
a. Social entrepreneur
b. Lifestyle entrepreneur
c. Growth entrepreneur
d. Gazelle

Self Test (continued)

5-3 One of the first things someone needs to do before starting a business is to write which of the following?

a. A business plan

b. A loan application

c. A partnership statement

d. A franchise agreement

5-4 Which of the following is not a characteristic of a small business?

a. They generally have between 500 and 1,000 employees.

b. On average, the annual revenue is no more than $7 million.

c. It is independently owned and operated.

d. It is not considered a dominant player in its industry.

5-5 Steven Ye wants to start a company. He has a rough draft of his business plan and some tentative funding but needs some additional advice and guidance to help him through the start-up process. The best source for Steve is

a. an angel investor.

b. a SCORE volunteer.

c. his parents.

d. a bank loan officer.

5-6 Kazuto is interested in starting a new business. Which is a reason Kazuto should consider buying an existing business versus starting one from scratch?

a. He will operate a tried and tested business.

b. He will need to work fewer hours.

c. He will need less capital up front.

d. All of the above

5-7 Wayland wants to open up a deli but doesn't want the risk of opening one up from scratch. He knows about a deli that's for sale, but the owner has put too high a value on the business's goodwill. Goodwill is

a. the value of the leftover products the deli gives to the local food pantry.

b. the value of the donations the deli gives to charity.

c. the value of the business's reputation with the current owner.

d. All of the above

5-8 Rebecca has been operating a pet grooming business for several years and has already maxed out her personal credit and savings. She has designed a device that will make the pet grooming process more efficient but needs about $125,000 to take the idea further and perhaps sell it to other pet groomers. Which is the most likely source of financing that Rebecca could use?

a. Credit cards

b. Line of credit

c. Funds from an angel investor

d. Venture capital financing

5-9 Which of the following factors commonly leads to the failure of a small business?

a. Not enough planning

b. Too much accumulated debt

c. Unanticipated personal sacrifices

d. All of the above

5-10 Rashid is starting a consulting business. He doesn't want to rent an office right now, but he needs a receptionist, a place to meet clients, and other aspects of an office. A good solution for Rashid to consider would be a(n)

a. mentoring group.

b. advisory board.

c. business incubator.

d. entrepreneurial team.

True/False *You can find the answers on the last page of this book.*

5-11 Being part of a franchise allows you to have access to tried-and-true marketing strategies.

☐ True or ☐ False

5-12 A social intrapreneur is someone who provides funding for those in Third World countries who want to begin their own businesses but have no capital with which to do so.

☐ True or ☐ False

5-13 According to the SBA, to be considered a small business, a company can have only one location.

☐ True or ☐ False

5-14 Small businesses help large businesses by providing the parts and services required in large manufacturing processes.

☐ True or ☐ False

5-15 Crowdfunding is putting a request for funds on your Facebook page.

☐ True or ☐ False

Critical Thinking Questions

⚙ **5-16** Companies that encouraged their employees to pursue entrepreneurial activities within an existing business created products such as Post-It Notes and Sony PlayStation. What aspects of the corporate environment promote intrapreneurial activities?

⚙ **5-17** Discuss how social media has affected small businesses at all stages of their development, such as financing, marketing, and communications.

⚙ **5-18** Compare the different sources of funding available to small business owners. What types of funding are better at the beginning stages of a business? What types of funding may be better once the business is better established and is looking to expand?

Team Time

STARTING A BUSINESS: BRAINSTORMING

Assemble into groups of four or five.

5-19 Before meeting as a group, think about what you are passionate about and whether there is a potential market involving your interests. Develop one or two ideas for potential businesses based on your passions.

    a. Consider if there is unfulfilled demand for what your business will sell. For example, are you passionate about locally grown organic vegetables but frustrated that there isn't a place nearby to purchase them? If so, you've developed an idea for a local farmers' market.

    b. Consider community service ideas. When school has a half day or full day off, consider having high school students form a daytime child care service for elementary students.

    c. Consider business ideas that have potential but aren't doing very well now. Are there ways to make them better?

5-20 Gather your group and go over each other's ideas. Refine the list to two or three ideas.

5-21 Have each group member refine an idea even further, identifying the target market and outlining the business goals and objectives.

5-22 Meet as a team one more time to pick one business idea.

5-23 If time permits, the group can develop this idea further by using the Business Plan project template. See Mini Chapter 2 for more information.

Ethics and Corporate Social Responsibility

SOCIAL ENTREPRENEURSHIP: START SOME GOOD

Alex Budak and Tom Dawkins created StartSomeGood to help raise money for social entrepreneurs. Similar to the crowdfunding sites Kickstarter and IndieGoGo, people who invest in the projects on StartSomeGood are rewarded with products and other incentives.

Step 1. Visit StartSomeGood.com to see the types of projects that are being proposed. Read through the "How it Works" section to learn more about how to submit an idea on StartSomeGood.

Step 2. In groups, discuss the needs your school or community has and create a list of ideas that your group feels would be good candidates for a StartSomeGood campaign. Decide on the levels of support required and appropriate rewards to be given to funders.

Step 3. Each group should present their idea to the class; as a class, vote on the best idea to send to StartSomeGood.

Web Exercises

5-24   Do You Have What It Takes to Be an Entrepreneur?
In this chapter, you learned that there are several personality traits common to successful entrepreneurs. Do you possess any of these traits? Using a search engine, find an entrepreneurial quiz that will help you determine if you have what it takes to be an entrepreneur. What aspects of your personality make you a good candidate to be an entrepreneur? What is holding you back?

5-25   Franchise Owner
You want to start a business but not from scratch. Go to Entrepreneur.com and research three franchise opportunities you would consider pursuing. Make sure these franchises are within your financial reach. Write up a brief summary of each franchise, noting the pros and cons of owning/operating each one.

5-26   Angel Investor for a Day
Congratulations! You just won the lottery! You are looking for some start-up businesses in which to invest some of your winnings. Go to Angel List (https://angel.co) and research the types of businesses that have received funding or are looking for funding. Pick three different businesses and discuss why you would or would not invest in them.

5-27   Build a Business with a Conscience
What does it take to create a socially conscious business? Play The New Heroes game on PBS to see if you have what it takes. Go to PBS.org and click on "The New Heroes" under the "Programs" link. To play the game, click "Engage."

5-28   Small Business Owners: Where to Go for Help
If you were a new small business owner, where would you go for help? Many colleges have a small business development center (SBDC). These centers, which are affiliated with the SBA, provide information and guidance to current and prospective small business owners. Go to the SBA's site and use the "SBDC Locator" link to identify the nearest SBDC in your area. Then research the services your area's SBDC can provide.

MyBizLab

Go to **mybizlab.com** for Auto-graded writing questions as well as the following Assisted-graded writing questions:

5-29   Why would someone want to buy an existing business rather than start a business from scratch? What are the drawbacks of buying an existing business?

5-30   Discuss the benefits of using an incubator when beginning a small business. Are there drawbacks to using an incubator?

References

1. From U.S. Small Business Administration, "Small Business Size Standards," www.sba.gov/size.
2. U.S. Census Bureau, "Statistics about Small Business from the Census Bureau," www.census.gov/econ/smallbus.html.
3. U.S. Small Business Administration, "Summary of Size Standards by Industry Sector," www.sba.gov/content/summary-size-standards-industry (accessed March 27, 2014).
4. National Federation of Independent Business, "NFIB's Small Business Growth Agenda for the 113th Congress | NFIB," www.nfib.com/Portals/0/PDF/AllUsers/IssuesElections/nfib-growth-agenda-congress.pdf.
5. John Tozzi, "Small Business's Shrinking GDP Contribution," *Bloomberg Businessweek*, February 16, 2012, www.businessweek.com/articles/2012-02-16/small-businesss-shrinking-gdp-contribution.
6. Tozzi, "Small Business's Shrinking GDP Contribution."
7. International Monetary Fund, "World Economic Outlook Database September 2011," www.imf.org/external/pubs/ft/weo/2011/02/weodata/index.aspx.
8. U.S. Census Bureau, "Profile of U.S. Exporting Companies: 2008–2009," April 12, 2011, www.census.gov/foreign-trade/Press-Release/edb/2009/index.html.
9. Anthony Breitzman and Diana Hicks, "An Analysis of Small Business Patents by Industry and Firm Size," November 2008, http://archive.sba.gov/advo/research/rs335tot.pdf.
10. "About Omnipod," www.myomnipod.com.
11. GigaBiter, "Our Company and Mission," www.gigabiter.com/about/index.aspx.
12. "Fabric: Recycled Polyester," www.patagonia.com/us/patagonia.go?assetid=2791.
13. Keith Giard, "GM Bankruptcy Spells Disaster for Small Suppliers," *Washington Post*, May 28, 2009, http://allbusiness.washingtonpost.com/government/elections-politics-campaigns/12344120-1.html.
14. Thomas H. Klier and James M. Rubenstein, "The U.S. Auto Supplier Industry in Transition—The New Geography of Auto Production," May 2006, www.chicagofed.org/digital_assets/publications/chicago_fed_letter/2006/cflmay2006_226.pdf.
15. Klier and. Rubenstein, "The U.S. Auto Supplier Industry in Transition."

16. Small Business Administration, Office of Advocacy, "Economy: A Report to the President," www.sba.gov/sites/default/files/sb_econ2010.pdf.

17. "The ASC Story," www.animatedspeech.com/Story/story_founders.html.

18. Bruce Freeman, "Fired? Start a Business!," www.prolinepr.com/Fired.html.

19. Rieva Lesonsky, "Customers Say Small Business Social Media Efforts Failing: Survey Says," *Huffington Post*, February 6, 2012, www.huffingtonpost.com/2012/02/06/social-media-efforts-fail_n_1210447.html.

20. Dan Tynan, "The 25 Worst Tech Products of All Time," May 26, 2006, www.pcworld.com/article/id,125772-page,6/article.html.

21. Jake Kilroy, "Wahoo's Has a Birthday Party (and I Get Invited)," *Entrepreneur Daily Dose*, February 27, 2009, http://blog.entrepreneur.com/2009/02/wahoos-has-a-birthday-party-and-i-get-invited.php.

22. "Pete's Wicked," www.petes.com.

23. "Citizen Wayne—The Unauthorized Biography," *Miami New Times* 9, no. 33 (December 1–7, 1994), www.corporations.org/wmi/huizenga.html.

24. Peter Drucker, "Quotations from Famous Entrepreneurs on Entrepreneurship: Inspiring Words from the Best of the Best," in *Innovation and Entrepreneurship* (New York: Harper & Row, 1985), 19.

25. "Henry Ford," http://inventors.about.com/library/inventors/blford.htm.

26. Adapted from Jack Kaplan and Anthony Warren, *Patterns of Entrepreneurship*, 2nd ed. (New York: John Wiley & Sons), 27; U.S. Small Business Administration, "The State of Small Business: A Report of the President," (Washington, DC: U.S. Government Printing Office, 1995), 114.

27. "Nimble and Quick: Entrepreneurs That Move, Adapt and Change Are Winners," February 3, 2010, http://nesheimgroup.typepad.com/my_weblog/2010/02/nimble-and-quick-entrepreneurs-that-move-adapt-and-change-are-winners.html.

28. "McDonald's Corp.," http://finance.yahoo.com/q/pr?s+MCD+Profile.

29. "Lifestyle Entrepreneurs: RV-Based Businesses Can Be Going Concerns," www.entrepreneur.com/franchises/franchisezone/startupjournal/article64548.html.

30. StartUpNation, "How PJ Jonas Turned a Bar of Soap into a Championship Business," May 21, 2013, www.startupnation.com/articles/how-pj-jonas-turned-a-bar-of-soap-into-a-championship-business (accessed March 28, 2014).

31. Leena Ray, "Facebook for Latinos Quepasa Buys MyYearbook for $100 Million in Cash and Stock," July 20, 2011, http://techcrunch.com/2011/07/20/facebook-for-latinos-quepasa-buys-myyearbook-for-100-million-in-cash-and-stock.

32. Miguel Helft, "The Class That Built Apps, and Fortunes," *New York Times*, May 7, 2011, www.nytimes.com/2011/05/08/technology/08class.html?_r=1&pagewanted+all.

33. John Case, "The Gazelle Theory," *Inc. Magazine*, May 2001, www.inc.com/magazine/20010515/22613.html.

34. James Rosen, "Economists Credit Small Business 'Gazelles' with Job Creation," April 25 2011, www.foxnews.com/us/2011/04/25/economists-credit-small-business-gazelles-job-creation.

35. "Creativity Overflowing," *Bloomberg Businessweek*, www.businessweek.com/magazine/content/06_19/b3983061.htm?chan+searchand.

36. "How Whirlpool Defines Innovation," *Bloomberg Businessweek*, www.businessweek.com/innovate/content/mar2006/id20060306_287425.htm?chan+search.

37. Jake Swearingen, "Great Intrapreneurs in Business History," www.bnet.com/2403-13070_23-196888.html?tag+content;col1.

38. J. Gregory Dees, "The Meaning of Social Entrepreneurship," www.caseatduke.org/documents/dees_sedef.pdf.

39. "Meet the New Heroes: Mimi Silbert," www.pbs.org/opb/thenewheroes/meet/silbert.html.

40. Ashley Jablow, "2010 Conference: The Business of Corporate Citizenship: Becoming a Social Intrapreneur," http://blogs.bcccc.net/2010/04/the-business-of-corporate-citizenship-becoming-a-social-intrapreneur.

41. Josh Cleveland, "Creating a Company Culture That Engages Social Intrapreneurs," June 29, 2009, www.greenbiz.com.

42. Karsten Strauss "$250 Million for a 14-Year-Old's Big Idea: Origami Owl," *Forbes*, October 22, 2013, www.forbes.com/sites/karstenstrauss/2013/10/22/250-million-for-a-14-year-olds-big-idea-origami-owl.

43. "Franchise Law: What Is a Franchise Business?," copyright by and used with permission of Freeadvice.com.

44. "Franchise Business Economic Outlook: 2013," January 13, 2014, http://franchiseeconomy.com/wp-content/uploads/2014/01/Franchise_Business_Outlook_January_2014-1-13-13.pdf (accessed March 28, 2014).

45. "Franchise Business Economic Outlook."

46. "Home-Based Franchises for 2013," www.entrepreneur.com/franchises/homebased/index.html.

47. "2010 Low Cost Franchises," www.entrepreneur.com/franchises/lowcost/index.html.

48. U.S. Census Bureau, "BDS Database List," www.census.gov/ces/dataproducts/bds/data.html.

49. Chart derived by author from data retrieved from Bureau of Labor Statistics, "Business Employment Dynamics: Entrepreneurship and the U.S. Economy," www.bls.gov/bdm/entrepreneurship/bdm_chart3.htm.

50. Stacy Perman, Jeffrey Gangemi, and Douglas MacMillan, "Entrepreneurs' Favorite Mistakes," *BusinessWeek*, http://images.businessweek.com/ss/06/09/favorite_mistake/source/1.htm.

51. National Business Incubator Association, www.nbia.org.

52. "About Us: History," www.subway.com/subwayroot/about_us/history.aspx.

53. "Financing Options for a Small Business: Finding the Right Funding," www.startupnation.com/articles/financing-options-for-a-small-business-finding-the-right-funding.

Chapter 6
Forms of Business Ownership

▶ Sole Proprietorships

When an entrepreneur starts a business, choosing the proper business structure is vital to the company's success. When Patty Jacobs decided to start her own cleaning business, she became a sole proprietor. Her business began growing so fast, and she now doesn't know if being a sole proprietor is the right business structure for her new venture. Do you know when it's best to operate as a sole proprietorship?

▶ Partnerships

Trying to do a job alone can sometimes be overwhelming. Because of this, entrepreneurs may partner together to share resources and talents for the benefit of everyone involved. Partners Daniel Ramirez and Stephan Brown brought their skills and finances together to begin a new venture. Why might a partnership be a good business structure for a business? What difficulties should new partners prepare for?

▶ Corporations

Brandon Jacobson and his sister, Sonya, found themselves unexpected landlords when they inherited properties that were owned and operated by their mother. Their mom reported the rental income on her personal income taxes as a sole proprietor. Brandon and Sonya were looking into creating a partnership, but they were advised that a partnership may not be the best corporate structure for them to operate under. Why isn't a partnership a good choice for Sonya and Brandon? What are their other options?

▶ Not-for-Profits and Cooperatives

Darrell Hammond knew he could make a difference in the life of inner-city children by giving them safe places to play. He quickly outgrew his modest volunteer activities and knew he wanted to expand to help more children. He needed a corporate structure that would allow him to take his profits and put them back into communities nationwide. What type of alternative business structure would work best for him?

▶ Mergers and Acquisitions

Companies constantly search for opportunities to expand by adding to their product lines, to enter into different geographic areas, or to gain a competitive advantage. The rationale behind mergers and acquisitions is that the resulting combined firm will be more valuable than the individual companies on their own. What is the difference between a merger and an acquisition? When do they occur?

OBJECTIVES

1 What are the advantages and disadvantages of a sole proprietorship? (pp. 160–163)

2 What are the advantages and disadvantages of a partnership and a partnership agreement? (pp. 163–167)

3 How is a corporation formed, and how does it compare with sole proprietorships and partnerships? (pp. 167–170)

4 What are the major differences between a C corporation, an S corporation, and a limited liability company? (pp. 170–173)

5 What are the characteristics of not-for-profit organizations and cooperatives? (pp. 173–175)

6 What are the different types of mergers and acquisitions, and why do they occur? (pp. 175–178)

Sole Proprietorships pp. 159–163

Patty Jacobs runs a small cleaning business from her home. She has no employees, and she reports the business's income and expenses on her personal income taxes. However, the business has begun to grow quickly, and she is considering hiring a few employees. She is concerned about the added liability she faces with an expanded business and new employees. As a sole proprietor, she knows that she is held responsible for any and all damages her company commits. In addition, now that Patty's small business is becoming successful, it may make more sense to report its earnings on a separate tax return rather than running them through her personal tax return. She realizes that being the owner of a growing company requires more decisions than she had anticipated. ∎

Source: Tatyana Gladskih/Fotolia.

Patty Jacobs chose to begin her company as a sole proprietorship because it was quick and easy to establish. No legal paperwork is required to begin a sole proprietorship, and all the financial information related to it can be reported on the owner's personal tax returns. Because of these advantages, a sole proprietorship is a common form of business ownership for start-up businesses. Many businesses also start out as sole proprietorships simply because their owners are unfamiliar with other forms of business ownership.

Choosing the right legal structure for Patty's business may have initially been a simple decision, but has her fast business growth outgrown a sole proprietorship? How do you know which form is best for your company? Choosing a form of ownership depends on many factors, including the personal liability you face, the amount you pay in taxes, your ability to borrow money, and the amount of paperwork your business is required to file.

The U.S. economy—as well as the global economy—is based on a variety of enterprises, including sole proprietorships (businesses owned by one person), partnerships (where two or more people legally share ownership of a business), and corporations (businesses that are formed as separate legal entities). More businesses in the United States are structured as a sole proprietorship. On the other hand, corporations, while fewer in number, generate the most revenue. Besides sole proprietorships, partnerships, and corporations, there are other classifications of corporations to consider, such as limited liability companies and S corporations. In this chapter, we'll explore each of these forms of business ownership in greater detail.

MyBizLab®
⭐ **Improve Your Grade!**
Over 10 million students improved their results using the Pearson MyLabs.
Visit **mybizlab.com** for simulations, tutorials, and end-of-chapter problems.

Why is a sole proprietorship a popular form of business ownership? A sole **proprietorship** is an unincorporated business owned (and usually controlled) by a single individual. Because no legal paperwork is necessary to establish a business as a sole proprietorship, many small business owners are sole proprietors without even knowing it. Although a sole proprietorship has only one owner, it can have any number of employees. For example, you can be the owner of a plumbing business with several other plumbers working for you and still operate as a sole proprietorship. Other characteristics of a sole proprietorship are listed in ■ **FIGURE 6.1**.

Starting a Sole Proprietorship

How do I start a sole proprietorship? The minute you begin doing business by yourself—that is, collecting income as a result of performing a service or selling a good—you are operating as a sole proprietor. There are no special forms to fill out, and there are no special filing requirements with state and federal governments. At a minimum, you might need to obtain a local license or permits, or you might have to ensure that you're operating in an area zoned for the type of business you are running. If you're hiring employees, you will need to register your company name and obtain an employer identification number (EIN) from the Internal Revenue Service (IRS).

Advantages and Disadvantages

Are there advantages to being a sole proprietor? There are several advantages of forming your business as a sole proprietorship—one of which we have already discussed: ease of formation. With only one person making all the decisions and no need to consult other owners or interested parties, sole proprietors also have great control and considerable flexibility to act quickly. Another advantage is that there are no specific corporate records to keep or reports to file, including tax reporting. Because there is no legal distinction between the owner and the business, no separate tax return is required. As a result, the income and expenses of a sole proprietorship flow through the owner's personal tax return. This can be an advantage, especially in the start-up phase of the business when it's likely that the operating costs of the business are greater than the incoming revenues. In this case, the excess expenses (or net loss) can help offset the taxes you owe on any other sources of income you might have.

For example, imagine you run a landscaping business during the summer in addition to your regular job. If the lawn mower breaks down and needs to be replaced, that expense could be more than all the earnings you collected, generating a loss for your lawn-mowing business. You can subtract that loss from the income earned

■ **FIGURE 6.1**
Characteristics of a Sole Proprietorship

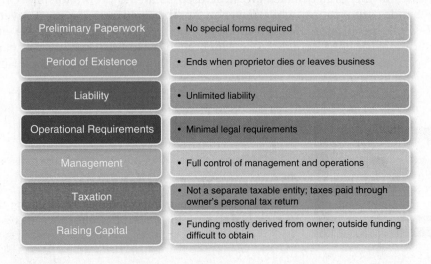

Preliminary Paperwork	• No special forms required
Period of Existence	• Ends when proprietor dies or leaves business
Liability	• Unlimited liability
Operational Requirements	• Minimal legal requirements
Management	• Full control of management and operations
Taxation	• Not a separate taxable entity; taxes paid through owner's personal tax return
Raising Capital	• Funding mostly derived from owner; outside funding difficult to obtain

from your regular job, reducing your income tax obligation. ■ **TABLE 6.1** and ■ **FIGURE 6.2** show how a business loss can reduce your tax payment. In this example, a business loss of $3,000 reduces by $450 the federal taxes you would have to pay.

Why wouldn't I want to run my business as a sole proprietorship? One of the biggest disadvantages of a sole proprietorship is that it leaves you exposed to personal liability. A **liability** is the obligation to pay a debt, such as an account payable or a loan. Liabilities can also include a breach of contract or losses associated from damages. **Unlimited liability** means that if business assets aren't enough to pay business debts, then personal assets, such as the sole proprietor's house, personal investments, or retirement funds, can be used to pay the balance. In other words, the proprietor can lose an unlimited amount of personal assets. As a sole proprietorship, the business is not a separate legal entity, and all business debts and liabilities are your personal obligations. You are personally responsible for the business's contracts, taxes, and the misconduct of employees who create legal

TABLE 6.1	Personal Income and Taxes Due with and without a Business Loss from a Sole Proprietorship	
	With Business Loss	**Without Business Loss**
Wage income	$14,500	$14,500
Business loss	−$3,000	
Net income	$11,500	$14,500
Taxes due	$2,437	$2,887
	Difference: $450	

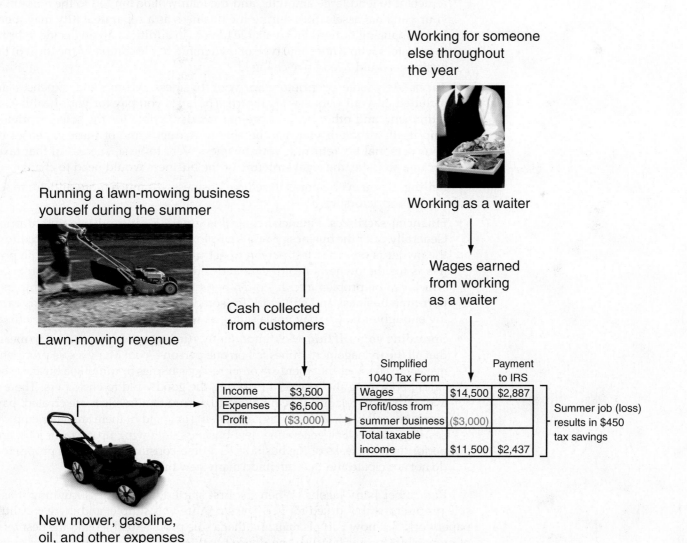

■ **FIGURE 6.2**
The Effect of a Business Loss on Personal Income
Sole proprietors can deduct business losses from their personal taxes, reducing their overall tax burden.

liabilities while acting within their employment. Therefore, if the type of business you're running has the potential for someone to sue you because of damages caused by your business, you may not want to operate as a sole proprietorship.

Imagine that you own a catering business. While you're preparing food in someone's house, the oven catches fire because you forgot to take the egg rolls off the paper tray. You are personally responsible, or liable, for paying for any damages if the assets of your business (or your insurance) are not sufficient to cover the damages. If the damages are severe enough—perhaps your client's entire house burns down—you could lose all your assets, including your own home and savings. If you decide that a sole proprietorship is the right business form for you for other reasons, buying insurance—such as errors or omissions insurance, disability insurance, and insurance to protect your assets—will help protect you against unforeseen situations.

Are there other things to consider with running a sole proprietorship?
Unlimited liability is perhaps the most critical reason for not operating as a sole proprietorship. However, there are other reasons why you might not want to operate your business as a sole proprietorship:

- **Financing/investment.** A drawback of a sole proprietorship is that it can make it more difficult for you to borrow money to help your business grow. Banks will be lending to you personally, not to your business, so they will be more reluctant to lend large amounts, and the loan will be limited to the amount of your personal assets. Structuring the business as a separate entity may mean more financing options are available to you. In addition, if you decide to bring in investors who want some type of ownership in the company, the form of the business would need to be changed.

- **Taxes.** As a sole proprietorship, your business income and expenses are included on your personal tax return. The costs you pay for your health care, retirement, and other benefits are not tax deductible for the sole proprietorship itself, although you may be able to deduct some of these expenses on your personal tax return. If your business were to be so successful that taxes became an issue, the legal structure of the business would need to change.

- **Selling.** If you ever wanted to sell the business, it's much more difficult to sell a sole proprietorship.

- **Financial sacrifices.** Financial control is great, but it can come with a price. Generally, after the business pays its employees, suppliers, and other creditors, the owner is often the last person to get paid. If the budget is tight, the payments for the owner's health care and retirement sometimes get postponed, which can be problematic. It's often helpful to run a sole proprietorship as a part-time business and still work for someone else until the business is earning enough money to pay you a salary as well as provide you with benefits.

- **Spreading yourself thin.** Most importantly, running a sole proprietorship means that all the management duties fall on one person—you! Many a sole proprietor neglect to consider that there are other responsibilities to running a business besides performing the services or making the goods sold to customers. There is a lot of paperwork and time involved to ensure that invoices are created, payments are collected, and salaries and benefits are paid (if there are other employees). This, as well as generating new business, following up on prior jobs, and performing the tasks of the business, is a time-consuming task that proprietors do not anticipate and that can undo many new businesses quickly.

Remember Patty Jacobs? When she first started her business, running it as a sole proprietorship worked for her. The structure was simple, and there was little paperwork. But now Patty is realizing that a sole proprietorship isn't the best form of ownership for her because she doesn't want to risk losing her personal assets in the event of an employee error. Patty, like many other small business owners, is realizing that making decisions about choosing the correct corporate structure is complex. After getting advice from other business owners, Patty decided that her business needed to undergo some corporate restructuring so that the company's business form would be more conducive to her needs.

Partnerships pp. 163–167

Daniel Ramirez had his eye on a piece of property for a storefront in an up-and-coming neighborhood. The property was affordable but still slightly out of his reach. It also needed some renovations—skills that Daniel did not have. Stephan Brown, a friend of Daniel's college roommate, had some construction and carpentry experience and was also looking for a business opportunity but didn't have as much capital. After much thought and conversation, Daniel and Stephan agreed to form a partnership, buy the property, and embark on the renovations together. What contributions did Daniel and Stephan each bring to the partnership? What difficulties should the two new partners prepare for? ■

Source: Ljupco Smokovski/Fotolia.

The saying that two brains are better than one may explain why many small businesses have two or more owners working together. There are some distinct advantages to these types of business arrangements, but there are also some potential disadvantages to be aware of.

Advantages and Disadvantages of Partnerships

When is it good to bring in a partner? A **partnership** is a type of business structure in which two or more entities (or partners) share the ownership and the profits and losses of the business. Joining forces with someone else can help a businessperson share the costs of starting and running a business as well as the managerial responsibilities and workload associated with it. Having a partner whose skills complement your own can be quite advantageous. For example, if you're great at numbers but hate making sales calls, bringing in a partner who loves to knock on doors would be beneficial for your business.

Another advantage of a partnership relates to time: Because more owners are involved in the business, there is more time available for the owners to increase the firm's marketing and sales efforts to generate more income. A partner can also help come up with new ideas and projects for the business as well discuss major decisions with you and help you make them. And because partners have a stake in the business, unlike employees, they are more likely to be willing to work long hours and go the extra mile.

Are there disadvantages to adding partners? For every advantage a partner can bring, adding the wrong partner can be equally problematic. Obviously, adding partners means sharing profits and control, so if you don't want to give these up, a partnership may not be the right structure for you. Your partner may also have different work habits and styles from you. If the person's style doesn't complement your own, the differences can be challenging. In addition, as the business begins to grow and change, your partner might want to take the business in a different direction than you had envisioned. Like entering into marriage, you want to consider carefully the person(s) with whom you will be sharing your business.

As a business form, how does a partnership compare to a sole proprietorship? Partnerships and sole proprietorships are very similar; in fact, the biggest difference between the two is the number of people contributing resources and sharing the profits and the liabilities. It's just as easy to form a

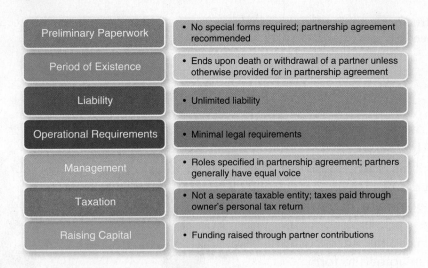

Preliminary Paperwork	• No special forms required; partnership agreement recommended
Period of Existence	• Ends upon death or withdrawal of a partner unless otherwise provided for in partnership agreement
Liability	• Unlimited liability
Operational Requirements	• Minimal legal requirements
Management	• Roles specified in partnership agreement; partners generally have equal voice
Taxation	• Not a separate taxable entity; taxes paid through owner's personal tax return
Raising Capital	• Funding raised through partner contributions

■ **FIGURE 6.3**
Characteristics of a Partnership

partnership as to form a sole proprietorship. The government does not require any special forms or reports, although some local restrictions may apply for licenses and permits. For example, suppose you and your brother-in-law form a small partnership called "All in the Family Electricians." Before you are able to do business, you might have to apply for a license, but you do not need any special papers to create the partnership itself. Also, like a sole proprietorship, partnerships do not file a separate tax return. All profits and losses of the partnership flow directly through each partner's individual tax return. ■ **FIGURE 6.3** outlines other characteristics of a partnership.

Elements of a Partnership Agreement

What goes into a partnership agreement? A partnership can begin with a handshake, and many of them do. Although no formal documents are required to form a partnership, it's a good idea to draw up a **partnership agreement** that formalizes the relationship between partners. Think of a partnership agreement as a prenuptial agreement. It helps settle conflicts when they arise and may prevent small misunderstandings from erupting into larger disagreements. Many points can be included in a partnership agreement; however, the following items should always be included:

1. **Capital contributions.** The amount of **capital** (money), equipment, supplies, technology, and other tangible things of value each partner contributes to begin the business should be noted in the partnership agreement. In addition, the agreement should also address how additional capital can be added to the business—who will contribute it and whether there will be a limit to a partner's overall capital contribution.

2. **Responsibilities of each partner.** To avoid the possibility of one partner doing more or less work than others or a conflict arising over one partner assuming a more controlling role than the other partners desire, it is best to outline the responsibilities of each partner from the beginning. Unless otherwise specified, any partner can bind the partnership to any debt or contract without the consent of the other partners. Therefore, it is especially important to spell out the policy regarding who assumes responsibility for entering into key financial or contractual arrangements.

How Do You Find the Right Business Partner?

Business partners are like spouses: Finding each other is often through circumstance and happenstance. Because of the high financial stakes, many look to partner with those whom they trust most: spouses, friends, or relatives. Hiring friends or relatives can have its benefits, but what do you do if your best friend doesn't do the job well?[1] You might instead want to turn to your casual acquaintance network—your gym buddy, a parent of your child's friend, or a classmate—to find a business partner. If your network isn't turning up any promising leads, turn to others' networks. Similar to finding a job, write a description of the "perfect partner" and send it to as many people as you can. Make sure you interview the candidates and look for those who have similar goals but complementary skills. And by all means, "date" (get to know) the prospective partner before jumping into a business marriage; there is too much at risk to proceed too quickly.

3. **Decision-making process.** How will decisions be made? Knowing whether decisions will be the result of mutual consent of all or several partners or whether just one or two partners will make the key decisions will help the partners avoid disagreements. What constitutes a key decision should also be defined in the agreement. In a partnership of two, where the possibility of a deadlock is likely, some partnerships provide for a trusted associate to act as a third "partner" whose sole responsibility is to be the tiebreaker.

4. **Shares of profits or losses.** The agreement should specify not only how to divide profits and losses between the partners but also how frequently this will be done. For example, it might stipulate that the profits and losses will be proportional to each partner's initial contribution to the partnership, as reflected in ■ **FIGURE 6.4**. Or, the agreement might split the profits evenly. It is also important to detail how adjustments to the distributions will be made—if any at all—as the partnership matures and changes.

5. **Departure of partners.** Eventually, the composition of partners may change as original partners leave and new partners come onboard. The partnership agreement should have rules for a partner's exit, whether voluntary, involuntary, or due to death or divorce. Provisions to remove a partner's ownership interest are necessary so the business does not need to end (liquidate). The agreement should include how to determine the amount of ownership interest and to whom the departing partner is permitted to transfer his or her interest. It is important to consider whether a partner can transfer his or her ownership solely to the remaining partners or whether individuals outside the existing partnership can buy the departing partner's share of the business.

6. **Addition of partners.** The partnership agreement should spell out the requirements for new partners entering the partnership. Also included should be how the profits will be allocated once a new partner is taken on and whether there will be a "junior partner" period during which the person must prove himself or herself before obtaining full partner status.

Types of Partnerships

Are there different types of partnerships? There are two common types of partnerships: *general partnerships* and *limited partnerships*. The distinction between the two types involves who accepts most or all of the business liability.

What is a general partnership? A **general partnership** is the default arrangement for a partnership and is, therefore, the simplest of all partnerships to form. For instance, if two friends, Juan and Franklin, set up an ice cream stand at the local park, sell ice cream cones, and split the profits at the end of the day, they have created a general partnership. For Juan and Franklin, this is a

■ **FIGURE 6.4**
Share of Profit and Loss in a Partnership
Partners' shares of profits and losses can be dependent on the capital contribution and the assumed responsibilities of each partner.

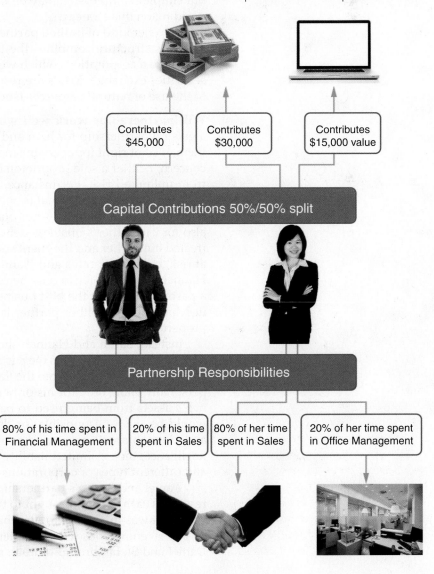

Contributes $45,000 | Contributes $30,000 | Contributes $15,000 value

Capital Contributions 50%/50% split

Partnership Responsibilities

80% of his time spent in Financial Management | 20% of his time spent in Sales | 80% of her time spent in Sales | 20% of her time spent in Office Management

logical arrangement because they share the profits equally, and there is little worry about liability. In a general partnership, each partner has unlimited liability for the debts and obligations of the partnership, meaning every partner is liable for his or her own actions as well as the actions of the other partners and the actions of any employees.

What is a limited partnership? Sometimes, a business can bring on additional "limited" partners who mostly provide capital and earn a share in the profits but who are not involved in operating the business. To encourage investors to contribute capital to a business without risking more capital than they have contributed, a **limited partnership** is created. In a limited partnership, there are two types of partners. **General partners** are full owners of the business, are responsible for all the day-to-day business decisions, and remain liable for all the debts and obligations of the business. **Limited partners** are involved as investors and, as such, are personally liable only up to the amount of their investment in the business. They must not actively participate in any decisions of the business. To continue our example, suppose Juan and Franklin don't have enough money to purchase a new freezer for their business. So, they ask Juan's brother Carlos to invest enough cash in the business to buy the freezer. Because Carlos is already working full-time and cannot participate in the business's activities, he becomes a limited partner. Should something go wrong and the partners needed to cover the damages incurred by the business, Carlos will only lose the money he has contributed (the cost of the freezer). Limited partnerships can be much more complex to form than our simple example, so it may be worth exploring other business structures before deciding on this strategy.

Another kind of limited partnership is a *master limited partnership* (MLP). This business structure combines the tax benefits of a limited partnership, but it is similar to a corporation (which we discuss next) in that it is publicly traded on a securities exchange. MLPs are restricted mostly to certain businesses pertaining to the use of natural resources (such as petroleum or natural gas) and real estate.

Will partnerships work well when liability is a concern? Although forming a general partnership for Juan and Franklin's ice cream business makes sense for them, it's not right for every business. In some situations, especially if liability is a concern, neither a sole proprietorship nor a partnership will protect the owner(s) from unlimited risk. For instance, if Sarah and Hannah decide to form Personal Training Partners, a personal training and fitness motivation company, they know that each partner is liable—not only for her own business debts and actions but also for each other's business debts and actions. If a client claims that Sarah mistreated him or her and the client sues the business, not only are the business assets at risk, but both Sarah's and Hannah's personal assets are also at risk. Sarah and Hannah would prefer to only be responsible for their own mistakes. In this case, a partnership is not the best business structure because a partnership has unlimited liability. So, neither partner is protected against the losses of their personal property.

Instead, Sarah and Hannah should consider forming a *limited liability partnership* (LLP). An LLP protects the partners not only from any debt or liability incurred by the business but also from the liability of another partner. A partner in an LLP is personally liable only for his or her own negligence. An LLP would protect Hannah's assets from being used to pay for claims against Sarah's negligence. Sarah would be solely responsible for damages caused by her own mistakes. If Sarah and Hannah aren't concerned about being protected from each other's possible negligence, then a limited liability company is another option. We'll discuss this and different types of corporations next.

Daniel and Stefan's partnership benefited from the complementary skills and resources each partner brought to the table. Because Daniel had more financial exposure, it was important to him that he and Stefan sign a partnership agreement. After the renovations were complete and the space was ready for commercial use, Daniel and Stefan brought in one more partner, Lily Ye, who has extensive retail and marketing experience—just what they needed to move forward with their venture. But Lily suggested the partnership look into a corporate structure. Why does she think a corporation is the best structure for their business? We'll discuss corporations next.

Corporations pp. 167–173

Brandon Jacobson and his sister, Sonya, found themselves unexpected landlords when they inherited a couple of rental properties owned by their mother. She reported the rental income she received from the properties on her personal income taxes as a sole proprietor. Brandon and Sonya were looking into creating a partnership, but they were worried about liability issues and realized that a partnership might not be their best option. They would still like to report the income on their own personal tax returns if possible. Why won't a simple partnership work? What are their choices? ■

Source: Vlam1/Fotolia.

The American writer Ambrose Bierce once defined a corporation as "an ingenious device for obtaining profit without individual responsibility."[2] Unlike partnerships and sole proprietorships, corporations provide business owners with better protection of their personal assets. What is a corporation, and why might a business owner choose to form one? What are the different types of corporations? In this section, you'll find the answers to these questions and more.

What is a corporation? A **corporation** is a specific form of business organization that is legally formed under state laws. A corporation is considered a separate entity apart from its owners; therefore, a corporation has legal rights like an individual. Consequently, a corporation can own property, assume liability, pay taxes, enter into contracts, and sue and be sued—just like any other individual. Most of the time, a corporation is structured as a **C corporation**, which refers to Subchapter C of the Internal Revenue Code by which it is governed, though sometimes a corporation can be structured as an S corporation (which we discuss next). Some characteristics of a C corporation are listed in ■ **FIGURE 6.5**.

Advantages of Incorporation

When does it make sense to form a corporation? Some business owners incorporate just to be able to end a company's name with "Company," "Co.," "Incorporated," or "Inc." Having corporate nomenclature such as "Co." or "Inc." at the end of the business name can give a start-up business an air of legitimacy, which can be a perceived benefit to prospective clients and lenders and potentially a greater threat to the competition. More important, forming under a corporate structure provides many advantages other business structures don't.

How can a business owner protect his or her personal assets? Corporations are not just for big businesses. A C corporation can be the right choice for many small entities because it is a separate legal entity and is responsible for its own debts, obligations, and liabilities. It also can sue and be sued. This is one of the main reasons

■ **FIGURE 6.5**
Characteristics of a C Corporation

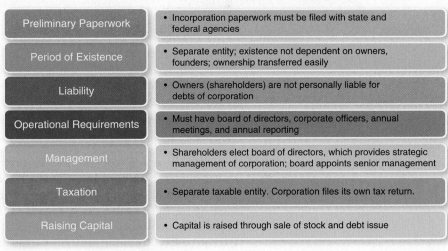

Preliminary Paperwork	• Incorporation paperwork must be filed with state and federal agencies
Period of Existence	• Separate entity; existence not dependent on owners, founders; ownership transferred easily
Liability	• Owners (shareholders) are not personally liable for debts of corporation
Operational Requirements	• Must have board of directors, corporate officers, annual meetings, and annual reporting
Management	• Shareholders elect board of directors, which provides strategic management of corporation; board appoints senior management
Taxation	• Separate taxable entity. Corporation files its own tax return.
Raising Capital	• Capital is raised through sale of stock and debt issue

owners incorporate their business. When a corporation runs into problems, only the corporation's assets can be used to remedy the situation; the owners are not personally liable for the business's debts.

What happens to a corporation when an owner leaves? Sole proprietorships and partnerships, by their nature, are dependent on their founding owners. When an owner dies or otherwise leaves the business, a partnership or sole proprietorship is usually terminated. On the other hand, corporations can theoretically live forever because their ownership can be transferred to different shareholders. Shares of ownership are easily exchanged, so the corporation will continue to exist should an owner die or wish to sell his or her interest in the business. As long as it is financially viable, a corporation is capable of continuing forever.

Is it easier for corporations to get funding and to raise capital? Corporations can raise money by selling shares of ownership to a specified group of individuals. Or, when a corporation has reached a significant size, it can extend its ownership by "going public"—selling shares of ownership in the corporation to the general public. A stock certificate is the tangible evidence of investment and ownership. And, as we noted earlier, lenders are more likely to loan money to an incorporated business because they are not limited to the credit profile of a sole proprietor or general partners.

Are corporations taxed the same as other types of businesses? Because sole proprietors and partners run their business income through their personal income tax statements, these two types of business structures pay taxes at the owner's or partners' tax rates. Corporations have separate tax rates. The corporate tax rate is 15 percent for the first $50,000 of net income a business earns, whereas the same amount of profits from a sole proprietorship or partnership would be taxed at a rate of 25 percent.[3] However, most corporations will generate more than $50,000 in net income. Businesses generating more than $50,000 in taxable income will pay taxes at an equal or higher tax rate than individuals.

Does it matter where a business is incorporated? The answer to this questions is more complex than it seems, but there are some general considerations that should be evaluated. If you have a corporation with fewer than five shareholders or members, it's usually much easier and often less expensive to incorporate in the state where your business has a physical presence. For some larger businesses, however, it may be more advantageous to incorporate in a state that is historically more favorable to businesses, such as Delaware, Nevada, and Wyoming. Delaware offers some of the most flexible and business-friendly statutes in the country. Nevada offers low filing fees and has no state corporate income, franchise, and personal income taxes. For similar reasons, Wyoming is also becoming a popular state in which to incorporate.

Structure of a Corporation

How is a corporation structured? In its simplest configuration, a corporation's organizational structure is comprised of shareholders, a board of directors, corporate officers, first-line managers, and employees, as ■ **FIGURE 6.6** shows. Each group has different responsibilities.

Shareholders

Whether or not a corporation is privately owned or publicly owned, it has shareholders. **Shareholders** (or **stockholders**) have an ownership interest in the company. For their investment, the corporation provides them with stock certificates identifying the number of shares (called *apportioned ownership interest*) they own. A **publicly owned corporation** is a corporation regulated by the U.S. Securities and Exchange Commission (SEC) because the shares of ownership can be traded on public stock exchanges. Although shareholders of a publicly owned corporation serve as the owners of the corporation, they have no involvement in the direct management of the corporation. Instead, they influence corporate decisions by electing directors, overseeing the laws and rules that govern the organization, and voting on major corporate issues.

In privately held (or closed) corporations, corporations are owned, in most cases, by the company's founders, a management team, or a group of private investors. The owners are generally involved in the management and daily operations of the business and have more decision-making responsibilities than do shareholders of publicly owned corporations. The owners of privately held corporations are generally the sole shareholders. Any shares of privately held corporations are not traded on public stock exchanges.

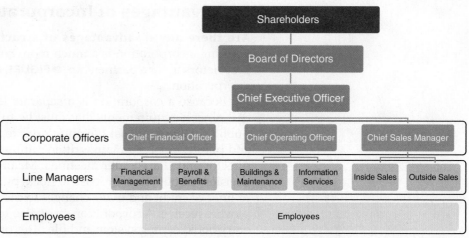

■ FIGURE 6.6

Organizational Structure of a C Corporation

Shareholders have the power to elect the board of directors of a C corporation. The board, in turn, has the ability to hire (or fire) the company's corporate officers.

Directors

The shareholders of a corporation elect its **board of directors**, and the members of the board select and hire the business's management team of corporate officers. Major financing and business decisions for the corporation are also made by the board of directors. For example, in addition to setting the corporation's policies, the board authorizes the issuance of stock, approves loans to or from the corporation, and decides on major real estate transactions. Consequently, because they vote for the board members, the firm's shareholders can influence the very nature of a corporation and how it is run.

Not only is a business's board of directors responsible for hiring the corporation's major executives, it is also responsible for ensuring they do their jobs. Not all boards are effective in doing so. Following a rash of corporate scandals, in 2002, the Sarbanes-Oxley Act was enacted. The act provides a new set of regulations designed to make boards of directors more accountable. If the members of a board of directors ignore their responsibility to manage the internal controls of a company, they risk going to prison and face huge fines.

Officers and Line Managers

The primary lineup of officers elected by a corporation's board of directors include the firm's CEO, CFO, and COO. The **chief executive officer** (CEO) is typically responsible for the entire operations of the corporation and reports directly to the board of directors. Sometimes the CEO is a member of the board of directors as well. The **chief financial officer** (CFO) reports directly to the CEO and is responsible for analyzing and reviewing the business's financial data, reporting its financial performance, preparing budgets, and monitoring the firm's expenditures and costs. The **chief operating officer** (COO) is responsible for the day-to-day operations of the organization and reports directly to the CEO. Often, there is a chief legal officer or general council, and, depending on the needs of the company, there might also be a chief information officer (CIO). In actuality, any "officer" position can be formed if it makes sense for the company. In smaller companies, only one or two people might play the roles of several different officers. For example, the CEO might also serve as the CFO. In large companies, the responsibilities of each officer are demanding enough that **first-line managers**, people who directly supervise lower-level employees, help run the business.

Disadvantages of Incorporation

Are there any disadvantages of structuring a business as a corporation? Forming a corporation is a much more cumbersome process than forming a sole proprietorship or a partnership. ■ **FIGURE 6.7** shows the steps involved in forming a corporation.

Because a corporation is a separate legal entity, there are many more filing and process requirements that must be fulfilled to maintain corporate status. All public companies must file an annual report, and all corporations, both private and public, must maintain written minutes of annual and other periodic board of director and shareholder meetings. Major decisions must be recorded, including decisions about whether to issue stock, purchase real estate, approve leases, loans, or lines of credit and make changes to the stock options and retirement plans employees receive. A corporation must also record financial transactions in a double-entry bookkeeping system and file taxes on a regular basis (quarterly or annually).

Because it is considered its own legal entity, a corporation files its own tax return. This results in the disadvantage of double taxation. **Double taxation** occurs when taxes are paid on the same income twice. The classic business example of double taxation is the distribution of dividends. A corporation is first taxed on its net income, or profit, and then distributes that net income to its shareholders in the form of dividends. The individual shareholder must then pay taxes on the dividends (which have already been taxed at the corporate level). Therefore, the same pool of money—corporate profits—has been taxed twice: once in the form of corporate profits and again as dividends received by the shareholders. Although this is a commonly mentioned disadvantage of corporations, it affects only those corporations that pay dividends to their shareholders.

Can a business have the protection of a corporation but not pay corporate taxes? When choosing a legal structure for their businesses, most entrepreneurs want to achieve two goals: protect themselves from personal liability and have the income of their businesses flow through to their individual tax returns so they don't face double taxation. A corporate structure protects an owner's personal assets from being touched if the corporation is in financial difficulty, but the corporation is taxed as a separate entity without flow-through to the owner's returns. Fortunately, there are other forms of business structures in which both goals can be met: the *S corporation* and the *limited liability company*.

S Corporations

What is an S corporation? An **S corporation** is a regular corporation (a C corporation) that has elected to be taxed under a special section of the Internal Revenue Code called Subchapter S. Like C corporations, S corporations have shareholders, and they must comply with all the other regulations involving traditional C corporations.

How is an S corporation different from a C corporation? Unlike C corporations, S corporations do not pay corporate income taxes. Instead, as with a partnership or a sole proprietorship, shareholders in an S corporation owe income taxes based on their proportionate share of the business profits they receive and pay taxes through their own individual tax returns. Passing taxes through personal tax returns is one of the primary advantages of forming a business as an S corporation. However, even though S corporations do not pay corporate taxes like C corporations, they still must file a corporate tax return every year. In addition,

■ **FIGURE 6.7**

Steps in Forming a Corporation
Corporations provide owners with more protection than other business structures, although forming a corporation is a more complex process.

Choose a Name → Appoint Directors → File Articles of Incorporation → Draft Bylaws → Hold a Meeting of the Board → Issue Stock → Obtain Licenses and Permits

S corporations must comply with the meeting and reporting requirements established for C corporations. Other characteristics of an S corporation are shown in ■ **FIGURE 6.8**.

How does an S corporation handle personal liability? The beauty of an S corporation is that it offers the best of both worlds: Profits and losses pass through to the shareholders, *and* the corporate structure provides some limitations on the personal liability of the owners. Although an owner's personal assets will be protected in case of a large claim against the corporation, the S corporation does not assume liability for an owner's personal wrongdoings. This is true for any corporate structure—whether it is a C corporation, an S corporation, or a limited liability company (discussed later). So, if an owner directly injures someone or intentionally does something fraudulent, illegal, or reckless that causes harm to the company or someone else, he or she will be held personally responsible and is not protected under the corporate umbrella.

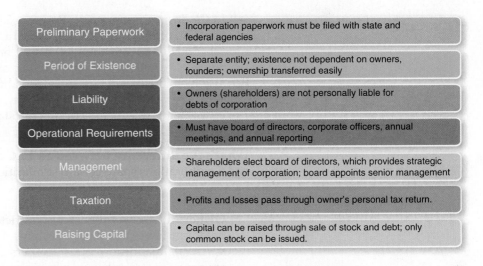

■ **FIGURE 6.8**
Characteristics of an S Corporation

For example, suppose William is the owner of a boating business that offers day cruises in the San Francisco Bay. Unfortunately, one foggy day, William's boat collides with another boat, causing his boat to capsize. Before leaving the dock, William knew there were not enough life jackets for each passenger. If any of his passengers were harmed because there were not enough life preservers, William most likely would be held personally liable for his negligent actions, even though he had structured his company as an S corporation. William not only would be in danger of losing the business but also may be forced into personal bankruptcy if his personal assets were needed to help satisfy the claims on the company.

Can any business elect to be an S corporation? There are certain qualification requirements a business must meet to elect an S corporation status. According to the Internal Revenue Code,[4] an S corporation must have the following characteristics:

- The company must not have more than 100 shareholders.
- Shareholders must be U.S. citizens or residents.
- The company must issue only one class of stock.
- The company must distribute proportionately all profits and losses to each shareholder based on each one's interest in the business.

S corporations are an appropriate business structure for small business owners who want the legal protection of a corporation but also want to be taxed as if they are sole proprietors or partners in a business. However, if a business does not meet the IRS standards required for an S corporation but the owner stills wants personal liability protection along with pass-through tax benefits, a limited liability company might be a suitable alternative corporate structure.

Limited Liability Companies

What is a limited liability company? A **limited liability company** (LLC) combines the corporate advantages of limited liability with the tax advantages inherent in sole proprietorships and partnerships. Similar to creating an S or a C corporation, an LLC requires articles of organization, so it is a separate legal entity (thus providing limited liability). But an LLC is free of many of the annual meetings and reporting requirements imposed on C and S corporations, so it is simpler to maintain.

LLCs do not issue stock. Rather, each member's ownership is determined by the value of his or her capital account. A capital account tracks the member's capital contributions to the LLC. Profit and loss distributions also flow through the capital accounts in proportion to the ownership percentage each member has. Because there are fewer corporate formalities, limited liability provisions, and the reporting of taxes at the individual level, an LLC is a popular business structure choice for many new businesses. Some states restrict the types of businesses that can form as LLCs. Other characteristics of an LLC are outlined in ■ **FIGURE 6.9**.

What's the difference between an LLC and an S corporation? Although LLCs and S corporations share certain similarities, there are several differences between the two:

- **Ownership.** S corporations are restricted as to the number of owners the company can have, but LLCs can have an unlimited number of owners (called *members*). In addition, LLC members are not limited to just U.S. residents and are not subject to other ownership restrictions imposed on S corporations.

- **Perpetual life.** When a member leaves an LLC, the LLC must dissolve, unless all remaining members agree to continue the business. Some states require a dissolution date be listed in an LLC's articles of organization. Consequently, an LLC has a limited life span.

- **Stock transfer.** Stock in an S corporation, like a C corporation, is freely transferable, whereas the ownership interest in an LLC is not, and the transfer generally requires the approval of other members.

- **Profit and loss distributions.** An LLC can allocate its profits in whatever way its owners agree on, but the profits of an S corporation are allocated in proportion to a shareholder's interest. So, if two members own a business and one contributes 75 percent of the capital but does only 25 percent of the work whereas the other member contributes 25 percent of the capital but does 75 percent of the work, the two members can decide that a fair allocation of profits is 50/50. This arrangement would be possible with an LLC, but with an S corporation, the profits would need to be distributed based on the 75/25 ownership interest in the business.

- **Owner and employee benefits.** An S corporation can offer fringe benefits to its owners, such as qualified retirement plans, employee-provided vehicles, and educational expenses related to the job. Because S corporations have stock, they can also offer their employees stock options and other stock bonus incentives. LLCs are limited in the benefits their members can be offered, and because LLCs do not issue stock, they cannot offer stock benefits to their employees.

What kinds of businesses are best suited as an LLC? There are many types of businesses in which an LLC structure is appropriate. LLCs may be a good choice for start-up businesses, not only for the tax benefits but also because it is easier to obtain financing because the number of investors (owners) is not restricted.

Comparing Forms of Ownership

Which form of ownership is best? There is no one entity that works for everyone. A certified public accountant or a tax attorney should be able to help you choose the right structure for your business.

■ **FIGURE 6.9**
Characteristics of an LLC

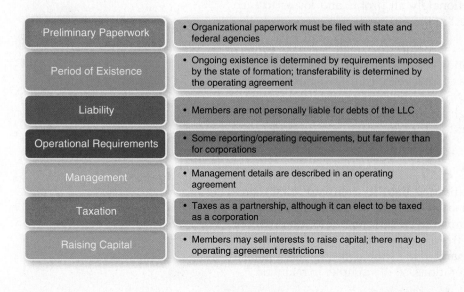

Preliminary Paperwork	• Organizational paperwork must be filed with state and federal agencies
Period of Existence	• Ongoing existence is determined by requirements imposed by the state of formation; transferability is determined by the operating agreement
Liability	• Members are not personally liable for debts of the LLC
Operational Requirements	• Some reporting/operating requirements, but far fewer than for corporations
Management	• Management details are described in an operating agreement
Taxation	• Taxes as a partnership, although it can elect to be taxed as a corporation
Raising Capital	• Members may sell interests to raise capital; there may be operating agreement restrictions

	Sole Proprietor	General Partnership	C Corp	S Corp	LLC
Preliminary paperwork required for business startup			☆	☆	☆
Business ceases after owners departure or death	☆	☆			
Owners have limited liability for business debts and obligations			☆	☆	☆
May have an unlimited number of owners		☆	☆		☆
Must have board of directors, corporate officers, annual meetings, and annual reporting			☆	☆	☆
Owners can report business profit and loss on their personal tax returns		☆		☆	☆
May issue shares of stock			☆	☆	

■ **FIGURE 6.10**
Comparing the Forms of Business Ownership

The important considerations are the operational, legal, and tax aspects of each structure as they apply to your unique situation. ■ **FIGURE 6.10** shows how the most common forms of ownership stack up to one another.

Brandon and Sonya were looking to form a partnership structure around their inherited real estate properties, but they have been advised that a partnership will not protect their personal assets if something terrible goes wrong and they are sued by a tenant. The siblings decided an LLC would be the best choice, as it would give them the protection of a corporation but the ability to report the business income through personal tax returns.

Not-for-Profit and Cooperatives pp. 173–175

While attending college, Darrell Hammond had volunteered to make playgrounds. Several years later, he read about two inner-city children who had suffocated while playing in an abandoned car and realized that if the children had had a safe place to play, the tragedy could have been avoided. Shortly afterward, Darrell and his friend Dawn Hutchinson built a community playground for a day of service they led, and a year later they founded KaBOOM!, a not-for-profit organization that helps communities build playgrounds.[5] How could he structure KaBOOM! to protect himself financially, gain credibility, and continue to serve the community? ■

Source: Nuwatphoto/Fotolia.

The goal of some business ventures is not to generate a profit but rather to make a difference in people's lives and their communities. These businesses can be

educational, scientific, religious, or charitable. What forms of businesses do organizations such as these use, and what are their benefits and drawbacks? We'll answer these questions next.

Not-for-Profit Organizations

What is a not-for-profit organization? Legally, a **not-for-profit organization** (or nonprofit organization) is a business that does not seek a profit. Not-for-profit organizations generate their revenues primarily through fund-raising and donations. After paying normal operating expenses—such as salaries, rent, and purchases of inventory, supplies, materials, and equipment—a not-for-profit organization uses the remaining revenue for the business's declared cause and mission rather than paying stockholders. Not-for-profit organizations must apply for tax-exempt status with the federal government and sometimes with the states in which they operate. To maintain their tax-exempt status, not-for-profit organizations must demonstrate that a substantial portion of their income or revenue is spent on services to achieve their goals.

Can not-for-profit organizations act like corporations? Not-for-profit organizations are incorporated and, as such, are subject to most of the laws that govern for-profit corporations. Not-for-profit organizations receive limited liability protection when they become incorporated and are established as a separate legal entity. Similar to a for-profit corporation, a not-for-profit is required to hold board meetings and keep complete books and records. Not-for-profit organizations do not issue shares of stock, and their members (or owners) may not receive personal financial benefit from the organization's profits (other than salary as an employee). However, some not-for-profit organizations do provide employee benefits, such as health insurance. In addition, should the not-for-profit organization dissolve, the organization's assets must go to another not-for-profit organization with a similar mission.

Are there advantages to being tax exempt? An organization that has met the qualifications in section 501(c)(3) of the IRS code is considered a not-for-profit. It is therefore exempt from paying most federal and/or state corporate income taxes. It may also be exempt from state sales and property taxes. Not-for-profit organizations are also able to apply for grants and other public or private distributions and get discounts on postal rates and other services. People who donate to not-for-profits can deduct their donations on their tax returns. This encourages people to contribute to not-for-profits.

Cooperatives

What structure would be best for groups of businesses with common goals? A **cooperative** is a business not owned by investors but rather governed by members who use or benefit from the products or services provided by the organization. The members of a cooperative have common interests and needs and can be individuals, such as individual farmers in an agricultural cooperative, or businesses, such as individual hardware stores, florists, or hotels that come together to form it. For example, Florida's Natural Growers is a cooperative of citrus growers who own their own groves in Florida. A group of growers formed the cooperative in 1933 to market their crops.[7]

How are cooperatives structured? Members are the most important part of a cooperative. They buy shares to help finance the cooperative, elect directors to manage the cooperative, and create and amend the bylaws that govern the cooperative. Cooperatives depend on their members to volunteer for projects supported by the cooperative and serve on boards and committees. The board of directors in a cooperative appoints committees for specific purposes, such as member relations and special audits. The board of directors also hires the cooperative manager who handles the daily affairs.

Are cooperatives not-for-profits? Although their members may be motivated by profits, the cooperatives themselves are not. Any profits made by a cooperative are reinvested in the organization to continue to maintain it and improve its functioning. Or, the profits are returned to members in proportion to their use of the cooperative, not their investment or their ownership share.

Cooperatives are incorporated under state co-op statutes as businesses organized to serve their members. The status of a cooperative is also recognized by state and federal tax codes. Consequently, any distributed profits to its member-owners are taxed at the owner's level.

What are the advantages of cooperatives? Cooperatives form because a group of individuals or businesses become dissatisfied with how the marketplace is providing the goods or services they need, the prices at which they are being sold, or their quality. By uniting, the members have more bargaining power to negotiate within the marketplace and enjoy reduced costs.[8]

Some businesses don't fit the mold of a sole proprietorship, partnership, or corporation due to the underlying cause or purpose of the business. When this occurs, the business's owners might form not-for-profit organizations or cooperatives. Darrell Hammond did not care about his personal profit; he just wanted to create an organization that would help improve communities, so he found that forming a not-for-profit organization was best for him.

Mergers and Acquisitions pp. 175–178

Google began in 1998 as a search engine, but nearly two decades later, the company has expanded to include many other businesses. Today, Google makes its mark as a Web browser (Google Chrome), mapping and directional service (Google Maps and Google Earth), online productivity and communications center (Google Docs and Gmail) and social media facilitator (Google+). In addition, Google runs the Android mobile platform, Picasa image manager, Blogger, and YouTube. How did Google expand into all these products and services? ■

Source: Photoedit/Alamy; NetPics/Alamy; Eric Carr/Alamy; Eric Carr/Alamy; Anatolii Babii/Alamy; Ingvar Björk/Alamy; PhotoEdit/Alamy.

Sometimes, in the evolution of a business or in response to market forces, companies seek opportunities to expand by adding new product lines, spreading out into different geographic areas, or growing the company to increase their competitive advantage. Often, product or market expansion is done gradually by slowly adding new product lines or penetrating new areas. However, it takes time and money to research and develop new products or to locate and build in new areas. Sometimes, especially to remain competitive, a business needs to expand more quickly. In that case, it may be easier to integrate another established business through the process of mergers or acquisitions. Acquiring or merging with another company are strategies companies can use to gain synergy and increase their competitiveness.

Mergers versus Acquisitions

What is the difference between a merger and an acquisition? The terms *merger* and *acquisition* are often used interchangeably, but there is a difference. When two companies come together cooperatively to form one company, a **merger** takes place. Generally, a merger implies that the two companies involved are about the same size and have mutually agreed to form a new combined company. An **acquisition**, on the other hand, occurs when one company completely buys out another company. In some instances, companies claim a merger has occurred, but in reality, one company has acquired the other. The term *merger* has a better connotation than acquisition and therefore is used to allow the acquired company to "save face." Often, the combined organization reflects the names of the individual companies, such as when Chase Manhattan Corp. acquired JPMorgan to form JPMorganChase & Company. In other situations, just one company name is kept. For example, when American Airlines and USAirways merged, the combined airline decided to operate under American Airlines. Sometimes, a completely new name is derived, such as when Bell Atlantic acquired GTE to form Verizon Communications.

Are all mergers and acquisitions mutually desired by both companies? Often, acquisitions are friendly, as was the case when Google purchased Android in 2005. At the time, Android was just a start-up but had demonstrated its ability to produce a working operating system for mobile devices. Postmerger, Android continues to be run by its cofounder Andy Rubin but benefits from the significant resources that Google offers. In turn, Google benefits by having a viable mobile operating system that it uses to challenge industry giants Apple and Microsoft.

Some acquisitions are "unfriendly." An unfriendly acquisition occurs when one company tries to purchase another company against the wishes of its shareholders or managers. Unfriendly acquisitions are referred to as *hostile takeovers*. In an unfriendly acquisition or hostile takeover, the acquiring firm makes a *tender offer*, which is an offer to buy the target company's stock at a price higher than its current value. The higher price is offered to persuade the shareholders of the target company to sell their stock.

Another method of acquiring a company against its wishes is through a *proxy fight* in which the acquiring company tries to persuade the shareholders of the target company to vote out the firm's existing managers and replace them with managers who are sympathetic to the goals of the acquiring company. This is the strategy Microsoft pursued when it unsuccessfully tried to take over Yahoo! in 2008.[9]

Some takeovers that are initiated by an outside group of investors, employees, or management are financed with debt. The acquiring group borrows as much as 90 percent of the funds necessary for the acquisition, using the assets of the acquired company as collateral. This type of transaction is called a *leveraged buyout* (LBO). LBOs can be either friendly or hostile, and companies of all sizes have been the targets of LBO transactions. Some of the more recent and largest LBOs involved the Hertz Corporation, Metro-Goldwyn-Mayer, and Toys "R" Us. While LBOs may be a good strategy in some instances, the practice has received much criticism because jobs are often lost due to LBOs, and the companies often fail due to the high debt loads resulting from the LBO.

Advantages of Mergers and Acquisitions

Why do mergers and acquisitions occur? *Synergy* is the business buzzword often used to justify a merger or an acquisition. **Synergy** is the effect achieved when two companies combine and the result is better than each company could achieve individually. Synergistic value is created when the new company can realize operating or financial economies of scale. Combined firms often lower costs by trimming redundancies in staff, sharing resources, and obtaining discounts accessible only to a larger firm.

In other instances, synergy is achieved by combining resources that could not have been created independently by either party. Such was the case with the merger of satellite radio providers Sirius and XM. Each satellite radio provider had exclusive contracts with different sports programmers. Customers were having a hard time choosing between one and the other. The merger gives customers the benefit of both.

Is competition a driving force for mergers and acquisitions? Achieving a greater competitive advantage is another reason mergers and acquisitions take place. Often, companies join to become a more dominant force in their market. For example, the merger between Office Depot and Office Max will improve the company's ability to compete with Staples, the market leader, as well as with online and discount stores, such as Amazon.com and Walmart.[10]

AOL-Time Warner Merger

OFF THE MARK

Although it took place more than a decade ago, the merger between America Online (AOL), an Internet services company, and Time Warner, a media and communications company, is still viewed as one of the worst mergers in U.S. history. Valued at $111 billion, the merger also was (and still is) the largest merger in the United States. At the time, it was believed that the combination of an Internet giant and a media behemoth would, in the words of Gerald Levin, then the CEO of Time Warner, "create unprecedented and instantaneous access to every form of media and to unleash immense possibilities for economic growth, human understanding and creative expression."[11] According to AOL cofounder Stephen Case, the merger was "a historic moment in which new media has truly come of age."[12]

However, the deal began to sour almost immediately, as it was soon quite apparent that the two companies had very different cultures. In addition, AOL, "the crown jewel of the transaction," ran into great financial difficulty when the dot-com bubble burst only months after the merger.[13] Moreover, investigations by the SEC and the Department of Justice revealed that AOL had been improperly inflating its advertising revenue. In 2009, Time Warner spun off AOL as an independent company.

Do companies add value to their product lines by merging? Many times, larger companies acquire smaller companies for their innovativeness, and a smaller company will agree to merge or be acquired if it feels it wouldn't have the opportunity to go public and couldn't survive alone otherwise. Much of Google's growth can be attributed to their innovative creativity within the company, but some has also come from its acquisitions of small, innovative companies, such as Feedburner, Like.com, Applied Semantics, Postini,[14] and drone maker Titan Aerospace.[15]

Types of Mergers

Are there different types of mergers? The rationale and strategy behind every merger is different. However, as ■ **FIGURE 6.11** shows, mergers fall into a number of categories that are distinguished by the relationship between the two companies merging:

- **Horizontal merger.** A merger in which two companies sell the same types of products and are in direct competition with each other. The merger between Exxon and Mobil and the merger between USAirways and American Airlines are examples.

- **Vertical merger.** A merger between two companies that have a company/customer relationship or a company/supplier relationship, such as Walt Disney and Pixar or eBay and PayPal.

- **Product extension merger.** A merger between two companies selling different but related products in the same market, such as the merger between Adobe and Macromedia.

- **Market extension merger.** A merger between two companies that sell the same products in different markets, such as when NationsBank, which had operations primarily on the East Coast and in southern areas of the United States, merged with Bank of America, whose prime business was on the West Coast.

- **Conglomeration.** A merger between two companies that have no common business areas but instead merge to obtain diversification. For example, Citicorp, a banking services firm, and Travelers Group Inc., an insurance underwriting company, combined to form one of the world's largest financial services group, Citigroup Inc.

Horizontal Merger

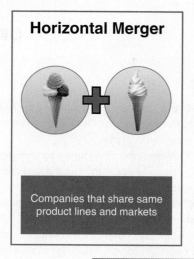

Companies that share same product lines and markets

Vertical Merger

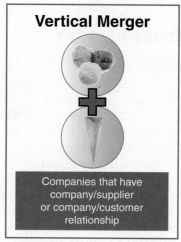

Companies that have company/supplier or company/customer relationship

Product Extension Merger

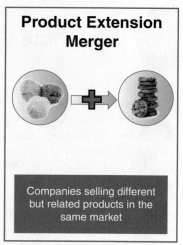

Companies selling different but related products in the same market

Market Extension Merger

Companies selling same products to different markets

Conglomeration

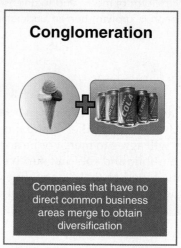

Companies that have no direct common business areas merge to obtain diversification

■ **FIGURE 6.11**
Different Types of Mergers

Disadvantages of Mergers

Are there disadvantages with mergers? Despite the perceived advantages of mergers, more than one-half of all mergers fail completely or don't live up to their financial expectations.[16] The primary culprit of a failed merger is poor integration following the transaction. After an exhausting process that may cause top executives to take their eyes off business, little energy or motivation may be left to plan and manage how the two companies will come together to work as one. Although cost cutting may be the initial primary focus of some mergers, revenues and profits may ultimately suffer if day-to-day activities are neglected. Additionally, the corporate cultures or the organizations may clash, and communications may break down if the new division of responsibilities is vague. Conflicts may also arise due to divided loyalties, hidden agendas, or power struggles within the newly combined management team. Employees may be nervous because most mergers result in the elimination of jobs and more turnover if employees whose jobs are not being eliminated seek employment in more stable organizations.

Google, like many technology companies, acquired other companies, helping to extend and complement Google's existing product line. Some acquisitions didn't work out, but others did. Google, once just a company with a great search engine, is striving to maintain its market dominance and maybe then some by acquiring firms in different markets.

Summary

1 What are the advantages and disadvantages of a sole proprietorship? (pp. 160–163)

- A **sole proprietorship** (p. 160) is a business owned and usually operated by a single individual.

- The sole proprietorship is a common form of business ownership because it is the easiest to establish, but there are both strengths and weaknesses inherent in this business form.

- The advantage of establishing a business as a sole proprietorship is that there are no formal, legal requirements for starting the business, and the revenues and expenses are reported directly on the business owner's personal income tax return.

- The primary disadvantage of a sole proprietorship is that the owner's personal and business assets are at risk in the event of a business catastrophe.

2 What are the advantages and disadvantages of a partnership and a partnership agreement? (pp. 163–167)

- A **partnership** (p. 163) is a business structure that is easy to establish and has no formal, legal requirements.

- In a partnership, two or more individuals share aspects of the business, including its financial management and sales and marketing responsibilities. Income and expenses flow directly through each partner's individual tax return.

- People entering into a partnership should create a **partnership agreement** (p. 164), which is a formal document that outlines the responsibilities of each partner and how the business's profits will be divided and disputes among the partners settled.

- Problems can occur when partners do not agree on the nature of the business or have different work ethics.

- Partners' personal and business assets are at risk, with each partner being solely liable for any part of the business. Responsibility is not limited to each partner's financial contribution to the business.

- A **general partnership** (p. 165) is an arrangement in which all partners have equal liability. In a **limited partnership** (p. 166), some partners do not participate in the daily operations of the business, and their liability is limited to the amount of capital they contributed to the business.

- A *limited liability partnership* (LLP) protects the partners from any debt or liability incurred by the business as well as each partner from the liability of another partner. A partner in an LLP is only personally liable for his or her own negligence.

3 How is a corporation formed, and how does it compare with sole proprietorships and partnerships? (pp. 167–170)

- **Corporations** (p. 167) are businesses structured as separate legal entities. Corporations are structured with different levels of managers, including shareholders, board of directors, and corporate officers, such as the **chief executive officer** (CEO) (p. 169), the **chief financial officer** (CFO) (p. 169), the **chief operating officer** (COO) (p. 169), and **first-line managers** (p. 169).

- Corporations differ from sole proprietorships and partnerships in the following ways:

  - Corporations are difficult to set up.

  - Corporations require much ongoing paperwork, including annual reports, corporate minutes, and formal financial records.

  - Corporations must file separate tax returns.

  - Corporations can sue and be sued.

  - Corporations protect an owner's personal assets.

4 What are the major differences between a C corporation, an S corporation, and an LLC? (pp. 170–173)

- Both **S corporations** (p. 170) and **C corporations** (p. 167) offer the protection of limited liability, but S corporations allow their shareholders to flow the corporate revenues and expenses through their personal tax returns so they don't face double taxation.

- S corporations face certain restrictions, including having no more than 100 shareholders, requiring shareholders to be residents of the United States, allowing for the issuance of only one class of stock, and basing profits and losses on the proportional interest of each shareholder.

- The corporate structure **a limited liability company (LLC)** (p. 171) offers the protection of limited liability like an S corporation does. LLCs differ from S corporations because they can have unlimited members, they must dissolve when any member leaves, and profits do not have to be distributed in direct proportion to a member's financial contribution.

5 What are the characteristics of not-for-profit organizations and cooperatives? (pp. 173–175)

- **Not-for-profit organizations** (p. 174) are corporations whose purpose is to serve the public interest rather than to seek to make a profit. Not-for-profit organizations are tax exempt, and donors to the organization can deduct their contributions on their tax returns.

- **Cooperatives** (pp. 174) are businesses that are owned not by outside investors but are governed by members who use its products and services.

- Cooperatives are motivated to provide services or goods to people with common interests or needs.
- All profits generated by the cooperative are returned to the members in direct proportion to their share of ownership.
- Cooperatives use the benefit of the power of their groups' to negotiate within the marketplace.

6 What are the different types of mergers and acquisitions, and why do they occur? (pp. 175–178)

- Firms sometimes use mergers and acquisitions to legally combine their companies for the purposes of achieving **synergy** (pp. 176) and economies of scale, expanding their product lines and geographic areas they serve, or gaining a competitive advantage.
- An **acquisition** (pp. 175) occurs when one company buys another company outright. The purchased company ceases to exist and starts to operate under the buying company's name and management. Acquisitions can be friendly (mutually agreed on) or unfriendly

(one company buys the other against the wishes of the management and/or the owners).

- A **merger** (pp. 175) occurs when two companies of similar size mutually agree to combine to form a new company. Some types of mergers are as follows:
  - **Horizontal mergers** (pp. 177): Two companies that share the same product lines and are in direct competition with each other merge.
  - **Vertical merger** (pp. 177): Two companies that have a company/customer relationship or a company/supplier relationship merge.
  - **Product extension merger** (pp. 177): Two companies selling different but related products in the same market merge.
  - **Market extension merger** (pp. 177): Two companies that sell the same products in different markets merge.
  - **Conglomeration** (pp. 177): Two companies that have no common business areas merge to obtain diversification.

Key Terms

acquisition (p. 175)	first-line managers (p. 169)	partnership (p. 163)
board of directors (p. 169)	general partners (p. 166)	partnership agreement (p. 164)
C corporation (p. 167)	general partnership (p. 165)	product extension merger (p. 177)
capital (p. 164)	horizontal merger (p. 177)	publicly owned corporation (p. 168)
chief executive officer (p. 169)	liability (p. 161)	S corporation (p. 170)
chief financial officer (p. 169)	limited liability company (p. 171)	shareholder (p. 168)
chief operating officer (p. 169)	limited partner (p. 166)	sole proprietorship (p. 160)
conglomeration (p. 177)	limited partnership (p. 166)	stockholder (p. 168)
cooperatives (p. 174)	market extension merger (p. 177)	synergy (p. 176)
corporation (p. 167)	merger (p. 175)	unlimited liability (p. 161)
double taxation (p. 170)	not-for-profit organization (p. 174)	vertical merger (p. 177)

MyBizLab
Go to **mybizlab.com** to complete the problems marked with this icon .

Self-Test

Multiple Choice *You can find the answers on the last page of this book.*

6-1 Omar and Sam are physical therapists who work together. Their office is on the first floor of a building Omar owns. They need protection of their personal assets. Which business structure would best suit their company?

a. A general partnership

b. A sole proprietorship

c. A not-for-profit organization

d. An LLC

6-2 Why might a potential business owner want to establish a business as a sole proprietorship?

a. The owner can use personal assets to satisfy any business liabilities.

b. The owner can take into consideration the opinions of other business owners.

c. The owner can generate a separate tax return for business expenses.

d. The owner is not required to file legal paperwork to start up the business.

6-3 Trudy and Yvonne have come together to run Salford Children's Center. The center receives state and federal grants, and whatever is left over is put back into the center to improve and expand its services. Salford Children's Center would best be described as a(n)

a. partnership.

b. LLC.

c. not-for-profit organization.

d. sole proprietorship.

6-4 Jackson Eats is a partnership owned by Jesse and Robert Jackson. They need additional capital to expand to a new location, so they have decided to bring in Sean, who will not only contribute some capital but will also manage the new restaurant. Sean would best be considered as a(n)

a. general partner.

b. limited partner.

c. owner.

d. None of the above

6-5 Which of the following is *not* an advantage of a C corporation?

a. The owner's personal assets are protected.

b. The owner can raise greater sources of funds by selling shares of ownership.

c. The corporation can continue to exist even if the owner leaves the business.

d. There is little paperwork involved.

6-6 Warren Buffet runs Berkshire Hathaway which owns companies such as GEICO insurance, Dairy Queen, Fruit of the Loom, and Helzberg Diamonds. Berkshire Hathaway is considered to be which of the following?

a. A conglomeration

b. An acquisition

c. A merger

d. A cooperative

6-7 A group of people elected by a firm's shareholders to oversee the operation of a corporation are

a. the firm's CEO, CFO and COO.

b. the firm's board of directors.

c. the firm's line managers.

d. All of the above

6-8 Which is a benefit of cooperatives?

a. The power of the group enables them to negotiate for goods and services at favorable prices.

b. They are exempt from paying federal and state taxes.

c. They are established to serve the public interest rather than make a profit.

d. They provide services to people with a variety of interests and needs.

6-9 If Mom's outdoor clothing store combined with Dad's camping equipment store to form Mom & Dad's Outdoor Store, which of the following best describes the type of transaction that occurred between the two companies?

a. A vertical merger

b. A product extension merger

c. A horizontal merger

d. A conglomeration

6-10 The management team of Company A decides to offer to buy the stock from all the shareholders of Company B at a higher price than current market value. Company A is launching a

a. proxy fight.

b. tender offer.

c. friendly acquisition.

d. friendly takeover.

True/False *You can find the answers on the last page of this book.*

6-11 Any business can elect to be an S corporation.
☐ True or ☐ False

6-12 Liabilities do *not* include losses associated with breaches of contract or from damages.
☐ True or ☐ False

6-13 A small, privately owned company can be structured as a corporation.
☐ True or ☐ False

6-14 A significant disadvantage of forming a corporation is the amount of paperwork and reporting it requires.
☐ True or ☐ False

6-15 A partnership agreement should include procedures that outline how a partner's departure from the business will be handled as well as how new partners are to be brought in.
☐ True or ☐ False

Critical Thinking Questions

6-16 Why might it be important to structure your business as a C corporation, even if you are the only person running the business?

6-17 What are the similarities and differences between a general partnership and a limited partnership?

6-18 Approximately 70 percent of all businesses are sole proprietorships. Why is sole proprietorship a popular form of business ownership? What are the circumstances when it might be important to consider a different form of ownership?

Team Time

WHAT'S THE PLAN?

Imagine that you work for the U.S. Small Business Administration and have the opportunity to advise new business owners on the form of ownership their businesses should take. Form groups of three to five people and choose one of the business ideas below. Work as a group to create an outline of a business plan for each business idea (see Mini Chapter 2 for some sample outlines). What kind of business forms would you suggest for each idea and why? Be sure to consider the potential risks and liabilities, the potential income tax situations, and the current and future investment needs of each business. Assume that in five years, the business needed additional capital to expand by adding a new building in a different location. Would your business structure support raising the necessary capital? Why or why not?

Business Ideas

- Roofing and siding company
- Ice cream parlor
- Yoga instruction
- Lawn mowing company
- Clothing donation company

Process

Meet as a group to discuss your business idea. Remember that you must prepare an outline of a business plan. Use what you know about the forms of business ownership to create the business plan.

Step 1. Prepare an individual report that explains the form of ownership your business should take and why.

Step 2. Determine who will be the group's primary spokesperson for your business plan.

Step 3. Your group will have five minutes to present your recommendations.

Step 4. After each group has presented, discuss any differences of opinion about the proposed business structures.

Ethics and Corporate Social Responsibility

CODE OF ETHICS

Many companies establish a code of ethics or a code of values. These codes are used to communicate to all the company's stakeholders—directors, management, employees, suppliers, and customers—a company's values and business style. Kraft, for example, has 10 rules of ethical behavior that all employees must follow. Verizon's code of ethics is a lengthy document outlining a variety of rules and guidelines.

Questions for Discussion

6-19 Research other codes of ethics from three different organizations. List any common values sited in these codes. Note any differences between organizations and comment on why you think the unique codes are necessary for that particular organization.

6-20 Do you think establishing a code of ethics is sufficient to ensure ethical behavior in an organization? What other forms of action or behavior might be necessary to ensure ethical business behavior?

Web Exercises

6-21 Business Combinations

Look on the Internet for a current example of a business merger, takeover, or acquisition. Explain the circumstances of the event. What companies are involved? Was the event friendly or unfriendly? What are the reasons given for the combination? What is your opinion of this business combination? Do you think it is a good business decision? Why or why not?

6-22 Student-Friendly Businesses

You have decided to start your own business. You want it to be something you can do while you're still a student. Research on the Web ideas for small businesses for students. Describe at least three different ideas and include what form of business ownership you would use to structure each business.

6-23 The Perfect Partner

Search the Web for information on how to pick the perfect business partner. Write a list of rules for picking the perfect business partner based on what you have learned. What factors should be taken into account? What can you do to avoid trouble in the future?

6-24 Plan with the End in Mind

Beginning a business requires a lot of planning, but even still, the business often fails. However, most business owners do not have an "exit plan" in mind when they start the venture. Research the main causes of business failures and what kind of exit strategies can be set in place at the beginning to ease the pain if the business needs to close.

6-25 Cooperatives and You!

Can you identify and or manage a cooperative? Go to www.coops.wisc.edu and play the "Find the Co-op" and "You're the Boss!" games. Write a brief summary of what you learned while playing both games.

MyBizLab

Go to **mybizlab.com** for Auto-graded writing questions as well as the following Assisted-graded writing questions:

⊘ **6-26** Discuss the various types of mergers and give examples of each.

⊘ **6-27** Describe a corporation's organizational structure. What are the three basic groups, and what are their roles?

References

1. Nan Mooney, "When Good Friends Make Poor Colleagues," *Inc. Magazine*, September 2006, www.inc.com/resources/women/articles/20060901/nmooney.html.
2. From Ambrose Bierce, "Corporation," in *The Devil's Dictionary* (New York: Neale Publishing, 1911).
3. A/N Group Inc., "Tax Facts for Individuals—2010," www.smbiz.com/sbrl001.html#pis10.
4. Internal Revenue Service, "S Corporations," www.irs.gov/businesses/small/article/0,,id=98263,00.html.
5. "Our Story," http://kaboom.org/about_kaboom/our_story.
6. From "The 2013 NPT Top 100," *The Non Profit Times*, www.thenonprofittimes.com/wp-content/uploads/2013/11/11-1-13_Top100.pdf.
7. "Florida's Natural," www.floridasnatural.com.
8. National Cooperative Business Association, "About Co-ops," www.ncba.coop/abcoop.cfm.
9. Intology, "Intology—Intelligent Technology NewsComputers Technology Internet Arts Business Science Sports," April 29, 2008, www.intology.com/business-finance/microsoft-vs-yahoo-hostile-take-over-explained.
10. "Office Depot and OfficeMax Complete Merger," http://news.officedepot.com/press-release/corporatefinancial-news/office-depot-and-officemax-complete-merger.
11. Gerald Levin, quoted in "AOL & Time Warner Will Merge to Create the World's First Internet-Age Media & Communications Company," January 10, 2000, www.timewarner.com.
12. Stephen Case, quoted in "AOL & Time Warner Will Merge to Create the World's First Internet-Age Media & Communications Company."
13. Ted Leoniss, quoted in Tim Arango, "How the AOL-Time Warner Merger Went So Wrong," *New York Times*, January 11, 2010, www.nytimes.com.
14. Matt Rosoff, "Google's 15 Biggest Acquisitions and What Happened to Them," *Business Insider*, March 2011, www.businessinsider.com/googles-15-biggest-acquisitions-and-what-happened-to-them-2011-3?op=1.
15. McNeal, Greg. "Google's Acquisition of Drone Maker Titan is About Imagery and Internet," *Forbes*, 14 April 2014. Retrieved from http://www.forbes.com/sites/gregorymcneal/2014/04/14/fight-for-internet-drones-heats-up-as-google-buys-drone-company-originally-sought-by-facebook.
16. Cartwright, Susan. Why Mergers Fail and How to Prevent It, *QFinance.com*. Retrieved from www.qfinance.com/mergers-and-acquisitions-best-practice/why-mergers-fail-and-how-to-prevent-it?page=1.

Chapter 2

Constructing an Effective Business Plan

From the moment you received money for mowing your neighbor's lawn or baby-sitting your neighbor's child, you've been interested in starting your own business. But where do you begin? Do you purchase business cards? Do you create and distribute flyers? Although these might be good ways to get your business moving, they are not the first things you should do when starting a business. The Small Business Association (SBA) suggests that the very first step in starting a business is *planning*. Writing a business plan is usually the first step in that planning process. A business plan is a written document that details a proposed or existing venture, describing the vision, current status, the markets in which it operates, and the current and projected results of a business.

Traditionally, a potential business owner writes a business plan *before* a business is launched, but it can be written after a business has been established. In some instances, and especially in industries in which change occurs rapidly, a business opportunity might be lost if you do not start operations immediately; you may not have time to take the weeks or months often required to write a business plan. In this situation, you should still begin by answering a few discrete and pointed questions, such as those shown in ■ **FIGURE M2.1**. This will help you determine whether the business you're pursuing will be worth the effort. Eventually, a formal business plan should be written to more thoroughly define the goals and objectives of the business and the means to achieve them.

Planning—It's Never Too Late

In 1958, college-aged brothers Dan and Frank Carney borrowed $600 from their mother to open a pizza parlor in Wichita, Kansas. This venture marked the inception of the Pizza Hut empire. The brothers had neither a formal business plan nor a clear vision of the path their business would take. In fact, the Carneys simply gave away pizza on their opening night to garner the public's interest. Although their gimmick was impulsive, it worked. Less than a year later, the boys incorporated and opened their first franchise unit in Topeka, Kansas. Within the next 10 years, more than 150 franchises opened nationwide, and one international franchise opened in Canada. However, in 1970, the company's growth became explosive. Pizza Hut went public, and the brothers quickly became overwhelmed. "We about lost control of the operations," Frank Carney said. "Then we figured out that we had to learn how to plan."[1] Ultimately, Frank and Dan developed a plan that kept operations constant and under control. They also created a corporate strategy that enticed PepsiCo to purchase Pizza Hut in 1977. At that time, Pizza Hut sales had reached $436 million a year.[2] The Carneys' story is a success; however, if they had developed a clear business plan from the beginning, they may have been better prepared to handle their company's incredible growth.

Source: Feng Yu/Alamy.

Step One: Write a mission statement. To help explain the purpose of your business answer the following questions:
- Why should this business exist?
- Who will be the target customer?
- How will the customer benefit from the business?

Step Two: Find the key to your success. To help figure out how your business will be successful, answer the following questions:
- Where will your operations take place?
- What three or four critical factors will be essential to your business's survival?
- What obstacles will you have to overcome?

Step Three: Perform a simple market analysis. To help determine how many potential customers your business will have, answer the following questions:
- At which businesses are your customers current patrons?
- Who are your main competitors?
- Are there enough potential customers?

Step Four: Perform a simple breakeven analysis. To help figure out how much money your business must produce to cover your costs, answer the following questions:
- What is the total cost of your operations?
- How many units of sales will you need to cover your costs?
- Are your sales goals realistic?

Step Five: Really think about it. To help decide if you are prepared to start a business, answer the following questions:
- Do you feel ready to start a business?
- Are you willing to commit long hours to making your business work?
- Have you discussed your idea with a business counselor or coach?

Considering your answers to these questions, do you still feel prepared to start a business? If so, get started, but find time to create a thorough business plan to use as a guide as your business develops.

The Purpose of a Plan

A business plan is your "business story"—a story that you will tell to a wide variety of people, from personal friends and casual acquaintances to potential partners, suppliers, customers, and investors. There are three purposes to writing a business plan: development, management, and communication.

- **Development.** Writing down your business plan solidifies and defines your intentions. It forces you to think through many aspects of a business that might otherwise be overlooked, identify roadblocks and obstacles, and determine ways to resolve or avoid them. Business plans can be used to get the entire management team and perhaps the employees of the company to understand where the company is and where it is heading.

- **Management.** Of course, the goal of most businesses is to make money, so a business plan should summarize how a business opportunity will translate into profits. A business plan also helps in the management of a company. Because it is a living document, it should be modified as the business changes and reaches certain milestones. It can be used to track and monitor the progress of the company as well as evaluate projections with respect to the actual performance.

Although Pizza Hut owners Dan and Frank Carney launched a successful business without a formal business plan, they soon found that planning was necessary for continued success.
Source: Glyn Thomas/Alamy.

185

- **Communication.** A business plan is often used to attract investors or obtain loans. It can also be used to attract strategic business partners, additions to the management team, or high-quality employees. As such, the plan needs to communicate that you have taken an objective and realistic view of your company and thought through all the potential problems and determined reasonable alternatives.

While some business plans are lengthy, formal documents that can take weeks or months to prepare, others are short, informal outlines. Regardless of when or how it is written, a business plan is a crucial part of a successful business operation.

Business Plan Competitions

The Massachusetts Institute of Technology is the site of one of the most famous and lucrative business plan competitions.
Source: Philip Scalia/Alamy.

A business plan can help you determine whether your idea is feasible, to pitch your idea to others, and, in some cases, help you win a bit of necessary start-up cash. Many top business schools and colleges in the United States offer business plan competitions, with cash prizes that range from $10,000 to $100,000.

Business plan competitions, once deemed as the culmination of an academic exercise, are now sources of serious money. Rice University hosts at business plan competition that offers over $1 million in prizes. The Massachusetts Institute of Technology Entrepreneurship Competition has launched over 160 companies. By bringing together new thinkers who are armed with a detailed business plan and venture capitalists, these competitive events can be win/win for all.

Before the Business Plan: Finding the Right Fit

Before you begin to think about writing a business plan, you should do some soul-searching to determine your own goals and objectives and whether they match those of the business that you've imagined. You might want to visit the SBA's website to find questionnaires and quizzes that can help you focus your ideas.

Not everyone wants to be (or can be) the next Bill Gates. Some individuals are quite content running a successful business that consists of a few employees and that never sees revenues in the millions. However, some ambitious entrepreneurs would like to have their ideas realized on a much larger scale. Regardless of the size of business you would like to own, it is important to articulate your own personal business plan by answering questions like the following:

- Do you want to have a balance between your business life and your personal life? Or is it okay for your business to be your life?

- How do you define "success"? Is it a monetary goal, a production goal, or a lifestyle goal?

- What is your time line for "success"? Do you want to achieve it quickly, or is it acceptable to work slowly toward graduated markers of success?

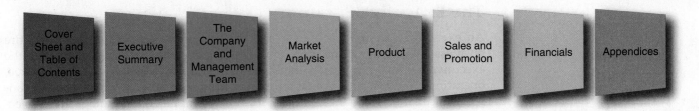

■ **FIGURE M2.2**
Basic Components of a Business Plan

Determining the answers to these questions will help to crystallize your focus, realize what your priorities are, and clarify your business goals and objectives. Once this preparation is complete, you're poised to begin writing your business plan.

Components of a Business Plan

There is no one right way to write a business plan. Each business is unique, so business plans can be drawn up in a variety of ways. Still, most business plans share a few basic components. A typical business plan for a start-up company is about 35–60 pages in length and contains eight key elements, as illustrated in ■ **FIGURE M2.2**. The order in which the key elements are included is not random; they should be in the order of importance to the person reading the document. Therefore, although a complete description of your product may be of utmost importance to you, your investors and key contributors first need to know about the market before the specifics of your product. Let's look at each of the basic components of a business plan in more detail.

■ **FIGURE M2.3**
Sample Business Plan Cover Sheet

The Cover Sheet and Table of Contents

The *cover sheet* of a business plan is like the cover of a book; it provides the first impression of your plan and your business. This component is crucial, but many business planners don't include the right information on the cover sheet, turning off potential investors. As shown in ■ **FIGURE M2.3**, the cover sheet should include the following:

- Basic company information (name, address, phone number, and Web address)
- The company logo (if applicable)
- Contact information of the owner(s) and any officers (name, titles, addresses, phone numbers, and e-mail addresses)
- The month and year the business plan was created
- The name(s) of those who prepared the plan
- A unique record number so that you can track who received which copy so you can easily follow up with him or her

The *table of contents* follows the cover sheet. It should be well organized so that the reader can quickly find information on any aspect of the business. It should also include the page number of the first page of each section, and all pages in the document should be numbered.

AB Environmental Consulting
21 N. LaSalle Street
Chicago, IL 60611
(312) 555-6439
www.abenvironmentalconsulting.com

Business Plan

Prepared by:

Adam Bernard
President & Owner
(312) 555-6438
abernard@abenvironmentalconsulting.com

January 2013

#AB5336

The Executive Summary

An **executive summary** is a clear and concise (abbreviated) form of the entire business plan, generally no more than two or three pages long. After reading the executive summary, a person should understand the business's purpose, value, operating methods, and profitability outlook. An executive summary should contain information about the company's unique competitive advantage and projections for future sales, growth, and profits. If the business plan is to be presented to potential investors, the executive summary should also include a statement regarding the amount of and uses for capital as well as plans and a timetable for repaying investors.

Ultimately, the executive summary should convey excitement and entice the reader to want to read more. Because this is often the only part of a business plan that is read completely, it is the most critical and, as a result, requires more of your time, thought, and attention than the rest of the business plan. Executive summaries are especially important when presenting your business plan to potential investors. If investors don't get excited about your business and the prospects of success after reading the executive summary, they'll stop reading and most likely file your plan in the trash. Because the executive summary is meant to condense the entire plan into a few pages, many people often write the summary as the last step in the business plan process. Writing your summary after completing the rest of your plan ensures that you've worked out all the kinks and made sure the other sections of the plan are sound.

The Company and Management Team

The next section of the business plan presents the "big picture" and defines the company and its purpose. The company section should include the following elements:

- **Mission and vision statements.** As discussed in Chapter 7, the *mission* and *vision statements* should spell out what the founder ultimately envisions the business to be with respect to growth, values, and contributions to society. They may also offer the company's business strategy that defines the business, identifies the intended customer, and explains how the business will benefit them.

- **Industry profile.** The *industry profile* describes the context in which the business will operate. This section discusses economic trends that affect the business and provides background on the industry, the current outlook for the industry, and future growth potential.

- **Company profile and strategy.** The *company profile* provides details regarding how the business works and why it has a unique chance to impact the industry. The *company strategy* summarizes the company's plans for growth and profits. It is important to be optimistic while also being realistic in discussing goals and strategy. It is even more important to back up the strategy with details of the company's past and present conditions so that the strategy is convincing.

- **Anticipated challenges and planned responses.** This section discusses potential vulnerabilities from competition, suppliers, resources, industry, or economic situations. It also discusses legal factors that might affect the business—either positively or negatively—including changes to legal restrictions, pending lawsuits, expiring patents, copyrights, and the like. This section should also state possible resources the company could make available should the need arise. Finally, the section should mention any protection from copyrights, trademarks, or patents.

- **Management team.** This section should list the members of the management team—finance, marketing, and production specialists—and the pertinent experience, knowledge, or creative ability that each member brings to the team.

If your company is large enough to have a board of directors, those members should be listed in this section as well. Because résumés of key personnel will be attached to the back of the business plan, keep this section brief and dedicate only a paragraph or two to each individual.

Market Analysis

The **market analysis** section identifies who your customers are and explains how you will reach them. The main purpose of this section is to explain the *benefits* of your product. It should answer the question "What is it about your product that creates a competitive advantage?" For example, your product might be homemade pasta. Your customers might benefit from an authentic Italian taste at a price that is lower than the competition's price. Or, your product could be made with all organic ingredients, which benefits health-conscious consumers. Consumer benefits are those things that do something better for the customer. They affect a person's feelings, pocketbook, or both. The market analysis section should include an assessment of the general market and, more specifically, the competition, as follows:

Market analysis is the section of your business plan that details whether customers exist for your product—and who they are.
Source: Zoonar/Ranczandras/Alamy.

- **Market research.** This section should contain an analysis of the market to determine whether enough customers exist and will continue to exist to make your business profitable now and in the future. First, you need to describe exactly what you see as the target market for your product—that is, identify your customer. For example, is your ideal customer teenagers heading off to college, owners of pets with little time to walk them, or those needing a great meal in a relaxing location? Once you've identified and described your customer, you need to determine whether the market is growing or shrinking. Your analysis should reach the conclusion that the market is big enough for your business to enter with adequate growth potential to make your time and investment worthwhile.

- **Assess the competition.** It is important to show that you have a clear understanding of your competition. Therefore, you should list your main competitors and their perceived strengths and weaknesses. You should then clearly articulate your plan to take advantage of their weaknesses and respond to their strengths.

The Product

In the next section of the business plan, you describe your product and list its important details. Your product's description should include any testing you've conducted and approvals you've received as well as trademarks, copyrights, or patents to protect your product. It is also important to discuss ongoing service aspects that are provided with the product, such as warranties and repairs. Your business plan should articulate how the product will be produced. If part of your product is dependent on outside suppliers, you should list those suppliers and verify their reliability. If your business is a service, you should discuss how you intend to find and train personnel who will deliver your service.

Most important, whether for a good or a service, this section should cover your pricing strategy. In your pricing discussion, detail any aspects of the product that require a higher price, such as using premium materials. Additionally, you must conduct a thorough analysis of what the competition is charging for

How will you promote your business? A business plan will help you decide whether to post a flyer on a busy street corner or place an ad in a popular magazine.
Source: Art Kowalsky/Alamy.

a similar product, noting the differences in their product or your product that justify a price differential. Finally, the section should list what you expect customers will be willing to pay for your product.

Sales and Promotion

The sales and promotion section of the business plan explains how you intend to implement the marketing plan. It should describe the approaches you'll take to promote the product. This should include promotional avenues beyond basic advertising. Include your social media strategy, such as using blogs, Facebook, Twitter, Foursquare, or YouTube, and also how you are monitoring the feedback derived from your social media strategy.

This section should also describe your selling approach. For example, are you selling the product with a sales force, over the Internet, through direct mail, via retail outlets, or simply by word of mouth? Include evidence of promotional success, such as current newspaper articles, customer referrals, or letters of satisfaction.

Financials

This section includes several pages of financial statements: the income statement, the balance sheet, and the cash flow statement. In addition, you should cover the financial history of the company to date and have several different forecasts and scenarios projecting the anticipated performance of the business in the next several years. You should put your financials through a stress test by showing how you expect the business to perform under worst-case, expected-case, and best-case scenarios. If one of the primary purposes of this business plan is to seek outside financing assistance, then another component of this section is a statement of funding requirements indicating information such as the amount of capital needed, the type of funding, the term of loan, and how funds will be used. Investors will also want to see how you intend to pay them back—the timing, the return on investment, and an exit strategy that you might want to suggest to investors.

Don't underestimate the importance of preparing the financial information or be misled into thinking that developing the financial information will or should be easy. This exercise forces you, as a new business owner, to face up to the reality of your business's finances beyond daily cash flow. The numbers need to show that you can be successful in the short term as well as over the long term.

Oddly, more is not better in presenting the financials of a company. More important, if you use a software program to generate financials, make sure you understand and can defend and explain every number in every line. It's not uncommon for someone who is reviewing the financials of a business plan to ask very specific questions, such as "What does the figure on line 24 in the income statement mean?" If your answer is "I'm not sure, the software program generated that number," you are not creating investor confidence in your ability to understand and manage the financial aspects of the business. If necessary, consult an accountant to help you prepare and/or interpret the financial statements and projections included in the business plan.

Including the actual financial statements, forecasts, and scenarios in the business plan is not enough. You need to explain and summarize the key information from those statements and specifically state how they relate to the marketing, sales, and production plans already discussed.

Appendices

The final pages of a business plan should be devoted to appendices. Any additional information that adds to the credibility of your business, the management team, or the industry that is not included in the body of the business plan is included in the appendices. Appendices will include information such as the following:

- Résumés of key managers
- Pictures of the product, facilities, production, and so on
- Letters of recommendations, professional references
- Published information
- Contracts and agreements; copies of patents, copyrights, trademarks
- Media, articles

Writing a business plan can seem like a formidable task. But if you have a clear idea and vision of your business venture, your task will become a little easier. It is also important to know that you're not alone. The SBA and SCORE provide a wealth of information and resources for the potential small business owner.

Remember, your business plan should be exciting, dynamic, and compelling. The plan's purpose is to make others as excited about your business idea as you are. If you carefully follow the steps for writing a business plan and strongly believe in your idea, you may soon have investors beating down your door to be a part of your project.

References

1. "Pizza Hut Inc.," www.fundinguniverse.com/company-histories/Pizza-Hut-Inc-Company-History.html.

2. Pizza Hut, "Our History," www.pizzahut.co.uk/restaurants/our-history.aspx.

Chapter 7
Business Management and Organization

▶ The Foundations of Management

Xerox Corporation CEO Ursula Burns started her career at Xerox in 1980 as a mechanical engineering intern. What kind of management skills did she display over the years to rise to the top of a multibillion-dollar corporation?

▶ The Functions of Management: Planning

Planning is critical as a business gets off the ground, and every day after that. How does a tattoo artist take his skills forward into a real business? What sequence of planning stages and what tools can he use to accomplish his ultimate goals?

▶ The Functions of Management: Organizing

Carrie Witt and Mark Healy have the same position at competing firms, but their day-to-day experiences differ greatly. Why is this?

▶ The Functions of Management: Controlling

It all sounded so good. The planned reorganization was going to push the company to the next level of competition. So why was everything such a mess now?

OBJECTIVES

1 What are the levels of management, and what skills do managers need to be successful? (pp. 193–197)

2 How are the strategic plan, the corporate vision, and the mission statement defined for a business? (pp. 197–201)

3 Why do managers need tactical plans, operational plans, and contingency plans? (pp. 201–203)

4 What is the significance of organizing, and how are most companies organized? (pp. 203–207)

5 How do managers ensure that the business is on track and moving forward? (pp. 208–211)

MyBizLab®

⭐ Improve Your Grade!

Over 10 million students improved their results using the Pearson MyLabs. Visit **mybizlab.com** for simulations, tutorials, and end-of-chapter problems.

The Foundations of Management pp. 193–197

Ursula Burns, the current CEO of Xerox Corporation, didn't start at the top. Instead, she rose from a position as a mechanical engineering summer intern at Xerox in 1980 to assume the role of chairperson and CEO in 2010. This was a historic event: It was the first time that a female CEO of a major U.S. company, Anne Mulcahy, handed the reins of a company over to another woman. Burns's personal story is dramatically American. She was raised by a single mother in a New York City housing project and now heads a $21 billion company.[1] It hasn't been all smooth sailing for Burns, however. Xerox Corporation faces serious challenges as business moves increasingly into electronic communication, therefore printing and copying less. But Burns has a track record for pushing forward new products. In 1997, she helped lead Xerox into the field of color copying. Her vision moved Xerox out of the manufacturing industry and diversified the set of products it offers. She is also willing to take the company in entirely new directions. One of her early moves as the company's CEO was to acquire Affiliated Computer Services. This led Xerox into the arena of providing full solutions to business data processing and document management problems. In addition, many people note Burns is able to effectively communicate her understanding of technology to Xerox's board of directors and other key members of the company's management team, which is an important trait. ■

Source: Paul Morigi/Getty Images.

What makes Ursula Burns such a talented and effective manager? What skills does she possess, and how does she apply them? In this chapter, we'll study what management is and discuss the skills successful managers must have.

Business Management

What exactly is management? Have you ever been in a team situation in which one person has been instrumental in making the group work more effectively? That person could have been a peer or a superior, but somehow he or she knew exactly what had to be accomplished, assessed the resources available to achieve the goal, and organized and led other group members to accomplish that goal. If so, you've seen management in action.

Management is the process of working with people and resources to accomplish the goals of an organization. An organization can be a simple working group, a corporate department, or a multi-billion-dollar company. The size of the group doesn't matter, but the skills of a manager and the process a manager goes through are similar across all management levels.

PLANNING
- Setting Goals
- Developing Strategies
- Determining Resources

ORGANIZING
- Allocating Resources
- Creating an Organizational Structure
- Recruiting and Placing Employees

CONTROLLING/ MONITORING
- Measuring Results Against Goals
- Monitoring Performance
- Correcting, When Necessary
- Rewarding

LEADING
- Guiding and Motivating
- Achieving Results and Milestones
- Maintaining Unit or Organization's Focus on the Goal or Vision

■ **FIGURE 7.1**
The Four Functions of Management

What are the four functions of management? As ■ **FIGURE 7.1** shows, a manager performs four primary functions: planning, organizing, leading, and controlling/monitoring. In the rest of this chapter, we'll examine three of these functions in more detail and explain how they integrate all of a company's resources, including its human, financial, and technological resources. In Chapter 8, we'll examine leadership as a function of management.

Levels of Management

What are the different levels of management? Within a company, there are different levels of managers, each with increasing levels of responsibility. ■ **FIGURE 7.2** shows a traditional managerial pyramid with examples of jobs held by managers at each level and the tasks they perform.

What do top managers do? At the peak of the pyramid are **top managers**, who are the corporate officers of the firm and are responsible for an organization as a whole. Most corporations have a chief executive officer (CEO) or president. Depending on the company's size and complexity, it might also have a chief financial officer (CFO), a chief operations officer (COO), and a chief information officer (CIO).

Top managers develop the "big picture" for a company. In other words, they outline its long-term goals and strategic vision. Then they create plans that will take the company in that direction. They establish the culture of an organization and inspire employees to adopt the vision they have for the organization. In smaller corporations, especially small start-up companies, top managers may also be responsible for planning and carrying out the day-to-day tasks of a company. But as the business grows, companies such as these usually need to hire more employees

■ **FIGURE 7.2**
The Managerial Pyramid

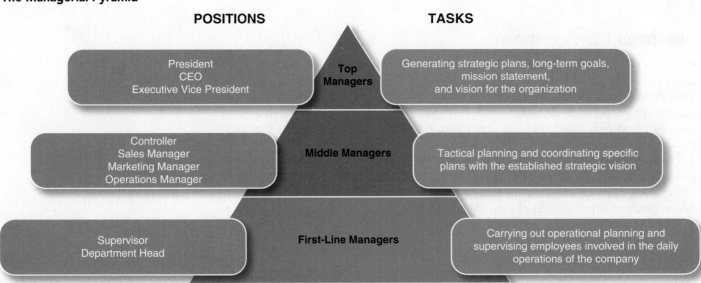

POSITIONS

TASKS

President
CEO
Executive Vice President
— **Top Managers** — Generating strategic plans, long-term goals, mission statement, and vision for the organization

Controller
Sales Manager
Marketing Manager
Operations Manager
— **Middle Managers** — Tactical planning and coordinating specific plans with the established strategic vision

Supervisor
Department Head
— **First-Line Managers** — Carrying out operational planning and supervising employees involved in the daily operations of the company

How Are Managers Responsible for Employee Behavior?

For two years, Ani Chopourian was a physician assistant on a cardiovascular team at Mercy General Hospital in Sacramento, California. During that time, Chopourian filed numerous complaints about sexually inappropriate workplace conduct by male physicians on the team. All of her complaints were ignored. After filing her eighteenth complaint, she was fired. In the legal action that followed, a jury awarded her $168 million in damages.[2]

The jury heard from a parade of employees who depicted a culture that allowed female employees to be humiliated and bullied, even to the extent that it put patients at risk. What responsibility do the managers of the hospital have to provide a safe workplace culture? Are they able to control cardiac surgeons, who know that they bring in the most money to the hospital? What kind of tools do managers need to be able to navigate these challenges?

and divide the work into smaller tasks and areas of responsibility, which usually requires hiring a new layer of managers.

What do middle managers do? Middle managers manage individual divisions or segments of an organization and are responsible for creating the specific plans to implement the strategic vision set by the firm's top managers. Included in this management layer are division managers of the firm's functions, such as finance, marketing, sales, operations, and information technology (IT). Also included in this layer are team leaders who are not arranged by function but are responsible for cross-functional groups of employees who work on projects or other tasks of the organization.

Are the people who supervise the day-to-day operations also managers? The bottom of the managerial pyramid includes **first-line managers**. These managers supervise the individual employees who carry out the day-to-day operations of a company.

Does every company have all these different managers? Not all companies have all three layers of management; some have more, and some have fewer. Typically, you'll find the extra layers are middle managers.

The Skills of Successful Managers

What skills should a manager have? Because managerial tasks are so varied, a successful manager needs to possess the following types of skills:

- **Conceptual skills.** The ability to think abstractly
- **Technical skills.** The specific knowledge for the discipline
- **Time management skills.** The ability to be effective and productive with one's time
- **Interpersonal skills.** The ability to motivate and communicate easily with others
- **Decision-making skills.** The ability to analyze options and implement the best plan of action

It is a rare person who masters all of these skills. Moreover, because they are responsible for a variety of jobs and because these jobs can change quite rapidly, managers must assess the skills that are required in any given situation. Managers must also be willing to acquire these skills if they are lacking in a specific area by studying, undergoing training, or finding mentors to help them.

What do we mean by conceptual skills? To make good decisions, a manager must have **conceptual skills**—the ability to think abstractly and to picture the organization as a whole and understand its relationship to the business community. Conceptual skills also include understanding the relationships between the parts of an organization itself. Whenever new market opportunities or potential threats arise, managers rely on their conceptual skills to help analyze the impending outcomes of their decisions. Conceptual skills are extremely important for top managers and often develop with time and experience.

What technical skills do managers need? **Technical skills** include the abilities and knowledge that enable employees to carry out the specific tasks required of a discipline or a department, such as drafting skills for an architect, programming skills for a software developer, or market analysis skills for a marketing manager. How to operate certain machinery is also a technical skill. Managers must be comfortable with technology and possess good analytical skills to interpret a variety of data. In addition to having the skills pertinent to their own jobs, managers must also know how to perform or at least have a good understanding of the skills required of the employees they supervise.

What time management skills does it take to succeed as a manager? Managers who possess **time management skills** are able to be effective and productive with their time. As a manager, how do you do this? Eliminating time wasters, such as constant interruptions, setting aside time each day to return phone calls and e-mail, ensuring that meetings have a clear agenda, and successfully delegating work to others, can increase the productive use of your available time. Tracking how you spend your time each day can also improve your time management.

Why are interpersonal skills important for managers? Managers achieve their goals by working with people both inside and outside an organization. **Interpersonal skills** enable managers to interact with other people to motivate them and develop their trust and loyalty and get them to work together well.

Top managers need good interpersonal skills to successfully communicate with the firm's board of directors, investors, leaders in the business community, and middle managers. Middle managers need good interpersonal skills to communicate with all levels of management and act as liaisons among groups. Lower-level managers need good interpersonal skills to motivate employees, build morale, and train and support those who perform the daily tasks of an organization. And all managers need good interpersonal skills to communicate with and motivate people who are different than themselves. Because the workplace is becoming more diverse, this is becoming an increasingly important managerial skill.

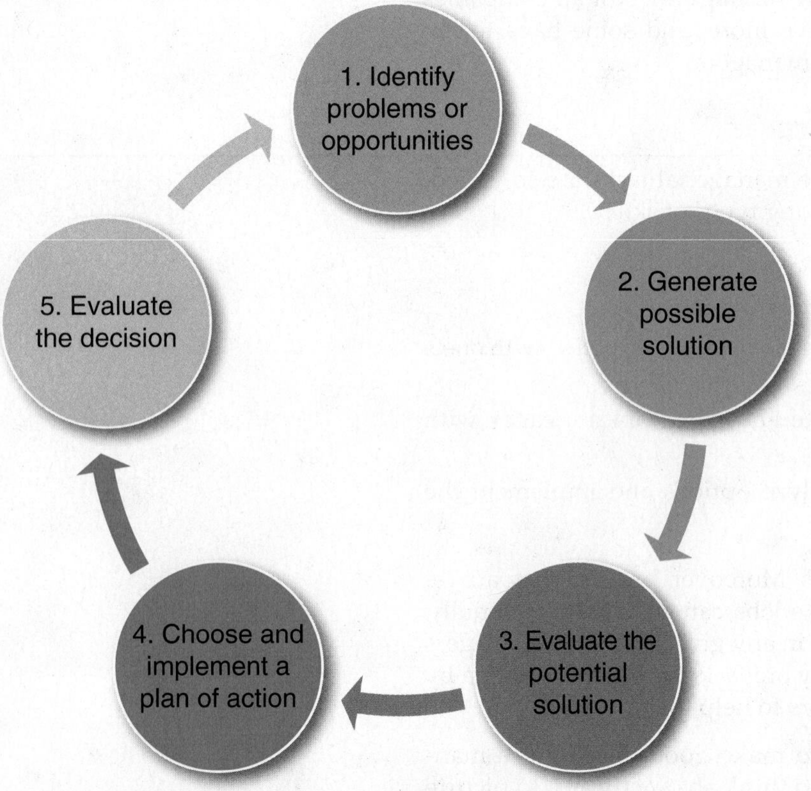

Why do some people consistently make better decisions than other people? It is critical that managers have good **decision-making skills**—the ability to identify and analyze a challenge, identify and examine the alternatives, choose and implement the best plan of action, and evaluate the results. When making important decisions, managers often go through a formal decision-making process similar to that shown in ■ **FIGURE 7.3**. Analyzing data and looking for trends allow a manager to identify unseen problems or opportunities.

■ **FIGURE 7.3**
Stages of Decision Making

1. Identify problems or opportunities
2. Generate possible solution
3. Evaluate the potential solution
4. Choose and implement a plan of action
5. Evaluate the decision

Social Media: How Do Web-Based Tools Make Time Management Easier?

Calendars have traditionally been a tool used by individuals to manage their personal schedules. But with modern social media tools, Web-based calendars can be used to synchronize and manage the schedules of many people simultaneously. Multiple people can add new events to the calendars, thus making the scheduling of meetings easier and faster. For example, using Meeting Wizard, you can send out e-mail invitations that contain a poll of suggested meeting times. The application then creates a report for you with the group's responses and sends everyone a confirmation e-mail with the final time chosen. NeedtoMeet is another application that allows you to have everyone in the group enter their available times on a Web-based calendar. Doodle (also available for iPhone or Android) is scheduling software that lets you check out the yes/no votes for suggested meeting times on your phone.

Such tools have proven useful to many managers, but some people argue that Web-based tools can make simple tasks more complicated and can make us actually less productive. What do you think? Do we rely too much on fancy electronic tools to manage our lives and our time?

Examples may include poor growth in sales, an increase in customer dissatisfaction, or an opportunity to expand into a new market. Next, managers work with their teams to generate possible solutions. They can then evaluate each potential solution based on various criteria, such as cost, feasibility, and time and resources needed. Once they have evaluated the potential solutions, managers select the best plan of action. At this point, managers often seek the opinions of customers or other people in the marketplace before completely committing to this choice. If the feedback is not positive, another alternative might be pursued. When the final choice has been made, plans are established to implement the plan of action. Finally, managers evaluate the results of their decisions. If changes need to be made, the entire process begins again.

Think back to Ursula Burns, the CEO of Xerox Corporation. How did her education equip her with the technical skills she uses to achieve success? Do you think her success reflects strong interpersonal skills? What does the direction in which she is taking Xerox say about her decision-making and conceptual skills? How might time management skills come into play in terms of her ability to manage a giant corporation? Clearly, Burns's prominence and success in business demonstrate that a combination of management skills is vital.

The Functions of Management: Planning pp. 197–203

Source: Dominique Faget/Afp/Getty Images.

William Lee knew his skills as a tattoo artist could lead into his own business if he did the right things. But where does he start? First, he sat down and wrote down his vision of the business and what he hoped to see it add to the world: "To inspire self-expression and creativity through fine arts tattoos." Even though it seemed like a grandiose statement, seeing it written on a page helped William solidify some of his ideas. Next was the *how*—how could he create a business from this idea? What were his goals for the future? How would he find a space to rent, the money to set up shop, and the expertise to help him run it? What was his competitive advantage over other tattoo artists, and how would he communicate it? There was a lot of work ahead for William. ∎

In today's busy world, it is easy to become distracted, just as William Lee felt when beginning to plan for his business. Goals and plans focus our intentions in a way that leads to results. **Planning** is the process of establishing goals and objectives and determining the best ways to accomplish them. **Goals** are broad, long-term accomplishments an organization wants to achieve within a certain time frame—in most companies, usually about five years. **Objectives** are short-term targets designed to help achieve the goals. Planning happens at all levels of an organization. In this section, we'll discuss the different levels of planning that occur in an organization.

Strategic Planning

What is the highest level of planning in an organization? A strategic plan is the main course of action created by top-level managers. A strategic plan helps to answer three questions:

1. Where is the company going?
2. What should the company focus on?
3. How will the company achieve its goals?

Simply put, a strategic plan points an organization to where it wants to be in the future and identifies how it will get there. Although individual goals sometimes contribute to the plan, the overall strategic plan is focused on an entire organization or an entire department.

How is a strategic plan developed? A good strategic plan reflects what is happening inside and outside an organization and shows how those conditions and changes will affect the organization in the future. Those making strategic plans must pay attention to the capabilities and resources of an organization as well as changes in the environment. There are several steps to the process of developing a strategic plan, as ■ **FIGURE 7.4** shows.

Consider the strategic plan development for the Wikimedia Foundation (WMF). WMF supports the online collaborative encyclopedia Wikipedia as well as nine other projects with a common goal (Wikibooks, Wikiquotes, Wikiversity, and so on).[3] In 2009 and 2010, WMF began to modify its strategic plan out to 2015.[4] WMF found that only about 15 percent of the world was using Wikimedia's products—far fewer than it wanted. Even in the United States, only about one-third of online users had ever accessed a Wikimedia product.

One problem was that participation and contributions to WMF projects had begun to decline—in fact, over 50 percent of the content was coming from about 1 percent of the contributors. In addition, the organization wanted to enhance the ability of the WMF community to think strategically and focus on the organization's strategic plan long term.

To develop a plan that could address these problems and challenges, WMF asked its community of contributors and asked for proposals. Every submission was available for the entire WMF community to view and comment on. Together

■ **FIGURE 7.4**
Strategic Planning Process

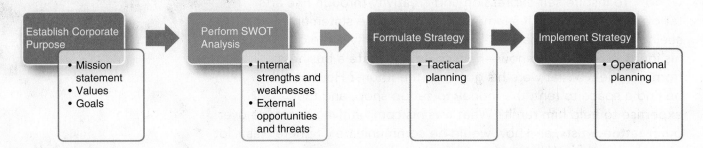

the community created goals and decided how to achieve these through specific actions. The process was conducted primarily online and involved over 1,000 people using over 50 different languages. The content of about 1,500 wiki pages of input was consolidated into a 19-page strategic report. While this process wouldn't work for every business, it seems very appropriate for the tech-savvy WMF community.

Vision and Mission Statement

What helps define the direction of a business? The first step in creating a strategic plan is to establish a corporate purpose through a clearly defined *vision*. A **vision** identifies what the business wants to be in the future, what you would like to see as the end result of all your work. The vision should be made clear to all employees and stakeholders. The vision statement for General Electric (GE) under the former CEO Jack Welch read as follows: "To become the most competitive enterprise in the world by being number one or number two in every business in which we compete."[5] A single clear vision worked for GE—during the 20 years Welch was CEO, the company's market value went from $14 billion to more than $410 billion.[6]

What helps define the purpose of a business? People often confuse the vision of a company with its mission statement. The vision statement sets the long-term objective of a company and tells where the company is headed. A **mission statement** is a description of an organization's current purpose, basic goals, and philosophies. A mission statement not only helps management remain focused but also lets employees understand the core values of the company for which they work.

Mission statements reflect the personality of a company, so even companies in the same industry can have mission statements that vary greatly in design and content. Some use scientific jargon in a no-nonsense manner directed specifically to a certain target audience. Others may try to reach a larger audience by using a simple, direct statement that inspires the average consumer. You may find that a company uses its mission statement to highlight its environmental awareness or to set an abstract goal for the firm's employees, like working to make the world better able to communicate. Other companies may discuss only their own business goals. The mission statement is a chance for consumers and employees to get a peek into the central values of a company.

What makes an effective mission statement? If employees feel an owner's passion for the business through the mission statement, it has a positive impact. Employees then incorporate the goals and objectives of the mission into their daily work and pass these on to customers and suppliers through their words and actions.

An effective mission statement does not to be flowery. Even simple mission statements can be very effective if they are written clearly and convincingly. Read over several mission statements at www.missionstatements.com. The Culver's restaurant chain has a concise statement of mission: "Every guest who chooses Culver's leaves happy."[7] In contrast, the cosmetics firm Avon has a 240-word mission statement. But both statements are effective and reflect a passion for excellence.

What are some benefits of well-defined vision and mission statements? The vision and mission statements lead to important benefits like the following:

- Keeping management on track by ensuring strategies are consistent with the organization's goals
- Inspiring employees
- Giving investors insight into the values of the organization

Are mission statements only for businesses with a profit? No, mission statements are useful for not-for-profit companies as well. The mission statements of not-for-profit organizations are focused on outreach to the community or a specific public service rather than on investor return. For example, the American Cancer Society's mission statement reads, "The American Cancer Society is the nationwide, community-based, voluntary health organization dedicated to eliminating cancer as a major health problem by preventing cancer, saving lives, and diminishing suffering from cancer, through research, education, advocacy, and service."[8] This statement reflects the organization's commitment to serving the community, the range of goals they have, and the set of avenues they use to accomplish their goals.

Where can I find a company's vision and mission statements? Both the vision and mission statements are usually found on an organization's website. However, because the mission statement is directed toward customers—unlike the vision, which is directed toward employees—the mission statement is often used alone on advertising materials or on actual products.

SWOT Analysis

How does the management team begin to move a company toward achieving its vision? Once a company's vision and mission statement have been articulated, the firm's managers must assess the company's strengths and weaknesses as well as its position among its competitors. What changes are anticipated to occur both inside and outside the organization? Is the company poised appropriately to respond to such changes? These are questions that must be answered first.

What is a SWOT analysis? The acronym *SWOT* stands for the following:

> Strengths
>
> Weaknesses
>
> Opportunities
>
> Threats

A **SWOT analysis** is an analysis of the strengths, weaknesses, opportunities, and threats a company is facing. It helps managers determine the strategic fit between an organization's internal, capabilities, and external possibilities relative to the business and economic environments. ■ **FIGURE 7.5** provides a brief explanation of each component of the SWOT analysis.

When evaluating a company's internal *strengths* and *weaknesses*, managers have to analyze a company's internal resources, including such elements as its financial health, the strengths of its employees, and its marketing, operations, and technological resources. For example, a company's strength might be its strong marketing department, but its weakness could be an unfavorable location.

To evaluate the *threats* and *opportunities* facing a company, managers assess various external elements, such as the economic, political, and regulatory environments as well as social, demographic, macroeconomic, and technological factors that could affect the company. Managers also analyze the state of the firm's industry and its market as well as its competitors. For example, a recession could threaten an alternative energy company, whereas increasing awareness of global warming may provide greater opportunity for market growth.

What happens after a SWOT analysis is completed? After conducting a SWOT analysis, managers establish a set of goals and objectives based on the information. To help ensure they actually get accomplished, the acronym SMARTER is helpful when designing and wording them: Goals should be **S**pecific, **M**easurable, **A**cceptable (to those working to achieve the goals), **R**ealistic, **T**imely, **E**xtending (the capabilities of those working to achieve the goals), and **R**ewarding to

SWOT Analysis

Internal Strengths	**Internal Weaknesses**
Potential internal assets that give a company a competitive advantage	Lack of internal capability or expertise compared to the competition
Examples for Walmart:	**Examples for Walmart:**
• Powerful brand • Reputation for value, convenience • Wide range of products in one store	• Not as flexible as competitors who sell just one type of product (clothing) • Global but still in only a few countries
External Opportunities	**External Threats**
Foreseeable external changes that could favorably affect a company's competitive capability	External conditions that could negatively affect a company's competitive capability
Examples for Walmart:	**Examples for Walmart:**
• Expand to new locations and new types of stores • Take over or form alliances with other global retailers in Europe or China	• Intense price competition increasing • Global retail exposes Walmart to political problems in the countries where it operates • Being Number 1 makes Walmart the target of competition

■ **FIGURE 7.5**
SWOT Analysis

employees as well (see ■ **FIGURE 7.6**).[9] So if you are conducting a fund-raiser as a student government project, having the goal of "Collecting 500 coats before the end of December by advertising our clothing drive through social media" works better to focus action than stating "We plan to collect clothing for the needy."

Tactical and Operational Planning

How do managers decide how to execute a strategic plan? The next part of the process of creating a strategic plan is to have middle managers generate *tactical plans* to carry out the goals of a company. **Tactical plans** specifically determine the resources and the actions required to implement particular aspects of a strategic plan. Whereas strategic plans have a long-term focus, tactical plans are made with a one- to three-year horizon in mind. Determining a company's annual budget, for example, is one function of a tactical plan. Let's say one goal of the strategic plan of a paper supply company is to sell more products to large offices on the East Coast. One part of this company's tactical plan might be to determine how much money should be allocated to advertising in that area.

How is a tactical plan translated into instructions for employees? The specifics of carrying out tactical plans are *operational plans*. In an **operational plan**, first-line managers precisely determine the process by which tactical plans can be achieved. Operational plans depend on daily or weekly schedules and focus on

■ **FIGURE 7.6**
SMARTER Design of Goals

S	M	A	R	T	E	R
Specific	Measureable	Acceptable	Realistic	Timely	Extending	Rewarding
Clear and concise statement	Success can be defined and monitored	To those working toward the goals	Reasonable given resources available	Time frame is reasonable	Extends the capabilities of those working to achieve goals	To the employees

specific departments or employees. For example, once the paper supply company determines how much of its budget can be allocated to advertising, specific department managers might have to determine which employees will travel to advertise the product.

Contingency Planning

What if unforeseen events occur? Contingency planning is a set of plans that ensures that an organization will run as smoothly as possible during an unexpected disruption (see ■ **FIGURE 7.7**). What happens if a company's best-selling product is recalled due to a defect or if it experiences more sales of a good than it can produce? How should a company fight off an unpredictable takeover threat from a competitor or a rapidly spreading computer virus that threatens to shut down all internal and external lines of communication? Sometimes, extreme circumstances occur that force a company to alter its plans and find alternative ways to survive. For example, the massive earthquake and tsunami in 2011 that left 20,000 people dead and devastated Japan, led to power shortages and disrupted supply chains and drastically impacted the output of factories worldwide that relied on Japanese parts.[10] All the best corporate strategies can be negated quickly if an unexpected crisis occurs and a plan is not in place to deal with it adequately.

How can planning help companies weather unexpected events? Part of contingency planning includes how a company will communicate, both internally and externally with all of its stakeholders during a crisis. Internally, employees need to be informed about how they should continue to do their jobs. Externally, an organization must have a plan in place to deal with requests for information either from employees, the families of employees, or even the media.

Contingency planning also involves determining what departments within a company are vital to the immediate needs of the organization when an unexpected crisis occurs. The particulars of each plan differ depending on the size and function of a company and the magnitude of crisis for which the plan is needed. For example, the Vanguard Group, an investment management company, has in place specific, formal business contingency plans to respond to a range of incidents—from worst-case scenarios, such as the loss of a data center, buildings, or staff, to more common occurrences, such as power outages.[11]

■ **FIGURE 7.7**
Contingency Planning—Are You Ready?

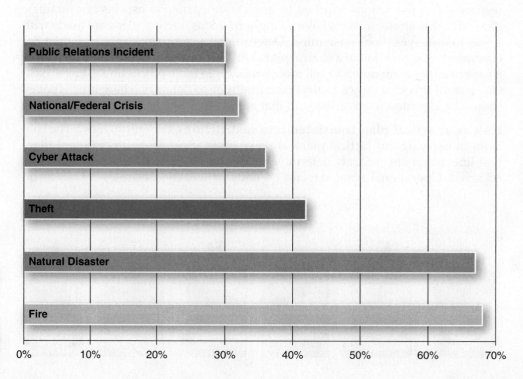

As important as it is to have plans in place, it is just as important to ensure that the plans are tested and that key individuals know exactly what is expected of them. Similar to fire drills in school, companies should periodically review and rehearse their plans. Vanguard officials put their contingency plans through rigorous testing, including full-scale practice drills in which the company closes a building and works from a remote location. The company also conducts mock disaster drills together with local, state, and federal authorities. Because Vanguard's business would be impacted significantly should a disruption in any of its technical systems occur, it also conducts tests to determine how quickly its IT systems can be made operational in the event of a disruption. ■ **FIGURE 7.8** summarizes the types of contingency plans that companies such as Vanguard use.

Now that a few years have passed, William Lee smiles when he thinks of the early planning of his business. He had to make hundreds of decisions along the way before opening the tattoo shop he now owns. At many points, he needed to think tactically, and he had to conduct a full SWOT analysis to determine where his strengths and weaknesses were so he could set the long-term and short-term goals for the shop. He also has contingency plans in place if he runs into problems in the future. "You never know what the future will bring," he says, "but you know if you don't plan, you won't win."

Strategic Plan — Top Management

- Sets the approach for achieving an organization's long-term goals and objectives
- Acts as a framework for decisions
- Assists in setting corporate benchmarks

Tactical Plan — Middle Management

- Determines resources and actions necessary to implement strategic plan
- Made with a one- to three-year horizon in mind

Contingency Plan — Middle Management

- Keeps an organization running in the event of a disruption
- Details internal and external communication procedures for such an event
- Determines which departments are most vital to an organization during a crisis

Operational Plan — First-Line Management

- Involves planning the execution of the tactical plan
- Depends on daily or weekly schedules
- Focuses on specific department or employees

■ **FIGURE 7.8**
The Four Types of Management Plans

The Functions of Management: Organizing pp. 203–207

Carrie Witt and Mark Healy have a lot in common: Both graduated with degrees in business, and both acquired jobs as marketing associates at medium-size firms that design solar energy panels for commercial use. Nevertheless, their professional experiences have been markedly different. At her firm, Carrie is part of the marketing department. She is undergoing training to help her firm acquire new clients within a specific region of the state. She reports directly to the department head, but her work is also overseen by several middle managers, including the marketing department supervisor and the marketing manager. They, in turn, take their orders from top managers: the executive vice president, the CEO, and the president. At his firm, Mark works on a team with individuals from a variety of areas, including marketing, research and development (R&D), finance, and operations. They work on a variety of projects as a comprehensive unit. One manager supervises his team and coordinates the team's efforts directly with the goals and instructions from the firm's CEO and president. ■

Source: MG/Getty Images.

Carrie's and Mark's jobs seem similar, yet their everyday experiences contrast significantly. Why is this? It's all about organization structure. Which structure does Carrie's firm use? Which one does Mark's firm use? Why are these structures necessary, and what are the benefits of each? Every company, regardless of its size or specialty, needs a solid organization structure. Without one, employees may have trouble making decisions and assigning responsibility. But this doesn't mean there's just one way to organize a company. In this section, we'll explore different aspects of organization.

Organization Structures

How do managers put their plans into action? Once goals have been finalized and plans have been made, the next step in the management process is to put those plans into action. **Organizing** is the process of structuring the capital, personnel, raw materials, and other resources to carry out a company's plans in a way that best matches the nature of the work. Part of organizing is to establish an organization structure. What structure an organization chooses depends on a variety of factors, such as the number of employees it has, the speed at which decisions need to be made, how vulnerable the business is to rapid changes, and the collaborative nature of the work.

How do companies document the structure of an organization? Smaller companies tend to use simpler organization structures compared to large companies. Regardless, to accomplish many tasks at the same time, organizations have some division of labor and allocate work into smaller units. An **organization chart**, like that shown in ■ **FIGURE 7.9**, shows how groups of employees fit into the larger organization structure. The organization chart is a visual representation of several ideas that reflect the structure of the company. The **span of control** of a specific position is the number of employees being supervised by a specific person. **Departmentalization** consists of the decisions made to structure the company into smaller groups. Sometimes this is done by function or by product and sometimes by geography or even the type of customers served.

How is power distributed in an organization? There are two common approaches:

1. **Vertical organization** (or a *tall organization*). The power belongs to a few, and most people are in positions in which they report to a supervisor.
2. **Horizontal organization** (or a *flat organization*). Power is distributed, with many people organized in teams or groups.

In a vertical organization, decision making is centralized, and the power to make decisions lies with a smaller number of people. The firm's organization chart tends

■ **FIGURE 7.9**
Organization Chart

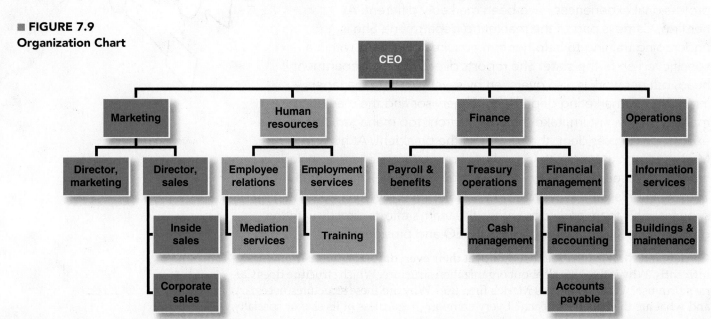

to have many layers and long vertical columns showing who reports to whom. The vertical organization has been the primary structure of businesses since the industrial revolution.

In a horizontal organization, the traditional managerial pyramid is flattened, and there are fewer layers of management. Decision making is decentralized and spread out across many more people than in it is in a vertical structure. A horizontally structured organization still has some of the pyramidal aspects, including a CEO and perhaps another layer of middle managers, but most of the remaining employees work in teams or groups. The organization chart for a firm such as this is flat and wide because there are many people with authority. ■ **FIGURE 7.10** illustrates the basic differences between vertically structured organizations and horizontally structured organizations.

What are the pros and cons of vertical organization? In a vertical organization, a company is organized by specific functions, such as marketing, finance, purchasing, IT, and human resources. Levels of expertise within the functions are developed, and managers have direct authority and reporting responsibility for their area. Integrating the functions and divisions is not always easy because communication and decisions have to travel up and down long chain-of-command lines. This makes it difficult for a company to respond quickly to changes in a market. Nonetheless, the structure has its benefits because there is ultimately one person in charge and a clear point of authority for decision making. However, in the early 1990s, vertical organization structures were criticized as being overspecialized, fragmented, and inflexible. Some businesses, such as Ford Motor Company and Barclay's Bank, found that they were more successful when they organized differently and formed management groups around areas of specific production.[12]

What are the pros and cons of horizontal organization? The benefit of a horizontal organization is that each team has more responsibility for the outcome of its work. There is less of a sense of competition for power and more of a push toward

■ **FIGURE 7.10**
Vertically and Horizontally Structured Organizations

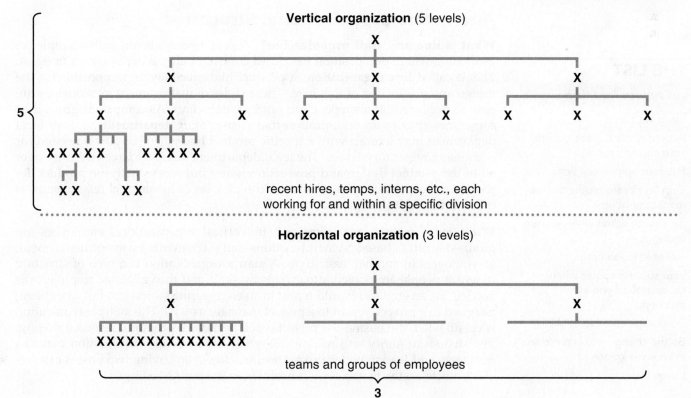

Vertical organization (5 levels)

5 { recent hires, temps, interns, etc., each working for and within a specific division

Horizontal organization (3 levels)

teams and groups of employees

3

collaborative work. Each employee is empowered to have more responsibility and decision-making authority. Because there are fewer layers of managers, if needed, approvals from them can be sought and received much faster.

Horizontal structures have been deemed the model for the knowledge age. Because employees today have better access to information in their firms, whereas previously only their bosses did, many people argue horizontal structures are more effective. They are suitable for industries that require rapid responses to quick changes.

Changing Structures

Does a company's organization structure ever change? Yes. Sometimes companies grow so large that their product lines, geographic regions, or manufacturing processes can become difficult to manage. So, the firms restructure from a vertical organization to a horizontal one. In these situations, managers often try to reorganize by function. For example, they might structure the organization into divisions of employees who work on just one product line. Or they might divide a company into teams to specialize in one geographic region or work through one manufacturing process. In essence, these divisions work like separate mini-companies. Each division has its own set of functional expertise, so separate managers are in charge of financing for that division, marketing for that division, and so on. In today's business environment, there are fewer and fewer organizations structured vertically by function.

One company that made the shift from being a vertical organization to a horizontal one is Xerox. It was once had a traditional vertical structure, organized by function, such as R&D, manufacturing, and sales. To more closely connect with its customers, the company realigned itself in the early 1990s around individual business markets, such as small businesses, office document systems, and engineering systems. Each individual group had its own set of financial reports, and factories were focused on individual product lines. Today, the company continues to maintain a flat organizational structure organized by product category as well as by region to take into account the company's global presence.

Alternative Organizational Structures

What is line and staff organization? Most companies begin with a simple organization where one position has direct control of all the departments under it. This is called **line organization**. A product manager may be responsible for the design and production of that item. These styles of management relationships are easy to document in a single, clean organization chart. As companies grow, they sometimes shift to an organization that creates **staff departments**. A staff legal department may interact with a specific product line when support is needed for addressing regulatory issues. The legal department does not have authority over all of the product design and production issues but works with the product department on specific topics. This more complex set of managerial relationships is called **line and staff organization**.

What is a matrix organization? In vertical organizations, employees are grouped together based on their functions—all accountants are in one department, all engineers in another, and so on. A **matrix organization** is a type of structure in which people are pooled into groups by skills and then assigned to projects as needed. So, an engineer would report to an engineering supervisor but, after being assigned to a project, report to a project manager as well. The matrix organization is useful when the business is project based because it promotes resource sharing. The shared authority and responsibility can mean better coordination between managers and lead to better project results. However, having two bosses can create conflicts, so the matrix style is useful only in specific settings.

▶ **THE LIST**

Bits of Advice for Managers

1. Keep your cool.
2. Accept opportunities outside your comfort zone.
3. Put your employees first.
4. Earn loyalty from others. Give respect to others.
5. Be able to admit when you are wrong.
6. Never stop learning.
7. Your success comes when those around you are successful.
8. Encourage creative thinking.
9. Be the change you want to see in your workplace.
10. Listen first.

What is an inverted organization? A vertical hierarchy can be mated with another structure that is quite different, the **inverted organization**. In this structure, managers must answer, or be accountable, to their employees. The goal of an inverted organization is to enable, encourage, and empower employees to do what they do best. Empowered employees can make decisions on the ground without the delay of forwarding requests upward through layers of management. Most firms end up implementing inverted structures along with the traditional vertical structure. So, although employees still have supervisors and supervisors answer to managers, managers are equally accountable to their employees. The rationale for this approach is that the core business of the company is to create value. The value creators in the company are the frontline employees. So, managers contribute to the company's success by empowering these people and putting them first.[13]

One company that has grown with this philosophy is HCL Technologies, a provider of IT services that has ranked as India's best employer. Founded by Vineet Nayar, HCL adopted an inverted organization in 2005. Afterward, the company began growing by more than 20 percent annually, even amid the global recession.[14] HCL's Nayar believes that in order for a business to satisfy its customers, its employees must feel valued and must trust their managers. Managers must be held accountable to their employees and vice versa.

Nayar wrote a book documenting the experience, titled *Employees First, Customers Second*. The result of taking care of employees was that customers were more satisfied and received better services and products. Many other companies, such as Southwest Airlines, have employed elements of the inverted organization.

What organizational structure works across multiple companies? Today, a new business structure has emerged: the network organization. A **network organization** is a collection of independent, mostly single-function firms that together produce a product or a service instead of one company being responsible for all functions. Boeing uses a network organization to build its 787s. In the past, the company's airplanes were built mostly by Boeing employees. With the 787, Boeing relies on the expertise of hundreds of manufacturers worldwide to independently manufacture the components of the plane. They then ship the individual subassemblies to Boeing's main plant in Everett, Washington, where they are assembled into a single 787.

Other companies that use a network organization include Nike, which owns only one manufacturing plant, and Reebok, which designs and markets but does not produce any of its products. Operating with a network structure requires that companies have the following characteristics:

- Be highly flexible and innovative
- Be able to respond quickly to threats and opportunities

Companies that successfully operate in a network structure find that they can save time and can reduce costs and risks.

Reflect back on Carrie and Mark. Carrie works under the supervision of the marketing department head and several middle managers in the same department, who in turn report to top management. Mark works on a team with people from various departments at his company. Is it clearer now why their experiences were so different despite the seeming similarity between their jobs? Carrie's company is a vertical, or tall, organization. The company is organized around specific business functions, and there are several levels of first-line and middle managers. Mark, however, works at a horizontal, or flat, organization. There are fewer middle managers, and employees work in groups. How would their work lives change if their companies reorganized to a matrix organization style? To an inverted organization?

Source: Izabela Habur/Getty Images.

The Functions of Management: Controlling pp. 208–211

It wasn't supposed to end like this. Company executives had worked together to make plans for the reorganization of the company. Matt Finley remembered the excitement of it; everyone knew moving toward a horizontal organizational structure would benefit managers, employees, and customers alike. It felt like great times were ahead. That was six months ago. Now sales are down, morale is low, and no one knows quite why. Matt believed in the goals the management team had established. What went wrong? ■

The best-laid plans are meaningless if they aren't put into place effectively. As managers form plans and carry out strategies to meet the goals of an organization, they must also determine whether their plans and strategies are generating the desired results. In this section, wvie'll look at how managers *control* (or *monitor*) their organizations and why doing so is so important.

Controlling to Stay on Course

Why does a company need to adapt to stay on course? Controlling (or **monitoring**) is the process by which managers measure performance and make sure the company's plans and strategies are being or have been properly carried out. Through the control process, managers ensure that the direction a company is moving toward aligns with its short- and long-term plans. The controlling process also can detect errors in systems, so if a plan is not meeting its goals, it can be modified.

■ **FIGURE 7.11**
The Monitoring/Control Cycle

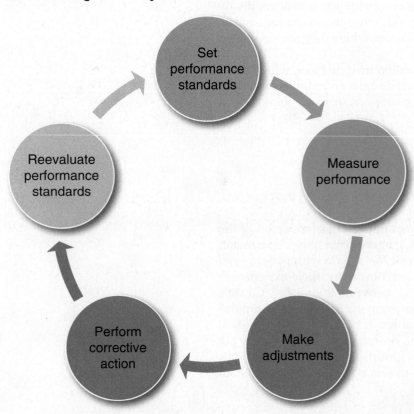

Control Strategies

How is moving toward the corporate vision measured? Most companies have control systems that help measure how well the plans they put in motion are working. In general, the control system forms a cycle, as shown in ■ **FIGURE 7.11**. Performance standards are set, and actual performance is measured and compared against the standard. To measure a firm's performance, reporting tools such as financial statements and sales reports are used. These reports help determine whether the firm's products are competitive and being produced efficiently and whether the company is using its capital wisely. Based on this information, adjustments are made, and the cycle begins again.

Are financial, production, and sales measures the only tools for assessing performance? No. Another measure of performance is quality—the goods or services a company provides must meet and exceed customer expectations. Many managers use **total quality management** (TQM), an integrated approach that focuses on quality from the beginning of the production process up through the final monitoring to detect and correct problems.

Pest Control Company Controls Its Fleet

Anchor Pest Control is a small pest control service with a fleet of 15 vans and trucks. When a van is down for repairs, the company experiences a serious loss of income. So keeping the entire fleet in top operating condition with a minimum of cost and downtime is an important business goal.[15] Another key goal is customer satisfaction. This includes drivers arriving on time, driving to and from sites carefully, and completing their work in a timely manner. Initially, Anchor owner Don Wolf tried using GPS devices in each van to monitor whether these business goals were being met. But he soon realized these systems would track the vehicles but were not helping him answer the business questions he had: When did each van need to go in for maintenance? How hard was the engine working? Which driver was making the most stops in a day?

Wolf found a monitoring device called CarChip that he could afford to install in each vehicle. By downloading the information from CarChip to a software program, each vehicle can be sent in for maintenance at just the right moment: before it breaks down but not before it is required. CarChip can set a top speed for each vehicle so that he knows drivers are being careful on the road. Wolf is able to rank top performers by safety rating or total miles driven and give rewards accordingly.

As a good manager, Wolf had to know what his goals were for Anchor and then investigate the right products and tools to monitor performance. Using data to check the business's progress toward meeting those goals has helped the company be the most efficient and profitable it can be.

What are the basic tools managers use for monitoring quality? There are seven basic tools managers use to monitor quality-related goals:

1. **Check sheet.** A simple sheet recording the number of times certain product defects occur (■ **FIGURE 7.12A**).

2. **Control chart.** A graph that shows the average and fluctuations of a process being monitored to determine whether it is behaving within the limits of proper functioning. ■ **FIGURE 7.12B** shows the average weld strength (35.5) and the fluctuations around the average according to the lot number.

3. **Histogram.** A graph that displays the count of the number of times a specific event occurs (for example, the number of times the smoothness of a tube produced was in the range 5 to 10) (■ **FIGURE 7.12C**).

4. **Pareto chart.** A combination bar and line graph that shows different categories of problems and the total (cumulative) number of problems. The Pareto chart in ■ **FIGURE 7.12D** shows the breakdown of types of complaints leading to returned merchandise.

5. **Scatter plot.** A graph that displays the values of two variables to see if there is a relationship between them. For example, the scatter plot in ■ **FIGURE 7.12E** would help a firm decide if more time in the kiln creates tiles that have a higher smoothness value.

6. **Run chart.** A graph that displays the value of some data across a specific set of dates. Managers can then identify problems that occur in a certain cycle, for example, once a month. Does the run chart in ■ **FIGURE 7.12F** show there is a pattern to the production of higher-brilliance bulbs?

7. **Cause-and-effect diagram.** Also called a fishbone diagram, this illustrates all of the contributing factors in the product design that might lead to faulty production (■ **FIGURE 7.12G**). For example, if the defect being analyzed is a soldering defect, the cause-and-effect diagram would show that contributing factors could be from the machinery operator, materials, or methods.

■ **FIGURE 7.12A**
Check Sheet

Name of Data Recorder: Jigme Patel
Location: Bowie, AZ
Data Collection Dates: 10/1–10/15

Defect Types/ Event Occurrence	Sunday	Monday	Tuesday	Dates Wednesday	Thursday	Friday	Saturday	TOTAL
Overheated		IIIIIII	IIIIIII	IIII	II			20
Cooled too long			II	I		II		5
Weak welds								0
Misaligned			I	II				3
Broken								0
Discolored		II		IIII				6
Spotting					II			2
Paint defect								0
Irregular shape				I				1
Inaccurate measurements						IIIII		5
TOTAL		10	10	12	4	7		

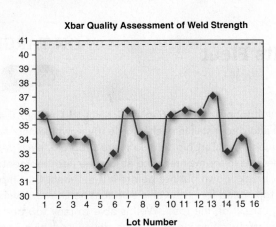

■ FIGURE 7.12B
Control Chart

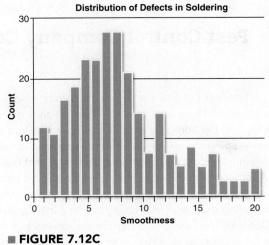

■ FIGURE 7.12C
Histogram

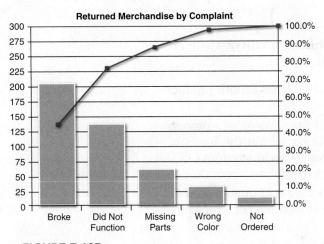

■ FIGURE 7.12D
Pareto Chart

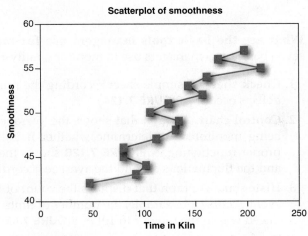

■ FIGURE 7.12E
Scatter Plot

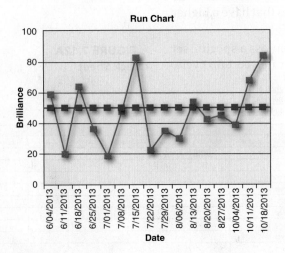

■ FIGURE 7.12F
Run Chart

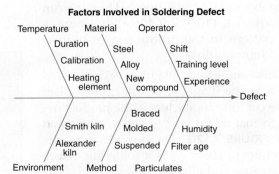

■ FIGURE 7.12G
Cause-and-Effect Diagram

There are many more advanced statistical tools available, but managers often begin their drive toward TQM with these seven basic tools.

What is the Six Sigma strategy for quality? Another well-known quality initiative is **Six Sigma**, a statistically based, proactive, long-term process designed to examine the overall business process and prevent problems. To achieve the "Six Sigma standard," a business must not allow more than 3.4 defects per million opportunities. To achieve such levels, it can take years to train and implement a staff that understands the approach. The techniques of Six Sigma produce results that are consistent and repeatable, which translates into very few defects and very consistent high levels of customer satisfaction.

Jack Welch, CEO of GE from 1981 to 2001, was a huge proponent of the Six Sigma method and pushed it into every corner of the company with great success. However, there is controversy around the proper use of Six Sigma monitoring in the business community.[16] For example, Robert Nardelli worked under Jack Welch and left GE to become the CEO of Home Depot, where he applied Six Sigma practices with great fervor. Home Depot initially saw great growth in profits, but the huge amount of paperwork and data collection began to take a toll on store workers. It left them less time for customer interaction, causing customer satisfaction to plummet. After having been in first place on the American Customer Satisfaction Index, the company fell to last. The current CEO of Home Depot, Frank Blake, has modified Six Sigma's approach to allow store managers to make more decisions independently.

The missing piece for Matt Finley's company, which was struggling despite a promising reorganization plan, turned out to be a lack of adequate control. The company began its reorganization with well-designed goals but never chose which tools it would use to monitor the results. Matt recognized this and established a set of procedures so managers could measure both the firm's financial progress and product quality. He had to learn about some new tools for quality reporting—Pareto charts and cause-and-effect diagrams—but once the processes for collecting and reporting data were in place, the picture became clear. The new organization structure began working once these important adjustments were made.

Summary

1 What are the levels of management, and what skills do managers need to be successful? (pp. 193–197)

- **Management** (p. 193) is the process of working with people and resources to accomplish the goals of an organization by performing four primary functions: **planning** (p. 198), **organizing** (p. 204), leading, and **controlling/monitoring** (p. 208).

- **Top managers** (p. 194) are the corporate officers who are responsible for the organization as a whole. **Middle managers** (p. 195) are the top managers of the major divisions or segments of an organization. **First-line managers** (p. 195) supervise the employees who carry out the day-to-day operations of a company.

- Successful managers need to possess a variety of skills, including **conceptual** (p. 195), **technical** (p. 196), **time management** (p. 196), **interpersonal** (p. 196), and **decision-making skills** (p. 196).

2 How are the strategic plan, the corporate vision, and the mission statement defined for a business? (pp. 197–201)

- Managers use planning, goals, and objectives to help achieve the corporate vision and stay on task. **Planning** (p. 198) is the process of establishing goals and objectives and determining the best ways to accomplish them. **Goals** (p. 198) are broad, long-term accomplishments an organization wants to achieve in about a five-year time frame. **Objectives** (p. 198) are the short-term targets that are designed to help achieve goals.

- Top managers put together a **strategic plan** (p. 198), or a main course of action, that maps out the way in which the corporation will achieve its goals.

- Before the strategic plan is in place, a firm's managers must define the organization's purpose, basic goals, and philosophies through **vision** (p. 199) and **mission statements** (p. 199). The corporate vision is what the business wants to be in the future. A mission statement is a description of the organization's current purpose, basic goals, and philosophies.

- Part of the strategic planning process includes conducting a **SWOT analysis** (p. 200) to help management determine the strategic fit between an organization's internal capabilities and external possibilities. SWOT stands for strengths, weaknesses, opportunities, and threats.

3 Why do managers need tactical plans, operational plans, and contingency plans? (pp. 201–203)

- **Tactical plans** (p. 196) specifically determine the resources and the actions required to implement particular aspects of a strategic plan. Tactical plans are made with a one- to three-year horizon in mind and are formulated by middle managers.

- **Operational plans** (p. 201) determine the process by which tactical plans can be achieved. Operational plans depend on daily or weekly schedules and focus more on specific departments or employees. Operational plans are formulated by first-line managers.

- **Contingency planning** (p. 202) is planning that ensures that an organization will run as smoothly as possible during a crisis or disruption and determines how a firm's managers will communicate, both internally and externally.

4 What is the significance of organizing, and how are most companies organized? (pp. 203–207)

- **Organizing** (p. 204) is the process of structuring the capital, personnel, raw materials, and other resources needed to implement a company's plans in a way that best matches the nature of the work. An **organization chart** (p. 204) shows how groups of employees fit into the larger organization structure and to whom they report.

- A **vertical organization** (p. 204) is organized by specific functions, such as marketing, finance, purchasing, IT, and human resources. However, integrating the functions and divisions is not always easy because communication and decision making must travel up long chain-of-command lines.

- A **horizontal organization** (p. 204) is flatter, and there are fewer managerial levels. Most employees work in teams or groups and have more responsibility for the outcome of their work. Because the chain of command is shorter, approvals for decisions can be sought and received much faster.

- **Matrix organization** (p. 206) is type of management system in which people are pooled into groups by their skills and then assigned to projects as needed.

- **Network organizations** (p. 207) are collections of independent, mostly single-function firms that collaborate with one another to produce a product or a service.

- In an **inverted organization** (p. 207), the role of managers is to empower and encourage employees to do what they do best and to be accountable to them.

5 How do managers ensure that the business is on track and moving forward? (pp. 208–211)

- **Controlling** (also called **monitoring**) (p. 208) is the process by which managers measure a company's performance and ensure that its plans and strategies are working.

- Performance standards are measured with reporting tools, such as financial statements and sales reports. Quality measures are also in place to ensure that products or services meet customer requirements. **Total quality management (TQM)** (p. 208) focuses on quality control throughout the entire production process. Basic mathematical and graphical tools, such as scatter plots and Pareto charts, are used to monitor quality goals.

Key Terms

conceptual skills (p. 195)
contingency planning (p. 202)
controlling (monitoring) (p. 208)
decision-making skills (p. 196)
departmentalization (p. 204)
first-line manager (p. 195)
goal (p. 198)
horizontal organization (p. 204)
interpersonal skills (p. 196)
inverted organization (p. 207)
line organization (p. 206)
line and staff organization (p. 206)

management (p. 193)
matrix organization (p. 206)
middle managers (p. 195)
mission statement (p. 199)
network organization (p. 207)
objective (p. 198)
operational plan (p. 201)
organization chart (p. 204)
organizing (p. 204)
planning (p. 198)
Six Sigma (p. 211)
span of control (p. 204)

staff department (p. 206)
strategic plan (p. 198)
SWOT analysis (p. 200)
tactical plans (p. 201)
technical skills (p. 196)
time management skills (p. 196)
top managers (p. 194)
total quality management (p. 208)
vertical organization (p. 204)
vision (p. 199)

MyBizLab

Go to **mybizlab.com** to complete the problems marked with this icon .

Self Test

Multiple Choice *You can find the answers on the last page of this book.*

7-1 The four primary processes of management are

a. planning, optimizing, leading, and controlling.

b. organizing, controlling, planning, and leading.

c. prioritizing, leading, controlling, and organizing.

d. planning, leading, organizing, and deciding.

7-2 A SWOT analysis

a. is an important part of developing a strategic plan.

b. is one type of contingency planning.

c. helps translate the tactical plan in instructions for employees.

d. leads to an effective mission statement.

7-3 A well-defined corporate vision benefits a company by

a. keeping managers focused on strategies that are consistent with the company's goals.

b. illustrating the company's values to investors.

c. inspiring employees.

d. All of the above

Self Test (continued)

7-4 The organization you work for just hired a new CEO. Within the first week in her new position, the CEO sent a memo to the firm's board of directors and senior managers that defined the purpose of the business as well as the basic goals and philosophies of the business. This document serves as a draft of a new

a. vision.

b. mission statement.

c. goals and objectives statement.

d. tactical plan.

7-5 A good strategic plan

a. determines the best ways to accomplish goals of an organization.

b. is specific and tactical.

c. concentrates only on what is going on inside an organization, not outside an organization.

d. is wide ranging.

7-6 The controlling function of management is best described as

a. keeping employees in line.

b. watching employees carefully by monitoring their e-mail and phone usage.

c. measuring the firm's performance to make sure the company's plans are on track.

d. All of the above

7-7 A horizontal organization requires

a. more use of collaborative teams.

b. a strict chain of command.

c. a tall organization chart.

d. None of the above

7-8 The seven basic tools for monitoring a business include all of the following except

a. Pareto analysis.

b. Monte Carlo statistical simulations.

c. scatter plots.

d. cause-and-effect diagrams.

7-9 Shauna is the sales manager for a regional chain of bookstores. She reports to the executive vice president of sales and marketing, and each sales manager reports to Shauna. Shauna would be considered a

a. top manager.

b. middle manager.

c. first-line manager.

d. Both b and c.

7-10 A corporation with a matrix organizational system

a. pools people into groups by skills.

b. makes sure teams have more responsibility for the outcome of their work.

c. organizes based on functional area.

d. collects single-function firms into a network that collaborates on a product.

True/False *You can find the answers on the last page of this book.*

7-11 A company with a vertical organization cannot use an inverted organization.
☐ True or ☐ False

7-12 A SWOT analysis is used to determine the strategic fit between an organization and its internal and external environments.
☐ True or ☐ False

7-13 Conceptual skills mean a person has the ability to think abstractly.
☐ True or ☐ False

7-14 Contingency planning helps a business weather a disruption or a crisis.
☐ True or ☐ False

7-15 The Six Sigma initiative is focused on improving communication.
☐ True or ☐ False

Critical Thinking Questions

⊙ **7-16** Recall your own personal working experiences and the managers with whom you have had interaction. Discuss the skills that define the best manager with whom you have worked and discuss the skills that define the worst manager with whom you have worked.

7-17 Would you prefer to work in an organization with a vertical structure or a flat, horizontal structure? Would your answer change if you were the CEO instead of a new hire? How would you feel about working in an inverted organization as a manager?

⊙ **7-18** Review the tools presented for monitoring quality. How would this kind of data-driven decision making help managers make decisions? Could too much data make it difficult to decide on a course of action? Would it depend on the type of problem? The type of manager?

Team Time

ON A MISSION

Research and print out several mission statements. Be sure to choose statements from both not-for-profit organizations and for-profit organizations. Bring these mission statements to class.

Process

Step 1. Assemble into groups of four or five.

Step 2. As a group, evaluate the similar components in each mission statement, such as the following:

- The statement of the product or service being offered
- The primary market it's being offered to
- An indication of the organization's commitment to quality
- An indication of the organization's commitment to social responsibility
- A declaration of organization's philosophy

Step 3. Make note of the components that are included in most mission statements and those that are included in only a few of them.

Step 4. As a group, decide which mission statement is the most inspiring. Why? Which is the least inspiring? Why?

Step 5. As a class, compare the statements deemed most inspiring from each group and determine which is the most effective. Finally, openly discuss with your classmates how the winning statement would affect their inclination to work for this organization.

Ethics and Corporate Social Responsibility

ASSESSING SOCIAL RESPONSIBILITY

One of the functions of management is control, which includes measuring financial performance. But how often and with what tools does a manager assess an organization's social responsibility?

Process

Step 1. In small groups, discuss the following:

- The planning and organizational changes that might need to be implemented
- The controls that a manager might use to measure and monitor the results of his or her social responsibility initiatives

Step 2. After this discussion, research companies that are known for their social responsibility efforts. Then discuss what impact their efforts have had on management.

Web Exercises

♻ 7-19 Project Oxygen
Google invested a great deal of time mining its own internal data to determine what type of person makes a good Google manager. Dubbed Project Oxygen, researchers made over 10,000 observations of managerial behaviors at Google. Find articles about Project Oxygen on the Web and read them. What were the researchers' conclusions? Who makes a good manager, and who does not? Are the researchers right? Or are there other key factors that do not appear in the final eight qualities the researchers identified good managers as having? Are the results valid only for Google, or do you think they are general truths?

♻ 7-20 Tools for TQM
Using online resources like YouTube and Office .Microsoft.com, see if you can teach yourself to create a Pareto chart in Excel. Can you create a histogram? A scatter plot? Can you find a PowerPoint template for a cause-and-effect diagram?

7-21 How Well Do You Manage Your Time?
Time management skills are important for a manager to have to work efficiently and accomplish all the tasks a manager is expected to handle on any given day. How are your time management skills? Even as a student, you are your own manager and can benefit from being more in control of your time. Find a quiz online that assesses your ability to manage your time. Write a brief report answering the following questions:

- What online assessment did you find?
- What were the results?
- How can you improve your time management skills?

7-22 Predictably Irrational
Visit the Ted.com website and search for the 20-minute video "Are We in Control of Our Own Decisions?" by Dan Ariely, a behavioral economist. Watch the video and concentrate on the example of the doctor and the patient. Are there business decisions that managers make where factors outside their decision-making process influence the outcome?

7-23 Get SMARTER
The acronym SMARTER reminds us that goals should be specific, measurable, acceptable, realistic, timely, extending, and rewarding. Do some research on the Web to see how other people have implemented SMARTER goals. Then create two goals for yourself for next semester. Document how they are SMARTER goals.

MyBizLab

Go to **mybizlab.com** for Auto-graded writing questions as well as the following
Assisted-graded writing questions:

✪ 7-24 Contingency plans are important in any business. Describe what kinds
of plans your school might have in place to recover from a disaster.
How would these plans differ, if at all, from those of a local business in
your area? What are a few possible scenarios that would require contingency plans in your school or at a local business?

✪ 7-25 How does the complexity of a project impact quality control? As software projects grow to have many millions of lines of code, can that industry still achieve Six Sigma quality? What kind of tools and processes
would it require?

References

1. "At a Glance: Ursula Burns," *Forbes*, August 2011,
www. forbes.com/profile/ursula-burns.
2. L. Bohm, *Work Harassment—Ani Chopourian's Story*,
www. youtube.com/watch?v=ZJMWaalwrcU.
3. Wikimedia Foundation, "Vision Statement," http://
wikimediafoundation.org.
4. *Wikimedia Strategic Plan*, February 1, 2011, http://upload
.wikimedia.org/wikipedia/foundation/c/c0/WMF_
StrategicPlan2011_spreads.pdf.
5. Quoted in Pete Johnson, "Best Vision Statement,"
September 25, 2008, http://blog.nerdguru.net.
6. "Our History: Our Company: GE," www.ge.com/
company/history/bios/john_welch.html.
7. P. Pitas, *Culver's Fact Sheet*, March 24, 2014, http://
culvers-bece73af.s3.amazonaws.com/media-documents/
Culvers-MediaKit-fact.pdf.
8. From American Cancer Society, "About the American
Cancer Society," www.cancer.org/AboutUs/WhoWeAre/
acsmissionstatements.
9. Carter McNamara, "Strategic Planning (in Nonprofit or
For-Profit Organizations)," www.managementhelp.org/
plan_dec/str_plan/str_plan.htm.
10. Rie Ishiguro and Shinji Kitamura, "Japan Quake's
Economic Impact Worse Than First Feared," April 12,
2011, www.reuters.com/article/2011/04/12/
us-japan-economy-idUSTRE73B0O320110412.
11. The Vanguard Group, "Business Contingency Planning
and Disaster Recovery Programs at Vanguard," www
.vanguard.com/pdf/ccri.pdf.
12. Frank Ostroff, *The Horizontal Organization* (Oxford: Oxford
University Press, 1999), 25–57, 102–50.
13. "Vineet Nayar's Scrapbook: In Search of New Leaders: Interview with Fox News," June 23, 2010, www.vineetnayar
.com/interview-with-fox-news.
14. Harichandan Arakali, "HCL Tech Exceeds Expectations,
Records 29% Jump in Net Profit," www.livemint.com/
2012/04/18085442/HCL-Tech-exceeds-expectations
.html.
15. Anchor Pest Control, "Pest Control Company Extermi-
nates Business Problem," www.carchip.com/Product_
Docs/CS_PestControl.pdf.
16. "Six Sigma: So Yesterday?," *Bloomberg Businessweek*,
www.businessweek.com/magazine/content/
07_24/b4038409.htm.

Chapter 8
Motivation, Leadership, and Teamwork

❯ Motivation

At Ana Gutierrez's public relations firm, employees were suffering from a severe case of demotivation. Translating motivational theories into practical applications is a challenge many business managers face. How can Ana use abstract concepts about human behavior to inspire her workforce and turn around her struggling company?

❯ Leadership

Every young person dreams big—but dreaming of changing the world's transportation systems and economic systems and creating the tools for space travel seems like too much for any one person. But Elon Musk is accomplishing it all with the help of his leadership skills.

❯ Teamwork

Teamwork can bring about great success. For all teams, teamwork is important, but for some teams, it is essential. If a surgical operating team does not work together effectively, patients can suffer complications or even die. How could one surgeon make a difference worldwide by studying the dynamics of his operating room team?

OBJECTIVES

1 How do motivation and the work environment encourage "flow"? (pp. 219–221)

2 What are the main theories of motivation, and how are they applied to the workforce? (pp. 221–225)

3 How have motivational theories and industrial psychology changed the work environment since the early twentieth century? (pp. 225–226)

4 What are the various identifiable leadership styles and traits, and how do they affect business leadership? (pp. 226–233)

5 What are the best ways to create, manage, and participate in teams? (pp. 232–237)

MyBizLab®

⭐ **Improve Your Grade!**

Over 10 million students improved their results using the Pearson MyLabs.
Visit **mybizlab.com** for simulations, tutorials, and end-of-chapter problems.

Motivation pp. 219–226

"All of my employees were so . . . uninspired," Ana Gutierrez laments. "People seemed to be just 'showing up'; the sense of apathy in the office was almost palpable. The quality of our work was suffering. I wasn't sure what to do."

Ana, the founder and CEO of a small public relations firm, was facing a crisis of motivation within her workforce. The sales team hadn't scored a new account in months, and existing clients were complaining about their sales representatives. "You're not delivering on your promises," one client, the leader of a local not-for-profit organization, blurted during a particularly tense conference call. "A recent event was poorly advertised and poorly attended. There were errors in your latest press release. And your associates take two days to respond to my e-mails."

Ana had already tried a variety of tactics to motivate her employees. She dangled the possibility of additional bonuses and free dinners to her company's salespeople—to no avail. She instituted a new policy requiring all employees to work nine hours a day, plus two weekends a month. It didn't work. She told her associates she was prepared to promote at least three of the highest-performing employees among them to more lucrative positions within six months. No one was interested.

How could Ana apply what she knows about motivational theories to light a fire under her employees and save her business? ■

Source: Tim Pannell/Thinkstock.

We hear the word *motivation* **often.** When students seek out extra learning opportunities to go beyond a course's general requirements, they are described as motivated learners. But what does motivation have to do with working in a business? Are all of a business owner's actions motivated solely by profit? Does an employer who pays well always have strongly motivated employees? In this section, we'll examine motivation in detail and look at techniques used in the past and the present to motivate employees.

Personal Motivation

What drives you to do your personal best? Even when pursuing their personal goals, different people retain and lose motivation for very different reasons. Think of times you have pushed to be your best, whether at school, in sports, or in other activities. Is it easier for you to build enthusiasm for tasks you're sure you can accomplish? Or do you set difficult goals and draw energy from the challenge of attaining them? Some people need immediate gratification to stay motivated. Others are able to postpone short-term success in pursuit of long-term gains. Which setting motivates you more?

Now think about how hard you work when you receive positive feedback—either financial or emotional. Are you driven more by the values of the place where you work, by your beliefs, or by the rewards from doing a job well? For some people, being part of the accomplishments of a team is what motivates them. Are you one of those people?

What does it feel like to be optimally motivated? Have you ever been working on a project in which you were so immersed in what you were doing that, when you looked at your watch, four hours had gone by? Psychologist Mihaly Csikszentmihalyi refers to this state of rapt attention as **flow**.[1] A flow state happens when you are completely involved and focused on what you are doing. Often, people produce their best work, make the best use of their skills, and feel the most pleasure when they are in flow. They feel a strong match between their own abilities and the challenge of a task: It is neither too difficult, which can lead to frustration, nor too simple, which can lead to boredom. They report a sense of control over what is happening and a feeling of effortlessness in their work. How do you create this sense of flow? This is the subject of **organizational psychology**—the study of how to create a workplace that fosters motivation and productivity among employees.

Motivating Employees

How motivated is the U.S. workforce? The Q12 is a 12-question survey of employee engagement administered by the Gallup Organization. Based on respondents' answers to a series of questions, the survey classifies employees as "engaged," "not engaged," or "actively disengaged." According to Q12 survey results, 73 percent of U.S. employees are not engaged or are actively disengaged in their work[2] (see ■ **TABLE 8.1**). Imagine a workplace in which three out of four employees are complaining or even disrupting other workers during the day. This statistic makes it clear that encouraging flow in the workplace is an important challenge.

How does a work environment encourage "flow"? There is no fixed recipe, but there are companies that have succeeded in building motivated, engaged environments that support workers and support the creative experience of flow.

One such company is SAS, a business software firm in North Carolina. With an incredibly low employee turnover rate of just 2 to 5 percent,[3] SAS has achieved 38 straight years of record revenues.[4] The company has achieved this in large part due to the policies of its CEO, Jim Goodnight. Goodnight lists the following as ways in which SAS works to foster a creative environment:

- It keeps employees intellectually engaged.
- It removes distractions so employees can do their best work.
- It makes managers responsible for sparking creativity.

TABLE 8.1	Motivation Levels of Employees		
Engaged	**Not Engaged**	**Actively Disengaged**
• Work with passion	• Work with minimal effort	• Work in a disruptive manner
• Feel connected and obligated to the company	• Are indifferent to the company	• Are unhappy with the company
• Add to the success of the company	• Make little or no contribution to the company	• Combat the efforts of engaged workers

Source: Based on Gallup Organization, "American Workplace Report," 2013, www.gallup.com.

- It has managers eliminate the arbitrary distinctions between administrative "suits" and more abstract "creatives."
- It engages customers to be creative partners.

In addition to fostering the professional lives of its employees, SAS supports their private lives as well. On the SAS campus, you'll find medical facilities for employees and their families, a Montessori day care center, and a cafeteria where families can eat lunch together. "The corporate philosophy is, if your fifth grader is in his first school play, you should be there to see it," says Goodnight. Such a philosophy has led to SAS earning a top spot on *Fortune* magazine's Best Companies to Work For list.[5]

What are the benefits of keeping employees motivated? Both employers and employees benefit from motivated workforces. Employers find that workers are more productive and creative when provided with a motivating environment and motivating tasks. According to Gallup's calculations, disengaged employees cost their firms up to $300 billion a year in reduced productivity.[6] In contrast, companies with high engagement levels have four-times-greater earnings growth rates compared to companies in the same industry struggling with disengaged workers.

The Atlanta-based chain Chick-fil-A is an example of a company that has benefited from strong employee motivation. The company fosters employee motivation with strong monetary rewards like scholarships and free cars to the operators of strong-performing stores. The chain has never allowed any store to be open on Sunday. Remaining closed on Sundays is both a practical and a spiritual decision, centered on the belief that employees should have an opportunity to rest and spend time with their families each week so they can return to work motivated on Monday mornings.[7] Chick-fil-A employees respond with highly engaged behavior by going out of their way to refill customers' drinks and watching to see if they need extra napkins delivered to their tables. The results of that are seen in the chain's explosive growth, with total sales now exceeding $4 billion.[8]

Traditional Theories of Motivation

What are the traditional theories describing what motivates people?
Several theories have been proposed to explain how and why people are motivated:

- Maslow's hierarchy of needs
- McClelland's "three needs" theory
- Herzberg's motivator-hygiene theory

What is Maslow's hierarchy of needs? One early researcher in the area of human motivation was Abraham Maslow (1908–1970), who published the book *Motivation and Personality* in 1954. In his theory of motivation, Maslow suggests that humans have a **hierarchy of needs** and that primary needs must be met first before higher-level needs can be addressed (see ■ **FIGURE 8.1**). The first needs that must be met are basic needs—termed **physiological needs**—such as the need for water, food, sleep, and reproduction. This means that before we as humans can think about anything else in our lives, we must ensure that these basic physiological needs are met.

Once our physiological needs have been met, Maslow's theory holds that people strive to satisfy their **safety needs**. This includes establishing safe and stable places to live and work.

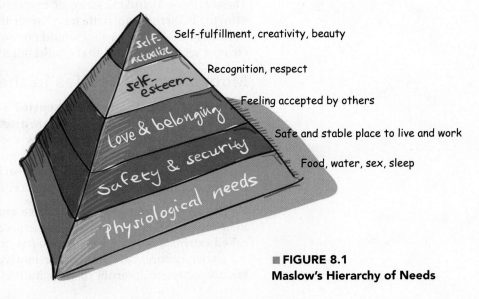

Self-fulfillment, creativity, beauty

Recognition, respect

Feeling accepted by others

Safe and stable place to live and work

Food, water, sex, sleep

■ **FIGURE 8.1**
Maslow's Hierarchy of Needs

Once these needs have been met, people try to meet their social or **belonging needs**. These include the need to belong to a group and feel accepted by others. The next level in Maslow's hierarchy includes **esteem needs**. These are satisfied by the mastery of a skill and the attention and recognition of others. Finally, **self-actualization needs** are at the top of the hierarchy. These needs include the desire to maximize your own potential through education and self-fulfillment as well as experiences of beauty and spirituality. Self-actualization needs cannot be met unless and until all of a person's lower-level needs have been met.

Maslow suggested that different people find themselves at different places in the hierarchy, and so their motivations may be different. An offer to work overtime for a higher hourly wage might motivate a person concerned with his or her safety needs but have the opposite effect on someone trying to fulfill his or her need for self-actualization.

What is McClelland's "three needs" theory? Other researchers have proposed different models to map human needs to motivation. Psychologist David McClelland's (1917–1998) **three needs theory** suggests there are three main motivators:

1. **The need for achievement.** To accomplish something difficult on your own
2. **The need for affiliation.** To form close personal relationships
3. **The need for power.** To be able to control the behavior of others

Although an individual may have multiple needs, McClelland suggests that one tends to be dominant over the others. Which need we try to satisfy depends on a variety of complex factors, including our cultural background. For example, in the workplace, a person whose main need is for affiliation may have little motivation to perform a solitary task, whereas a person with a high need for achievement may be highly motivated to perform a difficult task alone.

How does Herzberg's motivator-hygiene theory explain motivation? In 1959, psychologist Frederick Herzberg (1923–2000) proposed a theory of job satisfaction called **motivator-hygiene theory** (or **two-factor theory**). According to this theory, two factors influence a person's motivation.

Hygiene factors are factors such as a safe working environment, proper pay and benefits, and positive relationships with one's coworkers. People rarely notice hygiene factors if they are present. However, if hygiene factors are absent or inadequate, people tend to be dissatisfied. If there suddenly is no heat in the place where you work or if your pay is cut, you may be motivated to find a way to meet these needs. But if these factors are already in place, they are taken for granted and may not serve to motivate you.

Motivator factors represent the second set of factors in Herzberg's theory. These factors include a sense of responsibility, recognition, promotion, and job growth. If there is no path for growth in your job or little recognition of your achievements, you probably would not immediately quit, but their absence would create a set of conditions that would fail to motivate you.

Motivational Theories in the Modern Workplace

Do managers actually use theories of motivation? Theories of motivation can be very abstract. So, how can a team leader at a software development company take what researchers know about motivation and use it to increase the productivity and satisfaction of employees? The theories of human motivation you have just read about have given rise to several different approaches for organizing and motivating people in the workplace.

What can a manager do to enhance employee motivation? In the workplace, there are some external motivating factors managers can control. These motivators, called **extrinsic motivators**, include pay, promotion, and verbal praise.

Other factors, called **intrinsic motivators**, are beyond a manager's control because they are internal to each individual employee. Intrinsic motivators are based on a person's actual interest in his or her work and stem from the sense of purpose or value the person derives from the work being done. A manager will have difficulty motivating an intrinsically motivated employee to take on unsatisfying work by using offers of just bonuses or promotions.

Researchers are investigating if there are some intrinsic motivators common to all of us. At Cornell University, Evan Polman and Kyle Emich studied a large number of undergraduates to see if the motivation and the quality of their work would change depending on whom the work benefited.[9] Two separate groups of students were given puzzles and creative projects. One group was told that they were solving the puzzle to save themselves and that they were illustrating a story they would later publish themselves. The second group was told that they were doing the work to benefit someone else—solving the puzzle would save the life of another person who was imprisoned—and that they were illustrating a story someone else would publish. In each case, the group working for someone else produced better results—66 percent of the altruistic group solved the puzzle versus less than 50 percent of the self-focused group, and the creative level of the work for an unknown author was of much higher quality. If decisions for others are more effective and creative than decisions we make for ourselves, can managers structure their organizations in ways that promote that?

What other motivational models exist? In addition to the theories proposed by Maslow, McClelland, and Herzberg, several models have been developed that provide theoretical explanations of what motivates employees specifically in a business or workplace context:

- Theories X, Y, and Z
- The Vroom model
- Strength-based management

What are the Theory X and Theory Y models? In 1960, social psychologist Douglas McGregor proposed the Theory X and Theory Y models of behavior (see ■ **FIGURE 8.2**). The **Theory X** model suggests that people inherently dislike work and want to avoid it. Managers who subscribe to this model

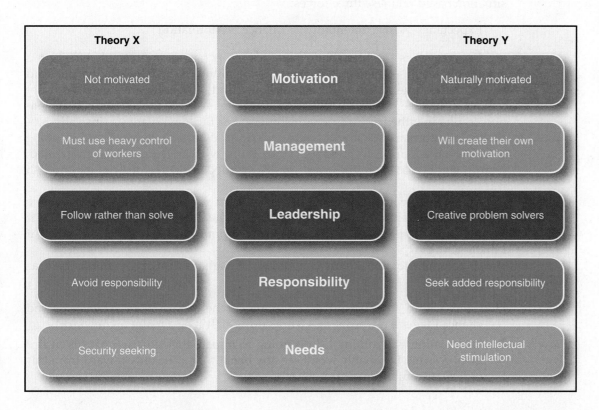

■ **FIGURE 8.2 Comparison of Theory X and Theory Y**

Theory X	Motivation	Theory Y
Not motivated	**Motivation**	Naturally motivated
Must use heavy control of workers	**Management**	Will create their own motivation
Follow rather than solve	**Leadership**	Creative problem solvers
Avoid responsibility	**Responsibility**	Seek added responsibility
Security seeking	**Needs**	Need intellectual stimulation

believe employees must be coerced and controlled to be productive and therefore use an authoritarian, hard-line style of management. In contrast, the **Theory Y** model suggests that people view work as being as natural as playing and resting. According to Theory Y, people are naturally motivated and will work to further the goals of an organization if they are satisfied with their jobs. Theory Y managers believe that, on average, people will accept and seek out responsibility and therefore have a softer, more collaborative style of management.

Clearly, Theories X and Y would not work equally well in all situations. Theory X style management—which is authoritarian and hard line—is often seen in large-scale operations such as mass manufacturing. In the knowledge industry, in which a mix of professionals work together to solve complex problems, Theory Y style management is more likely to be used.

How is the Theory Z model different? In 1981, William Ouchi, a professor at the University of California, Los Angeles, put forward a **Theory Z** model based on a Japanese management style that relied heavily on collaborative decision making. In many corporations in Japan in the 1980s, one person might be responsible for many different aspects of a single project. Employees tended to become generalists rather than specialists who were trained to do very narrow sets of tasks. Theory Z style management offers long-term employment with an emphasis on individual responsibility. Workers tend to show a desire to cooperate and be loyal to an organization. As a result, companies that apply Theory Z management often reap the benefits of low turnover, high productivity, and strong morale among the workforce. Morale, a sense of purpose and enthusiasm toward one's work, is an important factor in an employee's level of motivation.

Do any motivational models describe an individual person's motivation? Although Maslow's hierarchy and other theories describe human motivation, they do so in terms of an overall model for all employees. In 1964, Victor Vroom proposed a theory named **expectancy theory**, which has since been developed by other researchers. Expectancy theory suggests an individual's motivation can be described by the relationship between three psychological forces. He put forward the following formula to describe the motivation a person feels in any given situation based on these three forces:

Expectancy × Instrumentality × Valence = Motivation

Expectancy is the idea that a person's effort has an appreciable effect on a situation's result—whether it is a success or failure. Does working harder lead to a more positive outcome for an employee and/or a company? Or does it not make a difference? **Instrumentality** refers to the idea that the outcome of a situation results in either reward or punishment. For those who are extrinsically motivated, instrumentality answers the question "What are the chances I'm going to be rewarded if I do a good job?" For those who are intrinsically motivated, instrumentality answers the question "How good will I feel if I can accomplish this task?"

Valence is the importance that the individual places on the expected outcome of a situation. It answers questions such as "How great a reward will there be if my performance is exemplary?" and "How serious a punishment do I expect if I underperform?"

In common terms, Vroom's formulas for high and low motivations read as follows:

High motivation = (My work actually affects the outcome.) × (There's a good chance I'll get a reward if this works out.) × (It'll be a really big reward!)

Low motivation = (Nothing I do is going to impact this situation.) × (Even if it does go well, I probably won't see any benefit.) × (The only reward from this will be incredibly small.)

The Vroom formula can be used to analyze factors such as how satisfied employees are with their jobs, how likely it is they will remain in their jobs, and how hard they will work in them. Unlike Maslow's and McClelland's models, which address the typical needs of groups of people, Vroom's model, with its three independent variables, can generate a much more specialized result, attuned to the mental state of a specific individual.

Closely related to expectancy is **equity theory**—the idea that people expect to be rewarded on par with other people they feel their performance equals or else their motivation will suffer. People in an organization want to feel their contribution is recognized in a manner that fits with how they see the other coworkers being rewarded.

What is unique in strength-based management? Strength-based management is a system based on the belief that, rather than improve employees' weak skills, the best way to help them is to determine their strengths and build on them. This system is supported by research that shows that people can learn the most about areas in which they already have a strong foundation. Strength-based programs identify employees' current talents and skills and then provide additional training and support to develop them into areas of excellence. By designing a match between an employee's strengths and his or her daily activities and working around his or her weaknesses, the employee becomes more motivated and engaged.

Evolution of Motivational Theories

How have motivational theories changed? During the industrial age, large corporations were created, and researchers like Frederick Taylor (1856–1950) began to study ways to make workers more efficient and cost effective. In 1911, Taylor published his findings in *The Principles of Scientific Management*. He encouraged managers to scientifically study their employees to determine the best way for them to complete tasks and then train their employees to use these methods. Many of his ideas were implemented in factories. By the 1920s and 1930s, a field of academic study called **industrial psychology** was created to further address these issues. Other researchers, such as Frank and Lillian Gilbreth, used photography to study employees' work patterns. For example, they used **time-motion studies** to analyze factory jobs. These involved recording the actual movements and positions of workers, along with the timings, as they performed common tasks. Then workers could be trained in the precise sequence of steps that would make them most productive.

Another famous study of the period was conducted at the Hawthorne plant of the Western Electric Company in Illinois by Elton Mayo, a professor at Harvard University. The study ran from 1927 to 1932 and examined physical influences on the workplace (such as lighting and humidity) as well as psychological aspects (such as group pressure and working hours). Mayo's major finding, known as the **Hawthorne effect**, was that regardless of the experimental changes made, the production of the workers improved. Researchers concluded that the increase in productivity was based on the attention the workers were receiving. Because they knew they were being studied, the employees felt special and produced more, regardless of the conditions Hawthorne studied. The Hawthorne effect is used now as a term to describe the increase in productivity caused by workers being given special attention. After World War II, the direction of research in management theory shifted from the management of individual workers toward the management of entire organizations, their structures, and policies.

What motivational theories fit the modern workplace? Research continues to be conducted in the field of organizational psychology, and new theories about motivation and management continue to emerge. A recent motivational theory has been developed as a result of examining the *open-source movement*—software

For knowledge workers, autonomy, mastery of skills, and a sense of purpose in their work are key motivators.
Source: Fotolia.

projects that are developed, tested, and maintained for free by a worldwide network of volunteers. Wikipedia and the Linux operating system are examples of these projects. Both have been hugely successful and were created by professional people working many hours for free—outside of their regular jobs.

What is causing people to behave this way? Four academic economists tried to find out by running an experiment where people were recruited to perform a range of tasks that required motor skills, creativity, or concentration. Monetary rewards were promised to people doing the tasks, depending on how well they performed on them. Top performers were promised the equivalent of five months' pay if they did well on the creative tasks or the ones that required concentration. Surprisingly, the higher the incentives were, the *worse* people performed. Similar results were seen when the London School of Economics reviewed corporate pay-for-performance plans.[10] The researchers concluded that using economic rewards to motivate employees can actually lead to poorer performance when the work being done is creative or requires concentration. At least one additional study has shown that today's knowledge workers value three things much more highly than money:[11]

- **Autonomy.** Having some control over the key decision in their work lives
- **Mastery.** Feeling skilled and having time to develop and improve their skills
- **Purpose.** Wanting their lives and work to have a higher meaning

Companies that utilize knowledge workers and are able to provide them with incentives such as these will see great benefits.

Remember Ana Gutierrez and her team of uninspired public relations professionals? "I realized that extrinsic motivators didn't have much of an effect on my employees, nor did a hard-line management style based on the Theory X model," she says. "So I changed my approach, and I soon saw positive results." In an attempt to increase the level of intrinsic motivation among her employees, Ana met with her salespeople and asked them which accounts they found most meaningful and satisfying to work on. She then rearranged the salespeople's accounts based on this information and found that they were more motivated when they worked with clients with whom they felt a personal connection. Ana also eliminated the nine-hour-day mandate but soon found that many of her newly motivated employees voluntarily worked at least that many hours—if not more! The company, once struggling, now flourishes: Sales are up, and clients are thrilled. With experimentation and careful thought, Ana achieved the goal of all business managers: translating motivational theory into business success.

Leadership pp. 226–233

Elon Musk showed his technical talents early, selling a computer game he designed at age 12 for $500. After he finished his undergraduate education with degrees in economics and physics at the University of Pennsylvania, he made plans to attend Stanford and study physics. But his interests spanned more than one field. He wanted to impact the future of the planet through the revolution of the Internet by generating solutions to the energy crisis—and by exploring the possibility of mass space travel. How could one person hope to accomplish such lofty goals in two different industries? ■

Source: Jerry Lampen/ANP/Newscom.

An organization is often successful when employees have a strong leader to demonstrate what it takes for a company to achieve its goals. Leading is the process of influencing, motivating, and enabling others to contribute to the success and effectiveness of an organization. As we discussed in Chapter 7, leading is one of the four functions of management (other functions include planning, organizing, and controlling/monitoring).

Are all managers leaders? Famed management researcher and author Peter Drucker once noted that "management is doing things right; leadership is doing the right things."[12] Both leaders and managers strive to motivate people, but they have different scopes. Typically, managers spend their time making sure specific tasks are done well and completed on time. The leadership of a company, on the other hand, is focused on establishing the long-term vision and strategies a company will need to survive and flourish. Truly great leaders are able to be both managers and leaders: They define a vision, foster agreement across the company, and then implement the strategy.

What styles of leadership exist? Many different leadership styles exist, and leaders often employ different styles in a given situation depending on a complex mix of their own personalities, the types of companies they work in and their corporate cultures, and the employees they manage. ■ **TABLE 8.2** lists four of the most common leadership styles:

- Democratic
- Autocratic
- Affiliative (laissez-faire)
- Visionary

TABLE 8.2	**Styles of Leadership**			
	Democratic	**Autocratic**	**Affiliative (Laissez-Faire)**	**Visionary**
Leader characteristics	• Listens well • Is a team worker • Collaborates • Influences	• Commands—"Do it because I say so" • Threatens • Has tight control • Monitors studiously • Creates dissonance • Contaminates everyone's mood • Drives away talent	• Promotes harmony • Empathizes with others • Boosts morale • Solves conflicts	• Inspires • Believes in own vision • Is empathetic • Explains how and why people's efforts contribute to the "dream"
Benefits to style	Values people's input and gets commitment through participation	Soothes fear by giving clear direction in an emergency	Creates harmony by connecting people to one another	Moves people toward shared dreams
When style is appropriate	To build buy-in or consensus or get valuable input from employees	In a crisis, to kick-start an urgent turnaround; with problem employees; traditional military	To heal rifts in a team; to motivate during stressful times or strengthen connections	When changes require a new vision or when a clear direction is needed; radical change

Photo Sources: Tribalium81/Fotolia; Kikkerdirk/Fotolia; NLshop/Fotolia; Freshidea/Fotolia.

What are democratic and autocratic leaders like? A democratic leader delegates authority and involves employees in the decision-making process. An **autocratic leader** makes decisions without consulting others.

Consider Henry Chang, who runs the kitchen of a large restaurant. Henry allows his staff to offer opinions as he develops the menu. He also lets them experiment with different recipes and food presentations and features their work on the main menu when possible. The kitchen staff members love working with Henry because he allows them to be creative and innovative. He also encourages them to cultivate the skills they will need to run their own restaurants someday. However, Henry's restaurant often attracts important political dignitaries and famous entertainers. Sometimes, the restaurant becomes unexpectedly busy. In these circumstances, Henry doesn't leave anything to chance and dictates exactly what needs to be done and who should do it. Henry knows he might hurt someone's feelings in the process, but ultimately, his staff trusts him to make the right decisions to obtain the best results for the restaurant.

For the most part, Henry is a democratic leader because he knows that by involving his employees, they become more invested in the process. The trade-off, Henry recognizes, is that his democratic style of leadership requires more time and advanced planning. When such time is not available, Henry must take complete charge. In those instances, he becomes an autocratic leader. A good leader knows that such commanding leadership can be an effective style in certain circumstances when quick decisions need to be made or when it seems as if the group cannot come to a consensus.

What are affiliative leaders? Some leaders take a more hands-off approach to management and act more as consultants than participants. **Affiliative (or laissez-faire) leaders** are more advisory in style, encouraging employees to contribute ideas rather than specifically directing their tasks. This style of leadership is often best used with groups and teams. Affiliative leadership implemented properly can give employees a sense of challenge, commitment, and renewed energy as they are left to handle tasks on their own. As businesses continue to reduce the layers of management, affiliative and democratic styles are becoming the leadership styles of choice. However, it is possible for affiliative leaders to lose too much involvement in the group's processes. If the group or team members feel that management is virtually absent, the members may choose actions and strategies that are easy and not in line with the goals of a company.

What makes a leader a visionary? **Visionary leaders** are able to inspire others, believe in their own vision, and move people toward a shared dream. John Lasseter was an animator in Disney's computer animation department when George Lucas's company Lucasfilm opened a computer animation division. Intrigued by the advances in technology he saw in use at Lucasfilm, Lasseter left Disney in 1984 to spend a month at Industrial Light and Magic (ILM), a division of Lucasfilm. The division was later purchased by Steve Jobs and became its own company, Pixar. Lasseter is currently Pixar's chief creative officer. He has assembled a uniquely creative group of employees who have produced animated-film classics such as *Toy Story*, *The Incredibles*, and *Frozen*.

As a visionary leader, Lasseter had to create the special environment giving creative people the freedom to be inventive but also the structure to meet the deadlines required to produce a multi-million-dollar film on schedule. His leadership came into play in the production of *Toy Story*. At that time, Pixar had never produced anything longer than a short, five-minute film. It wasn't clear whether the company could actually produce a full-length film. *Toy Story* was being produced and distributed by Disney (in a partnership with Pixar), which called a meeting to see a segment of the film to check its quality. Lasseter remembers the meeting: "I

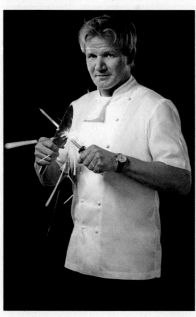

Gordon Ramsey is an accomplished chef, famous for an autocratic style of leadership in his restaurants.
Source: AF archive/Alamy.

was pretty much embarrassed by what was on the screen. I had made it. I directed everybody to do this . . . but it was a story filled with the most unhappy, mean people." Disney wanted to shut down production and fire the staff. But Lasseter negotiated a two-week reprieve and returned to lead his team of cowriters and animators. "Let's make the movie we wanted to make," he told them, and the story took on a gentler, sweeter tone. The team had to work nonstop during the two-week reprieve, with the threat of massive layoffs hanging over their heads. The ending of the story is well known: *Toy Story* went on to achieve $190 million in domestic box office receipts, and Lasseter earned an Honorary Oscar for the achievement.[13]

Traits of Leadership

What are the traits of great leaders? As illustrated in ■ **FIGURE 8.3**, the best leaders share some common traits:

- Great leaders *challenge the process* by not always accepting conventional beliefs and practices as the only way to accomplish tasks. Leaders are not afraid to alter their methods or plans if the situation calls for change. They continually brainstorm for solutions to problems and more effective ways of reaching goals.

- Great leaders *inspire a shared vision* and motivate people to care about the mission and goals of an organization. Leaders influence in a positive and moral way (rather than in a selfish and destructive way) and garner trust, respect, and commitment to the vision.

- Great leaders *model the way* by serving as a living example of the ideals they are asking their employees to emulate. Leaders have a good handle on their businesses and industries. They are willing to admit mistakes and constantly seek more information to make informed and reasoned decisions. Good leaders base their decisions on facts. They are well organized and detail oriented and through their speech and action choices set the ethical tone for their firms.

- Great leaders *exhibit emotional intelligence.* Most successful leaders possess a high degree of **emotional intelligence**—the ability to understand both one's own and others' emotions. It is a term for a set of skills that includes self-awareness, self-management, social awareness, and relationship management. Leaders can use their awareness of others' emotional states to inspire people to feel more positive and connect with others by being honest and open about their own ideals, concerns, and goals. In working with these types of leaders, people tend to feel secure and free to explore and share their creative ideas.

- Great leaders *enable others to act* by giving people access to information and empowering them to perform to their fullest potential.[14] Leaders need to achieve and have high energy levels. However, successful leaders also delegate authority and responsibility to others so they are successful as well.

These traits are essential to effective leadership and are common to most good leaders.

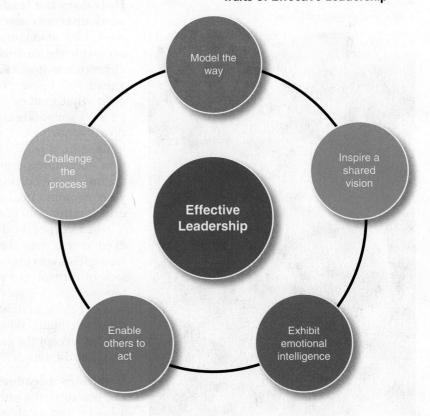

■ **FIGURE 8.3**
Traits of Effective Leadership

Masataka Shimizu

Masataka Shimizu, the head of the Tokyo Electric Power Company (Tepco), faced a horrible situation when an earthquake rocked the company's Fukushima nuclear reactor complex in Japan in 2011. The subsequent meltdown of three of the complex's reactors resulted in a massive release of radiation and more than $100 billion in damages. Japan's economy was disrupted for over a year, and plans to increase the role of nuclear power in the country were derailed.

It is hard to rise to such a challenging set of events, but in the investigations that followed, much troubling information came to light. The amount of radiation released was over twice what had initially been reported by the company. Moreover, senior Tepco engineers had known for years that half of the reactors had a dangerous design flaw, but the company failed to make upgrades to them.[15]

After the disaster struck, Shimizu disappeared for days, and his communication about it with the government created confusion. At stake was a complete evacuation of Tokyo if all six of the reactors at the Fukushima were to melt down. Although that did not occur, Shimizu resigned amid scandal within the year.

Masataka Shimizu, formerly the president of the Tokyo Electric Power Company, kneels and bows in apology to the people who had to evacuate the Fukushima region after the company experienced a power plant disaster there following an earthquake and tsunami.
Source: Sankei via/Getty Images.

Are there systems for measuring leadership potential? There are many personality tests that can provide information to assess people's leadership potential and improve their leadership skills. Popular personality assessments include the *Big Five*, the *Cattell 16 PF*, and the *Thematic Apperception Test*. Although no one personality test is recognized as the perfect tool, all of them strive to provide us with a better understanding of the traits that are the foundation of successful leadership.

Leadership and Corporate Culture

How does the leadership style of a firm's managers affect the work environment? The collection of values, norms, and behavior shared by managers and workers in a firm defines the character, or **corporate culture**, of an organization. What style of dress is appropriate at work, the work environment itself, rules for getting ahead and being promoted, what is valued, who is valued, and even what kind of work/life balance is expected are all aspects of a firm's corporate culture. Typically, this information isn't written down anywhere. Instead, it is communicated via an attitude of "this is how we do things here." Employees aren't explicitly told how to behave, but nonetheless they generally conform to the norms of the corporate culture. This is why it is important that your personal goals and style match the corporate culture of the organization you choose to work for.

In a corporation in which the culture is not well defined—or, even worse, one that supports questionable behavior—problems result. This was the case for the natural gas giant Enron. A significant lack of control and poor ethical behavior on the part of the firm's top managers resulted in an accounting scandal at the firm. The scandal came to light in 2001, and the company later collapsed. On the other hand, when the corporate culture is strong and all employees accept the culture as their own, they are motivated to maintain it and monitor their own behavior.

How does a leader establish corporate culture? Tony Hsieh of Zappos.com, the online shoe giant, is a powerful example of how a leader can establish corporate culture. Hsieh started Zappos at

Do You Have to Be Tall to Be a Leader?

Do taller people have more charisma and self-confidence? And what does height have to do with successful leadership in business? A lot, according to many industry experts and observers. Several studies have found that height is a tool business leaders try to use to appear powerful.[16]

What do you think? Does height affect success in business? Would the answer be the same for men and women? Or is the idea that height, rather than skills and talents, leads to promotion a myth?

a time when selling a product like shoes online was thought to be impossible. But he was sure top-notch customer service could make selling shoes on the Internet a successful venture. In his book *Delivering Happiness*: *A Path to Profits, Passion and Purpose*, he explains how first establishing a corporate culture naturally led to the customer service levels he wanted, the profits he wanted, and the purpose he wanted in his life and the lives of his employees. Hsieh and the two other founders developed a list of 10 core values and the slogan "What would Core Values Frog do . . . ?" ■ **FIGURE 8.4** shows the company's 10 core frog values.[17]

The corporate culture of Zappos shines through, even in the hiring process. For example, value 10 is "Be Humble." Candidates are picked up from the airport with a Zappos shuttle bus. Later, the bus driver is interviewed to see how the candidates treated the driver. In this way, the interview started before the candidates realized it. Another key interview question relates to value 3, "Create Fun and a Little Weirdness." Candidates are asked, "How weird are you on a scale of 1 to 10?" Zappos is looking for employees who are willing to bring some personality to the office, not hide behind what they think is expected of them. (You can see evidence of this at http://blogs.zappos.com, where a video from a "Zappos Prom" is posted.) One week after they have been hired, employees are offered $2,000 to leave Zappos if they don't think the company is right for them.[18]

Hsieh was also willing to take his corporate culture out of the office and into downtown Las Vegas, where the company is now located. Zappos has invested $350 million in what it calls the Downtown Project. The Downtown Project, which supports educational initiatives, new small businesses, and technology start-ups, has generated new jobs and retail centers like Container Park, a new shopping area built from dozens of shipping containers. Instead of following the model of building a corporate campus that meets all the employees' needs, Hsieh envisions building the perfect community—complete with artists, musicians, yoga shops, and cheese stores—so his employees will want to live and work in the area.

■ **FIGURE 8.4**
Zappos Core Values Frog
The corporate culture at Zappos shines through its Web page describing the company's core values using the Zappos Core Values Frog!
Source: "Introducing Core Values Frog!" Zappos.com.

Deliver Wow through Service

Embrace and Drive Change

Create Fun and a Little Weirdness

Pursue Growth and Learning

Be Adventurous, Creative and Open-Minded

Southwest Airlines

One company that has benefited from strong leadership and employee motivation is Southwest Airlines, one of the most admired companies in the world. Southwest Airlines has an amazingly low turnover rate for its industry, which the firm credits to allowing its employees to express their individuality. Singing flight attendants and comedic reports from pilots are common on Southwest flights. The company's charismatic CEO, Gary Kelly, outlines the three key criteria a Southwest employee must have: "a Warrior Spirit, a Servant's Heart, and a Fun-LUVing Attitude."[20] Managers encourage input from employees at all levels—one's position does not prevent anyone from contributing a new idea.

Southwest has never furloughed employees, a common industry practice where more people are hired to cover busy travel seasons but are then not given any work when traffic drops. Because they know their jobs are secure, Southwest employees are confident they can grow into new positions. The largely union environment has a similar pay structure to other airlines but also a profit-sharing plan. Employees own 5 percent of the company.[21] The company's stock has soared to such heights over the years that a number of longtime Southwest employees have become millionaires as a result. Not surprisingly, the company has repeatedly made *Fortune* magazine's annual "100 Best Companies to Work For" list.

What did all this focus on building a corporate culture do for the company? Zappos has become a company with a "higher purpose of vision that is more than just about money or profits or being No. 1 in the market," describes Hsieh.[19] Along the way, the staff has become renowned for outstanding customer service, being friendly, and even spending hours on the phone with a single caller if needed. That has translated into over $1 billion in annual sales for Zappos.

Elon Musk, the founder of the online service PayPal, has proven to be a visionary leader. Musk is the CEO and chief designer of the first company that sent a spacecraft to the International Space Station (SpaceX). He is also CEO of Tesla Motors, whose award-wining line of electric cars has revolutionized the automotive industry. How can one person create disruptive change in three industries? By being a powerful, transformative leader.

Musk has consistently been willing to challenge the status quo. For two years, pumped millions of dollars of his own money into Tesla Motors because no one else was willing to imagine that a business selling all-electric vehicles would be successful.[22] He inspires others with his vision and lures talented engineers from other great companies. The engineers know that at SpaceX and Tesla, they will get to push the envelope and create products never seen before. Musk's clarity of vision and dedication to creating important and beautiful products serves as a model of what is expected and what is possible at his companies.

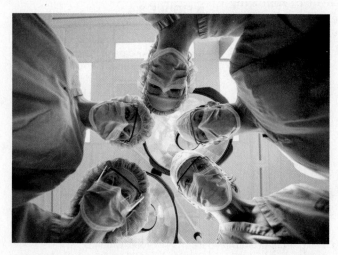

Source: Tyler Olson/Fotolia.

Teamwork pp. 232–237

There is probably no team you want to be more efficient, communicative, and effective than an operating room team performing surgery on you. It's not uncommon for an operating room team to be comprised of seven or more members who have never met each other before the day of the surgery. As medicine has become more sophisticated, even the most routine tasks have become so complicated that mistakes are all too common. Dr. Atul Gawande saw this happening and wanted to develop a way to make his operating teams function better. But where to begin? ■

It's challenging to develop effective teams, but the benefits can be extraordinary. In this section, we'll discuss teamwork and how it affects organizations.

The Advantages of Teams in the Workplace

What is the value of using teams in the workplace? Although the different personalities of people have the potential to create conflict within a team, they can also produce unique ideas. Successful teams ultimately agree on the objectives they need to accomplish, and the members depend on one another's ideas and efforts to develop successful plans and implement them. There is a sense of accountability, and the members are committed to one another's success.

One product that benefited from team development is the Microsoft Kinect. A breakthrough product for the video gaming industry, the Kinect allows video game players to play games without handheld devices. Players use voice commands and gestures instead. The Kinect was not designed by a single team but was made up of seven teams from seven different disciplines. A very small team began exploring ways to track player's body movements. Another small team of computer vision experts from Microsoft Research worked on the key algorithms. Once demos of the team's work began spreading through the company, engineers began to volunteer to come in and work nights on the project. In its first 60 days on the market, the product sold 8 million units and set a Guinness world record as the fastest-selling consumer electronics device.[23]

The Challenges of Teams in the Workplace

Do teams always improve the development process? Although teams have been shown to be effective in many situations, some people suggest that teamwork does not always result in more creativity. Research conducted by Barry Staw at the University of California, Berkeley, found that when college students were asked to think of business ideas—either individually or in teams—the individuals came up with more ideas than the teams did. In addition, the individuals' ideas were voted as more creative than were the teams' concepts. Staw concluded that collective thinking does not lead to increased creativity and can, in fact, hamper it. One possible reason, Staw proposes, is that team members often want to "fit in," but creativity demands a person take risks and "stand out."[24]

If the members of a team are not carefully selected, "wanting to fit in" can lead to narrow-mindedness within the group, a phenomenon referred to as **groupthink**. People who are from similar backgrounds and sectors of a company tend to have the same ideas and work with the same set of unspoken assumptions, which can lead a group to reject different ideas without fair examination.

Groupthink can hamper the creativity of teams, although this challenge can be minimized by carefully designing them, a topic we will discuss shortly.

Another challenge is the fact that there is now a wide mix of generations in the workforce (see ■ **TABLE 8.3**). It's now possible for people from three or even four generations to be assigned to a single team. Having grown up with different social and educational experiences, each generation exhibits distinct styles in the workplace and in teams.

TABLE 8.3	Three Generations in the Workplace		
Generation	**Birth Years**	**Famous Man**	**Famous Woman**
Boomer	1943–1960	Steven Spielberg	Oprah Winfrey
Gen-X	1961–1981	Matt Damon	Jennifer Lopez
Millennial	1982–2002	LeBron James	Miley Cyrus

Source: Neil Howe and William Strauss, *Millennials Rising: The Next Great Generation* (New York: Vintage, 2000).

There are challenges in having three generations of employees in the workplace.
Source: Adrian Weinbrecht/Alamy.

Are generational differences really that significant in the workplace? In their book *Millennials Rising: The Next Great Generation*,[25] researchers Neil Howe and William Strauss discuss the three dominant generations in the workplace today:

- **Baby boomers.** Those born between 1943 and 1960. Baby boomers are the veterans in the workforce. Many have been with their same companies for decades.

- **Gen-Xers.** Born between 1961 and 1981. Gen-Xers, who are independent thinkers and hanker for change, are the first generation of workers to value family life over work life.

- **Millennials.** Born between 1982 and 2002. Like Gen-Xers, Millennials want their jobs to accommodate their personal lives, but they also have very high expectations for achievement in their careers.

Millennials, who are now entering college campuses and the workforce, believe in their own self-worth and value.[26] They feel they have the capability to change the companies they work for and the world. According to Howe and Strauss, members of this generation expect to make their mark on society by using technology to empower the community. Teamwork, good behavior, and citizenship are much more important to Millennials than to earlier generations, and they see equality between different races and genders.

How will this affect business? How will businesses react to the needs of younger workers, who are juggling work demands along with the demands of their new families? How will older employees respond to their sense of confidence and their tendency to work toward team-based solutions?

Best Practices for Teams

What kinds of practices set the stage for the best team performance? Psychologist Mihaly Csikszentmihalyi has applied his idea of flow, discussed earlier, to teams. **Group flow** occurs when a group knows how to work together so that each individual member can achieve flow. The characteristics of such a setting are as follows:

1. **Creative spatial arrangements.** Pinning ideas on the walls and using large charts to combine ideas from the entire group tend to lead to the open consideration of ideas. Tables are used less because working while standing and moving promotes more discussion and interaction.

2. **Playground design.** This begins with creating a space where it's safe to divulge ideas that normally people might just keep to themselves. Often, a large number of charts display information inputs, graphs, and the project summary. Wall space can be used to collect results and lists of open topics.

3. **Constant focus on the target group for the product.** At Amazon.com, CEO Jeff Bezos has the nickname "the empty chair" because he often keeps a seat open at team meetings. The empty seat is the most important one in the room because it represents the customer.[27]

4. **Visualization.** Visualization and prototyping are used to construct initial models for product and service models, which are later refined.

How do managers create the best teams? Some important aspects a manager should consider in forming a team include the following:

- **Size.** A team that is too large may struggle with cohesiveness. At the same time, a large group can offer the benefit of diverse perspectives.

- **Time frame.** Some teams are put together to work on a specific problem or project within a short time frame, whereas others may work together for longer time periods on everyday tasks.

- **Status.** A team formally created by a company may be required to provide progress reports and updates, and it often has access to company resources. Less formal teams may need to take the initiative when it comes to communicating their progress to other people and groups.

Red Teamers in the Military

Teamwork is a critical part of business, but one place you might not think of team decision making occurring is in the military. The military is organized around the chain of command: Commanders call the shots, and the rank and file must obey their orders without question.

Recently, the U.S. military has become sensitive to how this conditioning could contribute to groupthink. So, a program of study was developed to produce "Red Teamers," officers trained to analyze problems from a wide range of points of view—including how a decision will impact the military's allies and how people in occupied countries will respond to the decision. Red Team students study military theory but also Eastern philosophy, for example. The goal is to expand their worldview. In Iraq, Red Team officers were used to decide how military dogs would be used. Why? Because Iraqi citizens generally consider dogs unclean and even evil.

A Red Teamer is responsible for raising issues that the group might not have considered but then stepping out of the way and not obstructing the decision making. The same idea of injecting a skeptic into a group to promote a variety of points of view is used in other government agencies. For example, the Federal Aviation Administration uses Red Teams to conduct airport testing to find and resolve security weaknesses. Is there a Red Teamer in your group—or do you need one?

According to business writer and theorist R. M. Belbin, effective teams are comprised of people with diverse skills, talents, and points of view. Team members' respective skills and talents should complement one another so the team can perform at an optimum level. For example, what if all of the members of a team are extremely creative yet inexperienced in effective time management? What if five of six team members are all aggressive leaders? Clearly, a balance of people who embody different team roles is the key to the success of a team.

Belbin's model of nine team roles is outlined in ■ **TABLE 8.4**. Considering both the personality traits of potential members and the roles they can play can be helpful when designing teams.

What are cross-functional teams? In the past, the members were often from the same department and reported to the same supervisor. But today, cross-functional teams have become more common. In a **cross-functional team**, members are selected across a range of critical functional divisions of a business. For example, in 2004, the LEGO Group was near bankruptcy. The company's investment in LEGO theme parks weren't yielding a good return, and some products like

TABLE 8.4	Belbin's Nine Team Roles
Role	**Personality Traits**
Plant	Creative and imaginative
Resource investigator	Extroverted and communicative
Coordinator	Mature and confident
Shaper	Challenging and dynamic
Monitor evaluator	Serious and strategic
Teamworker	Cooperative and diplomatic
Implementer	Disciplined and reliable
Completer/finisher	Painstaking and conscientious
Specialist	Dedicated and self-starting

Source: Adapted from R. M. Belbin, "Team Role Descriptions," Belbin Associates, www.belbin.com/content/page/731/Belbin_Team_Role_Descriptions.pdf. Adapted with permission from Belbin Associates, www.belbin.com.

Clikits had struggled in the marketplace. To turn things around, LEGO created a cross-functional team of employees to help the company push through new product innovations, pricing models, business processes, marketing plans, and community building efforts. The group ushered through modifications to existing product lines as well as new products, such as the series of LEGO board games. Now, for several years in a row, LEGO has been growing its revenues by over 20 percent per year.

What effect does technology have on team design? In a **virtual team**, members are located in different physical locations but work together via telecommunications technology to achieve a goal. The need for virtual teams has grown out of the increased globalization of business. Familiar tools like conference calls and e-mail have evolved to include videoconferencing and live broadcasting of key meetings and events over the Web. Webcasts can now support interactive participation of the viewing audience. In real time, audience members can ask questions, exchange electronic files with the group, and record the presentation for repeated viewing. Web conferencing software like Cisco WebEx and Microsoft Lync allow participants in any geographic location to brainstorm together in real time on a common "virtual whiteboard," watch demos and presentations live, and record and annotate these discussions for later playback.

How can social media tools like wikis help modern teams? Modern tools for collaboration are now often replacing endless streams of e-mails with file attachments. Wikis are one example. *Wikis* are websites that support editing by multiple authors. Team members can work on one common document all at the same time, watching each other make editing changes and having a live chat window open at the same time. Changes are archived and can be recalled; if a member of the team later reads the document and wants to revert back to an earlier version, he or she can do so with just one click. The problem of having multiple versions of a document is eliminated, so there are no concerns about synchronizing the different versions between all team members; the most current version is always available on the wiki.

One of the best-known public wikis is the encyclopedia project Wikipedia. Wikipedia is not the only use of wikis, however. Wikis can be run and maintained by individuals or within a specific corporation. Sites like www.wikimatrix.org can help identify the type of wiki software best suited to a specific virtual team. Products like Blackboard and Microsoft Windows SharePoint contain wiki tools.

Is designing a strong virtual team the same as creating a strong face-to-face team? Most successful virtual teams include some periodic face-to-face meetings. Very few virtual teams are 100 percent virtual. Although technology allows teams to communicate without ever meeting face-to-face, it is still important to have the group occasionally meet with each other in the same space to build social connections. Keeping the team connected is a key priority for a virtual team, and it can be difficult to keep contacts strong from a distance. There can be communication delays from working across time zones or using e-mail as a primary mode of communication. Establishing team rules, such as agreeing to respond to e-mail messages within a certain window of time or initiating global office hours, can minimize these problems. (For more on communicating with teams, see Mini Chapter 3.)

Your Role on a Team

How can I be a valued team player? It is important to begin now to build the skills that will make you successful in a team. Preparing yourself to contribute in a team setting may be the most important thing you can do to increase your value to an organization, no matter what position you hold.

What habits will give me the best chance to contribute to a team? There are many skills that you can build to enhance your success as a member of a team. One model that organizes these skills is the **Seven Habits model** developed by famed management author Stephen Covey.[28] Covey has found that there are seven habits of behavior exhibited by successful people:

1. **Be proactive.** This is the ability to control your environment rather than have it control you. Proactive team members are constantly looking "down the road" in terms of their time management, work, and obstacles that could impede the success of a project.

2. **Begin with the end in mind.** This means you are able to see the desired outcome and the activities that need to be done to achieve it. Staying focused on the ultimate goal allows you to avoid taking a team in the wrong direction or a direction that will cause divisiveness and waste resources and energy.

3. **Put first things first.** Manage your time and energy so that the required tasks are prioritized. This skill works together with the second habit to push you toward success in your team role.

4. **Think win-win.** This is the most important aspect of interpersonal leadership because most achievements are based on cooperative effort; therefore, the aim needs to be win-win solutions for all.

5. **Seek first to understand and then to be understood.** Good communication is critical to developing and maintaining positive relationships. Listening to your teammates and giving them the chance to be heard will be the key to your own success when it comes to being understood and contributing.

6. **Synergize.** This is the habit of creative cooperation—the principle that collaboration often achieves more than could be achieved by individuals working independently toward attaining a purpose.

7. **Sharpen the saw.** This catchphrase comes from the metaphor for chopping down a tree. If you are constantly sawing and never take time to stop and sharpen the saw, you'll feel as if you're investing tremendous energy, but the results will not be what they could be if you just stopped to sharpen the saw first. Strong team contributors take time to develop their skills, step back from "the grind," and reanalyze the task at hand so that they can work more efficiently.

If you work to develop and use these habits, you will find that both you and the teams you are a member of will become more successful—and that you will be in demand for increasingly more important team assignments.

The key to promoting better team function for Dr. Gawande was to develop a checklist. His book, *The Checklist Manifesto*, describes how he worked with his staff to create a checklist used during surgeries. Issues were identified, like the need for a mandatory introduction of each person on the team before the procedure was performed, and giving a clear authorization to nurses to stop the surgery if an item on the checklist was missed. By having every member of the team involved in developing the checklist, critical items were included that could easily be overlooked. The result? At a multihospital study, the number of surgical deaths dropped by 47 percent.

Summary

1 How do motivation and work environment encourage "flow"? (pp. 219–221)

- **Flow** (p. 220) is a state of feeling completely involved and focused on a task. Managers can increase motivation and foster flow by keeping employees intellectually engaged, removing distractions, encouraging creativity and flexibility, and supporting employees in all aspects of their lives.

2 What are the main theories of motivation, and how are they applied to the workforce? (pp. 221–225)

- Maslow's hierarchy describes motivation as a response to a progressive set of needs for **physiology** (p. 221), **safety** (p. 221), **belonging** (p. 221), **esteem** (p. 221), and **self-actualization** (p. 221).
- McClelland's **three needs theory** (p. 222) states the main motivators are the need for achievement, affiliation, and power.
- Herzberg broke the idea of motivation into two categories: **hygiene factors** (p. 222) and **motivators** (p. 222).
- **Extrinsic motivators** (p. 222) are factors external to the employee, such as pay or promotions, which improve their engagement at work.
- **Intrinsic motivators** (p. 222) are internal factors inside of a person that come from his or her actual interest in the work or from a sense of purpose and value in the work being done.
- **Theory X** (p. 223) posits that humans inherently dislike work and will try to avoid it if they can. As a result, managers should adopt a hard-line, authoritarian style.
- **Theory Y** (p. 224) proposes that people view work as natural and will be motivated to work as long as they are satisfied with their jobs. Thus, managers should implement a softer style that involves ample employee participation.
- **Theory Z** (p. 224) suggests that workers want to cooperate and be loyal to an organization and emphasizes collaborative decision making.
- The **Vroom model (expectancy theory)** (p. 224) states that an individual's motivation can be described by the relationship between three factors: expectancy, instrumentality, and valence.

3 How have motivational theories and industrial psychology changed the work environment since the early twentieth century? (pp. 225–226)

- **Industrial psychology** (p. 225) is a field of academic study developed to scientifically understand how to optimally manage people and work.

- A 1932 study by Elton May concluded that when workers feel important, productivity increases. This is called the **Hawthorne effect** (p. 225). After World War II, research began to focus on the management of entire organizations rather than individual workers.
- Studies that have shown that today's workers value autonomy, mastery, and purpose at least as much or as more as they do economic rewards. Studies of people engaged in creative work show they are often demotivated by traditional financial incentives and highly motivated by offers of autonomy, mastery, and purpose.

4 What are the various identifiable leadership styles and traits, and how do they affect business leadership? (pp. 226–233)

- Leaders may exhibit a **democratic** (p. 228), **autocratic** (p. 228), **affiliative (laissez-faire)** (p. 228), and/or **visionary** (p. 228) style. Many top executives demonstrate one or more of these styles.
- Certain traits are common among effective leaders. They challenge conventional beliefs, inspire a shared vision, model by example, use emotional intelligence, and enable others to perform to their fullest potential.

5 What are the best ways to create, manage, and participate in teams? (pp. 232–237)

- Teams can benefit the workplace by encouraging collaboration, which can lead to greater innovation and the speed with which organizations are able to respond to changes in the marketplace.
- Effective teams must be designed and managed thoughtfully. Today's workplace includes employees from three or more generations, and it takes care and insight to make them mesh well on a single team.
- **Group flow** (p. 234) is achieved when a group knows how to work together so that each individual member can achieve flow. Best practices for creating strong teams include considering the size, the life span, and the status of the team.
- R. M. Belbin outlined a model of nine team roles. An effective team requires a variety of roles, and the members must be matched carefully to the team needs.
- E-mail, videoconferencing, Webcasts, wikis, and other technology allow for virtual teams in which members are in different locations around the country or the world. However, most virtual teams meet face-to-face periodically.
- Stephen Covey's **Seven Habits model** (p. 237) can help employees enhance their success as members of a team.

Key Terms

MyBizLab

Go to **mybizlab.com** to complete the problems marked with this icon .

Self Test

Multiple Choice *You can find the answers on the last page of this book.*

8-1 Which of the following does not describe a type of leadership style?

a. Visionary

b. Autocratic

c. Democratic

d. Affluent

8-2 When employees are motivated,

a. they often take more time to be with their families.

b. they often move on to other companies.

c. net profits tend to decline.

d. they are more productive and creative.

8-3 Maslow's hierarchy of needs

a. is a theory of why people are motivated.

b. uses three factors to compute the motivation of a person in a situation.

c. was developed to address the Hawthorne effect.

d. was displaced when Theory Z was introduced.

8-4 With creative and abstract work, studies find that the principal motivators are

a. financial incentives.

b. autonomy, mastery, and purpose.

c. competitive push for advancement.

d. reduction in hours involved at work.

8-5 Teams improve creativity

a. when the phenomenon of groupthink sets in.

b. no matter what the makeup of the team.

c. when best practices for selecting the team members and roles are followed.

d. when individuals work with others who are just like them.

8-6 An example of Herzberg's hygiene factors is

a. feeling of belonging.

b. creativity.

c. safe working environment.

d. respect.

8-7 Theory Z is different than Theory X or Theory Y because

a. it relies heavily on collaborative decision making.

b. it is authoritarian and hard line.

c. it is often seen in mass-manufacturing settings.

d. managers believe people will seek out responsibility.

Self Test (continued)

8-8 Virtual teams are teams that

   a. are incomplete and need to be dissolved.

   b. communicate only through face-to-face meetings.

   c. primarily focus on technology-based projects.

   d. work in different physical locations.

8-9 A laissez-faire leader would

   a. challenge every decision.

   b. take a very hands-off approach to management.

   c. believe in strong involvement in employee teams.

   d. be very important to a company experiencing a crisis.

8-10 Extrinsic motivators include such things as

   a. doing work that you enjoy.

   b. believing your opinion matters.

   c. knowing there is a large financial bonus for good work.

   d. working for a company whose mission is meaningful to you.

True/False *You can find the answers on the last page of this book.*

8-11 Corporate culture is the set of sports and extracurricular activities promoted at work.

   ☐ True or ☐ False

8-12 Autocratic leaders cannot manage large companies effectively.

   ☐ True or ☐ False

8-13 Intrinsic motivators come from a sense of purpose and value in the work employees are doing.

   ☐ True or ☐ False

8-14 Strength-based management believes the best way to develop talent is to help employees add skills and knowledge that build on their existing strengths.

   ☐ True or ☐ False

8-15 Groupthink is the convergence of the group on the best idea.

   ☐ True or ☐ False

Critical Thinking Questions

✪ 8-16 When in your life have you been motivated by external factors like rewards, money, or promotion? In what kind of setting would the combination of autonomy, mastery, and purpose be more successful in focusing you to go above and beyond?

✪ 8-17 Consider the traits of effective leaders presented on (p. 229) in the chapter. Then consider your own personality traits. How could you strengthen the leadership traits you do not currently see in yourself?

8-18 You have just been assigned a position on a virtual team. What specific strategies would you focus on to be a strong, contributing member of the team? Are there specific skills you would need to learn? How would your role be different than if the team were physically meeting on a regular basis instead of virtually meeting?

Team Time

FORMING A SUCCESSFUL TEAM

A shoe manufacturer wants to diversify its successful product line of hiking boots. The company wants to appeal to young people, a rapidly growing consumer base with increasing amounts of disposable income. The company has decided to give one team almost unlimited resources and freedom to develop a flip-flop sandal for modern, gadget-loving youth.

You need to apply the best-practices principles in team formation to determine the personalities and strengths of each member and assign roles in which the members will be motivated to contribute.

Process

Step 1. Break up into teams of three or four individuals.

Step 2. Begin by deciding what tool you will use to evaluate each member for personality traits, strengths, and weaknesses.

Step 3. Develop a strategy for assessing what work needs to be done and then how your team will assign appropriate responsibilities to each member.

Step 4. How will you evaluate the level of motivation and creativity for the team? What changes can be made if the team's performance is not adequate?

Step 5. Present your findings to the class for discussion.

Ethics and Corporate Social Responsibility

ETHICS IN TEAMWORK

Being a member of a team means you are accountable for your actions and the actions of your fellow teammates. Review the following scenario.

Scenario

Imagine you work at an advertising firm. You're on a team that is developing an advertising campaign proposal for a chain of fitness centers. The firm has been struggling and needs your team to land this account. At a meeting, one of your teammates reveals that he has hacked into a competing firm's network and has a draft of its proposal for the same account. Your teammate wants to steal the idea and use it in your team's proposal. Most of your teammates agree with this idea, but you think it is unethical.

Questions for Discussion

8-19 How would you handle this situation? Would you voice your objection or go along with the team?

8-20 If you decide to voice your objection, do you address the entire team or speak to members individually? Why?

8-21 How would you reconcile your role as a loyal employee and team player with your need to uphold ethical standards?

Web Exercises

8-22 Testing 1, 2, 3 . . .
Find three online leadership, team roles, and/or personality assessment tools. Go to http://testyourself .psychtests.com for examples. How consistent are the results in describing your personality or tendencies? How accurate would you rate the results?

8-23 Great American Leaders
Do an online search for the "20th Century American Leaders Database," which is a database maintained by the Harvard University Business School (www.hbs.edu). Select one leader from your state, one of your gender, one leader of the same ethnicity as you, and two additional people profiled from different industries. What similarities and differences do you see in this group of five great leaders?

Web Exercises (continued)

8-24 Drive and Inspiration

Go to YouTube and view Daniel Pink's animated video on intrinsic motivation titled "Drive." Describe the presentation in terms of what motivates you in school and in your free time. Then watch Simon Sinek's talk on "The Golden Circle" of why, how, and what and explain how it relates to inspiration. How could you use these ideas to inspire the next group project in which you participate?

8-25 Too Much Collaboration?

Review the materials published by Susan Cain on the value of being introverted. Cain argues that some people are more creative and productive when given the space to work alone. Has our culture overvalued collaboration? Examine the story of the founding of Apple computer and the research of the Coding War Games to delve into this idea further.

8-26 Measuring Your Team's Health

Consider a team that you are part of and complete the Team Effectiveness Assessment form at www.mindtools .com. Submit the form and examine the summary for your score. Do you agree with the analysis of your team's dynamics? Use the material following the score interpretation to spark useful discussion in your team. What action steps can you take personally and as a group to become more effective?

MyBizLab

Go to **mybizlab.com** for Auto-graded writing questions as well as the following Assisted-graded writing questions:

✪ 8-27 Is it better for a business to respond to a changing climate by hiring a different style of leader or to expect the current leadership to adapt its style to new conditions?

✪ 8-28 What factors are the most important for creating a team that works efficiently together? What problems have you seen in your own academic career when working in group settings, and how could they be prevented?

References

1. Mihaly Csikszentmihalyi, *Flow* (New York: HarperCollins, 1990).
2. Gallup, *State of the American Workplace*, 2013, www.gallup .com/strategicconsulting/163007/state-american-workplace.aspx.
3. Ian Tan, "Why Work for SAS," www.sas.com/offices/ asiapacific/singapore/press/why-sas.html.
4. "SAS Surpasses $3 Billion in 2013 Revenue, Growing 5.2% over 2012 Results," January 23, 2014, www.sas.com/ en_us/news/press-releases/2014/january/2013-financials.html.
5. "Fortune 100 Best Companies to Work For," February 3, 2014, http://money.cnn.com/magazines/fortune/ best-companies/2014/snapshots/2.html.
6. Gallup, *State of the American Workplace*.
7. Casey Slide, "9 Leadership Lessons & Quotes from Truett Cathy, Founder of Chick-fil-A," www.moneycrashers .com/leadership-lessons-from-truett-cathy-founder-of-chick-fil-a.
8. "Chick-fil-A: Company Fact Sheet," www.chick-fil-a.com/ Company/Highlights-Fact-Sheets.
9. E. Polman and K. J. Emich, "Decisions for Others Are More Creative Than Decisions for the Self," *Personality and Social Psychology Bulletin*, 2011 (PMID: 21317316).
10. Daniel Pink, *Drive: The Surprising Truth about What Motivates Us* (New York: Riverhead Books, 2009).
11. Ibid.
12. Peter Drucker, "Quotation Details," http://quotationspage .com/quote/26536.html.
13. *Black Friday*, a seven-minute video on the *Toy Story* Blu-Ray DVD, www.youtube.com/watch?v=bk8a_C0ao9Y.
14. James M. Kouzes and Barry Z. Posner, *The Leadership Challenge*, 4th ed. (San Francisco: Jossey-Bass, 2008).
15. Aaron Sheldrick, "Former Tepco Chief to Be Grilled over Fukushima Disaster," *Chicago Tribune*, June 7, 2012, http://articles.chicagotribune.com/2012-06-07/news/ sns-rt-us-japan-nuclear-shimizubre85703w-20120607_1_ fukushima-plant-masataka-shimizu-tepco-executives.

16. M. Hamstra, "'Big,' Men: Male Leaders' Height Positively Relates to Followers' Perception of Charisma," *Personality and Individual Differences* 56 (2014): 190–92, www.melvyn-hamstra.com/wp-content/uploads/2013/10/Hamstra-PAID-2014.pdf.

17. From "Introducing Core Values Frog!," www.zappos.com.

18. Based on "Our Unique Culture" and various blogs, www.zappos.com.

19. Tony Hsieh, quoted in Venuri Siriwardane, "Zappos CEO Adds Happiness to Corporate Culture," July 7, 2010, www.nj.com/business/index.ssf/2010/06/zappos_ceo_adds_happiness_to_c.html.

20. "Culture," 2014, www.southwest.com/html/about-southwest/careers/culture.html.

21. Southwest Corporate Fact Sheet," 2014, www.swamedia.com/channels/Corporate-Fact-Sheet/pages/corporate-fact-sheet.

22. Moryt Milo, "Executive of the Year," *San Jose Business Journal*, 24 December 24, 2010, www.teslamotors.com/sites/default/files/blog_attachments/elon_musk_ceo_of_the_year.pdf.

23. Matt Rosoff, "The Story behind Kinect, Microsoft's Newest Billion Dollar Business," *Business Insider*, January 19, 2011, www.businessinsider.com/the-story-behind-microsofts-hot-selling-kinect-2011-1?op=1.

24. National Association of College Stores, "Teamwork Concept Questioned," August 11, 2006, www.nacs.org/news/081106-teamwork.asp?id=cm.

25. Neil Howe and William Strauss, *Millennials Rising: The Next Great Generation* (New York: Vintage, 2000).

26. Stephanie Armour, "Generation Y: They've Arrived at Work with a New Attitude," *USA Today*, November 6, 2005, www.usatoday.com/money/workplace/2005-11-06-gen-y_x.htm.

27. George Anders, "Jeff Bezos Gets It," *Forbes*, April 25, 2012, www.forbes.com/global/2012/0507/global-2000-12-amazon-jeff-bezos-gets-it.html.

28. Based on Stephen R. Covey, *The 7 Habits of Highly Effective People* (New York: Free Press, 1989).

Chapter 9
Human Resource Management

▶ Human Resource Management

H and R—two simple letters that together represent a vital component of any successful business. Indeed, a well-managed human resource (HR) department is essential to the smooth operation of all organizations. HR managers like Leslie Booth are responsible for many tasks, from hiring to firing and everything in between. Why is human resource management so important?

▶ Training and Evaluating Employees

Training allows a business to leverage the talents of its employees across a whole company. George Hensel knows how to run the perfect meeting. How can his company use him most efficiently to train others?

▶ Compensating, Scheduling, Promoting, and Terminating Employees

To attract high-caliber applicants, companies need compensation packages that are comparable to their competitors or better. Kathy Sanchez is a full-time graphic designer but is struggling to afford health insurance. What other types of benefits are important in a good compensation package?

▶ Managing Workplace Diversity

Diversity is encouraged because it benefits a company, but it has been a challenge for Chandraki Patel to manage the widely diverse group she is responsible for. What issues do companies and managers face when establishing more diversity in the workplace?

▶ Labor and Union Issues

College athletes at Division I schools are key contributors to athletic programs that generate millions of dollars for the school. Does this make them employees, or does their academic status mean they cannot unionize to negotiate for better working conditions?

OBJECTIVES

1 What processes are involved in human resource management (HRM)? (pp. 245–251)

2 How are employees trained and evaluated? (pp. 251–255)

3 How are employees compensated and scheduled? (pp. 255–259)

4 How does an employee's status change as a result of promotions, termination, and retirement? (pp. 259–261)

5 How does incorporating diversity affect the workforce? (pp. 261–263)

6 What are the objectives, structures, and future of labor unions in the global business environment? (pp. 263–265)

MyBizLab®

⭐ Improve Your Grade!

Over 10 million students improved their results using the Pearson MyLabs.
Visit **mybizlab.com** for simulations, tutorials, and end-of-chapter problems.

Human Resource Management pp. 245–251

When HR manager Leslie Booth needed to hire a new senior account executive for her firm, she weighed her options carefully. Filling a senior position required patience. She hired a recruiter to find outside candidates to interview for the position, and, to keep her options open, she also ran job advertisements in local newspapers and top accounting journals. After no one with the right qualifications applied, she began to feel pressured by her boss to get the position filled. What should she do? ■

When you think about the resources required to run a business, you probably think about things like money, space, equipment, and supplies. Although those resources are key components, the "human" resource—people—is often taken for granted but is arguably the most important. People provide the ideas, creativity, knowledge, and ingenuity that make a business run.

Source: Robert Nickelsberg/Alamy.

Human resources—the people in an organization—need to be managed just as carefully as the material and financial resources of a business. **Human resource management** (HRM) is the organizational function that deals with a firm's employees. As ■ **FIGURE 9.1** shows, HRM encompasses every aspect of the "human" in a business, including the hiring, training, motivating, evaluating, and compensating of personnel, as shown. In this chapter, you'll learn the ins and outs of human resource management.

Managing Staffing Needs

How does planning for staffing needs change as a company evolves? A small business may initially have one person working for it—the person who launched the business. Once the business begins to grow, new people are brought into the organization. Although keeping track of HR needs at small businesses can be fairly simple, companies that add employees and continue to grow require more specific HR planning.

Poor staff planning can be costly. Being overstaffed burdens a company with the unnecessary expense of maintaining salaries, benefits, and training for surplus employees. An understaffed organization can lead to a loss of sales and competitiveness if customer needs are not met. A key part of human resources planning includes the following:

- Determining the optimal number of employees a business needs
- Clearly identifying the exact job positions and the requirements of those positions

How does a company determine whether it has the correct number of employees? The process begins with gathering information on a firm's current workforce and on the future demand for workers within the company. The current supply of employees is determined by developing a workforce profile. A **workforce profile** is a personnel inventory that includes information about each

■ FIGURE 9.1
The Functions of HRM

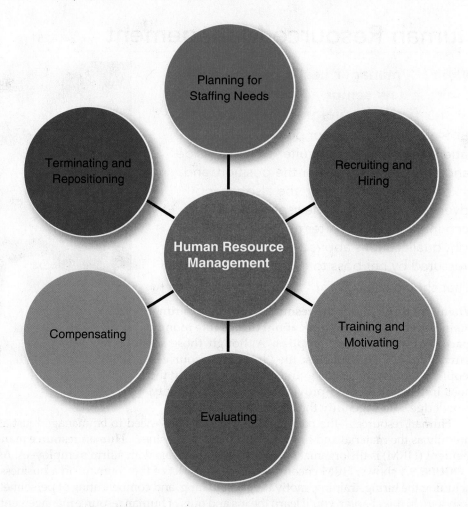

employee, such as his or her age, education, training, experience, specialized skills, and current and previous positions held within the company.

The future demand for employees is determined by a process called **forecasting**. Forecasting is based on several factors, such as the predicted sales of a company's goods or services, the current skill level of employees, whether a firm plans to contract or expand, how technology is changing or will change a firm's staffing needs, and available employment alternatives, such as outsourcing, offshoring, or using part-time or temporary employees. In addition, staffing changes that are expected to occur through normal turnover, retirement, and any planned reassignments are also taken into consideration. If the forecast indicates an imbalance between the supply of and the demand for employees, adjustments can be made, for example, by recruiting, training, or retraining employees, making labor force reductions, or changing the extent to which the workforce is utilized by increasing or decreasing the hours employees work.

How do companies identify the exact jobs they need to staff? The HR department also completes a study of the tasks to be performed within the organization. A **job analysis** defines in detail the duties and requirements of the tasks an employee is required to perform. A job analysis includes the following:

- A **job description**—a formal statement that summarizes what the employee will do in that role. It includes the responsibilities of that position, the conditions under which the job will be performed, and its relationship to other functions in the organization. Job descriptions are important because they define job objectives that are used later in performance appraisals. They also can become a part of the legal contract between the employee and the employer.

- **Job specifications**—the knowledge, skills, education, experience, personal attributes, and physical requirements a person needs to successfully do the job.

Job Analysis	
Company: Nelson Wireless	
Position title: Marketing manager	
(a) Job description	**(b) Job specifications**
Join a team of marketing professionals focused on mobile technologies in the consumer market segment. The marketing manager is responsible for coordinating and/or implementing marketing projects designed for the consumer market segment. Working in cooperation with the sales team, product offers, and other headquarters marketing teams, the marketing manager will coordinate public relations projects and other promotional activities to drive Nelson Wireless brand awareness and product demand and generate consumer purchases. The marketing manager will provide strategic oversight for regional-level industry events, and be responsible for planning and executing customer events. The marketing manager will be responsible for coordinating budgets and timelines, maintaining accurate records of expenditures, and compiling reports of activity results. Additionally, he/she will be responsible for managing a team of 8–10 marketing associates. The marketing manager role will also include administrative elements such as invoice processing, event scheduling, and maintenance of a promotional calendar.	• College degree required with emphasis in marketing, business administration, or communications preferred • 3+ years marketing/communications experience required • Excellent demonstrated verbal and written communication skills • Demonstrated experience in event execution • Demonstrated ability to coordinate cooperative working relationships across multiple parties • Ability to work well under pressure • Extremely well organized, strong project management and time management skills and strong ability to multi-task • Proven ability to operate in a fast-paced, high-growth professional environment

■ **FIGURE 9.2** shows a job analysis with a sample job description and the job specifications.

Once a job is well defined, how does HR find the best candidates to interview? Matching the right person for each job depends on a well-devised recruiting plan. **Recruitment** is the process of finding, screening, and selecting people for a specific job using a variety of methods and resources.

Internal recruiting, or filling job vacancies with existing employees from within a business, is the first choice of many companies. Often, companies post job openings on the company intranet, in in-house newsletters, or bulletin boards in break rooms or announce them at staff meetings. Internal recruitment has several advantages. It tends to be a morale booster for employees because they know that the company has an interest in promoting its own employees. In addition, because employer and employee have established a working relationship, the risk of filling a position with an unsuitable candidate is lessened. Filling jobs internally is also generally quicker and less costly because it reduces the costs associated with outside recruiting and often shortens the length of the training time new hires need.

Internal recruiting has its disadvantages, however. This includes the possibility of not getting the best candidate due to the limited search process. In addition, when a firm hires from within, another internal vacancy is created that must be filled. Moreover, relying on internal employees can result in "inbreeding" and leave a firm with fewer new perspectives and ideas that people coming in from outside a firm often have to offer. As a result, businesses also rely on external recruiting to meet staffing.

External recruiting is the process of searching outside of a firm to fill job vacancies. Posting ads in newspapers, in trade magazines, on Internet job sites, or on social media sites such as LinkedIn, Facebook, and Twitter are methods used to reach a wide audience. ■ **FIGURE 9.3** lists various resources HR staff use when recruiting externally.

Depending on the type of position, employment agencies may be used. Employment agencies often specialize in specific sectors, such as accounting, sales, or clerical services. They provide a pool of screened candidates, which reduces the hiring company's administrative burden of recruitment. Recruitment consultants, often referred to as "headhunters," conduct more specialized searches, usually for senior managers or key employees. Using external firms to help with the search is often expensive, but the costs of finding the wrong candidate can be even higher.

How do social networking sites impact recruiting? Social media sites specifically for the professional community include LinkedIn, Data.com, Connect, and Spoke. LinkedIn has become a primary source recruiters turn to find candidates. Most people would like to hire or work with someone they know, and LinkedIn can provide helpful colleague and customer recommendations. Using applications such as SlideShare and Google Docs, LinkedIn members can post presentations they have given as well as showcase their portfolios of work. This helps recruiters quickly evaluate and sort prospective candidates. With versions available on

■ **FIGURE 9.3**
External Recruitment Resources

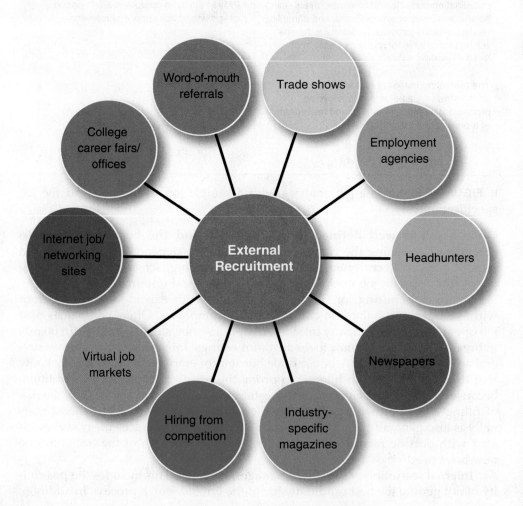

mobile devices, LinkedIn is always there when an HR recruiter wants to follow a lead. Additionally, LinkedIn, along with Glassdoor.com, can help job seekers by providing them with "insider" information on companies and employees. For example, before an interview, LinkedIn might be able to provide background information on the person with whom you are meeting. Knowing more about the interviewer and the company can provide good conversation during the interview.

Does technology help or complicate recruiting? There are both opportunities and challenges that come with the use of technology. Compared to older methods of recruiting, candidates can be recruited much more quickly, and different types of candidates—often those who are technologically savvy—are more likely to be recruited. For example, by ensuring all of its jobs were viewable on mobile platforms, UPS has been able to recruit younger employees in inner cities who might not have regular access to computers at home and must go to their schools or libraries to look for jobs. By searching sites like LinkedIn, recruiters can also find talented employees who might not be actively searching for work but who would consider leaving their jobs for the right opportunities.

The drawback of online job postings is that they yield many responses and thus a large pool of candidates, so sifting through these responses to find the right person for the job can be a time-consuming process for HR professionals. The challenge of finding qualified candidates for critical positions is significant. Therefore, HR managers must know how to skillfully use technology. At a basic recruiting level, this means learning how to make a posted job description appeal to the most qualified candidates as well as stand out from competitors in the online environment so the right person can find the open position more readily. In addition, HR departments are using software systems to scan résumés and help screen applicants to weed out those who are unqualified. The software program Unicru is used by many retail stores to screen candidates for dependability, honesty, and other qualities. Some firms have successfully reduced their employee turnover rates using electronic screening methods. Other people argue that electronic screening eliminates strong candidates with interesting backgrounds because they don't fit job profiles programmed into the software. Strong candidates who simply don't use words in their résumés that the software is searching for can also get eliminated.

Social Media and Privacy

What are the risks of posting information on social media sites if you are trying to find a job? As a job applicant, don't be surprised if the people considering hiring you review public information you post—such as reading your Facebook Wall and checking out the Facebook pages of your friend. What if during an interview an employer asks that you "friend" them into other areas of your Facebook site?

The proper workplace use of public information is not yet clearly defined, so some employers watch public postings to see what kind of comments employees are making about the company. What if confidential information that is sensitive to the company appears on your Twitter feed—can the company take action against you? If you are using geolocation apps like Four-Square, your location becomes public information that might give away important clues to a technologically savvy recruiter or hiring manager who wants to know where you "hang out."

Even if the recruiter or hiring manager doesn't personally conduct a search, he or she can hire an outside firm, such as Social Intelligence, to do so. For a fee, firms like Social Intelligence scour social media sites and other sites and, based on the information they find, create reports on candidates.

For legal and other reasons, companies are finding it important to establish policies for employees on how to use social networking. The site Social Media Governance provides the current policies of many major corporations. For example, Intel has set of Social Media guidelines that require employees to disclose employment relationships when commenting on Intel's products/services on social media.[1]

On a positive side, social media can be used as your own personal marketing agency, creating a "brand" for you as a prospective employee. Does your Facebook page attract a second look from a professional recruiter? Consider including presentations and videos that show your abilities and potential.

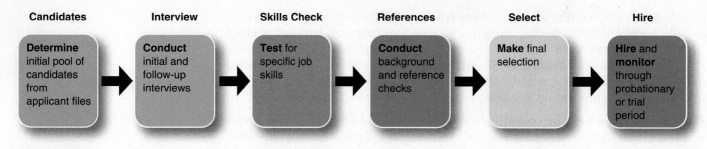

■ FIGURE 9.4
The Hiring Process

Hiring

What happens in the hiring process? As **■ FIGURE 9.4** shows, hiring is a multistep process. The first step is to select a pool of qualified candidates from the original group of applicants. To do this, HR managers compare the applicants' qualifications to the job specifications. Some firms use *applicant-tracking system* software to screen résumés and narrow down the pool. The software also tracks applicants' progress through the hiring process and can notify them and hiring managers about where each person stands in the process.[2]

After identifying a small pool of appropriate candidates, department and HR managers generally interview them to gauge their strengths and weaknesses, clarify information in the candidate's résumé, and determine whether he or she is a good match for the position. Candidates might also need to complete some skills-related tests and be asked how they have handled specific job-related situations in the past. Qualified candidates are then asked to interview with the job's manager and his or her employees.

Once a candidate is selected, a conditional offer will be made. If the candidate accepts, the company completes thorough background and reference checks and drug and medical tests if the firm requires them. It's not uncommon to hear stories about companies that failed to conduct background checks and were later sued by their employees and other people because the person became violent on the job and injured them. It's also not uncommon for someone to falsify his or her educational or professional experiences or to have been in trouble with the law. For example, Dennis O'Riordan, a high-powered lawyer and partner in the London firm Paul Hastings, was disbarred when it was revealed he has falsely claimed he had degrees from Oxford and Harvard.[3] After accepting a position, it is typical for the employee to have probationary status for a certain period of time to make sure the hiring is a good fit.

What legalities must be considered when hiring? Several federal laws must be observed during the hiring process:

- **Federal equal employment opportunity.** Established in 1965, the Federal Equal Employment Opportunity Commission (EEOC) enforces federal legislation prohibiting employment discrimination. This legislation consists of a number of different acts and laws known as equal employment opportunity (EEO) laws. The EEOC investigates discrimination claims made by job applicants and employees and files lawsuits against companies when necessary.

- **Civil rights act of 1964.** The Civil Rights Act of 1964 prohibits discriminating based on a person's race, color, gender, religion, and national origin. Title VII of the act also established the EEOC to enforce antidiscrimination laws.

- **Americans with disabilities act.** The Americans with Disabilities Act of 1990 (ADA) prohibits discrimination based on disabilities (or perceived disabilities). It also requires employers to make reasonable accommodations to the known disability of a qualified applicant or employee as long as it does not impose an "undue hardship" on the operation of an employer's business. Reasonable accommodations might include providing wheelchair accessibility, modified equipment, or interpreters.

- **Age Discrimination in Employment Act.** The Age Discrimination in Employment Act (ADEA) of 1967 makes it unlawful to discriminate against a person because of his or her age with respect to employment. It also prohibits the inclusion of age preferences in job notices or advertisements, except in specific circumstances where age is considered necessary to the job's function.
- **Fair Labor Standards Act.** In addition to establishing the minimum wage and how overtime pay must be calculated, the Fair Labor Standards Act (FLSA) governs the use of child labor—what jobs minors are allowed to do and what hours they can work.

HR departments take care of a company's biggest resource—its employees. HR managers like Leslie Booth must possess a variety of skills to capably oversee a wide array of complex tasks. Although these tasks—planning, recruiting, and hiring—may not seem directly related to the overall success of a company, they are, in fact, closely entwined. After not finding a strong candidate for four weeks, Leslie decided to rewrite the job description to more carefully match the job specifications. She expanded the search into virtual job markets and LinkedIn and offered a bonus to employees for word-of-mouth referrals. Applications began to arrive that were from higher-caliber candidates, and she is confident her firm will hire someone for the position soon.

Training and Evaluating Employees pp. 251–255

George Hensel is an expert at running meetings—and everybody knows it. A meeting with George in charge will be just the right length, everybody will have their voice heard, and creative results often emerge. Employees throughout the national company would love to run a meeting like George does, but there is no time or budget to send him around the country to train them on how to do so. How can George's skills be leveraged to help the entire company? ■

Source: Eric Audras/PhotoAlto/Alamy.

Companies that emphasize training and development experience greater employee productivity, loyalty, and retention—all of which are good for the bottom line. In this section, you'll learn about how training and evaluating employees can enhance the success of a business and ensure that employees stay in top form.

Training Methods and Requirements

What kind of training do new employees receive? Initially, when an employee is hired, an organization uses an **orientation program** to integrate a new employee into the company. Orientation can be as simple as an overview of an organization and the distribution of basic information, such as company procedures and expectations. Today, however, many companies are going beyond the traditional orientation program of explaining rules and regulations, as reflected in the orientation checklist in ■ **TABLE 9.1**. Orientation is more effective when it familiarizes the employee with a company's mission and discuss how a new employee's contribution can add to a company's success.

What other training is required of new and current employees? Training begins where orientation ends. Training should teach employees new skills or ways to improve their existing skills. For example, a salesperson might know how to sell a product but may not know all the intricacies of selling a new product. Often, other employees in the department or the recent hire's mentor can conduct **on-the-job training**. With on-the-job training, employees learn skills by performing them.

TABLE 9.1   New Employee Orientation

Introduction	To Fellow Workers and Supervisors	Tour of Work Area	To Organizational Mission	To Health Unit
Employee's job	Role of supervisor	Position description	Employee responsibilities	Sources of assistance
Hours of work	Schedule (flextime/ compressed)	Breaks and lunch periods		
Performance	Probationary period	Job elements and standards	Appraisals and evaluations	
Leave	Employee responsibilities in application	Reporting illness or emergency	Signing in/out	
Training and advancement	On-the-job; classroom	Schedules	Individual development plan	
Ethics	Training			
Security	Use of property	Safeguarding passwords/IDs	Security awareness training	

The Center for Advanced Medical Learning of the University of South Florida draws 30,000 health professionals to practice skills on simulators.
Source: Chris O'Meara/AP Images.

For example, there are many training and certification programs to become a pharmacy technician. But the specialty of nuclear pharmacy technician, a position that requires dispensing radiopharmaceuticals for use as therapies or for diagnostic testing in hospital settings, requires 500 additional hours of on-the-job training.[4]

Some jobs require an apprentice training program. In an **apprentice training program**, people go through classroom or formal instruction and get on-the-job training. For example, there is a growing need for underwater welders to repair the infrastructure of bridges and other underwater structures. To be an underwater welder, you need to complete a surface welder program and a commercial diving program. Next you would apply to a commercial diving company that offers underwater welding as a service. You would begin your career as a diver tender (apprentice diver) to gain experience. Once you gain enough experience, you can advance to welder-diver status, at which point your wage rate would increase.

A **programmed learning approach** is one in which an employee is asked to perform step-by-step instructions or respond to questions, often in the form of computerized multiple-choice tests that provide immediate feedback. The benefit of programmed learning is that an employee can progress at his or her own pace, picking up information piece by piece. For some settings, though, this kind of training may not match the type of complex decision making needed to teach employees. A firm must also provide computer access to employees and acquire and maintain the software needed for this type of a training program.

What kind of impact does technology have on training? Improvements in technology provide companies with other training options, such as simulated training and interactive multimedia training. *Gamification*, the application of game design concepts to nongame settings, has led to some training tools that are very engaging. Cold Stone Creamery, the U.S. Army, and Hilton are all turning once-dull training into an interactive video experience by using games to train their employees. One study by the Entertainment Software Association showed that 70 percent of major U.S. employers have used interactive software and games for training.[5]

Other companies offer **simulation training**. Simulations provide employees with realistic experiences they would face on the job without having to worry about the catastrophic consequences that would result by making a wrong move. Simulation training is suitable for airline pilots, astronauts, and medical professionals for whom making mistakes during training is not an option or is too costly.

Online training allows employees to get training on the Internet either delivered live or at their own convenience. Instructors in one location can train groups of employees at remote locations via Webcasts, Webinars, and videoconferencing technology. These technologies allow users to share documents, share application software, swap control of meetings, and, depending on the type technology, allow trainers to take over an attendee's desktop for demonstration purposes. Attendees can ask questions in real time, comment to the group as videos are being shown, and archive the session for later viewing.

Videoconferencing and teletraining allow employees at various remote locations to train and work together easily.
Source: Monty Rakusen/Getty Images.

Electronic Performance Support Systems (EPSSs) contain online modules employees can access when they need training instead of attending long, formal training sessions disconnected from their daily work. Organizations are finding that EPSSs can be very cost effective. One case study reported that after a client implemented an EPSS, a year later, the firm's employees had made more than 300,000 requests for training. By being able to be train its employees on the spot and electronically, the company saved $2.6 million.[6]

Do managers need training? Yes, but because of their roles in the organization, managers require different types training. Managerial training often focuses on leadership, communication, teamwork, and relationship-building skills. In addition, managers need to keep abreast of changes in employment laws, such as laws related to discrimination and harassment, as well as updates in using new tools for electronic communication.

Management development programs prepare managerial trainees to become managers. These programs may have trainees participate in an on-the-job training program, which might include *job rotation*, whereby an employee rotates through different departments to learn firsthand the various aspects of the business, or a *coaching/understudy program*, in which an employee works directly with the company's senior managers to learn how to plan, lead, and make decisions at the corporate level. With *action learning*, another management development training approach, trainees work alone or together on teams to analyze real-time corporate problems that extend beyond their areas of expertise. Companies such as Microsoft, DuPont, and Boeing have successfully implemented action-learning teams as part of their management development programs.

Some companies use **off-the-job training and development** techniques that require employees to participate in outside seminars, university-conducted programs, and corporate universities. Hamburger University, McDonald's system of 22 corporate training facilities, trains employees for management roles. Nineteen full-time professors offer training for restaurant managers, department heads, and executive development. Through interpreters, McDonald's trainers can deliver courses in over 28 languages.[7]

How are experienced managers developed? Senior managers often use *executive coaches* to further develop their effectiveness. Executive coaches identify a manager's strengths and weaknesses by interviewing those who work closely with the manager. They then meet with the manager to minimize their weaknesses and further develop their strengths.

Mentoring is another option companies use. A **mentor** is an employee with more experience who takes a less experienced coworker under his or her wing. The mentor

Annual Employee Performance Evaluation

Employee's Name:		Supervisor:	
Job Title:		Date Hired:	
Department:		Date of Review:	

Evaluation

This form is designed to assess your current performance and to help in setting goals for the future. This form is considered confidential and will only be reviewed by you and your supervisor(s).

Overall Job Knowledge/Experience Level

	Consistently meets requirements
	Generally meets requirements
	Does not meet requirements

Comments:

Quality of Work

	Exceeds expectations
	Meets expectations
	Does not meet expectations

Comments:

Attendance

	Rarely tardy or absent
	Sometimes tardy or absent
	Frequently tardy or absent

Comments:

Cooperation

	Consistently participates and contributes to the team
	Generally participates and contributes to the team
	Does not participate or contribute to the team

Comments:

Future Goals:

■ FIGURE 9.5
A Sample Performance Appraisal

shows the person how to perform specific tasks, creates opportunities for him or her to learn new skills, and counsels him or her about the consequences of particular actions and decisions. A new practice named **reverse mentoring** is beginning to show up in the workplace as well. In reverse mentoring, older employees, often executives, are trained by younger ones on how to use technology and on new trends in the marketplace. It benefits both as the younger employees garner experience and time with higher-level management. Like other forms of training and management development, mentoring increases employee performance, satisfaction, and loyalty.

Performance Appraisals and Alternatives

Why are performance appraisals necessary? A **performance appraisal** is a formal evaluation, usually done annually or biannually, that provides an employee with feedback about how well he or she is doing on the job. A sample appraisal form is shown in ■ **FIGURE 9.5**. Managers use the results of performance appraisals to make decisions about promotion, raises, additional training, or reassignments. The performance appraisal process is important for both employees and the organization as a whole and includes three aspects:

- *Evaluating the performance* of an employee relative to the job's performance standards
- *Providing feedback* to reduce and eliminate poor performance and improve or enhance positive performance
- *Setting goals* toward which employees should aim in their work

When employees are hired, they should have a good understanding of what is expected of them. These expectations become the performance standards on which they'll be measured. Appraisals act as a confirmation of these standards and help employees establish quantifiable and measurable goals for improvement in the upcoming year.

Are there problems with performance appraisals? Performance appraisals, when conducted properly, are very helpful to an employee and ultimately an organization. However, they are often not effective. Many managers shy away from them because they are uncomfortable delivering negative comments. Managers also sometimes have a difficult time objectively appraising the performance of employees because they often do not see all of the aspects of the employees' performance. The use of a **360-degree appraisal** can help in this instance. Input for the appraisal is solicited, usually anonymously, not from just a person's managers but also from coworkers, customers, and subordinates.

Although performance appraisals are way to provide feedback to an employee about how to improve a weak performance or enhance a solid one, the process does not always result in follow-up to ensure the feedback has been acted on. Typically, it is not until the next performance appraisal that a manager and employee reluctantly admit that the needed training and development did not occur. And when the next appraisal can be a year away, more immediate crises can take time away from the focus on an appraisal's recommendations.

What alternatives exist for performance appraisals? An alternative to a performance appraisal is performance management. **Performance management**

TABLE 9.2	Aspects of Performance Management
Direction sharing	Communicating an organization's higher-level goals, such as vision, mission, values, and strategy
Role clarifying	Defining roles in terms of daily work tasks
Goal setting and planning	Translating organizational or departmental goals into specific employee goals, which includes an employee's development of the steps necessary to achieve goals
Ongoing performance monitoring and feedback	Periodic performance reports about an employee's progress toward meeting his or her goals as well as feedback about how better to achieve them
Coaching and support	Ongoing feedback and support for the employee
Performance assessment (appraisal)	An element in the performance management process that offers specific information about how an employee's performance is improving the company's results
Rewards, recognition, and compensation	Given as appropriate to motivate an employee toward achieving current and future goals
Work flow, process control, and return on investment	Making sure an employee's measurable performance is linked to measurable goals of company

Source: Adapted from Gary Dessler, *Human Resource Management*, 14th, © 2015. Printed and electronically reproduced by permission of Pearson Education, Inc., Upper Saddle River, New Jersey.

is an approach that combines goal setting, performance appraisals, and training and development into a unified and ongoing process. As such, it is more of a cyclical and fluid process than the single occurrence of a performance appraisal. Employees are constantly receiving feedback and given opportunities for training and development to ensure that they have the right tools with which to perform their jobs. ■ **TABLE 9.2** summarizes several aspects of the performance management process. The concept, while often applied to employees, is also applicable to other components of an organization, including an entire department, a product or a service, or an organization as a whole.

Performance management, appraisals, and training can play a significant role in keeping a business productive and efficient. George Hensel's company decided that knowing how to run and participate in a productive meeting are skills all employees should have. They therefore created online learning modules that featured videos in which George explained how people often allow meetings to go off track. The company then created a game that allowed players to conduct a virtual meeting and be scored based on how well they did. Employees who watched the online training and attempted the simulation a certain number of times received credit for doing so in their performance appraisals. The commitment to training created more productive meetings throughout the company.

Compensating, Scheduling, Promoting, and Terminating Employees pp. 255–261

Kathy Sanchez loves what she does. Since graduating from college two years ago, she has worked for a small start-up company as a graphic designer, creating brochures and other materials for a wide variety of clients. Because the company is so small, she gets to work on projects she would never have a chance to work on in a bigger company. She also loves the

Source: Stockbroker/Alamy.

relaxed atmosphere of the office and feels like her coworkers are actually her friends. So what's the problem? Because the company is still finding its footing in the marketplace, it isn't able to offer her much in the way of pay or benefits. Although she loves her work, she is tired of reaching the end of each pay period with no money left. And don't even ask her about her retirement plan or dental insurance! What should she do? ■

Having the right pay system in place is very important for a company to become and remain competitive. A good compensation package attracts high-quality employees and keeps them from leaving. But compensation is not just about monetary rewards. In today's workplace, employees frequently receive compensation in a variety of forms, including work/life benefits, health insurance, and retirement plans. Because there are many ways to compensate employees, deciding how to structure a competitive compensation package is not an easy one. It's often a delicate balance between paying employees enough to attract, motivate, and retain them while keeping a company financially sound and providing its owners with a return on their investment.

Compensation Strategies

Are all employees paid in the same way? There are many ways to pay workers for their time and effort.

Compensation, payment for work performed, is generally offered in the form of fixed **salaries** (annual pay for a specific job) or **wages** (payments for hourly work). Usually, on an annual basis, an employee's compensation level has the potential to increase based on the results of the person's performance evaluation.

Incentive-based payment structures are better compensation strategies for some positions, such as those in sales. A salesperson typically has a lower base salary, which can be enhanced with **commissions** based directly on the employee's sales levels or performance. Incentive-based compensation rewards employees who achieve strong measurable results.

Bonuses, compensation based on total corporate profits, help tie employees' efforts to the company's bottom line. Higher corporate profits mean higher bonuses.

What types of retirement plans do companies offer employees? The most popular retirement plan offered today is the 401(k) plan. A **401(k) plan** is a retirement plan in which an employee invests pretax dollars in a bundle of investments generally managed by an outside investment company, such as the Vanguard Group or Fidelity Investments. The amount of the annual contribution is determined by the employee as a percentage of salary up to a specified legal limit. In some cases, a company will match a portion of the employee's contribution to the account. A 401(k) is referred to as a *defined contribution plan* because the amount an employee receives at retirement depends on the amount of the contributions and the fund's investment earnings. The burden of risk falls on employees because they decide how much to contribute to their plans and how the money will be invested.

An employer that has a **pension plan** regularly contributes a certain amount of money to a retirement fund for its employees. Employees know ahead of time exactly how much pension money they will receive when they retire based on their years of service to the company. A pension plan is a *defined benefit plan*. Defined benefit plans are not popular with employers because they entirely fund them and take on financial risks if the fund's investments do not perform as expected.

A **profit-sharing plan** is a term used for a range of different types of compensation options. If the company hits certain profit targets, then there is a bonus structure for employees. Sometimes the term *profit sharing* is used for company contributions to an employee retirement plan. Profit-sharing plans are often offered as a part of executive compensation in larger companies, but in many small companies, they are a way to motivate employees, especially during the start-up phase when cash is tight and salaries may be low.

What other financial incentives do companies offer as compensation? Stock **option** agreements allow an employee to purchase a specific number of shares of stock at a specific price but only at a specific point in time. If the stock's value increases beyond that point, the employee can reap a huge financial reward. If not, however, the employee gains little. Facebook used stock options as part of a compensation package designed to lure top engineers. When the company began selling shares to the public, the engineers were able to exercise their stock options, and thousands of employees at Facebook became millionaires as a result.[8]

Employee stock purchase plans allow employees to buy company stock at a discount (usually at 85 percent of their market value). Companies typically limit the amount of stock an employee can purchase this way to 10 percent of their total salary. **Employee stock ownership plans** (ESOPs) are plans whereby employees are given stock in a company based on the amount of time they have worked for it. The stock is held in the ESOP's trust fund until the employees either retire or leave the company. In 1994, United Airlines was failing and needed to negotiate dramatic wage reductions with its unions (pilots, flight attendants, and so on). The employees formed the United Airlines ESOP and then agreed to 8 to 15 percent wage cuts for the next five years. In return, via the ESOP, employees were given a 55 percent ownership of United Airlines. An advantage of providing employees with ownership in a company via stock transactions is that employees feel more connected to the business and are motivated to ensure that the business succeeds. For United Airlines, the first year under ESOP was the best for stockholders in the 70-year history of the company.

Benefits

What are noncash forms of compensation? Employee benefits are indirect financial and nonfinancial rewards employers provide their employees to supplement their wages and salaries. Some benefits are mandated by law. For example, the Affordable Care Act, passed in 2010, requires firms with more than 50 full-time employees to provide them with health care coverage or else pay a penalty. Other benefits are voluntarily provided by employers. Vacation time, holidays, and pensions are examples.

Some companies offer **flexible benefit plans** (or **cafeteria plans**) that allow employees to pick from a menu of several choices of taxable and nontaxable forms of compensation. Flexible benefit plans allow employees to choose the benefits that are most important to them while reducing the cost of offering all benefits to all employees.

What are work/life benefits? Work/life benefits are benefits that help an employee achieve a balance between the demands of life both inside and outside the workplace. Work/life benefits include flexible schedules, relaxed atmospheres, and child care and fitness/gym programs. For example, the SAS Institute, the largest privately held software developer in the United States, offers employees unlimited sick leave, an on-site fitness club with indoor pool, on-site car detailing, massages, and a hair salon. There are four subsidized child care centers on-site and pantries stocked with free food. Although seemingly expensive, this strategy of keeping its employees happy saves the company approximately $70 million per year because it experiences low turnover. In fact, compared with an industry average of 20 percent turnover, SAS has kept its turnover rate below 5 percent.[9]

The Googleplex, Google's Mountain View California campus, has amenities including swimming pools, 11 free gourmet cafeterias, volleyball courts, and massage services.
Source: Justin Sullivan/Getty Images.

What are some other trends in employee benefits? In the early 1980s, the *Village Voice*, a free alternative weekly newspaper in New York City, began offering *domestic partner benefits*. These benefits provide for an employee's unmarried partner of the same or opposite sex. Since then, domestic partner benefits have become increasingly common components of compensation packages. In fact, almost 62 percent of Fortune 500 companies offer domestic benefits to their employees.[10] Benefits such as health care and family leave policies are extended to domestic partners.[11]

The Family and Medical Leave Act states that companies with more than 50 employees must allow all eligible employees to take up to 12 weeks of unpaid time off to be with family because of medical issues, births, or adoptions. Upon the employee's return, the act guarantees that the employee can return to his or her job or a comparable job. This benefit compares weakly to those of other countries. At least 178 countries have laws that guarantee paid leave for new mothers; more than 50 countries offer paid leave for new fathers as well.

Rising health care costs are impacting businesses and bringing changes to the medical benefits employees can expect. A rising trend is for employers to provide employees with a fixed amount of money to purchase health care on their own in the marketplace instead of providing a choice of specific plans. Some companies are dropping working spouses from eligibility, requiring them to negotiate health care with their own employer.

Alternative Scheduling and Work Arrangements

What work schedules are possible outside of the traditional workday? An increasing number of employees are finding that keeping up with the demands of their work and personal lives has left them doing neither well. The added stress employees today face from child care, elder care, commuting, and other work/life conflicts have led to a decrease in productivity and an increase in employee absenteeism and tardiness.

Due to these demands, more and more employers are offering alternatives to the traditional 9-to-5, Monday-to-Friday workweek. In addition to benefiting employees, flexible work schedules can also benefit employers. A study conducted by the Gallup research group looked at employees with flexible schedules who were allowed to work from home and found that they actually worked an additional 4 hours per week.[12]

The most popular flexible work arrangements include the following:

- **Telecommuting. Telecommuting** allows employees to work in the office part-time and work from home part-time or to work completely from home and make only occasional visits to the office. Cisco employees work remotely an average of two days per week, a practice that the company estimates has saved it $277 million.[13] The disadvantages of telecommuting include monitoring employees' performance at a distance, servicing equipment for off-site employees, and communication issues. Additionally, employees who telecommute can become isolated from other employees. Yahoo! used to allow telecommuting but ended the practice because its CEO believed it was leading to less collaboration and idea generation among employees.

- **Alternative scheduling plans (flextime).** When a company implements **flextime**, it specifies a core set of hours that define the workday and is flexible with the starting and ending times employees can work.

- **Compressed workweek.** A **compressed workweek** allows employees to work four 10-hour days instead of five eight-hour days each week or nine days instead of 10 in a two-week schedule for a total 80 hours. However, firms need to check their state labor laws. Many states, for example, prohibit minors from working in excess of eight hours per day.

- **Job sharing. Job sharing** is an arrangement in which two employees work part-time to share one full-time job. Those who share a job are often very motivated to make the arrangement work, and productivity and employee satisfaction can increase. However, job sharers must carefully coordinate and communicate with one another and their employers to ensure that all of the responsibilities of the job are met.

- **Permanent part-time. Permanent part-time employees** are hired on a permanent basis to work a part-time week. Unlike temporary part-time workers who are employed to meet a firm's short-term needs, permanent part-time employees in some firms enjoy the same benefits full-time employees do.

What benefits do employers see from supporting alternative work schedules? Despite the costs associated with designing and implementing flexible working arrangements, employers can expect positive bottom-line results due to increases in employee satisfaction, decreases in absenteeism, and increases in worker productivity. Similarly, reductions in employee turnover lead to a decrease in time and costs associated with employee recruiting and replacement training.

Contingent Workers

Why does a company hire contingent workers? Contingent workers are people who are hired on an as-needed basis and lack status as regular, full-time employees. These workers often fulfill important and specific functions. Contingent workers are most likely hired by companies in business and professional services, education and health care services, and construction industries. Companies hire such temporary workers to fill in for absent employees or augment the staff during busy periods. Long-term temporary employees are often hired for indefinite periods of time to work on specific projects. In many cases, temporary staffing is part of a company's HR "temp to perm" strategy in which temporary employees are evaluated and then moved to permanent positions if they are found to be reliable and skilled.

Independent contractors and **consultants** are examples of contingent workers who are generally self-employed. Companies hire them on a temporary basis to perform specific tasks. Often, contractors are hired for jobs that involve state-of-the-art skills in construction, financial activities, and professional and business services. For example, it might be most cost efficient to hire a Web page developer as an independent contractor rather than keeping one on staff permanently. Consultants are hired to assist with long-term projects, often at a strategic level, but also with a specific end in sight. For example, a company that is reviewing its executive management compensation arrangements might hire a compensation consultant.

Is temporary work a common situation for people? The U.S. Bureau of Labor Statistics estimates that the temporary workforce accounts for more than 2 percent of the U.S. workforce.[14] Temporary staffing is a $70 billion industry. Kelly Services and Manpower are two prominent temporary agencies. Temporary workers often get the opportunity to work in many different companies, do different jobs, and meet numerous people. Recent college graduates and college students may find that temporary work is a good way gain real-world experience in an industry they are interested in pursuing on a full-time basis and see if they companies they are temping at are employers for whom they would like to work full-time. But temporary workers are often paid less than full-time workers and are less likely to receive benefits. The temporary agencies they work for may provide them with some benefits, however.

Promotions

How can employees increase their levels of responsibility in a company? After performing successfully in a position, many employees look to increase their responsibility levels and pay in a company or a department by seeking a promotion. Employers like to promote from within because it allows them to reward exceptional behavior and fill positions with tested employees. However, a promotion may not always result in a positive situation if it was made in secrecy or arbitrarily. Sometimes

UPS offers a permanent part-time package handler position in which employees work about four hours per day, Monday through Friday. UPS offers permanent part-time employees health insurance, vacation time, a stock purchase plan, and, in certain locations, tuition assistance.
Source: David R. Frazier/Alamy.

▶ **THE LIST**

Top 10 Ways to Get Promoted

1. Get a mentor.
2. Learn outside of work.
3. Self-promote your successes.
4. Volunteer.
5. Ask questions.
6. Be consistent.
7. Help your colleagues.
8. Tell your boss you want to be promoted.
9. Be a team player.
10. Create your own opportunities.

employees are promoted to new positions without other employees being given a chance to apply for them, which can lead to hard feelings. Therefore, management must ensure that promotions are based on a distinct set of criteria, such as seniority or competency, and that HR protocols are followed.

Do promotions always move you into management positions? Consider an engineer who succeeds on the job but has no desire to manage. Some companies provide two career paths: one toward management and the other for "individual contributors" with no management aspirations. Engineers with a desire to manage can pursue one track, and other engineers without managerial aspirations or capabilities can be promoted to "senior engineer" positions. Alternatively, it's always possible to keep employees in their same job but give them more responsibility, thus enriching their experience while continuing to prepare them for further advancement.

Terminating Employees

Why do companies lay off workers? At times, it becomes necessary to reevaluate an employee's contribution or tenure at a company or the composition and size of the workforce altogether. Downsizing and restructuring, the availability of outsourcing and offshoring, the pressures of global competition, and the increased uses of technology are also reasons companies look to reduce the number of employees. **Termination** refers to the act of permanently laying off workers due to poor performance or a discontinued need for their services. Companies often offer a set of benefits for terminated employees, including the continuation of health care coverage for a period of time, severance pay, and outplacement services, such as résumé writing and career counseling.

Terminating employees due to poor performance or illegal activities is a complex process. Most states support **employment at will**, a legal doctrine that states that an employer can fire an employee for any reason at any time. Likewise, an employee is equally free to resign at any time for any reason. Regardless of the employment-at-will doctrine, employers cannot discriminate or fire someone because of the person's race, religion, age, gender, national origin, disability, or childbearing plans. In addition, companies cannot terminate employees for whistle-blowing (revealing company wrongdoing to authorities), engaging in legal union activities, filing a worker's compensation claim, performing jury duty, or testifying against a company in a legal proceeding.

How does a manager prepare to terminate an employee? Before firing an employee for wrongful acts or incompetence, managers must take steps to avoid a wrongful discharge lawsuit. These steps include maintaining solid records so that they can build a documented case for dismissal that's legally defensible. Courts have sided with the terminated employee, especially when not enough evidence of poor behavior is brought forth. Hearsay and rumors of wrongdoing often do not stand up in legal proceedings. Consider Monique Drake, a medical secretary in the same physician's practice for 12 years. The doctor married, and his new wife began running the office. This new office manager told Drake that due to a poor performance, her salary was being cut from $54,000 to $40,000, her sick days would be eliminated, and her vacation time would be cut. A month later Drake was terminated. She sued and won her case for wrongful dismissal. Part of the reason why she won was because there was a lack of documentation showing that her performance was weak and because her employers clearly had no ongoing discussion with her about improving her performance.[15]

Retirement

Is there a set age when employees retire? It **Retirement** is the point in one's life where one stops participating full-time in a career. It used to be that employees retired when they were 65 years old. However, the legal age at which workers can collect Social Security is gradually rising. Workers born after 1959 must now work until age 67 before then collect it.

Many older employees are continuing to work to stay active and engaged and remain on their firm's health care insurance plans. Other employees are remaining on the job because they haven't saved enough money to retire or their savings haven't grown as much as they hoped for as a result of the last recession. One impact of this shift in workforce demographics is that younger employees are experiencing greater competition for jobs and promotions than they have in the past.

For employers, an aging workforce may present other challenges, such as age-discrimination lawsuits if they aggressively lay off older workers. To encourage older workers to retire, some companies offer them **worker buyouts** (or *golden parachutes*), which are one-time payments to leave a company. For example, in recent years, the U.S. Postal Service has offered its employees several buyouts to reduce its operations and costs. Phased employment is another option. Longtime employees are moved to part-time basis for a period of time and then shifted into retirement. That practice offers the company the chance to avoid a sudden draining of experience from the company.

Remember Kathy Sanchez? She loved her job but wasn't sure what to do because of her low pay and benefits. After some serious soul-searching, Kathy decided to stay on at the small company, but she has set a limit of two more years before she starts looking for a job elsewhere. She is hoping that within that time frame, the start-up company will find solid footing and be able to offer its employees a more attractive and competitive compensation package that could include stock options.

Managing Workplace Diversity pp. 261–263

Source: michaeljung/Fotolia.

Chandraki Patel always thought of herself as someone who was familiar with a range of types of people and cultures. Although she was born in Detroit, her parents came from India, and she has often traveled abroad for vacations. But now that she is a manager at an international marketing firm, she is faced with issues she never anticipated. She has a staff that includes men and women from six different nationalities with five different religions (each with different holiday calendars). In addition, she is responsible for remotely managing a site in Dublin, Ireland, and one in Beijing, China. The language and cultural differences there have caused misunderstandings more than once. How could anyone manage so many different types of people and locations? ∎

The workforce is becoming more diverse. In this section, you'll learn why and how diversity creates both challenges and benefits for organizations.

Benefits and Challenges of Diversity

Why has the modern workplace become so diverse? The changing demographics of the United States is a major reason why the workplace is becoming more diverse. Workers of Hispanic origin, for example, make up about 15 percent of the workforce today. But due to the rapid growth of this segment of the population, by 2050 it is estimated they will make up 30 percent. The percentage of people of Asian descent in the workforce is also expected to double by 2050.[16] Advancements in technology have made it possible for businesses to operate with relative ease on a global basis. It's not unusual for companies to outsource or offshore work to other countries to decrease labor costs or establish operations in other countries to broaden their market reach. Hiring patterns are adding to the diversity of the workforce as U.S.-based companies hire workers who have emigrated from other countries. European and Middle Eastern companies are experiencing similar increases in immigration.

More women are now in the workforce than in decades past. And, as we indicated, many more employees than ever are indicating that they plan to work beyond the traditional retirement age, meaning increased age diversity in the workforce. For all these reasons, the modern workplace is now very diverse in age, gender, and ethnicity.

How is a diverse workforce beneficial? Diversity is an important component of the modern workplace. For many companies, hiring to diversify the workforce initially meant fulfilling an **affirmative action** requirement by filling positions with a certain number of women, Hispanics, or African Americans. Some criticized this strategy as unfair and bad for a company if the best candidate was not hired in favor of meeting such a requirement. Over time, however, many companies have come to embrace the idea of diversity beyond just satisfying a requirement. It's now becoming clear that companies should embrace diversity to improve their competitiveness. A diverse workforce helps companies offer a broad range of viewpoints that are necessary to compete in a world that is more globalized.

In addition, products and services need to be tailored to customers and clients with diverse backgrounds, so it's vital to have a workforce that understands the cultural needs of different customers. When PepsiCo's Frito-Lay division launched a Doritos guacamole-flavored tortilla chip to appeal especially to Latino consumers, its Latino employees provided valuable feedback on the product's taste and packaging. The new chip variety generated more than $100 million in sales in its first year, making it the most successful product launch in the company's history.

What issues do companies face while managing diversity? Despite its many benefits, a diverse workforce can pose challenges. For example, a more culturally diverse population naturally brings about a wider variety of religious beliefs and practices, with more employees trying to integrate their religious practices into the workday. As employers struggle to accommodate workers' religious needs, they must also try to avoid the potential friction that open demonstrations of religious practices might provoke. Many employers strike a balance by allowing employees to take prayer breaks and time off to observe religious holidays, catering to dietary requirements, and permitting differences in dress. Surveys show that 64 percent of companies now use floating religious holidays to accommodate employee needs, and 70 percent have introduced on-site religious accommodations, such as prayer rooms.[17]

Although the number of women in the workforce is growing, women are still battling some of the same issues that their mothers and grandmothers faced: sexism, salary inequities, and sexual harassment. Historically, women in similar positions as their male counterparts were paid less and experienced fewer promotions despite documented higher performance ratings. Many gender-discrimination and sexual harassment lawsuits continue to receive national press and indicate that gender-related challenges have not gone away. Moreover, men still dominate top managerial positions. Fewer than a dozen Fortune 500 companies are headed by women.

The aging workforce also creates several challenges. Compared with younger workers in the same position, older workers often expect higher salaries and better benefits. Health care costs, for example, are higher with an older workforce. However, many employers find that there is less turnover and absenteeism among older workers and that they are willing to learn new skills as well as help and train their younger coworkers. These benefits can offer enough savings to a company to negate the higher costs of retaining more senior workers.

Harley-Davidson realized that to remain competitive, it needed to understand the needs and wants of customers beyond the traditional stereotype of the white male. The motorcycle manufacturer has made a significant effort to hire and retain women and minority managers. *Source:* David Gee/Alamy.

One Diversity Training Does Not Fit All

Diversity training workshops and seminars that teach managers and their employees about the benefits of having a diverse workforce can be quite costly. And yet, according to a recent study, most of these programs don't work.[18] After analyzing years of national employment statistics, a major study concluded that standard diversity training rarely had an effect on the number of women or minority managers employed by companies where it was used. Why not? Some people theorize that mandatory training inevitably leads to backlash; others say that altering people's inner biases is a nearly impossible task.

Hope for promoting diversity in the workplace is not lost, however; the study also found that two techniques had significant, beneficial effects on workplace diversity: (1) The appointment of a specific person or committee accountable for addressing diversity issues within the company led to 10 percent increases in the number of women and minorities in management positions, and (2) mentoring increased the number of African American women in leadership positions by 23.5 percent.

How can employees improve their understanding of each other's differences? Differences can create misunderstandings and conflict despite the most well intentioned actions. Therefore, it is important that employers provide effective **diversity training** for their employees. It is also important for coworkers to learn to look at situations from perspectives that are different than their own. Ultimately, managing diversity means developing a workforce that has the capacity to accept, incorporate, and empower the different talents, backgrounds, and perspectives people have.

Recall that Chandraki Patel was responsible for managing people with different cultural backgrounds, languages, and beliefs and was unsure how best to do it. To see if she could improve her performance in this area, she began researching all the ways that the diversity of the group she managed had led to innovative solutions to problems for her company. As she counted the many benefits of working with such a varied range of people in the group, she felt more motivated to manage some of the challenges. She began a training program to help employees become more adept at examining issues from a variety of perspectives. Not only did that help the group she headed up, it also resulted in the group working better with the company's Chinese and Irish divisions.

Labor and Union Issues pp. 263–265

Are college football players employees of the schools they play for? College football player across the country have begun wearing wristbands with the letters *APU* printed on them. APU stands for "All Players United" and is a slogan of protest against the National Collegiate Athletic Association (NCAA). Some players feel they should be compensated with some fraction of the money from the television rights, merchandising, and ticket sales their play generates. They also believe the NCAA is not doing enough to protect players from head injuries or to provide them with medical insurance and care for injured players. When athletes' images are used in ads or in video games, they earn none of the profits. Should the athletes be allowed to form a union to have a single voice in these issues? ■

Source: Barbara J. Perenic/MCT/Newscom.

Have you ever passed a picket line and wondered why the workers were on strike? A **strike** occurs when workers agree to stop work until certain demands are met. In this section, you'll learn about organized labor and its effect on the workplace.

Organized Labor

What is a labor union? A **labor union** is a legally recognized group dedicated to protecting the interests of workers. Unions represent many types of workers, such as teachers, nurses, and firefighters in the public sector; employees in the manufacturing industries; and engineers, plumbers, and roofers in the construction industry. Entertainers such as actors and writers also have unions. Labor unions negotiate various employment issues on behalf of the workers they represent, such as their salaries, benefits, and working hours.

What are the objectives of organized labor? Labor unions were formed to protect workers from the terrible injustices employers inflicted on their workers in the nineteenth century during the U.S. industrial revolution. During that time, employers subjected workers to long hours, low pay, and health risks. Women and children were often treated even worse and paid less. Labor unions formed to fight for better working conditions and employee rights. A number of these unions later united to gain more power to negotiate better working conditions. Two of the more influential unions are the **American Federation of Labor** (AFL), founded in 1886 to protect skilled workers, and the Industrial Workers of the World, founded in 1905 to represent mainly unskilled workers.

The **Congress of Industrial Organizations** (CIO) was formed in 1935 to represent entire industries rather than specific workers' groups. The CIO was initially a separate organization within the AFL but soon split to form its own organization. In 1955, the two were reunited to form the AFL-CIO, which is still in effect today as a federation comprised of 56 member unions. The Change to Win Federation, formed in 2005 as an alternative to the AFL-CIO, is the newest organized labor union. Other prominent unions include the United Auto Workers (UAW), the International Brotherhood of Teamsters, and the Service Employees International Union.

How are labor unions structured? To form a union, a group of workers must either have their employer voluntarily recognize them as a group or have a majority of workers form a **bargaining unit** for union representation. A bargaining unit is a group of employees that negotiates with an employer for better working conditions or pay. When a union forms, workers join and pay membership dues. Most unions have paid, full-time staff members as well as substantial numbers of volunteer workers. In addition to the dues they collect from their members, some unions create strike funds that help support workers should they strike. Union members elect officers and shop stewards who make decisions for the entire body and represent the members in dealings with management. So that unions can better represent specific interests, union **locals** are created by workers of the same industry, company, region, or business sector.

Collective Bargaining

What is the collective bargaining process? **Collective bargaining** is the process that occurs when a union negotiates with an employer. The union's goal is improve the wages, insurance and benefits, working hours, pensions, and grievance procedures for its members as a group (collectively) rather than each of them having to negotiate individually with their firms. A collective bargaining agreement is the result of such negotiations, and it forces an employer to abide by the conditions specified in the agreement. Change can be made only through subsequent negotiations.

What happens if an agreement cannot be reached through collective bargaining? If negotiating does not produce a collective bargaining agreement and both parties seem to be at an impasse, then other methods are used to settle their differences before workers go on strike. One method is **mediation**, a process in which a neutral third party helps the two parties reach an agreement. The mediator works with both sides to understand their genuine interests and helps each side generate proposals that address those interests. Another method is **arbitration**, whereby a dispute is sent to an arbitrator to resolve. An arbitrator hears both sides of a dispute, and the parties involved agree in advance that the arbitrator's decision is final. Sometimes, arbitration is nonbinding, meaning that neither party is required to accept the arbitrator's decision.

What happens when negotiations break down? When negotiations reach an impasse, union workers have several ways to persuade a firm to accept their demands. For example, the workers and people who are sympathetic to their cause can boycott the firm. A **boycott** occurs when people refuse to buy or distribute a company's products or services. Companies have their tactics as well. One is a lockout. In a **lockout**, union members are not allowed to enter the firm's premises. Lockouts are legal only if negotiations have come to an impasse and the company is defending a legitimate position.

As a last resort, union workers may vote to go on strike and agree to stop working. Strikes jeopardize the productivity of an organization, so they are used to force management into making concessions that they might not have made otherwise. Strikes also gain considerable media publicity, especially when workers **picket** a workplace by walking outside a company's entrances with signs that reflect the employees' grievances.

It is not easy to persuade a union's members to go on strike because they risk losing income throughout the strike period. For example, a six-week strike would cost a worker earning $700 per week a total of $4,200 in lost wages. If the new contract negotiated a weekly wage increase of $1, it would take about two years to recover the lost wages. Additionally, strikers might be replaced by a firm temporarily or permanently with workers, known as **strikebreakers**, or scabs. Some states prohibit public safety workers, such as police officers and hospital workers, from going on strike. In these cases, workers often have "sick-outs," during which union members are not officially on strike but instead call in sick and refuse to come to work.

The State of Labor Unions

Are labor unions still effective today? In the United States, the role of labor unions is declining. Today, only a little more than 10 percent of the nation's workers are unionized.[19] Many private-sector unions, such as the automobile workers and construction trade unions, have experienced dramatic reductions in their membership. This decline is the result of several factors, including a reaction to their own success by fighting for better working conditions, higher wages, and more benefits. Additionally, the introduction of technology has resulted in a shift from blue-collar–based industries to professional white-collar, service-based industries, for which unions are less common. Employers are also in a better position to outsource and offshore jobs done by union members. Despite their declining numbers, labor unions continue to be influential in many industries as well as in other countries. Efforts are under way to organize retail workers and service-sector workers, such as those in the fast-food industry.

What is the future of unions and labor–management relations? U.S. unions have begun to build alliances with unions in other countries. They recognize that when multinational corporations decide to move production abroad, for example, there might be a negative impact on local and international workers. Consequently, in an effort to protect their interests, unions must broaden their reach to try to achieve international labor solidarity. Immigration is another issue affecting unions. Immigrant workers are crossing borders and threaten to take jobs traditionally done by the members of labor unions. Unions, especially in California and Florida, continue to grapple with integrating and embracing these potential new members into their organizations. Finally, and perhaps most important, unions will need to transform themselves to survive the effects of globalization.

Remember the athletes wearing those "All Players United" wristbands? A group of football players from Northwestern University brought a case to the National Labor Relations Board, requesting the right to form a union. The board ruled strongly in their favor, stating that they are employees of their universities. The decision could fundamentally change the structure of college sports in the United States.

After the negotiations the snack-food maker Hostess had with its unionized employees broke down, the company filed for bankruptcy. A reorganized, nonunion Hostess emerged, with new workers making far less.
Source: Kevork Djansezian/Getty Images.

Summary

1 What processes are involved in human resource management (HRM)? (pp. 245–251)

- **Human resource management (HRM)** (p. 245) is the organizational function that encompasses every aspect of the "human" in a business, including hiring, training, motivating, evaluating, and compensating personnel.

- Staff planning involves determining how many employees a company needs. A **workforce profile** (p. 245) is compiled as a form of "personnel inventory" and includes information about each employee. The future demand for employees is determined by a process called **forecasting** (p. 246).

- **Recruitment** (p. 247) is the process of finding, screening, and selecting people for a job.

- Hiring begins by narrowing down the number of applicants who are qualified for a job. They are then interviewed by human resources personnel and the job's manager and sometimes the other people he or she supervises. Often a firm will make a conditional offer to the candidate selected, who then must first pass background and reference checks and sometimes medical and physical tests before officially being hired.

2 How are employees trained and evaluated? (pp. 251–255)

- **Orientation** (p. 251) integrates new employees into an organization so they become productive faster, feel part of the organization, and do not quit shortly after being hired. Other forms of training include **on-the-job training** (p. 251), **apprentice training programs** (p. 252), and **simulation training** (p. 253).

- **Management development programs** (p. 253) prepare management trainees to become managers within an organization by having them participate in on-the-job training programs, such as job rotation, coaching/understudy programs, action learning, and mentoring.

- **Off-the-job training and development** (p. 253) require the employee to participate in outside seminars, university-conducted programs, and corporate universities.

- A **performance appraisal** (p. 254) is a formal evaluation of an employee's performance. Providing feedback and suggestions to employees for improvement, coaching and encouraging them, and helping them set goals are parts of appraisals. They are useful when done properly, but many managers avoid performance appraisals because they do not feel comfortable critiquing employees and do not see all aspects of their performance. A **360 performance appraisal** (p. 254) in which input is solicited from an employee's coworkers, customers, and subordinates and incorporated into the appraisal, can help in this regard.

- **Performance management** (p. 254) is an alternative to performance appraisals. It approaches employee evaluations as ongoing and systematic.

3 In what ways are employees compensated and scheduled? (pp. 255–259)

- **Compensation** (p. 256), or payment for work performed, consists of financial and nonfinancial payments.

- **Salaries** (p. 256) and hourly **wages** (p. 256), **bonuses** (p. 256), **commissions** (p. 256), and retirement **pension plans** (p. 256) constitute financial compensation.

- Defined benefit plans specify the amount of retirement benefits employees will receive, and defined contribution plans identify the maximum contribution employees can make to their retirement plans. **401(k) plans** (p. 256) allow employees to contribute pretax dollars to their retirement plans.

- Noncash **employee benefits** (p. 257) come in many forms, including health and disability insurance, vacation and sick pay, and retirement plans. Some benefits are mandated by law. Others are provided voluntarily by employers.

- **Work/life benefits** (p. 257), such as gym memberships, are important for those employees who are trying to balance busy lives both in and out of work.

- Alternative scheduling arrangements enable employees to have more flexibility in their lives. **Flextime** (p. 258), **job sharing** (p. 258), **permanent part-time** jobs (p. 258), **telecommuting** (p. 258), and **compressed workweeks** (p. 259) are alternative scheduling methods.

4 How does an employee's status change through promotions, termination, and retirement? (pp. 259–261)

- Employees increase their level of responsibility through promotions—taking on a job that has more responsibility and greater status and pay in a company or a department.

- **Termination** (p. 260) is when companies permanently lay off workers due to poor performance or a discontinued use for their services. Downsizing and restructuring, outsourcing and offshoring, pressures of global competition, and increased uses of technology are reasons companies look to reduce the number of employees through termination.

- **Retirement** (p. 260) occurs when employees decide to stop working on a full-time basis or stop working altogether. Financial security, staying active and engaged, and learning something new are reasons seniors cite for deferring retirement.

5 **How does incorporating diversity affect the workforce?** (pp. 261–263)

- The workforce today consists of employees from many different cultures and religions, which can lead to challenges in helping employees understand one another.

- More women are now in the workforce than in decades past, but few are reaching executive management levels. Sexism, salary inequity, and sexual harassment remain prominent issues.

- The workforce is getting older as more baby boomers work beyond typical retirement age. An aging workforce increases a firm's health care costs but also can increase a firm's productivity and decrease its training costs.

- A diverse workforce has proven to be more creative and innovative than a nondiverse workforce. Diversity keeps companies competitive by helping them develop products and services tailored to diverse customers.

6 **What are the objectives, structures, and future of labor unions in the global business environment?** (pp. 263–265)

- **A labor union** (p. 264) is a legally recognized group organized to protect the interests of workers. Labor unions typically negotiate various employment terms, such as the salaries, health benefits, and work hours of their members.

- Representatives of the labor union form a **bargaining unit** (p. 264) that negotiates with an employer. The negotiations are referred to as **collective bargaining** (p. 264).

- If satisfactory terms cannot be agreed on by both sides, **mediation** (p. 264) is used. A neutral third party assists both sides and generates a proposal that addresses each party's interests.

- In the **arbitration** (p. 264) process, a third party settles the dispute after hearing all of the issues.

- If negotiations break down, unions and their supporters may choose to **boycott** (p. 265) a company (not do business with it).

- As a last resort, union members may vote to go on **strike** (p. 263) and agree to stop working altogether.

- As the business community continues to expand globally, unions will need to increase their numbers by allying themselves with international workers and workers and immigrant workers.

Key Terms

360-degree appraisal (p. 254)

401(k) plan (p. 256)

affirmative action (p. 262)

American Federation of Labor (p. 264)

apprentice training program (p. 252)

arbitration (p. 264)

bargaining unit (p. 264)

bonus (p. 256)

boycott (p. 265)

collective bargaining (p. 264)

commissions (p. 256)

compensation (p. 256)

compressed workweek (p. 258)

Congress of Industrial Organizations (p. 264)

consultants (p. 259)

contingent workers (p. 259)

diversity training (p. 263)

employee benefits (p. 257)

employee stock ownership plan (p. 257)

employee stock purchase plan (p. 257)

employment at will (p. 260)

external recruiting (p. 248)

flexible benefit plan (cafeteria plan) (p. 257)

flextime (p. 258)

forecasting (p. 246)

human resource management (p. 245)

incentive-based payment (p. 256)

independent contractors (p. 259)

internal recruiting (p. 247)

job analysis (p. 246)

job description (p. 246)

job sharing (p. 258)

job specifications (p. 246)

labor union (p. 264)

locals (p. 264)

lockout (p. 265)

management development programs (p. 253)

mediation (p. 264)

mentor (p. 253)

off-the-job training and development (p. 253)

online training (p. 253)

on-the-job training (p. 251)

orientation program (p. 251)

pension plan (p. 256)

performance appraisal (p. 254)

performance management (p. 254)

permanent part-time employee (p. 259)

picketing (p. 265)

profit-sharing plan (p. 256)

programmed learning approach (p. 252)

recruitment (p. 247)

retirement (p. 260)

reverse mentoring (p. 254)

salary (p. 256)

simulation training (p. 253)

stock options (p. 257)

strike (p. 263)

strikebreakers (p. 265)

telecommuting (p. 258)

termination (p. 260)

wages (p. 256)

worker buyout (p. 261)

workforce profile (p. 245)

work/life benefits (p. 257)

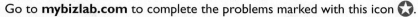

MyBizLab

Go to **mybizlab.com** to complete the problems marked with this icon ⭐.

Self Test

Multiple Choice *You can find the answers on the last page of this book.*

9-1 Human resource management requires expertise in
   a. managing staffing needs as a company evolves.
   b. training and evaluating employees.
   c. compensation, disciplinary actions, and promotion of employees.
   d. All of the above.

9-2 When interviewing candidates for an administrative assistant's job, which of the following interview questions is legally inadvisable?
   a. What church do you attend?
   b. What are your strengths and weaknesses?
   c. What are your hobbies?
   d. Who do you think will win the Super Bowl?

9-3 Types of training required in some careers include
   a. an on-the-job mentor.
   b. time spent as an apprentice.
   c. programmed learning.
   d. All of the above.

9-4 The performance review process often includes all of the following except
   a. an evaluation of the employee's social standing in the work environment.
   b. an assessment of the employee's relative to the job's performance standards.
   c. specific feedback on how to enhance a positive performance.
   d. the employee's job expectations.

9-5 Amit Patel, as part of his compensation package, was offered an opportunity to purchase his company's stock at a later date at its current, lower price. Which of the following was Amit given?
   a. A stock option
   b. A stock ownership plan
   c. A stock purchase plan
   d. None of the above

9-6 James Rodriguez wants to spend more time at home with his two-year-old granddaughter and is considering leaving his company. He could receive three months' pay and the same retirement package he will be eligible for in three years' time if he leaves now. This type of offer is called a(n)
   a. independent consultant status.
   b. worker buyout.
   c. retirement.
   d. compressed workweek.

9-7 Which one of the following is *not* a reason to hire a contingent worker?
   a. To fill in for absent employees
   b. Not enough office space for a full-time employee
   c. To supplement staff during particularly busy times
   d. To evaluate how a person performs on the job before hiring permanently them

9-8 Which of the following are benefits that companies experience by employing a diverse workforce?
   a. Cultural differences result in alternative perspectives and lead to better problem solving.
   b. They fulfill expected affirmative action standards.
   c. Companies become more competitive in the global marketplace.
   d. All of the above.

9-9 The AFL-CIO, the UAW, and the Teamsters are examples of
   a. illegal organizations.
   b. labor unions.
   c. labor relations.
   d. union locals.

9-10 In the United States today, labor membership is
   a. increasing because of a shift toward service industries.
   b. declining because of a shift toward service industries.
   c. no longer legal in many states.
   d. decreasing because unions are being replaced by bargaining units.

True/False *You can find the answers on the last page of this book.*

9-11 Federal laws like the ADA and the ADEA must be followed by every business when hiring.
☐ True or ☐ False

9-12 Profit sharing could mean that in a good year, employees get bonuses, or it could refer to the company's contributions to an employee retirement plan.
☐ True or ☐ False

9-13 Some companies use an alternative to performance appraisals called performance management.
☐ True or ☐ False

9-14 Employment at will means workers have increased job security.
☐ True or ☐ False

9-15 A diversified workforce adds creativity and a variety of viewpoints to the workforce, which often helps improve a company's competitiveness and its bottom line.
☐ True or ☐ False

Critical Thinking Questions

9-16 Performance management is one alternative to a traditional performance appraisal. Which style of evaluation would you prefer as an employee? Which would be more useful to you as a manager?

9-17 An inefficient hiring process can cripple a company because the costs of turnover and retraining employees are so high. Does electronically collecting and evaluating résumés help companies? Job seekers?

9-18 Describe the "perfect" benefits package. How would your salary and pay level affect your decision? Would you accept a lower pay level for better benefits?

Team Time

SEEING BOTH SIDES

Walmart has been both praised and criticized for many of its HR policies. Form teams of four students. Divide each team into two subgroups.

a. Subgroup 1—Good HR Practices: Research articles about the positive HR policies and practices Walmart has implemented. Prepare a summary paper outlining your findings.

b. Subgroup 2—Bad HR Practices: Research articles about the negative HR policies and practices Walmart has implemented. Prepare a summary paper outlining your findings.

Process

Step 1. As a group, compile your findings, comparing the positive and negative policies. Were there instances in which a policy started out as a positive and ended up being negative or vice versa? How did the policies work with Walmart's strategic goals? How have the policies affected Walmart's stock price and bottom line?

Step 2. If you were employed as an HR consultant for Walmart, what kind of advice would you give the company based on your findings?

Ethics and Corporate Social Responsibility

THE ETHICS OF INTERVIEWING

The interview and hiring process is fraught with ethical concerns. Form a small group and discuss the ethical implications of the following scenario.

Scenario

Where does a candidate's right to privacy end and a company's right to know begin? As you learned in this chapter, federal laws protect potential employees from discrimination. Hiring managers must observe these laws by refraining from asking certain questions during the interview process, such as direct questions about candidates' ages and physical disabilities. However, to uncover this information legally, managers have devised alternative questions.[20] For example:

Instead of asking . . .	They ask this legal alternative . . .
Which religious holidays do you observe?	Can you work our required schedule?
Do you have children?	What is your experience with "X" age-group?
Do you have any disabilities?	Are you able to perform this position's specific duties?

Process

With your group, discuss your opinions on the use of these "legal alternatives" as an HR strategy. They are legal, but are they ethical? Do managers undermine the laws by finding ways around them? Or does a company have a right to know this information to make the best hiring decision?

Web Exercises

9-19   Analyzing Annual Reports
Using the Internet, access the annual reports of three companies in different industries. How are human resources issues handled in the annual report? What kind of HR issues do the reports discuss? Are the issues similar or different among the companies?

9-20   Social Media and HR
It is happening more and more that a candidate's social media profile has caused him or her not to be hired. Review all of the online materials available about you—Facebook, LinkedIn, blog postings you have made, photographs uploaded—from the perspective of a potential employer. Do you have any materials that might keep you from being hired? What do you think of the privacy issues surrounding this practice?

9-21   Battle of the Superstores
Costco directly competes with Sam's Club, the bulk-sales retailer owned by Walmart. Costco and Sam's Club approach labor in very different ways. This can be seen in the salaries they pay, in the benefits they provide, and in their relationship with unions. How do labor rates at Costco compare to those at Sam's Club? What about the profit per employee, turnover cost per employee, and turnover rates? Try to compare the overall labor costs for each of the businesses in contrast to just the labor rates they pay workers.

9-22   Benefits Packages
Many companies have determined that their biggest asset is their employees, so taking care of employees is a mission-critical objective. Research companies that use benefits packages as a way to make their employees feel cared for and that retain a high percentage of employees. Consider both small and large businesses.

9-23   A Student and an Employee
Research several colleges' policies on student employees. How many hours can students work, and what types of employee behaviors and disciplinary actions do the policies specify? How do the rules at specific schools overlap with federal and state laws? Do you see specific rules that need to be revised to better accommodate student workers?

MyBizLab

Go to **mybizlab.com** for Auto-graded writing questions as well as the following Assisted-graded writing questions:

✪ **9-24** Job analysis is an important part of human resource management. How does the job analysis work with the development of a workforce profile? How would HR help a company move to innovate in a quickly changing industry?

✪ **9-25** Labor unions were born at a time when working conditions were quite exploitive and even dangerous in many parts of the United States. Do labor unions serve a purpose in today's workplace environment? Discuss what functions unions provide that benefit a company as a whole.

References

1. *Intel Social Media Guidelines*, April 8, 2014, www.intel .com/content/www/us/en/legal/intel-social-media-guidelines.html.
2. Peter Cappelli, "How to Get a Job? Beat the Machines," June 11, 2012, http://moneyland.time.com/2012/06/11/how-to-get-a-job-beat-the-machines.
3. D. Weiss, "Resume Lies Lead to Disbarment for Former Paul Hastings Partner," January 23, 2014, http://www .abajournal.com/news/article/resume_lies_lead_to_ disbarment_for_former_paul_hasting_partner.
4. "Nuclear Pharmacy Opportunities with Cardinal Health," *RXInsider*, www.allpharmacyjobs.com/nuclear_ pharmacy_cardinal_health_nuclear.htm.
5. Scott Steinberg, "Video Games Are Tomorrow's Answer to Executive Training," March 14, 2012, www.fastcompany.com/1824740/ video-games-are-tomorrows-answer-to-executive-training.
6. L. Lanese and F. Nguyen, "The Journey from Formal Learning to Performance Support," *Performance Improvement*, May 11, 2012, http://frankn.net/Publications/ PI2012-JourneyFormal2Ps.pdf.
7. McDonald's, "Our Curriculum," www.aboutmcdonalds .com/mcd/corporate_careers/training_and_development/ hamburger_university/our_curriculum.html.
8. Alexei Oreskovic and Sarah McBride, "Facebook IPO Sparks Dreams of Riches, Adventure," December 9, 2011, www.reuters.com/article/2011/12/09/ us-facebook-millionaires-idUSTRE7B72NK20111209.
9. "Why Work for SAS," www.sas.com/offices/asiapacific/ singapore/press/why-sas.html.
10. Human Rights Campaign, "The Domestic Partnership Benefits and Obligations Act," March 10, 2014, www .hrc.org/laws-and-legislation/federal-legislation/ the-domestic-partnership-benefits-and-obligations-act.
11. "Domestic Partner Benefits: Grossing Up to Offset Imputed Income Tax," April 8, 2014, www.hrc.org/ resources/entry/domestic-partner-benefits-grossing-up-to-offset-imputed-income-tax.
12. S. Sorenson, "Don't Pamper Employees—Engage Them," July 2, 2013, http://businessjournal.gallup.com/ content/163316/don-pamper-employees-engage.aspx.
13. Cisco, "Transforming Employee Engagement," www .cisco.com/en/US/solutions/collateral/ns340/ns1176/ business-of-it/Cisco_IT_Trends_in_IT_Article_Employee_ Engagement_V2.html.
14. U.S. Bureau of Labor Statistics, *Current Employment Statistics Highlights*, April 4, 2014, www.bls.gov/web/empsit/ ceshighlights.pdf.
15. "Medical Practice Messes Up Secretary's Termination," *Canadian Employment Law Today*, May 23, 2012, www.employmentlawtoday.com/articleprint .aspx?articleid=2731.
16. U.S. Census Bureau, "Table 4. Projections of the Population by Sex, Race, and Hispanic Origin for the United States: 2010 to 2050," April 23, 2014, http://www.census.gov.
17. DiversityInc, "Ask DiversityInc: How Does Your Company Handle Religious Holidays?," April 22, 2014, http:// diversityinc.com/diversity-and-inclusion/ask-diversity-inc-how-does-your-company-handle-religious-holidays.
18. Lisa Takeuchi Cullen, "Employee Diversity Training Doesn't Work," *Time*, April 26, 2007, www.time.com/ time/magazine/article/0,9171,1615183,00.html.
19. U.S. Bureau of Labor Statistics, "Union Members Summary," January 24, 2014, www.bls.gov/news.release/ union2.nr0.htm.
20. HR World Editors, "30 Interview Questions You Can't Ask and 30 Sneaky, Legal Alternatives to Get the Same Info," November 15, 2007, www.hrworld.com/ features/30-interview-questions-111507.

Chapter 10
Online Business and Technology

▶ Online Business

Sonja Pettingill is launching a start-up venture to sell a specialty vest to new moms. Sonja can sell her product through local boutique stores, but she knows she needs a strong online business component to succeed. How does being online change her marketing strategy? How does she take advantage of the latest online technologies?

▶ Technology in Business

When Ian McGregor started working for a hardware store, he was amazed that the technology it used was so outdated. There was no website or customer database, and the cash registers weren't even connected to an information system. How could advancements in technology benefit the store? Who is responsible for keeping the store's technology current?

▶ Security

Although Kevin Fossbenner's business, Flatland Frames, is doing well, he's worried that a suspicious e-mail sent to his employees on any given day could result in the firm being hacked. How do businesspeople protect themselves against problems like this?

▶ Impact of Social Media and Mobile Technology

You make the effort to stay up on current technologies. You add a social media component to your business. It begins to take off, but then one upset customer seems to begin to drive customers away. There are positive and negative ways to incorporate new technologies into your business, and they can make or break you.

OBJECTIVES

1 What does the online environment offer to help market a business? (pp. 273–275)

2 What types of business transactions are supported by online commerce? (pp. 276–278)

3 What are the functions of a company's chief information officer (CIO) and information technology (IT) department? (pp. 279–280)

4 How do businesses transform data into useful business intelligence? (pp. 280–283)

5 What security challenges arise with the increase of technology? (pp. 283–287)

6 How have new advances in social networking and mobile technologies impacted business? (pp. 287–291)

MyBizLab®

⭐ **Improve Your Grade!**

Over 10 million students improved their results using the Pearson MyLabs.
Visit **mybizlab.com** for simulations, tutorials, and end-of-chapter problems.

Online Business pp. 273–278

When Sonja Pettingill decided to start a business, she knew she had a great idea. Her Mom Utility Vests (MUVs) would give mothers a place to store all the things they need for a day out with their babies but leave their hands free while toting all of that gear. Sonja knows the idea is a solid one. But how should she to kick off the business for such a product? She could travel from one small boutique to another in the area, but she'd never recoup the cost of developing and producing the products. She realizes she needs to take her marketing message to a national audience and take her storefront online—but how? ■

Online marketing and selling, social networking, and mobile technologies are increasingly being used by firms to grow their businesses, even if they have brick-and-mortar stores. But doing business electronically requires firms and their employees to have a wider set of skills—they need to understand the marketing techniques that work in the cyber environment, possess technical skills to maintain and support the online business, and have security knowledge to recognize and respond to online threats. In this chapter you'll explore the challenges and opportunities technology brings to businesses.

Source: Sonja Pettingill.

Growth of Online Business

Has online shopping hit its peak? You have likely shopped online. More than 89 percent of consumers say they prefer to shop online because it saves them time, makes it easy to compare prices, and offers more variety.[1] By 2017, 60 percent of U.S. retail sales will involve the Web in some way, and $100 billion of those sales will be made on mobile devices alone, the experts predict.[2]

Marketing Online

How can the online environment support a firm's marketing efforts? Marketing is an aspect of business that has responded to changes in business technology by redefining itself. In today's world, a marketing department must consider the Internet as a tool for both collecting information about its customers and distributing information about its products and services. Companies such as Lyris, Topica, and Constant Contact can organize and control mass e-mail campaigns by providing templates for e-mail newsletters or advice on how to create e-mail surveys. They also provide services that generate reports to track the number of people who read the e-mail message, how many followed the links inside, and how many forwarded the e-mail to another contact.

How does having an online presence change a firm's marketing strategies? For marketing experts, taking advantage of new advertising outlets offers many new opportunities. **Online advertising** refers to any form of advertising that uses the Internet to market its message to customers. This includes everything from banner ads to Facebook campaigns to spam e-mails and messages sent on Twitter. The insurance

▶ THE LIST

Brought to You by PayPal[3]

Each of the following people spent time working at PayPal, the company that pioneered a new style of online purchasing transactions. After leaving PayPal, they founded or invested in all the wildly successful businesses listed after their names. What did PayPal teach them?

1. Elon Musk—SpaceX and Tesla
2. Reid Hoffman—LinkedIn
3. Chad Hurley—YouTube
4. Steve Chen—YouTube
5. Jawed Karim—YouTube
6. David Sacks—Yammer
7. Keith Rabois—Square
8. Premal Shah—Kiva
9. Max Levchin—Slide
10. Peter Thiel—funded Facebook, Palantir, Zynga

Google AdWords allows you to reach potential customers already searching for products like yours.
Source: Digitallife/Alamy.

company Esurance exploited this shift toward online-based advertising during the 2014 Super Bowl. A single television ad run during the Super Bowl costs a whopping $5 million. Esurance instead ran a short ad after the game letting viewers know they could enter a $1.5 million drawing by sending a tweet to #EsuranceSave30. The hashtag was used over 3.8 million times and increased the company's profile significantly.

As the number of households with high-speed broadband Internet access and mobile devices has increased, online advertising has become much more sophisticated. QR codes that can be scanned with mobile devices take consumers from magazine ads and counter displays directly to a company's Web content. Flash and Java technologies allow advertisers to embed animated ads and full-motion video. Apple's iPhone operating system iOS includes a feature called iAds. Instead of redirecting a user out of the application he or she is in and into a Web browser, iAds are integrated into the iPhone app so they fade up, interact with the user, and then fade away—all while the user is still in the original app.

More often than not, an online ad is hyperlinked to another website and tracks how many "clicks" are registered. The ability to track how many eyes have viewed an ad is, in fact, one of the great allures of Internet advertising. Programs such as Google's AdWords service are successfully generating revenues for companies with **pay-per-click (PPC) advertising**. With PPC advertising, advertisers pay only for the number of times a Web surfer clicks on their ads. PPC ads are effective because they are associated with key words and are highly relevant to what potential consumers are searching for.

Google's popular AdSense network takes PPC ads to the next level. By placing PPC ads on third-party sites, such as blogs and Web forums, they reach readers depending on the content of a particular page instead of search results. Also known as **contextual advertising**, these ads are automatically generated by the content on a specific site. This way, readers of a popular snowboarding blog might see ads with Shaun White promoting Red Bull. Moreover, the AdSense network also allows individual bloggers to generate revenue by hosting these ads on their site. Blogs with a significant readership can earn a great deal of money by giving such ads visibility.

Are there any drawbacks to online advertising? *Click fraud* is one drawback. It occurs when a competing company clicks on ads to run up the cost of its competitor's advertising. Spam annoys people and fills up their in-boxes. Web surfers also complain about pop-up ads, which open their ads in new browser windows, and interstitials, pages that appear before a viewer can get to their desired content. Also, many people have grown so used to seeing Web ads that they may not even notice them. ■ **TABLE 10.1** summarizes the pros and cons of online advertising.

How does technology change marketing in a global marketplace? Internet technology allows every company with a website to advertise to anyone in the world with Internet access. In the modern world any site must support multiple languages and, more importantly, make sure its content is customized to those different cultures. Every marketing campaign is now global.

What is viral marketing? To get people to notice their advertisements, many marketers are turning to a technique known as **viral marketing**. This practice involves using social networks, e-mail, and websites to spread the awareness of a particular brand. Rather than being an overt advertising campaign that relies on airwaves with commercials, a viral campaign is more subtle and dependent on the user to be an active participant in spreading a message. It's designed to appeal to consumers who may be resistant to traditional advertising. Essentially, viral marketing is a Web 2.0 version—that is, a more consumer-engaged, interactive, and collaborative type—of old-fashioned word of mouth.

Table 10.1	**Pros and Cons of Online Advertising**
Pros	**Cons**
Reasonable cost: With PPC advertising, the cost of advertising depends on frequency of use.	Fear of spam: Web users may avoid clicking ads to avoid receiving spam.
Hitting target markets: Contextual advertising allows for high probability of reaching intended viewers.	Annoyance factor: Rather than be drawn in, Web users can become annoyed with flashing ads or pop-ups.
Tracking: Companies are able to keep records of who is clicking ads and where they are located—essential information for designing future campaigns.	Click fraud: Companies who invest in PPC advertising may receive unexpectedly large invoices if a competitor purposefully clicks on its ads repeatedly.

Viral marketing gives a company more than the opportunity to promote a product or brand; it allows potential consumers to feel a personal connection to the brand by becoming a part of a communal experience. Hollywood movie studios have been on the forefront of this kind of viral advertising. Consider the marketing campaign for the science fiction film *District 9*. Before the film's release, public service announcements began to appear in the 15 largest U.S. markets. Bus benches were plastered with signs reading "Bus bench for humans only" followed by a note, "Report nonhumans," and a phone number as well as a website address that took visitors to information about the movie.[4] In two weeks there were over 33,000 phone calls as people on the street agreed to play along with the premise that alien beings were residing in their community. The site had language support for both human and nonhuman visitors as well as games and simulations. By generating interest about the extensive campaign, the $30 million film took in over $37 million its first weekend.

This dedication to using advertising as a means to develop content and create an entertainment experience is one way the Internet and viral marketing are shifting the paradigm of advertising's capabilities.

■ **FIGURE 10.1**
The Global Web
Thanks to Internet technology, every company with a website is now capable of advertising globally. This page markets Pearson publishing products to a Japanese audience.
Source: Pearson Education, Inc.

The movie *Contagion*, about a rampant virus, put a twist on viral marketing. Custom Petri dishes and specifically colored bacteria were created that grew into a living billboard.
Source: CB2/ZOB/WENN.com/Newscom.

Types of Online Business Transactions

What types of business transactions occur online? Interaction between business and the consumer has also changed radically since the introduction of the Internet. The most common modes of transactions are business to business (B2B), business to consumer (B2C), and consumer to consumer (C2C).

What is the focus of B2B transactions? Business-to-business (B2B) transactions involve the exchange of products, services, and information between businesses on the Internet. B2B websites can be classified as follows:

- *Company websites* target other companies and their employees. These websites are designed to sell goods or services to business clients rather than household consumers. For example, UPS has a B2B site for business owners looking for shipping solutions, which is different than the website consumers use for their personal shipping needs.

- *E-procurement*, or electronic procurement, refers to the online purchase and sale of products and services between businesses. For example, most states have e-procurement websites companies can use to bid on state projects. The companies can register, examine current bidding opportunities, and enter online bids for contracts through the site.

- *Procurement exchanges* are marketplaces where companies can buy and sell goods or services at lower prices. Sometimes they are run by a group of companies and sometimes by third parties. Alibaba.com, a Chinese site that's similar to eBay, has a B2B section on its website. It was launched in 1999 to help Chinese manufacturers sell products to overseas business buyers.

- *Specialized industry portals* are online gateways to major sources of information, discussion forums, and product listings. To see an example, view the portal page for CEOs at www.ceoExpress.com. These are also known as *niche portals* or *vertical portals* because they provide expanded information on a specific product or market.

- *Brokering sites* are third-party sites that act as liaisons between providers and potential buyers of goods or services. Brokering sites can be found for a variety of rental goods that businesses may need, from projectors and video equipment to backhoes and excavators.

- *Information sites* provide information about a particular industry. Also called an *infomediary*, an information site gives businesses information about current standards and developments. For example, TheMedica.com is an infomediary that posts news about the health care and medical industries. It also includes information about trade shows, links to medical publications, and a directory of health care businesses and products. Infomediaries help facilitate and originate B2B traffic.

Do businesses work directly with customers online? Yes, business-to-consumer (B2C) transactions refer to e-commerce that takes place directly between businesses and consumers. In fact, it's becoming essential for almost all businesses to sell or at least promote their products to customers online. "Click and mortar" refers to B2C businesses that have both an online presence and brick-and-mortar stores. This combination is ideal for customers who like the convenience of online shopping but who want to be able to look at products before buying them as well as return products purchased online without incurring shipping costs.

To stay in business, B2C companies have gotten savvy with regard to how they access and network with their customers and distribute and advertise products. Some models that have accelerated B2C e-commerce include the following:

- *Online intermediaries* are businesses such as Travelocity and Amazon.com that are not direct producers of products but instead buy goods and/or services and sell them to customers.

- *Advertising-based models* rely on banner ads on other websites to attract customers. The two main approaches that advertisers use are *high traffic* and *niche*. The high-traffic approach is designed to reach a wide audience, with ads placed on popular sites, such as Yahoo!. The niche approach best serves companies that target a small, specific audience.

- *Community-based models* allow users with similar interests to interact with each other worldwide. Steam is an example of a community-based gaming website where users can purchase and play online games produced by both small, independent video game makers as well as large ones. With over 65 million active accounts, Steam members always have someone to play with—and someone to encourage them to buy a new game!

- *Fee-based models* require users to pay a subscription fee to view their content. In these systems, website content is restricted until a user registers and pays either a flat monthly rate or a pay-as-you-go fee. Netflix.com and Internet dating sites, such as Match and eHarmony, and online journals, such as *Consumer Reports*, are examples of fee-based B2C sites.

What kind of business happens between customers? Transactions that take place between individual consumers, sometimes with the involvement of third parties, are called **consumer-to-consumer (C2C) transactions**. In this e-commerce model, consumers sell goods and services to other consumers, sometimes with the involvement of a third party. The artsy storefront Etsy is an example of a business based on C2C transactions. A popular C2C marketplace with an intermediary is eBay. File and music sharing are types of C2C exchanges, sometimes referred to as *P2P*, or *peer-to-peer*. Social networking sites, including Facebook and LinkedIn, can fill this role as well. The wide variety of business transactions happening online is summarized in ■ **TABLE 10.2**.

Table 10.2	**Types of Online Business Transactions**		
Business-to-Business (B2B) Examples	**Business-to-Customer (B2C) Examples**	**Customer-to-Customer (C2C) Examples**
Company websites: UPS	Online intermediaries: Amazon.com	Exchange through intermediary: eBay
Procurement exchange: Kentucky e-procurement	Advertising-based models: Ads on Yahoo!	Peer-to-peer exchange: Music files
Specialized industry portals: CEOExpress.com	Community-based models: Steam	
Brokering sites: Excavating broker	Fee-based models: *Consumer Reports*	
Information sites: TheMedica.com		

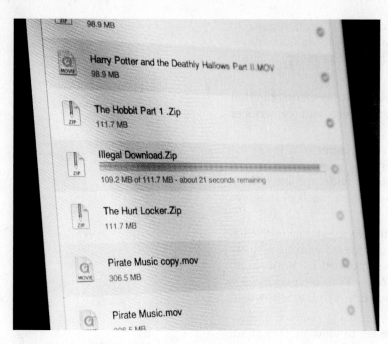

Source: Matthew Lloyd/Contributor/ Getty Images.

Challenges of E-Commerce

How are taxes applied to e-commerce sales? Most Internet sales are tax free, which causes major problems for states that rely on sales taxes to fund their public institutions. The laws regarding e-commerce taxation have been debated since Congress passed the Internet Tax Freedom Act (ITFA) in 1998. This law expired in 2003. The Internet Tax Freedom Forever Act has been introduced in the Senate but as of this writing has not yet passed.[5]

Online sales tax requirements also vary depending on the business. For example, if an e-business also has a physical presence, such as a store, office, or warehouse in a state, the state might require it to impose a sales tax on customers. Target, for example, has some stores in Maryland, so a customer living in Maryland must pay sales tax on a purchase from Target's website. However, if a customer in Georgia orders a bouquet from the 1800Flowers website, he or she does not have to pay sales tax because 1-800-Flowers doesn't have a brick-and-mortar store in Georgia.

Because consumers like tax-free shopping, being able to offer it can give a firm a competitive advantage. For this reason, some large companies have created online stores that are separate legal entities from their brick-and-mortar stores. This allows customers to purchase from their online stores without paying sales taxes. However, the practice has outraged many retailers that must collect taxes from their customers. Some state governments have instituted a "use tax." For example, in Pennsylvania, you have one month to pay the 6 percent use tax on anything you purchase over the Internet if the seller did not collect state taxes.

Who has legal jurisdiction over an online business? Jurisdiction is the authority of a government to legislate and enforce its many laws. It is usually territorial, but because the Internet has a geographic territory that is too broad to define, it is difficult to address legal jurisdiction issues for online-only businesses. Disputes over the legal jurisdiction of e-commerce have been occurring since the dawn of the Internet. A large corporation might have offices or stores in several different countries, and it becomes very difficult to comply with the laws of all those countries. In addition, to protect the rights of buyers and sellers and protect copyrighted material, the Digital Millennium Copyright Act, passed in 1998, must be followed. In 2000, the World Intellectual Property Organization assured e-businesses that they would have to comply with laws only where the companies are based.

Sonja decided to start with a significant investment in an online presence. She hired Web developers from India to construct a viral advertising campaign, placing videos and images in a number of popular forums and websites for new moms and those throwing baby showers. While those were building interest in the new product, she began researching how to use Google Analytics to gather useful information about the visitors to her newly opened Web storefront. It requires a lot of time to put all these aspects of the business in place, but she knows she is building a business that can compete in the twenty-first century.

You think you found a great deal shopping online. But do you know if your state taxes Web purchases?
Source: Silroby/Fotolia.

Technology in Business pp. 278-283

When Ian McGregor began working for a hardware store, he thought all he'd be doing was updating its website and maintaining its computer system. But when he saw the outdated technology the store was using, he was amazed that the place was still in business. No orders could be placed on the website, and there was no central storage of sales information and no way to send out targeted marketing messages to customers. The store owner told him that he wanted to give the store a makeover and update the technology so he could increase his profits. Ian didn't know where to begin. What role does information technology play in business? ■

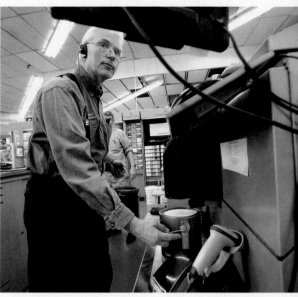

Source: John Patriquin/Portland Press Herald/Getty Images.

Try to imagine a type of business that doesn't use computer systems for at least some of its primary functions—it's hard to do! To remain competitive, businesses need to reach their consumers via electronic communication media such as texting, Facebook, websites, and email. Accounting information can be managed electronically so that taxes are filed easily and budgets prepared and monitored, and word processors and databases are vital. In retailing businesses, point-of-sale terminals collect information that is fed into inventory and sales computer systems so that stock can be reordered, fast-moving products can be identified, and accounting information can be kept current and accurate.

At Apple's retail stores, employees roam the store with mobile "cash registers" in hand. They complete credit card transactions, e-mail sales receipts, and have customers in and out of the stores in no time. Customers can check themselves out of the stores using their own phones. Many grocery stores, as well as Home Depot warehouses, provide self-service automated checkout systems, reducing the need for cashiers. It's clear that technology is changing the fundamental aspects of how business is conducted.

The Information Technology Organization

Who is in charge of business technology? **Information technology** (IT) is the design and implementation of computer-based information systems. The person responsible for such technology in an organization is its **chief information officer** (CIO). This is typically a position at the same level as the CFO of a firm, for example. As ■ **FIGURE 10.2** shows, the CIO is in charge of overseeing a firm's information processing, including how the firm's IT system is designed and developed. Typically, he or she is responsible for making decisions about what hardware and software the company purchases and when it should be updated. In addition, CIOs are involved in creating business and e-business opportunities as well as defining governing policies for the company in areas such as privacy and security.

What is a typical decision a CIO has to make? IT demands can pose a financial burden placed on companies trying to stay up to date. The CIO must manage a budget that balances the benefits of technology against the ever-rising costs of upgrading to the latest systems. The full cost of any new piece of technology includes not only the purchase of the software and hardware itself but also potential hardware upgrades required to make the new product useful. For example, suppose a company wants to upgrade its operating system. This requires that the firm buy not only licenses for the operating system software but also memory upgrades for computer systems. In addition, the IT department will need to take time to test the software prior to deployment, establish a support staff, install the software, and train users on how to interact with the programs.

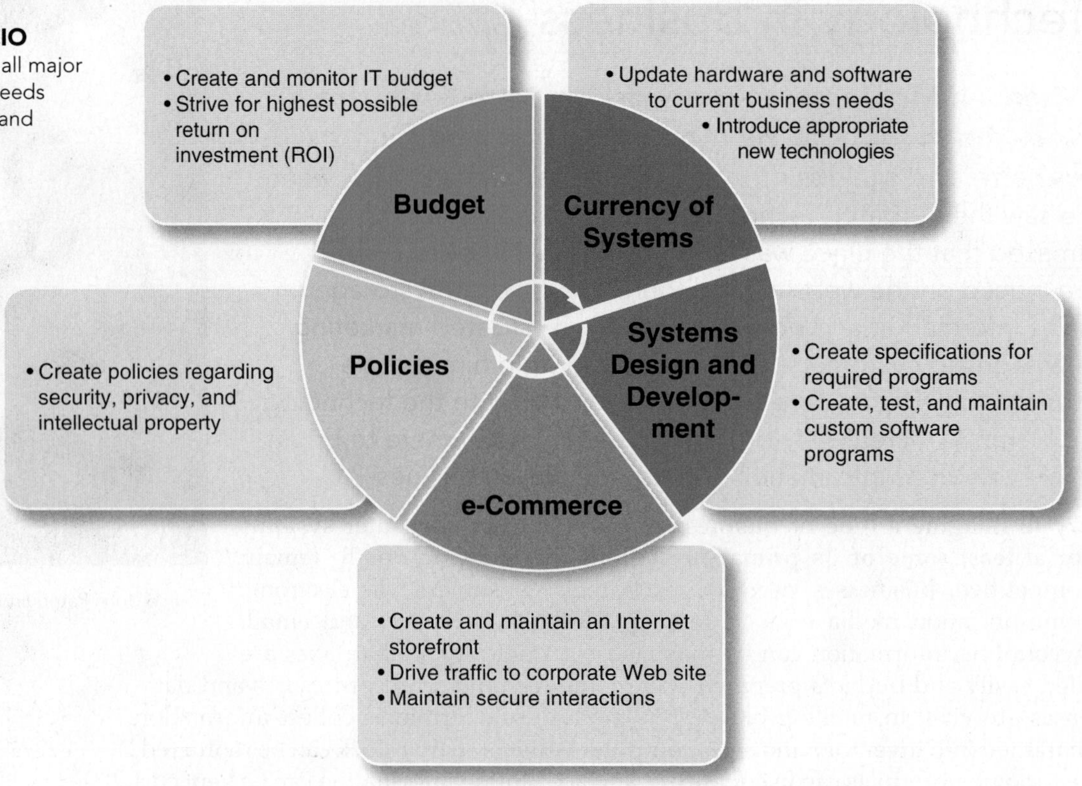

■ **FIGURE 10.2**

The Many Functions of a CIO
Because technology is used for all major functions of a business, a CIO needs excellent technical, leadership, and organizational skills.

- Create and monitor IT budget
- Strive for highest possible return on investment (ROI)

Budget

- Update hardware and software to current business needs
- Introduce appropriate new technologies

Currency of Systems

Policies

- Create policies regarding security, privacy, and intellectual property

Systems Design and Development

- Create specifications for required programs
- Create, test, and maintain custom software programs

e-Commerce

- Create and maintain an Internet storefront
- Drive traffic to corporate Web site
- Maintain secure interactions

Sometimes managers feel pressured to upgrade software or hardware because the entire market has switched to a new product or because customers or vendors have already moved to a new version of a program or device. In such circumstances, the CIO must determine whether the new software or hardware will truly make the return on investing in it worthwhile. For example, when Microsoft released its Windows 8 operating system, many companies found it hard to efficiently upgrade their computers and systems. The touch-screen interface in Windows 8 required firms to upgrade their hardware upgrades and train their employees to use it. Some firms decided not to upgrade to the new operating system because they didn't think the increases in productivity from using it would offset these costs.

What happens in an IT department? The IT department is comprised of many professionals responsible for everything from hardware components and software programs to networking strategies. Members of this department are also responsible for security in response to both computer virus attacks and emergency recovery from power outages and system failures. In addition, the department keeps all of a firm's computers, printers, and other equipment operational and current. The IT department manages the design of a company's networks and databases where information is stored, helps the CIO select appropriate hardware and software programs, and provides training to employees.

Sometimes, IT professionals must create custom software to bridge the gaps between the software available on the market and the needs of a firm. The IT department also maintains and manages the use of mobile computing devices in a firm, such as notebook computers, tablets like the iPad, smart phones, and other devices. Finally, the IT department is responsible for ensuring that employees have remote access to computing resources, such as their files and e-mail, when they are working outside the office.

Information Systems

What's an information system? The main difference between an IT system and an **information system** (IS), also called a **management information system** (MIS), is that an MIS is focused on applying IT to solve business and economic problems.

For example, the payroll department may need to upgrade to a new accounting system or software package. It is the role of the MIS professionals to investigate the impact of that change on the other technology systems in the company and rate the amount of gain against the cost required for the new software. So, MIS staff bridge the gap between purely technical knowledge and how it will impact a business.

What is the difference between data and information? In common usage, the terms *data* and *information* are often used interchangeably, but they have different meanings. **Data** are the representations of a fact or idea. Data can consist of numbers, words, images, or sounds. **Information**, however, is data that have been organized or arranged in a way that makes the data useful (see ■ **FIGURE 10.3**).

The extraction of information from raw data is critical to the success of many business enterprises. Businesses try to use all the resources at their disposal to gather raw data. For example, media, credit bureaus, and information brokers often purchase data made public in court proceedings. These data are processed into useful information for that business or later resold to other companies. So, a health club in Massachusetts may request a list of recently divorced women from the family court. The health club's plan is to process that raw data into a mailing list of a specific target audience for its membership services.

What are databases? Database programs allow businesses to quickly enter data, filter and sort information, and generate reports. Forms can be easily designed so that data can be entered and validated for accuracy. These forms, such as weekly time cards or customer surveys, can be delivered through e-mail and the responses automatically added into tables in the database. The collected data can be queried to create reports that describe specific conditions, such as the ZIP codes of all customers who purchased gardening supplies in the past week.

As the amount of data grows, how is it managed? Data are stored in **database management systems** (DBMSs). DBMSs are collections of tables of data that organize the data and allow people to analyze and run reports on those data. As companies begin to store vast amounts of data in database systems separate from their production databases, **data warehouses** are created. These can hold petabytes of transaction data. (A single petabyte can hold over 13 years' worth of high-definition television video.) Sometimes, subsets of data are created to isolate one product or one department. These smaller data sets are called **data marts**. Exploring and analyzing the data mart to uncover relationships and patterns in the data that can help a business is referred to as **data mining**. Data mining can be used in many ways. For example, suppose a supermarket uses data mining to help decide whether to restock a product that isn't selling well. If data mining reveals that the few people who typically buy the product are among the supermarket's most profitable customers, it's probably worthwhile to keep the product in stock to retain their business. New advances in hardware and software are making data mining a larger part of business decision making.

What Is "Big Data"? The availability of gigantic data sets for analysis to improve business has only recently become inexpensive and reliable. It is now

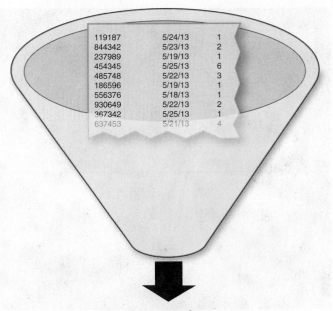

Processing

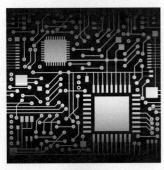

Products Purchased		5/18/13 thru 5/25/13		
Item code	Item name	Units	Date	Time
630649	KMF 2% Milk	1	5/18/13	6:15:55
234342	Luc Chd Cheese	2	5/18/13	6:34:15
937553	Yp Straw Yogurt	6	5/18/13	6:34:20
630649	KMF 2% Milk	1	5/18/13	6:59:03
237989	WF Doz Eggs	1	5/18/13	7:55:07
119187	Kft Strg Cheese	2	5/18/13	7:55:17
630648	DN 1% Milk	2	5/18/13	8:03:43
485748	BKS Sour Cream	1	5/18/13	8:06:51
867362	LDLK Butter	4	5/18/13	8:11:13

Information

■ **FIGURE 10.3**
The Processing of Data into Useful Information
The raw data from a grocery store's sales log can be processed into information that helps the store's owner know when to schedule milk shipments.

Many businesses use software programs to organize and analyze the data they collect.
Source: Wavebreak Media ltd/Alamy.

possible to gather free, public information, like the page view statistics for all articles in Wikipedia, hour by hour. The use of very large data sets and special software tools that can extract information from them is named **Big Data analysis**. Companies are using Big Data analysis to find new trends. Merck has used it to spot specific genetic traits in cancer survivors. The company Evolv uses more than 500 million data points, measuring things like gas prices, unemployment rates, and social media usage, to help clients like Xerox predict when an employee is most likely to leave his or her job.

Does Big Data create threats to our privacy? Now that very large data sets can produce useful information, there is new value in collecting the billions of clicks, purchases, and behaviors of consumers. Data brokers are companies that gather and sell this kind of information. It might include tracking a person's usage of social media or phone networks or purchase histories—both data that are publicly available and data collected from marketing efforts like surveys or loyalty programs. Software systems then combine pieces of data to make certain inferences or guesses about you—whether you like sports or whether you have children.

There is growing concern about the impact of this trade in information and how to best protect the kind of data people want to maintain, such as private medical status or credit standing. While your medical records are private, if you purchase specific medications or search for certain terms online, that can be a clue that you have a health-related issue. For example, recently a health insurance company bought data on 3 million members' purchases to check for things like the purchase of plus-sized clothing. Legal restrictions governing the collection and use of data are becoming more popular. The proposed Consumer Privacy Bill of Rights is one attempt at detailing legislation to define what is permitted in the digital age.

What kinds of tools are used to analyze business data? Businesses can easily collect and store large amounts of data, but turning them into useful information, or "business intelligence," is a challenging task. Several software systems help in this regard:

IT departments have a range of responsibilities, including choosing and installing hardware, software, and networks.
Source: Wavebreak Media ltd/Alamy.

- A **decision support system** (DSS) is a software system that enables companies to analyze collected data so they can predict the impact of business decisions. A DSS can also retrieve data from external sources and display results tied to business decision making.

- An **executive information system** (EIS) is a software system that is specially designed for the needs of management. This system can consolidate and summarize the transactions within an organization by using both internal and external sources. The terms *DSS* and *EIS* are sometimes used interchangeably, but usually an EIS has a more graphical interface compared to a DSS, which often uses spreadsheets and can show only one department or product at a time.

- An **online analysis package** (OLAP) is a software application designed to help people combine multiple pieces of information to get a clear picture of the state of a business. For example, OLAPs are often used for tasks such as reporting sales, budgeting, and forecasting figures. OLAP products in the marketplace include MS Analysis Services, the open-source product Openi (pronounced "open eye"), and Jedox software.

What kinds of questions can business intelligence software answer? **Business intelligence software** can further assist managers by helping them analyze not only the financial state of the firm but also answer other questions, such as the following:

- Who are my top 10 revenue-generating customers?
- What factors (for example, regions, products, or customers) are the greatest contributors to bad debt?
- Which vendors have unpaid invoices, and how much money do these vendors owe?
- How many days' worth of inventory is in each warehouse?
- Which plants have completed the highest number of work orders on time?

Even small businesses, like the hardware store where Ian McGregor works, need someone with IT experience to bring it into the modern age. Ian's boss recognized the store's technology needed upgrading, but he wasn't sure where to begin. To help him, Ian played the role of a chief information officer and began by collecting data on the demographics and purchasing habits of the store's customers. He analyzed the data using a suite of business intelligence software and developed a marketing strategy and campaign that included giving the company a presence on Facebook and a Twitter. He then tied the campaign to an online store at the company's website and marketing materials sent out via e-mail. Ian showed his boss that he would better be able to stay in touch with his customers by using this technology. As the store's business improves and the owner begins to realize benefits and profits from these initial changes, Ian hopes to have the opportunity to make additional IT changes.

Security pp. 283–287

Kevin Fossbenner, who grew up competing in BMX races, always wanted to own a bicycle manufacturing company. His dream came true—his company, Flatland Frames, produces both custom frames and full custom design race bicycles. Like most businesses, the company receives thousands of e-mails a day, many of them spam. One day an employee received a "phishing" e-mail that looked like it came from the firm's IT department. New passwords were being assigned, the message explained, and the employee was asked to confirm her "administrator password." The employee hesitated—something just didn't seem right. But she had so much other work to get done. ■

Security issues are important for our personal lives but are even more vital for businesses. Employers need to protect their business but balance that protection with their employees' need for privacy. In this section we'll examine these issues in more detail.

Threats to Online Business

What special security threats do online businesses face? Although online businesses and businesses with an online component have the most potential for growth and expansion, they are also the most vulnerable to threats, such as security breaches and viruses. If you've ever clicked on a banner ad or downloaded a

Source: Keith Morris/Alamy.

Phishing is using e-mail impersonating a real business to trick you into divulging your personal and financial information. *Source:* Newscom.

Celebrity Ashton Kutcher's Twitter account, which has over 16 million followers, was hacked with the posting "Ashton, you've been Punk'd. This account is not secure. Dude, where's my SSL?" *Source:* Chelsea Lauren/WireImage/Getty Images.

program, you've run the risk of allowing adware or spyware onto your computer. **Adware** is any software application that displays banner ads or pop-up ads while a program is running. At best, this is annoying. At worst, the software installs **spyware**, which tracks your personal information and passes it on to a third party without your knowledge.

Spyware operates in the backchannel of an Internet connection, collecting data and relaying that data to interested parties for the purposes fraud or identity theft. This can cripple businesses. Hackers can use spyware to steal money, erase valuable information, or even crash an entire company's system. The most insidious spyware can capture keystrokes, thereby stealing passwords and other confidential information, which can grant hackers unlimited access to company networks.

Can a business protect its online identity? Any business that processes transactions online is at risk of having its customers' credit card information stolen by hackers. Spyware is not the only method that hackers use to obtain private information. **Phishing** is a common way to trick online users into sending their personal information, like credit card numbers, straight to hackers.

Suppose you have a credit card account with Bank of America and you receive an e-mail from the company informing you that your online passwords need to be updated. The e-mail requests that you fill out a secure form with your personal information so Bank of America can reactivate your online access. The e-mail has Bank of America's logo and background, and it includes a link to the secure form to be filled out. You click on the link, which takes you to an online form on the Bank of America website. After completing the form, which asks for your name, address, password, credit card number, and credit card expiration date, you click the submit button and send all of that information to Bank of America.

Surprise! You've just been phished. That e-mail was not from Bank of America but from hackers who broke into Bank of America's network and copied its logo and e-mail design. The link you clicked took you to a fake website that was designed to look like an authentic registration form. You just sent your banking information to phishers, who can now use your credit card to make fraudulent purchases in your name and potentially destroy your credit rating. It also hurts Bank of America because the bank will have to track and cancel any illegal transactions and issue you a new credit card account. If you find yourself in this situation, be sure to report it to the company's fraud or abuse center.

Banks are not the only businesses that suffer from phishing. Online retailers, such as eBay, or payment services, such as PayPal, have been the victims of spyware and phishing. This can cost them dearly because customers may no longer trust these websites after they have been scammed. Businesses that have been hacked often spend thousands of dollars on reclaiming lost information and updating their antivirus programs and security systems to prevent future break-ins. Although these security breaches remind us of the risks of online transactions, they also force online businesses to keep their networks protected with the latest technology and take extra precautions to protect consumers.

What risks does a breach of security pose for management? With so much of the value of a modern business stored in electronic material—whether as documents, software programs, or e-mail files—a company can be vulnerable to hackers. **Hackers** are individuals who gain unauthorized entry into a computer system.

Their goal may be to disrupt the operation of the system or gain access to protected data. The retailer Target had a breach to its data records that impacted over 70 million people. Information stolen included customer names, credit card numbers, e-mail addresses. Secret Service investigators believe it may take years to identify the hackers responsible. Analysts estimate the cost to Target at nearly half a billion dollars.

Another large security breach occurred when the Sony PlayStation Network was illegally hacked a few years ago. The online gaming service had over 77 million members, all of whom had personal information and credit card numbers exposed to an unknown hacker. The network was down for 44 days while the company's IT professionals worked to revamp the system to provide better protection, at a cost of about $170 million.[6] Customers were angry at Sony's handling of the break-in—it took over a week for the company to acknowledge that the system had been compromised. Sony ultimately responded with a "Welcome Back" campaign, giving customers a range of free games, free rentals, and free upgrades. It was not enough to stop a series of class-action lawsuits over its failure to protect customers' information.

Sometimes it is not an attack from the outside that jeopardizes business stability. The business can also be vulnerable if technology is not implemented reliably. Even a short blackout of vital services, such as internal e-mail or customer access to a corporate website, can damage a company's reputation and value. For example, when the Hawaiian airline Go! attempted to sell 1,000 tickets for $1 each, the promotion crashed the company's website, and buyers couldn't purchase the tickets. To assuage the upset customers, the airline was forced to double the number of $1 tickets it was offering.[7]

Can technology also be used to support ethical conduct? Part of the Sarbanes-Oxley Act of 2002 mandates that all public companies have procedures for handling the concerns of whistle-blowers—persons who report on illicit activities. Several corporations now use their intranet to allow whistle-blowers to make anonymous reports. Organizations such as the Occupational Safety and Health Administration (OSHA) and the American Civil Liberties Union also have designed their websites to allow people to file reports easily and safely, shielding them from possible retaliation.

This type of reporting system is common in hospitals and medical centers. Staff members can report "near misses"—mistakes that could have occurred but were caught and corrected—through the organization's intranet. This allows an organization to learn from possible mistakes but safeguards the employee from embarrassment or disciplinary action. Without the benefit of anonymity, many mistakes and unethical actions might go undetected.

How a Simple Mistake Can Lead to a Major Data Breach

The U.S. government experienced one of the largest data breaches to date. This occurrence wasn't the result of savvy hackers, though. Rather, an employee for the Department of Veterans Affairs (VA) violated the VA's computer policies and took home a laptop, which was later stolen during a burglary. The laptop contained the names and Social Security numbers of over 26 million veterans. It was eventually recovered. Fortunately for the VA and the vets involved, sensitive information on the computer had not been accessed.

Another kind of data breach happened when Apple was developing the iPhone 4. One of the company's engineers was at a local brew house for his birthday and left a prototype of the device on his barstool. The person who found the phone realized what it was, and the phone eventually ended up being featured on the Gizmodo website, months before its official release. Threats of legal action came from a number of directions, but any excitement Apple wanted to build before announcing the phone's new features was already compromised.

Spying Scandal at Hewlett-Packard

A serious case of spying occurred at Hewlett-Packard (HP) when the company violated the privacy of its employees and journalists in an attempt to discover the source of an anonymous news article that leaked company information. Chairwoman Patricia Dunn hired private investigators and allegedly authorized them to use illegal tactics to uncover the source of the leak. Among other things, the private investigators used pretexting, or lying about one's identity, to gain access to employees' personal phone records. The investors also used tracer e-mails containing spyware and even discussed planting physical spies in a newsroom. Dunn resigned from HP over the scandal, as did board member George Keyworth, who was discovered to be behind the information leak. Several other board members also quit, and the scandal ended up costing the company millions of dollars in legal bills and bad press.

Although HP engaged in illegal methods of observation, companies can legally screen the e-mail, Internet, and phone histories of employees. Do you think they should be allowed to do so? Employee privacy is a big issue today.

Other websites are more controversial in how they support similar activities. The site WikiLeaks describes itself as "a multi-jurisdictional public service designed to protect whistleblowers, journalists and activists who have sensitive materials to communicate to the public."[8] But it has sparked several controversies because it has made public confidential documents from the U.S. military, the Central Intelligence Agency, the U.S. Embassy, and a variety of private corporate reports and e-mails. For example, WikiLeaks made public a video of a U.S. Army helicopter strike in Iraq against a group that included children and two Reuters journalists.[9]

Privacy

How has technology impacted employees? Some uses of technology in the workplace have brought about difficult changes. The increasing volume of e-mail can contribute to a breakdown in communication as fewer personal exchanges take place. Communication experts agree that in face-to-face discussions, up to 93 percent of the meaning of the messages exchanged is communicated in nonverbal ways—through gestures, glances, body position, and facial expression. As more office discussions take place via e-mail, the chance of misunderstandings and errors continues to rise.

The boundary between work and home has also blurred because of the increase of technology. Once a worker has access to office files from home and the office has access to employees via smart phones or live video-conferencing, the workday can extend dramatically.

How does technology affect employee privacy? At home, U.S. citizens are guaranteed specific levels of privacy and freedoms. In the workplace, however, the expectation of privacy is quite different. **Electronic monitoring** is commonly used to track employees' keystrokes and e-mails, examine their Internet browsing histories, and even monitor their mobile phones and text and instant messages. Camera surveillance is also used.

Electronic surveillance can help companies prevent theft, fraud, and employees from loafing on the job and improve a firm's security. The practice is also generally legal as long as employers inform their workers they are being monitored. However, if the monitoring is extensive,

Employee monitoring can feel like an invasion of privacy in the workplace.
Source: J. R. Bale/Alamy.

employees can begin to feel stifled to the point where they no longer do their best work. Researchers have found that employees experience an increase in stress and anxiety when their work is being monitored, which in turn can lead to health problems and job dissatisfaction.[10] Finding the balance between an appropriate level of monitoring and an optimal work environment is a continuous challenge.

Flatland Frames escaped disaster this time. The employee realized the e-mail was an unusual request for sensitive protected data and called the firm's IT manager before responding. But phishing schemes and other threats to Flatland's data will continue, and the company will need to stay vigilant in terms of being aware of the latest types of attacks and how to defend against them.

Impact of Social Media and Mobile Technology pp. 287–291

When he first opened his restaurant 10 years ago, Philippe Durand was sure that no advertising was bad advertising. Even bad word of mouth would make people curious enough to try the restaurant, and he would win them over once they did. But in the new age of blogging and Facebook, what is said in cyberspace can have a real negative impact. For a long time, Philippe's restaurant was the only place to get French American cuisine, but a new competitor just opened across town. Philippe decided to go on the offensive and began posting little quips about his competitor on his restaurant's Facebook page. The reaction was quick—people hated the fact that Philippe was being negative and started complaining about his postings and then about his restaurant's service and food. How did this all go wrong so fast? And how was Philippe going to make things right? ∎

Source: Mario Proenca/Bloomberg/ Getty Images.

New technologies emerge every day, and they are changing the face of business in unexpected ways. Social networking, for example, has created new employment opportunities, new marketing opportunities, and new dangers when it comes to marketing a business or brand. So have mobile devices. Understanding how social networking and mobile technology can be used to enhance the success of a business and anticipating how it will be used by consumers can make or break a businessperson's future.

Social Networking

How is social networking changing businesses? Firms are using social networks to communicate throughout their organizations, and managers and marketing professionals use social networks to generate interest in their firms' products and increase their revenues. Dell entered the Chinese computer market by becoming a popular brand on the country's top social networking site Ren Ren. Social networks are also being used to generate funding, and human resources departments use social media to recruit employees. Let's take a closer look at the specific impact this technology is having.

Are social media apps used within businesses? **Enterprise social networking** refers to the application of products like Facebook in a corporate setting. Today, enterprise versions of products such as Facebook and Twitter and workplace wikis such as Yammer are

Social media sites are important to our personal lives but also to the functioning of good businesses. *Source:* Anatolii Babii/Alamy.

To find out what people are saying about the company's products and services, Dell employees monitor more than 25,000 posts on the Web every day.
Source: Business Wire/Handout/Getty Images Publicity/Getty Images, Inc.

ModCloth's "Be the Buyer" program is one example of crowdsourcing a business decision.
Source: http://www.inc.com/magazine/20100201/using-crowdsourcing-to-control-inventory.html and company is mod cloth.

becoming more common in the office. Companies hope the tools will increase collaboration and speed up decision making in their organizations and improve the customer's experience and ultimately their profits. For example, @DellOutlet, a Twitter account the computer maker Dell uses to advertise discounts, has generated millions of dollars of sales for the company.

How are companies using social media to monitor their business? Social media monitoring—keeping watch on the external messages and information being spread about their products in cyberspace—is critical and a relatively new activity for businesses. There are many products now being sold, like Brandwatch and UberVU, which collect social media mentions of a specific product or company and then analyze and report on patterns and trends.

Many companies are doing much more than purchasing software for social media monitoring software, however. The computer manufacturer Dell is a good example. A number of years ago, the blogosphere was in a furor over Dell's poor products and service. "Dell Hell" rants on the Web continued for more than a year before Dell figured out what to do about the bad publicity.

In 2010, Dell opened the Social Media Listening Command Center, where employees monitor over 25,000 Web posts daily. The average daily number of mentions of Dell on Twitter alone is more than the combined circulation of the top 12 daily newspapers in the United States. The company also has thousands of staff members who work on more than 40 Facebook pages worldwide for Dell as well as handle the firm's Twitter account.

What new jobs have been created with the rise of social media? Firms large and small are now hiring *social media managers*, who are also sometimes called *social media marketing specialists*. A person in a position such as this is responsible for monitoring social networks and generating "buzz" on them about a company and its products. Social media managers also listen to what is being said about their firms to identify problems and opportunities. For example, the social media manager watches over Facebook groups who have "liked" a product and makes sure they get special updates, offers, and the latest news on promotions and events. Other social media–related jobs include *social media strategists*, *social media copywriters*, and *search engine optimization specialists*.

Can social media provide information that is directly useful to a business? It is important to use social media for marketing, but using it as an avenue for more specific business decision making is happening as well. Using information solicited from people on social media and the Internet to help make a decision is referred to as **crowdsourcing**. Dell uses crowdsourcing to help develop its products. Its IdeaStorm website allows customers to post ideas for products, promote others' ideas, and then see how the company puts them into action. Likewise, since many manufacturers require that large minimum orders be placed, Susan Gregg Koger, the owner of the clothing franchise ModCloth, faced tough buying decisions. So, ModCloth introduced a "Be the Buyer" program that encourages customers to vote online on clothing styles. By evaluating their feedback and responses to a particular item, Gregg Koger knows whether she should risk placing a large order to have it manufactured.

How can social media help with technical support services? Companies can use social media to head off potential technical problems that might turn into public disaster. The company iRobot, manufacturer of home robots like the

Tasteless Tweet

To avoid backlash, businesses need to carefully think about how their customers are going to respond to information they broadcast on the social media. For example, shortly after the singer-songwriter Amy Winehouse died from alcohol poisoning in 2011, Microsoft sent out a tweet encouraging fans to remember the singer by buying her last album from Zune, the company's digital marketplace. Thousands of Twitter users responded with tweets of their own that included "utterly tasteless," "vile-leaches—seriously?," and "Microsoft—failing at social media."[11]

Roomba vacuum cleaner, realized the importance of this when one customer posted to YouTube a video account of the trouble he was having and very quickly racked up 60,000 views. Now iRobot uses software to match social media comments with specific customer records and respond quickly to problems to help solve them.

How is social media helping people start and fund new businesses? For several years, the microlending movement, begun by Muhammad Yunus, has been used to connect many people in need of funding for very small businesses with those who can loan small amounts. The Grameen Bank became a microcredit lending institution by making extremely small loans with very low interest rates to the poor of underdeveloped countries. The website Kiva combined this idea with the interconnectivity of the Internet to allow investors to make a loan as small as $25 to borrowers worldwide.

As we explained in Chapter 5, social networking is becoming a mechanism for funding start-ups in a variety of business arenas in a similar manner. **Crowdsourced funding** (crowdfunding) allows a great number of people who believe in a company or a product to contribute a small amount of money to help a company get started. In most cases the company gives them something back in return—a free copy of the product or a signed card from the founder. Some of the projects crowdfunded through Kickstarter include five films that premiered at the Sundance Film Festival. The virtual-reality headset project Oculus Rift began with a Kickstarter campaign to raise $250,000 to get the device off the ground. Oculus, its maker, was later bought by Facebook for more than $2 billion. Other sites, like RocketHub, Indiegogo, and Funding4Learning, are continuing the crowdfunding trend.

Nobel Prize winner Mohammed Yunus developed microlending, which has allowed millions of the world's poorest people to borrow small amounts of money to begin businesses.
Source: Alexander Klein/Stringer/AFP/ Getty Images, Inc.

Mobile Devices

Why do businesses need mobile devices? Most business organizations today find it critical to have a mobile component both to support their employees and to attract and serve customers. Customers demand a way to find the closest locations at which to shop and to place orders from their smart phones. A firm's sales staff requires constant access to e-mail, calendar and contacts, and Internet resources. Being able to make video phone calls with applications like Facetime, see data mapped to their current locations, and create and send photos and videos all can serve the larger mission of the company if implemented well.

Jackson Kayak is a small business that designs, manufactures, and sells kayaks in Tennessee. The firm has its own kayaking social network on its website, a Facebook page, and its own mobile app. The app allows users to browse the latest kayak industry news, upload photos and status information, and, of course, shop at Jackson Kayaks. The company also uses mobile analytics, which allow its sales representatives to quickly display and analyze the company's site traffic when working with kayak dealers in the field. The analysis can point to specific customer behaviors that support stocking certain items, for example.

How does a business select which mobile devices to purchase? There are a number of issues a firm has to consider when it comes to selecting the mobile devices it buys. For example, what kind of mobile devices—phones, tablets, and so forth—should the firm have, and what brand? What kind employees should use them, and what kind of devices are customers using? Should employees be able to use their personal mobile phones for work? How easily can the devices be rolled out to the entire company if a smaller trial of them is successful? How do they integrate with existing mail systems? IT also needs to think about what kind of encryption and data protection is available and whether the right applications exist or can be developed in-house.

Externally, a company would ideally provide mobile solutions for the various platforms customers may have, whether an iPhone, an Android device, or a non–smart phone. The expense of developing and maintaining multiple applications, though, means that a business must thoroughly understand its own client base before deciding which mobile products to deploy.

What kinds of mobile apps are useful for business? There are over 1 million apps available for the iPhone, and other smart phone devices have impressive stores of content as well. For business, many useful apps focus on communications, task management, and managing data. For example, phone applications can allow users to conduct a WebEx conference, integrating a slide show, file transfer, and multiple voice and audio feeds. Products like Omnifocus organize a schedule beyond a simple calendar format, displaying tasks that require resources that are nearby geographically or listing which tasks can be run concurrently and which are on hold for input from someone else. Mobile apps for the sales force organize new leads and customer requests, help manage salespeople's expense reports, or process invoices right from their tablets or phones.

The Oculus Rift virtual reality headset started as a Kickstarter project.
Source: Robyn Beck/Staff/AFP/Getty Images, Inc.

How has cloud computing helped grow the mobile device market? Cloud computing refers to the practice of storing and retrieving information, resources, and software on remote servers accessed via the Internet rather than a local server or personal computer. Using cloud computing, online backup systems can work through a "cloud" so that files are automatically backed up and made available instantly to a whole set of users. Cloud backup makes a business free from worries that data could be lost due to a flood or a corrupted server. The instant synchronization of data can make employees more productive, especially when they are out in the field. With Apple's iCloud service, for example, a photograph taken on someone's iPhone is instantly available on his or her iPad as well as on his or her home PC. As more services beyond just storage begin to take advantage of cloud computing, businesses will become more agile and efficient.

As you read at the beginning of this section, Philippe Durand tried to become part of the social media revolution. His first foray into marketing his business using social media didn't work out the way he'd hoped, but he learned from that. Specifically, he learned that discrediting the competition not only didn't hurt the competition but also hurt his own business. Instead, he began to study more closely who was using his Facebook page and who was responding to the QR codes he used in his new ad campaign. He found that his restaurant was attracting a specific demographic of affluent, well-traveled people. He decided to try to appeal to their sense of interest in new cuisines and new experiences. His Facebook page began to highlight the ingredients he used and the stories behind his suppliers. He also offered customers a new way to pay at the end of their meals, using a custom mobile app that keeps track of their reward points earned.

Summary

1 What does the online environment offer to help market a business? (pp. 273–275)

- Online shopping continues to grow. **Online advertising** (p. 273) and marketing through e-mail campaigns are critical, as is managing viral marketing techniques.

- With **pay-per-click (PPC) advertising** (p. 274), advertisers pay only for the number of times a Web surfer clicks on their ads. PPC ads are effective because they are associated with key words and are highly relevant to what potential consumers are searching for.

- **Viral marketing** (p. 274) involves using social networks, e-mail, and websites to spread the awareness of a particular brand.

2 What types of business transactions are supported by online commerce? (pp. 276–278)

- There are three common types of transactions—**business to business** (B2B), **business to consumer** (B2C), and **consumer to consumer** (C2C):

  - **B2B** (p. 276) sites facilitate transactions between businesses through the exchange of information and brokering of services.

  - B2C (p. 276) sites refer to e-commerce that takes place directly between businesses and consumers.

  - C2C (p. 277) sites facilitate transactions between individual people rather than businesses.

3 What are the functions of a company's chief information officer (CIO) and information technology (IT) department? (pp. 279–280)

- A company's **chief information officer (CIO)** (p. 279) is the executive in charge of information processing, including systems design and development and data center operations. He or she is also responsible for the following:

  - Determining how systems should be designed and developed and the software programs installed on it

  - Deciding whether a firm's should update or replace its computer systems and software

  - Managing a budget that balances the benefits of technology against the ever-rising costs of having the latest systems

  - Setting policy for privacy and security concerns

- The IT department consists of a number of professionals responsible for everything from hardware components to software programs to networking strategies. The IT department also has the following tasks:

  - Maintaining security both in response to computer virus attacks and emergency recovery from power outages and system failures

  - Keeping all of an organization's computers, printers, scanners, and other equipment operational and current

  - Designing networks used within a company and databases where information is stored

  - Selecting or creating software programs used by the business and providing software training to employees

  - Maintaining and managing the use of mobile computing throughout a company

  - Implementing remote access to computing resources, such as employees' access to work files or e-mail when they are working from home

4 How do businesses transform data into useful business intelligence? (pp. 280–283)

- **Information technology (IT)** (p. 279) is the design and implementation of computer-based information systems.

- **Information systems (ISs)** (p. 280) focus on applying IT to the solution of business and economic problems. IS professionals bridge the gap between purely technical knowledge and how it will impact business.

- Raw **data** (p. 281) must be organized and arranged into useful **information** (p. 281). IS professionals and other decision makers can then use this information to determine which IT solutions to implement.

5 What security challenges arise with the increase of technology (pp. 283–287)

- **Adware** (p. 284) and **spyware** (p. 284) can cause annoyance for online customers or even contribute to theft of their identity information and credit card data.

- **Phishing** (p. 284) is an illicit means of obtaining secure private information by imitating a communication from a legitimate site.

- Businesses of all sizes must protect against data breaches from **hackers** (p. 284), which disrupt business operations and can open the door to expensive legal action against the company if customer data are compromised.

- Technology can support ethical conduct within the workplace. Many organizations have websites that allow employees and people with complaints or allegations of misconduct to file reports easily and safely, shielding them from possible retaliation.

6 How have new advances in social networking and mobile technologies impacted business? (pp. 287–291)

- Businesses need to know what is being said about them in cyberspace, so many use **social media monitoring** (p. 288). Software products are available for this purpose, but firms are also hiring social media managers and similar types of employees to help maximize their effectiveness in this sphere.

- **Crowdsourcing** (p. 288) is the process of using the suggestions of customers and people online to help a business make decisions.

- **Crowdsourced funding** (p. 289) is the use of social networks and the Internet to raise money to help start and grow small businesses.

- The increase in the number of mobile devices and the advent of **cloud computing** (p. 290) are supporting a large increase in the growth of mobile technology.

Key Terms

adware (p. 284)

Big Data analysis (p. 282)

business intelligence
  software (p. 283)

business-to-business
  transactions (p. 276)

business-to-consumer
  transactions (p. 276)

chief information officer (p. 279)

cloud computing (p. 290)

consumer-to-consumer
  transactions (p. 277)

contextual advertising (p. 274)

crowdsourced funding (p. 289)

crowdsourcing (p. 288)

data (p. 281)

database management
  system (p. 281)

data mart (p. 281)

data mining (p. 281)

data warehouse (p. 281)

decision support system (p. 282)

electronic monitoring (p. 286)

enterprise social
  networking (p. 287)

executive information
  system (p. 282)

hacker (p. 284)

information (p. 281)

information system (p. 280)

information technology (p. 279)

management information
  system (p. 280)

online advertising (p. 273)

online analysis package (p. 283)

pay-per-click (PPC)
  advertising (p. 274)

phishing (p. 284)

social media monitoring (p. 288)

spyware (p. 284)

viral marketing (p. 274)

Self Test

Multiple Choice *You can find the answers on the last page of this book.*

10-1 IT is

  a. internship technology opportunities.

  b. company-wide investigations of office conduct.

  c. building a networking plan for the flow and use of information.

  d. the design and implementation of computer-based systems.

10-2 MIS differs from IT because

  a. MIS focuses on applying IT to solve business problems.

  b. MIS is the branch of IT focused on Internet usage.

  c. IT focuses on hardware, and MIS focuses on software.

  d. MIS is applied, and IT is theoretical.

10-3 DSSs are used most often by

  a. managers who make decisions based on current data.

  b. employees who decide how to solve technical problems.

  c. clerical staff who organize and format documents and reports.

  d. trainers who teach staff and employees new software products.

10-4 Data warehousing is

  a. the storing of terabytes of transaction data.

  b. not used when DBMSs are in place.

  c. is not used now because data marts have replaced it.

  d. is the management of large quantities of paper records.

Self Test (continued)

10-5 Tools used to analyze data include

a. DBMSs, ERP, and ROI.

b. DSSs, OLAPs, and executive information systems.

c. OSHAs and C2Cs.

d. PPCs, ISs, and B2Bs.

10-6 Hackers can infiltrate systems

a. only if they use cookie files to store information.

b. if the systems are isolated as a single corporate extranet.

c. All of the above.

d. None of the above.

10-7 Social media monitoring is best described as

a. planning events where the sales force mingles with potential clients.

b. regulating the use of e-mail and messaging in the workplace.

c. staying aware of the messages posted about your products in cyberspace.

d. eavesdropping on personal communications.

10-8 Phishing can be used to

a. minimize the taxes owed to the federal government.

b. steal identity information from unsuspecting clients.

c. record the keystrokes typed in when someone is logging into a password-protected site.

d. help save storage space on mobile devices.

10-9 Business-to-business transactions include

a. brokering sites.

b. social networking sites.

c. specialized industry portals.

d. Both a and c.

10-10 Technology has forced businesses to focus on security issues like

a. phishing.

b. adware and spyware.

c. disruption by hackers.

d. All of the above.

True/False *You can find the answers on the last page of this book.*

10-11 The CIO is the director of IT and reports to the CFO.
☐ True or ☐ False

10-12 Business intelligence software supports decision making by presenting visual, interactive views of the state of a business.
☐ True or ☐ False

10-13 Viral marketing can be prevented by using the proper spyware.
☐ True or ☐ False

10-14 Enterprise social networking is the application of social network tools to education.
☐ True or ☐ False

10-15 Crowdsourced funding is the use of social networking to acquire capital for a new venture.
☐ True or ☐ False

Critical Thinking Questions

✪ **10-16** Businesses have experienced several major data breaches in the last few years. How do you see these lapses in corporate security affecting consumers? Does it make you less likely to purchase from certain companies or to purchase certain products? Has it changed how you protect your identity information?

10-17 What responsibilities accompany the new volume of information we can collect with information technologies? If airlines can cross-reference travel data with bank records and identify suspicious patterns, do they have a responsibility to alert authorities? Or should it be illegal for companies to look for patterns in data in order to "profile" people (extrapolate data about their psychological and physical characteristics, spending patterns,

and so forth in order to make judgments about them)? What if a college IT department finds a threatening message that has been sent from a student e-mail account? What if it is not "threatening" but in very bad taste? Where is the boundary of the college's responsibility?

10-18 The growth in online and mobile shopping has forced many businesses to dramatically adjust their sales and marketing strategies. What kind of brick-and-mortar bookstores have survived the move to electronic media and online shopping? What unique qualities have they focused on to demonstrate the value their products have in the digital age? Has Amazon.com promoted interest in reading, which helps brick-and-mortar stores, or has it eliminated them?

Team Time

THE WINDS OF CHANGE

Assemble into groups of three. Each member of the group should select one of the following areas to explore:

a. The social impact of business technology

b. The ethical impact of business technology

c. Thee global impact of business technology

Process

Step 1. As a group, determine what innovation in business technology will have the most impact on people over the next year, five years, and 10 years. After the group has selected a specific innovation, each group member should prepare a short presentation on why that particular technology change will be significant in his or her area.

Step 2. Evaluate the innovation by asking the following:

- What proportion of businesses will be impacted by the technology?
- What aspects of business activity will be impacted?
- What proportion of consumers and/or vendors will be impacted?
- Will the innovation lead to additional changes in the business in the future?

Step 3. Optional: As a class, compare the groups' results. Determine which innovation has the most likelihood of coming to fruition. How will it change your career and the world you will be part of in the future?

Ethics and Corporate Social Responsibility

COMPUTER HACKING: A HIGH PRICE TO PAY

Read the following case study. Then, as a class, discuss the questions that follow.

One night, 21-year-olds Brian Salcedo and Adam Botbyl were driving around in Adam's car with a couple of antennas hanging out the window and a laptop. Salcedo and Botbyl were looking for open wireless networks they could access. As they drove past a Lowe's home improvement store, they found it had an open network. Lowe's had set it up to be open so the company's employees could use scanners and other handheld devices to connect wirelessly to it.

Six months later, Salcedo and Botbyl used the Lowe's network to upload a modified program onto Lowe's computer system. The program was designed to transmit customers' credit card numbers to the men. Fortunately, the FBI investigated the incident and arrested Salcedo and Botbyl before they ever saw a single credit card number. They pleaded guilty and worked with Lowe's to boost its security. Nonetheless, Salcedo was sentenced to nine years in prison, one of the longest sentences in U.S. history for computer hacking. Botbyl was sentenced to 26 months.

Ethics and Corporate Social Responsibility (continued)

Questions for Discussion

10-19 Who is responsible for keeping the credit card numbers of Lowe's customers secure?

10-20 How can consumers know if it's safe to use their credit cards to make a purchase?

10-21 Were Salcedo's and Botbyl's sentences appropriate? Why or why not?

Web Exercises

10-22 WikiLeaks
Visit the WikiLeaks website and select two of the most current leaks posted. Evaluate the effect of the information being made public. Does it violate the privacy rights of the individuals involved? Is WikiLeaks a good way to expose a criminal act? Do the benefits of leaking the information outweigh the associated privacy and confidentiality violations, or not?

10-23 To Censor or Not to Censor
In 2010, Google reversed its previous position and stopped allowing the Chinese government to censor the search engine results its citizens received on Google. Instead, Google began to redirect users to an uncensored search engine based in Hong Kong. What led to the change in Google's corporate position? What response did Google receive from the Chinese government? Contrast this to the deal Microsoft signed with Baidu, the biggest search engine in China.

10-24 Online Business Is Global Business
Visit BMW's website. This international portal redirects customers to one of many hundreds of country-specific

sites. Select three countries and investigate the websites presented. What elements are kept the same? How does BMW maintain a unified international marketing message? Which components are different? How does your Web browser handle the differences in character sets for different languages?

10-25 After the Data Breach
Research the data breach at Maricopa County Community College, where information for 2.4 million current and former students was exposed. How the college's IT department responded after the breach was critical. How expensive was the response effort? How timely? What kind of actions can reestablish confidence in the college's IT department and the college itself?

10-26 The Power of Your Likes
Examine the PBS *Frontline* episode "Generation Like" at www.pbs.org. Are young people and their social media sites being exploited by marketing professionals? Or is this generation especially skilled in how to use social media to advance themselves and open doors to new opportunities?

MyBizLab

Go to **mybizlab.com** for Auto-graded writing questions as well as the following Assisted-graded writing questions:

✪**10-27** Many people are concerned about the "digital divide," the gap in IT resources among industrialized countries and developing countries. The explosive growth of smart phones may be a path that allows developing countries to move quickly into the digital age. What advantages would there be to supporting the use of smart phones versus the use of computers in a developing country? What infrastructure and other devices might help minimize the digital divide?

✪**10-28** What kinds of business functions could benefit from input from consumers? How would you collect the best-quality data for that purpose?

References

1. "Eighty-Nine Percent of Consumers Prefer Online Shopping to Store Shopping According to Part II of Survey by Online Retailer Safe Home Products.," January 1, 2014, www.prnewswire.com/news-releases/eighty-nine-percent-of-consumers-prefer-online-shopping-to-store-shopping-according-to-part-ii-of-survey-by-online-retailer-safe-home-products-58656737.html (accessed April 27, 2014).

2. C. Jones, "Ecommerce Is Growing Nicely while Mcommerce Is on a Tear," *Forbes*, www.forbes.com/sites/chuckjones/2013/10/02/ecommerce-is-growing-nicely-while-mcommerce-is-on-a-tear (accessed April 27, 2014).

3. Eric M. Jackson, "Why 'the PayPal Mafia' Is Killing It," *Huffington Post*, December 1, 2011, www.huffingtonpost.com/eric-m-jackson/why-the-paypal-mafia-is-k_b_1121899.html.

4. Chris Lee, "'Alien' Bus-Stop Ads Create a Stir," *Los Angeles Times*, June 19, 2009, http://articles.latimes.com/2009/jun/19/entertainment/et-district19.

5. R. Wyden, "S.1431," August 1, 2013, http://beta.congress.gov/bill/113th-congress/senate-bill/1431 (accessed April 27, 2014).

6. Ned Potter, "Sony PlayStation Network Hacked Again," October 12, 2011, http://abcnews.go.com/blogs/technology/2011/10/sony-playstation-network-hacked-again-closes-93000-accounts.

7. "United Airlines Sells 'Free' Tickets on Website," September 13, 2013, www.cnn.com/2013/09/12/travel/united-free-tickets (accessed April 27, 2014).

8. WikiLeaks, "About Us," www.wikileaks.org.

9. Megan Chuchmach, "WikiLeaks Preparing to Release Video of Alleged U.S. 'Massacre' in Afghanistan," June 18, 2010, http://abcnews.go.com/Blotter/wikileaks-preparing-release-video-alleged-us-massacre-afghanistan/story?id=10954929.

10. A. Semuels, "Tracking Workers' Every Move Can Boost Productivity—and Stress," *Los Angeles Times*, April 8, 2013, http://articles.latimes.com/2013/apr/08/business/la-fi-harsh-work-tech-20130408 (accessed April 27, 2014).

11. Tweet from unknown user, quoted in Cooper Smith, "Microsoft Sorry for 'Insensitive' Amy Winehouse Tweet," *Huffington Post*, July 26, 2011, www.huffingtonpost.com.

Chapter 11
Production, Operations, and Supply Chain Management

▌ The Production of Goods and Services

Steve Schmidt loves his job making custom bicycles. He and his business partner, Ralph Brinsdorfer, take pride in providing the best customer service by ensuring that the bikes are delivered on time, offering financing, and providing friendly and efficient repair service. Their goal, like the goal of all businesses, is to deliver a quality good or service to their customers. What is involved in the production of goods and services? How important is production to the U.S. economy and also to world economies?

▌ Production Management

Kristi Kwan and Yuan Martin run a fitness and nutritional consulting firm. For all of their clients, especially those with specific food allergies or dietary requirements, they recommend the YouBar, a nutrition bar with customizable ingredients that cater to the tastes and nutritional needs of each of their clients. How does the YouBar provide for such product customization without making each bar by hand?

▌ Operations Planning and Management

Arthur Ridder's furniture manufacturing company has had great success in northern Washington and he's considering expanding operations to a new location. What factors does Arthur need to consider before choosing a new location? How should the facility be arranged, and how does he determine the best suppliers to use?

▌ Operations Control

Jeanette Pae's daughter hurt herself when the tray of her high chair unexpectedly separated from the rest of the chair. The chair was later recalled, but Jeanette's confidence in the product was shaken. Similar situations happened to her friends and family members, who had experienced the recall of toys, medicine, computer batteries, and cars. What can companies do to ensure the production of a high-quality product?

▌ Suppliers and Supply Chain Management

Sylvia Ackerman loves the simple lines and clean design of IKEA products and can't wait to furnish her new apartment with IKEA merchandise. Moreover, she knows she'll be able to afford what she needs and can assemble the furniture on her own with minimal help from others. How does IKEA manage the process of producing inexpensive, high-quality goods for its stores around the world?

OBJECTIVES

1 How is manufacturing and production important to the U.S. economy and to global economies? (pp. 229–301)

2 What is production management, and what common production processes are used by businesses? (pp. 301–304)

3 What is operations management, and what is important in determining a facility's location and layout? (pp. 304–308)

4 What types of technology are used in production facilities? (pp. 308–311)

5 How are operations controlled and quality standards achieved in a firm? (pp. 311–317)

6 What is supply chain management, and how does it help companies create and deliver their goods and services more effectively? (pp. 317–319)

The Production of Goods and Services pp. 299–301

Steve Schmidt builds bicycles by hand for a growing list of professional cyclists and triathletes. His customers appreciate the attention to quality each bike receives during the production process. His growing list of customers are mostly professional cyclists and triathletes who appreciate the attention to quality each bike receives during the production process. In fact, the firm's sales have begun to rival those of some of the leading custom-bike manufacturers. As a result, to help produce the bikes, Steve has hired and begun training apprentices with the same fine eye for detail he has. Meanwhile, Ralph Brinsdorfer, Steve's co-owner, has established relationships with parts suppliers as well as customers, to whom he provides impeccable service. He ensures that each bike is delivered damage free and on time and offers repairs and other services customers need.

Source: Photographee.eu/Fotolia.

Although Steve and Ralph like the how they produce the bikes, as the company grows, they are concerned that the production process might need to change. What challenges do Steve and Ralph face as their business expands? What processes can they put in place to maintain the high quality and customer-service standards the business has been known for? These questions are common production and operations concerns for all manufacturing and service-based companies that want to remain competitive in the changing global environment. ■

All businesses, whether they produce strictly manufactured products, strictly services, or a combination of both (which most do), utilize production processes. Production is the process of getting a good or a service to the customer; it is a series of related activities, with value being added as each activity or stage is completed.

How efficiently a company handles the production process can either help or hinder the overall success of the business and the competitiveness of the good or the service in the marketplace.

MyBizLab®

⭐ Improve Your Grade!

Over 10 million students improved their results using the Pearson MyLabs.
Visit **mybizlab.com** for simulations, tutorials, and end-of-chapter problems.

The Importance of Production

Why is production a critical component of any business? Companies strive to make a profit by providing goods or services to consumers. To increase their profits and decrease their production costs, businesses must find the most efficient production process possible. To remain competitive in the global economy, U.S. manufacturers and service organizations in particular need to continue to improve their operations and production processes to become more customer focused, quality driven, economically efficient, and technologically savvy. This necessitates managing each component of the production process from beginning to end, including developing tighter relationships with suppliers, if a company wants to remain profitable and competitive.

How important is manufacturing in the United States? Manufacturing remains a fundamental component of the U.S. economy. In fact, manufacturing was the largest contributor to the U.S. real gross domestic product (GDP) in 2012, according to the Bureau of Economic Analysis.[1] This is true even though the country has been hit hard in the past two decades by significant increases in imported goods and related job losses.

Part of the reason why manufacturing contributes significantly to GDP is the substantial amount of commodities and services the manufacturing sector requires to produce goods. Manufacturing also generates many other service-based economic activities: the transportation of goods, the production of software needed to assist with the processes used to make the goods, and their marketing, advertising, and selling.

Moving to a Service-Based Economy

How important are services to the U.S. economy? Despite the ongoing importance of the manufacturing sector, the United States, like most developed nations, has transitioned from an industrial-based, manufacturing economy to a service-based economy. Services make up nearly three-fourths of the U.S. GDP, and over 75 percent of jobs are in the service sector.[2] Service businesses, such as bookkeeping, child care, and even retail operations, are easier to start because they require less capital than manufacturing businesses, which generally need to or rent or purchase real estate, factories, and equipment.

We may think of service businesses as being the small mom-and-pop stores in our neighborhood, but not all service businesses are small. Ten of the 30 firms that currently make up the Dow Jones Industrial Average (DJIA) are in the service sector. They include American Express, AT&T, Bank of America, Cisco, McDonald's, JP Morgan Chase, Travelers, Verizon Communications, Walmart, and Walt Disney.

Some companies are considered to be both manufacturing and service based. GE and IBM, also on the DJIA, are considered to be the largest and most competitive service operations in the world. Both have manufacturing components. Additionally, transportation and utility companies are service based and are very important to the U.S. economy.[3]

The Global Production Landscape

How does U.S. manufacturing compete globally? When you look at the country-of-origin labels on the products you use, most of them have probably been made in a foreign country. Consequently, it is hard to imagine that the United States is still a globally important manufacturing country. Although the United States is the world's largest importer, it is also the third-largest exporter. In 2013, the U.S. exported $1.5 trillion worth of goods.[4] Even though the United States doesn't manufacture as many low-dollar products as it used to, it continues to manufacture a lot of high-dollar products. According to the authoritative *CIA World Factbook*, the United States has "the largest and most technologically advanced economy in the world."[5] Nearly one-half of U.S. exports are goods such as transistors, aircraft, motor vehicle parts, computers, and telecommunications equipment. Industrial supplies, such as organic chemicals, account for another one-fourth of U.S. total exports, and consumer goods, such as automobiles and medicines, make up another 15 percent.[6]

How does manufacturing affect the global economy? Over the past few decades, U.S. companies reduced their costs of manufacturing by offshoring production to Third World or developing countries, such as those in Asia and Africa, to take advantage of lower wage rates. Outsourcing has contributed to the decline in U.S. manufacturing and the increase in unemployment. However, on a global basis, the outsourcing the production of products to Third World countries has helped to improve their standards of living and contributed to the world's economic growth. Despite offshoring and outsourcing, the United States still has a higher GDP than any other nation in the world.[7]

In recent years, some changes in the global manufacturing competitiveness of many countries, including the United States, have occurred. According to the Global Manufacturing Competitive Index, China remains the most competitive manufacturing nation and is poised to remain in that position for the next five years. The United States, Germany, and Japan rank among the top 10 most competitive manufacturing nations, although their relative positions have slipped. Lower-wage countries, such as India and Brazil, which haven't traditionally been large manufacturing nations, now make the list.[8]

What are the changes in production to keep the United States competitive? The forecast is for the U.S. manufacturing sector to continue shifting. Some foreign-based companies, such as Lenovo, the Beijing-based computer manufacturer, are opening new facilities in the United States, and American companies, such as Caterpillar, GE, and Ford, are bringing some manufacturing operations and jobs back to the nation. In addition, to produce better products more economically and faster, U.S. manufacturers are utilizing newer practices, such as enterprise resource planning, computer integrated manufacturing, flexible manufacturing, and lean manufacturing, which we will discuss later in the chapter. Service-based organizations, including Nordstrom and the Ritz-Carlton, have learned from manufacturers and are using modified versions of the same practices to improve their offerings. McDonald's, Disney, and Federal Express, for example, have well-developed quality management programs similar to quality improvement techniques found in manufacturing firms.

In many respects, companies like the one run by Steve Schmidt and Ralph Brinsdorfer are significantly different from their larger competitors, such as Schwinn, Trek, and Cannondale. But all companies share similar concerns with regard to producing quality products. As Steve's and Ralph's business continues to expand, they will need to determine the best location for the business so they are accessible to their customers, good workers, and suppliers. These are concerns of every business—whether they are big or small.

Production Management pp. 301–304

Kristi Kwan and Yuan Martin have known each other since high school. They became great friends mainly because of their shared interests in sports. While they went their different ways in college, they met years later and started a fitness and nutritional consulting firm. One of the main products they recommend, especially to their clients with food allergies or dietary requirements, is the YouBar, a nutrition bar with ingredients customized to the tastes and nutritional needs of each customer. Customers can choose a number of the ingredients (including the vitamins the bars contain) and customize the name of their bars. The bars are available only via online orders and are sold around the world. How does the YouBar provide for such product customization? ■

Source: DragonImages/Fotolia.

Goods and services don't just appear; they are created. As you learned earlier in this chapter, production is the process through which resources are converted into finished products and given value. **Production management** refers to the planning, implementation, and control measures used in the process to convert resources into finished products. Production managers are in charge of setting schedules, choosing what parts and supplies are necessary for production, overseeing quality control, and managing other important issues. Production managers who plan effectively are able to increase their firms' productivity, reduce their costs, and improve the satisfaction of customers.

The Make-or-Buy Decision

What is a make-or-buy decision? It is not always necessary for a company to make everything in-house. When starting the production process, one of the first decisions that operations managers make is determining if the company will make the entire product or if the product will be assembled from a combination of parts manufactured in-house and parts manufactured or purchased outside the organization. This is commonly called a **make-or-buy decision**. If it is less expensive to outsource the production of certain parts elsewhere, that may be the best decision. However, it is important that a company can trust the quality of any parts that are outsourced since the product ultimately will bear the company's name and its reputation depends on it.

Customers perceive a product as a single entity—not as component piece-parts provided by different suppliers. Customers will hold the company responsible even if an individual supplier is to blame for making a faulty part or missing a deadline and causing a delay. For example, Mattel had to recall close to 1 million toys because its supplier in China had coated the toys in paint that contained lead. Mattel was later fined $2.3 million by the Consumer Product Safety Commission because, ultimately, the company was responsible for the quality of the finished product.[9] So, having a good supplier that meets a company's needs and cares about a company's customers as if they were its own is an invaluable asset. Understanding these needs before choosing a supplier is important. We will discuss choosing suppliers in more detail later in the chapter.

Of course, a firm's decision as to whether to make or buy some or all of the products it intends to sell will affect the rest of its operations management process, including its production processes, capacity planning, the size of its facilities, where to locate them, and often the technology used in the facilities.

Common Production Processes and Techniques

What production processes are used in business? Henry Ford introduced the concept the assembly line to meet the increased demand for his automobiles. The assembly line utilized **continuous flow production**, a method that produces discrete units of products in large numbers one by one continuously and rapidly. Although it's a cost-effective method, it is doesn't allow for products to be customized. In fact, one of Ford's most famous quotes is the following: "Any customer can have a car painted any color that he wants so long as it is black."

Over time, firms in the United States began to feel the pressures created by foreign competitors producing customized high-quality products and selling them at reasonable prices. To stay competitive, manufacturers in the United States had to implement new production processes that were both flexible and cost effective. With **intermittent processes**, production runs are shorter, so machinery can be changed over between them to accommodate product changes.

Retailers emptied their shelves of Mattel toys, which were recalled after it was determined that one the company's suppliers had used lead paint on the toys.
Source: Ross D. Franklin/AP Images.

There are several types of production processes that manufacturers use. The type that is chosen depends on the company and what types of goods or services it produces. Some common production processes and techniques are listed in ■ **FIGURE 11.1**.

How are large quantities of goods produced? Producing large quantities of goods at a low cost is referred to as **mass production**. As noted earlier, the **assembly line** is a mass production process. Mass production relies on machines and automated assembly lines to produce goods that are identical to each other and adhere to certain standards of quality. The cost to run an assembly line is kept low because machines do most of the work, and the laborers don't need to be especially skilled to perform their repetitive tasks. Mass production cuts down on production time, allowing a large quantity of goods to be produced very quickly. Because machinery is the main component, the risk of human error is virtually eliminated. A major disadvantage, however, is that mass production is inflexible. After a production line is established, it is very difficult to change or alter the process if a change is required.

What production process is best when customization is desired? Mass customization is the production of goods or services tailored to meet customers' individual needs cost effectively. It ranges from bulk customization of industrial supplies, such as valves, switches, and instruments, to individual customization that is most often seen with clothing, shoes, glasses, and bicycles. For example, Cafepress and Zazzle enable users to place their own designs on clothing, books, and other accessories and to buy, share, or sell them in their own online shops. Blank Label allows customers to design their own shirts online for nearly the same price as a store-bought shirt. The benefit of this process is that Blank Label does not need to produce shirts of every size and style, thus incurring additional warehousing and shipping expenses. This is the same model that Dell Computers began in the 1990s. Rather than warehouse potentially unused parts that soon would be obsolete, Dell allowed customers to design their computers to the specifications that best met their needs. Now, most PC manufacturers offer online customization for their products.

How is mass customization achieved? A flexible manufacturing system (FMS) enables manufacturers to produce large quantities of customized products. Victory Motorcycles, a division of the off-road vehicle manufacturer Polaris, uses an FMS to create motorcycles that customers design online to their specific needs and tastes. In an FMS system, several machines are linked together by one central computer. All the machines in the system can process different part types simultaneously. Unlike a mass production system, an FMS can adapt to changes in schedules and product specifications.

Can mass customization be used in service industries? The technologies of mass customization have enabled many service-based organizations to meet the individual needs of their customers. Burger King is famous for its "Have It Your Way" method of production and associated advertising campaign, which, unlike McDonald's, allowed customers to "tweak" their hamburger toppings to meet their specific tastes.[10]

Most hotel chains offer a preference of bed size and perhaps room location, but the rest of the stay is pretty standard no matter which city or country you are in. But the Ritz Carlton trains its staff to record the unique habits, preferences, and dislikes of each guest, which they enter into a database used to further customize a guest's current stay and also make the person's next stay filled with personal touches. Each guest is greeted by name, and the hotel knows whether the person

Mass Production

- Machines and automated assembly lines

Mass Customization

- Customized mass production through flexible manufacturing systems

Lean Production

- Aimed to increase efficiency by eliminating waste along the production process

■ **FIGURE 11.1**
Common Production Processes and Techniques

CafePress uses mass customization to produce customized products.
Source: NetPhotos/Alamy.

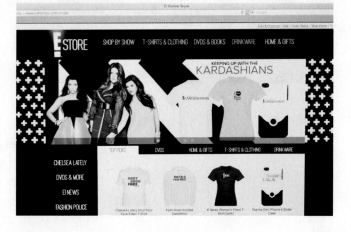

Victory Motorcycles uses an FMS to produce customer-designed made-to-order motorcycles.
Source: Michael Doolittle/Alamy

has a preference for feather or nonallergenic pillows and ens that the guest's favorite newspaper is placed at his or her door e morning. The results of this customized program have been a 23 cent increase in guest retention.[11]

What type of production focuses on efficiency? Lean produ is a set of principles concerned with reducing waste and impro the flow of processes. Eliminating overproduction, long wait t as products move through production, needless transportation cess inventory, superfluous motions, and redundant processes a aspects of lean production. Toyota first began using lean produ methods in the 1980s with great success. Although lean produ originally was used for manufacturing, it is also used in se industries, such as hospitals and restaurants.

Social Networking and Its Effect on Production

How has social networking impacted production? Not only does social n enable consumers to directly influence what companies develop and produce give instant feedback on whether their initiatives are worthwhile, it has also cr a ready-made distribution system for more creative consumers who want to "h their way." Using social media tools, such as blogs, Web videos, and podcasts, as as social networking sites, such as Facebook and Twitter, consumers can design own products and also have direct influence on what companies develop and duce. The website Trendwatching.com has coined this new process *customer-m* Although Blank Label is a relative newcomer to this growing genre of busine Adidas with its "mi Adidas" campaign and Converse's "Make One Yours" prog are proven examples that this design-your-own trend is part of our society.

Kristi and Yuan were committed to offering high-quality nutrition bars tha each customer's specific tastes and nutritional needs. They developed a website allowed their clients to select the type of bars that met their tastes and nutrit needs. Then Kristi and Yuan passed this information directly to the manufac which produced the customized product and shipped it directly to the client. Th of mass customization techniques enabled them to incorporate an ever-expandir ray of flavors, nutrients, and ingredients to satisfy customers from around the g

Operations Planning and Management pp. 304–311

Arthur Ridder is the operations manager for a furniture company in northern Washington. The company has enjoyed a great deal of success; its close proximity to natural resources and dependable suppliers, as well as a large employee base, has allowed it to produc large quantities of high-quality furniture. Shipping has bee efficient, as the factory is located three miles from a major highway and 20 miles from a port for international delivery

Due to the company's ongoing success, it is considering opening a new location in Europe to expand its internation presence. Arthur is considering a site near the Alps in Switzerland. Na resources are amazingly abundant there, but finding an adequate num of skilled employees may be difficult. Shipping and receiving are also concerns, as the area is not centrally located. What should Arthur do?

Source: Big_tau/Fotolia.

Operations management is the administration and planning of business operations to produce and distribute goods and services as efficiently as possible. Operations managers are focused on the big picture: the acquisition, development, and utilization of the resources needed to create and deliver goods and services successfully to the customer.

In this section, we'll look at some important operational issues that an operations manager must consider, such as figuring out how much production capacity will be needed to produce a product, finding the ideal location to make it, and determining how the facility will be organized.

Capacity Planning

How big should a facility be? Operation managers use production forecasts to help estimate the future demand for the company's products. These forecasts are drawn from past sales as well as current or anticipated sales orders, customer feedback, market research, and industry analyses.

Once a "best guess" for a firm's future demand is determined and the firm has decided which parts of the product it will make and which it will buy, the company's operations manager turns to the next step: capacity planning. **Capacity planning** is the process of determining how much of a product an organization can produce to meet its demand. Capacity planning requires balancing the maximum amount of product an organization is capable of producing and the quantity of the good or service demanded by its customers. The overall size of a facility, as well as efficient utilization of resources, dictates production capacity.

Capacity can be increased by introducing new technologies or equipment, increasing the number of workers or machines or improving the efficiency of existing workers or machines, or expanding a firm's production facilities. Conversely, capacity can be decreased by reducing the number of workers and machines.

Warehousing goods is also a key part of capacity planning. For example, most toy makers work throughout the year to produce toys, most of which are warehoused until the holiday season. Since services can't be stored as products can be in inventory, service firms often use tactics to manage their demand, which has a direct impact on capacity. For example, restaurants offer early-bird and after-hour specials to generate business in off-peak hours. Applebee's campaign of half-price appetizers after 9:00 P.M. increases demand in the after-dinner hours. In addition, capacity management for service businesses can include hiring new workers or retraining current workers so they have new skills.

Determining Where to Locate Facilities

Where do businesses decide where to locate their facilities? Where an organization locates its offices, factories, or retail outlets can have a significant

Tate Steel factories, located throughout the world, are situated near raw-materials sources and transportation facilities.
Source: Thomson Reuters.

Solar panel manufacturer SunPower provides green-collar jobs. Here a 150-acre solar installation uses panels to generate more electricity than conventional systems. This solar system delivers electric power to approximately 8,000 homes.
Source: Thomson Reuters.

effect on the firm's overall efficiency, profitability, and success. Beyond the cost and availability of a location, several other factors have to be looked at:

- **Proximity to the market.** Service businesses, such as restaurants, supermarkets, and retail operations, must choose their locations based on how convenient they are to their potential customers. A restaurant that is easily accessible to cars and pedestrians has an advantage over a restaurant tucked away in a remote part of town where few people visit. However, many businesses have found they can use e-commerce and social media to make their services more accessible and where they locate less of an issue. For example, the Internet has made the location decision less critical for education, banking, and other service businesses.

- **Proximity to raw materials.** To reduce their spoilage costs, manufacturing businesses try to locate close to the raw materials they need as well near transportation systems. Transportation costs are a major cost and can be as much as five times the cost of operating a production facility.[13] Tata Steel, headquartered in India, is one of the world's leading steelmakers. One factor that has contributed to Tata's success is that it has located it facilities in close proximity to raw-materials sources.[14] Tata secured the iron ore mines in India, and its overseas operations in Southeast Asia, Australia, and parts of Africa are focused on securing raw-materials sources at these locations.

- **Proximity to utilities.** Even if land were cheap, a company that is establishing a large facility, such as a plant or a warehouse, would be reluctant to situate it in a remote location that lacks utilities, such as electricity, natural gas, water, and telecommunications lines. The cost to establish this infrastructure if it didn't exist could be enormous.

- **Proximity to hazardous waste disposal.** Many businesses, as part of their day-to-day operations, generate large amounts of hazardous waste that must be disposed of in ways that comply with state, county, and municipal hazardous waste disposal guidelines. Even everyday materials, such as paint and cleaning fluids, are considered hazardous waste and must be disposed of properly.[15] The proper disposal of hazardous waste has ramifications on a business's location. Responsible organizations must be aware of the disposal options that are available in their areas.

In addition to disposing of hazardous wastes, companies are becoming increasingly more aware of ways to manage other forms of production waste and trash, such as returned defective, broken products and leftover scraps. Dealing with and managing returned products and material so as to add value to them is a process referred to as *reverse logistics*. BestBuy sells its returned defective products to Genco, a company that specializes in reverse logistics, which then finds buyers for the material. Patagonia recycles used fleece vests that customers return to the company into fiber used to make new vests.[16] In addition to adding value to waste, this process helps companies operate in an environmentally friendly way.

How does labor affect location decisions? The availability of labor and the right types affects where a company will locate as well. Companies need to hire employees to maintain their operations, but they also need to be aware of how the communities they locate in affect their ability to attract employees. Let's look at some of these factors:

- **Skilled labor.** Choosing a location for virtually any business requires finding an area with an abundance of workers who possess the necessary skills. California's famed Silicon Valley is a top hub for the tech industry's software and hardware manufacturing businesses because of its proximity to Stanford

University, its abundance of local engineers, and the area's history in developing technology.[17]

- **Affordable labor.** Seeking skilled workers is only part of the decision-making process. Many businesses need to find employees who are both highly skilled and affordable. India is the primary destination for these types of workers.[18] A company need not necessarily locate to India to hire these workers, though. Affordable, skilled labor has become more globally accessible through the use of the Internet and communications technologies. For example, many clinics and radiologists in the United States scan patients during the day and then transmit the scans to specialists in India, where they are analyzed overnight.

- **Living conditions.** Businesses can alter an area's living conditions either positively or negatively. A business brings opportunities to a community by creating jobs, and this can result in a higher standard of living. Conversely, a business can have negative effects on a community by exploiting workers, consuming limited resources, or increasing local traffic. Many businesses try to locate in areas where the quality of life is already high (for example, areas with good schools, pleasant weather, or low crime rates) to attract a better caliber of employees. Some social entrepreneurs might take it on themselves to locate their business in impoverished areas to revitalize them.

- **Tax incentives.** Environmentally aware politicians often try to attract green businesses to their communities precisely for their ability to rejuvenate economically depressed communities. Many U.S. state and local governments offer cash grants, tax credits, tax abatements, and other incentives to entice companies to locate to their areas. Pitt County, North Carolina, offers site and utility improvement grants, funds and services for employee screening, testing and training, and low-cost industrial revenue bonds for qualified new and existing manufacturing facilities in the area.

- **Laws and regulations.** To maintain a balance between business and community interests, governments have created many laws and regulations to protect individuals and the environment. Laws and regulations may vary by state or country; therefore, companies, as part of their location assessment process, must consider how any government intervention will affect the organization.

Facility Layouts

Why is facility layout important? Facility layout refers to the physical arrangement of resources and people in the production process and how they interact. The design of a facility's layout is important to maximize efficiency and depends greatly on the processes or tasks to be performed. It involves everything from the arrangement of cubicles in an office space to the position of robotic arms in an automobile manufacturing plant.

When planning facility layouts, operations managers must anticipate and plan for future changes in them, such as how they might be expanded or contracted as demand changes. Additionally, the facility layout should be in accordance with Occupational Safety and Health Administration guidelines to ensure worker safety.

How does facility layout affect production? A facility layout should be designed so that raw materials are handled efficiently to ensure a smooth flow of production and to maximize the efficiency of employee flow throughout the facility. The distance that a work-in-progress item must travel within a facility must also be taken into account. This is true not only for the production of goods but also in the production of services. For example, the layout of a fast-food restaurant should help the employees involved in the different parts of the operation work quickly an integrated fashion.

The layout of a fast-food restaurant helps employees prepare food and serve customers in an integrated fashion.
Source: David Levenson/Alamy.

Crayola Crayons are produced using a product layout, which is suitable for high-volume, standardized products.
Source: Dennis Lowe/KRT/Newscom.

What are the different types of facility layouts? Different manufacturing processes require different types of facility layouts. There are four common types: process layouts, product layouts, cellular layouts, and fixed position layouts:

- A **process layout** is used mostly to produce low-volume, or batches, of customized products. Cakes made on the reality show *Cake Boss* are produced in a process layout: Each cake is assembled according to specific customer orders. Although different processes are done in different work stations, the flow from one to the next is not necessarily uniform and instead varies from product to product. For example, some cakes may get baked, but other cakes, such as cheesecakes, may not be baked. Similarly, some cakes may get icing, whereas others may not, depending on what customers order.

- A **product layout** is used generally used for high-volume, standardized products made sequentially on an assembly line. Crayola Crayons are an example. Batches of crayons go through parallel processes sequentially: Wax is melted, colored, shaped into molds, and wrapped with paper, and then the individual crayons are assembled into boxes.

Both process and product layouts are organized by function. However, functional arrangements are not always efficient because production can stall if a problem occurs at one station. Workers are also likely to get bored doing repetitive tasks. To overcome the shortcomings of process and product layouts, some manufacturers have adopted cellular and fixed-position layouts:

- In a **cellular layout**, small teams of workers are grouped together in work stations and handle all aspects of the assembly of a product. Each station is equipped with the parts and tools necessary to produce a product from start to finish, and the worker moves through the work station as he or she conducts the assembly process.

- A **fixed-position layout** is used to manufacture large items, such as ships, airplanes, and modular homes. With a fixed-position layout, the product stays in one place, and the workers move around the product to complete its assembly.

Technology Used in Production Facilities

What is the role of technology in the production process? Up-to-date technologies can improve any or all aspects of the production process by increasing productivity and the quality and variety of products and reducing their costs. This in turn can affect the buying decisions of customers. Customers are more likely to buy a product that is not only low priced compared to other similar products but also of high quality and readily available in many varieties.

What has helped automate the production process? Humans are sometimes at a disadvantage when it comes to performing a task repetitively for many hours and with great precision and accuracy. This is where *industrial robots* come in. Not only can robots work around the clock tirelessly and with accuracy, but they can also work in potentially hazardous conditions, thereby protecting human workers from dangerous environments. The two biggest industries employing robot are the automotive industry, which uses robots to weld, paint, assemble, and handle various materials, and the household appliances industry, which uses robots to seal and paint appliances such as microwave ovens. Industrial robots may eliminate some production-related jobs, but the technology has also created many new jobs for technicians and engineers. Companies that can effectively apply robotic technology in their production processes are more likely to gain an economic advantage in the global marketplace.

How does technology improve the design process? **Computer-aided design** (CAD) refers to using a computer and software to create two-dimensional or three-dimensional computer models of parts or products. A product designer first translates the design into a geometric model for the CAD system to display. Once the data for the model are received, the CAD system provides the designer with tools and a flexible environment so the product can be modified in size or shape, viewed internally, and rotated on any axis. CAD also facilitates the testing of parts in simulated environments before they are manufactured. By programming a simple design change into a CAD system, a manufacturer can produce custom-designed products, such as clothing and cars, without incurring extra costs. CAD systems are used to design tools and other small products as well as houses, machinery, and commercial structures.

Robots play a big part in automobile manufacturing, but they are also used to weld, paint, assemble, package, inspect, and test many other types of products.
Source: Rainer Plendl/Shutterstock.

Some manufacturing processes that are more complicated, such as those for motor vehicles and airplanes, need more than one CAD program to design and incorporate all the different components. For example, the design of a ship may require one CAD application for the steel structure and another CAD program for the propeller. A disadvantage of this method is that it requires knowledge of all the different software applications used as well as how to integrate them in the end.

How does CAD information get incorporated into the manufacturing process? Once a design is approved, **computer-aided manufacturing** (CAM) uses the design data to control the machinery used in the manufacturing process. The integration of CAD and CAM systems with the various aspects of a production process is referred to as *simultaneous engineering*. Ford Motor Company's engine division, for example, successfully integrated all its production and design systems into one database that is accessed by employees and suppliers involved with design and production.[19] This type of facilitated communication is a huge benefit for firms with complex systems. One of the main disadvantages of using CAD/CAM systems is that they require considerable time and investment to set up and to learn the necessary software, hardware, communications, and integration processes.

Technology: Too Much of a Good Thing?

OFF THE MARK

In 1995, the new Denver International Airport boasted a fully automated baggage-handling system. The technology, however, turned out to be too much of a good thing. The system was designed to move luggage along an automated track between airport terminals and baggage claim areas, some of which were as far as a mile apart in the large airport. A centralized computer system would control the entire operation, eliminating the need for human baggage handlers to physically move bags from one point to another. But after 10 years of misplaced luggage, glitches in the system, and soaring maintenance costs, the error-prone system was finally shut down. In 2005, the only airline to ever use the system, United Airlines, went back to using baggage handlers to complete the tasks previously handled by the automated system. In a test run before the switch was made, human baggage handlers beat the automated system's error rate hands down. With the help of mobile devices, such as handheld scanners, United Airlines is now able to track luggage better than the automated system ever could.

CAD uses computer technology for the design of objects in two or three dimensions.
Source: Marzky Ragsac Jr/Fotolia.

Can an entire production facility be automated? Computer-integrated manufacturing (CIM) systems combine design and manufacturing functions with other automated functions, such as order taking, shipment, and billing, for the complete automation of a manufacturing plant. The printing company VistaPrint uses CIM not only to manufacture its products but also to help customers create and place orders for custom-designed business cards, brochures, and even T-shirts. Through the use of CIM, the company has expanded its business and is able to serve more customers while continuing to offer affordable prices.[20]

What effect has automation had on overall productivity? CAD, CAM, and CIM have dramatically improved the process of producing goods by reducing the time between design and manufacturing, thus making a significant impact on productivity. These systems have also increased the scope of automated machinery in the production process. Through the rapid pace of technological advancement, CAD, CAM, and CIM systems are not limited to large mass production facilities; they are entering smaller companies as well.

3D Printing: An Industrial Revolution?

Who would have thought that the simple process of printing could potentially change the manufacturing industry? Thanks to a convergence of ingenious technologies, a new twist on printing has emerged: 3D printing. A 3D printer makes objects from a digital file with a process that is similar to inkjet printing. However, the objects are made from layers of resilient, durable plastic. One the printing is complete, you have a plastic object you can hold in your hand. The objects can be complex in design, such as a toy car with movable wheels and different-colored parts. The potential of these 3D printers is that they allow for the mass customization of items specific to an individual's wants and needs in virtually any environment: at home, at work, or on a remote island. Moreover, since a 3D machine can be purchased for as little as about $1,000 (and will undoubtedly become even more affordable over time), 3D printing may change outsourcing decisions. For example, it's possible that manufacturing of small parts and objects may return to the United States and may even be done in people's homes rather than in large facilities. 3D printers also allow prototypes of products to be created much more quickly, thereby speeding up the research-and-development process for new products. What do you think? Could 3D printing change the world?

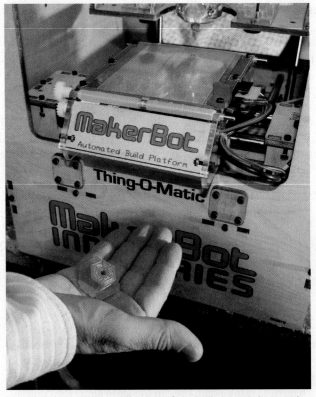

The Thing-O-Matic is a 3D printer from MakerBot Industries that enables users to produce small plastic objects at home as simply as printing from an inkjet printer.
Source: James Emmett/Associated Newspapers/Alamy.

Given what you know now about operations management, capacity planning, and locating and laying out facilities, do you think Switzerland is the best location for Arthur Ridder's furniture company? What type of facility layout should the operation use? What type of technology and equipment?

Operations Control pp. 311–317

Source: Purestock/Getty Images.

Jeanette Pae could hardly stop her daughter, Rihanna, from crying or stop her own self from shaking after her daughter fell out of her high chair. The activity tray of the high chair unexpectedly separated from the rest of the chair, and Rihanna tumbled out onto the tile kitchen floor, hitting her head and cutting her lip.

Shortly after the incident, Jeanette received a product recall notice from the manufacturer. Jeanette and her family were no strangers to recalls. Recently, she had to throw away several pounds of ground meat because of E. coli contamination, and the cherished family Toyota was recalled. What was going on? What controls are used in the production process to ensure that a product is produced on time and is of high quality? ■

Inventory management is a factor in profitability but also in customer satisfaction to ensure that the product or service is delivered on time. The quality of a product is best determined and controlled at every step of the production process. In this section, we'll look at some important areas of control in the production process, beginning with key project management and scheduling techniques.

Controlling the Production Process

How does scheduling shape the production process? When it comes to production, **scheduling** refers to the efficient organization of equipment, facilities, labor, and materials. There are two different types of scheduling: *forward* and *backward*. With *forward scheduling*, you start with the date that materials are available, create the most efficient production schedule, and then determine a shipping date based on that schedule. *Backward scheduling* is the exact opposite: you are given a shipping or due date, and you need to determine the start date and the most efficient production schedule based on when everything must be finished.

What tools are available to help with scheduling? Two major components go into making an effective schedule: loading and sequencing. *Loading* is assigning a job to a specific machine or an entire work center. *Sequencing* is assigning the order in which jobs are processed. Software systems are used to put together a cohesive schedule of loading and sequencing to ensure that all the right tools are working on the right jobs at the right times. But no matter how complex the system, all configurations are just estimates based on the data input into the system and the rules it uses. Having a person oversee scheduling is still invaluable because that individual can bring experience and judgment that cannot be programmed into a computer.

How are the individual tasks of a process tracked? One method for keeping tabs on the progress of a given project is a **Gantt chart**, a tool developed by Henry Gantt in the 1920s. A Gantt chart is formatted similarly to a horizontal bar graph. It is used to lay out each project task, the order in which each task must be completed, and how long each task should take.

■ **FIGURE 11.2** shows an example of a Gantt chart for a remodeling project. Originally used for large-scale construction projects, such as building the Hoover Dam in the 1930s, Gantt charts are used to manage a variety of both large-scale and small-scale projects. At any point in the process, project managers and manufacturers can see at a glance which tasks have been completed,

■ FIGURE 11.2
Sample Gantt Chart

Remodeling Project

Remodeling Project Job No.: 980015.05	Jul '12			Aug '12				Sep '12					Oct '12	
	15	22	29	5	12	19	26	2	9	16	23	30	7	14
Project Summary														
Soft Demo														
Soft Demo-Structural														
Structural Steel-Fab														
Framing-Rough														
Skylights														
Roof Curbs & Patch														
Electrical-Rough/Finish														
Overhead Doors														
Inspection-Structural Rebar														
Structural Concrete-Pour														
Service/Repair Elevator														
Plumbing Rough														
Data/Phone Cabling														
Structural Steel-Install														
T-bar Grid Repair														
Inspection-Walls														
Inspection-Drywall Screw														
Mud & Tape														
Mezzanine Demo														

which tasks are in the process of being completed, and which tasks have yet to begin. In addition, a Gantt chart helps to identify whether tasks were completed on schedule.

What is a PERT chart? The **program evaluation and review technique** (PERT) maps out the steps involved in a project, differentiating tasks that must be completed in a certain order from tasks that may be completed simultaneously. A PERT chart is like a flowchart (see **■ FIGURE 11.3**) and to a greater extent emphasizes the relationships between tasks than the time line of the tasks.

■ FIGURE 11.3
Sample PERT Chart

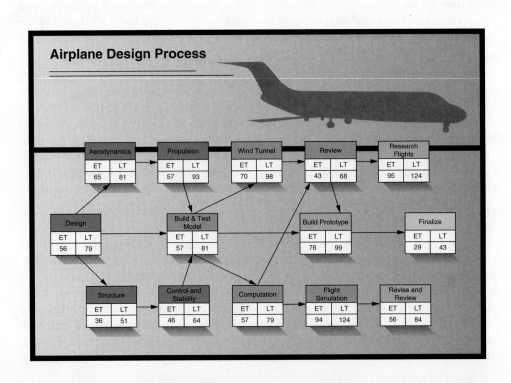

A PERT chart identifies the *critical path*, or the path of sequential tasks that will take the most time to complete. This helps managers determine an overall time line for completing a project or, from a manufacturing standpoint, producing a particular good or service. However, because delays can cause the critical path in a project to change, PERT charts are limited in their ability to predict project completion times.

Purchasing and Inventory Control

How are materials used in the production process acquired? Purchasing is the task of acquiring the materials and services needed in the production process. Production managers need to find reliable suppliers who can provide high-quality resources at the best price. The Internet has made purchasing a much more competitive process. Just like you might use the Internet to search for the best price before buying a particular product, purchasing managers can compare prices and services between suppliers online before embarking in a service agreement.

How does a company maintain inventory control? Inventory control includes the receiving, storing, handling, and tracking of everything in a company's stock. There are four main types of stock: raw materials, unfinished products, finished products, and consumables (such as pens and paper), from raw materials to finished products. Inventory often makes up a large portion of a business's expenses. Therefore, maintaining records on each type of stock is a way to keep it from being wasted and costs low while ensuring that all necessary materials are in stock and stored in the proper places. Ensuring the firm's adequate supply of finished products or other types of stock is further complicated when customer demand is variable. Proper inventory management also helps a company manage products with specific shelf lives that could deteriorate as well as products that have become obsolete. Good inventory management also helps prevent the pilferage (theft) of inventory.

What methods are used to manage inventory? Inventory can be managed in a number of different ways. No single method works best for every business, and sometimes multiple methods are used to manage different types of inventory. Factors such as the size of a business, the amount of inventory it needs and its proximity to suppliers, the amount of storage space available for the inventory, and its perishability will all affect which inventory control method will work best:

- The least complicated way to manage inventory is to simply visually assess it. When the supply is low, it's time to reorder. This method works really well for smaller companies or companies that don't maintain large amounts of stock.

- When an accurate count is necessary, a *stock book solution* may be the best solution: The stock on hand is tallied in a book along with the stock that has been ordered and the stock that has been sold.

- A less complicated management system is a *reserve stock system*. With this method, stock is set aside in reserve so that it cannot be used. The company goes through its inventory as it regularly would, and when it has to dip into the reserve stock, it knows it is time to reorder that item. It is important for managers to keep in mind when using this system that however much stock is in reserve should be enough to last the length of time it takes to resupply it.[21]

What inventory system is most efficient for large companies? The inventory management systems just described can work well for smaller businesses. However, larger businesses often require more efficient inventory management systems, such as just-in-time inventory management. With **just-in-time (JIT) inventory management**, a firm maintains the smallest amount of inventory possible, with inventory being ordered as it is actually needed. With JIT, rarely is inventory

With bar codes and RFID tags, inventory is monitored electronically.
Source: Mr.Zach/Shutterstock.

sitting around without a specific purpose. Dell Computers made its mark in the PC manufacturing industry by embracing JIT inventory control. Because the company adopted a build-to-order system, the huge expense of holding in inventory components that may not be used and subsequently become obsolete and useless was reduced. Over a four-year period after adopting this system, Dell's revenues grew from $2 billion to $16 billion.[22] Storing fewer items for shorter periods of time will also reduce a firm's storage costs.

JIT systems are not without their drawbacks. To work properly, a company must have a very good relationship with its suppliers to ensure that appropriate quantities of the right goods arrive on time and are delivered to where they are needed.

How is technology used to streamline the control of inventory? Many organizations rely on computerized inventory systems that utilize bar codes or **radio frequency identification** (RFID) tags attached to products. Both bar codes and RFID tags store all the specific information for each item, such as its cost, stock number, and storage location. The tags are electronically scanned as the items come into and go out of a firm's facilities or the facilities of the firm's supply chain partners. Using these systems, items in inventory can be scanned when they are used or sold, and the computer continuously updates the information for each item as the quantities of it change. Computerized inventory makes it easier to analyze the quantitative factors of managing stock, such as how quickly each item is sold, how much really needs to be held in inventory at one time, and how often inventory is restocked.

What is materials requirement planning? More appropriate to the production side of inventory management is **materials requirement planning** (MRP), a computer-based program used for inventory control and production planning. When an order is made, the specifics of that order are input into the MRP system. It uses previous manufacturing data to break the job into components, then the MRP system determines which parts will be needed to complete the job and compares these findings to current inventory. Based on this information, the MRP highlights what parts need to be obtained, either through production or a supplier, as well as when the parts will be needed. Knowing these estimates helps determine if a firm has a shortage of the parts and labor needed for the project before it even starts.

There are many limitations to MRP, the biggest being that it is only as effective as its data. So if the data are not well maintained, the estimates that it provides will become increasingly useless. Another limitation to MRP is its scope: It focuses only on the management of needed component parts in the manufacturing processes of a company and not in any other business areas.

What is enterprise resource planning? One way around the limitations of MRP is to use **enterprise resource planning** (ERP).[23] Like MRP systems, ERP systems are used to monitor a firm's inventory and process schedules but can integrate these functions with other aspects of the business, such as a firm's finance, marketing, and human resources functions. A typical ERP system consolidates information into a central database, and different types of information are accessible to different types of functional areas of a firm. Information can be shared across departments, which can streamline work flows and improve the productivity of employees. Various departments of an organization can work together without worrying if their software is compatible. Oracle, SAP, and Microsoft are companies that make ERP systems.

Quality Management

Has quality control always been part of the operations control process? The techniques, activities, and processes used to guarantee that a certain good or service meets a specified level of quality is referred to as **quality control**. In the past, most firms had separate quality control departments that would inspect and test products for flaws at the *end* of the process after products had been manufactured.

But this system creates several problems. For one, it is expensive in terms of time and labor. Because inspection is performed by outside people instead of by the workers making the product, each inspector can pass or fail a product using his or her own standards and procedures. Moreover, if not inspected until after they are finished, products with defects have to be scrapped or completely reworked, and this can be costly.

What methods are used to improve quality? Merely controlling for quality by monitoring employees and inspecting products after they are finished is like a doctor treating the symptoms of an illness as opposed to remedying it. So, since the 1980s, firms have been focusing on building quality into every step of the production process instead of scrapping products or fixing them after they are produced. Building "total quality" into a product at every stage of production was fully embraced by U.S. companies only after Japanese manufacturers had done so and strengthened their presence in the global market.[24] The market for cars is an example. Japanese models gained a reputation for quality that American car manufacturers were finding hard to compete with. The Japanese produced exports not only at higher levels of quality but also at lower prices. In response, and to remain competitive, companies in the United States began to demand that everyone involved in the production process, including managers, customers, employees, and suppliers, adopt a **total quality management (TQM)** approach.

How is TQM carried out? TQM involves making ongoing improvements to products, services, and processes. This can be accomplished by undertaking a plan-do-check-act (PDCA) cycle, created by American statistician W. Edwards Deming (see ■ **FIGURE 11.4**).[25] Using the PDCA cycle, organizations first formulate a plan to reduce potential errors, carry out the plan on a small scale, check the outcome and effectiveness of the change, and then implement the plan on a larger scale while monitoring the results continually.

What other tools are used to implement TQM? **Statistical quality control (SQC)** describes the set of statistical tools used to analyze each stage of the production process to ensure that quality standards are being met. **Statistical process control (SPC)** is one of the tools used with SQC. With SPC, random samples of products are checked at each phase of production to see if there are any variations that need to be corrected. If there is, this signals to managers that something is wrong with that phase of the production process and must be corrected.

■ **FIGURE 11.4**
Total Quality management uses the plan-do-check-act methodology.

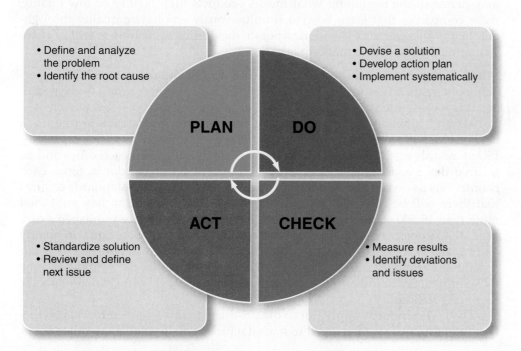

- Define and analyze the problem
- Identify the root cause

- Devise a solution
- Develop action plan
- Implement systematically

PLAN   **DO**

ACT   **CHECK**

- Standardize solution
- Review and define next issue

- Measure results
- Identify deviations and issues

The Baldrige Awards

The Malcolm Baldrige National Quality Awards recognize public and private U.S. organizations for their performance excellence. The awards are named for Malcolm Baldrige, the U.S. secretary of commerce during the Reagan administration, and were established in 1987. They are the only award of the kind given by the president of the United States.

To be eligible for a Baldrige Award, an organization has to fit into at least one of six sectors: education, manufacturing, service, small business, health care, and nonprofit. The award does not focus on a particular product or service; rather, its focus is on overall organizational quality. To receive a Baldrige Award, an organization must exemplify role model management that focuses on continuous improvement in delivering quality products and/or services, an organization that demonstrates efficient and effective operations, and a demonstrated means of engaging and responding to customers and other stakeholders.

The most recent Baldrige Award recipients are the Pewaukee School District for education and the Baylor Regional Medical Center and Sutter Davis Hospital for health care. There have been six repeat winners of the award: MESA Products Inc. for small business; North Mississippi Health Services for health care; Solectron Corp. for manufacturing; Sunny Fresh Foods, Inc., for small business and manufacturing; Texas Nameplate Company, Inc., for small business; and the Ritz-Carlton Hotel Co. for service.

Another common quality control method is **Six Sigma**, a method that seeks to virtually eliminate defects by implementing a quality focus in every aspect of the organization. Six Sigma strives for *continuous improvement*. Employees are trained in the Six Sigma methodologies and are responsible for implementing any necessary changes in the production process to ensure that total quality is met. A company with Six Sigma quality produces at a low defect rate of just 3.4 defects per 1 million opportunities. Motorola managed to achieve Six Sigma quality in 1992 after adopting continuous quality improvement methods in the 1980s.[26] Other large corporations, such as GE and Honeywell, followed suit.

How does TQM cater to the customer? It's not enough to simply implement quality management tools. A significant aspect of TQM is catering to customers' needs and desires. SGL Carbon, a manufacturer of graphite specialties, adheres to a TQM approach by giving its customers the final say in determining whether a product meets their requirements of high-quality standards. Although firms may define in the beginning what makes products high quality or low quality, those companies that learn how to simultaneously emphasize quality throughout the production process and incorporate the desires of customers will be more competitive in the global marketplace.

What is the International Organization for Standardization? The International Organization for Standardization (ISO) is an organization dedicated to creating worldwide standards of quality for goods and services. ISO was created in 1947 and is headquartered in Geneva, Switzerland. As barriers to free trade between markets began to be removed among the European countries especially, ISO standards enabled markets and companies to trade with each other and be assured that goods and services meet a consistent set of standards. Since each country has its own set of standards, companies adopting ISO standards ensures that there will be consistency across borders. The organization has published more than 19,500 standards, and over 1,000 new standards are published every year.[27] ISO's objective is to develop production processes that are equal in quality and capability in all participating countries.[28] More than 161 countries have adopted these standards, and thousands of companies require their products to be ISO certified. Some industries have even developed their own industry-specific set of ISO standards.

The ISO standards apply not to the products themselves but to the production methods and systems used to manufacture them, as well as to other areas, such as communication within the company and leadership. Such a standardized system is necessary to avoid trying to comply with various conflicting systems. Most of the standards generated by the ISO are product specific, but there are two "generic" standards that can be applied to any organization regardless of size, product/service, sector, or type of business enterprise. These standards are ISO 9001 and ISO 14001. **ISO 9001** implements a quality management system, and **ISO 14001** implements an environmental management system.

What is the ISO certification process? Certification is usually done by a third-party registrar. This registrar conducts an assessment of a company's quality assurance manuals and practices. First, a preliminary assessment is conducted during which the registrar reviews the documents that outline a company's standards and processes. If the manual and other printed documents pass the review, a company can proceed with the rest of the assessment. If the registrar finds errors in these documents, further review is delayed until the mistakes are corrected. During the formal assessment, the registrar reviews the corrected documents and interviews employees and administrators in the company. The goal of this part of the assessment is to ensure that written policies and procedures are being implemented in the company's production methods. Finally, the registrar issues an audit report that summarizes the results of the assessment and lists any areas that need improvement. If corrections are required at this stage, the company can make them and document them in a report to the registrar. After satisfactory corrections have been made, the registrar can then award certification to the company. Once it has earned certification, the company can put the ISO seal on its promotional materials and its letterhead.

After certification, the registrar returns to the company twice a year to make sure the company is still in compliance with ISO standards. These spot checks are conducted without advance warning, and the registrar focuses on areas that were notably weak during the initial assessment. Every three years, the registrar will complete another assessment and issue a new audit report. The company must also establish an internal auditing program that is responsible for keeping ISO standards in practice.

What are the benefits of ISO certification? Companies that have successfully gone through the ISO certification process have indicated significant benefits, including improved customer satisfaction and international recognition. More tangible benefits include increased efficiency, procedural consistency, and a factual approach to decision making, all of which are due to the guidelines and training that need to be established to obtain certification. Companies with ISO certification also enjoy marketing advantages because they can now easily publicize that their company has reached this quality standard to attract new and maintain existing customers. As a result, companies have reported increased revenue due to improved financial performance and increased productivity and a boost in customer satisfaction. After implementing ISO 14001 environmental standards, Ford Motor Company reduced its water consumption by nearly 1 million gallons per day and saved over $65,000 in electricity costs by no longer using fluorescent lightbulbs. The company also began to recycle paint waste, thus reducing disposed paint sludge, and began to use reusable plastic or metal containers instead of cardboard and plywood boxes.[29]

It's no surprise that Jeanette Pae's confidence in the quality of her daughter's high chair was shaken. The loss of consumer confidence in a company to produce quality products is costly. Lost sales result in reduced revenues, but the process needed to repair a company's reputation and earn back the customer's respect can be even more expensive. Mattel, Merck, and Dell each experienced the repercussions of poor quality management, even though some of the problems were due to supplier error. Putting the focus on quality management at the beginning of the production process and adopting a quality orientation throughout the company can ensure that a consistent product is produced.

Source: Iain Masterton/Alamy.

Suppliers and Supply Chain Management pp. 317–319

The ink was barely dry on the lease as Sylvia Ackerman drove to IKEA to pick out furniture for her new apartment. Sylvia loves the Swedish furniture manufacturer because of the simple lines and clean designs of its products. In addition, because she has only herself to rely on, she can move her purchases into her apartment without much help from others because the products are packaged in flat boxes. Sylvia also loves the challenge of assembling the products herself. More important, Sylvia knows that it is hard to beat IKEA pricing; she will always get quality products at a low cost. ■

What sets IKEA, the Swedish home products retailer, apart from other furniture companies is the packaging and storage of its products. Most of the furniture it produces is shipped in flat boxes that can be economically transported and then assembled at the consumer's home. The condensed packaging minimizes shipping and storage costs, in turn lowering the retail cost of IKEA products. The company has many factories worldwide and is constantly opening new locations to supply its growing number of franchised stores.

How does a company decide which suppliers to use? Most companies don't make all of the components they use in their goods and services. Instead, they contract with other companies to supply these components. Establishing a business relationship with a supplier is like entering into a partnership. To find suppliers that truly fit its requirements, a firm must first clearly define and understand its needs relative to its competitive strategy. Cost is always a factor, but it should never be the sole factor. For example, one supplier might offer to manufacture a part for significantly less but of such poor quality that later repairs or recalls would end up costing a company more than the higher cost of producing quality parts. As a result, the firm's reputation would also be affected. This is particularly problematic if the firm is attempting to differentiate itself from the competition by offering higher-quality products.

The challenge for operations managers is in finding the best suppliers that offer optimal solutions for your firm's production needs. Some companies, such as Patagonia, the activewear clothing company, chooses and manages its supply chain partners to ensure that each step of the supply chain—from crop to finished garment—reflects Patagonia's commitment to be as environmentally conscious and conservative as possible. The company publishes articles about its supply chain process, called "The Footprint Chronicles," on its website (www.patagonia.com/us/footprint).

A vast collection of resources is available to help businesses connect with suppliers. These resources include the Better Business Bureau, local chambers of commerce, exhibitions, trade magazines, the Internet, and old-fashioned recommendations from friends and business acquaintances. In addition, as explained earlier, to find good, reliable suppliers at home and abroad, many companies look for supply chain partners certified by the ISO.

What is a supply chain? Virtually every product that reaches an end user, whether or not it's completely manufactured in-house, is derived from an accumulation of efforts from multiple organizations around the globe. A **supply chain** consists of all of the suppliers, business partners, and service providers, as well as sourced manufacturers, distributors, retailers, and transporters, that take part in the producing a product and delivering it to the customer. The supply chain also includes all the major departments within an organization. And, of course, at the end of the supply chain is the customer.

Companies acquire raw materials from global vendors to be used in their factories located in different continents. The finished goods then pass through different distribution networks involving exports to different countries or local markets, warehouses, distributors, and retailers before finally reaching the end customer. The information and communication systems needed to coordinate these activities are also a significant part of the supply chain system. The proliferation of new telecommunications and computer technology has made instantaneous communications a reality. Such information systems can link together suppliers, manufacturers, distributors, retail outlets, and, ultimately, customers, regardless of location.

A supply chain is fluid and constantly changing, and demands great communication and coordination between all involved parties to achieve the greatest efficiencies. Supply chains are a part of every business—service, manufacturing, profit, and not-for-profit.

Why is supply chain management important? **Supply chain management** is the management of activities from all organizations involved in the production process. The goal of supply chain management is to maximize value and achieve a sustainable competitive advantage. Moreover, supply chain management helps companies reduce their carbon footprints by critically looking at each component of the supply chain (see ■ **FIGURE 11.5**). Until recently, companies didn't consider the chain of activities that ultimately delivered their product to the final customer. The chain is as strong as its weakest link. A poor relationship within any link of the supply chain can have disastrous consequences for all other supply chain members.

Supply chain management is important to improving efficiencies not only within the organization but also among all the components of the production and distribution process. In addition, companies are seeking ways to strengthen their global presence by positioning inventories so products are available when customers want them, regardless of location, in the right quantity for the right price. This can happen only if all components along the supply chain are working together. The partnering in manufacturing and design with other companies involved along the supply chain has increased the need for better sharing of product information and collaborative product development. Companies like IKEA have been forced to become global enterprises as they seek the lowest-cost suppliers, making the supply chain a more complicated process and ripe for inefficiencies if not managed well.

Is supply chain management only for manufacturing companies? Supply chains also exist in service organizations. The goal is the same for service organizations: to maximize value in the delivery process to achieve a competitive advantage; however, instead of managing "things," supply chain management for service organizations (sometimes referred to as service chain management) manages the time and actions of the labor force required to perform the service. Supply chain management also measures and forecasts the responses and needs of the customer. In addition, it involves planning, scheduling, workforce management, and enterprise resource planning. Finally, supply chain management focuses on establishing strong relationships with customers through enhanced communication technologies.

In an effort to remain competitive and to keep their retail prices low without sacrificing quality or customer service, IKEA looked for opportunities to improve operational efficiencies. To achieve cost reduction, quality, and customer satisfaction, IKEA focused on its supply chain management, from product design phase through distribution.[31] With stores and franchise operations, warehouses, and suppliers in all major regions of the world, IKEA's supply chain has a global spread.

■ **FIGURE 11.5**
As companies try to reduce their carbon footprints, they need to take a closer look at each component of the supply chain.

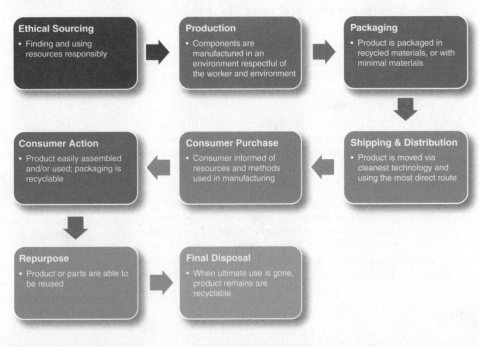

Summary

1 How is manufacturing and production important to the U.S. economy and to global economies? (pp. 299–301)

- **Production** (p. 299) is the process of getting a good or a service to the customer; it is a series of related activities, with value being added at each stage. Companies are in business to provide a service or a good to consumers. The more efficiently a company can produce and deliver the product or the service, the greater the profit it will generate.

- Although the U.S. manufacturing industry has been declining over the years, it still generates a major portion of the U.S. GDP. Moreover, manufacturing uses services and commodities as inputs, so manufacturing is actually responsible for a bigger share of total output.

- The service industry is very important to the U.S. economy and accounts for nearly 75 percent of the U.S. GDP and about 80 percent of jobs. Service businesses range from small start-ups and home-based businesses to large corporations that are represented on the DJIA.

- Despite the push to outsource and offshore jobs and manufacturing to low-cost locations, the U.S. manufacturing industry is still globally important. The United States is still the leading industrial power in the world. Even though the nation doesn't manufacture as many low-dollar products as it used to, the nation continues to manufacture a lot of high-dollar products and is the world's third-largest exporter of goods and services.

2 What is production management, and what production processes are used by businesses? (pp. 301–304)

- **Production management** (p. 302) refers to the planning, implementation, and control measures used to convert resources into finished products. These activities are similar to those in operations management but are more focused on the product.

- When starting the production process, one of the first decisions that operations managers make is what needs to be manufactured and what needs to be purchased from outside suppliers. This is commonly called a **make-or-buy decision** (p. 302).

- **Mass production** (p. 303) is the method of producing large quantities of goods at a low cost. The benefits of mass production include low cost, decreased production time, and virtually no human error due to the reliance on machinery. A major disadvantage is that mass production is inflexible, making it difficult to alter the process if an unexpected problem occurs.

- **Mass customization** (p. 303) is the production of goods or services tailored to cost-effectively meet customers' individual needs. Mass customization is achieved with a **flexible manufacturing system (FMS)** (p. 303)—a system in which machines are programmed to process different part types simultaneously—allowing a manufacturer to mass-produce customized products. The primary benefit of an FMS is that it provides the flexibility to make products with many slight variations. A challenge of an FMS is that it is not well suited for goods that are in high demand.

- **Lean production** (p. 304) is a set of principles concerned with reducing waste and improving flow. The basic tenet of lean production is to do more with less through the elimination of wasteful overproduction, unnecessary wait time, needless transportation, excess inventory, superfluous motion, redundant overprocessing, and careless defective units.

3 What is operations management, and what is important in determining a facility's location and layout? (pp. 304–308)

- **Operations management** (p. 305) consists of managing the activities and processes to produce and distribute products and services. Operations management includes how the facility should be organized, what supplies to purchase, what materials and inventory to keep on hand, and how quality is measured and controlled.

- When determining a location for a facility, companies consider their proximity to market, the cost of transporting raw materials, the presence of highways and other transportation systems, and utilities, hazardous waste disposal, labor availability, living conditions, and laws and regulations.

- **Facility layout** (p. 307) refers to the physical arrangement of resources and people in the production process and how they interact. The design of a facility's layout is important to maximize efficiency and satisfy employees' needs.

- Although operations management has been traditionally associated with manufacturing goods, many of the concepts also apply to the service industry.

4 What types of technology are used in production facilities? (pp. 308–311)

- Robots offer consistency in reducing production costs, raising productivity, and producing high-quality products.

- **Computer-aided design (CAD)** (p. 309), **computer-aided manufacturing (CAM)** (p. 309), and **computer-integrated manufacturing (CIM)** (p. 310) have dramatically improved the process of producing goods by reducing the time between design and manufacturing, thus making a significant impact on productivity. These systems have also increased the scope of automated machinery in the production process.

- The social networking structure of the Internet, along with hardware and software tools, has created a ready-made distribution system for more creative consumers who want to "have it their way." Beyond design, social media capabilities enable consumers to directly influence what companies develop and produce as well as to give instant feedback on whether their initiatives are worthwhile.

5 How are operations controlled and quality standards achieved in a firm? (pp. 311–317)

- Effective **scheduling** (p. 311) can help managers control the production process. Gantt and PERT charts are scheduling tools to ensure that all the right tools are working on the right jobs at the right times.
- **Purchasing** (p. 313) is the task of acquiring the materials and services needed in the production process. In doing so, production managers must find reliable suppliers who can provide high-quality resources at the best price.
- **Inventory control** (p. 313) includes the receiving, storing, handling, and tracking of everything in a company's stock, from raw materials to finished products. A **just-in-time (JIT) inventory control** (p. 313) system keeps the smallest amount of inventory on hand as possible, and everything else that is needed is ordered so that it arrives when it is needed.

- **Quality control** (p. 314) is the use of techniques, activities, and processes to guarantee that a certain good or service meets a specified level of quality.
- **Total quality management (TQM)** (p. 315) involves every factor in producing high-quality goods—management, customers, employees, and suppliers. At any point, employees and leaders are aiming to produce high quality.
- The ISO has created worldwide standards of quality for goods and services. ISO standards apply not to the products themselves but to the production methods and systems used to manufacture them as well as to other areas, such as communication within a company and leadership.

6 What is supply chain management, and how does it help companies create and deliver their goods and services more effectively? (pp. 317–319)

- **Supply chain management** (p. 319) is the management of activities from all organizations involved in the production process. The goal of supply chain management is to maximize value and achieve a sustainable competitive advantage. Supply chain management is important to improve efficiencies not only within the organization but also among all the components of the production and distribution process.
- A **supply chain** (p. 318) is made up of information and communication systems that work together to coordinate the path of the product and its components from raw material to finished product delivered to the consumer.

Key Terms

MyBizLab

Go to **mybizlab.com** to complete the problems marked with this icon .

Self Test

Multiple Choice *You can find the answers on the last page of this book.*

11-1 **Capacity planning refers to**
- a. how much inventory can be warehoused.
- b. the potential output of a robot.
- c. how much product an organization is capable of producing.
- d. how many workers can fit in a facility.

11-2 **Mass customization is achieved by using which type of system?**
- a. Flexible manufacturing system
- b. Lean production
- c. Forward processing
- d. Backward processing

11-3 **Which production process strives to reduce waste and improve production flow?**
- a. Mass customization
- b. Mass production
- c. Lean production
- d. Assembly line production

11-4 **If the Ford Motor Company wants to understand the aerodynamics of a new auto body, which of the following would be used to create a virtual three-dimensional model of the auto body?**
- a. CAD
- b. Simultaneous engineering
- c. CIM
- d. Robotics

11-5 **Which of the following is a set of environmental quality standards that can be applied to any organization?**
- a. Six Sigma
- b. ISO 14001
- c. ISO 9001
- d. TQM

11-6 **An inventory system that keeps the smallest amount of inventory on hand is called**
- a. a just-in-time system.
- b. radio frequency tagging.
- c. materials requirement planning.
- d. enterprise resource planning.

11-7 **Which feature distinguishes a PERT chart from a Gantt chart?**
- a. A PERT chart creates a time line of production tasks.
- b. A PERT chart creates a work flow for production equipment.
- c. A PERT chart identifies the critical path of tasks in a project.
- d. A PERT chart predicts the completion time of a project.

11-8 **Radio frequency identification is used to**
- a. keep track of the status and quantity of each inventory item.
- b. keep track of the customer base for a product in the store.
- c. stay in touch with other workers in a factory.
- d. keep track of natural resources as they ship to the factory.

11-9 **Which type of facility layout would be best used for the production of custom-designed bicycles?**
- a. Product layout
- c. Cellular layout
- b. Process layout
- d. Fixed position layout

11-10 **TQM is geared toward**
- a. producing the largest quantity of goods in the time allotted.
- b. reducing errors throughout the production process.
- c. eliminating humans from the workplace.
- d. meeting government standards for emissions.

True/False *You can find the answers on the last page of this book.*

11-11 **Robots can work around the clock with good accuracy and in potentially hazardous conditions.**
☐ True or ☐ False

11-12 **CAD refers to using a computer and software to create two- or three-dimensional models of parts or devices.**
☐ True or ☐ False

11-13 **Supply chain management refers to the process of delivering the supplies necessary for manufacturing.**
☐ True or ☐ False

11-14 **The make-or-buy decision comes at the end of the production process if a product has not turned out as planned.**
☐ True or ☐ False

11-15 **Because the United States is more of a service-based economy, manufacturing is not a contributor to the GDP.**
☐ True or ☐ False

Critical Thinking Questions

11-16 Supply chain management is the management of activities from all organizations involved in producing and delivering a good or service. Describe the supply chain that delivers education at your college. What internal and external components does it involve? What improvements might be made?

11-17 Providing quality customer service is an important factor in any service organization, yet we often have to wait extended periods of time to be seen by a doctor or have had bad service at a restaurant, for example. Think about a time when you had a bad experience from a service provider. Describe the experience and then list some suggestions as to improving the service.

11-18 A sports equipment company is known for a special grip on its tennis rackets that is imported from South America. The cost of shipping these grips has grown steadily more expensive, and the business would like to produce the grips in-house. What factors does the business need to consider before adding another step to the production process?

Team Time

TO OUTSOURCE OR NOT TO OUTSOURCE . . . THAT IS THE QUESTION

Divide into two teams to represent both sides of the issue:

a. One group thinks the company should make the component.

b. One group thinks the company should outsource the component.

Scenario

The Grindstone Supply Company of New Jersey is attempting to expand its manufacturing of large wall clocks. In years past, the company has outsourced the manufacturing of clock springs to a company in Nebraska. This has been cost effective in the past, but now that demand for the springs has increased, Grindstone is considering manufacturing the springs in-house. Although the cost of producing the springs in-house is lower, it is unclear whether it will be profitable in the long run, as the manufacturing process will change greatly. New machines for the production of springs will be needed, as the factory works exclusively in wood and plastic. With the new machines comes the need for new technicians to monitor and service them. Should the Grindstone Supply Company alter its manufacturing process to include the production of clock springs, or should it continue outsourcing to Nebraska as it has in the past? What factors contribute to this decision? Will this be more profitable in the long run? How will the decision affect employee morale and relations?

Process

Step 1. Record your ideas and opinions about the issue presented in the scenario. Be sure to consider the issue from your assigned perspective.

Step 2. Meet as a team and review the issue from both perspectives. Discuss why the position of your group is the best decision.

Ethics and Corporate Social Responsibility

ENVIRONMENTAL SHIPPING CONCERNS

You have just been promoted as the head of the shipping department for your office supply company, and it is now your responsibility to determine routing. The company is located on the eastern seaboard near major highways as well as the ocean. In the past, trucking has been the preferred method of shipping, as it was deemed the most cost effective. Shipping by boat, however, would greatly reduce the negative effects on the environment caused by truck emissions. After calculating the cost on paper, you realize that shipping by sea would have a negative effect on the overall profit margin, but the company would still generate solid profits.

Questions for Discussion

11-19 What decision would you make in this situation—land or sea?

11-20 If you were told that you would take a personal pay cut from switching to the more environmentally friendly route, how would that affect your decision?

11-21 What kind of impact do you think one company switching to less environmentally damaging practices could have on the general atmosphere of the shipping world?

Web Exercises

11-22 Have It Your Way
Burger King introduced mass customization to its fast-food offerings in the mid-1970s, thus revolutionizing how fast food could be delivered. Today, mass customization is aided by the Internet and other technologies. Search the Internet and find five companies that use mass customization. Is customizing a product to your specific needs important to you? Why or why not?

11-23 Greening America
Although the United States has become more of a service-based economy, many feel that the focus on creating new, environmentally friendly technologies may bring manufacturing back to the country and help power an economic recovery. Research what kinds of environmental technologies are being manufactured in the United States today. Do you think a greater investment in these technologies could result in the return of a significant number manufacturing jobs to the country? Why or why not?

11-24 Radio Frequency Identification
The use of chips to track goods during the shipping process is becoming more widespread. Use the Internet to research options for RFID. What are some of the options for tracking goods? What kind of range can these products cover?

11-25 How Everyday Things Are Made
The Alliance for Innovative Manufacturing at Stanford University has put together short videos on how certain products, such as jelly beans, airplanes, and bottles, are made. These products use various manufacturing processes, including forging, casting, and injection molding. Type "manufacturing.stanford.edu" into your Web browser and click on the "How Everyday Things Are Made" link. Watch a few videos and click on the "Test Your Knowledge," "Think About It," and "Apply It" links. Write a brief summary of your experience and outcomes.

✪ 11-26 Award-Winning Quality Providers
There have been six companies to receive the Malcolm Baldrige National Quality Award. They are listed in the "On Target" feature in this chapter. Research at least two of these companies and discuss the quality initiatives each company has in place to enable them to receive the Baldrige Award multiple times.

MyBizLab

Go to **mybizlab.com** for Auto-graded writing questions as well as the following Assisted-graded writing questions:

- ⊙ **11-27** What technological changes have enabled mass customization to take place? What are the advantages and disadvantages of this type of production process compared to mass production?

- ⊙ **11-28** Give an example of how the TQM process could be implemented in a restaurant. What steps can restaurants take to ensure that a high level of quality is maintained consistently in their food delivery process?

References

1. Bureau of Economic Analysis, U.S. Department of Commerce, "Widespread Economic Growth in 2012," June 6, 2013.
2. U.S. Bureau of Economic Analysis, "National Data," http://bea.gov/iTable/iTable.cfm?ReqID=9.
3. Douglas B. Cleveland, "The Role of Services in the Modern U.S. Economy," http://trade.gov/td/sif/PDF/ROLSERV199.PDF.
4. Ibid.
5. Central Intelligence Agency, "United States Economy," *CIA World Factbook*," May 7, 2012, www.cia.gov/library/publications/the-world-factbook/geos/us.html.
6. Ibid.
7. World Bank, "World Development Indicators, GDP," http://data.worldbank.org/indicator/NY.GDP.MKTP.CD?order=wbapi_data_value_2012+wbapi_data_value+wbapi_data_value-last&sort=desc.
8. Deloitte, *2013 Global Manufacturing Competitive Index, Summary Brief*, www.deloitte.com/view/en_US/us/Industries/Process-Industrial-Products/manufacturing competitiveness/mfg-competitiveness-index/index.htm.
9. Christopher W. Hart, "Creating Competitive Advantage through Mass Customization," www.spiregroup.biz/pdfs/06-04-07%20Creating%20Competitive%20Advantage%20through%20Mass%20Customization.pdf.
10. "Customer-Made," May 31, 2012, http://trendwatching.com/trends/CUSTOMER-MADE.htm, reprinted with permission.
11. Tim Feemster, "A Step-by-Step Guide to Choosing the Right Site," November 2007, www.areadevelopment.com/Print/siteSelection/nov07/stepByStep.shtml.
12. "Tata Steel Ranked World's Best Steel Maker by World Steel Dynamics," *Tata*, June 22, 2005, www.tata.com/media/releases/inside.aspx?artid=nAIH2iibp8Q=.
13. Local Hazardous Waste Management Program in King County, "Does Your Business Produce Hazardous Waste?," www.lhwmp.org/home/BHW/index.
14. Reverse Logistics: From Trash to Cash. *Bloomberg Businessweek*, July 28, 2008, www.businessweek.com/stories/2008-07-23/reverse-logistics-from-trash-to-cash.
15. Paul Graham, "How to Be Silicon Valley," May 2006, www.paulgraham.com/siliconvalley.html.
16. N. Shivapriya, "India Remains World's Top Outsourcing Destination," *Bloomberg Businessweek*, July 10, 2009, www.businessweek.com/globalbiz/content/jul2009/gb20090710_974200.htm.
17. Ibid.
18. Tim Mullaney, "An IPO That Might Print You Some Money," November 9, 2005, www.businessweek.com/the_thread/dealflow/archives/2005/11/vistaprint.html?chan=search.
19. SCORE (Counselors to America's Small Business), "Inventory Control," www.ct-clic.com/Newsletters/customer-files/inventory0602.pdf.
20. Jonathan Bymes, "Dell Manages Profitability, Not Inventory," in *Working Knowledge for Business Leaders*, Harvard Business School, http://hbswk.hbs.edu/archive/3497.html.
21. "What Is ERP?," www.tech-faq.com/erp.html.
22. American Society for Quality, "The History of Quality—Total Quality," www.asq.org/learn-about-quality/history-of-quality/overview/total-quality.html.
23. American Society for Quality, "Continuous Improvement," www.asq.org/learn-about-quality/continuous-improvement/overview/overview.html.
24. Motorola, Inc., "Motorola University: Six Sigma in Action," www.motorola.com/Business/US-EN/Motorola=University.
25. International Organization for Standardization, "ISO Standards," www.iso.org/iso/iso_catalogue.htm.
26. International Organization for Standardization, "Discover ISO: ISO's Mame," www.iso.org/iso/about/discover-iso_isos-name.htm.
27. Fielding, Stanley. "ISO 14001 Brings Change and Delivers Profits," *Quality Digest*, www.qualitydigest.com/nov00/html/iso14000.html.
28. "The Gartner Supply Chain Top 25 for 2013," May 22, 2013, www.gartner.com.
29. "Reducing Costs through Production and Supply Chain Management," *QFINANCE*, www.qfinance.com/operations-management-best-practice/reducing-costs-through-production-and-supply-chain-management?page=1.

Chapter 3
Business Communications

Source: Alamy.

We communicate and interact with others all day, every day. In fact, people in organizations spend at least 75 percent of their time in interpersonal situations—one-on-one, in groups, intraorganizational, or with customers, suppliers, investors, and advisers.[1] Communicating effectively is critical in the business world, yet it can present significant challenges. When you consider the impact poor communication can have on business—such as a loss of customers from poor customer service, a lack of focus on business objectives, and stifled innovation—it becomes clear why effective communication is an important business goal. In this mini chapter, we'll discuss how you can improve your communication skills in the workplace.

Improving Your Presentation Skills

In business, you often need to persuade, educate, or inform a group about your ideas. If you don't have strong presentation skills, your audience won't be receptive. Good presentation skills begin with good oral communication skills, so you need to make sure you speak loudly and clearly. Change your vocal intonation to add emphasis or interest when appropriate. It is important to engage audience members by looking directly at them as well as at different individuals around the room. Relax and smile, just as you would if you were talking to your friends.

Presentation software, such as Microsoft's PowerPoint, can be a great addition to a presentation if it is used correctly. We have all sat through boring presentations where the speaker read directly from the slides or used too many distracting graphics, animations, and blinding color schemes. When used to its best capabilities, PowerPoint can be a very effective tool. In this mini chapter, you'll find some tips to make your next PowerPoint presentation successful.

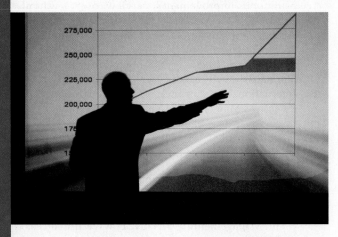

Delivering effective presentations requires planning and practice.
Source: John Crum/Alamy.

The complement to good oral communication skills is active listening skills. To ensure that you're being attentive when listening, repeat back or summarize the points you believe were made. Good listening also means asking good questions, but avoid becoming distracted by trying to think of what you're going to say next. If you need clarification, try to respond with statements such as "Tell me more." Finally, keep an open mind to others' ideas and suggestions. You do not necessarily want to have a solution or outcome defined in your mind before you hear what everyone else has to say.

POWERPOINT TIPS

1. **Keep it simple.** Just because the software is capable of doing amazing things, don't feel as if you have to use all the bells and whistles. Keep the design clean and charts simple and easy to understand. Limit the number of animations and special effects. In addition, use graphics to illustrate or highlight what you're saying—not to serve as the focus.

2. **Follow the 6 × 6 × 24 rule.** Remember, PowerPoint slides should consist of an outline of the key points you are making. Don't include everything you plan to say on the slides. Include only those key words or thoughts you want your audience to remember. As you speak, fill in the other details. To help keep the content of your slides to a minimum, presentation experts suggest you use no more than six words in a bullet point, six bullet points on a slide, and a font size that is at least 24 points. Also try to keep the total number of slides to a minimum.

3. **Use graphics and media to convey ideas.** Combining a strong oral presentation with visual cues on slides can make PowerPoint a very effective part of your delivery. We better remember what someone is saying if we see key words at the same time as we hear them. We remember even better when the right graphic or image is used to convey an entire idea. Consider incorporating short video pieces into your presentation to add a bit of humor, bring in a different "speaker," or convey a message in a different way. YouTube and Google Video are useful storehouses of video, as are Vimeo, Ustream, and Ted.com.

4. **Use color sparingly but effectively.** A light background with dark text is the best color combination for most lighting conditions. Adding color sparingly will help add visual interest and bring special attention to key areas of the presentation. Too much color can be distracting.

5. **Edit and proofread.** Typographical and spelling errors as well as grammatical mistakes make it appear as if you didn't review your presentation slides and leave a bad impression with your audience. If you know that grammar is a weak area for you, ask a friend who is a good editor to review the slides for you.

6. **Practice.** Practice giving your presentation several times aloud before giving it live in front of an audience. If you find yourself stumbling through a part, think more about the exact idea you need to communicate—additional examples you could use, analogies that might explain it better to your audience, and so on. When you practice your presentation, use PowerPoint's Rehearse Timings function to record how many seconds you spend on each slide. Review these numbers and make sure you are spending the most time on the sections most critical to your message.

Improving Your Writing Skills

In business, written communication is often in the form of a business letter or memo. Let's look at each of these forms of writing.

Business Letters

There is still a place in the business world for nonelectronic communication. For example, when a company offers you a position, it will often mail a business letter documenting the responsibilities and benefits of the offer. Communications sent via the U.S. Postal Service are also often used when a formal, documented series of actions is being conducted between two people. A business typically has a supply of paper with the company's letterhead and logo printed on it for purposes such as these.

■ **FIGURE M3.1**
A Traditional Business Letter

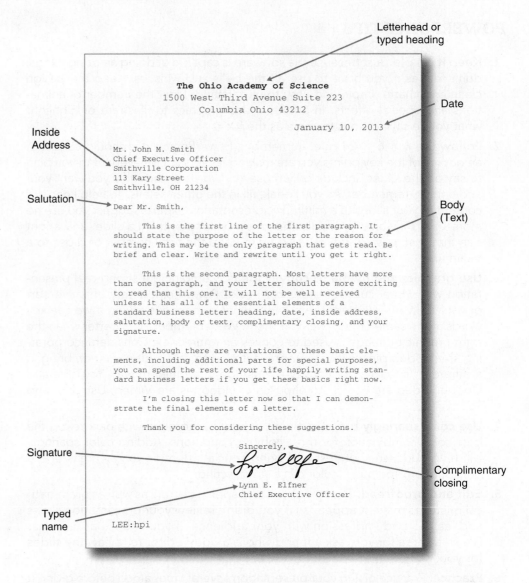

Letterhead or typed heading

Date

Inside Address

Salutation

Body (Text)

Signature

Complimentary closing

Typed name

As ■ **FIGURE M3.1** shows, a traditional business letter has a specific format that includes the date at the top, the address of the person receiving the letter, and a formal salutation. If you are on a first-name basis with the intended recipient, then your salutation can use the first name, such as "Dear Rebecca." In other cases, use a title and last name such as "Dear Mr. Consuelas." Letters can be more descriptive and include more detail than other types of communications, but they still need to be clear and to the point. Assume that the recipient doesn't have time to read through flowery prose. As with any other piece of writing, a business letter should have a beginning, a middle, and an ending. State the purpose of the letter in the first paragraph: "As you requested, I am providing more information . . . ," "I regret to inform you that . . . ," or "I am enclosing. . . . The paragraphs that follow should add supporting details. The final paragraph should offer information about what actions will follow or what actions the recipient should take. End the letter with a formal closing, such as "Sincerely," followed by your full name and title. You may include your contact information after your title if it's not included in the letterhead information. It is important that information in a business letter be written precisely and that the language be clear and simple.

Memos

Memos are used to make announcements, summarize facts from a conversation or a meeting or request or exchange information. They are either formal or informal,

To: All Employees

From: Evan Galvez. CEO

Re: Welcome to our new Vice President of Social Media Communications

---

I would like to announce that Jerry Spangler will be joining the Digital Strategies family as our new Vice President of Social Media Communications.

We are very excited to have Jerry leading our social media communications. He brings with him a wealth of experience having been a social media consultant to many well-known firms in the Silicon Valley area.

Please join me in welcoming Jerry to Digital Strategies!

depending on the content. Typically, they're used for communications within an office or a company, not between companies and external contacts or clients. As ■ **FIGURE M3.2** shows, memos have a standard heading format that contains the date, the person(s) to whom the memo is addressed (the To: line), the name of anyone else receiving a copy (the Cc: line), the name of the sender (the From: line), and a concise statement of the memo's topic (Subject: or Re:). You can find a large number of predesigned memo templates for Microsoft Word on the Microsoft Office website. The following tips provide some points to remember when writing memos.

MEMO WRITING TIPS

- Be concise.
- Use headings, bullets, and/or numbered lists to highlight key points.
- Keep each paragraph short and focused on one main idea.
- Always proofread carefully. Check all facts for accuracy.
- Identify any attachments so they don't go unnoticed.
- Closings are unnecessary. The "From" line eliminates the need.
- Remember that memos should be professional in tone and appearance.

What Form of Communication Should You Use?

There are many options when it comes to getting your message across. Should you send an e-mail? Write a letter? Visit your client face-to-face? Let's investigate the specific strengths and weaknesses of each type of communication so you can better match your delivery choice to the situation.

Oral communication allows participants to assess the meanings of the speaker's words and voice intonations. When speaking in person, participants also use "unspoken" messages sent by body language and facial expressions when interpreting the message. The speaker can adapt his or her message by assessing a listener's attentiveness. However, oral communication is not perfect. To deliver your message accurately, especially to those with whom you're not very familiar, it is important to offer clear, unbiased language and avoid clichés, negative metaphors, and culturally specific references. For example, using the expression "down to the last out" is meaningful to an American baseball fan but perhaps not to someone from another country.

Written communication has more permanency than oral communication. You can revise it before sending or review it at a later date. In addition, the receiver has more time to analyze the content before responding. On the other hand, the sender has no control over when the recipient chooses to read the message and does not benefit from immediate feedback. Neither is the sender given the opportunity for further clarification. Finally, written communication can lead to misunderstandings due to the lack of face-to-face interaction. Albert Mehrabian from the University of California, Los Angeles, found that 55 percent of meaning in an interaction comes from facial and body language and that 38 percent comes from vocal inflection. The words convey only 7 percent of meaning.[2] Therefore, if the nature of a written communication contains anything sensitive or complicated, it might be wise to follow up with a quick phone call or an in-person meeting.

E-Mail

E-mail is perhaps the most used form of digital written communication, although social networks, wikis, podcasts, and blogs are becoming increasingly popular in the business world. E-mail is quick and convenient, and the sender and receiver don't need to be available at the same time to communicate. Popular mobile devices, such as smart phones, and Internet tablets, such as the iPad, enable people to read and reply to e-mail any time they have a phone signal or Wi-Fi connection.

In the business world, your e-mail is all that many people see of you. It is important to take time to understand the audience to whom you're sending the e-mail and structure it accordingly. Obviously, an e-mail to a friend will be different from one to your boss or a client. A friend may expect a loosely formatted e-mail—full of slang and spelling errors. However, in a business context, such an e-mail will give people a negative impression of you. Your e-mails represent you and your organization, which is why you need to send clear, organized, and thoughtful messages. The following list has some pertinent tips for effective business e-mail writing.

TIPS FOR WRITING AN EFFECTIVE BUSINESS E-MAIL

1. **Use a meaningful subject line.** Subject lines help the reader prioritize and organize e-mail messages. Instead of "Here's what you're asking for," try to be more specific, such as "3/3/13 Client X Update." Create agreed-on acronyms for use in subject lines that help to better identify messages and/or actions required, such as AR (Action Required) or MSR (Monthly Status Report). Using consistent identifications helps people prioritize and organize e-mail. If possible, condense the entire message into several words that fit in the subject line, such as "2 P.M. meeting on 2/15/13 confirmed."

2. **Watch slang and offensive or potentially damaging content.** E-mails are business documents. Err on the side of being utterly conservative in your language and content. You don't want to offend anyone by using the wrong words or including something deemed inappropriate. Do not use texting abbreviations.

3. **Proofread and edit.** Quickly firing off an e-mail without proofreading can lead to big mistakes or misunderstandings. Make sure the message is free of grammatical and spelling errors.

4. **Keep it brief and focused.** Your e-mail may be one of 200 (or more!) read by the recipient that day, so keep the content brief and focused. Organize it with bullets or short sentences so the reader can clearly understand the key points. Be specific. If you send a 20-page attachment, for example, tell the recipient that the important information is on pages 2 and 17.

5. **Consider the format of attachments and their sizes.** When you don't know if the recipient has the right software to view an attachment, use a universal format, such as a PDF. Also, most e-mail servers will not allow an e-mail through if it has an exceptionally large attachment. If large files need to be exchanged, consider placing the information on a firm's intranet if the person has access to it. Free Web services, such as Dropbox and Hightail, can also be used for this purpose. They allow you people to share large files by uploading and downloading them to and from their websites.

6. **Include previous messages in a reply.** Even if you copy only a phrase from a previous e-mail, including messages in a reply helps when responses are not immediate. You wouldn't pick up a phone and say "I agree" and expect the person on the other end to understand what you're agreeing with if you hadn't spoken in a day or two. However, be careful when including an entire message if you're adding someone new to the e-mail. Long threads of e-mail exchanges may contain information that is not appropriate for a new person to see.

7. **Use a signature line.** The line should include your title and full contact information.

E-mail has other limitations, so users need to be aware of them to avoid problems. Be considerate of the size for attachments. Apply caution when using e-mail because it is not as private as a regular letter. E-mail is more like a postcard that can be read, copied, saved, shared, and exchanged by anyone. Work e-mails can be legally monitored by your boss and may be subject to review if a lawsuit is filed against your company. In addition, serious mistakes have occurred when users have mistakenly "replied to all" with comments about one of the people on the distribution list or have forwarded the message to the wrong person. Because of its ease of use and access, many users have found themselves in trouble after shooting off an e-mail in frustration or anger rather than waiting to cool off and responding in a calmer and more professional state of mind. The bottom line is that e-mail should be used with care and should not be used to communicate secure, private, or potentially damaging information.

Companies are beginning to recognize the problems erupting from the high volume of e-mail employees receive daily. A number of companies are adopting "no e-mail" days in an effort to reduce the e-mail overload and encourage employees to get out from behind their digital devices and actually talk to their colleagues and customers, whether in person or on the telephone. The results have been astonishing. When U.S. Cellular enforced a no-e-mail Friday, two coworkers who had been communicating with each other exclusively by e-mail found out that instead of being across the country from each other, they were only across the hall. Now, their working relationship is much stronger due to their in-person interactions.

Instant Messaging

Instant messaging (IM) is catching on in the business community as a means for conducting personal chats. Because of its immediacy and streamlined efficiency, many business users prefer IM to phone calls and e-mail. However, like e-mail,

Texting has become part of business in many settings.
Source: XiXinXing/Alamy.

IM should not be used to communicate confrontational, sensitive, or confidential information. IM messages can be copied and saved to a Word document or archived in their entirety, so discretion is important. IM is great when used to convey simple messages, clarify a point, confirm a meeting, and the like.

Texting

Texting is another popular form of digital communication. As a means of exchanging quick messages via a cell phone, texting can be as useful as IM. Many businesses also use text messaging as a means to "push" information to users via their cell phones. For example, airlines use texting to confirm flight information, and real estate agents use it to inform buyers when new listings that fit their specifications come on the market. Advertisers are also finding text messaging a convenient way to alert users to new product information. However, avoid using informal texting abbreviations in business texts.

Using Collaborative Communication Tools

In addition to presentations, memos, e-mail, and so on, there are a variety of tools to aid collaborative business communications.

Videoconferencing

Videoconferencing uses two-way audio and video technology to allow people in two or more locations to interact simultaneously. This means that people in different parts of the country or the world can have virtual meetings in which they can see each other and interact face-to-face. In addition to reducing travel costs, companies that use videoconferencing have found that increasing face-to-face time between employees is beneficial. Videoconferencing has also been implemented as a means of following up with clients and as a mode of effectively training workers in multiple locations.

Most mobile devices now support videoconferencing. Smart phones typically have two cameras, one pointing to the speaker's face and one pointing out the back of the camera. Apps for videoconferencing allow you to switch between cameras, showing the user your expression using the front-facing camera or switching to the rear camera and showing them the surroundings. Other features, like Skype's ability to also exchange files at the same time or ooVoo's four way video display, have pushed videoconferencing to new levels of usefulness and ease.

There are other technologies that offer efficient and effective collaborations in a virtual workplace. Online meeting software, such as WebEx, allows users to run and archive meetings with users from any location. Each person can stream in video from a webcam or just join in through voice. They can participate whether they are at a computer work station, on a laptop, or using a smart phone. Meeting participants can present slide shows, take live questions, run software applications, and share documents. A remote desktop control function allows anyone in the meeting to take control of another person's desktop to make a point or illustrate a feature. Tools like WebEx are used for conferencing but also for interactive customer training, sales presentations, and customer support.

Videoconferencing allowed Edward Snowden to join the Austin SxSW festival from Russia, where he was exiled after revealing details of the U.S. National Security Agency's surveillance efforts.
Source: Tammy Perez/Getty Images for SXSW.

Wikis

A wiki is a collaborative website that allows users to create, add, edit, or remove Web content using any Web browser (see ■ **FIGURE M3.3**). It's like a shared work-space where everyone has full and equal access to the same project, only better. Because all versions of the Web content are saved, users can revert back to a previous version of a document as well as track all edits and who made the edits. Wikis provide an excellent way for multiple authors to draft and edit a single document.

Unlike exchanging e-mails and attachments, there are no timing and version issues when a Wiki is used. Moreover, all users can see and comment on the document at any time, thus making the process more collaborative and accessible to all. The cost of using wikis is virtually negligible because the software for wikis is free, and little—if any—additional hardware or information technology support is required.

Beyond team collaboration, businesses are using wikis to ask questions, offer help, correct and add information to documents and presentations, brain-storm, and keep everyone informed about projects. Although some wikis, such as Wikipedia, the wiki-based online encyclopedia, are available and accessible to the general public, it is possible to make wikis private and available to only a select group of individuals, thus reducing privacy and confidentiality issues. Wikis can contain a variety of different file formats, such as documents, spreadsheets, and presentations, and they can be arranged into different pages for better content organization.

Blogs

A blog is a Web log that is usually authored by an individual and cannot be changed or edited by visitors. Visitors can, however, add comments to the original content. In some instances, blogging and business have not mixed well, such as when bloggers have written unflattering tales about their employers and other people. Consider what happened to Natalie Munroe, a Philadelphia high school English teacher who blogged about her students. Munroe didn't reveal the name of her school or the names of her students but vented about them on the blog

■ **FIGURE M3.3**
Professional Collaboration
Wikis are great collaboration tools.

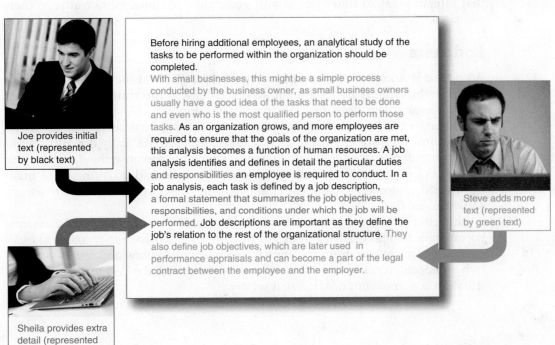

Joe provides initial text (represented by black text)

Sheila provides extra detail (represented by red text)

Steve adds more text (represented by green text)

Before hiring additional employees, an analytical study of the tasks to be performed within the organization should be completed.
With small businesses, this might be a simple process conducted by the business owner, as small business owners usually have a good idea of the tasks that need to be done and even who is the most qualified person to perform those tasks. As an organization grows, and more employees are required to ensure that the goals of the organization are met, this analysis becomes a function of human resources. A job analysis identifies and defines in detail the particular duties and responsibilities an employee is required to conduct. In a job analysis, each task is defined by a job description, a formal statement that summarizes the job objectives, responsibilities, and conditions under which the job will be performed. Job descriptions are important as they define the job's relation to the rest of the organizational structure. They also define job objectives, which are later used in performance appraisals and can become a part of the legal contract between the employee and the employer.

Blogging, often done with the tool WordPress, is a way to reach a wide audience and solicit feedback.
Source: M4OS Photos/Alamy.

by using term such as "frightfully dim" and "rat-like" to describe them. She was suspended for doing so, but her school district later returned her to the classroom rather than engage in an expensive legal battle.[3] The legal boundaries between the workplace and what people write and post on the Web about their jobs are still evolving.

Many companies recognize that blogs afford them an opportunity to reach a wide audience and elicit feedback via commenting sections. Today the Internet abounds with business blogs. Dr. Laundry is a blog created by the Clorox Company about bleaching tips. When Bob Lutz, vice chairman of GM, began his FastLane blog, readers bombarded it with their critiques and suggestions. Blogs offer companies the opportunity to interact with their customers in ways that other forms of communication do not. Because companies can sift through blogs to determine the "pulse" of the public—what they are talking about, what is important to them, and what they like and dislike about current trends or products—blogs are a valuable marketing research tool. They are also a good way to promote a company and its products. One study found that businesses that blog at least 20 times per month generate five times more traffic to their websites.[4]

Podcasts

A podcast is another form of digital communication that the business community is embracing. A podcast is an audio (or video) file stored on the Internet that customers can download to their computers or MP3 players and listen to whenever they want. Podcasts are unique in that customers can subscribe to programs they are interested in and have them automatically downloaded to their computers every time new content is available. Because the downloading process is quick and automatic, podcasts are simple and convenient for businesses and customers alike. Best of all, most podcasts, as well as the necessary software, are free.

Effective, efficient communication is key in today's dynamic global economy. Fortunately, there are many options from which to choose when it comes to business communications, from traditional phone conversations and letters to high-tech videoconferencing and wikis. Remember to choose the best form for a given situation and, most important, use it wisely.

References

1. Edward G. Westheim, "The Importance of Effective Communication," http://windward.hawaii.edu/facstaff/dagrossa-p/ssci193v/articles/EffectiveCommunication.pdf.

2. Alan Chapman, "Mehrabian's Communication Research," www.businessballs.com/mehrabiancommunications.htm.

3. K. Araiza, "Teacher Suspended for Blog Posts about Students," February 9, 2011, www.nbcphiladelphia.com/news/local/Teacher-Suspended-for-Blog-Posts-About-Students-115655164.html.

4. B. Gaille, "How Many Blogs Are on the Internet," November 20, 2013, www.wpvirtuoso.com/how-many-blogs-are-on-the-internet.

Chapter 12

Marketing and Consumer Behavior

❚ Marketing Fundamentals

Ford Motor Company started production of the first Model T in 1913. Nearly 100 years later, the automobile manufacturer is still producing vehicles. Part of the company's success is that it has changed its marketing concepts to meet the times. How has marketing evolved? How does marketing benefit the customer, the seller, and even society?

❚ Marketing Tactics

Aaron Hoffman has a business idea to start a mobile pet-grooming service. An adviser told him that he needs to create a "marketing strategy." What is a marketing strategy? Why is it necessary?

❚ The Marketing Environment

Amelia Russo runs an exclusive store that sells interesting and unique dress shoes and handbags for women. She gets much of her stock from Europe. However, the value of the U.S. dollar has fallen, increasing the cost she must pay for European products. In addition, the area in which the store is located is experiencing an influx of young, professional women who currently do not shop at her store. Amelia's marketing environment is forcing her to change the way she does business. What is a marketing environment, and how can it constrain a business?

❚ Marketing Research and Planning

Tiara Watson has decided to start a salon supply business. She knows that there is a demand for her service, but she wants to draw up a carefully organized marketing plan to ensure the success of her business. There are over 100 salons in her region. What steps must she take to get her name known in the salon supply world? What can she do to ensure success in her new business?

❚ Consumer Behavior

Will Giusto needs to buy a computer and is overwhelmed at the selection in front of him at the store. His girlfriend has a Mac, and his best friend has a top-notch gaming machine. Will isn't looking for a name-brand computer or one with lots of features. What factors will help him choose one computer over another?

OBJECTIVES

1 How has marketing evolved over time? (pp. 338–340)

2 What are the benefits and criticisms of marketing? (pp. 341–343)

3 What are the elements of a marketing strategy and the components of the marketing mix? (pp. 343–345)

4 How do firms implement a marketing strategy by applying the marketing process? (pp. 345–347)

5 How does the marketing environment influence a firm's ability to manipulate its marketing mix? (pp. 347–350)

6 What is the marketing research process, and what are the elements of a good marketing plan? (pp. 350–355)

7 How do the buying decisions and marketing processes in the business-to-business market compare to those in the business-to-consumer market? (pp. 355–359)

Marketing Fundamentals pp. 337–343

The innovation of the assembly line enabled Ford Motor Company to mass-produce millions of Model Ts when their production began in 1913. When customers' needs and tastes changed and the Model T did not, production of the Model T stopped in 1927. Ford learned its lesson that it needed to respond to the customer. Ford's new Model A, which hit the market in 1928, appealed to more affluent consumers by offering them both style and comfort. Two decades later, an improved economy and more sophisticated customer tastes sparked an interest in the 1949 Ford, which was offered in a wide range of body styles, so it had "something for everyone." The Ford Thunderbird was released in 1955, capturing the free spirit of that era.

Ford continued along the "road to postwar prosperity"[1] over the next several decades despite stiff competition and financial pressures from economic and gas crises. And although the firm did not declare bankruptcy like GM and Chrysler did, Ford was nonetheless hard hit during the Great Recession. But today the company is back—some say better than before. As this brief history indicates, the company's marketing strategies have evolved over time. Will it be able to continue its marketing success into the future? ■

In its broadest sense, *marketing* **can be thought of as identifying and meeting human needs and wants.** The American Marketing Association (AMA) defines **marketing** as "the activity, set of institutions, and processes for creating, communicating, delivering, and exchanging offerings that have value for customers, clients, partners, and society at large."[2]

Source: Stock Montage/Contributor/Archive Photos/Getty Images, Inc.

Source: Print Collector/Contributor/Hulton Archive/ Getty Images, Inc.

Source: Print Collector/Contributor/Getty Images.

MyBizLab®

⭐ **Improve Your Grade!**

Over 10 million students improved their results using the Pearson MyLabs.
Visit **mybizlab.com** for simulations, tutorials, and end-of-chapter problems.

FIGURE 12.1
Functions of a Marketing Department

What does a marketing department do? Marketing departments serve a variety of functions (see ■ **FIGURE 12.1**). First and foremost, marketers are responsible for keeping an eye on what people need and want and then communicating these needs and desires to the rest of the organization. Marketing departments help develop pricing strategies and persuade customers that their firms' products are the best. As you've learned, a **product** is a tangible good, service, or idea available for purchase in a market, as well as any intangible benefits derived from its consumption. Marketing departments are also responsible for distributing products to customers at places and times most suitable to them. But perhaps the most important aspect of marketing is successfully establishing meaningful relationships with customers to gain their loyalty and ensure repeat business. In this chapter, we'll present some basic aspects of this important corporate function, including marketing strategies, the marketing mix, and consumer behavior. We'll start by looking at how marketing has changed over time.

The Evolution of Marketing

How has marketing evolved over time? The nature of marketing has evolved over five general eras (see ■ **FIGURE 12.2**):

1. The production era
2. The sales era
3. The marketing era
4. The societal marketing era
5. The customer relationship era

Although each concept experienced a peak in popularity during a specific time period, today's most successful marketing campaigns are a sophisticated combination of the best of each of the concepts.

What was the production era? From the industrial revolution until the 1920s, most companies focused solely on production—thus the *production* era evolved.

FIGURE 12.2
The Evolution of Marketing

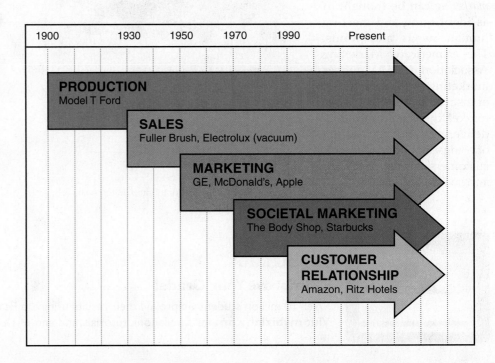

The prevailing mind-set was that a good-quality product would simply sell itself. This approach worked for many organizations during this era because of strong demand and a limited supply of products. Whenever demand exceeds supply, it creates a seller's market. This type of economic climate may have motivated Henry Ford to remark that his Model T cars could be painted "any color, so long as it's black."[3]

What was the sales era? From the mid-1920s through the early 1950s, technological advances accelerated production. In the first part of the era, however, the United States was in the middle of the Great Depression, during which unemployment was nearing 30 percent, and people bought only what they absolutely needed. Supply far exceeded the demand for most products, so the competition for customers was intense. Businesses focused on selling existing products and used aggressive sales tactics to "push" them, including door-to-door salesman who sold everything from hairbrushes and vacuum cleaners to encyclopedias. Companies also began advertising heavily in all available forms of media. Thus began the *sales* era. During this era, marketing generally took place only after a product was developed and produced. Today, many people associate marketing with selling or advertising; however, it has become much more than that.

What was the marketing era? By the 1950s, production continued to expand more quickly than the demand for goods and services. In addition, there were more companies producing similar products competing for a buyer's attention. This created a buyer's market and the start of the *marketing* era. Soldiers returning from World War II were getting married, starting families, and willing to spend their money on goods and services. Consumers were beginning to tire of the "hard-sell" tactics companies were using to force them to buy products they didn't necessarily want or need. Eventually, businesses began to realize that simply producing quality products and pushing them onto customers through clever advertising and promotional campaigns didn't guarantee sales.

Companies needed to determine what customers wanted and then produce products that met those wants and needs as opposed to producing products and then trying to convince customers to buy them. The **marketing concept** changed the focus from finding the right customer for a product to producing the right product for a customer and doing it better than the competition. As you can see in ■ **FIGURE 12.3**, the marketing concept also focuses on aligning all functions

■ **FIGURE 12.3**
The Marketing Concept

of the organization to meet or exceed the customer's needs by providing superior products and customer service. In addition, the marketing concept focuses on satisfying customers over the long term.

General Electric (GE) was one of the first companies to implement this new marketing strategy. GE's 1952 annual report outlined its new marketing philosophy, which stated that GE would provide a product the customer wants at the price the person is willing to pay and have it delivered to him or her at the right time and location. To do this, GE's marketing team had control of the product through all phases, from planning, through production scheduling and inventory control, as well as sales, distribution, and servicing.[4]

The marketing concept requires a company to constantly take the pulse of changing customer needs and wants and then quickly adapt to meet them. Moreover, it may mean anticipating customers' changing preferences—before they are expressed or even known by the customer—and satisfying these preferences before competitors do. Companies such as Apple have had great success following this philosophy. Apple has become a master of anticipating customers' desires and fulfilling them with its range of iPods, iPod accessories, iPhones, iPhone apps, and the iPad.

Does marketing also take into consideration what's best for society?
Companies began to realize that they must also consider the long-term interests of society. *Societal marketing*, an offshoot of the marketing concept and corporate social responsibility, began in the late 1960s and early 1970s. It challenged companies to profit by working for the benefit of both consumers and society. The Body Shop, a skin and cosmetics company, sells products made with only 100 percent natural ingredients. The company also actively does business with highly skilled but small-scale farmers, craftsmen, and rural cooperatives.[5] Patagonia's 2013 Black Friday campaign that encouraged shoppers to rethink consumerism is an example of the societal marketing approach in action. The clothing maker's "Don't Buy This Jacket" advertisement went on to articulate the actual environmental cost of producing the company's best-selling jacket, and concluded, "There is much to be done . . . don't buy what you don't need."[6] Other industries are influencing healthy behavior and discouraging unhealthy practices, such as the new health-conscious menu additions at fast-food restaurants.

What marketing philosophy encourages customer loyalty?
During the marketing era, firms focused on offering customized products to acquire customers initially. But in the late 1990s, the *customer relationship* era began, and organizations began focusing on continuing to satisfy customers over the long term by pleasing them after the sale. The result has been the creation of **customer relationship management** (CRM), the process of establishing long-term relationships with individual customers to foster loyalty and repeat business (see ■ **FIGURE 12.4**). CRM combines customer service and marketing communications to *retain* customers in order to stimulate future sales of similar or supplementary products. For example, most stores send e-mails with coupons and information about their sales and promotions to customers who join their mailing lists or who "like" them on Facebook. Amazon.com uses its massive database to automatically offer suggestions for future purchases to customers based on their prior purchases or browsing interests. CRM enables a company to offer products tailored to specific customers' needs and desires.

Customer loyalty programs revolve around learning as much as possible about customers and their shopping behaviors so as to create a meaningful one-on-one interaction with each of them. Often a firm's sales force gathers information about specific customers to create a customer database outlining their wants, needs, and preferences. Other companies use CRM software to personalize communications to their customers.

■ **FIGURE 12.4**
Customer Relationship Management
CRM involves marketing, sales, customer feedback, and support to ensure that customers are satisfied long term.

Source: Steve Skjold/Alamy

Marketing for Not-for-Profits and Others

How do not-for-profit organizations market their products? Many not-for-profit organizations also have an interest in marketing. Rather than a product or a service, these organizations look to market an event, a cause, a place, or a person. Not-for-profits, such as the Sierra Club and the Red Cross, rely on marketing to raise awareness of and increase donations to their causes. Countries, states, and cities run marketing campaigns to attract tourists and businesses to their locations. You may be familiar with the public service advertising campaigns run by the Ad Council, such as the Buzzed Driving Is Drunk Driving campaign.[7]

Is it possible to market a person? Political parties market candidates for elected office. Agents market their clients on television shows, cereal boxes, and magazine covers. We market ourselves when we interview for a job. You may have marketed yourself for acceptance to your college or university.

Regardless of what is being marketed, the essence of marketing remains the same: delivering value to customers and managing customer relationships. The only differences between marketing practices are the stakeholders involved and their objectives.

Benefits of Marketing

How does society benefit from marketing? Society in general benefits from successful marketing because scarce resources are more efficiently channeled into the production of the goods and services most desired by society. The market mechanism ensures that resources, such as raw materials and labor, flow into the production of those goods and services in greatest demand and away from low-value products with falling demand.

How do investors and employees benefit from marketing? Investors receive financial rewards for investing in organizations with good marketing departments that help make the firms successful. Indeed, more and more investment capital flows to those businesses that are most successful in satisfying customers because investors earn higher returns. Employees benefit from successful marketing because their jobs and livelihoods are more secure. In addition, new job opportunities are created as production expands to satisfy the growing demand for high-value products.

How do sellers benefit from marketing? Of course, a company also benefits by successful marketing because it sells more products. As long as the costs of producing and marketing them are less than the revenue generated by their sale, a company generates a profit. Profits enable the organization to not only sustain itself but also to prosper and continue to provide value to customers—ideally, it's a win/win arrangement.

How does marketing benefit consumers? As consumers, we have many needs—food, clothing, housing, medical care, and transportation, to name a few. Marketers *respond* to needs in an effort to *satisfy* them, but sometimes they also

Form Utility
- Creating a finished product

Task Utility
- Performing a desired service

Time Utility
- Delivering product when customer wants it

Place Utility
- Delivering product where customer wants it

Ownership Utility
- Freedom to use product as needed

■ **FIGURE 12.5**
Marketing Generates Five Types of Utility for Customers

can *create* needs. Subway and Quiznos go to great lengths to convince you to buy their sandwiches to satisfy your need for food, just as Toyota and Ford try to convince you to purchase their vehicles to fulfill your transportation needs. When needs are satisfied, *utility* is created.

Are there different types of utility? There are five kinds of utility that marketing provides to customers (see ■ **FIGURE 12.5**):

- **Form utility.** When a company produces a product from raw materials, such as a swimsuit is made from fabric and supplies. The product takes on a form that is useful to the customer.
- **Task utility.** When someone performs a service for someone else, such as when a seamstress alters a swimsuit.
- **Time utility.** When a business makes a product available at a time when it is most needed, such as having the swimsuit available in time for summer.
- **Place utility.** When the product is made available for purchase at a place that's convenient for buyers, such as when the swimsuit is stocked and placed on display at your local department store.
- **Ownership utility.** When a store transfers ownership to the customer by selling the swimsuit.

How is a product's value measured? Whenever a business satisfies a need or a want, it creates value for a customer. But how do customers measure value? The **value** of a product is the ratio of a product's benefits to its costs. Benefits far exceed costs for a high-value product. A low-value product has few benefits in relation to its costs. Successful marketers finds ways to increase the value customers get—by either increasing the real or perceived benefits of a product or minimizing customers' costs by reducing the product's price or maximizing the consumer's convenience. Organizations that offer the highest-valued products win the most customers and thrive. Those organizations that offer low-value goods and services lose market share or go out of business entirely.

Criticisms of Marketing

What are the criticisms of marketing? Over time, certain social shortcomings have emerged from marketing techniques. Some of the questionable tactics include price gouging (setting a price that is widely considered unfair), high-pressure selling, the production of shoddy or unsafe products, planned obsolescence (the product becomes outdated after a period of time planned by the manufacturer), poor customer service, the misuse of customer information, confusing and deceptive labeling, and hidden fees and charges.

Let's consider some examples of the costs to society of questionable marketing:

- **Misuse of personal information.** Marketing often involves the collection of customers' personal information. Companies track what people do online and conduct marketing surveys to determine the marital status, annual income, age, sex, race, and other characteristics of current and prospective customers. Information brokers collect and sell user data for targeted ads and market research. The Internet has become

Source: Apic/Hulton Archive/Getty Images.

a hotbed for this type of activity. Many of us feel violated when this personal information is not adequately protected or is resold without our permission.

- **Hidden fees.** Many of us feel taken advantage of when we must pay hidden fees and charges not included in the advertised price. Products that require additional parts or shipping and service fees often make customers upset.

- **Consequences of purchase.** Unscrupulous marketers sometimes take advantage of people who are not knowledgeable about certain features of a product. To what extent is it reasonable to hold buyers responsible for being aware of the consequences of their purchases? This is especially important when purchasing expensive or sophisticated goods and services, such as a car or a mortgage on a home. Similar concerns emerge when marketing is directed at children.

The many criticisms of marketing should not be taken lightly. They help explain the strong support for laws protecting consumers and other regulations governing business behavior. Too often the social costs of marketing stem from unethical business practices. As we discussed in Chapter 3, all companies should have a code of ethics and policies in place to curb unethical behavior within their organizations. However, not all companies do, which allows for questionable products to be marketed or questionable marketing tactics to be used. On its website, the AMA has a posted a statement of ethics that contains guidelines on ethical norms and values for marketers.

The marketing landscape has changed over the past 100 years or so. Companies that have managed to stay in business—such as Ford Motor Company—have changed their products and marketing strategies to match changes in consumers' wants and needs. Ford went from mass-producing one model of a car to producing dozens of models and styles today in an effort to meet the individual preferences, tastes, and budgets of different consumers.

Marketing Tactics pp. 343–347

Aaron Hoffman is determined to work for himself. He knows he can do that with his own mobile pet-grooming service. Because Aaron worked as a pet groomer for seven years, he has enough experience to branch out on his own. Aaron has already found a van to hold all his equipment, and he knows a few of his previous customers are interested in his services, but he isn't sure what the next step should be. Someone suggested he come up with a marketing strategy. What does a marketing strategy do? And how should Aaron develop one? ■

All organizations can benefit from a well-developed marketing strategy. In this section, we'll discuss the factors that are involved in the marketing process.

Source: Willee Cole/Fotolia.

Marketing Strategy: The Four Ps of Marketing

What is a marketing strategy? A marketing strategy consists of two major elements:

- The **target market**. A specific group of potential customers on which a firm focuses its marketing efforts.

- The **marketing mix**. The combination of controllable elements of a product's marketing plan designed to serve the target market.

We'll discuss target markets in more detail later in the chapter. Let's first turn our attention to the marketing mix.

■ **FIGURE 12.6**
The Marketing Mix
The ideal marketing mix blends the four
Ps in a way that best meets the needs of
targeted customers.

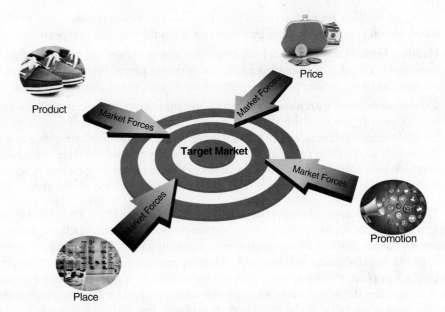

What elements are included in the marketing mix? Traditionally, there have been four elements in the marketing mix, which are known as the four Ps: product, price, promotion, and place. The idea is to provide the *product* customers need and want at an appropriate *price*, *promote* its sale, and then *place*, or distribute, the good or the service in a convenient location for the customer to purchase. Some feel there is a fifth P that should be added to the marketing mix: people. Particularly when a service is being offered, the people involved can add significant value.

The elements of the marketing mix need to be blended in a way that best meets the needs of the target market. As you can see in ■ **FIGURE 12.6**, finding the best blend is constrained by environmental factors beyond a firm's control. We'll discuss these constraints found within the broader market environment later in this chapter. Let's first look at each of the four Ps in a bit more detail.

Product

The perfect product is one that provides value for the customer. Companies must determine what a customer wants from a product, or how a product satisfies a particular need. Additionally, distinguishing a product from that of the competitors is critical. If a product isn't different from or superior to the competition, then why should customers buy it? *Product differentiation* is the creation of a real or perceived difference in a product designed to attract customers. Product differentiation is critical for most businesses and will be discussed in greater detail in Chapter 13.

Price

There's a lot to consider when deciding on the price for a product. The price has to be high enough for a firm to profit from it but be low enough to appeal to customers. The cost of warranties and returns must also be factored into the price.

Pricing a product competitively doesn't always mean selling it at the lowest price in the marketplace, though. Sometimes when it's difficult to offer a consistently low price, coupons, discounts, or other services can help reduce the cost to the customer. However, this strategy must be evaluated periodically to assess its overall effectiveness. We'll investigate the price component of the marketing mix in more detail in Chapter 13.

Promotion

Promotion consists of all the methods used to inform customers about a product's benefits and persuade them to buy it. Promotions are also used to build positive customer relationships. Communicating the benefits of your good or service to customers is done through advertising, sales promotions, personal selling, public relations, direct marketing, and publicity. We'll explore promotion more fully in Chapter 14.

Place

The **place (or distribution)** component of the marketing mix refers to all the methods involved in getting a product into the hands of customers. A product isn't beneficial to a customer if it can't be purchased when and where it is needed. When a business is providing a good instead of a service, the delivery component is often more complicated. Many goods, such as grocery store items, go through a *distribution channel*, which is a series of firms or individuals that participate in the flow of a product from the manufacturer to the consumer. The middle players in a distribution channel are sometimes called *distributors* or *wholesalers*. Some goods, such as food products, go through many wholesalers before reaching a retail outlet (for example, a grocery store) and, finally, the consumer. Other goods, such as automobiles, typically move from the manufacturer to just one wholesaler, the car dealership, and then the consumer. Still other goods bypass wholesalers altogether and move from the manufacturer directly to the consumer, such as L.L. Bean clothing products, when they are ordered from a catalog and shipped directly to consumers.[8] In Chapter 14, we'll examine finding the appropriate distribution channel and managing it efficiently to get the product to the right place at the right time, in the proper quantity, and at the lowest cost.

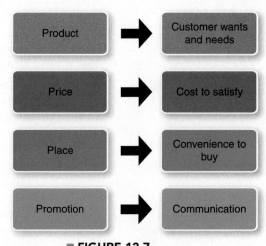

■ **FIGURE 12.7**
The Four Cs of Marketing
The four Cs reflect a movement to a more customer-oriented marketing approach.

The Four Cs of Marketing: Marketing from the Consumer's Perspective

Can the marketing mix be represented a different way? The four Ps present marketing from the producer's perspective. As ■ **FIGURE 12.7** shows, a more recent revision to the four Ps model looks at marketing from the consumer's perspective:

- *Customer* replaces product: This represents a shift toward niche marketing and creating individual solutions for customers rather than forcing them to buy a standard product solution.

- *Cost* replaces pricing: The price of a product is only a portion of the total cost of owning it. Other factors include the costs a consumer incurs by changing to a new product or service, such as driving to the place where it can be purchased, taking time to decide to buy it, and learning how to use it.

- *Convenience* replaces place: Online shopping and other hybrid models of purchasing have reduced the importance of place. Convenience, instead, factors in the ease with which information about a product or where it is located can be communicated and how the actual purchase transaction takes place.

- *Communication* replaces promotion: The proliferation of mobile devices and social networking platforms allows companies and consumers to be in constant communication with each other. Companies need to "listen" to their customers as much as they want their customers to listen to their marketing messages.

The Marketing Process

How does the marketing process work? ■ **FIGURE 12.8** shows the five steps in the marketing process. As the figure indicates, marketing isn't just about advertising a product in the marketplace. A great deal of marketing research and analysis occurs before the final message about the product is communicated as well as afterward:

1. **Identify a market need.** Think back to Aaron Hoffman's mobile pet-grooming service. Aaron has his own pets, and before he became a groomer himself, he took his dogs to the pet-grooming service at which he was later employed. Transporting his dogs was a huge hassle, and he felt horrible about leaving them in a cage for part of the day. He didn't know it at the

■ **FIGURE 12.8**
The Five Steps in the Marketing Process

time, but Aaron had identified an unfilled market need: a mobile pet-grooming service that eliminates the hassle and guilt that trouble pet owners when they take their pets to a grooming service. This is the first step in the marketing process.

2. **Conduct market research and develop a marketing plan.** By analyzing the marketing environment, Aaron can determine if any political, economic, societal, and/or technological factors could affect his business and its profitability. In addition, he conducts an internal analysis that includes evaluating his potential customers, competitors, and collaborators. These analyses form the foundation for his marketing plan. Aaron discovers that sufficient demand already exists for the services of his potential business. We'll discuss how to analyze the marketing environment, as well as how to conduct market research and develop a marketing plan, in more detail later in the chapter.

3. **Identify target customers.** If Aarons skips this step, he will waste effort and money promoting a service to people not interested in his service. Therefore, Aaron must consider who his ideal customers are and what they think and want and then use this information to inform his marketing decisions. Identifying a target market is discussed in more detail later in the chapter.

4. **Implement the marketing mix.** Next, Aaron needs to implement the marketing mix. He has already identified a customer need and has developed a product that not only meets that need but also fulfills it better than the competition. Then he will want to contemplate his pricing strategy to ensure that a profit is made *and* that he remains competitive. In developing his pricing strategy, Aaron needs to be sensitive to any other direct or indirect *costs* that the customer may incur from using his service.

   The place component of the marketing mix involves deciding how his product will be distributed to his customers. The initial size and mobility of Aaron's business affords him great flexibility. He will be delivering his product to his customers, within a reasonable distance, with little or no inventory management required. This service offers his customers much convenience. Are there other conveniences Aaron might also consider offering? Can he make scheduling appointments any easier?

   Promotion, which can be very expensive yet very fruitful, is the most visible part of the marketing mix. Aaron should begin promoting his service by creating a memorable brand name for the business to distinguish it from all others. How should he communicate with the marketplace to engage with his current customers and attract new ones? Should he create a Facebook account, generate a mobile app, or set up a website? Should he blog or tweet about pet grooming and other care tips?

5. **Maintain good customer relationships.** The final step in the marketing process is to establish and nurture long-term, trusting relationships with customers to foster their loyalty and get repeat business. Aaron must develop a rapport with his customers and their pets. He should know which customers are returning clients and note any of their particular grooming preferences. He should also solicit suggestions from customers as well as respond to their complaints by continuing to improve his services. To build customer trust, he might also offer customers their money back if they are unsatisfied. To maintain and foster interest in his services, he may want to use social media. Aaron may also want to establish relationships with veterinary clinics and dog breeders. Personalizing and maintaining good customer relationships is critical to a business's ongoing success.

The marketing process may seem simple when it is written on paper, but it's as much an art as it is a science. It is a continuous process of tweaking business strategies to satisfy customers, to ensure quality products are delivered, and to garner repeat business. Aaron Hoffman's mobile pet-grooming service will have a completely different marketing strategy than a business that produces and sells a good. Each product needs to be looked at individually to tailor an appropriate marketing mix for it.

The Marketing Environment pp. 347–350

Amelia Russo runs an exclusive store that sells interesting and unique dress shoes and handbags for women. She gets much of her stock from Europe, so the value of the U.S. dollar makes a big difference in terms of her total costs. However, the value of the dollar has fallen recently, taking a toll on Amelia's bottom line. In addition, her shop caters to a wealthier and older demographic, but Amelia would like to attract more young professionals to the shop. What environmental influences are affecting Amelia's business? How can she respond to these effects? ■

A business can directly control the variables in its marketing mix. By contrast, the **marketing environment** in which the firm operates is beyond its control, constraining its ability to manipulate its marketing mix. These influences include the competitive, economic, technological, and sociocultural environments as well as the global, political, and regulatory environments shown in ■ **FIGURE 12.9.**

Marketers must be keenly aware of the marketing environment when determining the marketing mix. In fact, one of the key responsibilities of managers in any organization is to do **environmental scanning**, which is the process of surveying the marketing environment to assess external threats and opportunities. A successful business detects changes in the marketing environment and adjusts its marketing mix quickly inasmuch as the overall marketing environment will allow the firm to do so. Let's study each element of the marketing environment in more detail.

Source: Adisa/Fotolia.

■ **FIGURE 12.9**
The Marketing Mix and the Marketing Environment
The marketing mix can be controlled by marketing managers, but the marketing environment consists of external forces they cannot control.

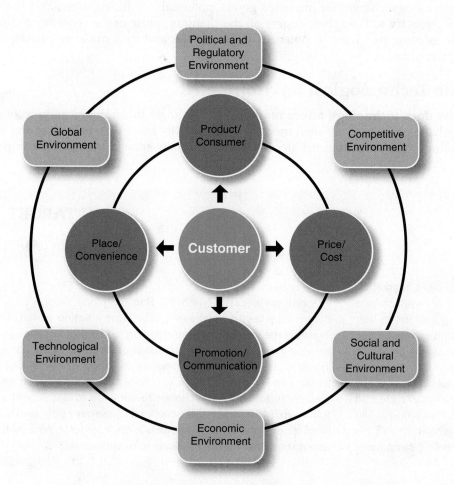

The Competitive Environment

Why is analyzing the competition important? The degree of competition facing a firm is critical to creating an effective marketing mix. Recall that the varying degrees of competition are perfect competition, monopolistic competition, oligopoly, duopoly, and monopoly. The degree of competition affects a firm's marketing strategies. A company operating in a monopolistic competitive environment will have a different marketing strategy than one operating in an oligopoly. A successful business must be aware of its competition and try to stay one step ahead of them. Amelia Russo's shoe store had an edge on the competition due to her unique products. As a result of the dollar's weakness, however, Amelia may need to rethink her strategy to maintain a competitive advantage.

The Economic Environment

How does the economic environment affect a marketing strategy? Marketers must keep abreast of changes in the economy. Why? Because the economic environment, including inflation, interest rates, unemployment, economic growth rates, and consumer confidence levels, can affect a firm's marketing strategy in many ways. For example, a rising inflation rate reduces the purchasing power of money, and sales may fall. A recession will reduce the demand for some products. Even the best-laid marketing plans will fail when customers can no longer afford to buy a company's product. If interest rates are low, then the cost of borrowing drops, and consumers who buy on credit, especially big-ticket items such as houses and automobiles, may purchase more. Because of globalization, prudent firms follow global economic trends as well.

As a final example, suppose the value of the dollar falls (gets weaker) in foreign exchange markets. This will cause imported goods to become more expensive, like Amelia Russo's French dress shoes. This means Amelia may have to increase the prices she charges for imported goods, potentially reducing their sales. Savvy marketers try to keep their fingers on the changing pulse of the economy to forecast looming problems or potential opportunities and then make any necessary adjustments.

The Technological Environment

How does technology affect marketing? Advances in communication technology have profoundly affected modern marketing. By being able to market and sell products online, the Internet alone has enabled many small businesses to compete

---

Viral Marketing

ON TARGET

Viral marketing has become an efficient marketing tool. It is the digital version of word of mouth. Like a virus, this form of Internet marketing spreads to vast audiences quickly. A successful viral marketing campaign can have a much larger impact than a traditional campaign, which explains why many companies are including viral marketing as a part of their overall marketing strategies. Some of the most successful viral marketing campaigns have been created by Dos Equis beer (Most Interesting Man in the World[9]), Old Spice men's grooming products (the Old Spice guy), and the innovative and popular Blendtec (Will it Blend?[10]) campaigns.

More recent campaigns include Geico's "Hump Day," AT&T's "It's not complicated," and the Ron Burgundy Dodge campaigns. The key to great viral marketing is creating a marketing message that is novel, entertaining, and intriguing enough to get people to notice it and then to "talk about it" by passing it on to others. What makes a message good enough to go viral? It's harder than you think, but most include an unexpected theme, an incentive to continue to watch, and a follow-up. Most important, good viral messages rarely sell the product directly. What are your favorite viral ads? What is it about them that makes you want to pass them on?

with large corporations around the world. The Internet has also helped companies deliver marketing messages, often in the form of video, more quickly and to broader audiences. This can give a firm exponential exposure almost instantaneously. Moreover, the onset of social media and Web-based communications has been a key influence in changing the focus of the marketing mix from the product to the consumer.

As a result of technological improvements, manufacturing innovations have enabled firms to more easily customize their products to meet individual needs and to offer them at dramatically reduced prices to satisfy the varying tastes of targeted customers. Technology has enhanced CRM by facilitating the creation and use of computer databases. Successful marketing requires using the latest technologies to reach and satisfy target customers wherever they may be.

The Social and Cultural Environment

How do cultural and social trends affect marketing? In Chapter 4, we examined the critical effect the sociocultural environment has on businesses. Demographic shifts—such as age, gender, ethnicity, and marital status—and changing values can signal opportunities for businesses. For example, we can expect the demand for medical care, pharmaceuticals, and nursing homes to increase as the average age of the population increases. Amelia Russo recognized the demand for high-quality dress shoes from a younger, professional crowd.

The Political, Legal, and Regulatory Environments

How do politics and legislation affect marketing? It has been said that in a democracy, the squeaky wheel gets the grease. Special interest groups try to influence the political process in various ways. Businesses are no exception. They try influence the laws and regulations affecting them by making contributions to political parties, individual candidates, and political action committees. In addition, a variety of regulatory agencies, such as the Environmental Protection Agency, the Consumer Product Safety Commission, the Food and Drug Administration (FDA), and the Federal Trade Commission, enforce laws and regulations constraining the marketing efforts firms can engage in. Kellogg's was forced to stop using the terms "All Natural" and "Nothing Artificial" on certain Kashi and Bear Naked products. The FDA states that few products are "natural" since they have probably been processed at some point

---

The Hard Lessons of Social Media

OFF THE MARK

Although social media has given many companies the opportunity to create some great branding campaigns, unfortunately, there are also some not-so-good campaigns. Take, for example, Kmart. The company had just run the very successful "Ship My Pants" and "Big Gas Savings" television ad campaigns that also went viral. But the success of the campaigns was quickly marred when a Kmart staffer tweeted a response to customers complaining about the retailer's decision to remain open on Thanksgiving Day: "Kmart is staffing w/teams & seasonal associates when possible, giving them opportunity to make extra money during holiday," the tweet read. Many people thought the tweet was rude and dismissed customers' concerns.

Recently, the banking conglomerate J.P. Morgan decided it would use Twitter to allow customers to #AskJPM. But when the campaign was announced, people began tweeting questions such as the following: "How do you decide who to foreclose [sic] on? Darts or a computer program?" and "As a young sociopath, how can I succeed in finance?" Hours later, J.P. Morgan tweeted, "Tomorrow Q&A is cancelled. Bad Idea. Back to the drawing board."

Most social media blunders occur when a person neglects to consider the different ways in which campaigns can be viewed. Clearly, neither Kmart nor J.P. Morgan had a good read on the public's sentiments and how best to respond to them. There are many other examples of good social media intentions turning into public relations problems. What do you think of these social media events and each company's response? Are there other poorly managed campaigns that you can think of?

and that, since these products had added chemical forms of vitamins, "nothing artificial" was also a misnomer. Businesses are consequently forced to consider the political and legal environment when making marketing decisions, as these factors can play a major role in overall success of a marketing campaign.

The Global Environment

How does the global environment affect marketing? Thanks in part to the Internet, world trade has increased significantly. Customers can search globally for attractively priced products, and businesses can search globally for suppliers. To tap new markets, companies have expanded internationally. The marketing efforts that accompany efforts to globalize are not without their difficulties, though. Marketers need to be aware of cultural and social differences before launching their products and their marketing campaigns. Political landscapes with differing policies and regulations can also affect how a company does business in another country. Businesses must also be aware of the complications involved in shipping products to foreign countries.

So what did store owner Amelia Russo decide to do to address the changing market environment she was facing? To deal with the weakened dollar, Amelia found some great start-up domestic shoe and handbag designers who were thrilled to have their products featured in her shop. Amelia promoted her change with a "Designed and Made in the USA" campaign. The campaign, as well as the unique, fresh designs of the products, lured in the young professionals she had been wanting to attract. Successful businesses like Amelia's are constantly on the lookout for changes in the market environment and are prepared to adjust their products and marketing efforts accordingly.

Marketing Research and Planning pp. 350–355

Source: Tatty/Fotolia.

Tiara Watson noticed that the owner of the hair salon she went to constantly complained about one of her suppliers located several states way. The owner was frustrated with the supplier's ever-increasing delivery costs and long delivery times. In addition, the supplier didn't carry products that could meet the needs of the increasingly diverse clientele moving into the area.

Tiara recognized an opportunity to launch a local supply company that could do the job better. Her initial research revealed that there were more than 100 salons in her immediate area. Casual conversations with some of the owners of these salons that used the same supplier indicated that many would be willing to switch to a new supplier. Tiara knows she can't start out selling supplies to every salon in the area. How can she determine which salons to target initially for a successful start of her new business? ∎

Look back at the five-step marketing process shown in Figure 12.8. You'll notice that after a market need is identified, a firm needs to conduct *market research* to determine the profitability of a venture, develop a marketing plan, and determine its target market. In this section, we'll explore each of these processes in more detail.

The Market Research Process

What is market research, and what are the steps involved in the process? **Market research** is the process of gathering and analyzing market information for making marketing decisions. Market research can be as simple as including a brief survey with an invoice or via e-mail, or it can be as complex as conducting a full-blown market analysis before launching a new product. Although there are dozens of intermediate steps in conducting marketing research, they all fit into the basic process shown in ▪ **FIGURE 12.10**.

Why is it important to define the marketing needs or opportunity? Although a new marketing need or opportunity seems apparent, it's important to really define the opportunity carefully because other hidden issues might actually be the real opportunity. For example, Tiara has identified the need for a salon supply company located closer to salons in her area. But is distance the real problem, or could other factors, such as poor service or insufficient product offerings, really be the problem?

The first step in the marketing research process is to define the problem, which could include doing more research to further identify or enhance the perceived need or opportunity. Marketing managers and researchers work together to determine what kind of data need to be gathered and how. Doing so helps the researcher determine the research's approach, establish a budget for it, and collect the right type of data.

What kind of data should be collected? Determining which types of data will be collected and how the information will be collected is critical. Two general types of data exist: primary and secondary:

- **Primary data** are raw data collected by a researcher. The data are frequently collected through observation, questionnaires, surveys (via mail, e-mail, or telephone), focus groups, interviews, customer feedback, samples, and controlled experiments. A **focus group** is typically a group of 8 to 10 potential customers who are asked for feedback on a good or a service, an advertisement, an idea, or a packaging style.

- **Secondary data** are data that have already been collected and processed. A great deal of potentially useful data exist within the firm itself, including sales and production data. External sources of secondary data can include data collected from national or international institutions, government statistics, trade publications, and the like. Recently, social media have become great tools for gathering secondary data not only on your product but also on competing products. Because this information already exists, it is usually much cheaper than primary data to obtain.

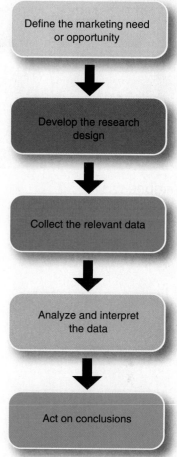

▪ **FIGURE 12.10**
The Marketing Research Process

Examples of primary and secondary data sources are summarized in ▪ **TABLE 12.1**.

By contacting current salon owners, Tiara Watson has begun to collect primary data about how eager salon owners might be to switch to a closer, cheaper supplier. She also has collected secondary data about the location of the closest salon supply companies and data regarding the demographics of potential salon customers in her region.

TABLE 12.1	Primary and Secondary Data Sources
Primary	Observations
	Questionnaires and surveys
	Experiments
	Interviews and focus groups
	Customer feedback
Secondary	Internal corporate information
	Trade associations
	Commercial sources
	Government data
	Magazines and newspapers
	Social media, Internet databases, and search engines

■ **FIGURE 12.11**
Benefits of Using Social Market Research

How are social media used in market research? Social media sites, such as Facebook and Twitter, are becoming invaluable tools for businesses to get in touch with the public at large (see ■ **FIGURE 12.11**). Not only can companies find out what is being said about their products, but they can also find out what is being said about the competition. Both types of information are invaluable—regardless of whether the opinions are good or bad. Honest feedback can be gathered from people who are eager to voice their opinions. There are two advantages of collecting information using social media rather than traditional focus groups: size and immediacy. Focus groups are limited in size, and a researcher can never be sure whether he or she has picked the right individuals. Because of the formality of a focus group, the event often requires much planning and can be quite expensive to implement. Alternatively, social media networks gather quick results from substantial numbers of consumers. Not every company or marketing research project will lend itself to social media tools. But if a fit is determined, social media give marketers another valuable tool for obtaining consumer insights.

How are the data analyzed and interpreted? Once the data have been collected, they must be assembled into a format that can be easily analyzed and interpreted. The person analyzing the data must understand various statistical techniques and how to use them (a discussion of which goes beyond the scope of this book). The ultimate goal is to conduct careful analyses that will lead to conclusions about what marketing strategies to implement. The analysis must also be honest; researchers should never adjust data to get the results they want. Through surveys and personal interviews, Tiara discovered that about 30 salons in the area were willing to switch suppliers, indicating she had a strong potential target market. Her research also uncovered buyers' concerns about the current supplier's product offerings, prices, and its relationship with area salons.

What happens when the research is completed? Once the information is collected and analyzed, it is usually presented in an organized manner to decision makers. The purpose of marketing research, after all, is to help managers make better marketing decisions. A formal presentation may be given to the sales and marketing teams, or a plan outlining a new advertising strategy may require hiring an advertising agency. Changing market conditions require businesses to continually adapt and constantly search for better ways to provide value to customers. As a result, marketing research should be ongoing.

The Marketing Plan

What is a marketing plan? Part of acting on the conclusions of marketing research is creating a marketing plan. A **marketing plan** is a written document that specifies the marketing activities that will take place to achieve an organization's objectives. It is the road map that will help carry out the strategies as determined by marketing research.

What are the elements of a good marketing plan? Four elements emerge from all good marketing plans:

- A clearly written marketing objective
- A situational analysis
- The target market
- A description of how the marketing mix will be implemented, evaluated, and controlled.

Why is a marketing objective necessary? A **marketing objective** is a clearly stated goal to be achieved through marketing activities. It should be realistic, quantifiable, and time specific.[11] A marketing objective of having every home in the United States purchase a specific product is unrealistic. Selling 100,000 units in a year is a more realistic, quantifiable, and time-specific marketing objective. When objectives are realistic, they are attainable and can motivate employees toward the goal. When they are measurable, a firm can determine whether they are being achieved. If deadlines are also imposed, then firms know whether they are reaching their goals in a timely manner.

What is a situational analysis? Creating clearly stated objectives is the first step in any good marketing plan. The next step is conducting a *situational analysis*. There are several methods that can be used to conduct a situational analysis, which is similar to the SWOT analysis discussed in Chapter 7, in that it includes an evaluation of internal *strengths* and *weaknesses* as well as the *opportunities* and *threats* found in the external environment; however, it focuses on marketing only rather than on the entire organization.

What do we mean by internal strengths? In terms of marketing, a company's internal strengths refer to the competitive advantages or core competencies a company has at its disposal to meet a specified marketing objective. Core competencies set a company apart. They enable a firm to provide customers with benefits that can't be easily imitated by other firms. For example, Deere and Company has been very successful in expanding its business by transferring the strength of its John Deere brand-name reputation for superior-quality agricultural equipment into lawn tractors and mowers for urban dwellers and earthmoving equipment for the construction industry. Indeed, a significant portion of Deere and Company's revenues now come from nonagricultural sales.[12]

How does a company assess its weaknesses? Assessing internal weaknesses means a company must perform an audit of its current managerial expertise, manufacturing and financing capabilities, and ability to successfully implement a product's marketing mix. By honestly assessing its weaknesses, a company can determine a realistic marketing objective. For example, a company that makes handmade watches and has only three employees cannot expect to produce 75,000 watches a week.

Why look to the external environment? The dynamic and ever-changing external environment offers many opportunities and creates many threats. Changes in the degree of competition facing firms, the economy, technology, and sociocultural forces, as well as changes in the global, political, and regulatory environments, have caused some firms to thrive while others suffer. This is especially true for international businesses because the number of market environments compounds the analysis. Rapid changes in technology create new opportunities, such as expanding sales over the Internet, but also pose new threats and challenges. Eastman Kodak, once the leader in cameras and photographic film products, was forced into bankruptcy because of its failure to transition to digital photography more quickly. Successful companies continually evaluate environmental factors as part of their situational analysis to match their strengths with opportunities and address their weaknesses to avoid threats.

Are there other ways to perform a situational analysis? Another way to conduct a situational analysis is by analyzing the factors shown in ■ **FIGURE 12.12**. This type of situational analysis requires gathering information about a company and its collaborators and the climate of the economy and industry and then extending the information by including an analysis of its customers and its competitors.

Target Markets

How are target markets determined? Determining a target market begins with **market segmentation**, the process of separating the broader market into smaller markets segments. A **market segment** is a subgroup of potential customers who share similar characteristics and therefore have similar product needs and preferences. A market segment should be identifiable, accessible, substantial, and stable and have unique needs. So, for example, rather than selling to all the salons in the state, Tiara decided to focus on a smaller market segment of just those salons

Company	Collaborators	Customers	Competitors	Climate
• What does my company do? • What are we selling? • What are our strengths and weaknesses?	• Who am I working with to make my business operate? • How can I grow and foster these relationships?	• Who is my target audience? • Who are my current customers? • Am I selling what they want?	• Who are my primary competitors? • Are there substitutes for my product? • Are there emerging businesses or technologies that might impact me? • What is my uniqueness, and am I leveraging it?	• What's going on in the industry? • Are there laws or regulations that impact me? • How is the current economic situation affecting buying behaviors?

■ **FIGURE 12.12**
Factors to Consider in a Situational Analysis

in the local area. Some markets, called **niche markets**, are even more narrowly defined. For example, a company that sells specialized gear shifters for racing bicycles is operating in a niche market.

Marketers choose the market segments that offer the greatest profit potential, and they become the target markets. For each target market, a company tries to blend the marketing mix to best satisfy its targeted customers. The process of developing a unique marketing mix that best satisfies a target market is known as **positioning**.

How are consumer markets segmented? Consumer markets can be segmented based on many variables or characteristics of customers. Four of the most common market segmentation classifications are geographic, demographic, psychographic, and behavioral and are summarized in ■ **TABLE 12.2**.

How are markets defined by location or region? Segmenting markets according to geographic characteristics is called **geographic segmentation**. For example, clothing apparel, skis, snowblowers, four-wheel-drive vehicles, air conditioning, and heating needs differ according to regional climate differences. Food preferences also vary by region. As a result, McDonald's offers special menu items to cater to the tastes and preferences of people in particular regions and countries. McLobster Rolls are served in Canada and the northeastern region of the United States; because people in India do not eat beef, the Maharaja Mac, which is made of lamb or chicken meat, is a big seller there. For Tiara Watson's salon supply company, the prominent hairstyles in her region may require specialized products that are not as popular in other locations.

How are markets defined by different population characteristics? Often, products are best received by men, or athletes, or seniors. **Demographic segmentation** is the process of segmenting a market by age, race, religion, gender, ethnic background, and other demographics. For example, by 2020, one in five Americans is estimated to be of Hispanic origin.[13] Few businesses want to miss out on this growing market segment. It's now common to find labels or instructions written in

TABLE 12.2	**Consumer Market Segmentation**		
Geographic	**Demographic**	**Psychographic**	**Behavioral**
• Region • Suburban • Rural • City • County • Population density • Climate • Terrain	• Age • Race • Religion • Family size • Ethnicity • Gender • Income • Education	• Lifestyle • Personality traits • Motives • Values	• Benefit sought • Volume usage • Brand loyalty • Price sensitivity • Product end use

both English and Spanish, and the number of Spanish-language television stations and newspapers is increasing.

Can a market be segmented based on opinions or interests? Harley-Davidson offers a wide variety of motorcycles, and each model attempts to cater to a particular lifestyle.[14] Cat food ads cleverly focus on "cat lover" personalities, whereas many beer commercials target men and sports enthusiasts. Segmenting markets based on people's lifestyles, personality traits, motives, and values is called **psychographic segmentation**. For example, Whole Foods Market and Trader Joe's focus on consumers interested in healthier, organic foods, and Planet Fitness sells memberships to customers concerned with their health but who are also price conscious.

Sophisticated marketers closely examine their customers' lifestyles, personality traits, motives, and values because, unlike geographic and demographic variables, these psychographic variables can be manipulated by marketing efforts. Whatever consumers may value, whether it be quality, social status or affiliation, safety, health, privacy, technology, or appearance, you can bet that businesses will offer a good or service to satisfy that real or perceived need and will be rewarded with profits for doing so.

How can consumer behaviors define a market segment? Do you buy only one particular brand of toothpaste regardless of price? Do you buy cranberry sauce only at Thanksgiving? These types of behaviors define **behavioral segmentation**, the market segmentation based on certain consumer behavior characteristics, such as brand loyalty, price sensitivity, the benefits sought from a product, occasions that stimulate purchases, and the ways in which a product is used.

Brand loyalty, which can affect a buyer's price sensitivity, is a type of behavioral segmentation. The more loyal the customer, the less sensitive he or she is to a price increase. If a customer has been using the same brand of toothpaste for 12 years and has had no cavities, a small price increase will most likely not be an issue to that customer.

Finally, knowing how a product is actually used can help companies develop packages that appeal to customers. For example, packaging vitamins in containers with lids easily turned by arthritic hands can appeal to some adult consumers.

The marketing process may involve only a few steps, but each of these takes some time and plenty of focused effort. Tiara Watson has given much thought as to which salons she wants to target. However, without performing a market analysis, she wasn't sure where to start. Once she stepped back and took time to go through the research process, she identified smaller salons that would appreciate her personal service, quick deliveries, and unique product offerings. Tiara is off to a good start, but she still has some work ahead of her in implementing her marketing mix and nurturing good customer relationships. The next two chapters explore the implementation of the marketing mix in more detail to nurture good customer relationships.

Consumer Behavior pp. 355–359

Will Giusto is standing in front of a display of laptop computers. He has to buy one for school but has left the task to the last minute, and he really can't leave the store without one. Not knowing much about computers, they all look pretty much the same to him, so how is he to decide? His girlfriend has a MacBook Pro and loves it, but she loves everything Apple makes. His best friend has a top-of-the-line HP and raves about how awesome it is, but he's a gamer. His sister has a Surface tablet and swears by it, but it seems so small. Will isn't looking for a fancy label or a "tricked out" machine. He just needs something to type his papers on and access Facebook from. But staring at the row of similar looking laptops is just plain

Source: Fotolia.

intimidating. How can Will make the best purchasing decision? What factors will influence his decision? ∎

Virtually every consumer faces numerous sources of influence while making any purchasing decision. The term **consumer behavior** refers to the ways individuals or organizations search for, evaluate, purchase, use, and dispose of goods and services. Notice that consumer behavior involves the study of individual consumers or business organizations as buyers in the market. Most of us intuitively think of a market as being a consumer market. In **business-to-consumer (B2C) markets**, individuals purchase goods and services for their personal consumption. But there are also business-to-business markets. In **business-to-business (B2B) markets**, businesses purchase goods and services from other businesses. In this section, we'll explore both markets and examine the buying behavior differences between consumer markets and B2B markets.

B2C Markets

Why study consumer behavior? Understanding how consumers behave helps marketers select the most profitable target markets and guides the implementation, evaluation, and control of the marketing mix for these groups. For example, consumers are becoming increasingly concerned about the environment. Automobile manufacturers that realize this concern may offer more gas-efficient vehicles or drop the prices on less efficient models to compensate for their poor gas mileage.

How does a consumer make a buying decision? The consumer buying process involves five steps:

1. Need recognition
2. Information search
3. Evaluation of alternatives
4. Purchase or no purchase decision
5. Postpurchase evaluation

Not all consumers go through each step in the process, and the steps do not need to be completed in the same order. The process can be interrupted at any time with a "no purchase" decision.

Consider your decision to purchase the educational services of your college or university. You first recognized the need for higher education. You likely obtained information about colleges from many sources, including your friends, family, counselors, and perhaps even the annual college rankings of *U.S. News & World Report*. You may have also visited a few college campuses to gather firsthand information. You then evaluated your choices based on a variety of factors, including a college's tuition (price), geographic location, or perhaps where your friends were going to college. Your final choice may have been based on rational analysis or the result of an emotional decision (based on some gut feelings). After making a purchase, we also evaluate our decisions in terms of how well our expectations are being met. You'll likely continue to evaluate your college choice long after you graduate.

What influences consumer decision making? The consumer decision-making process is part of a broader environmental context that influences each step. Marketers should be aware of these factors when developing an appropriate marketing mix for the target market. These environmental forces are shown in ∎ **FIGURE 12.13**.[15]

How does culture affect a person's buying behavior? *Culture* is the set of learned attitudes, beliefs, and ways of life that are unique to a society and handed down from generation to generation. Subcultures are specific groups within a culture that share attitudes and life experiences. Some examples of subcultures include churches, community organizations, and online communities like Facebook and Pinterest. Together, a buyer's culture, subculture, social class, family, and peers comprise the *sociocultural influences* that affect his or her buying decisions. Cultural values change over time. For example, the obesity epidemic has led many people today to value healthier lifestyles, which in turn has changed their buying patterns.

Social class refers to a combination of factors, such as education, income, wealth, and occupation, common to a group of people. Social class can have an impact on purchasing decisions, as some possessions are considered status symbols, like the MacBook Pro that Will's girlfriend owns. Apple computers are often viewed as just being "cooler" than other types of computers.

What unique personal influences shape buying behaviors? *Personal influences* on a buyer's consumption choices are often shaped by his or her age, gender, economic situation, lifestyle, and personality. Knowing that there is a difference between how men shop and how women shop can help influence a sales strategy. Women often like to browse, linger, and socialize, whereas men often prefer to get in and get out of a store. The owner of a Canadian women's clothing boutique recognized these patterns. To cater to her female customers, she hosts "trunk shows," during which her customers get together with their friends to have a glass of wine while reviewing a designer's new line. Similarly, she caters to her male customers' more efficient buying preferences by keeping a database of their spouse's or partner's personal information and preferences. Prior to special occasions, she'll contact her male customers and let them know she has the perfect gift for their spouse or partner.[16]

How do attitudes affect buying decisions? One goal of marketing is to shape the perception of a product in the minds of consumers. Attitudes toward a product put customers in a frame of mind that either predisposes them to favorably view a product or not. *Psychological influences* include differences in a buyer's motivation, perception, attitudes, and learning. Equally important is an effort to create positive product experiences. Good experiences with brands result in repeat business; bad experiences stunt future sales. It is more expensive to find new customers than to keep existing customers, so investing in methods to ensure that existing customers' needs are met and that they remain loyal to the brand is very important.

Can temporary conditions affect how buyers behave? *Situational influences* include the physical surroundings, the social surroundings, and the type of product purchased, and all of these can affect how a buyer behaves. Some factors, such as where products are placed or how a store is organized, can be easily controlled. However, other factors, such as adverse weather conditions or a consumer's negative mood, are not as easily managed, such as the hurried purchase Will Giusto was about to make because he had left his shopping to the last minute. He may not feel able to make a calm and informed decision due to the immediate pressure of the moment.

How does the marketing mix influence purchases? *Marketing mix influences* include putting forth a product that buyers want at an affordable price, promoting the attributes of that product, and placing the good or the service in a timely and convenient location for consumers to buy.

■ FIGURE 12.13

Major Influences Impacting a Consumer's Buying Decision
An effective marketing campaign helps consumers gather information about a product and evaluate alternatives.

Understanding consumer buying behavior and how it is influenced is critical to effective marketing. Some of these influences, like personal influences, are beyond the control of marketers, whereas other influences, like psychological influences, can be affected by businesses. All of these influences should be kept in mind when selecting a target market; implementing, evaluating, and controlling the marketing mix; and building customer relationships.

B2B Markets

What are the differences between B2C markets and B2B markets? The difference between B2C and B2B markets hinges on who's doing the buying. If a good or a service is purchased in a B2B market, it is purchased by a business for further processing, for resale, or to facilitate general business activity. The B2B market is larger than consumer markets because virtually all consumer products go through a number of distributors or wholesalers before reaching the final consumer at a retail outlet. In fact, a separate B2B market exists at each stage of the supply chain. Think of all the transactions involved in manufacturing and delivering a car. Most of the components are manufactured by separate firms, each of which needs to purchase from other companies the raw materials needed to make the part.

What are the characteristics of a B2B market? The first step in selling to a business market is the same as the consumer market: identify the customer and determine why the customer needs the product. However, the rest of the process is distinct for each market because of the inherent differences among the markets. B2B markets are generally more relationship driven than product driven. The quality of the product remains important, but the emphasis is on the relationship. Some other characteristics of B2B markets are as follows:

1. **A few buyers that purchase in large quantities.** B2B markets typically involve a few buyers that purchase very large quantities. For example, only a few airline companies buy most of Boeing's jets.

2. **Highly trained buyers.** Most business-purchasing agents are highly skilled at their jobs. They often weigh the benefits and the costs in a more systematic fashion and are less influenced by emotional factors than are buyers in consumer markets. This requires sellers to pitch their products at a much more sophisticated level.

Augmented Reality—A Passing Phase or the Future?

Augmented reality (AR) is a technology used on mobile devices that allows users to point their smart phones at an object and then watch a video or see a relevant graphic on top of the object on the smart phone screen. The technology has been around for years. Museums use AR to provide information about works of art and cities us the technology to provide useful information about public transportation. But AR has been slow to capture much attention from marketers looking to sell products in B2C markets.

However, the recent buzz surrounding Google Glasses, which use AR technology, has generated renewed interest. LEGO and Ford are using the technology to bring their products to life. LEGO uses AR in its stores to show the 3D version of the Lego structure shown on a product's box. And LEGO's Story Builder app lets children create interactive stories to go with their LEGO projects by using their iPads or iPhones. At the American International Auto Show, Ford introduced AR in a "Ford 4D" app. Users pointed their mobile device to a graphic on the cars to launch the 4D app. Then users could swipe the screen to open the back of a vehicle and see its storage capacity or to view the off-road suspension system.

Gartner, a technology research and advisory company, identified augmented reality and wearable devices that use AR technology as an up-and-coming mobile technology. But what do you think? Is AR be a viable marketing strategy of the future, or is it a passing phase?

3. **Group purchasing decision.** Teams of individuals within purchasing departments usually collaborate when making purchasing decisions. This means marketers must be patient and mindful of the concerns of all decision makers to seal a deal.

4. **Strong customer relationship.** Because there are only a few sophisticated buyers that purchase large quantities, marketers find it necessary to establish much closer relationships with customers compared to the relationships with buyers in consumer markets. As a result, B2B marketing is focused more on personal selling compared to the mass advertising campaigns that typify consumer markets.

5. **Geographically concentrated buyers.** Most buyers in B2B markets are concentrated in a few of the most industrialized states, where large businesses are located. This reduces the costs of reaching buyers.

6. **Direct purchasing.** Buyers in B2B markets often purchase directly from sellers, as opposed to consumer markets, where products typically go through many wholesalers before a product arrives at the end user.

These key differences between B2C and B2B markets are summarized in ■ **TABLE 12.3**. The differences can be organized by market structure, the nature of the buying unit, and the purchasing process.

How does a business make a buying decision, and what influences that decision? Similar to consumers, businesses begin by recognizing a need and then seek out information to aid them in the purchase decision, evaluate alternatives, decide to either purchase or not purchase, and do a postpurchase evaluation. However, business purchases are generally more rational, reasoned, objective decisions based on various influences, such as the state of the economy, technological factors, the degree of regulatory concerns, and organizational objectives, policies, and procedures.

Is the marketing process different for B2B markets? The marketing process remains the same for all markets: identify a need, conduct research to come up with a marketing plan, select a target market, implement and control the marketing mix, and nurture customer relationships.

Will Giusto finally made his purchase. After consulting with a sales clerk about each of the brands, he chose an HP laptop. Was it the quality and reputation of HP products that swayed his decision? The influence of his friend? Or something else?

TABLE 12.3	**Differences between B2B and B2C Markets**	
	B2B Market	**B2C Market**
Market structure	• Few customers • Large-volume purchases • Geographically concentrated	• Many customers • Small-volume purchases • Geographically dispersed
Nature of the buying unit	• More professional and rational purchase decision	• Less sophisticated and more emotional purchase decision
Purchasing process	• Highly trained buyers • Group purchasing decision • Complex buying decisions • Formalized buying procedures • Close and personal selling relationship between marketer and buyer • Personal selling	• Untrained buyers • Individual purchasing decision • Relatively simple buying decisions • Informal buying decision • Impersonal relationship between marketer and buyer • Mass advertising

Summary

1 How has marketing evolved over time? (pp. 338–340)

- During the production concept era (from the industrial revolution until the 1920s), most companies focused solely on production. Demand was often greater than supply, and the prevailing mind-set was that a good-quality product would simply sell itself.

- During the sales concept era (from the mid-1920s through the early 1950s), technological advances meant that production increased more sharply than demand for goods and services. "Push" selling and heavy advertising in all available forms of media became prevalent.

- During the marketing concept era (from the 1950s through the 1990s), production continued to expand more quickly than the growth in demand for goods and services. The **marketing concept** (p. 339) changed the focus from finding the right customer for a product to producing the right product for a customer and doing it better than the competition.

- During the societal marketing era (1960s to the present), companies began to realize that they must work for the benefit of both consumers and society.

- During the customer relationship era (from the late 1990s to the present), organizations have worked to establish long-term relationships with individual customers to foster loyalty and get repeat business.

2 What are the benefits and criticisms of marketing? (pp. 341–343)

- **Marketing** (p. 337) identifies and satisfies human needs and wants. It provides value to customers by providing them with benefits that exceed their costs. In turn, sellers benefit because marketing enables them to survive.

- Businesses that most successfully satisfy customers generate higher profits, and investors benefit from the profits earned. Employees benefit from successful marketing as well because their jobs and livelihoods are more secure.

- Society in general benefits from marketing because scarce resources are more efficiently allocated to goods and services most desired by society.

- Criticisms of marketing include price gouging, the production of shoddy or unsafe products, and confusing and deceptive practices. The criticisms of marketing should not be taken lightly. All companies should have a code of ethics and policies in place to curb unethical behavior within their organizations.

3 What are the elements of a marketing strategy and the components of the marketing mix? (pp. 343–345)

- The two basic elements of a marketing strategy are the **target market** (p. 343) and the **marketing mix** (p. 343).

- The four Ps of the marketing mix are **product** (p. 338), price, **promotion** (p. 344), and **place** (p. 345).

4 How do firms implement a marketing strategy by applying the marketing process? (pp. 345–347)

- The marketing process involves (1) identifying a need, (2) conducting market research and developing a marketing plan, (3) determining a target market, (4) implementing the four Ps of the marketing mix, and (5) nurturing good customer relationships.

- The application of the marketing process is as much an art as a science. Producing a high-quality product with a unique brand properly promoted that consistently delivers value to customers at a fair price when and where customers want a product are common ingredients for marketing success.

5 How does the marketing environment influence a firm's ability to manipulate its marketing mix? (pp. 347–350)

- The **marketing environment** (p. 347) includes environmental influences, such as the competitive, economic, technological, and sociocultural environments, as well as the political, legal, and regulatory environments. Because these factors are beyond a firm's control, they constrain an organization's ability to manipulate its marketing mix.

6 What is the marketing research process, and what are the elements of a good marketing plan? (pp. 350–355)

- **Market research** (p. 350) is an ongoing process of gathering and analyzing market information to gauge changing market conditions that may lead to better ways and opportunities to provide services to customers.

- The marketing research process involves (1) defining the marketing need or opportunity, (2) collecting relevant data, (3) analyzing and interpreting the data, and (4) acting on the research's conclusions.

- A **marketing plan** (p. 352) is a written document that specifies marketing activities designed to achieve an organization's objectives.

- Four elements emerge from a good marketing plan: (1) a clearly written marketing objective, (2) a situational analysis, (3) the selection of a target market, and (4) implementation, evaluation, and control of the marketing mix (the four Ps).

- Another type of situational analysis is looking at other factors of marketing: company, collaborators, customers, competitors, and the climate of the industry and economy.

7 How do the buying decisions and marketing processes in the business-to-business market compare to those in the consumer market? (pp. 355–359)

- In a **business-to-consumer market (B2C)** (p. 356), buyers are households that purchase final consumer goods. In a **business-to-business (B2B) market** (p. 356), businesses buy from other businesses. There are many more B2B markets than consumer markets. In B2B markets, purchases are often made by a small group of highly trained individuals who buy in large volumes and have much closer relationships with marketers. B2B buyers are also more geographically concentrated.

- Consumers and businesses use the same five-step decision-making process when making purchases. However, some of the factors that affect business purchases are different.

- The marketing process remains the same for all markets: identify a need, conduct research to come up with a marketing plan, select a target market, implement and control the marketing mix, and always remember to nurture good customer relationships.

Key Terms

behavioral segmentation   (p. 355)

business-to-business (B2B) market   (p. 356)

business-to-consumer (B2C) market   (p. 356)

consumer behavior   (p. 356)

customer relationship management   (p. 340)

demographic segmentation   (p. 354)

environmental scanning   (p. 347)

focus group   (p. 351)

form utility   (p. 342)

geographic segmentation   (p. 354)

market research   (p. 350)

market segment   (p. 353)

market segmentation   (p. 353)

marketing   (p. 337)

marketing concept   (p. 339)

marketing environment   (p. 347)

marketing mix   (p. 343)

marketing objective   (p. 352)

marketing plan   (p. 352)

niche market   (p. 354)

ownership utility   (p. 342)

place (distribution)   (p. 345)

place utility   (p. 342)

positioning   (p. 354)

primary data   (p. 351)

product   (p. 338)

promotion   (p. 344)

psychographic segmentation   (p. 355)

secondary data   (p. 351)

target market   (p. 343)

task utility   (p. 342)

time utility   (p. 342)

value   (p. 342)

MyBizLab

Go to **mybizlab.com** to complete the problems marked with this icon .

Self Test

Multiple Choice *You can find the answers on the last page of this book.*

12-1 **Which marketing era occurred during the Great Depression when manufacturers almost had to force consumers to purchase their products?**

  a. Production concept era

  b. Sales concept era

  c. Marketing concept era

  d. Customer relationship era

12-2 **When a car is purchased, *form utility* refers to the value customers receive from**

  a. owning the car.

  b. the styling and function of the automobile.

  c. ready availability and speed with which the dealer made the car available for purchase.

  d. close proximity to the car dealership.

12-3 **LinYee created a document that includes a situational analysis and a discussion of the target market. LinYee's document is called**

  a. marketing research.

  b. a marketing mix.

  c. a marketing plan.

  d. marketing segmentation.

Self Test (continued)

12-4 Tenitia Reynolds opened a small community bookstore several years ago. When a new book comes out, Tenitia e-mails clients she thinks will enjoy it based on their past purchases. Which part of the marketing process do Tenitia's actions reflect?

a. Conducting market research

b. Identifying a market need

c. Implementing the marketing mix

d. Nurturing customer relationships

12-5 Bill Wertz runs a transportation service that caters exclusively to the residents of retirement communities. Bill's business is taking advantage of which of the following marketing environments?

a. The competitive environment

b. The sociocultural environment

c. The technological environment

d. The economic environment

12-6 Which of the following does *not* define a B2B market?

a. The market consists of small-volume purchases in a geographically dispersed area.

b. Buyers make complex purchasing decisions, often with formal buying procedures.

c. The purchasing process involves much personal selling and requires a close relationship between the buyer and seller.

d. Buyers are more professional and make more rational purchasing decisions.

12-7 Market segmentation based on lifestyles, personality traits, motives, and values is called

a. geographic segmentation.

b. demographic segmentation.

c. psychographic segmentation.

d. behavioral segmentation.

12-8 Which of the following represents a shift from the four Ps to the four Cs of marketing?

a. Considering the complete cost of a product to the consumer

b. Making the product convenient to buy

c. Focusing on the consumer's wants and needs

d. All of the above

12-9 Identifying the internal strengths and weaknesses as well as the opportunities and threats found in the external environment with regard to the marketing functions of an organization is known as

a. a situational analysis.

b. a SWOT analysis.

c. a marketing analysis.

d. a competitive analysis.

12-10 Which is *not* an example of secondary data?

a. Census data

b. Customer feedback on Twitter

c. Focus group results

d. Data collected from company sales reports

True/False *You can find the answers on the last page of this book.*

12-11 The main difference between the B2B and B2C markets is that B2B markets have fewer buyers that purchase many more individual quantities.
☐ True or ☐ False

12-12 A product is defined as any intangible good, service, or idea available for purchase.
☐ True or ☐ False

12-13 A market niche is a narrowly defined market segment.
☐ True or ☐ False

12-14 Employees can benefit from successful marketing because new job opportunities may be created as production expands to satisfy the growing demand for highly-valued products.
☐ True or ☐ False

12-15 Sociocultural influences that affect buying decisions include a buyer's culture, social class, family, and peers.
☐ True or ☐ False

Critical Thinking Questions

✪ **12-16** Think of an example of how a specific organization (a for-profit or not-for-profit) tried to establish a better customer relationship with you. What did the organization do? Was it effective? Why or why not?

✪ **12-17** List as many brands of ice cream as you can think of. Include the brands sold by ice cream stores as well as brands sold in grocery stores. Group the ice cream brands into target markets. What features of each brand identify its target market.

12-18 Suppose you were hired by Apple to develop a marketing campaign for a new iPhone. Who would be the target market? List at least four characteristics and the corresponding market segment that define the ideal customer. Repeat the exercise for a Toyota Prius and a vacation package to a luxury spa in Arizona.

Team Time

BRAND ANALYSIS

Divide into teams of four or five. Each team should pick a different sports drink (such as Gatorade) or flavored water product (such as Vitamin Water).

Process

Step 1. Determine what the target market is for your brand. Discuss the segmentation approaches used by your brand.

Step 2. Discuss the marketing mix for your product.

Step 3. Discuss the specific elements and tactics the company uses to communicate a brand's message to prospective and current buyers.

Step 4. Conduct a brief situational analysis for your brand.

Step 5. Write a brief summary of your findings. What recommendations do you have for the brand based on your research and analysis?

Ethics and Corporate Social Responsibility

PATAGONIA AND COMMON THREADS PARTNERSHIP

Patagonia has long been a leader in environmental initiatives. As mentioned in the text, the company took out a full-page ad in major newspapers on Black Friday to urge its customers not to buy a jacket from the company unless they really needed it. This action was in keeping with the firm's initiative to reduce the company's carbon footprint. The company publishes their actions on The Footprint Chronicles, found on Patagonia's website. In addition, Patagonia started the Common Threads Partnership, which encourages people to take steps to help the environment by reducing the number of products they use and repairing, reusing, recycling, and reimagining products.

Questions for Discussion

12-19 Go to Patagonia's website and look at all the actions the company has taken and is currently pursuing in their efforts to become a responsible company. Briefly summarize their current campaign "The Responsible Economy."

Ethics and Corporate Social Responsibility (continued)

12-20 Discuss how Patagonia's environmental and corporate social responsibility practices drive customer loyalty.

12-21 In The Footprint Chronicles, the company lists ways other companies can use Patagonia's strategies to reduce their carbon footprint. Choose a local company or even your college and discuss how you think the organization could implement Patagonia's practices.

Web Exercises

12-22 Apple's Marketing Mix
Go to Apple's website and click on the iPad link. Describe Apple's marketing mix strategy for the product—that is, the product/customer, price/cost, promotion/communication, and place/convenience. How does Apple attempt to foster good customer relations? What marketing recommendations would you make to Apple?

12-23 Mobile Marketing
Marketers are offering coupons on mobile devices, sending alerts to them to announce special sales or discounts, using QR codes, and creating mobile shopping applications. Starbucks is a leader in mobile marketing. Research and comment on Starbuck's mobile marketing efforts. What is Starbucks doing in this regard that other companies can emulate, and what can it do better?

12-24 Organic Differences
Visit the websites of Trader Joe's and Whole Foods Market. Both companies are in the organic and health-conscious food industries. Compare the two websites.

What marketing techniques does each site use? Do you think the companies are targeting the same type of customer? Why or why not?

12-25 Daily Deals
Groupon and LivingSocial pioneered the concept of daily deals. Over time, many more daily deal websites, such as Woot and Google Offers, have evolved. Research three daily deal websites and comment on their marketing plans. How does each attract, retain, and communicate with its customers?

12-26 The Jeep Experience
The Jeep brand uses a nontraditional marketing approach by offering Jeep owners invitations to special events. Go to the Jeep website and research the events that this company offers to its customers. How effective do you think engaging customers in ongoing events is in getting them to be repeat buyers?

MyBizLab

Go to **mybizlab.com** for Auto-graded writing questions as well as the following Assisted-graded writing questions:

✪ **12-27** Briefly compare the marketing environments for a pizza parlor and a flower shop. What do they have in common? What is different?

✪ **12-28** Think of the last major purchase you made. Discuss how sociocultural, personal, psychological, situational, and marketing mix influences impacted this purchase.

References

1. Ford Motor Company, "Vehicle History," June 1, 2012, http://corporate.ford.com.
2. American Marketing Association, "Community: AMA Definition of Marketing". *Resource Library Dictionary*, June 12, 2012, www.marketingpower.com/_layouts/Dictionary.aspx?dLetter=M (reprinted with permission).
3. Henry Ford, quoted in Henry Ford Museum and Greenfield Village, "Showroom of Automotive History: The Model T," June 18, 2012, www.hfmgv.org.
4. From General Electric 1952 Annual Report, p. 21, as quoted in Rom Zemke and John A. Woods, *Best Practices in Customer Service* (Amherst, MA: HRD Press, 1998), 3.
5. The Body Shop, "About Us," www.thebodyshop-usa.com/about-us/aboutus.aspx?cm_re=Tyra_CrueltyFreeMakeup2012-_-Navigation-_-about-us.
6. Patagonia, "Common Threads Initiative," www.patagonia.com/email/11/112811.html.
7. Ad Council, "About Buzzed Driving," http://adcouncil.org.
8. L.L. Bean www.llbean.com.
9. Dos Equis, "Meet the Man," www.dosequis.com.
10. Blendtec, "Will It Blend? Home," www.willitblend.com.
11. Charles W. Lamb Jr., Joseph F. Hair, and Carl McDaniel, *Marketing*, 7th ed. (Stamford, CT: Thomson Publishing, 2004), 33.
12. John Deere, www.deere.com.
13. High Beam Research, www.omniglot.com/language/articles/spanishtranslation.htm.
14. "Will Harley-Davidson Hit the Wall? It Redefined the Motorcycle Industry as It Roared through 16 Years of Growth. But as Its Customers Age—and the Stock Market Slides—the Ride Could Get Uneasy," http://money.cnn.com/magazines/fortune/fortune_archive/2002/08/12/327029/index.htm.
15. Philip Kotler and Gary Armstrong. *Principles of Marketing*, 12th ed. (Upper Saddle River, NJ: Pearson/Prentice Hall, 2008), 131–47.
16. Women's Enterprise Centre, "Sales Savvy Series for Women Entrepreneurs: #6—Gender Differences in Buying Habits," www.womensenterprise.ca/enews/articles/Microsoft%20Word%20-%206%20-%20Gender%20Differences%20_2_.pdf.

Chapter 13
Product Development, Branding, and Pricing Strategies

▶ New Product Development

Jessica Smith wants to open a yoga studio in her neighborhood. She also wants to sell yoga supplies. The closest studio is 5 miles away and in poor condition, so she thinks her location would be great. What else does Jessica need to do to develop her studio? What steps are involved in the product development process?

▶ Products and Product Lines

Evelyn Robinson and Juan Delgado each drink zero-calorie soft drinks made by Coca-Cola. Evelyn drinks Diet Coke, and Juan drinks Coke Zero. Each thinks his or her soda is the best. Are the products really different, or are they basically the same with different labeling and names?

▶ Branding

Robin Green loves homemade bread. When her bread-making machine needed a new part, she contacted the manufacturer and, surprisingly, was told that the company didn't actually make the machine and would not service it. The company had licensed its name to a different manufacturer. Robin felt let down by the brand she thought was so good. When you go shopping, how important is the brand of a product?

▶ Pricing Goods and Services

When Gina Riviera wanted to increase the profits at the store she managed, she revisited the pricing strategies that the previous manager had relied on. How can Gina get customers to think differently about the unique items in her store so people will shop there instead of at a nearby chain store? What pricing approach should she take?

OBJECTIVES

1 What steps take place during new product development, and what is the product life cycle? (pp. 367–371)

2 How is a product distinguished from a total product offer? (pp. 371–372)

3 What is product differentiation, and what role does it play in product development? (pp. 372–373)

4 What are the different classifications of consumer products and business-to-business products? (pp. 373–376)

5 Why is branding beneficial to both buyers and sellers, and what are some branding strategies? (pp. 376–383)

6 What are some pricing objectives, and how do they relate to the marketing mix? (pp. 383–385)

7 What are the major approaches to pricing strategies? (pp. 385–389)

New Product Development pp. 367–371

Jessica Smith had a dream to open a yoga studio in her hometown. There was one other yoga studio nearby, but people were becoming dissatisfied with the studio's service. Jessica formerly taught classes there but quit because it was so poorly run and maintained. There weren't enough mats for students, the locker rooms were tiny, and the paint on the walls was peeling off. So Jessica decided it was time to open her own studio. Not only did she want to teach classes, but she also wanted to sell yoga equipment. How should Jessica go about creating her new offering? And what happens to her product after it's been created? ■

In Chapter 12, we saw that successful marketing requires identifying a need, using market research to determine a target market, and implementing a marketing plan that satisfies customers over time. This may sound easy, but it's not. Applying the marketing process is as much an art as it is a science.

Source: Pete Saloutos/Fotolia.

Making a high-quality product with a unique brand that is properly promoted and that consistently delivers value to customers at a fair price and is available when and where they want it presents significant challenges to marketers all over the world.

This chapter focuses on two of the four Ps of the marketing mix: *product* and *price*. The next chapter focuses on the other two components—*promotion* and *distribution* (place).

We begin by looking at the product because all marketing begins with a product and, in particular, how new products are developed. Most businesses must regularly modify their products or offer entirely new products to meet rapidly changing market conditions.

The New Product Development Process

What is involved in new product development? Companies need to introduce new products or else face losing market share and potential extinction. "Innovate or die" is a phrase often associated with new product development. The process of developing new, high-quality products involves several steps, which are as follows as well as outlined in ■ **FIGURE 13.1**:

1. **Idea generation.** New products start with an idea, like Jessica's idea to open a yoga studio. Ideas for entirely new products or improved versions of existing products

MyBizLab®

⭐ **Improve Your Grade!**

Over 10 million students improved their results using the Pearson MyLabs.
Visit **mybizlab.com** for simulations, tutorials, and end-of-chapter problems.

Step 1: Idea Generation
- Brainstorm new product ideas
- Think of ways to improve an existing product

Step 2: Idea Screening
- Ask yourself: will my target market benefit from this product?
- Ask yourself: can this product be competitive with similar products?

Step 3: Product Analysis
- Determine a desired sale price
- Assess the cost of production

Step 4: Development and Testing
- Produce a virtual or conceptual prototype
- Get feedback from potential customers

Step 5: Product and Marketing Mix Development
- Produce physical prototype
- Obtain more feedback from potential customers

Step 6: Market Testing
- Place product in select target market
- Virtual reality or simulated tools can help customers

Step 7: Commercialization
- Introduce the product to the market
- Begin the rollout process

■ **FIGURE 13.1**
The New Product Development Process
Source: Kotler, Philip; Keller, Kevin Lane, Marketing Management: Analysis, Planning, Implementation and Control, 12th Ed., © 2006. Reprinted and electronically reproduced by permission of Pearson Education, Inc., Upper Saddle River, New Jersey.

are often obtained by listening closely to customers or groups of customers, which includes monitoring social media. In Jessica's case, customer complaints signal a need for a new service. Similarly, SC Johnson, the maker of cleaning products, found that consumers were using a competing product, Lysol Disinfectant Spray, because they thought the spray killed bacteria in the air. However, since the spray kills bacteria only on surfaces, the company used this information to create a new product, Oust Air Sanitizer. They differentiated it from Lysol and other similar products by stating that Oust Air Sanitizer is different because it kills airborne bacteria.[1] Suppliers, employees, and salespeople also generate ideas by assessing the competition and visiting trade shows. Some companies foster internal innovation and brainstorming sessions to spur new ideas.

Still other companies search externally for innovations and product ideas and purchase them from other firms. Or they acquire the firms outright. Purchasing firms outright for new product development is done quite a bit in the technology industry. For example, Apple Inc. bought Beats Music to improve their own music streaming service.

2. **Idea screening.** The objective of idea screening is to identify the best ideas and eliminate unsound concepts before devoting costly resources to their development. Screening involves estimating the level of consumer demand for a product, its profitability, and its production feasibility given the company's current capabilities or costs to outsource the work. Acceptable ideas move on for further analysis.

3. **Product analysis.** The viable ideas are then analyzed further to determine the demand for the product and its financial feasibility. As part of this step, the costs of production are estimated, as are the product's selling price, sales volume, and profitability. The costs of production depend on the features of the product deemed necessary to meet the targeted customers' needs.

4. **Concept development and testing.** Concept testing involves soliciting customer responses to the new product idea. *Focus groups*, which are groups of customers brought together for this purpose, are asked to evaluate different features, prices, packages, and a host of other factors surrounding a product as well as to compare it to the competition. Often storyboards or a virtual mock-up of the product are used to present the concept. Sometimes advertising ideas are presented. Ultimately, the goal of the focus group process is to determine what the participants liked and disliked about the concept and whether they would purchase the product and at what price. The idea is to come up with the best, most profitable total product offering.

5. **Product and marketing mix development.** Once a product concept has gone through initial development and testing and after a business analysis indicates there is financial merit to the idea, an initial design or prototype is developed. Previously, the design and prototype were in conceptual or virtual format. At this stage, a physical product is developed and introduced for additional consumer feedback as well as aspects of the marketing mix, such as pricing, promotional techniques, and how and where the product should be distributed or sold.

6. **Market testing.** Sometimes this step is skipped if enough information and feedback has been obtained in the previous steps. But often a product is placed in trial phases to test its acceptance even further. Market testing is usually done by introducing the product in a specific geographic area, aimed at a select target market. Because of the unknown nature of the product, sometimes marketers must convince distributors or store managers to make shelf space available in order to test a new product. To avoid some of these complications and to reduce the expense with market testing, some companies and marketers have begun to use virtual worlds in which to conduct market testing. Simulation tools and virtual stores help to reduce development costs and the time required to bring a new product to market.

7. **Commercialization.** If a product concept makes it this far in the process, it is ready to be launched. Commercialization is the decision to market a product. Introducing a new product can be costly due to the research and manufacturing investments required to develop it and the advertising, personal selling, and other promotional activities needed to launch it. The returns from such investments can take time. This may explain why many companies introduce their new products in one region at a time, which is referred to as *rolling out the product*.

Despite the rigors of new product development, a large proportion of new products still fail. One of the most interesting cases of a new product failure was Coca-Cola's New Coke, launched in 1985. In an attempt to revitalize its brand, the company toyed with the formula of its popular soda and almost destroyed it. People didn't want their favorite soft drink modified, and New Coke was pulled from the shelves only three months after being introduced.[2] Coca-Cola returned to its original formula and renamed it Coca-Cola Classic. Netflix's attempt to spin its DVD-by-mail service into a separate company named Qwikster was met with immediately negative reaction and a loss of nearly a third of their subscribers. Many compared the proposed Qwikster launch to the similarly disastrous launch of New Coke.

The Product Life Cycle

What is a product life cycle? Once a product is developed, it begins the product life cycle. A **product life cycle** is a theoretical model describing a product's sales and profits over the course of its lifetime. During this cycle, a product typically goes through an introductory stage, a growth stage, a maturity stage, and a declining stage. The product life cycle can be applied to a specific product or an entire product category.

You can see how the theory works if you consider the life cycle of vinyl musical records. Vinyl records were first introduced in 1930 by RCA Victor but became popular in the 1950s as a replacement for the brittle and easily broken 78-rpm records. This was their introductory stage. Sales grew rapidly in the 1950s and the 1960s, representing the product's growth stage. In the early 1970s, vinyl records hit their maturity stage. By the late 1970s and early 1980s, cassette tapes gained wide acceptance, the sales of vinyl records fell drastically, and they entered their declining stage. After compact discs (CDs) and digital music were introduced, the decline continued. Vinyl records are now sold mostly as collectors' items.

The product life of fad items like Beanie Babies can be as short as a few months; for some products, such as automobiles, a product's life can be as long as a century or more. In addition, not all products strictly follow these stages. Some products are introduced but never grow in sales, whereas others never seem to decline. Also, companies often make adjustments to products, causing them to go back and forth between stages before continuing through the cycle. Like all models, the product life cycle model presents a simplified version of reality. Consequently, it should be used with caution when forecasting the future sales and profits of an actual product.

How do marketing decisions affect a product's life cycle? Knowing which stage of the product life cycle a particular product is in helps determine the appropriate marketing mix strategy for that stage. In fact, marketing decisions can affect

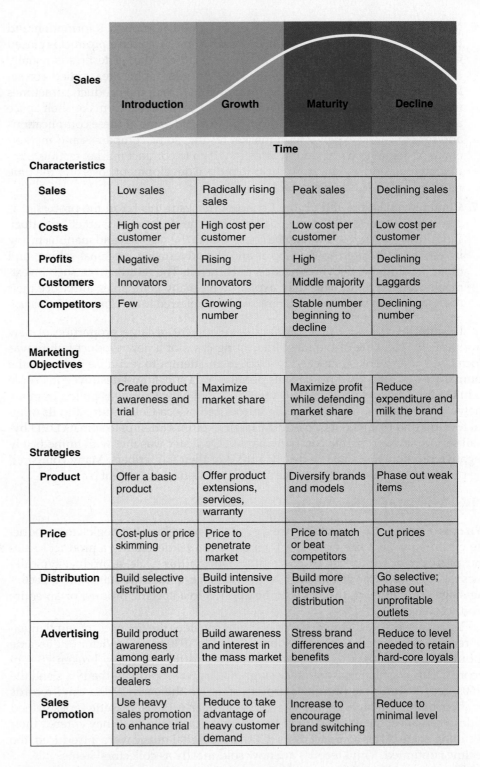

■ **FIGURE 13.2**
The Product Life Cycle Model
The product life cycle is a theoretical model describing a product's sales and profits over the course of its lifetime. Not all products strictly follow these stages. *Source:* Kotler, Philip; Keller, Kevin Lane, Marketing Management: Analysis, Planning, Implementation and Control, 12th Ed., © 2006. Reprinted and electronically reproduced by permission of Pearson Education, Inc., Upper Saddle River, New Jersey.

	Introduction	Growth	Maturity	Decline
Characteristics				
Sales	Low sales	Radically rising sales	Peak sales	Declining sales
Costs	High cost per customer	High cost per customer	Low cost per customer	Low cost per customer
Profits	Negative	Rising	High	Declining
Customers	Innovators	Innovators	Middle majority	Laggards
Competitors	Few	Growing number	Stable number beginning to decline	Declining number
Marketing Objectives	Create product awareness and trial	Maximize market share	Maximize profit while defending market share	Reduce expenditure and milk the brand
Strategies				
Product	Offer a basic product	Offer product extensions, services, warranty	Diversify brands and models	Phase out weak items
Price	Cost-plus or price skimming	Price to penetrate market	Price to match or beat competitors	Cut prices
Distribution	Build selective distribution	Build intensive distribution	Build more intensive distribution	Go selective; phase out unprofitable outlets
Advertising	Build product awareness among early adopters and dealers	Build awareness and interest in the mass market	Stress brand differences and benefits	Reduce to level needed to retain hard-core loyals
Sales Promotion	Use heavy sales promotion to enhance trial	Reduce to take advantage of heavy customer demand	Increase to encourage brand switching	Reduce to minimal level

each phase of a product's life cycle. ■ **FIGURE 13.2** summarizes the characteristics, marketing objectives, and strategies for each stage of the product life cycle.

How can a product's life be extended? Companies work hard to extend the lives of existing products to derive as much profit from them as possible. Some tactics used to extend the growth stage of a product include the following:

• **Lowering the price.** Some auto manufacturers have used discounted prices, rebates, and low-interest loans to extend the life of their models.

• **Creating a new use for the product.** Arm & Hammer, a company that produces baking soda, extended its product's life by advertising it as a refrigerator deodorizer.

- **Finding a new market for the product.** Crocs, the distinct footwear company, initially marketed their unusual clog-like shoe for its lightweight, odor-resistant, water-resistant qualities to recreational boaters. Several years later, the company came out with "CrocsRx," a line of shoes designed for special medical conditions. Now, the company produces more than 300 styles for all types of users.

- **Relabeling or repackaging the product.** Repackaging is another popular method to extend a product's life. Sally Hansen, the nail care company, put nail polish in a pen-like applicator that is portable and spill-proof.

- **Create a new vision.** A company can also reposition its product as Oldsmobile attempted to do with its "This isn't your father's Oldsmobile" campaign. These strategies are not always effective. The Oldsmobile brand, despite the revised campaign, has been discontinued.[3] Buick has also attempted to bring awareness back to its brand by showing moments in which people cannot find the Buick despite it being right in front of them.

As you've just learned, developing a high-quality product is not so much an end in itself as it is a beginning. Three years after opening her yoga studio and equipment store, Jessica Smith changed her marketing and pricing strategies for classes that were experiencing declining sales. At the same time, she expanded the offerings of her most popular classes to maximize their profits during the critical growth and maturity stages. She has also begun to offer organic snacks and light meal offerings. As Jessica has learned, a dynamic market calls for dynamic product development.

Products and Product Lines pp. 371–376

Evelyn Robinson and her boyfriend, Juan Delgado, were ordering lunch. "I'll have a Diet Coke," Evelyn added after placing their sandwich orders, "and he'll have a Coke Zero," pointing to Juan. Evelyn laughed at Juan. "You know, they're both the same. I don't understand why you won't drink Diet Coke."

"I've never liked Diet Coke. For some reason, Coke Zero tastes better," Juan quipped back. "If you think they're the same, why don't you just drink Coke Zero?"

"I couldn't imagine drinking anything besides Diet Coke. You can keep your Coke Zero; I have to have my Diet Coke," Evelyn replied.

Are the two zero-calorie cola products produced by Coca-Cola the same, with just different labels and names, or are the products really different? Why would Coca-Cola make two very similar products? What is the company trying to accomplish? ■

Source: Art Directors & TRIP/Alamy.

In addition to modifying existing products or creating new products, businesses need to differentiate their products from their competitors'. To accomplish these goals, a company needs to consider not only the product's physical components but the other attributes that make up the total product offer.

The Total Product Offer

What is the total product offer? Recall that a product is any good or service that might satisfy a want or a need. An Apple iPhone, a college education, a doctor's advice, and even a Caribbean vacation package are all products. Consumers buy products for a number of tangible and intangible benefits. The **total product offer** consists

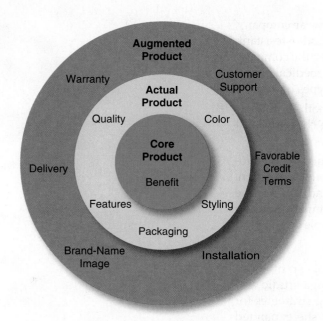

■ **FIGURE 13.3**
The Three Levels of a Product
The three levels of a product define the benefits to be derived from a total product offering.
Source: Based on "Three Levels of a Product." from Marketing Teacher. www.marketingteacher.com.

of all the benefits associated with a product that affect a consumer's purchasing decision. For example, when you buy a car, you're not just buying a mode of transportation; you're also buying some intangible benefits, such as style or image. Marketers know this. So, when they plan a total product offering, they think about the product on three levels: the *core product*, the *actual product*, and the *augmented product*. Each level adds more value to a product.

■ **FIGURE 13.3** summarizes the three levels of a product. The three levels of a product define the benefits to be derived from the total product offering.

What is the core product? The **core product** is the primary benefit or service that satisfies the basic need or want that motivates a consumer's purchase. For a car, the core product is convenient transportation. For a soft drink, it's the thirst-quenching capability. For a camera, it's the ability to capture memories. Notice that the core product is intangible. You can't touch it. Companies use the benefits of their products to lure customers. Think about Coke's "Have a Coke and a smile" campaign. What core benefit is it trying to convey?

What is the actual product? The **actual product** is the tangible aspect of the purchase that you can touch, see, hear, smell, or taste. It provides core benefits when it is used. Consumers often assess the tangible benefits of actual products by comparing brands, their quality (often associated with a brand's reputation), features, styling, or packaging. For a car, the actual product is the automobile itself. The core benefits of an automobile could be its numerous safety features, leather seats, or entertainment system. For a soft drink, the actual product is a refreshing taste or the caffeine buzz that consumers are looking for when they purchase some sodas.

What is the augmented product? The **augmented product** consists of the core product and the actual product *plus* other real or perceived benefits that provide additional value to a customer's purchase. These benefits might include customer service and support, delivery, installation, a warranty, or favorable credit terms. The value-enhancing elements of an actual product are an important part of the total product offering because they help provide a more satisfying customer experience. For a car, the augmented benefits might include a reasonable price, an easy payment plan, a 10-year warranty, or just the feeling of safety you get from owning a brand-new car.

Product Differentiation

How important is product differentiation? Product differentiation is critical for a product's success. **Product differentiation** is the process of distinguishing a product from its competition in real or perceived terms to attract customers. Products are differentiated by establishing concrete or intangible differences among similar products. For example, Southwest Airlines set itself apart from other airlines with its low-cost fares and fun and friendly service. The company's "bags fly free" campaign also distinguishes it from its competitors. If a product doesn't stand out, there is no motivation for customers to buy it rather than a competing product.

Hair care products are differentiated by packaging, scents, and perceived beauty benefits.
Source: Jeff Greenberg/people images/Alamy.

How does consumer input affect product development? Companies rely on customer input to help shape their products. Listening to customers and incorporating their suggestions are effective ways to foster good customer relationships, which is critical for getting repeat business and achieving long-term success. In fact, using customer feedback is one of the most important elements of sound customer relationship management. You have to know what your customers want in order to tailor a product offering to their needs.

Many a company has found that searching social media sites is a great way to learn what is on their customers' minds as well as the minds of those using competing products. Consumer input often provides information that prompts companies to divide a large market and focus on narrowly defined, targeted customers. For example, if a breakfast cereal company learns that most consumers buy its cereal because it is high in fiber, to target health-conscious adults and distinguish the cereal from other products, the company might run an ad campaign highlighting this fact.

Product Lines and the Product Mix

What are a product line and a product mix? Customer feedback can also lead to the creation of a **product line**, a group of similar products marketed to one general market. For example, Honda offers a number of different product lines: automotive products, plane and boat motors, and power equipment. Each product line is marketed to a different group of consumers. A **product mix** is the combination of all product lines offered for sale by a company. All of Honda's combined product lines constitute its product mix.

Does it matter how many products are in a product line? An important marketing decision involves product line length. **Product line length** is the number of items in any given product line. The addition or removal of items from a product line affects a company's profits. The Coca-Cola Company has found it very profitable to pursue a long product line length given the huge variety of drinks it offers for sale. The company offers 450 regular, diet, caffeine-free, and flavored varieties of Coca-Cola. People who do not want a soft drink can choose from the wide variety of non-soft drink beverage made by Coca-Cola, including fruit juice drinks, waters, sports and energy drinks, teas and coffees, and milk and soy-based beverages.[4]

Product mix width refers to the number of different product lines a company offers. This, too, is determined by profitability. General Electric (GE) has hundreds of product lines, ranging from light bulbs and home appliances to jet engines and medical machinery.[5] GE aims to achieve maximum profitability by stretching its capabilities across multiple markets. Product line length and product mix width are the result of companies striving to offer differentiated products to satisfy targeted customers. ■ **FIGURE 13.4** shows a small sample of Coca-Cola's product line lengths and product mix widths.

Consumer Products and Business-to-Business Products

What's the difference between consumer products and business-to-business products? In Chapter 12, we explored the differences between consumer markets and business-to-business markets. Similarly, there are differences between **consumer products**, goods and services purchased by households for personal consumption, and **business-to-business (B2B) products** (sometimes called *industrial products*), goods and services that are purchased by businesses for further processing or resale or for use in facilitating business operations. The distinction depends on whether the product is used for personal use or for business use. For example, if a home owner purchases a lawn mower for personal use, then it would be a consumer product. If a landscaper purchases the same lawn mower but uses it in his business, then it would be a B2B product.

It's convenient for marketers to classify consumer and B2B products differently because the buying behaviors of businesses and consumers are different. As a result,

■ **FIGURE 13.4**
Coca-Cola's Product Mix Width and Product Line Length

Product Mix Width			
Soft Drinks	**Energy Drinks**	**Juices/Juice Drinks**	**Water**
Coca-Cola	Full Throttle	Fuze	Dasani
Diet Coke	Rehab	Five Alive	Aquarius Spring
Coke Zero	TaB Energy	Minute Maid Juices	Glaceau Smartwater
Fanta			Glaceau Vitaminwater
Sprite			

Product Line Length (label at left of table rows)

Convenience
• Used often
• Consumed quickly

Shopping
• Bought less frequently
• Requires more effort and time for compensation

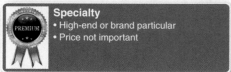
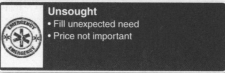

Specialty
• High-end or brand particular
• Price not important

Unsought
• Fill unexpected need
• Price not important

■ **FIGURE 13.5**
Consumer Product Classifications

the products in consumer and B2B markets have to be priced, promoted, and distributed differently. The shopping patterns of consumers help to establish classifications of consumer products. Industrial products are classified by how they are used in the production of other goods. The distinction between consumer and B2B products can also help a firm expand its product lines by crossing over from one category to the other. For example, the Cascade brand of dishwashing detergent is sold in consumer markets. However, the product's maker, Procter & Gamble (P&G), also makes a version of Cascade with phosphates for use in businesses such as restaurants. Let's now look more closely at these product classifications.

Consumer Product Classifications

What are the different consumer product classifications? Consumer products can be divided into four categories, as shown in ■ **FIGURE 13.5**:

- Convenience goods and services
- Shopping goods and services
- Specialty goods and services
- Unsought goods and services

What constitutes a convenience product? Products that customers purchase frequently, immediately, and without much deliberation are considered **convenience goods and services**. Because they are normally consumed quickly, they are also referred to as *nondurable goods*. Milk, soap, and newspapers are all considered convenience goods. A car wash is an example of a convenience service. These purchases are usually based on habitual behavior, meaning consumers routinely purchase particular brands with which they're familiar and comfortable. Convenience goods and services are also relatively low-priced items. They're usually promoted through brand awareness and image (which we'll discuss shortly) and are widely distributed through conveniently located stores or in high-traffic areas.

How are products purchased less frequently classified? Some products require more effort and time to compare and are typically purchased less frequently than consumer goods. These products are referred to as **shopping goods and services**. Shopping goods are typically *durable goods*—goods that can be used repeatedly over a long period of time. Examples of shopping goods include automobiles, clothes, furniture, and major appliances. Examples of shopping services include hotels, airlines, and other travel services. Consumers usually compare shopping products based on attributes such as their suitability, quality, price, style, and brand image.

Cars are examples of durable shopping goods.
Source: Happy Alex/Fotolia.

What if a consumer is very particular about the type of product he or she wants? Sometimes buyers are willing to spend a considerable amount of time and effort searching for particular brands or styles. These customers know exactly what they want, and they will not accept substitutes. These types of unique or specialized products are **specialty goods and services**. Examples of specialty goods and services include Ferrari sports cars,

Rolex watches, high-fashion designer clothing, and the services of prestigious medical and legal experts. Because there are no suitable substitutes, buyers of specialty products do not comparison shop. They already know the specific good or service they want, and they are willing to seek it out regardless of its price and location. Businesses that successfully differentiate their products to the point that they are considered specialty goods or services can charge higher prices for them than similar products that are considered shopping goods or services.

What about products that are purchased only when a special need arises? **Unsought goods and services** are products buyers don't usually think about buying, don't know exist, or buy only when a specific need arises. We don't usually think about or want to think about buying some products, such as life insurance or cemetery plots. Other unsought goods and services are products that are completely new to consumers. New and innovative products, such as pharmaceutical drugs, must be introduced to consumers through promotional advertising before they will actively seek them out for purchase. Emergency medical services and automobile repairs are also unsought purchases made without much prepurchase planning. In these cases, resolving the immediate problem is more important than comparison shopping. Sales of unsought products require personal selling or promotional advertising, and the price may not be an important consideration if the good or service is urgently needed.

B2B Classifications

What are the different B2B product classifications? B2B products can be divided into five categories, as shown in ■ **FIGURE 13.6**:

- Equipment
- Maintenance, repair, operating (MRO) products
- Raw and processed materials
- Component parts
- Specialized professional services

Each of these types of products requires different pricing, promotion, and distribution strategies.

What is considered equipment? *Equipment*, also known as *capital items*, includes all the physical facilities of a business. These physical items are further defined as *production goods* (factories, warehouses, and office buildings and heavy equipment) or *support goods* (computers, printers, and copiers). Many capital items are

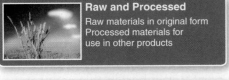

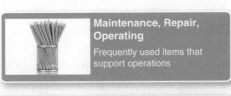

■ **FIGURE 13.6**
B2B Product Classifications

expensive, unique, and are intended to last for a long time. Therefore, selling them often requires long negotiations that stretch out over many months or even years and involve a firm's top managers. Marketers frequently offer a variety of services to help sell this type of equipment, including financial packages to ease the large price associated with the purchase, maintenance, and repairs after the sale.

How do you classify operating supplies? Products that facilitate production and operations but do not become a part of the finished product are classified as *MRO products*. These products include paper, pens, and cleaning materials. They are often marketed based on convenience, just like consumer convenience goods and services.

How are unprocessed products that are used to make other products classified? Materials sold in their original form before being processed for use in other products, such as crops, crude oil, iron ore, and logs, are examples of *raw and processed materials*. These products are the basic inputs that become part of a finished good. Raw and processed materials are usually purchased in large quantities at prices that are based on the quality of the materials.

How are parts used in an assembly process classified? *Component parts* are assembled portions of the finished product. Examples include brakes and engines for a car or drywall and electrical wire for a house. Businesses purchasing component parts make their decisions based on quality and brand-name recognition because, ultimately, the quality of a business's product will be based on the quality of its component parts.

Do specialized services have a separate classification? Businesses often require the use of services, just as individuals do. *Specialized professional services* help support a firm's operations. These services include advertising, management consulting, legal, accounting, and information technology services. Managers compare the costs and the quality of these specialized services with their in-house operations before deciding whether to outsource these activities. For example, a local grocery store owner might assess his or her ability to handle the business's financial records before hiring an outside accounting firm.

Considering the variety of types and classifications of products, it's clear that product development is an exciting yet challenging area of business. Remember Evelyn and Juan? Evelyn loved Diet Coke, and Juan preferred Coke Zero. Both products are zero-calorie cola-flavored soft drinks manufactured by the same company, but the two sodas have different marketing strategies and targeted demographics. Coke Zero was designed to appeal more to men.[6] The can is darker to convey a bigger flavor, and ads for the beverage are male dominated. Coke Zero shows it is important to differentiate products not only from their competitors but also to meet the needs of a broader market. The key is considering and understanding the many complex factors involved in creating a differentiated product.

Branding pp. 376–383

Robin Green loves homemade bread and has used her bread-making machine a lot. After baking many loaves of her favorite bread, honey whole wheat, the paddles started to slip and needed to be replaced. To her surprise, when she contacted the manufacturer, she was told that the company didn't make such products, nor did it service them. In fact, the company had licensed its brand name to a completely different manufacturer. The trust Robin had in this company and its products was tainted. Robin, like so many of us, bought a product based on the inherent trust she had in a brand name to deliver a quality product, but she didn't get quite what she expected. ■

Source: Robert McLean/Alamy.

Nike's Reuse-A-Shoe

Nike has manufactured millions of shoes. But did you know that those shoes (and others) when they are worn out and of no use to anyone as footwear still have a useful purpose? For the past 20 years, Nike Reuse-A-Shoe has been recycling worn-out shoes that would normally end up in landfills and repurposes them into Nike Grind. Nike Grind is the end result of ground-up rubber, foam, and fabric from worn-out shoes. Nike Grind is then used to manufacture athletic surfaces, such as tennis and basketball courts, and playgrounds. The entire athletic field at Concordia University in Portland, Oregon, is 100 percent Nike Grind from approximately 6 million pairs of shoes. Nike Grind is also beginning to be used in various footwear and apparel products. So when you think of the Nike brand, you might think of playgrounds and athletic fields in addition to athletic shoes, clothing, and sports equipment.

What are the benefits of a brand? Why are some brands perceived to be better than others? How is brand loyalty built and kept? These questions are important components of another complex aspect of product development—branding. In this section, we'll discuss branding, its benefits, brand loyalty, and branding strategies.

Branding Benefits

What are the benefits of branding? Branding is one of the most important tools of product differentiation, benefitting both buyers and sellers. A **brand** is a name, a term, a symbol, or a design that distinguishes a company and its products from all others. For buyers, well-recognized brands reduce the shopping time necessary to find the quality and consistency they desire in a product. Branding also reduces the risks involved in some purchases when buyers are unable to objectively determine quality. We rely on established brands to consistently deliver an expected level of quality. Comparing product descriptions and ingredients takes a lot longer than simply picking up a trusted brand. Consumers are also able to express themselves by buying brand names with which they wish to be identified. For example, some buyers seek prestige by buying exclusive brands, such as Mercedes-Benz cars, Rolex watches, Dom Pérignon champagne, or "cool" trendy items, such as Beats headphones.

Branding also helps sellers highlight the special qualities of their products, which can lead to repeat purchases as well as new sales at higher prices. Companies with trusted brands are also able to introduce new products quickly and at a relatively low cost. By expanding their brands, companies add length to their product lines, widen their product mix, and enhance their profitability. Marketing a product using the same brand name but in a different product category is known as **brand extension**. Because Kraft has a wide diversity in its product mix, the company can market its brand to just about any person in the world. There is something for everyone among Kraft's product lines.

Well-branded companies are generally recognizable by the trademarks they put on their products and the advertisements for them. A **trademark** is a name, symbol, or mark that is legally protected and cannot be used by anyone else without the owner's permission. Trademarks benefit sellers by distinguishing their brands from the competitors' *knockoff brands*, which are illegal copies or cheap imitations of another product.

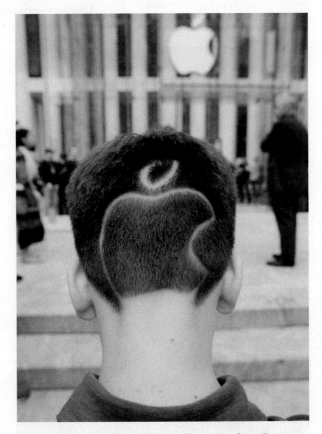

One benefit of branding for sellers is brand loyalty, such as that displayed by many users of Apple products.
Source: James Leynse/Corbis.

Can a company's trademark legally be put on another company's product?
Yes, if a brand license is obtained. A **brand license** is an agreement between the owner of a brand and another company or individual who pays a royalty to use the trademark in association with a new product, such as the bread-making machine in our opening story. Brand owners use licensing to extend a trademark or character onto different products. The Walt Disney Company is a good example. Characters such as Mickey Mouse appear on toys, books, and clothing that are not made by Disney. The national sports leagues are also big licensors and leading retail sellers of licensed products.

How does a logo help to build a brand? A **logo** is a graphic representation or symbol of a company name, trademark, or abbreviation. Sometimes trademarks and logos are the same, but sometimes a company can have a logo that isn't trademarked. Logos are an important element of a company's identity. They help make a company stand out from the competition, build trust and confidence about the brand, and increase customer loyalty. No doubt you can describe the logo for Starbucks, Apple, and Ralph Lauren. A good logo makes it easy for customers to associate products with a company's set of standards. When you are miles away from home and see McDonald's "golden arches" rising above the horizon, you know exactly the type and quality of food you'll be served.

Brand Loyalty and Brand Equity

Can branding promote customer preferences? Brand loyalty, the degree to which customers consistently prefer one brand to others, is another major benefit of branding. In fact, companies hope that customers recognize their brands by their attributes, such as the logo, slogan, or colors (*brand recognition*), and prefer them regardless of convenience or price (*brand preference*) and then eventually insist on them, not accepting a substitute or generic product in its place (*brand insistence*). When consumers insist on a brand, it is the highest degree of brand loyalty. It can turn a product into a specialty good or service that can command a much higher price. Ultimately, the degree of brand loyalty depends on satisfied customers. Perhaps the most significant contemporary example of brand loyalty is the fervent devotion of many Apple customers.

Companies understand the passion of NASCAR fans, so they display their logos on cars and driver's jumpsuits to associate their brand with the sport.
Source: Christa L Thomas/Cal Sport Media/Newscom.

What is brand equity? Strong brand loyalty contributes to **brand equity**, the overall value of a brand's strength in the market. Although this value may be difficult to measure, it represents the value of the brand to the organization. In addition to brand loyalty, perceptions of quality contribute significantly to brand equity. Quality products not only are free from defects but also consistently perform at high levels. For example, many customers purchase Levi's jeans because of the brand's high quality and durability. This reputation adds significantly to Levi's brand equity.

What also contributes to brand equity? Besides brand loyalty and quality, two other perceptions of a brand lead to a brand's equity: *brand awareness* and *brand association*.

- **Brand awareness** is the extent to which a particular brand name is familiar within a particular product category. Companies participate in mass advertising as a way to help their product's brand name become the most recognized and thought of for that category. For example, what brand first comes to mind when you think of laundry soap? If it's Tide, then P&G has succeeded in its brand awareness campaigns for laundry soap. Similarly, what brand do you

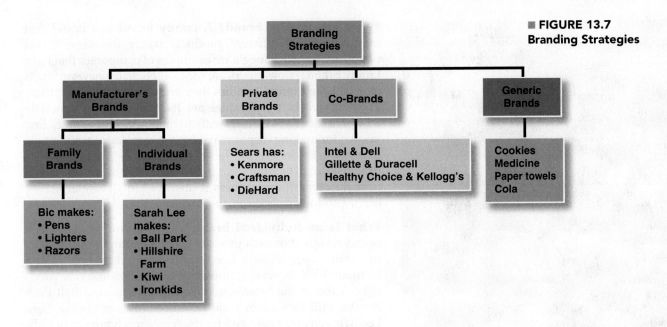

**■ FIGURE 13.7
Branding Strategies**

think of first when someone mentions coffee? You might think of Starbucks if you get your coffee on the go, or perhaps you might think of Maxwell House. Either way, those companies have succeeded in making you aware of their brand.

- **Brand association** involves connecting a brand with other positive attributes. Hiring celebrities to endorse a product can be an effective tool for nurturing brand associations. The success of Nike's Air Jordan line of sneakers is due to its association with Michael Jordan. Disney has been successful in associating its brand with wholesome family values. Images invoked by symbols and slogans can also be very powerful brand association techniques.

Branding Strategies

What strategies are used to brand products? There are several different branding strategies a firm can use, depending on how it wants to portray its products. Is the brand meant to convey thriftiness or luxury? A different branding strategy would be chosen for each of these objectives. Branding strategies also differ depending on the characteristics of the target customer.

There are several different types of brands that a product could be categorized into (see ■ **FIGURE 13.7**):

- Manufacturer's brands
- Family brands
- Individual brands
- Private brands
- Co-brands
- Generic brands

What is a manufacturer's brand? A **manufacturer's brand** is a brand created by producers. A manufacturer's brand is also known as a *national brand*, even though the brand may be distributed globally. Well-known brands, such as Ben & Jerry's and Google, are considered manufacturers' brands. Manufacturers spend a lot of money creating, promoting, and building their brands. There are two types of manufacturers' brands: *family brands* and *individual brands*.

> **THE LIST**
>
> **Retailers and Their Private-Brand Labels[12]**
>
> | Company | Private-Brand Labels |
> |---|---|
> | Best Buy | Insignia, Dynex, Geek Squad |
> | CVS Caremark | CVS, Fieldbrook Farms, Just the Basics |
> | Home Depot | Hampton Bay, PowerCell |
> | Kroger | Private Selection, Comforts, Kroger |
> | Lowe's | Kobalt, Allen & Roth |
> | Safeway | Eating Right, Lucerne, Captain's Choice |
> | Sears Holdings | Craftsman, Kenmore, DieHard |
> | Target | Archer Farms, Market Pantry, Sutton & Dodge |
> | Walgreens | Walgreens, Deerfield Farms |
> | Walmart | Equate, Sam's Choice, Great Value |

Glade's Home Fragrances candles teaming up with Betty Crocker is an example of how two organizations can come together to form a co-brand. *Source:* Derek Davis/Portland Press Herald/ Getty Images.

Generic brands often have very plain labels but may be made by a brand-name manufacturer. What might be the brand-name equivalent for this product? *Source:* Ted Foxx/Alamy.

What is a family brand? A **family brand** is a brand that markets several different products under the same brand name. Sony and Kellogg's are examples of companies that have family brands. Consumers are more likely to try new products in established brand families they are familiar with and trust. These established companies are therefore able to penetrate new markets successfully with their brand names. Bic, first known for making disposable ink pens, successfully added Bic disposable razors and Bic lighters to its family brand. There's a drawback of extending a company's brand name to new products, however: If one of them is unsuccessful, it can tarnish all of the products or even create a negative brand image.

What is an individual brand? An **individual brand** is a brand assigned to each product within a company's product mix. For example, Sara Lee uses individual brands among its many food, beverage, household, and personal care products. Some of the brands may be familiar to you: Ball Park Franks, Hillshire Farm meat products, and, of course, Sara Lee's frozen and packaged foods. A major advantage of individual branding is that if a new product fails, it won't damage the image of the other products.

What is a private brand? A **private brand** is a brand created by a distributor, or a middleman. Middlemen can be wholesalers, dealers, or retail stores. As a result, private brands are also called *distributor, wholesaler, dealer, store,* or *retail brands.* The key characteristic of a private brand is that the manufacturer is not identified on the product. Examples include Sears's line of DieHard batteries, Kenmore appliances, and Craftsman tools. These products are made by other well-known and recognized manufacturers but are sold under Sears's private-brand labels. Grocery stores often sell similar products under their own private labels. Safeway, the supermarket chain, has several private labels, including Open Nature (100 percent natural foods), Lucerne (dairy), and In-Kind (personal care products). In addition to putting a different label on the same product, a manufacturer may make special products just for the private brand. The advantage of private branding is that an individual distributor has more control over a product's price and promotion. The competition is heating up between manufacturers' brands and private brands, as many private brands have gained national recognition. Private labels are big business for many stores since they are generally perceived as being of similar quality to the national labels but more economical than the national labels since they are generally offered at a lower price.

What is a co-brand? A **co-brand** is packaging two or more brands affiliated with a single product, such as Gillette M3 Power shaving equipment with Duracell batteries. The objective is to combine the prestige of two brands to increase the price consumers are willing to pay. Co-branding is also used to foster brand loyalty for one product while extending loyalty to the contributing product.

What is a generic brand? A **generic brand** is a product that has no brand at all. The product's contents are frequently identified by black stenciled lettering on white packages. Generic brands often look nearly identical to branded products and, in fact, may be made by the branded products' manufacturers. So, a generic brand of cream-filled sandwich cookies may look like Oreo cookies, but they won't be called Oreo cookies or bear the Nabisco brand name, even if Nabisco produced them. However, because they are not advertised, generic products are typically priced lower than branded products.

By producing both types of products, a manufacturer can capture both cost-conscious and brand-loyal customers. Often consumers will buy generic brands of products they use routinely and do not have a brand preference for products they believe are exactly the same as the branded product, such as generic drugs.

Packaging

How does packaging help promote a product? Because it's the first thing they see when looking for a product, packaging often is the first criteria consumers use to make their purchasing decisions. Getting the consumer to notice a product and choose it from among many products on crowded shelves is extremely important. The package design, shape, color, and texture all influence buyers' perceptions and buying behavior. Packaging also sends a message about a product and brand. The makers of luxury items, such as jewelry or high-end cosmetics, typically package their products to create an impression of extravagance, sophistication, and exclusiveness.

Coca-Cola has an iconic package that defines the brand, the shape of which is distinctive and immediately recognizable. That contoured shape was initially created in 1915 to differentiate Coke from its competitors. It was such a success that the bottle design was trademarked in 1977. The little blue box from Tiffany & Co. is another example of an iconic package that promotes both a brand and a lifestyle. The robin's-egg-blue box has been a symbol of elegance and excitement since it was introduced in 1837. The packaging is so desirable that some consumers simply want to buy the box. However, it is an ironclad rule that no Tiffany & Co. blue box can leave the store unless it contains a purchased item.[8]

How does packaging protect a product? Packaging is intended to preserve and protect a product. This is the most obvious purpose of packaging. Most products are handled several times as they are distributed from the manufacturing site to the final consumer. Many of these products also need to be protected from adverse conditions. Additionally, packaging must protect a product from tampering. Products, such as medicines or infant formula, need to be tamperproof and must meet the minimum requirements set by the U.S. Food and Drug Administration (FDA).

Why is convenient packaging so important? Packaging should facilitate use and convenience. Sellers want packages that are easy to ship, store, and stock on

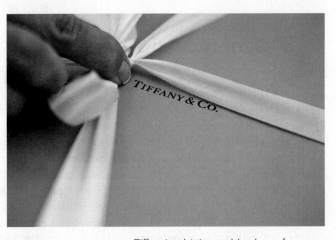

Tiffany's robin's-egg-blue box often makes the recipient happy without even looking inside.
Source: Simon Lord/Alamy.

Brand You: Creating a Personal Brand

What do Katie Perry and Mark Cuban have in common? Both are their own brands. Each celebrity has a unique image that is as much of a brand as are Nike, Apple, and Starbucks. But celebrities are not the only ones who can create a personal brand. Everyone, including you, can create a personal brand. Personal branding is the process by which we market ourselves to others. If we develop our personal brands carefully, they can build brand equity for us.

Business management guru Tom Peters actually coined the phrase *personal branding.* "We are CEOs of our own companies: Me Inc.," he writes. "To be in business today, our most important job is to be head marketer for the brand called You. It's that simple—and that hard. And that inescapable."[7] Enhancing your own personal brand is important to your success; it's what will give you a competitive edge in almost everything you do.

There are a variety of ways you can create your own personal brand, and many of them are similar to the ways companies promote their own brands. For example, you can start by using social media tools, such as Facebook, LinkedIn, and Twitter. Make sure your brand image is consistent and professional. Write a blog or have a website with your own name in the title or domain name and establish your brand in your e-mail address by using something like firstname.lastname@email.com. Take charge of your brand. It's the first step you can take toward your own success.

Genericized Trademarks

Branding acts as a tool to help differentiate one product from other similar products. However, what happens when the brand name or trademark gains such popularity that it becomes synonymous with the general product category? When was the last time you purchased a box of Q-tips? If you bought cotton swabs that didn't display the brand name Q-tips, then you didn't buy Q-tips, but you probably still referred to them as Q-tips. The Q-tips brand has become a genericized trademark—a trademark or brand name that has become synonymous with a general class of product or service. Someone shopping for Q-tips may actually buy another brand of cotton swabs because the competitor's price and/or packaging could convince a consumer to choose that particular brand over the Q-tips brand. All companies want to guard against their brand names becoming a generic description for a product category because then their brand name becomes public property. A trademark that has been genericized can lead to

the loss of trademark rights, enabling competitors to benefit by being able to use the term to describe their similar products. This happened to not only Q-tips but also to *Kleenex, Xerox, aspirin, escalator, shredded wheat, kerosene, Band-Aid,* and *Thermos.* The trademarks of technology firms are frequently at risk of being genericized. How many times have you "googled" something?

To try to protect a trademark from becoming generic, a firm will often use it as an adjective describing the category the product belongs to and then follow the trademark with the term "brand." *Jell-O Brand Gelatin* is an example. To help Google keep its brand name distinct, the Merriam-Webster dictionary worked with the company to provide a definition for the verb *google.* The dictionary defines the term as "using the Google search engine to obtain information on the Internet." What other genericized trademarks can you think of?

shelves. More importantly, consumers want products that handle easily, open, reseal, and store conveniently and that, for perishable items, have a long shelf life.

Packages that are convenient to use and that are also physically attractive sell better. Heinz ketchup experienced a significant increase in sales when it began offering ketchup in a squeezable bottle. Campbell's soup has responded to changing consumer tastes and preferences for greater convenience by offering pull-top lids and sippable soups, microwave soup lines, and ready-to-serve soups. Many sellers also offer different-sized packages depending on the serving size. For example, salt, sugar, and breakfast cereal packages come in many different sizes for added convenience.

How does packaging affect the environment? A growing concern among many consumers is whether a product and its package are environmentally sound. Some packaging, especially the single-serve packages, can be considered wasteful and environmentally unfriendly. Consequently, many companies are going green and developing new products that are eco-friendly, which can increase their sales. Puma developed an eco-friendly packaging concept for its shoes. Instead of the traditional cardboard shoebox, Puma packages its shoes in cardboard frames wrapped in reusable shoe bags. This repackaging saves nearly 8,500 tons of paper and reduces the resources required for production and transportation.[9]

The Importance of Labels

What does the government have to say about product labels? Labeling serves two functions: to inform and to persuade. Labels should inform consumers about a product, its uses and benefits, and any safety concerns. The government has initiated several acts that regulate what must go on a product's label. The Fair Packaging and Labeling Act of 1966 requires that companies communicate specific information about their products to consumers. The act requires that all

Source: Simon Dawson/Bloomberg via Getty Images.

labels include the name and place of business of the manufacturer, the packer or the distributor, and the net quantity of the contents. The Consumer Product Safety Commission (CPSC) has also established guidelines to ensure that manufacturers warn consumers about the hazards of various products, for example, if they are flammable, and the adverse consequences of using them improperly. The CSPC also requires that products have tracking labels. The tracking labels include batch and run numbers that identify the exact source of the product and its components. That way, if the product is defective or contaminated, the manufacturer can trace the source of the problem to more quickly to correct it.

Other government attempts to make labels more useful for consumers to evaluate products include the Nutrition Labeling and Education Act of 1990. This legislation requires that all nutrient content claims, such as high fiber or low fat, and health claims are consistent with agency regulations. However, labels can be confusing or misleading. For example, the FDA criticized General Food's claims that "You can lower your cholesterol 4 percent in six weeks" by eating Cheerios.[10] Now, the box carries a more general statement that the cereal helps to lower cholesterol. Businesses that wish to foster good customer relationships must be careful to label their products ethically.

Why is labeling important to establishing a brand image?
Labels are also used to promote and persuade customers to buy a product. Labels can educate consumers of the features and other benefits of a product. Many companies label their products with their brand logos to distinguish their products. If a label comes to represent consistent quality and dependability, then the label can perpetuate a positive brand-name image.

How are digital media and the Internet affecting branding strategies? More companies than ever are incorporating digital media into their branding strategies by advertising online, creating blogs, providing online customer chats, and using social networking. Zagat, the restaurant-ratings guide publisher, uses Facebook, Twitter, and YouTube and places tips and recommendations into Foursquare. This new set of technologies has caused some companies to rethink and reformulate their previous branding practices.

Robin Green was disappointed that the brand that she chose for its quality was not at all what she bought. The next time Robin needs to buy an appliance, it most likely won't be from that manufacturer. And she'll be sure to check out the servicing and warranty information before purchasing anything. Branding is important for both the buyer and the seller. Making products memorable and appealing is a priority for all companies, and branding helps them achieve this goal.

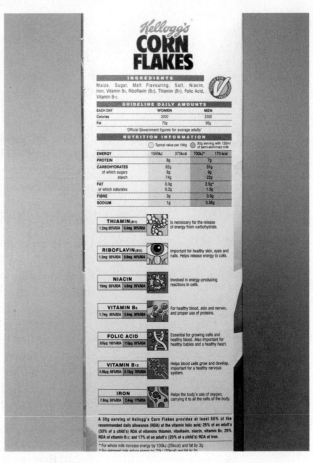

Labels are used to inform, such as to communicate nutritional value to the consumer.
Source: sciencephotos/Alamy.

Pricing Goods and Services pp. 383–389

Gina Riviera, the new manager of Bitsy Baby, badly needs to increase the store's profits. Under the previous manager, Bitsy Baby was barely surviving, and the owner was contemplating closing the doors forever. Gina is his last hope. The previous manager insisted on carrying many of the same items

Source: mangostock/Fotolia.

as a big chain store in a nearby mall sold but at lower prices. Bitsy Baby also carries a small assortment of unique baby items inconspicuously displayed in a back corner of the store. Gina thinks these items could be the stores "niche." The question she is struggling with is the pricing. Should she try to compete with the chain store on the items both of them sell? What pricing strategy should she use with the unique goods? ■

Pricing is important to consumers and producers alike, and it is an essential component in the marketing mix. We conclude this chapter by discussing the pricing component of the marketing mix. We'll discuss promotion and distribution strategies in the next chapter.

Product Pricing and Pricing Objectives

Why is a product's price an important component in the marketing mix? As consumers, we know a product's price represents what we must pay to acquire it. From the seller's perspective, the price is the only revenue-generating component of the marketing mix. Product, promotion, and distribution are all cost components. The price can also serve as a marketing tool and is often used in promotional campaigns.

Trying to set the right price can be a real challenge for marketers. The price of a product has to be low enough to motivate customers to buy it but high enough that a company can cover its costs and earn a profit from the good or service. In addition market and economic conditions are always changing, as are the prices of competing products. As a result, companies usually must constantly tweak their prices to remain competitive.

How does value affect a product's price? The price is what customers actually pay for a product, but the value is the derived benefit of the entire product offering. Recall that the total product offer consists of all benefits associated with a product, and each level of benefit (core, actual, and augmented) adds more value to the product. As you know, often the price affects how a customer views a product's value. In addition, there can be other costs associated with purchasing a product, such as the cost of learning how to use it or the costs associated with disposing of it later. These costs can also affect the product's overall value to the customer.

What are some pricing objectives? Setting the right price is more than simply calculating the cost of production and then tacking on a markup for profit. The price often impacts how consumers view a product and may determine whether they will purchase it. The price also helps differentiate the product from the competition. Setting a specific pricing objective is important to do before establishing the price point. There are a variety of pricing objectives. Some of the most common ones include the following:

- **Maximizing profits.** This occurs when the price is set so that the total revenue earned from the product exceed the total costs by the greatest amount.
- **Achieving greater market share.** A company's market share is the percentage of total industry sales or revenues it is able to capture. Unfortunately, achieving greater market share does not always translate into higher profits.
- **Maximizing sales.** Maximizing sales often means charging low prices that can result in losses. Firms cannot survive for long with losses. However, maximizing sales may be an appropriate short-run objective to rid the company of excess inventory, such as last year's models.
- **Building traffic.** Many retail stores, such as grocery stores and department stores, may advertise low sales prices on a few goods to increase traffic in their stores and build a stronger customer base. They also hope customers will purchase other, more profitable items while they are shopping for the bargains.
- **Matching the status quo prices.** The objective of status quo pricing is to match competitors' prices, possibly to avoid a price war that could be damaging to

all sellers. The airfare wars of the past hurt every airline carrier, so they have chosen to compete on nonprice factors instead.

- **Covering costs to survive.** If a company is struggling to build a customer base, it may set its prices to generate just enough revenues to cover its costs. However, this is not a suitable long-term objective. Survival prices might generate sales, but they will not generate profits.

- **Creating an image.** Some products are priced high because firms hope that consumers will associate high prices with high quality. This is the case for many specialty goods, such as luxury cars, perfume, and designer clothing, shoes, and accessories.

- **Ensuring affordability to all.** Some organizations charge low prices to enable more people to afford their products. For example, some insurance companies have low-cost automobile policies for people on tight budgets.

How do you choose the right pricing objective? The ideal pricing objective is determined by considering the business and financial goals of a product or a company. If one of the business goals is to become a market leader and amass the greatest market share, then maximizing quantity of sales may be a more appropriate choice over building traffic; if a business objective is aggressive production growth, then profit maximization will be important. Survival and status quo pricing may be better suited when market conditions are poor or unstable or when a firm is entering a market for the first time. The pricing objectives will change over the life cycle of a product as well. And because the price is only one element in the marketing mix, marketers must develop their pricing strategies in coordination with their product branding, packaging, promotion, and distribution strategies too.

Pricing Strategies and Price Perceptions

What are the major pricing strategies? After determining the pricing *objective*, choosing the best pricing *strategy* to achieve that objective is chosen next. Certain strategies work better with certain objectives. In addition, some pricing strategies are used at different times to accommodate changes in a firm's marketing strategies, market conditions, and product life cycles. Although there is no one right way to determine the price of a good or service, there are several strategies sellers can use. The most common pricing strategies include *cost-based pricing*, *demand-based pricing*, *competition-based pricing*, and *everyday low pricing*.

There are also several alternative pricing strategies and strategies that affect price perceptions. ■ **FIGURE 13.8** outlines these pricing strategies.

What is cost-based pricing? One of the easiest and simplest ways to price a product is to use **cost-based pricing**. This pricing strategy (also known as *cost-plus pricing*) is based on covering a firm's costs and providing for a set amount of profit. Suppose you manufacture 100 units of a product at a total cost of $2,000. This makes the average cost per unit produced $20. If you want to make a unit profit margin, or *markup*, of 20 percent, which is $4 (0.20 × $20), you would price the product at $24. The total revenue you would then generate would equal $2,400, and your profit would equal $400, which is 20 percent above your total costs.

There are many advantages of cost-based pricing. Besides being easy to calculate and easy to administer, it requires a minimum amount of information. However, it has several disadvantages as well. Cost-based pricing ignores whether a price is compatible with consumers' expectations or can compete with the prices of similar products. Cost-based pricing also provides a firm little incentive to operate more efficiently to hold its costs down. Many pharmaceutical companies use cost-based pricing to recover the expensive research and development costs associated with a new drug and to earn a targeted profit level. The monopoly power granted by patents on new drugs means there is no competition, so the pharmaceutical companies find little need to consider consumer demand when setting prices on the new drugs.

■ **FIGURE 13.8**
Pricing Strategies and Price Perceptions

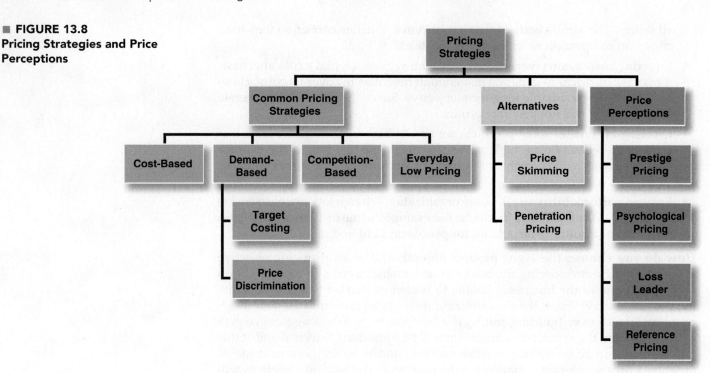

How does product demand impact pricing? Demand-based pricing (sometimes called *value-based pricing*) is the strategy of setting the price of a product based on its demand or its perceived value. A higher price will be charged when the demand or the perceived value of the product is high. A lower price will be charged when its demand or perceived value is low. This pricing strategy assumes firms can accurately estimate the perceived value or demand for their goods or services. Sometimes this is the case, but it's usually very difficult to do in practice. Nevertheless, many firms try.

Demand-based pricing can be defined further by other pricing strategies: target costing and price discrimination:

Early bird specials are a form of price discrimination.
Source: Richard B. Levine/Alamy.

- **Target costing** estimates the value customers receive from a product and, therefore, the price they are willing to pay for it. The firm then subtracts an acceptable profit margin to obtain an estimated cost for the product. Firms then work to get costs down to this targeted level. IKEA has successfully used target cost pricing. The company starts with a product need and its price in mind and then designs and manufactures the product to meet those goals.[11]

- **Price discrimination** occurs when a business charges different prices to different customers for an identical good or service for reasons not associated with costs. Customers who are price insensitive are charged higher prices, and customers who are more price sensitive are charged lower prices. For example, because senior citizens are often on fixed budgets, restaurants and movie theaters frequently offer them lower prices. Salespeople often charge different prices to customers based on their perceived demand for big-ticket items, such as cars and furniture, so don't tell them how much you value or love their good or service! For price discrimination to work, firms have to be able to successfully segment customers based on their differences in demand and how price sensitive they are. Moreover, the product must be a type of good or service that cannot be easily resold by the customers who are able to purchase it at the lower price. Many organizations price discriminate because it's profitable.

- **Competition-based pricing** is a pricing strategy that's based on the degree of competition in a market, which, in turn, affects a company's price-setting ability. Markets can be categorized based on their degree of competition:

  A *perfectly competitive market* is one with many suppliers and homogeneous products, such as gasoline, agricultural, and raw material commodities. All the products are virtually the same and sold at the same price, so individual sellers have little or no control over the prices they can charge.

  A *monopolistically competitive market* is a market in which there are many firms, but they have the ability to differentiate their products somewhat and can therefore charge different prices for them. For example, Oakley, Inc., which makes sunglasses and goggles for sports and fashion, has successfully differentiated its products and can charge higher prices.

  An *oligopoly* is a market in which there are only a few sellers. The airline, oil, and textbook industries are examples. To avoid price wars, rarely do these firms compete on the basis of price. Instead, they compete aggressively on product differentiation and charge higher prices if their total product offerings are unique. Periodically, a firm (usually the market leader) charges a different price, and all other firms follow with similar price changes.

  A *monopoly* is a market supplied by a single firm. Because there is no competition, the monopolist has great price-setting latitude. Sometimes monopolists capture their markets by using *predatory pricing*, the practice of charging very low prices with the intent of destroying the competition. Predatory pricing is illegal, but that hasn't prevented it from occurring.

What pricing strategy offers low prices all the time? Some retail stores rarely put individual products on sale and instead offer **everyday low pricing** on all of their products. Walmart has successfully used this strategy because it has been able to give the impression that its brand means everyday low cost.

Are there pricing strategies that work better in certain phases of the product life cycle? When launching a new product, companies may need to use a different type of pricing strategy than they would for an existing product (refer back to Figure 13.8).

- **Price skimming** involves charging a high price for a product when it's first introduced and there are few if any competitors. The idea is to initially skim off as much profit as possible to recoup the product's development costs. However, the high price is likely to encourage competitors to enter the market at a lower price. When they do, the firm then lowers the product's price.

- **Penetration pricing** involves charging the lowest possible price for a new product to quickly build market share for a product. If the increased production to satisfy growing sales results in lower per unit costs, then the product's profits can actually rise even though its price is lower. Penetration pricing is also appropriate during the growth stage of a product's life cycle and when customers are price sensitive. It may also create goodwill among consumers and inhibit competitors from entering the market. However, penetration pricing can may make it difficult to increase a product's price later and possibly lead to a poor-quality image for a brand or company.

What strategies are used to affect people's price perceptions? For many consumers, a high price indicates good quality. Consumers are more likely to associate price with quality when a product is complex and they are not familiar with it or its brand name. There are several types of pricing strategies that can be used to affect people's perceptions of a product:

- **Prestige pricing** (also known as *premium pricing*) is the practice of charging a high price to invoke perceptions of high quality and privilege. For those brands for which prestige pricing may apply, the high price itself is a motivator for consumers. The higher perceived value because of the higher price actually increases the product's demand and creates a higher price that becomes self-sustaining. Some people have called this the *snob effect*. Examples of this strategy include the pricing of luxury and designer items.

- **Psychological pricing** (sometimes called *odd* or *fractional pricing*) is the practice of charging a price just below a whole number to give the appearance of a significantly lower price. Charging $9.99 as opposed to $10.00 is an example of psychological pricing. Gas stations often use psychological pricing.

- A **loss leader** is a product that is priced below its costs. Stores use loss leaders to attract customers into the store and then motivate them to buy more expensive items.

- **Reference pricing** refers to using an inflated price (the regular retail price or the manufacturer's suggested retail price) that is then discounted to appear as if the product is a good value. A variation of this strategy occurs when stores provide both a more expensive "gold-plated" version of a product and a lower-priced alternative. This makes the alternative appear to be a bargain.

How might production be affected by pricing strategies? No matter which pricing strategy is selected, it is important to determine how much product can be produced at that price level before generating a profit. A **breakeven analysis**, which determines the production level at which total revenue is just enough to cover total costs, is useful to conduct with any pricing strategy. At the breakeven point, no profit has been made, and no losses have been incurred. The first step in conducting a breakeven analysis is to determine costs. There are two types of costs that make up the total product cost: fixed costs and variable costs. *Fixed costs* (sometimes called *overhead costs*) are any costs that do not vary with the production level. Fixed costs typically include expenses such as salaries, rent, insurance, and loan repayments. *Variable costs* are costs that vary with the production level. Examples include wages, raw materials, and energy costs. *Average variable costs* (or *per unit variable costs*) equal total variable costs divided by the production level. A convenient formula for calculating the breakeven production level is as follows:

$$\text{Breakeven volume of production} = \frac{\text{Total fixed costs}}{\text{Revenue per unit} - \text{Average variable costs}}$$

For example, suppose that the total fixed costs equal $600, the product's selling price is $24, and the average variable costs are $14. The breakeven volume of production is therefore $600/($24 − $14), or 60 units. Any production level below the breakeven volume will result in losses, and any production level above the breakeven level will result in profits. Any changes in the fixed or variable costs or in the price will affect the breakeven volume of production.

Adjusting Prices

What are common types of price adjustments? Most businesses adjust their prices periodically to promote their products. Several tactics are used to do this, as ■ **FIGURE 13.9** shows. One way is to use **discounts**, a deduction from the regular price charged. Discounts come in many forms:

- Cash discounts (discounts for paying with cash)
- Quantity discounts (discounts for buying large quantities)
- Seasonal discounts (discounts for buying goods and services out of season)
- Forms of allowance, such as a trade-in allowance (discounts for trading in old products for new ones)

Another way to adjust prices is to use rebates. **Rebates** are partial refunds on what a customer has already paid for a product. An example is a mail-in rebate. The customer mails the rebate to the manufacturer, which then sends the buyer a check or a debit card that can be used for future purchases.

Bundling is another type of price adjustment. With **bundling**, two or more products that usually complement one another are combined and sold at a single price. The single price is usually lower than the sum of the individual products' prices. Bundling is quite common in the fast-food industry, where products are bundled to make a complete meal. Cable, DSL, and satellite television companies bundle groups of channels sold at a single price as well as combine them with phone and Internet services. A vacation package is also a bundled product, consisting of airfare, car rental, hotel accommodations, and other amenities.

Dynamic pricing is another price-adjustment technique. Instead of a fixed price being charged, with **dynamic pricing**, it can quickly change at any time, depending on the interaction of buyers and a sellers. Auctions are a traditional form of dynamic pricing. eBay and Priceline.com are other examples.

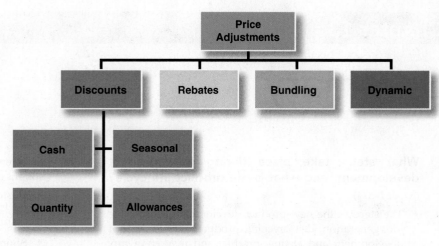

■ **FIGURE 13.9**
Price Adjustments (Tactics)

Can you determine the effect a change in price will have on demand? Before adjusting prices, it's always good to determine how consumers might respond to the price adjustment. For some products, a price adjustment can significantly affect consumer demand. For other products, demand might not be affected much at all. The degree to which the demand for a product will be affected by price changes is what economists refer to as the **price elasticity of demand**, or simply *price elasticity*. Products purchased in approximately the same quantities even when prices rise are said to be price inelastic. Essential items, such as gasoline and electricity, tend to be inelastic. Elastic goods, such as restaurant meals, movie tickets, and luxury or big-ticket items, usually will see a drop in demand when their prices rise. Consequently, producers should determine the price elasticity of demand for their products before they change their prices. If a price increase is being proposed, it's better if the demand for the product is relatively inelastic because the demand for it will fall less. Assuming costs are kept the same, the firm's profits will increase. By contrast, price increases for products that are more elastic will experience a decrease in demand, negatively affecting a firm's overall profits.

Of course, there are factors that affect the degree of elasticity besides a product's price. For example, products with fewer substitutes are more inelastic than products with more substitutes. Over time, the elasticity of an item may change since consumers have time to alter their buying habits.

Gina began to pursue a different pricing strategy at Bitsy Baby. She competitively priced items the chain store also carried and priced the unique items just high enough so customers would think they were special but not too high to deter interest in them. Gina also moved the unique goods to the front of the store and created a much nicer display for them. After making these changes, Gina began to notice that more customers were coming into Bitsy Baby to purchase the unique items as gifts. In addition, she had special bags, boxes, tissue paper, and ribbons designed with Bitsy Baby's logo and colors, so the store's items stood out even after they left the store. Ultimately, the pricing and packaging strategy paid off. Within two years, the store's financial woes were behind it. Bitsy Baby had found its niche.

Summary

1 What steps take place during new product development, and what is the product life cycle? (pp. 367–371)

- The steps in the new-product development process are idea generation, idea screening, product analysis, concept development and testing, product and marketing mix development, market testing, and commercialization.

- The **product life cycle** (p. 369) is a theoretical model describing a product's sales and profits over the course of its lifetime. Introduction, growth, maturity, and decline are stages in the product life cycle.

2 How is a product distinguished from a total product offer? (pp. 371–372)

- A *product* is any good, service, or idea that might satisfy a want or a need. A **total product offer** (p. 371) consists of all the tangible and intangible benefits associated with a good, a service, or an idea that affects a consumer's purchasing decision. Marketers know this. When planning a total product offering, they think about it on three levels:

  - The **core product** (p. 372) satisfies the basic need or want that motivates a purchase. Because it is the basic benefit provided by a product, you can't touch it; it is intangible.

  - The **actual product** (p. 372) is the tangible aspect of a purchase that you can touch, see, hear, smell, or taste. It provides core benefits when it is used.

  - The **augmented product** (p. 372) consists of the core and actual product plus other real or perceived benefits that provide additional value to the customer's purchase.

3 What is product differentiation, and what role does it play in product development? (pp. 372–373)

- **Product differentiation** (p. 372) is the process of attracting customers by distinguishing a product in real or perceived terms from competing products.

- Customer input and feedback guide product development and product differentiation and lead to the creation of a **product line** (p. 373), a group of similar products marketed to one general market. A **product mix** (p. 373) is the combination of all product lines offered for sale by a company. Product lines and mix result from trying to tailor total product offerings to unique targeted customers.

4 What are the different classifications of consumer products and business-to-business products? (pp. 373–376)

- The four classifications of **consumer products** (p. 373) are convenience goods and services, shopping goods and services, specialty goods and services, and unsought goods and services:

  - Customers purchase **convenience goods and services** (p. 374), such as gum, soap, and milk, frequently, immediately, and with little deliberation.

  - **Shopping goods and services** (p. 374) are products that are less frequently purchased and require that the customer spend more time and effort comparing them. Examples include clothes, electronics, and furniture.

  - **Specialty goods and services** (p. 374) have unique characteristics and no suitable substitutes. Examples include designer clothing or the services of prestigious lawyers.

  - **Unsought goods and services** (p. 375) are products buyers don't usually think about buying, don't know exist, or buy only when a specific problem arises. An example is funeral services.

- There are five categories of **business-to-business (B2B) products** (p. 373): equipment, MRO products, raw and processed materials, component parts, and specialized professional services.

5 Why is branding beneficial to both buyers and sellers, and what are some different branding strategies? (pp. 376–383)

- Branding reduces shopping time for consumers and helps them express themselves. Branding helps sellers define the special qualities of their products, encourages repeat purchases, and can result in new sales at higher prices.

- Marketing a product using the same brand name but in a different product category is known as **brand extension** (p. 377). A **brand license** (p. 378) is an agreement between the owner of a brand and another company or individual who pays a royalty for using the brand in association with a new product.

- For sellers, branding creates **brand loyalty** (p. 378) among consumers. Brand loyalty contributes to **brand equity** (p. 378), the overall value of a brand's strength in the market. **Brand awareness** (p. 378) refers to the extent to which a particular brand name is familiar to consumers. **Brand association** (p. 379) occurs when consumers connect a brand with other positive attributes.

- There are six different types of brands: **manufacturer's brands, family brands, individual brands, private brands, co-brands**, and **generic brands** (pp. 379–378).

- How a product is packaged and labeled sends a message about a product and a brand.

6 **What are some pricing objectives, and how do they relate to the marketing mix?** (pp. 383–385)

- Common pricing objectives include maximizing profits, achieving greater market share, maximizing sales, building traffic in stores, matching status quo prices, covering costs to survive, creating an image, and ensuring greater affordability.

- Price is the only revenue-generating component of the marketing mix. Marketers must carefully consider their pricing objectives to develop the best pricing strategy.

7 **What are the major approaches to pricing strategies?** (pp. 385–389)

- The major approaches to pricing strategies are **cost-based pricing** (p. 385), **demand-based pricing** (p. 386), **competition-based pricing** (p. 387), and **everyday low pricing** (p. 387).

- **Price skimming** (p. 387) and **penetration pricing** (p. 387) are tactics used for new products.

- **Prestige pricing** (p. 387), **psychological pricing** (p. 388), the use of **loss leaders** (p. 388), and **reference pricing** (p. 388) are pricing strategies that affect the price perceptions of consumers.

- **Discounts** (p. 388), **rebates** (p. 389), **bundling** (p. 389), and **dynamic pricing** (p. 389) are common types of price adjustments.

- Measuring how the demand for a product will be affected when its price changes is referred to as the product's **price elasticity of demand** (p. 389). Products that are purchased in approximately the same quantities when their prices rise are said to be price inelastic. By contrast, the demand for elastic goods falls when their prices rise.

Key Terms

MyBizLab
Go to **mybizlab.com** to complete the problems marked with this icon .

Self Test

Multiple Choice *You can find the answers on the last page of this book.*

13-1 The level of a product that satisfies the basic need or want that motivates a purchase is the

a. total product offering.

b. augmented product.

c. actual product.

d. core product.

13-2 Which of the following is *not* an example of a product line length?

a. Diet Coke, Cherry Coke, and Classic Coke

b. Quaker Instant Oatmeal, Quaker Oatmeal Squares, and Quaker Toasted Oats

c. Honda Civic, Honda lawn mower, and Honda marine engine

d. Crest 3D White toothpaste, Crest Baking Soda & Peroxide toothpaste, and Crest Pro-Health Clinical Gum Protection toothpaste

13-3 When companies compete aggressively on the basis of price, quality, and brand-name image because consumers carefully compare brands, these businesses are most likely selling _____ goods and services.

a. convenience

b. shopping

c. specialty

d. unsought

13-4 When businesses hire celebrities to endorse their products and connect their brands with positive attributes, they are focusing on enhancing their brand

a. loyalty.

b. awareness.

c. association.

d. extension.

13-5 A brand that markets several different products under the same brand name is a

a. manufacturer's brand.

b. family brand.

c. private brand.

d. co-brand.

13-6 Siobhan Clark just bought a Philadelphia Phillies jersey with player Cole Hamel's name and number on the back, as well as a hat and jacket that display the Phillies logo. The type of branding strategy used for these products is

a. generic branding.

b. manufacturer's branding.

c. private branding.

d. brand licensing.

13-7 In what stage in the product life cycle would you consider 3D televisions to be?

a. Introduction

b. Growth

c. Maturity

d. Decline

13-8 Stephanie Ling has been asked to conduct a breakeven analysis. Which of the following would be considered a variable cost?

a. Price of gasoline

b. Property insurance

c. Salaries

d. Interest on a loan

13-9 Rocco Valentino shops only at Walmart. Because Walmart rarely has sales, Rocco believes he'll receive the lowest price without further hassles. This type of pricing strategy is known as _____ pricing.

a. dynamic

b. everyday low

c. competition-based

d. penetration

13-10 Which pricing strategy sets prices just below a whole number to give the appearance of a lower price?

a. Predatory pricing

b. Price discrimination

c. Target costing

d. Psychological pricing

True/False *You can find the answers on the last page of this book.*

13-11 The augmented product provides additional value to a customer's purchase.
☐ True or ☐ False

13-12 A local pizza joint increased its prices, so now you buy pizza elsewhere. Pizza is therefore an inelastic good.
☐ True or ☐ False

13-13 Loss leader pricing is used to move a product quickly off the shelves.
☐ True or ☐ False

13-14 MRO B2B products are marketed much like consumer convenience goods and services.
☐ True or ☐ False

13-15 A product's packaging is used only to provide protection of the good's contents.
☐ True or ☐ False

Critical Thinking Questions

✪ **13-16** How are brand loyalty, specialty goods and services, and prestige pricing related?

13-17 Describe the core, actual, and augmented product benefits for the following goods and services: a hamburger purchased at McDonald's, a gym membership, and this textbook.

✪ **13-18** Describe when it might be appropriate to use each of the following pricing strategies: discounting, rebates, bundling, dynamic pricing, prestige pricing, psychological pricing, loss leader pricing, and reference pricing.

Team Time

DEVELOPING A NEW PRODUCT

Divide into teams of three or four. As a team, use what you have learned in this chapter to discuss how you would develop a new app for a smart phone or tablet.

Process

Step 1. Begin with the first step in the new product development process: idea generation. Work as a group to decide what your new app will be.

Step 2. Proceed through the idea screening, product analysis, product development and testing, and commercialization steps. What do you estimate the consumer demand and production feasibility for this product to be? What factors will affect production costs? How might you test-market this product? How will it be marketed? Discuss the answers to these questions as you address their corresponding steps.

Step 3. Prepare a summary of your findings and present them to the class.

Ethics and Corporate Social Responsibility

THE ETHICS OF RX

The pharmaceutical drug industry is an ethical minefield. The development of prescription medications is one topic among many that can present significant ethical challenges. Consider the questions raised by the following scenario. If possible, discuss your thoughts with a classmate or participate in a group debate on the topic.

Scenario

You are an executive at one of the top drug companies in the United States. At the most recent product development meeting, two teams of scientists reported that each is within one year of having a new drug ready for clinical trials. Team A is developing a drug to cure a rare but fatal bone disease. Team B is developing a drug to treat a common, non–life-threatening skin condition. To make the deadline, however, both teams need an additional $10 million in funding. You know that the company can afford to fund only one team. According to the product analysis, Team A's drug will be expensive to produce and difficult to market and yield only modest profits. Team B's drug has the potential to yield massive profits.

Questions for Discussion

13-19 Which team would you recommend the company fund? Why?

13-20 How do the potential profits of Team B's drug affect your stance from both financial/business and medical/ethical perspectives?

13-21 What about pricing? How might you reconcile the need to keep the drug company profitable with the ethical responsibility to make medications affordable for those in need?

Web Exercises

13-22 **The iPhone as a Product**
Go to Apple's iPhone website. Describe Apple's marketing mix strategy for its product and its price. When would an iPhone be a consumer product, and when would it be a B2B product? What does Apple do to augment its product? What type of branding strategy is Apple pursuing? What stage of the product life cycle is the iPhone in? Is Apple undertaking the appropriate strategies, given this stage of the product's life cycle?

13-23 **Organic Coke?**
Organic products are increasing in popularity. Suppose Coca-Cola came out with an organic soda product. Use the Internet to research other organic beverages and sodas. Where among Coca-Cola's product lines would this item fit? How would Coca-Cola's established branding help or hurt the product launch? What kind of pricing strategy do you think it would use to introduce the product?

13-24 **Research a Brand**
Choose a favorite brand of clothing or food and use the Internet to gather information about it. What type

of brand is it—manufacturer's, private, individual, or other? Is it part of a brand extension? Is it associated with a co-brand or a licensing arrangement? How do packaging and labeling affect the image the brand projects? Summarize your findings in a brief report.

13-25 **Toothpaste Differential**
Look at Walmart's website or a website for an online drugstore. List the various manufacturers of toothpaste. Then, under each one, list the various products they make. How are companies trying to differentiate their products from each other? How do you think consumers react to these various types of toothpaste?

13-26 **Comparison Shopping Websites**
Go to an online comparison shopping website such as mySimon, PriceGrabber, or DealTime and research the prices for at least three products. Describe the different prices for each product, noting the kind of stores that offer the lowest and the highest prices. Does there seem to be some consistency in their prices? Why or why not?

MyBizLab

Go to **mybizlab.com** for Auto-graded writing questions as well as the following Assisted-graded writing questions:

13-27   Why is it important for marketers to think of a good or a service in terms of the total product offering?

13-28   What part of the product life cycle would a product like the energy drink Red Bull be in?

References

1. SC Johnson and Son, Inc., "Most Frequently Asked Questions," www.oust.com/faq.aspx?oust=airSanitizer.
2. Michael E. Ross, "It Seemed Like a Good Idea at the Time," April 22,2005, www.msnbc.msn.com/id/7209828.
3. Robert E. Cannon, "A Tutorial on Product Life Cycle," www.mrotoday.com/progressive/online%20exclusives/productlifecycle.htm.
4. Coca-Cola, "List of Coca-Cola Products: Comprehensive Coca-Cola Brand List," www.thecoca-colacompany.com/brands/brandlist.html.
5. GE, "Products & Services Overview: Introduction, Businesses, Categories," www.ge.com/products_services/index.html.
6. Theresa Howard, "Coke Finally Scores Another Winner," *USA Today*, October 28, 2007, www.usatoday.com/money/advertising/adtrack/2007-10-28-coke-zero_N.htm.
7. Tom Peters, "The Brand Called You," August 31, 1997, www.fastcompany.com.
8. Tiffany & Co., "Welcome to Tiffany & Co.," www.tiffany.com/About/Default.aspx.
9. Puma,, "PUMA's New Packaging and Distribution System to Save More than 60% of Paper and Water Annually," April 13, 2010, http://about.puma.com/puma%E2%80%99s-new-packaging-and-distribution-system-to-save-more-than-60-of-paper-and-water-annually.
10. "FDA Takes Issue with Cheerios Health Claims," May 13, 2009, www.msnbc.msn.com/id/30701291.
11. "The IKEA Product Range: Democratic Design," http://franchisor.ikea.com/Theikeaconcept/Pages/The-IKEA-product-range.aspx.
12. "The NRF Top 100 Retailers Are Private Brand Stars," *My Private Brand*, July 1, 2010, http://mypbrand.com/2010/07/01/the-nrf-top-100-retailers-are-private-brand-stars. Copyrighted 2010 NRF Enterprises Inc. 69694-12mcd.

Chapter 14
Promotion and Distribution

▶ Promotion and the Promotional Mix

When Danny Corbett started his food truck business, he thought that being in a location with other food trucks and giving away samples would generate business. Unfortunately, things didn't turn out as he anticipated the first day. How can Danny create an effective promotional strategy?

▶ Advertising and Public Relations

Monica Garcia and Steven Alvarez have opened their own new interior design business. They have a website and are using Instagram and Facebook to connect with their customers and hear what people are saying about their business. But how can they monitor all the comments made in these social networking sites? Do they need other, more traditional means of advertising? What other advertising options are best for them?

▶ Personal Selling and Sales Promotion

Keith Jefferson works for a trucking company and is giving his first sales pitch alone. When his potential client asks a question about shipping rates, Keith freezes. He has no idea how to answer it. What is personal selling? What traits do good salespeople have?

▶ Distribution: Marketing Intermediaries

For her modern U.S. literature class, Liv Karlsen needed a book that was on the *New York Times* "best-seller list. The college bookstore had no more copies. What other sources does Liv have to find her book? Are all distribution processes the same?

OBJECTIVES

1 What is a promotional mix, and what is its function in a promotional campaign? (pp. 397–399)

2 What are the different categories of advertising, and what role do these categories play in business and society? (pp. 399–404)

3 What is public relations, and how is it used in the promotional mix? (pp. 404–406)

4 What are the steps in the personal selling process? (pp. 406–409)

5 What are the two types of sales promotions, and what types of tools are commonly used as incentives? (pp. 409–412)

6 Why are marketing intermediaries and distribution channels important elements of marketing? (pp. 412–414)

7 What types of services do wholesalers, agents, and brokers provide? (pp. 414–416)

8 Why are retailing and physical distribution key aspects of distribution? (pp. 416–420)

MyBizLab®

⭐ **Improve Your Grade!**
Over 10 million students improved their results using the Pearson MyLabs.
Visit **mybizlab.com** for simulations, tutorials, and end-of-chapter problems.

Promotion and the Promotional Mix pp. 397–399

Danny Corbett dreamed of having his own business. When he decided to take the leap and switch careers, he was nervous but excited. He loves to cook and wanted to get people to taste his food, but he didn't have the money to open a full-fledged restaurant. Instead, he decided to operate a food truck and was able to set up in a busy commercial area that already had several other food trucks. Danny's friend suggested he start a Facebook page and a Twitter account first, but Danny didn't want to waste time on those things until his business took off. Instead, he decided to begin by giving away samples of some of his menu items. Although many people took the free samples, few bought anything. In the end, he was out $400 in food the first day with nothing to show for it. Was it his food, his location, or how he promoted his product? Should he have taken his friend's advice about the social media sites? ■

Source: © Aurora/Aurora Photos/Corbis.

Danny's plan to promote his business was well intentioned, but it didn't work out quite the way he had hoped. What should he have done differently? What other options does he have? In this chapter, you'll learn about the promotion and distribution (or place) components of the four Ps of the marketing mix.

Promotion

What is promotion? Few products—no matter how well they are developed, priced, and distributed—will sell well if they are not properly promoted. **Promotion** involves all the techniques marketers use to inform targeted customers of the benefits of a product and persuade them to purchase it. Promotion is designed to increase brand awareness, brand loyalty, and sales and is, therefore, one of the most visible components of the marketing mix.

Finding the best way to communicate the benefits of a product and persuade customers to buy it is a critical job of marketers. Should a product be advertised, or is personal selling more appropriate? If advertising is used, is it best to advertise through newspapers, television, the Internet, or another source? Beyond advertising and personal selling, what types of public relations activities might be most appropriate? These are just a few of the questions that marketers must ask themselves when promoting a product.

What are the most popular tools marketers use to promote a product? The following four basic promotional tools are used to promote a good or a service:

- Advertising
- Public relations
- Personal selling
- Sales promotions

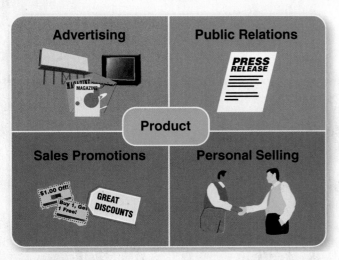

FIGURE 14.1
The Promotional Mix

The **promotional mix** is the strategic combination of the promotional tools used to reach targeted customers to achieve marketing objectives. The elements of the promotional mix are illustrated in ■ **FIGURE 14.1**. Notice that the product is also included as an element in the promotional mix. It can be a promotional tool because its features may be promoted by giving away free samples of the good or service, as Danny Perez did.

Efficient organizations search for the optimal or most cost-effective promotional mix given their marketing objectives and budgetary constraints. The optimal promotional mix for a given product will vary depending on the goals of the promotional campaign.

What are the steps involved in a promotional campaign? It's best to plan out a promotional campaign to determine the right balance of activities and their timing. Although each campaign will differ depending on the specific needs of the product, the basic steps are as follows:

1. **Identify the target market.** Recall that a *target market* is a specific group of potential customers on which marketing efforts are focused. The promotional campaign should devote its promotional activities to that market first.

2. **Determine the marketing objectives.** Is a business trying to maximize profits, sales, or market share? Is the goal to build traffic, build brand awareness, or bolster a brand image? Is a business trying to introduce a new product or respond to an attack by a competitor? Whatever the marketing objective is, the goal should be clearly understood and measurable.

3. **Determine the budget.** The best combination of promotional activities can be determined by finding the mix that results in the biggest bang for the buck—but it still needs to stay within a predetermined budget.

4. **Design the message.** The message should inform customers of the product's benefits and be echoed by all elements of the promotional mix.

5. **Implement the promotional mix.** It is important to ensure that the variety of tools and resources used in a promotional campaign all work together harmoniously. **Integrated marketing communications (IMC)** is a strategy to deliver a clear, consistent, and unified message about a company and its products to customers at all contact points. This strategy contrasts with allowing members of an organization to develop in isolation their own communications with customers, something that could give rise to conflicting messages, consumer confusion, and ultimately lost sales.

6. **Evaluate and adjust as needed.** The effectiveness of any promotional mix needs to be measurable. In addition, each element of the mix, as well as the entire combination of the mix, will need to be adjusted over time to continue to grow the product's sales as market conditions change, or to correct ineffective promotional techniques.

Source: Paul Italiano/Alamy.

Promoting a product involves choosing the best combination of promotional tools to persuade customers to purchase a good, a service, or an idea. As Danny Perez discovered, achieving this blend can be a challenge. Danny is now putting careful thought into each of the steps he needs to take to develop an effective promotional campaign and the best promotional mix for his business. How would you design the promotional mix if you were Danny?

Advertising and Public Relations pp. 399–406

After graduating from design school, Monica Garcia and Steven Alvarez rented a small studio and opened their interior design business. They already had several clients—friends and family connections—but they know they have to get the word out in a more formal and broader context if they want their business to grow. Steven designed the website and created a page on Facebook. Monica loves Instagram, so she posts daily images of her designs. They are concerned about how they will monitor all the conversations that are happening in response to their efforts. Monica and Steven also wonder whether their social media efforts are enough or whether they need to do some form of print advertising campaign. What kind of advertising would be best for Monica and Steven? ■

Businesses use methods to persuade an audience to purchase their products. This communication is better known as advertising. **Advertising** is paid, impersonal mass communication from an identified sponsor to persuade or influence a targeted audience. When we think of advertising, many of us first think of television commercials. But advertising is much more.

Source: Andresinfinite/Fotolia.

The Role of Advertising

What role does advertising play in the promotional mix? Advertising is one of the promotional tools designed to communicate with targeted customers. Businesses use advertising to do the following:

- Help build mass brand awareness and brand association, so it is especially important in the introductory and growth stages of a product's life cycle.
- Emphasize a product's differences, something that is especially helpful in its maturity stage.
- Build brand loyalty and brand equity.
- Inform consumers of the value inherent in products and educate the public about their uses. However, critics argue that advertisers often mislead the public by highlighting product qualities or benefits that may not exist. This debate continues. It also helps explain the existence of government laws and regulations that constrain advertising and other marketing practices.
- Lead to lower prices for consumers. The more people know about a product and like it, the more the sales of the product and its production increase. Increased volumes of production result in economies of scale, so consumers may get lower per unit costs and lower-priced products as a result.

What's the economic impact of advertising? Advertising has a major effect on the economy because of the huge sums of money spent on it. Nike alone spends $2.7 billion globally on advertising.[1] Advertising dollars are dispersed throughout the economy in a variety of ways. Commercials help pay for the television programming, and print ads help pay for the publishing of newspapers and magazines. A well-received campaign results in increased sales profits, which ultimately lead to business growth, more jobs, and more discretionary income available to spend. However, the opposite can also be true, so if a company doesn't spend money on advertising or has a poor campaign, sales can stagnate, resulting in corporate retrenchment and lost jobs.

What is an advertising agency? Often companies need help with their advertising needs. In these cases, an advertising agency is hired to help create, plan, and handle advertising (or other forms of promotion). Advertising agencies can range from small "boutique" firms to much larger national organizations and offer a wide range of services. Advertising agencies can handle some or all aspects of marketing campaigns, including market research, branding strategies, producing ads, and placing them in the appropriate media.

Types of Advertising

What are the different types of advertising? Virtually all organizations advertise, and there are many different types of advertising media to choose from. Some of the more common types of advertising are shown in ■ **FIGURE 14.2**.

Advertising Media

What are the different types of advertising media? Companies use a variety of media to implement their advertising strategies. Some of the more traditional media used include television, newspapers, the Internet, social media, and outdoor media. Outdoor media include billboards, signs in sports arenas, ads painted on the sides of vehicles, and even skywriting.

Direct-mail advertising remains one of the most frequently used form of advertising. You're probably familiar with direct-mail advertising; you just have a different name for it—junk mail. Direct-mail advertising ranges from coupon offers to brochures and catalogs. Surprisingly, nearly 80 percent of people who get direct-mail advertisements either read or skim them.[5] This type of advertising also allows companies to target their advertising dollars to customers who are most likely to buy their products depending, for example, on their ZIP codes and other demographic information.

Dove's Real Beauty

ON TARGET

Dove has been pushing the discussion of what real beauty is since 2004. The first two phases of the company's Campaign for Real Beauty featured real women with atypical "beauty" features: wrinkles, curves, and other "imperfections." The third phase in 2007 continued Dove's goal to widen the world's fairly narrow definition of beauty. The campaign also focused on how the self-esteem of young girls is likely to be adversely affected when they are constantly surrounded by unattainable beauty standards.

In 2013, Dove launched another phase of the campaign, Real Beauty Sketches, in which an FBI sketch artist drew images of women based on their own descriptions as well as that of a stranger. Remarkably, the self-described images were less attractive than the stranger descriptions, confirming that women are often the most critical of their appearances.[3] The video became the most viral ad of all time, being shared 3.74 million times.[4] The reaction to these campaigns has been mixed, however. Many people applauded the campaign and continue to give Dove credit for bringing forth a discussion to redefine beauty. Others criticized the campaign for being hypocritical since Dove

Source: Associated Press.

sells products to enhance or change a person's appearance. What do you think about the Campaign for Real Beauty?

Product advertising promotes a specific product's uses, features, and benefits. This is the type of advertising we most often think of.

Advocacy advertising promotes an organization's position on a public issue, such as global warming or immigration. We are familiar with advocacy advertising undertaken during political campaigns by organizations that are independent of a political party or candidate.

Corporate (or institutional) advertising focuses on creating a positive image toward a government, an organization, or an entire industry as opposed to a specific product.

Interactive advertising uses interactive media, such as interactive video catalogs on the Internet or kiosks at shopping malls, to connect directly with consumers in a personal and engaging way.

Comparative advertising compares a brand's characteristics with those of other established brands. Examples include television commercials comparing toothpaste, pain relievers, and detergents.

Internet advertising displays messages on websites as banner ads, pop-ups, videos, and the like. The advantages of online advertising are that it is immediately delivered, can be interactive and customized, and is reasonably cost-effective.

Retail (or local) advertising focuses on attracting customers to a fixed location, such as a department store or a grocery store.

Mobile advertising is delivering advertising messages via mobile phones or other mobile devices. Since more people own mobile phones than any other device, this form of advertising will continue to increase in the near future.

B2B advertising is directed to other businesses rather than to consumers. For example, Caterpillar, the earth-moving equipment company, advertises to construction companies.

Non-profit and public service advertising focuses on promoting organizations such as the Red Cross or on behalf of a good cause such as the prevention of wildfires.

■ **FIGURE 14.2**
Common Types of Advertising
Source for Comparative advertising: Alpha and Omega collection/Alamy.

What are the advantages and disadvantages of the different types of advertising media? Every type of advertising media has certain advantages and disadvantages. For example, television advertising reaches a huge audience, but it's very expensive. Social media also reaches large numbers but can demand a great deal of manpower to follow and interpret the results. ■ **TABLE 14.1** lists some of the advantages and disadvantages of each major medium.

Internet Advertising

How does advertising take place online? **Internet advertising** includes spam (junk e-mail), pop-ups, banner ads, and other links found at websites to attract potential customers to a company's Web page. Google's advertising services AdWords and AdSense are another form of Internet advertising. With Google AdWords, advertisers submit text-only ads to Google along with a list of relevant key words. When a user types one of the key words into the Google search engine, the text-only ad appears in a sidebar of the Google search results. The advertiser pays Google only when a user clicks on the ad. Google AdSense is a service that enables website owners to earn money by displaying relevant ads on their websites. Another more subtle form of Internet advertising is search engine optimization (SEO). SEO is used to improve a website's position in search results.

TABLE 14.1   Advantages and Disadvantages of Advertising Media

Media	Advantages	Disadvantages
Direct mail	High levels of segmentation; allows personalization; high flexibility; ad can be saved; measurable impact	High cost; can be rejected as junk mail and viewed as a nuisance
Television	Good mass-market coverage; low cost per contact; combines sight, sound, and motion; good audience attention span	High cost; low recall; channel surfing or digital video recorders (DVRs) skip over ads; short exposure
Newspaper	Timing and geographic flexibility; good local market coverage; high credibility and acceptability	Short life span; lots of competition for attention; poor-quality reproductions
Magazine	High market segmentation; high-quality color; long life; longer audience attention span; high credibility	Declining readership; lots of competition for attention; high cost; long ad-purchase lead time
Radio	High geographic and demographic selectivity; low cost; creative opportunities with sound	Low audience attention; short exposure time; information overload; limited coverage
Internet	Global and interactive possibilities; ease of segmentation; high audience interest; easy to measure responses	Audience controls exposure; clutter on each site; skewed demographically to surfers
Social media	Relatively inexpensive to set up; results in immediate consumer feedback; provides access to consumer feedback on competition; builds customer relationships	Can be difficult to monitor; not a passive strategy—must be actively maintained
Mobile	Good for immediate recognition; low cost; easy to reach target market	Easy to ignore
Outdoor	Able to select key geographic areas; low cost per impression; high frequency on major commuter routes	Short exposure time; brief messages; creative limitations; little segmentation possible

Image Sources: Top to bottom: raven/Fotolia; T/C; Patrikeevna/Fotolia; Studio 101/Alamy; Tengu/Fotolia; AMATHIEU/Fotolia; bloomua/Fotolia; Oleksiy Mark/Fotolia; magann/Fotolia.

What is the benefit of online advertising? The Internet has become a fast-growing advertising medium, in part because it allows firms to focus their advertising dollars on targeted customers. Once customers visit a company's website, the company can learn a lot about their preferences and shopping habits based on where and how often they click within the website. Businesses can also interact with their customers by offering a chat service, providing helpful videos, or posting a blog. If a business is able to consistently deliver high-quality value using these techniques, then Internet advertising can help businesses maintain positive customer relations.

Social Media

How is social media being used in advertising? Social media have caused many companies to rethink how they can connect and communicate with their customers and are part of many IMC plans. Companies create blogs and tweets to announce new products or corporate developments, post help tutorials and product demonstrations videos on YouTube, and create fan pages on Facebook that prompt interactions with their customers. Social media enable companies to build customer relationships rather than just advertise products.

Mobile Marketing

How is mobile marketing being used? Smart phones and tablets are the most pervasively used technology. Surprisingly, it's been documented that more people own mobile phones than they do toothbrushes.[6] Given their ubiquitous market penetration, mobile phones make the best platform for advertisers. Companies are embracing technologies such as QR codes, text messages, and mobile app platforms to connect with their customer bases 24/7.

Product Placement

What is product placement? When a company pays for its product to be prominently displayed in television shows, movies, and video games where they will be seen by potential customers, it's known as **product placement**. This promotional technique has been around as long as the media themselves. Companies have increased their product placements in television shows because so many viewers have DVRs that allow them to fast-forward through commercials. Another product-placement variant are the banners of brand names, symbols, and slogans displayed during sporting events on players' uniforms and equipment as well as within arenas. They are strategically placed so that camera shots of the televised games will frequently display the messages.

Infomercials

How are infomercials useful as an advertising technique? Infomercials (or **paid programming**) appear to be actual television programs, often in the form of talk shows, with little direct reference to the fact that they are actually ads. "Experts" or celebrities often appear as guests or hosts to endorse and push the products being advertised. Because they run longer than traditional commercials and many run as long as regular television programs, infomercials allow advertisers to show the features of products in great detail. Unlike normal commercials, infomercials are designed to elicit a specific, direct, and quantifiable response from viewers in terms of direct sales of products. In other words, advertisers don't have to wonder if the advertisement is working. The infomercial results in either a few sales or a lot of sales. Some successful infomercials include ads for workout products such as P90X, Proactiv Solution Acne Treatment, and Vitamix blenders.

P90X is sold successfully through infomercials.
Source: Splash News/Newscom.

Global Advertisements

How is global advertising conducted? Some products can be successfully exported to other countries without many changes. However, most products have to be customized to satisfy foreign customers. This means that products are tailored to meet the unique local tastes, preferences, and cultural sensitivities of foreign customers or satisfy the regulatory standards of different governments around the globe. Likewise, some advertising campaigns can be exported intact, while others have to be modified. Advertisers prefer to use the same ads for domestic and foreign markets because doing so is cheaper and allows for a more globally integrated message. But transferring domestically created, successful advertising messages abroad can be tricky. As we discussed in Chapter 4, marketers have to carefully consider how their messages will be interpreted by foreign consumers. Increasingly, marketers are realizing that customized advertising campaigns to globally segmented markets work much better, just as domestic market segmentation is more effective.

Public Relations

What is public relations? Another important part of the promotional mix is public relations. **Public relations** is the process of establishing and maintaining mutually beneficial relationships between an organization and its stakeholders, including consumers, stockholders, employees, suppliers, the government, and the public in general. In other words, public relations promotes the image of a company or an individual.[7] All organizations are interested in public relations.

Negative Political Ads: Do They Really Work?

We have all heard them, and they are prolific weeks before any election—campaign ads that criticize the opponent rather than praising the candidate. Why are negative messages used? Are they really more effective than positive ads? In certain circumstances, campaign strategists indicate that negative ads can be more effective because they initially create uncertainty and doubt about the candidate in question. Positive ads are most helpful to introduce first-time candidates whose attributes might otherwise be unknown to the voting public. Negative ads can quickly raise questions about a new candidate's character, so they are often used when the opposing candidate has used a positive ad introducing him- or herself early on in the campaign. Negative ads can also be more cost effective because they get more attention due to their inflammatory nature. As a result, they are more frequently shared via social media or discussed in the press. Thus, their exposure is increased without a candidate having to spend additional money.

The frequency of negative political ads is also important. Studies show that a negative political ad is most effective when shown in moderation. Otherwise, there could be backlash for the candidate who sponsored the ad.

So, during the next election cycle, pay particular attention to the campaign ads and your response to them. No doubt there will be at least one negative ad. Was it effective in helping you formulate your opinion about a candidate?

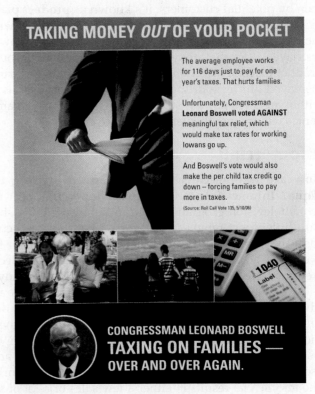

TAKING MONEY *OUT* OF YOUR POCKET

The average employee works for 116 days just to pay for one year's taxes. That hurts families.

Unfortunately, Congressman **Leonard Boswell voted AGAINST** meaningful tax relief, which would make tax rates for working Iowans go up.

And Boswell's vote would also make the per child tax credit go down – forcing families to pay more in taxes.

(Source: Roll Call Vote 135, 5/10/06)

CONGRESSMAN LEONARD BOSWELL
TAXING ON FAMILIES —
OVER AND OVER AGAIN.

Source: Economic Freedom Fund/AP images.

What steps are involved in developing public relations plans? There are three steps to a good public relations program:

1. **Consider public opinion.** The idea behind public relations is to create and maintain a positive image of an organization in the minds of stakeholders. This begins with assessing the public's attitudes and perceptions of the organization. Sometimes, they may be based on perceptions that have little to do with facts. In any case, an organization needs to conduct an audit of public opinion before formulating specific public relations programs to shape its image.

2. **Change the policies and procedures.** Once an organization has listened carefully to public concerns and interests, it needs to respond by changing its behavior or correcting the public's misperceptions about it. Sometimes, a public relations campaign is needed to correct or rebuild a corporation's reputation after a mishap. British Petroleum (BP), Toyota, and Netflix are among the many companies that have had to run public relations campaigns to regain the trust of their customers.

3. **Inform the public of actions planned or taken.** Finally, an organization needs to inform the public of any changes it has made or educate the public about the facts associated with it.

What are some common public relations tools? Several specific types of public relations tools exist to build a positive business image. They can be classified by whether the news transmitted is controlled, semicontrolled, or uncontrolled by the organization.[8] The degree of control hinges on how and when the message is delivered:

- *Controlled messages* include corporate (or institutional) advertising, advocacy advertising, and public service advertising. A company might also disseminate annual reports, brochures, flyers, and newsletters or provide films or speakers to send a controlled message to targeted audiences.

- *Semicontrolled messages* are placed on websites, in chat rooms, and on blogs. In these forums, what people say about a company is not strictly regulated. Other semicontrolled messages include sponsorships of sporting events and other special events because participation by the press and stakeholders is not under the control of the sponsoring company.

- *Uncontrolled messages* generally take the form of *publicity*.

How is publicity helpful? Information about an individual, an organization, or a product transmitted through mass media at no charge is called **publicity**. Publicity has two advantages over advertising. First, it is free. Second, it is more believable because it is often presented as a news story.

Publicity can be shaped by an organization but *not* controlled by it. Publicity is instead controlled by the media. Naturally, maintaining a friendly relationship with the press increases the probability that a "newsworthy" story will be covered and treated with a favorable spin. Nevertheless, public relations managers need to ensure that the information released to the press and to the public is timely, interesting, accurate, and in the public's interest.

An example of positive publicity is the favorable press companies receive when they contribute to some humanitarian purpose. Corporate philanthropy is generally good publicity, especially if it results in getting a company's name on a building or is associated with an annual event that is visible to the public. Many smaller companies make donations to local organizations to garner positive publicity.

LA Clippers owner Donald Sterling faced a significant public relations crisis after racist remarks went viral.
Source: Robyn Beck/AFP/Getty Images/Newscom.

How does a company respond to negative publicity? Another role of public relations personnel is managing a crisis. *Damage control* is a company's effort to minimize the harmful effects of a negative event. Negative publicity can, in a matter of days, tear down a firm's image that took decades to build up. For example, Donald Sterling, owner of the LA Clippers professional basketball team, faced a public relations crisis when racist comments he made went public.

Sometimes, bad news doesn't come from the media but from word of mouth, which is especially easy given the viral nature of social media. In the event of bad news, a company must stand ready to react—and react quickly. No easy remedies exist for crises, but being honest, accepting responsibility, and responding ethically are the first steps toward regaining credibility and reestablishing a positive image.

Monica and Steven consulted with a friend who is a public relations specialist and asked for advice on how best to get the word out about their new venture. For now, it seems they are generating just enough business with their current promotional efforts. They will continue to get the word out via their friends, relatives, and business contacts as well as work the social media sites. They can't afford to do too much more, but they also know they can't afford to do any less.

Source: Stokkete/Fotolia.

Personal Selling and Sales Promotion pp. 406–412

Keith Jefferson is nervous about giving his first big sales pitch alone. He's trying to convince an electronics wholesaler to switch from its current trucking company to his company. Despite his nerves, the presentation goes well, and the client seems receptive. After the presentation, the client asks him how fluctuating oil prices will affect shipping rates. Keith has no idea what to say, and the client defers closing the deal. The sales encounter was much more difficult than he imagined. How could he have been more effective with his potential client? ■

Personal selling is more complicated than simply suggesting to a customer that he or she should buy your product. It's a complex process that involves several steps, each of which must be executed with great planning and care.

Personal Selling

What is personal selling? Personal selling, another component of the promotional mix, is direct communication between a firm's sales force and potential buyers to make a sale and build good customer relationships. Good salespeople don't just want to sell products; they want to serve customers. A salesperson should help customers with their buying decisions by understanding their needs and presenting the advantages and disadvantages of a product. Salespeople must effectively represent their companies by establishing good customer relationships that foster repeat business and lead to a company's long-term success.

Why is personal selling important? A company's salesperson is often the first contact point for many customers. To build good customer relationships, a salesperson should be customer oriented, competent, dependable, honest, and likable. The best salespeople aren't fast talkers. Instead, they listen carefully to customers' needs and find solutions for them. In many B2B sales, millions of dollars are involved in a single purchase, such as buying an airplane or constructing an office building. You can see why businesses want nothing less than truly professional salespeople—people who can deliver carefully prepared presentations, establish rapport with customers, and negotiate details with skill. The demand for well-educated, well-trained professional salespeople explains why some salespeople are top earners in their companies.

What are the advantages and disadvantages of having a sales force? Personal selling is the most expensive part of the promotional mix for most companies. In addition to salespeople's direct compensation (salaries and commissions) and employment benefits, firms must spend money to train their sales forces and purchase the tools they need to track and maintain customers in their territories. This can include buying or leasing company cars, paying for salespeople's travel, and expenses to entertain customers. Generally, personal selling is preferred to advertising when a high-value, custom-made, or technically complex product is being sold. Advertising is more cost effective when a firm is selling a low-value, standardized product that is easily understood.

What other different sales roles are there in organization? There are four general roles taken on by salespeople. Of course, some salespeople, especially in smaller businesses, may be required to fulfill some or all four roles.

1. **Order getters.** An **order getter** increases a company's sales by selling to new customers and increasing a firm's sales to its existing customers. These salespeople use current customers as sources for leads on new prospects. Telemarketers are order getters.

2. **Order takers.** An **order taker** handles repeat sales and ensures that buyers have sufficient quantities of products when and where they are needed. This is especially true in B2B sales. Retail clerks are order takers in B2C markets. They generally handle routine orders for standardized products that do not require a lot of technical sales expertise. So are customer service representatives who sell customers products to help solve their problems.

3. **Order influencers. Order influencers** are not engaged in direct selling; rather, they concentrate on selling activities that target people who influence the purchases made by the final customer. For example, pharmaceutical salespeople discuss products with doctors (the order influencers) who then write a prescription for the patient (the final customer). Similarly, your college professors act as the order influencers recommending specific textbooks for you to purchase.

4. **Support personnel. Support personnel** may obtain new customers but focus on assisting current customers with technical matters. Support personnel are most common in B2B sales and include the office personnel who assist salespeople.

All salespeople, whatever their specific role at any given time, are ambassadors for a business. They need to listen carefully, act as sounding boards, and relay customer feedback to an organization. This allows firms to improve existing products or create new products to better meet customer needs and preferences. Serving customers better is a large part of what building good customer relationships and promotion are all about.

What are the steps in the selling process? The steps involved in the selling process are essentially the same for selling a consumer product and for selling a B2B product, though the sale of a B2B product is usually more complex. In all cases, a salesperson has to be knowledgeable about his or her product and the competitors' products.

Personal selling is the preferred method used to sell complex products that require explanation or demonstration.
Source: Blend Images/Fotolia.

No two salespeople are alike, and no two selling situations are the same. However, six steps emerge from all personal selling: prospecting, approaching the prospect, presenting, overcoming objections, closing the sale, and following up. This six-step personal selling procedure is outlined in ■ **FIGURE 14.3**.

How are customers identified? The first step in the personal selling process is to identify qualified potential customers. This is known as **prospecting**. Businesses need to not only find potential customers but also identify those who are *qualified* to buy. To be qualified to buy means that a potential customer has the ability and the authority to purchase. Prospecting can be a daunting task; it often involves cold calling. Cold calling is approaching prospects without their expecting it. Some salespeople find leads at trade shows, from those who have scouted a company's website, or, better yet, from currently satisfied customers who are willing to recommend them to others because of their superior product and service.

What is the best way to approach a prospect? The second step of the personal selling process involves two parts: the *pre-approach* and the *actual approach*. The pre-approach involves salespeople doing their homework. This is especially critical if they are trying to sell a B2B product, such as an inventory software system. Salespeople must learn as much as possible about their potential customers to determine their likely needs and think about how they might be able to satisfy those needs. The timing decision of the actual approach should also be carefully planned not to catch the prospect at a busy time or at an off time in a firm's budget cycle.

When it comes to approaching a potential customer, the idea is to meet, greet, and put the prospect at ease. First impressions are lasting impressions! This is the salesperson's first chance at building a long-lasting relationship. Good salespeople present themselves as knowledgeable and friendly professionals who are genuinely interested in serving customers. The first impression is followed by asking some questions to learn about a potential customer's needs. Then the salesperson must listen carefully to those responses.

How are the details of the product explained? The next step in the personal selling process is the actual presentation of the product to the prospective customer. Often salespeople demonstrate the product and let the prospect use it as

■ **FIGURE 14.3**
The Personal Selling Process

Prospecting	Approaching the Prospect	Presenting	Overcoming Objections	Closing the Sale	Following Up
• Identify qualified potential customers	• Preapproach: gathering information • Approach: Initial contact	• Tell the product's "story" • Conduct demonstrations	• Provide additional information to answer questions or resolve doubts	• Conduct physical purchase	• Answer questions • Provide training or solutions

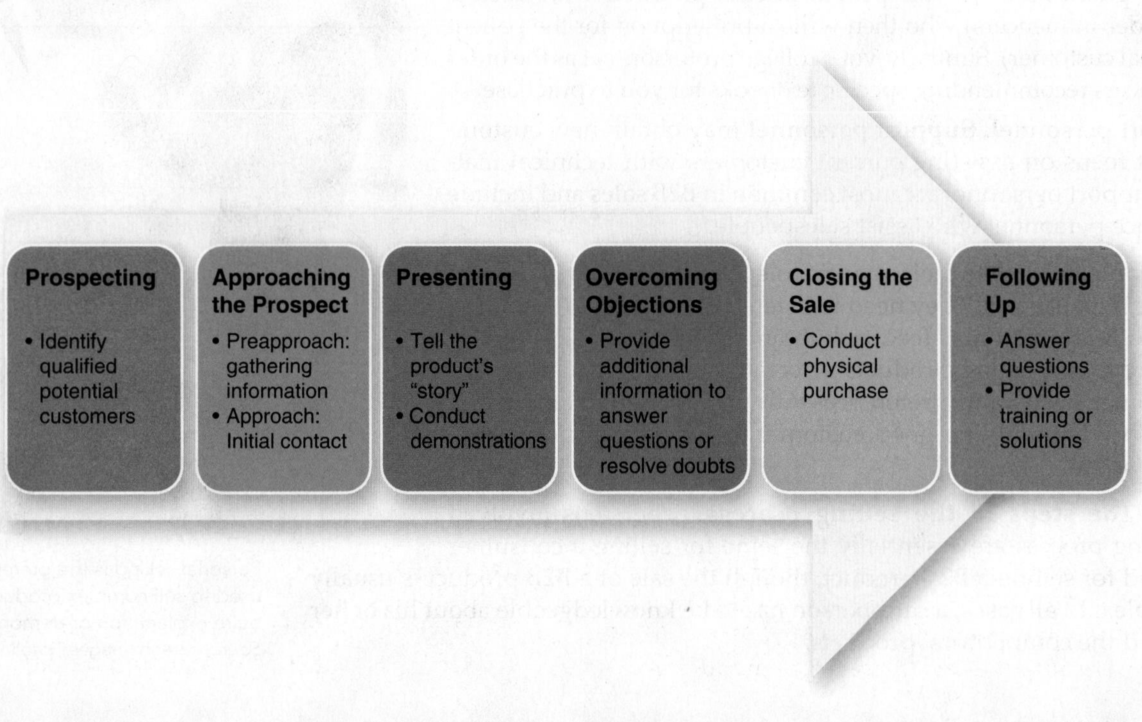

well. The presentation should be carefully planned using the most advanced presentation technologies that allow for the full use of multimedia effects. The salesperson asks probing questions during the presentation, and the prospect's responses are listened to carefully. Listening is more important than talking to fully understand the customer's needs.

What happens if the prospect has an objection? Objections to buying are common. Good salespeople anticipate objections and are prepared to counter them. Once objections surface, a salesperson will provide more information about the product and turn these objections into reasons to buy. Bringing in other people from the company who have additional expertise to address the prospect's objections can be helpful.

How is the sale finalized? After overcoming the prospect's objections, the next step is to close the sale. Great salespeople know the physical cues, comments, or questions that signal the time to ask the buyer for an order. This is also the time to review any buying agreements, ask the buyer which model he or she prefers or how many units are needed or to sweeten the deal by offering more favorable credit terms or throwing in extra quantities of the product free of charge. Closing the sale is an art that is learned with practice.

What happens after the sale is made? To ensure a long-term relationship and repeat business, the salesperson must follow up with the customer to ensure that he or she is happy with his or her new product. Any feedback from the new customer is relayed back to the company as input for improving existing products or designing new ones. Good follow-up service and rapport can give rise to referrals or testimonials that can be used to enhance future sales. Following up is all about building and nurturing relationships.

Sales Promotions

What is a sales promotion? The final element of the promotional mix is sales promotion. A **sales promotion** is a short-term activity that targets consumers and other businesses for the purpose of generating interest in a product and selling it. As consumers, we see sales promotions almost everywhere: coupons in newspapers, rebate offers on a new car purchase, e-mail announcements offering discounted prices on airline tickets, and end-of-aisle displays of potato chips at a local grocery store tempting impulse purchases.

What are the two general types of sales promotions? Most companies' products go through a distribution system before they reach the final consumer. These companies encourage wholesalers (middlemen) to push their products through to end users. Any incentives to push a product through the distribution system to final consumers are called **trade (B2B) sales promotions**. In addition, **consumer sales promotions** are incentives designed to increase final consumer demand for a product. Coupons, contests, and free samples are examples. The whole idea behind all sales promotions is to generate interest and excitement around a product. Businesses need to create a reason why stores should not only carry their products but also encourage their purchase by consumers. Companies want consumers to be so excited about their products that they seek the products out and ask for them by name. In short, companies want all involved to opt for their products instead of competitors' alternatives.

What are some consumer sales promotional tools? Some of the most common consumer promotional tools are listed in ■ **FIGURE 14.4.** Consumer sales promotions are aimed at the end users, or final consumers. Consumer promotions are intended to increase demand for a good

IKEA offered "free samples" of its products by leaving displays of their furniture in several busy Paris subway stops. *Source:* Laurent Garric/Newscom.

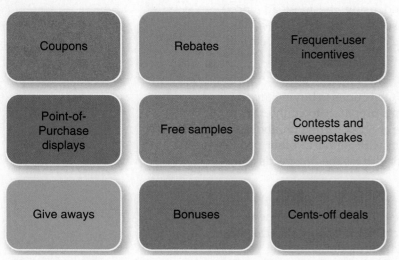

FIGURE 14.4
Common Sales Promotion Techniques

or a service by providing that extra incentive to tip consumers in favor of a specific brand. They are also aimed at providing customers with another reason to feel good about their purchases. The timing of consumer sales promotions is important to get maximum impact. They need to be strategically coordinated with other elements in the promotional mix. Using promotional tools is becoming more common because it helps segment markets and is cost effective.

What are some trade sales promotional tools? Some of the specific tools used to promote a product to other businesses are listed in ■ **FIGURE 14.5**. However, if you want other businesses to become interested and excited about carrying your product, it is important to generate in-house enthusiasm. Fully educate the sales staff about the product and its many uses, features, and benefits. This also may require some formal training on how to best present the product. To generate leads, it is often beneficial to participate in trade shows equipped with sophisticated multimedia presentations, full-color brochures, and giveaways embossed with your product logo. Creating some internal buzz and excitement for your product is necessary to get other businesses interested in carrying and promoting your product. Finally, the same level of energy and excitement should be created with distributors. When it comes to trade sales promotional techniques, firms have many options from which to choose. If one doesn't work, they can easily adopt new strategies until they find the best combination.

Social Media Promotions

How is social media used to promote products? In essence, social media are today's form of word-of-mouth communication. If you had a wonderful meal at a restaurant, you can Tweet about it, post a picture of the dessert on Pinterest, or check in on Facebook to let all your friends immediately know of your great experience. Similarly, news of a bad experience can travel just as fast. Companies are well aware of this and are using social media not only to hear from their customers but also to communicate with them.

The term **viral marketing** (viral advertising or marketing buzz) refers to using social media tools and techniques to spread a marketing message quickly. As important as it was two decades ago for a company to have a website, it's equally important now for a company to have a presence on at least one but generally several social media sites. Accordingly, companies have begun to shift their marketing and promotion budgets from traditional print and broadcast advertising to social media and website initiatives.?

FIGURE 14.5
Common Business-to-Business Sales Promotion Techniques

What are the advantages and disadvantages of the promotional mix? As you've learned, when developing the best promotional mix for a product, companies must weigh the advantages and disadvantages of each of the four main options—advertising, public relations, personal selling, and sales promotions. ■ **TABLE 14.2** summarizes some of these key advantages and disadvantages.

Recall Keith Jefferson? He wasn't prepared to answer questions about the service he was offering when giving his sales pitch to a potential

TABLE 14.2	The Advantages and Disadvantages of Promotional Tools	
Promotional Tool	**Advantages**	**Disadvantages**
Advertising	• Builds brand awareness and brand loyalty • Reaches a mass audience	• Expensive • Impersonal • Not good at closing a sale
Public relations	• Often seen as more credible than advertising • Inexpensive way of reaching many customers	• Risk of losing control • Cannot always control what other people write or say about your product
Personal selling	• Highly interactive communication between the buyer and the seller • Excellent for communicating a complex product, information, and features • Good for building customer relationships and closing a sale	• Expensive • Not suitable if there are thousands of buyers
Sales promotions	• Can stimulate quick increases in sales by targeting promotional incentives on particular products • Good short-term tactical tool	• If used over the long term, customers may get used to the effect • Too much promotion may damage the brand image
Social media	• Reaches a large group of people quickly and with low cost • Can be used to establish customer relationships	• Often difficult to maintain and manage all conversations • Negative news travels fast

KFC Marketing Campaign Gone Wrong

OFF THE MARK

Chinese customers mob a KFC restaurant in Beijing, angry that a coupon deal has gone awry.
Source: AFP/Getty Images/Newscom.

Not to be outdone by a free Grand Slam Breakfast promotion by Denny's, KFC offered a free grilled chicken meal on the *Oprah* show. The coupon was available on both Oprah's and KFC's websites for the following 24 hours. Simple enough, but the company underestimated the power of the Internet (and *Oprah*) to make the KFC meal coupon one of the top trends on Twitter. Four million people printed the coupon!

KFC had not expected this amount of interest, so their stores were not prepared. In some areas, customers wanting to redeem their coupons were lined up out the door and around the block. Stores ran out of chicken, and staff refused to honor the coupons. Pandemonium followed. Police had to break up riots of unhappy customers.

KFC had a huge problem on their hands. The entire situation reflected terribly on KFC. In response, the president of KFC announced on *Oprah* two days later that the company would offer rain checks and add a free drink, too! In the end, this episode cost KFC nearly $42 million in free food.

Amazingly, however, the story does not end there. Nearly a year later, KFC offered a similar deal in China. This time, the offer was for half price but still available for only 24 hours. When coupons were brought in, some were rejected, with the KFC staff offering varying excuses. Once again, KFC posted a compromised response, but the majority of customers left feeling cheated and mishandled.

You would think KFC would have learned the first time around!

client. As a result of his lack of preparedness, he wasn't able to land the account. In retrospect, he should have done more homework and researched the potential concerns his prospect might have. Or he could have offered to get back to the client with the answer. Next time, he will be more prepared. As Keith's story shows, determining which promotional tool to use is merely half the battle. Effective execution—whether it is an ad campaign, a public relations event, a sales pitch, or a sales promotion—is equally important.

Source: Kadmy/Fotolia.

Distribution: Marketing Intermediaries pp. 412–420

Liv Karlsen listened as her modern U.S. literature class professor rattled off the book requirements for the new semester. Most were from the *New York Times* best-seller list, and Liv was required to have the first book read by the end of the week. After class, she ran over to the campus bookstore, only to find that the bookstore had run out. What other sources does Liv have to find her book? Are all distribution processes the same? ■

Most of us don't think about the transfer and storage of the products we buy— unless something goes wrong and we are unable to get the products we want, when and where we want them, like Liv Karlsen. Distribution is the process that makes products available to consumers when and where the consumers want them. The distribution (or place) function of the four Ps of marketing is often overshadowed by the more visible product, pricing, and sales promotional strategies. Distribution is a very complicated but essential process in business. You can imagine the challenges companies face trying to guarantee that customers have access to products at the right time and in the right quantities and places and are handled correctly if they are returned. As was discussed in Chapter 11, this process is known as supply chain management.

Distribution Channels and Marketing Intermediaries

How do companies get their products to customers? A channel of distribution is the part of the supply chain that focuses on getting the product to the ultimate consumers. More specifically, a **distribution channel** is a set of marketing intermediaries who buy, sell, or transfer title (or ownership) of products as they are passed from producer to consumer or business user. Some distribution channels involve several intermediaries, whereas others are shorter with fewer intermediaries.

What are marketing intermediaries? A **marketing intermediary**, formerly known as a *middleman* or *reseller*, is a business or person that moves goods and services between producers and consumers (in a B2C environment) or between business users (in a B2B environment). Marketing intermediaries, therefore, pass along products from manufacturers to end users. Sometimes no intermediaries are needed, such as when you buy a dozen ears of corn from the farmer down the road. But usually many intermediaries of different types work to ensure that a product reaches consumers.

What are the different types of marketing intermediaries? There are three main types of marketing intermediaries:

- **Wholesalers** buy and resell products to other wholesalers, retailers, and industrial users. For example, your local grocery store probably purchased Tide laundry detergent from a wholesaler who bought it from P&G, the manufacturer.

- **Agents/brokers** facilitate negotiations between buyers and sellers of goods and services but never take title (ownership) of the products traded. Examples include real estate agents and brokers, stockbrokers, and agricultural brokers. eBay also can be considered an agent/broker because the company facilitates the transfer of ownership from sellers to buyers.

- **Retailers** sell products directly to consumers. Many retailers sell products they manufacture themselves. In some instances, retailers purchase products from a manufacturer or directly from a wholesaler and then sell them to the consumer.

Why are marketing intermediaries needed? You might wonder why we need all of these intermediaries and whether they serve to only drive up prices. It's certainly true that each link in the distribution channel results in additional costs, and intermediaries must cover these costs and earn a profit to remain in business. Intermediaries' added value is efficiency.

To examine the efficiencies provided by intermediaries, review ■ **FIGURE 14.6**, which shows five consumers and five producers. Without an intermediary, each consumer would have to contact each producer to order the desired goods. Without intermediaries, if Juan, Shannon, Spencer, Ragish, and YunLi each wanted toothpaste, potato chips, soda, tissues, and soap, they would each have to go to the individual companies to get the items. That would involve 25 transactions (five transactions for each person). Now suppose a grocery store stocks and resells each of the five manufacturers' products. Now the five manufacturers and five customers have only one intermediary (the grocery store) to deal with. Each of the manufacturers makes one trip to the grocery store to deliver the items, and Juan, Shannon, Spencer, Ragish, and YunLi each make only one trip to the grocery store to get those products. This reduces the number of exchange relationships from 25 to 10. Intermediaries therefore reduce the time and costs of providing products to customers.

In short, intermediaries are a necessary part of the distribution process. If they are not available to do the job, someone else (ultimately the consumer) would need to perform the task of retrieving a product directly from a manufacturer. Intermediaries also help to transport and store goods and are often involved in other parts

■ **FIGURE 14.6**
The Efficiencies of Intermediaries
The introduction of an intermediary reduces the number of exchange relationships between manufacturers and retailers.

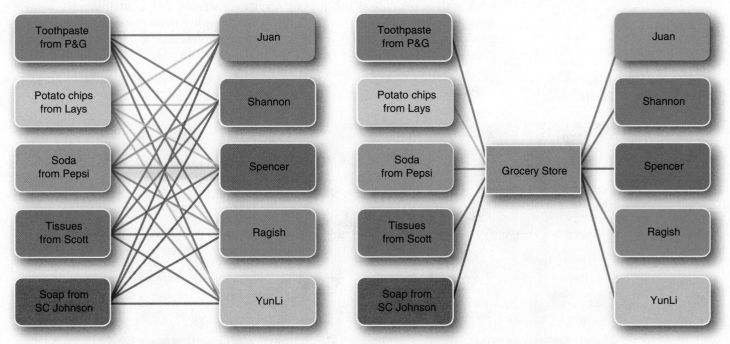

25 individual transactions required without an intermediary

10 transactions required with intermediary

of marketing, such as advertising and relationship building. Some intermediaries even serve as interim bankers by financing inventories or supplying credit to their supply chain partners. Historically, intermediaries have proven that they can add value, despite some additional costs.

What are the different types of distribution channels? Not all channels of distribution are the same. As ■ **FIGURE 14.7** shows, the type of distribution channel needed depends on the type of product being brought to the consumer. The number of intermediaries within a distribution channel depends on whether greater efficiency or additional value is provided by adding another link in the distribution system. For example, in Figure 14.7, Jeanne buys cosmetics directly from Avon without the need for any intermediary, but when Kevin buys a Goodyear tire, the tire is manufactured at a Goodyear plant and then delivered to TiresPlus, a Goodyear dealer that sells it to Kevin. Adding the extra component to this channel of distribution adds value to the product because the retail shop can provide information and service more easily than can the manufacturing plant and also provide convenience because Kevin lives closer to the store than to the plant.

Other products, such as food and clothing, have more complicated distribution systems and require the use of brokers, wholesalers, and retail stores to get the products to the consumer, but all are necessary to achieve efficiency. Similar channels of distribution also exist in B2B markets. Competitive markets determine what number of intermediaries will be required to achieve the greatest level of efficiency.

Wholesalers, Agents, and Brokers

What services do wholesalers provide? Wholesalers are intermediaries that buy and resell products to retailers, other wholesalers, and industrial users. They are different from retailers in that retailers sell products only to final consumers. One of the most effective ways to distinguish wholesalers from retailers is to remember that wholesalers sell *primarily* B2B products, while retailers sell *only* consumer products. Nevertheless, to their customers, wholesalers provide an array of services, some of which are listed in ■ **TABLE 14.3**.[9]

What are the different types of wholesalers? Wholesalers are independently owned businesses that take ownership (title) of the products they handle. Wholesalers include *full-service wholesalers* and *limited-service wholesalers*. **Full-service wholesalers** provide a full line of services: carrying stock, maintaining a sales force, offering credit, making deliveries, and helping their price, market, and sell products. There are two types of full-service wholesalers: *wholesale merchants* sell primarily to retailers, and *specialty distributors* sell to manufacturers and institutions, such as hospitals and the government.

■ **FIGURE 14.7**
Distribution Channels for Consumer Products

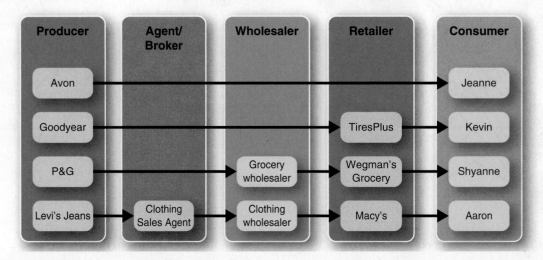

TABLE 14.3	**Services Provided by Wholesalers**
Service	**Description**
Bulk breaking	Wholesalers save retailers money by buying in bulk and breaking bulk packages down into smaller quantities.
Financing	Wholesalers finance retailers by giving credit, and they finance manufacturers by ordering early and paying bills on time.
Management service and advice	Wholesalers often help retailers train their sales clerks, improve store layouts and displays, and set up accounting and inventory control systems.
Market information	Wholesalers give information to manufacturers and retailers about competitors, new products, and price developments.
Risk bearing	Wholesalers absorb risk by taking title to merchandise and bearing the costs of the products' theft, damage, spoilage, and obsolescence.
Selling and promoting	Wholesalers' sales forces help manufacturers reach many smaller retailers at a low cost. The wholesaler has more contacts and is often more trusted by the retailer than the distant manufacturer.
Transportation	Wholesalers can provide quicker delivery to buyers because they are closer than manufacturers.
Warehousing	Wholesalers hold inventories, thereby reducing the inventory costs and risks of suppliers and retailers.

As intermediaries, **limited-service wholesalers** offer fewer services than full-service wholesalers. The major types of limited-service wholesalers include the following:

- *Cash-and-carry wholesalers* carry a limited line of fast-moving goods and sell to small retailers for cash. They normally do not deliver. For example, a small fish store may drive to a cash-and-carry fish wholesaler, buy fish for cash, and bring the merchandise back to the store.

- *Truck wholesalers* (or truck jobbers) sell and deliver directly from their trucks. They generally carry semiperishable items that regular wholesalers prefer not to carry. For example, trucks that deliver bread or snack food to convenience stores and restaurants are truck wholesalers.

- *Drop shippers* don't carry inventory or handle products. After receiving an order, they select a manufacturer that ships the merchandise directly to the customer. Drop shippers assume title and risk from the time of the order to delivery. They operate in bulk industries, such as lumber, coal, and heavy equipment.

- *Rack jobbers* sell mostly nonfood items in grocery stores and drugstores in which they set up racks and displays. Magazines are an example. Rack jobbers retain title to the goods and bill the retailer only for the goods sold to consumers.

Because of their limited functions, these limited-service wholesalers usually operate at a lower cost than full-service wholesalers.

What are some common types of agents? Agents and brokers are unique among intermediaries because they do not transport or take title to the products traded. They merely facilitate the buying and selling of products and earn a commission on their sale. What distinguishes agents from brokers is that agents represent the buyers or the sellers who hired them on a more permanent basis, whereas brokers are hired on a temporary basis.

Three common types of agents are manufacturers' agents, selling agents, and purchasing agents:

- *Manufacturers' agents* are independent contractors who sell products for more than one manufacturer. Generally manufacturers' agents represent two or more manufacturers of complementary lines. A formal written agreement with each manufacturer covers the pricing, territories, order handling, delivery service and warranties, and commission rates they earn. Manufacturers' agents are often used in such lines as apparel, furniture, and electrical goods. Most manufacturers' agents are small businesses with only a few skilled salespeople. Small manufacturers may hire an agent if they cannot afford their own field sales forces, while larger manufacturers rely on agents to open new territories or cover territories that cannot support full-time salespeople. Some manufacturers' agents work directly for the manufacturer and directly distribute the company's products to retailers. In some instances, these agents deal directly with the consumer, skipping the retail middleman altogether.

- *Selling agents* have the contractual authority to sell a manufacturer's entire product line when the manufacturer is either not interested in the selling function or feels unqualified to do so. The selling agent serves as the sales department for the manufacturer. Selling agents are common in the industrial machinery and equipment businesses; coal, chemicals, and metals industries; and real estate and stock brokerage industries.

- *Purchasing agents* generally have long-term relationships with buyers and make purchases for them, often receiving, inspecting, warehousing, and shipping merchandise for them. They provide helpful market information to clients and help them obtain the best goods and prices available.

Retailers

What are the important retail strategies? Retailers primarily sell products to the final consumer. Retailing constitutes a major sector of our economy. You're likely familiar with retail distributors because most of your personal shopping experiences take place at retail stores. All companies that sell products need to decide how intensively they wish to cover any geographic market. Companies can choose to sell either through all available retail outlets or only through a more selective distribution (see ■ **FIGURE 14.8**):

- An **intensive distribution** is most appropriate for companies selling convenience goods, such as newspapers, chewing gum, and milk. Companies want these products to obtain the widest possible exposure in the market and so strive to make these products convenient for purchase in as many convenience stores and supermarkets as possible.

- A **selective distribution** strategy uses only a portion of the many possible retail outlets for selling products. This approach is appropriate for the sale of shopping products and durable goods, such as stereos, televisions, and furniture. Buyers spend more time comparing competitors' prices and features when buying shopping products. A sale often depends on providing buyers with information on these features to successfully differentiate one brand's product from another. Naturally, producers want to selectively determine where their products will be sold to ensure successful differentiation. Moreover, customers often want other services, such as installation, to be properly distributed. Again, producers are selective in determining outlets and may provide training to outlets to ensure the best service.

■ **FIGURE 14.8**
Distribution Strategies

Intensive Distribution
Selling convenience products

Selective Distribution
Selling shopping products

BEST BUY

Exclusive Distribution
Selling specialty products

- An **exclusive distribution** strategy uses only one outlet in a geographic area. This is most appropriate when selling specialty products, such as high-quality cars or high-end jewelry and clothing. Because these products carry a certain degree of prestige, sellers often require distributors to carry a full line of inventory, offer distinguished high-quality service, and meet other exclusive requirements. Another common form of exclusive distribution exists with franchises. Often, to avoid competition between franchises within the same company, only one outlet is allowed in a given geographic area, and the retail distributors are required to meet strict quality and service standards to protect brand-name integrity.

What are the different types of retailers? There are two main types of retailers: *in-store retailers* and *nonstore retailers*. ■ **TABLE 14.4** describes the major types of retail stores and lists some examples of each.

What kinds of in-store retail organizations are there? In-store retail organizations consist of **corporate chain stores**, individually owned retail stores, cooperatives, and franchises:

- *Corporate chain stores* are two or more retail outlets owned by a single corporation. They attempt to realize economies of scale by buying large volumes at reduced prices. Corporate chains appear in all types of retailing.

- *Individually owned retail stores,* sometimes referred to as mom-and-pop stores, are prevalent.

- *Cooperatives* are formed when independent companies voluntarily band together and buy in bulk to experience economies of scale that reduce costs. Some cooperatives agree to use common merchandising techniques, such as the Independent Grocers Alliance (IGA) and True Value (hardware stores). Some cooperatives have created jointly owned, central wholesale operations, such as Associated Grocers (groceries) and Ace (hardware stores).

- *Franchises* are a distribution system where a *franchiser* sells a proven method of doing business to a *franchisee* for a fee and a percentage of sales or profits. Subway, Jiffy Lube, and Holiday Inn are familiar franchises. Franchisees

TABLE 14.4	Types of Retail Stores	
Type of Store	**Description**	**Examples**
Specialty store	A retail store that carries a wide selection of products in one category	Gamestop, Foot Locker
Department store	A retail store that carries a wide variety of products organized by departments	Nordstrom, Saks, Neiman Marcus, JCPenney
Supermarket	Large, low-cost, high-volume grocery stores that also sell household products	Safeway, Albertson's, Kroger
Convenience store	Small stores located near residential homes that are usually open long hours seven days a week and carry the most frequently purchased convenience goods	KwikTrip, 7-Eleven
Discount store	Stores that offer lower prices by accepting lower profit margins and sell at a higher volume than department stores	Target, Walmart
Factory outlet	Stores owned and operated by a manufacturer that normally carries surplus, discontinued, or irregular goods	Nordstrom Rack, Banana Republic Factory Outlet Stores
Warehouse club	Stores that sell a limited selection of brand-name food and nonfood items at deep discounts that usually require an annual membership fee	Sam's Club, Costco, BJs

Vending machines are not just for food. Best Buy has placed vending machines in airports that are stocked with frequently forgotten electronics.
Source: Christina Kennedy/Alamy.

are typically required to purchase necessary items from the franchiser and must meet strict rules and regulations to ensure consistency and quality.

What is nonstore retailing? Little has drawn as much attention in modern retailing as the growth of nonstore retailing. **Nonstore retailing** is a form of retailing in which consumer contact occurs outside the confines of a traditional brick-and-mortar retail store. Of course, the Internet is a big component of nonstore retailing, but there are other forms of nonstore retailing that you commonly interact with. For example, vending machines, kiosks, and carts are convenient and inexpensive ways of providing products and services. Some important nonstore retailers include the following:

- **Telemarketers** sell products over the phone. Sometimes the sales pitches are recorded messages. To avoid such sales pitches, many have signed up for the National Do Not Call Registry.

- **Direct sellers** sell goods and services door-to-door at people's homes and offices or at temporary or mobile locations. Direct selling is also known as *multilevel marketing* (MLM) because of the marketing structure that defines the corporate strategy of many of these organizations. Often MLM companies are referred to as pyramid structures because of the resulting hierarchy of compensation levels. Not only is the sales force compensated by the products sold, but they are also incentivized to bring other sales members to an organization. When they bring in other sales members, they receive a percentage of the sales generated by the new associates, creating multiple levels of compensation. Avon cosmetics, Pampered Chef kitchen products, and Herbalife health products are sold through MLM.

- **Direct marketers** are those retailing a good or a service and bypassing intermediaries. Such retailers include catalog sales and direct mail and infomercials.

How has the Internet impacted retailing? **Electronic retailing**, or the selling of consumer goods and services over the Internet, is a subset of e-commerce. It is now almost mandatory that any business, especially a retail store, have an online as well as a social media presence.

In addition, the Internet has enabled consumers to access data and information about products and competitors quickly. The ability to purchase products online has changed a consumers' expectation of an in-store experience. Often, consumers come into a store to touch and interact with a product before purchasing or to seek more information. If a sales associate is not familiar with a product or cannot access information more quickly than can the customer with his or her smart phone, the store risks losing a sale.

Stores are also keenly aware of other factors that can potentially turn customers away, such as long lines or insufficient store inventory. If customers have to wait too long or if the product is not on the shelf, they may decide to leave and order the product online when they get home—or they may ultimately not purchase the product or purchase it from somewhere else. Either way, the sale is lost.

Distribution Logistics

What do we mean by distribution logistics? **Logistics** refers to managing the flow of materials, information, and processes that are involved in getting a product from its initial raw stages to the point of consumption. Different kinds of logistics are involved at various stages of the production and distribution processes, as shown in ■ **FIGURE 14.9**. Bringing raw materials, supplies, information, and any other goods and services from suppliers to the producer is *inbound logistics*. Managing the movement of resources throughout the production process is *materials handling* and *operations control*. Finally, managing the **physical distribution** of produced products to customers in the quantities needed, when and where they want them, is *outbound logistics*. It is also important to properly manage *reverse logistics*, bringing products back to the producer when they are defective, overstocked, outdated, or returned for recycling. If part of the process is outsourced, then managing that process is *third-party logistics*.

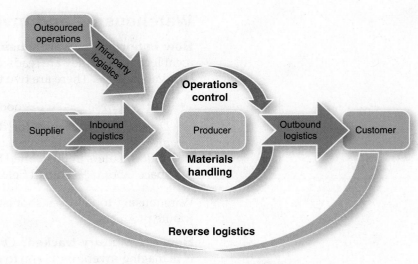

■ **FIGURE 14.9**
The Distribution Logistics Process

The Benefits and Costs of Transportation Modes

What are the benefits and costs of various transportation modes? Transportation is often the most expensive distribution cost. To keep costs as low as possible, a company looks for the most economical mode of transportation. However, companies also have to consider other factors beyond cost—such as speed, dependability, flexibility in product handling, frequency of shipments, and accessibility to markets. ■ **TABLE 14.5** outlines the benefits and costs of the five major modes of transportation according to these criteria. Businesses have to carefully weigh these benefits and costs in making a mode-of-transportation decision. They look at different transportation methods when receiving materials from suppliers as well as when delivering orders to customers. A firm might rely on one method of transportation or a combination of methods for each component.

How does a company determine the transportation method? Routing is simply the way in which goods are transported to a client, from suppliers, or anything in between. Proper routing ensures that any transportation of goods, be it with a company's own equipment or through a courier, is done at a minimum of cost, time, and distance without sacrificing quality. The best way to understand all the variables of each transportation option pertinent to a specific company is to develop a comprehensive *routing guide* that provides detailed routing solutions for a company's every possible shipping situation.

TABLE 14.5	Benefits and Costs of Various Transportation Modes					
Mode	**Cost**	**Speed**	**Dependability**	**Flexibility in Handling Products**	**Frequency of Shipments**	**Accessibility to Markets**
Railroads	Moderate	Average	Average	High	Low	High
Trucks	High	Fast	High	Average	High	Very high
Waterways	Very low	Very slow	Average	Very high	Very low	Limited
Airways	Very high	Very fast	High	Low	Average	Average
Pipelines	Low	Slow	High	Very low	Very high	Very limited

Warehousing and Inventory Control

How important is warehousing? Warehousing, or storing products at convenient locations so they are ready for customers when they are needed, is critical for customer service. There are two types of warehouses:

- *Storage warehouses* store goods from moderate to long periods of time.
- *Distribution warehouses* (or distribution centers) are designed to gather and move goods quickly to consumers. Walmart operates approximately 42 distribution centers in the United States. Each center is over 1 million square feet of space (about 29 football fields) under one roof.[10]

Warehousing today uses sophisticated technologies to effectively store and distribute products.

How is inventory tracked? One of the challenges in managing a supply chain is managing inventory levels to ensure that there is neither too much nor too little inventory on hand. Encountering either situation can be costly, as having too much inventory involves extra warehousing fees, and too little inventory means lost sales. As we mentioned earlier, companies use bar codes, or Universal Product Codes, on almost all products to help identify and track products.

RFID tags are intelligent bar codes. RFID technology, although more costly than bar codes, is more versatile and provides a richer amount of information about the movement and details of a product. Companies use bar codes and RFID tags to help reduce inventory costs by generating information on a real-time basis, thus providing accurate stocking information and reordering information.

Recall the dilemma faced by Liv Karlsen? She couldn't find the book she needed for class in her college's bookstore. Liv immediately used her smart phone to check for the book online. Fortunately, she was able to find several copies of the book, both used and new, from a variety of retailers—the large chain stores, online distributors, and a local independently owned bookstore. She also had her choice of paying to have the book delivered to her home or having the book shipped to her college bookstore store free of charge.

The bookstore is only one part of the channel of distribution for Liv's book. The channel of distribution for the book involves different marketing intermediaries, including a wholesaler and a retailer. Her online search revealed other channels through which she could obtain her book, one of which was a website with no retail stores. The distribution process is not the same for all products—some are longer and some shorter, but the process is carefully determined to be as efficient and cost effective as possible. Although it might not always work to ensure that all products are always available when needed, the distribution process ultimately adds value to the consumer.

Summary

1 What is a promotional mix, and what is its function in a promotional campaign? (pp. 397–399)

- A **promotional mix** (p. 398) is the strategic combination of promotional tools used to reach customers to achieve a product's marketing objectives. Included in the mix are advertising, public relations, personal selling, and sales promotions.

- Implementing the promotional mix is part of an effective promotional campaign. Promotional campaigns involve six steps:
  - Identify the target market.
  - Determine a product's marketing objectives.
  - Design the message.
  - Determine the budget.
  - Implement the promotional mix.
  - Evaluate and adjust the mix as needed.

2 What are the different categories of advertising, and what role do these categories play in business and society? (pp. 399–404)

- **Advertising** (p. 399) is paid, impersonal mass communication from an identified sponsor to persuade or influence a targeted audience.

- Advertising plays several important roles in business:
  - It helps businesses build brand awareness and differentiate products.
  - It has economic benefits because a great deal of money is spent on it, which creates jobs.
  - If advertising increases a product's sales volume, a firm can achieve economies of scale in terms of how the product is produced and potentially lower the price of the product.

- Advertising also plays a societal role:
  - Society benefits from advertising because it informs and educates us about new and different products.
  - Advertising can also persuade us in ways that can have positive or negative social ramifications.

- Many categories of advertising emerge from marketing: **product, corporate, comparative, retail, B2B, nonprofit, public service, advocacy, interactive, Internet,** and **mobile**. (p. 401)

3 What is public relations, and how is it used in the promotional mix? (pp. 404–406)

- **Public relations** (p. 421) is the process of establishing and maintaining mutually beneficial relationships between an organization and its stakeholders.

- Public relations tools consist of controlled, semicontrolled, and uncontrolled news messages. Information communicated about a person, organization, or a product transmitted through mass media at no charge is called **publicity** (p. 404).

- Damage control is the effort to minimize the harmful effects of a negative event.

4 What are the steps in the personal selling process? (pp. 406–409)

- **Personal selling** (p. 406) is direct communication between a firm's sales force and potential buyers to make a sale and build good customer relationships. Establishing and maintaining good customer relationships through personal selling is critical for a firm's success.

- Six steps are involved with personal selling:
  - **Prospecting** (p. 408) is identifying qualified potential customers.
  - Approaching the prospect has two parts. In the preapproach, the salesperson learns as much as possible about potential customers to determine their likely needs and think about how those needs might be satisfied. In the actual approach, the idea is to meet, greet, and put the prospect at ease.
  - Presenting involves telling a product's story, demonstrating its use, asking questions, and listening to customers' answers.
  - Overcoming objections involves countering customers' reasons for not buying with reasons to buy.
  - Closing the sale is when a salesperson asks for a purchase.
  - Following up is when a salesperson ensures that a customer is happy with a product and asks for feedback.

5 What are the two main types of sales promotions, and what types of tools are commonly used as incentives? (pp. 409–412)

- **Sales promotions** (p. 409) are short-term activities that target consumers and other businesses for the purpose of generating interest in a product, which have not already been undertaken by advertising, public relations, or personal selling.

- One type of sales promotion is a **consumer sales promotion** (p. 409). Tools used for consumer sales promotions include coupons, rebates, frequent-user incentives, point-of-purchase displays, free samples, contests, and sweepstakes.

- **Trade (B2B) sales promotions** (p. 409) include trade shows, trade allowances, cooperative advertising, free merchandise, sales contests, dealer listings, store demonstrations, quantity discounts, and training programs.

6 Why are marketing intermediaries and distribution channels important elements of marketing? (pp. 412–414)

- **Marketing intermediaries** (p. 407) are middlemen in the distribution process. Wholesalers, agents/brokers, and retailers constitute the different types of intermediaries.

- A **distribution channel** (p. 412) is a whole set of intermediaries. There are many different types of distribution channels, including consumer channels, consumer/business channels, and business channels. The type and length of the distribution channel depends on the type of product that is being brought to the consumer.

- Intermediaries are important because they reduce the costs of products to consumers by increasing the efficiency of the distribution of goods and services.

7 What types of services do wholesalers, agents, and brokers provide? (pp. 414–416)

- **Wholesalers** (p. 412) provide many services that add efficiency to the distribution of merchandise, including selling and promoting, warehousing, transporting, financing, and providing market information.

- **Agents/brokers** (p. 413) are intermediaries that facilitate negotiations between buyers and the sellers in B2B markets but never take title (ownership) of the products traded.

8 Why are retailing and physical distribution key aspects of distribution? (pp. 416–420)

- Several types of retailers exist: specialty stores, department stores, supermarkets, convenience stores, discount stores, factory outlets, and warehouse clubs.

- In **nonstore retailing** (p. 418) consumer contact occurs outside a traditional retail store. Examples include electronic retailing, vending machines, kiosks, carts, telemarketing, direct selling, and direct marketing.

- Retailers can cover their markets using an **intensive** (p. 416), a **selective** (p. 416), or an **exclusive distribution strategy** (p. 417).

- Physical distribution is one of the most expensive parts of marketing a product. In the broadest sense, it entails the management of the entire supply chain.

- Transportation options include railroads, trucks, waterways, airways, and pipelines. Careful measurement of the advantages and disadvantages of these options is important before selecting a mode of transportation.

Key Terms

advertising (p. 399)

advocacy advertising (p. 401)

agents/brokers (p. 413)

B2B advertising (p. 401)

comparative advertising (p. 401)

consumer sales promotion (p. 409)

corporate (or institutional) advertising (p. 401)

corporate chain stores (p. 417)

direct marketers (p. 418)

direct sellers (p. 418)

distribution (p. 412)

distribution channel (p. 412)

electronic retailing (p. 418)

exclusive distribution (p. 417)

full-service wholesaler (p. 414)

infomercials (paid programming) (p. 403)

integrated marketing communications (p. 398)

intensive distribution (p. 416)

interactive advertising (p. 401)

Internet advertising (p. 401)

limited-service wholesaler (p. 418)

logistics (p. 418)

marketing intermediary (p. 407)

mobile advertising (p. 401)

nonprofit advertising (p. 401)

nonstore retailing (p. 418)

order getter (p. 407)

order influencers (p. 407)

order taker (p. 407)

personal selling (p. 406)

physical distribution (p. 419)

product advertising (p. 401)

product placement (p. 403)

promotion (p. 397)

promotional mix (p. 398)

prospecting (p. 408)

publicity (p. 405)

public relations (p. 404)

public service advertising (p. 401)

retail (or local) advertising (p. 401)

retailers (p. 413)

routing (p. 419)

sales promotion (p. 409)

selective distribution (p. 416)

support personnel (p. 407)

telemarketers (p. 418)

trade (B2B) sales promotions (p. 409)

viral marketing (p. 410)

warehousing (p. 420)

wholesaler (p. 412)

MyBizLab

Go to **mybizlab.com** to complete the problems marked with this icon

Self Test

Multiple Choice *You can find the answers on the last page of this book.*

14-1 Which of the following is a step involved in a promotional campaign?
a. Identify the target market
b. Determine the budget
c. Implement an IMC
d. All of the above

14-2 Advertising that promotes a specific product's uses, features, and benefits is _____ advertising.
a. product
b. retail
c. comparative
d. corporate

14-3 Your college professors take on what kind of sales role when they select books for you to read for their class?
a. Order taker
b. Order influencer
c. Support personnel
d. None of the above

14-4 Bosch tools are sold in stores such as Home Depot and Lowe's. What kind of retail distribution strategy is being used?
a. Exclusive
b. Intensive
c. Selective
d. Franchise

14-5 Intermediaries that facilitate negotiations between buyers and sellers but never take ownership of the product are
a. wholesalers.
b. retailers.
c. agents/brokers.
d. distributors.

14-6 Which type of logistics is involved in bringing raw materials, supplies, and information from suppliers to the producer?
a. Inbound
b. Outbound
c. Reverse
d. Third-party

14-7 Which is *not* an example of a nonstore retail outlet?
a. A kiosk
b. A vending machine
c. A convenience store
d. A telemarketer

14-8 *American Idol* judges often have on their desks tall glasses embossed with Coca-Cola's logo. This advertising strategy is known as
a. product placement.
b. viral marketing.
c. an infomercial.
d. a direct pitch.

14-9 Which of the following is a consumer sales promotion tool?
a. A 10-percent-off coupon from the newspaper
b. A $10.00 mail-in rebate
c. A frequent buyer card
d. All of the above

14-10 QR codes, text messages, and apps are part of what kind of promotional strategy?
a. Viral promotions
b. E-commerce
c. Mobile marketing
d. Social promoting

True/False *You can find the answers on the last page of this book.*

14-11 The product itself can be considered part of the promotional mix because samples of it can be given away to demonstrate its features.
☐ True or ☐ False

14-12 Finding the best way to communicate the benefits of a product and persuade customers to buy it is a critical job of marketers.
☐ True or ☐ False

14-13 QR codes are similar to bar codes except that they do not need a physical scanner to process the information.
☐ True or ☐ False

14-14 Brokers work with buyers and sellers on a permanent basis, whereas agents are more temporary.
☐ True or ☐ False

14-15 The last step in the selling process is closing the sale.
☐ True or ☐ False

Critical Thinking Questions

⊘ **14-16** Describe *mobile marketing*. Why is it such a growing promotional trend? Describe a mobile marketing technique that has made you notice a product. Why did it work (or not work)?

⊘ **14-17** Discuss when it would be appropriate to use the following sales promotional techniques:

coupons, rebates, frequent-user incentives, free samples, and cents-off deals.

⊘ **14-18** Describe which distribution strategy—intensive, selective, or exclusive—would be most appropriate for each of the following products and explain why: laundry detergent, cigarettes, Mercedes sports cars, and Snickers candy bars.

Team Time

DEVELOPING A PROMOTIONAL MIX

The company you work for, Fit Foods, is launching a new product, Shine Breakfast Bars, which are all-natural, vitamin-fortified granola bars. The company has enlisted you and your teammates to design an optimal promotional mix for this product.

Process

Step 1. Assemble into teams of four. Each team member should be assigned as the "lead" for one of the four components of the promotional mix—advertising, public relations, personal selling, or sales promotions.

Step 2. Develop a promotional mix for Shine Breakfast Bars that integrates each promotional component. What will be the key aspects of the advertising campaign? What media will be used? What public relations tools will be used? What will a sales pitch for this product consist of? How will sales promotions be implemented?

Step 3. Summarize the key points of the promotional mix plan in a poster or PowerPoint presentation.

Step 4. Present your findings to the class for discussion.

Ethics and Corporate Social Responsibility

JUST WHAT THE DOCTOR ORDERED?

In Chapter 13, you considered the ethics involved with the pricing of prescription drugs. Now turn your attention to the promotion of these products and the ethical issues raised by their advertising.

Scenario

Currently, the United States and New Zealand are the only two countries in the world that permit the widespread use of direct-to-consumer (DTC) advertising for prescription drugs. Such advertising has become big business in the United States: Billions of dollars are spent on it each year. Some people argue that DTC advertising is unethical because it encourages the overuse of medications, preys on the elderly and/or the chronically ill, and does not fully inform consumers of the risks and side effects of drugs. Others say that DTC advertising puts the power where it belongs—in the hands of consumers—and allows people to be advocates for their own health.

Questions for Discussion

14-19 If you were a legislator voting on a bill that proposed a ban on DTC advertising of pharmaceuticals in the United States, would you vote for it or against it? Why?

14-20 Is DTC advertising more appropriate for certain drugs? For example, do the ethics of advertising cholesterol-lowering drugs differ from the ethics of advertising antidepressants? Why?

14-21 Consider the tactics pharmaceutical companies use in print and television ads. When and/or where are the side effects mentioned? Do the ads help raise the awareness of certain illnesses and treatments, or do they give false hope and/or incomplete information to people about powerful medications?

Web Exercises

⊙ 14-22 Getting to the Top of the List

Many companies spend a significant part of their marketing budget on search engine optimization (SEO). Research what SEO is. Why is it so important for companies to do? Discuss why you think companies feel it's worth spending millions of dollars to do.

⊙ 14-23 Viral Marketing

Find an example of a viral marketing campaign on YouTube. Discuss the features of this campaign that made it go viral. Research to see if the company reported any benefit from this campaign. Discuss whether you think viral marketing is an effective type of marketing.

14-24 Personal Selling

There are many different careers in sales. To determine whether sales is a good career path for you, use the Internet to research careers in sales. You might want to start by looking at the *Occupational Outlook Handbook* on the Bureau of Labor and Statistics

website. What are the pros and cons of a career in sales? Describe several of the sales careers. Is this a field you are interested in entering? Why or why not?

14-25 Multilevel Marketing

Suppose you want to earn a few dollars but don't want a full-time job. Research the benefits and requirements of working for a multilevel marketing company doing in-home product demonstrations. Some companies to consider are the Pampered Chef, Amway, Discovery Toys, Herbalife, or MonaVie. How does the compensation structure work for these companies? Is this something you can make a career out of?

14-26 Distribution Logistics

The text discussed the distribution channels for several products. Complete a similar diagram to Figure 14.7 using examples of other products with a one-step distribution channel (producer to consumer), a two-step distribution channel (producer to retailer to consumer), and so on.

MyBizLab

Go to **mybizlab.com** for Auto-graded writing questions as well as the following Assisted-graded writing questions:

⊙ 14-27 How has social media impacted the promotion and advertising processes?

⊙ 14-28 Discuss the value created by marketing intermediaries. Is their service worth the extra costs? Why or why not?

References

1. Natalie Zmuda, "Under Armour Adds Millions to Marketing Budget," *AdvertisingAge*, April 14, 2014, http://adage.com/article/cmo-strategy/armour-adds-millions-marketing-budget/292854.
2. www.forbes.com/sites/cherylsnappconner/2013/11/12/fifty-essential-mobile-marketing-facts.
3. Dove, "The Dove Campaign for Real Beauty," www.dove.us/Social-Mission/campaign-for-real-beauty.aspx.
4. Laura Stampler, "How Dove's 'Real Beauty Sketches' Became the Most Viral Video of All Time," *Business Insider*, May 22, 2013, www.businessinsider.com/how-doves-real-beauty-sketches-became-the-most-viral-ad-video-of-all-time-2013-5.
5. Nancy Dediemar, "Direct Mail Marketing Is Still the Most Effective Medium," October 1, 2013, www.myprintresource.com/article/11130249/direct-mail-marketing-is-still-the-most-effective-medium.
6. Cheryl Conner, "Fifty Essential Mobile Marketing Facts," *Forbes*, November 12, 2013, www.forbes.com/sites/cherylsnappconner/2013/11/12/fifty-essential-mobile-marketing-facts.
7. Scott M. Cutlip, Allen H. Center, and Glen M. Broom, *Effective Public Relations*, 9th ed. (Upper Saddle River, NJ: Pearson Prentice Hall, 2009), 1, 321.
8. Sandra Moriarty, Nancy Mitchell, and William Wells, *Advertising, Principles and Practices*, 8th ed. (Upper Saddle River, NJ: Pearson Prentice Hall, 2009), 517–26.
9. Philip Kotler and Gary Armstrong. *Principles of Marketing*, 12th ed. (Upper Saddle River, NJ: Pearson Prentice Hall, 2008), 386.
10. Walmart, "Distribution Center," http://careers.walmart.com/career-areas/transportation-logistics-group/distribution-center.

Chapter 4

Finding a Job

Clearly, the job search landscape is a challenging one. As a job seeker, it is essential that you stand out in a crowd. In this mini chapter, you'll learn how to effectively market yourself, search for jobs, and interview and negotiate with a company so that your job searches will be successful.

Source: Alamy.

Marketing Yourself

Standing out in a crowd requires that you sell yourself. This starts with developing a powerful résumé and cover letter.

Developing a Résumé

A **résumé** is a fact sheet that outlines your work history, experience, and accomplishments. It lets an employer know what you've done and what you want to do. There are two main types of résumés: chronological and functional. A *chronological résumé* lists your jobs in the order in which you held them, beginning with the present. Use this type of résumé if you're staying in the same field or just getting started in the job market. *Functional résumés* detail your work history by pointing out your skills and achievements, not your titles and the companies you've worked for. This is a good type of résumé to use when you're switching fields. Your skills show employers what you can do for them because your previous job experience may not be related.

Getting Started

Before you start typing, take some time to evaluate yourself. Consider the following:

- What are your strengths and weaknesses?
- What type of skills do you possess?
- What do you want from an employer?

Aside from technical skills, think about your soft skills. Soft skills include your personality traits and interpersonal skills, such as honesty, responsibility, leadership, and teamwork. Some employers find these traits more desirable than technical skills because technical skills can be taught, whereas soft skills are innate.

When you begin your résumé, remember that organization is key. Employers generally spend about 15 seconds reviewing a résumé,[1] so you need to quickly capture the attention of the reviewer. Organize your résumé clearly, with bold headings and bulleted information. No one will take the time to read a lengthy paragraph about your achievements. The following headings can help you organize a basic chronological résumé: Contact Information, Objective, Education, Experience or Work History, Skills/Interests, and References. Depending on how you format your résumé, you may or may not use all of these headings.

Contact Information

Your **contact information** is typically centered at the top of the page, with your name in the largest font. Include your mailing address, phone number, and e-mail address. Remember that prospective employers may hear your outgoing phone message, so be sure it's appropriate.

Objective

An **objective** is a short summary of the job you're seeking and how your skills will apply to that job. Objectives should be specific to the job for which you're applying. Generalized objectives don't tell a prospective employer anything about you and don't get anyone's attention.

Read the following objective and analyze it from an employer's perspective.

OBJECTIVE: To employ my advertising knowledge by working for a successful company that will help me get experience to kick-start my career.

What position is the applicant applying for? This objective doesn't specify the position. It also describes what the applicant wants the job to do for him or her, not what he or she can contribute to the company. Employers already know that you want to learn and gain experience. Reiterating it makes you look selfish.

A good objective is specific and short. Here's an example.

OBJECTIVE: To obtain a position at Doyle and Associates as an entry-level graphic designer where my creativity and technical ability will add value to the operations.

With this objective, an employer knows what position you want and why you think you're the right person to fill the opening. It also shows you're serious about the position because you took the time to tailor your résumé to this specific position and company.

Education

Begin your education list with your most recent educational experience. Be sure to detail your degree, major, minor, dates of attendance, and the name and location of the school. If you haven't graduated yet, list your expected degree and graduation date. Include your grade-point average (GPA) if it is 3.0 or higher. Including a GPA that is lower may inadvertently invite questions about your studying skills that you may not be comfortable answering. Or, you may get passed over altogether for the job.

If you don't have relevant work experience, list your educational background first. If you have pertinent work experience, reverse the sections so your work history comes before your education.

Experience or Work History

List your previous work experiences chronologically, starting with the most recent job, and include each company's name, its location, your dates of employment, and your title or position. For each experience listed, include at least three bullet points that highlight your achievements or undertakings. You don't have to put specific dates of employment but do list the month and year. If you include the years only, you may give the impression that you have gaps in your employment history. If possible, include specific, quantifiable data about your accomplishments and how you benefited your employer.

Skills/Interests

This section should include your hidden talents or skills, such as whether you speak a foreign language or are knowledgeable about a certain software package. Also include the extracurricular activities and professional organizations you belong to that relate to your career field. You don't want to restate anything you've said in your education and experience sections, so if you don't have anything to add, omit this section.

References

References can attest to your work ethic and skills and are important to have ready to go. You should have three professional references expecting to be called on to help you. If you have no professional references, obtain references from teachers, instructors, professors, clergy, and other people who know about your character. Avoid using family members and friends. Always ask permission to use someone as a reference before listing him or her. Be sure your references know you're engaging in an active job search in case a potential employer calls them so they can be prepared to answer questions accurately.

Employers generally won't need references until they interview you, so it's customary to include at the bottom of your résumé the line "References are available upon request." However, if you choose to provide information for each reference on your résumé, you should include for each reference the person's name, title, employer, contact information, the nature of your relationship, and the length of time he or she has known you. Including references shows that you have professional contacts with people willing to recommend you. When you are invited to an interview, bring additional copies of your references with you.

Résumé Showdown!

To get yourself noticed, you need to make your résumé pop. Look at the two examples (on the following pages) from the perspective of an employer who has a pile of résumés to look through. Both résumés are for the same person. Consider the strengths and weaknesses of each and which one you feel makes the best impression.

Which résumé do you think an employer would be more impressed with? Most likely the second one—right? It has a better organizational structure and a cleaner appearance. The résumé also focuses more on the candidate's achievements than on her responsibilities, with specific and detailed actions and outcomes. Overall, the second résumé gives a prospective employer a stronger idea of what the candidate can offer the company.

Writing a Cover Letter

Along with your résumé, you need to include a cover letter. A **cover letter** introduces you to a prospective employer. This is an opportunity for you to market yourself by demonstrating sound communication skills. A cover letter may be more important than a résumé in the eyes of a prospective employer because it gives you a voice. Even if you're the most qualified person for a job, a poorly written cover letter may end your chances before anyone ever looks at your résumé. If you follow these basic tips, your cover letter may get you an interview all on its own.

Tip #1: Tailor Your Cover Letter to Fit the Job You're Applying for.

There are three main types of cover letters: an application letter, a prospecting letter, and a networking letter. An *application letter* is sent as a response to a job opening. A *prospecting letter* is a letter asking about potential positions at a company where you want to work. A *networking letter* is sent to further a relationship with someone you think could help you in your job search.[2] Each cover letter you send out needs to be tailored to fit the job opening you're applying for or inquiring about. Look at the requirements in the ad. Find the key words and phrases used to describe the position and then describe your skills and experience using the same terms. Highlight your major relevant accomplishment in the terms used by the employer. Include how you have or will address the needs of the employer. Overall, demonstrate in your cover letter that you fulfill the specific requirements the company is looking for.

Tip #2: Indicate What You Can Do for the Employer.

All cover letters should explain to potential employers what you can do for them, not what they can do for you.[3] Don't tell them how the job will give you experience in a particular field. Instead, tell them how you have what it takes to perform the required tasks.

Jane Doefield
4117 Blank Street
Cincinnati, OH 45202
(513) 555-4529
Janedoefield@email.com

Education
Ohio State University, Columbus, OH, 2008–2013
BS, Biology with a concentration in Medical Technology
GPA: 2.57

Work History
Johnson and Webb, Columbus, OH, January 2013–May 2013
Intern
My main responsibilities were to organize a computerized file-retrieval system for research and create a tracking spreadsheet to keep track of tested drugs. I also worked hands-on in the lab testing cells for sensitivity to different drug treatments.

BookZilla, Columbus, OH, 2009–2012
Sales Associate
While working at BookZilla, I was responsible for stocking and straightening the magazine and stationery sections. When needed, I also worked on the cash register and sold BookZilla discount cards.

Pepe's Garments, Cincinnati, OH, 2007–2009
Sales Associate
I provided customer service by helping customers pick out garments and ringing up there purchases. I maximized sales by signing people up for Pepe's credit cards. I was also responsible for keeping an accurate sales drawer.

Skills/Interests
I am proficient in Microsoft Office and fluent in French. I enjoy playing the piano, painting, and swimming. While in college, I played on an intramural softball team.

References
Mario Rodríguez
Supervisor, BookZilla
(614) 555-7619

Andrea Zimmerman
Owner, Pepe's Garments
(513) 555-9723

Résumé #1.

Jane Doefield
4117 Blank Street
Cincinnati, OH 45202
(513) 555-4529
Janedoefield@email.com

Objective: To obtain a position as a quality-assurance technician in AIF's lab.

Education
Ohio State University, Columbus, OH, 2008–2013
BS, Biology with a concentration in Medical Technology

Work History
Johnson and Webb, Columbus, OH, January 2013–May 2013
Intern
· Tested cells for sensitivity to a variety of drug treatments at a rate of 4 assays per day, enabling our department to exceed company testing expectations
· Developed a tracking mechanism to organize drugs tested, preventing the inadvertent retesting of drugs, which saved our department over 10 hours of lost time per month
· Streamlined retrieval process for locating researched materials, adding 5 hours of additional analysis time per month

BookZilla, Columbus, OH, October 2009–December 2012
Sales Associate
· Organized and maintained periodical and stationery sections containing more than 200 items
· Marketed and sold five BookZilla discount cards a week to boost sales
· Provided excellent customer service while processing purchases

Pepe's Garments, Cincinnati, OH, June 2008–August 2009
Sales Associate
· Assisted customers with making purchasing decisions
· Used sales strategies to register customers for Pepe's credit cards
· Provided customer service to achieve sales goals

Skills
· Proficient in Microsoft Office
· Fluent in French

References
· Available upon request.

Résumé #2.

Tip #3: Clearly Explain Why the Company Should Hire You.

After you've explained that you can do the job, discuss why the company should hire you.[4] Think about what sets you apart from the competition. Be both assertive and descriptive. Instead of saying, "I'm flexible," say, "My years in customer service have taught me how to effectively interact with people of different ages and backgrounds. As a result, I have learned to be flexible, persuasive, and tactful.

These abilities have allowed me to maintain long-term customer relationships that have boosted sales for my previous employers." Use concrete examples to show how you can be an asset to the company.

Tip #4: Keep It Short.

Each cover letter you send out should be limited to one page with at least three paragraphs. The first paragraph explains why you are writing, whether it is to respond to a job opening or to ask about available positions. The goal of the first paragraph is to start strong and get the reader's attention. Here is an example:

> I am responding to your advertisement on Monster.com regarding an entry-level sales position. My background in customer service and advertising is a perfect fit for your company. I am interested in being part of a company that has a fast-paced environment, like ATI Corp. does, and feel I can be an asset to your expanding team.

The body of the letter lets the employer know your experience as it relates to the desired position. For example,

> My background includes three years of experience in sales. I have extensive experience working with customers and implementing sales strategies. I coordinated and advertised events, including fashion shows and cooking demonstrations that boosted my firm's sales over 20 percent and led to successful product launches. I am skilled at motivating teams and have consistently met or exceeded my sales goals.

The final paragraph thanks the reader and leaves contact information:

> I would appreciate an opportunity to sit down with you and discuss how I can become a valuable member of the ATI Corp. team. Feel free to call me at 443-555-2728. I look forward to hearing from you. Thank you for your time and consideration.

Because your résumé states only facts, your cover letter is a valuable opportunity to highlight your skills, show a bit of your personality, and sell yourself. Consider time invested in writing your cover letter as time invested in your future.

Multimedia Portfolios and Personal Websites

Because résumés and cover letters only *say* what you can do, creating a portfolio to *show* what you've already done may be beneficial. Don't worry if you're not an artist or a writer; anyone can have a multimedia portfolio. A **multimedia portfolio** is a collection of work displayed in the form of photographs, pictures, audio clips, and video clips. Choose your best work to include in your portfolio—papers, projects, posters, videos of presentations, or photos of you volunteering for a charitable organization. You can compile your work in a binder or save it on a portable storage device and bring it with you to interviews. You can also create your own website that has a list of all your accomplishments and give your interviewer the Web address to check out your work during or after the interview.

All these things show who you are and will help leave a mark in the mind of the interviewer. However, it takes time to create a good portfolio or an impressive website, so don't throw something together just to have it for an interview. The portfolio is meant to help you stand out and put you in a positive light, not hinder you by exemplifying rushed or shoddy work.

Search Strategies

When searching for a job, you need to use a variety of strategies and methods to be successful. Don't expect to e-mail a few résumés on Monday and be invited to an interview on Tuesday. In this section, you'll learn about how tools such as networking, online and newspaper job postings, recruiting companies, cold calling, college-campus career resources, and informational interviews that can help you get a job.

Networking is best done face-to-face but can take place online as well.
Source: Eric Audras/Alamy.

Networking

Networking is the process of building relationships that can potentially create business opportunities. Networking is best done face-to-face, but it can take place online as well. There are numerous social networking sites, such as LinkedIn, where you can connect with colleagues and professional acquaintances. Professional organizations also offer opportunities to connect through social networks. Other organizations hold regularly scheduled face-to-face social networking opportunities to generate job leads.

The benefit of networking in person is that it can happen anywhere. You can meet someone while you're grabbing a cup of coffee, or you can attend a formal networking event, a conference, or a job fair. No matter where it happens, you need to know what to say and how to say it to make a good first impression. The first thing you need to do is create an elevator pitch. An **elevator pitch** is a brief statement that clearly summarizes your skills and what you can offer. It's called an elevator pitch because it should be a crisp, concise statement you could make on a short elevator ride. You should focus on three or four key points and sound informal. Try practicing your pitch in front of a mirror or on your voicemail. Don't mistake a networking event for a party. Remember, networking is about making business contacts, not a new best friend.

When you attend networking events, be prepared. First of all, dress to impress. If you're going to a job fair, you may encounter people who may want to hire you, so dress the part. If others are dressed casually, you'll stand out as someone serious about your future. Don't forget to take along your business cards and copies of your résumé. Before attending an event, try to find out what companies or types of companies will be there. Research the companies that interest you so you'll have more to say than "What does your company do?" Representatives will likely be impressed by your initiative and enthusiasm for a particular job. Once you meet someone, don't ask for a job right away. Instead, if it seems appropriate, ask to meet him or her again to discuss possible opportunities.

Building a network takes commitment. You can't meet new contacts sitting around waiting for someone to call you. Get connected on some of the reputable online social networking sites. Attend a free social networking seminar. Check your local newspaper for conferences or jobs fairs. Enroll in classes to further your skills or meet other people with the same interests. Look for professional networking groups for people with your area of expertise. Be open to networking opportunities outside professional settings. You could meet a person who works in your desired field at the gym, at the grocery store, or in line at Starbucks. This is why it is important to always be prepared to present your pitch at a moment's notice. Finally, be patient. You can't expect to create a network overnight. It takes time, but know that after all your work, you'll have a solid group of people who can give you valuable support, advice, and perhaps the opportunity to get ahead.

SPOT THE TRUTH

Which of the following is *not* a myth related to job hunting?

a. Posting your résumé on websites will have employers lining up to hire you.

b. If you are in need of a job, take the first offer you get.

c. Most job openings are never publicized.

    Answer: c. Most jobs, especially higher positions, are never advertised. The key to finding out about these openings is through networking and, to a lesser extent, cold calling, which you'll learn about later in this mini chapter.

Internet Research

If you're sure of the field you want to work in, create a list of potential employers. Find each company's website and read about each company's history and its mission and vision statements. Consider setting up a RSS (real simple syndication) feed following those firms. This can keep you on top of new events and opportunities, making it easier to tailor a cover letter, for example.

    You want to know as much as you can about a company and the industry so that you can make an informed decision about where you want to work. Sites like Glassdoor allow you to prepare for an interview or evaluation of a company with information on salaries, other employees' experiences and lists of job openings.

    You can also look online for job openings and contact information. Looking at online job postings, such as those on Monster.com, is also a popular way to look for a job. You can search these sites and then e-mail your cover letter and résumé at any time—day or night. You can also post your résumé on sites such as Monster.com so companies can contact you if they think you're the right fit for a job. Many people view online job sites, so openings fill fast. Check the sites often for new postings and make sure your résumé really stands out.

Although you don't literally need to deliver your "elevator pitch" during an elevator ride, the pitch should be concise enough that you theoretically could.
Source: Denkou Business 2/Alamy.

Newspapers

As with online postings, classified ads can be a starting point for your job search. Generally, the Sunday paper has the most classified job ads, but that shouldn't stop you from looking in the paper every day. Once you find a position that sounds good, research the company. Check to see whether the position is still open and send your cover letter and résumé. Newspapers don't have the same number of postings as does the Internet, but you can look at a newspaper anywhere.

Recruiters

The job of a **recruiter** is to find qualified employees to work for a company. They can work full-time for a large corporation, or they can be contracted for part-time help at multiple companies. Recruiters may get in touch with you to learn more about your capabilities or determine whether you're a good fit for a particular company. If a recruiter contacts you, be sure to ask why he or she is interested and to which companies your résumé is being sent. If the recruiter has multiple positions to fill, be clear about the types of companies and jobs that work best for you. If you don't like a strict nine-to-five schedule or a corporate atmosphere, let the recruiter know. Once you're both on the same page, you can figure out whether the job available is right for you.

    You can contact a recruiter yourself if you're seeking help with your job search. His or her large pool of contacts can be useful; however, be aware that you may be one of many job seekers the recruiter is assisting. It is best to continue your job search on your own as well as with the help of a recruiter.

Cold Calling Pros and Cons

Cold calling is a method of job hunting in which you make unexpected and uninvited phone calls to potential employers to express your interest, inquire about

Cold calling is controversial as to its effectiveness and can end up producing mixed results.
Source: Lev Dolgachov/Alamy.

openings, and request interviews. It's a practice that is somewhat controversial because an uninvited contact may seem off-putting to some employers but resourceful to others. If you decide to make cold calls, there are some things you should do before you start dialing. First, make a list of companies that interest you. Then make preliminary calls to obtain the name, title, and phone number of the person in charge of the department you're interested in working for. You may also be able to find this information on a company website. Send your cover letter and résumé directly to the person you want to impress before you make a call. Don't forget to tailor your cover letter to the specific company and position. Finally, call the people you sent your résumé to and request an interview.

Cold calling is hard and can end up producing mixed results. An employer may view your call as bothersome or pushy, and an opportunity that could have been an option if you would have waited for the employer to contact you could then be lost. On the other hand, an employer may see your phone call as ambitious. He or she may view you as a self-starter who is motivated to reach your goals. Unfortunately, there's no easy way to tell which way the process will go. It is up to you decide whether cold calling is right for you and the situation.

College Campus Career Resources

Your college's career center can help you determine your skills and strengths, focus on your goals, explore potential career paths, and find current job openings. Most centers have manuals, informational books, and career-planning guides available. In addition, you can meet with a counselor to talk about your career goals and interests. Your counselor may administer an assessment test that can help you gain a deeper understanding about the kinds of jobs that would be a good fit for you. These tests don't tell you what you should do, but they can give you an idea about what kinds of preferences you have and provide career suggestions based on those preferences.

Also, check your career center's website for links to other informational sites that can help you. For example, the Bureau of Labor Statistics publishes the *Occupational Outlook Handbook* on its website, a publication that holds a wealth of information about various career fields. This is a great place to start researching a career field. There should also be listings for local job fairs and other career-related events on your college's career center's website. Career centers can also help you find internships that allow you to explore a career field and begin to build networking contacts. Many career centers can provide you with help writing résumés and cover letters and offer seminars on proper etiquette and how to dress for success.

Informational Interviews

The goal of an **informational interview** is to gain firsthand knowledge about a company or job from someone who currently works in the field. This gives you a chance to hear about the reality of what you think is your dream job. If you don't know anyone personally to interview, you can check your local career center or your school's alumni office for contacts. You can also contact a business directly and ask the human resources office to direct you to the best person to interview. Be sure that you're interviewing the right person, though. If you're just getting started, you shouldn't be interviewing the president; you should be speaking with a junior-level employee. The idea is to gain insight into what your job, not the boss's job, would be like in that field.

When you meet for the informational interview, you should have a list of questions to ask. The following examples are general questions you would have about any job. You may want to include one or two in your interview but try to formulate questions directly related to a specific field.

- What duties do you perform daily?
- What type of degree do you need to be considered for this job?

- What types of skills are employers looking for when filling positions? Technical? Soft?
- What do you enjoy most about your job? Least?
- Do you have any advice for me if I decide to pursue a job in this field?

If your interviewee is not forthcoming and gives vague or off-putting answers, don't jump to conclusions. Set up another interview with someone else in the same field. Also, although this isn't a formal job interview, you should dress professionally. An informational interview is another opportunity to network. Your interviewee may be impressed with you and give your name to someone higher up or know about an opening elsewhere. Try to make the best impression possible. One meeting could result in your landing your dream job.

Interviewing and Negotiating

Congratulations, you've landed an interview! Interviews can be a breeze if you're properly prepared or a nightmare if you're not. The goal of the interview is to convey that you're the best person for the position, so confidence is key.

Interview Red Flags

Not all interview questions are created equal. Some are even illegal. Interviewers cannot ask questions about your race, gender, sexual orientation, religion, age, national origin, marital status, or family matters.[5] If your interviewer asks you any of the following questions or makes any inappropriate comments, it may be a red flag, a warning signal that you should look elsewhere for employment:

- Where were you born?
- How old are you?
- Are you married?
- Do you attend church?
- Do you plan on having children soon?

Informational interviews enable you to gain firsthand knowledge from someone who currently works in the field.
Source: Monashee Frantz/OJO Images Ltd/Alamy.

Preparing for the Interview

There is so much to do before the big day, so if you have the option, give yourself a few days to prepare. Go over everything on your résumé. Be prepared to talk about anything listed, from previous jobs to your educational background. Research the company as much as you can. Look at its history, mission and vision statements, and current projects. Try to relate previous experiences to the position you're applying for, such as "While I served as vice president of the student body, I learned a lot about persuasion and compromise, which I know are two skills a marketing representative must have."

Next, practice your answers to standard interview questions, such as "What's your biggest weakness?" Think about the questions and jot down your answers. Stage a mock interview with a friend. You might feel silly, but practicing your responses will make you feel more confident.

Interview Questions

No matter which field you're in, certain interview questions show up everywhere:

- What can you tell me about yourself?
- Why do you want to work here?
- What kind of position are you looking for?
- Why did you leave your last job?

Preparation is key when it comes to interviews.
Source: A. Chederros/ONOKY - Photononstop/Alamy.

- What is your greatest strength? Weakness?
- Describe a problem you faced at your previous job and explain how you handled it.
- How do you handle stress?
- How do deal with interpersonal conflicts?
- What is your proudest accomplishment?
- Where do you see yourself in five years?
- How would you describe your work style?
- What motivates you?
- How do you evaluate success?

By preparing your responses ahead of time, you'll boost your confidence and give yourself a little room to relax.

Once you know what you want to say, work on looking the part. You want to make a good impression, so be careful what you choose. Because you don't know the person interviewing you, stick with a conservative look. Don't wear baggy clothes, tennis shoes, short skirts, funky jewelry, or other inappropriate attire and don't overload yourself with cologne or perfume. Also, be sure to consider the job and whether tattoos, body piercings, or extreme makeup will present a negative impression.

Make sure you know how to get to the place where you will be interviewing and how long it will take to you to get there, especially if the traffic can be heavy. Try to arrive about 30 minutes early, as you may have to fill out some paperwork before the interview. Being late is a signal to the person interviewing you that you're not serious about the job. If you know you're going to be late, call and apologize as soon as you realize it. Once you arrive, give another quick apology and sit down for the interview.

During the Interview

When you meet your interviewer, give a firm handshake, smile, and make eye contact. Have questions prepared to ask at the end of the interview. If you need to, write them down ahead of time and take them to the interview with you. Some examples of interview questions are as follows:

- Can you describe an ideal employee?
- What kinds of growth opportunities are available in the organization?
- Can you describe the company's management style and the type of employee that fits well with it?
- What do you consider to be the most important aspects of this job?

Also, ask about the overall responsibilities of the position, the day-to-day tasks associated with it, travel requirements, and any other questions you might have. Keep in mind that you are interviewing the company just as they are interviewing you. You need to determine if this is an employer you want to spend hours, days, weeks, and maybe years of your life working for. However, avoid asking directly about the salary in your initial interview. If you feel it is important and appropriate, though, ask about salary at the very end of the interview.

Interview Take-Alongs

There are some things you need to take to your interview besides your winning personality. Grab a briefcase or folder and include the following items:

- Copies of your résumé
- A list of your references
- A portfolio if you have made one

▶ THE LIST

Interview Tips

1. Be confident.
2. Listen carefully to the interviewer's comments and questions.
3. Think before responding to questions.
4. Don't feel rushed. If you are uncertain about what a question is asking and want clarification, ask for it.
5. Never interrupt anyone.
6. Answer questions succinctly yet thoroughly.
7. Avoid nervous habits, such as bouncing your leg, rolling your pen, or biting your nails; these things can be distracting and undesirable.
8. Keep a continuous yet natural level of eye contact.
9. Do not ask any questions that are clearly answered on the company website or in any literature provided to you.
10. Be sincere and genuine.

- Paper and a pen
- Directions
- A cell phone in case something happens, but leave it in the car or turn it off during your interview

At the end of the interview, if you still want the job and feel you're a good fit, say so directly. Ask the interviewer what the next step entails—a second interview, a background/reference check, and so forth—and when you can expect to hear from him or her again. Before leaving, remember to thank the interviewer for the opportunity. Following up with a personal thank-you note or e-mail is also highly recommended.

Negotiating Strategies

You aced the interview, and the company has offered you a job. Now you have to think about negotiating a salary. Negotiating may be uncomfortable, but it helps set the tone for your career. The following steps can help guide you through the negotiation process:

1. Before you negotiate, figure out a reasonable salary for the position you're interested in.
2. Using websites such as Salary.com, research the median salary for your profession based on your ZIP code, educational background, and experience.
3. Ask for a day to consider the salary offer. This will give you time to do further research and come up with a negotiating plan.
4. Don't forget that you can negotiate factors aside from salary, such as benefits, vacation time, or a more flexible schedule.
5. When you sit down to negotiate, make it clear you want the job, make reasonable requests, and have a positive attitude.
6. Sell yourself and defend your goal if there is a specific salary or benefits that you want and that are in line with the job.
7. If you succeed in getting what you want, be sure to obtain the agreement in writing. If you don't get what you want, consider how much you want the job. It may be beneficial to gain valuable experience even though you aren't getting paid what you want.
8. If you decide to turn down the offer, let the company know you are still interested in a position if something else opens up.

Marketing yourself, searching for employment, interviewing, and negotiating all present their share of challenges. Now you have the knowledge to successfully land a job that fits your skills, talents, and goals. Go for it!

Negotiating a salary may be uncomfortable, but it sets the tone for your career.
Source: Wavebreakmedia Ltd PH09/Alamy.

References

1. Ball State University Career Center, "Résumé Development," http://cms.bsu.edu/About/AdministrativeOffices/CareerCenter/MyCareerPlan/JobSearchDocs/Resumes.aspx.
2. Alison Doyle, "Cover Letters," http://jobsearch.about.com/od/coverletters/a/aa030401a.htm.
3. Pat Kendall, "Cover Letter Tips," www.reslady.com/coverletters.html.
4. Ibid.
5. Johanna Schlegel and Brian Braiker, "Inappropriate Questions," www.salary.com/Articles/ArticleDetail.asp?part=par284.

Chapter 15
Financing and Accounting for Business Operations

▶ Financial Management

In an effort to remain competitive, the company that Cindy Li works for needs to launch a new device to quickly match the competitor's latest gadget. As chief financial officer, Cindy was asked to assess the company's financial ability to pull this off. What kind of financial information does she need to pull together? What are her company's options for financing such a project?

▶ Financing Small Business Activities

Ginny McIntyre runs a small clothing tailoring business out of her home. She is so overwhelmed with business that she doesn't have enough space for her orders and equipment. She wants to expand her business into a small shop, but she doesn't have enough money. Where can Ginny find financing for her business?

▶ Financing Big Business Activities: Debt and Equity

Joseph Cortez is planning large growth for his company. He needs capital and outside investors for funds. Should he use stocks or bonds? What factors are involved when making the decision?

▶ Accounting Functions

Arnold Sawyer always thought he was good with figures, and for years he was able to help his niece manage the books for her catering business. Then, after an appearance on a local newscast, his niece's catering sales went through the roof. Can the company mobilize quickly enough to fill the requests? Where is the money going to come from?

▶ Financial Statements

Mateo Morales has just received a huge bonus check. After a great deal of excited contemplation about what "big-ticket item" he could purchase, Mateo has reined in his enthusiasm and decided a more prudent action would be best. He will invest the money. So, now he is trying to decide between two companies. Where should he begin? What numbers should he look at, and how should he make sense of them?

OBJECTIVES

1 What is financial management, and how do financial managers fulfill their responsibilities? (pp. 439–443)

2 How do companies finance their short-term business needs? (pp. 443–445)

3 What kinds of loans and grants are available to finance short-term business needs? (pp. 445–447)

4 What is the purpose of each type of long-term financing? (pp. 448–449)

5 What are the pros and cons of debt and equity financing? (pp. 449–453)

6 What are the functions of the different types of accounting? (pp. 453–456)

7 How is double entry bookkeeping used to maintain the balance of the fundamental accounting equation? (pp. 456–459)

8 What is the function of balance sheets, income statements, and statement of cash flows? (pp. 459–469)

Financial Management pp. 439–443

Cindy Li had no idea how her company was going to pull this off. In the past, board members had come up with some far-reaching projects, but this one was the most aggressive by far. As a part of the strategic plan, the board was suggesting the company launch a new kind of mobile eyewear computer to keep up with its competitor's latest gadget. Putting this together would require significant cash and capital investments. As chief financial officer, Cindy was asked if the company currently had the resources to pull off this venture and, if not, what its options for financing such a project were. Cindy knew that her days would be full for the next few months. ■

Source: Darren Baker/Fotolia.

Financial managers are vital to the success of any company. In this section, you'll learn about what financial management entails, what responsibilities a financial manager must fulfill, and how financial managers guide their companies to success.

The Financial Manager

What is financial management? You understand that a business is created to sell a good or a service and make a profit. Producing, marketing, and distributing products are important aspects of generating a profit. Even more important, however, is a company's ability to manage the financial resources required to accomplish these tasks. Without sound financial management, there is no business!

Situations like the one facing Cindy Li's company are not uncommon. Good financial controls and planning enable a company, regardless of its size or how long it has existed, to respond to unexpected challenges or planned expansions. Just as you might save money to ensure that you can pay next month's rent or make plans for a big purchase such as a car or home, businesses must also plan and save. To remain competitive, businesses make large strategic investments, such as buying or building new factories or investing in more advanced machinery or technology. At the same time, businesses also must ensure they can pay their monthly bills.

Financial management is the strategic planning and budgeting of funds for a firm's short-term needs (one year or less) and long-term needs (more than one year). Financial management requires a firm to implement controls to ensure its money and budgets are managed in a way that allows it to reach its financial goals. Tracking

MyBizLab®

⭐ Improve Your Grade!

Over 10 million students improved their results using the Pearson MyLabs.
Visit **mybizlab.com** for simulations, tutorials, and end-of-chapter problems.

past financial transactions, controlling current revenue and expenses, and planning for a company's future financial needs are the foundation of financial management.

All successfully run businesses have people designated to manage the financial decisions and transactions of the company. In many small companies, the owner makes most of the financial decisions and transactions, with or without the help of outside consultants. But as a company grows, it is often necessary to establish a finance department. Generally, the finance department has two divisions: accounting and financial management. Accounting, which we'll cover later in this chapter, is concerned primarily with creating historically accurate financial reports for investors and lenders and for those who make financial decisions for the company.

What is the role of a financial manager? A financial **manager** is responsible for the financial health of a company. In smaller companies, the financial manager may be the owner or someone who may have other responsibilities within the business. Eventually, companies may opt to have a *chief financial officer* (CFO). CFOs are brought on when a business's finances become complicated or when the business is in a high growth phase and extra financial expertise and planning is critical. As shown in ■ **FIGURE 15.1**, a financial manager is responsible for planning and managing a company's financial resources, including the following:

- Developing plans that outline a company's financial short-term and long-term needs
- Defining the sources and uses of funds needed to reach goals
- Monitoring the cash flow of a company to ensure obligations are paid in a timely and efficient manner and funds owed to the company are collected efficiently
- Investing any excess funds so those funds can grow and be used for future developments
- Raising capital for future growth and expansion
- Evaluating financial outcomes and expectations and generating financial reports

Planning for a Firm's Financial Needs

How does the financial manager plan for a firm's financial needs? Because a company's financial needs are both short term and long term in nature, a financial manager must plan for both by developing a financial plan. In addition, a financial manager must ensure the firm's funds are used optimally and the company is ultimately profitable. To meet these objectives, a financial manager oversees three important processes: forecasting financial needs, developing budgets and plans to meet those needs, and establishing controls to ensure that the budgets and plans are being followed.

What is involved in planning for and managing a firm's financial needs? Good financial management begins with a **financial plan**. As shown in ■ **FIGURE 15.2**, a financial plan uses information from a firm's overall corporate strategic plan, financial statements, and external financial environment to identify the amounts and types of capital the company will need in the short term and the long term.

For example, a priority among the goals Cindy Li's company's board of directors and management team discussed was to produce a new device to go head-to-head with a competitor's product. As the head financial manager, it is Cindy's responsibility to communicate with various departments of the company, such as production, marketing, and human resources, to determine the financial impact this strategy will have on these areas of the organization. Among the questions she will have to answer are the following: How much product do we need to sell? Do we need to expand to meet demand? Do we have the human and capital resources to expand our product line?

Cindy will then need to develop short- and long-term sales and other financial forecasts to ensure that her firm's strategic goals are financially feasible. Financial forecasts are especially important when a firm's strategic goals include large capital projects, such as acquiring new facilities, replacing outdated technology, or expanding into a new line of business. It's critical that such forecasts be as accurate as possible. If they aren't, serious consequences can result. Additionally, she'll need to manage revenue and expenses for the plan as it is carried out.

In addition, financial managers must anticipate the impact external factors will have on a company's financial situation. If, for example, a slowdown in the economy is looming, a financial manager knows it will affect his or her company in many ways. Steps may need to be taken to handle the possibility that customers' payments might be harder to collect or that sales could be lower. Because of the result from either or both of these possibilities, plans for expanding buildings or purchasing new equipment might have to be postponed.

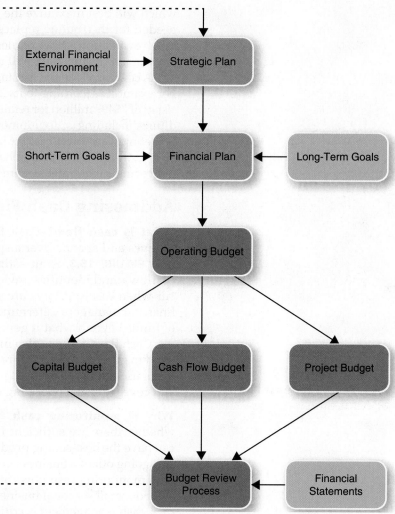

■ **FIGURE 15.2**
The Financial Planning Process

How does a company know it has enough resources to meet its forecasted needs? The accounting area of the finance department generates financial statements. These statements include the *income statement*, the *balance sheet*, and the *statement of cash flows*. We'll discuss financial statements in more detail later in the chapter, but for now you just need to know that together they create a financial picture that explains what a company has done over the current year and in past periods. Moreover, they serve as a basis for management to develop expectations of the company's financial condition in future periods.

Using these expectations, a financial manager develops a **budget**—a management tool that outlines a company's planned cash flows, expected operating expenses, and anticipated revenue. An **operating (master) budget** includes all the operating costs for an entire organization, including its inventory, sales, purchases, manufacturing, marketing, and operating expenses. The operating budget maps out the projected number of units the firm expects to sell, the income generated from them, and all of the operating costs incurred to produce and sell them.

How are funds obtained for large projects? Another component of the budgeting process is the capital budget. The **capital budget** outlines the financial needs for significant purchases, such as real estate, manufacturing equipment, plant expansions, or technology, as part of a company's long-range plans. Because large capital investments are often financed with borrowed money or money raised through the sale of stocks or bonds, it is important to plan ahead to ensure funds are available when they are needed. During the capital budgeting process, each department in an organization makes a list of its anticipated capital needs. The firm's senior managers and the board members evaluate these needs to determine which will best maximize the company's overall growth and profitability. Capital needed for the routine replacement of equipment or technology may not require much evaluation. Other requests for capital, such as those needed to take the company in a new direction, will require closer evaluation.

A company's actual capital expenditures are often outlined in its annual report. For example, according to its 2013 annual report, Apple's capital expenditures consisted of "$499 million for retail store facilities and $6.5 billion for other capital expenditures including . . . equipment and other corporate facilities and infrastructure."[1] Sometimes, a **project budget** is prepared to identify the costs needed to accomplish a project—an endeavor that has a specific start and end date, such as installing and upgrading a computer system or renovating an existing building.

Addressing Cash Flow and the Budget

What is cash flow? Cash flow is the amount of money a company actually receives and spends over a specific period. The **cash flow budget**, as illustrated in ■ **FIGURE 15.3**, is an estimate of a company's short-term cash inflows and outflows, and identifies any cash flow gaps for the business. Cash flow gaps occur when cash outflows are greater than cash inflows. Cash flow budgets help financial managers determine whether a business needs to seek outside sources of funds beyond what it generates by its own business operations.

Cash flow budgets also indicate whether a business will have enough cash on hand to grow and fund future investment opportunities. Moreover, financial managers use the cash flow budget to help plan for the repayment of the firm's debts and cover unusual operating expenses.

Why is monitoring cash flow important? Cash flow specifically measures whether there are sufficient funds to pay a firm's outstanding bills. A company can have the best-selling product on the market, but if the flow of funds coming in and going out of a business is not managed properly, the firm can easily fail. That's why monitoring cash flows are so important.

For small seasonal businesses, such as ski shops and pool installation companies, cash management is critical for carrying a business through the slow months. Seasonal business owners must be disciplined to not spend surplus cash generated during the busy season. Although many investors focus on a company's profitability, a company's *liquidity*—how quickly an asset can be turned into cash—is often a better indicator of a firm's strength. Companies go bankrupt when they cannot pay their bills, not because they are unprofitable; a firm can remain unprofitable for a period of time as long as it has enough cash on hand. As you'll read later in this chapter, accountants also play a big role in helping financial managers monitor cash flows using ratios such as the current and quick ratios.

How does a company know if it's staying on budget? After a budget is developed, it must be compared periodically to a company's actual performance.

■ **FIGURE 15.3**
Cash Flow Budget
Image Sources: Left to right, top to bottom: Texelart/Shutterstock; slaved/Fotolia; lucadp/Fotolia; Arthur Eugene Preston/Shutterstock; SDuggan/Fotolia; Pawel Burgiel/Fotolia; Paul Fleet/Fotolia; scusi/Fotolia; Stoyan Haytov/Fotolia.

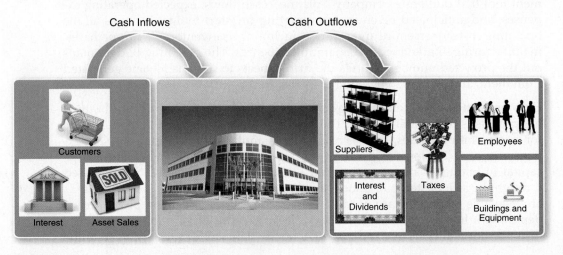

Ideally this happens every month. Without such a comparison, it's hard to determine whether a company is performing as expected. To understand this concept better, think about your personal financial situation. Let's say you decide to save some money, and at the end of the month, you have $50 in your savings account. Is that good or bad? It all depends on what you originally planned to save. If you intended to save only $35 during the month but end up with $50, that's great. If you intended to save $75, then the outcome is not as good, and you should modify your spending to bring you back into budget.

The same is true with the financial performance of a company. If the actual numbers generated by a company closely match the budget, this shows that the company is fulfilling its plans. However, if the actual numbers differ greatly from those projected by the budget, this indicates that corrective actions or adjustments should be taken.

What must financial managers consider when seeking outside funds? In your personal life, you most likely have different types of financing options to help you manage your financial needs. For example, you may have a checking account or credit card to pay for short-term expenses. You might have a savings account as well as some loans to pay for bigger, long-term expenses, such as your tuition, car, or home.

Likewise, companies have different financing options available to them. How do financial managers evaluate these options and choose the best one? They do so by assessing several criteria, including how much and how quickly the money is needed, how long the financing is needed, the cost of the financing, and the riskiness of the project being financed. Short-term financing options for small businesses and start-ups generally include grants, short-term loans, or lines of credit from banks as well as credit from suppliers. Long-term financing needs may be met with bank loans or mortgages, venture capital, or funds from an angel investor. Larger, more established companies that need to finance growth or expansion many need to determine whether it is best to finance by raising **equity**—ownership interest in the form of stocks—or issuing debt. We'll discuss all of these options later in the chapter.

To determine the feasibility of the company's planned launch of the eyewear device her company is considering, Cindy developed short- and long-term financial forecasts after assessing the impact this new strategy would have on the company as a whole. Taking into account the state of the economy, the projected sales of the new product, available financing sources, and the future plans of the company, Cindy found that while producing the new product would be challenging, it could be done. Next she would need to take a closer look at the capital budget and evaluate specific financing options to prepare for the specific financial needs this type of project will require.

Financing Small Business Activities pp. 443–447

Ginny McIntyre runs a tailoring business from her home. Her customers have been recommending her work to other people, so in the last six months her customer base has almost doubled. Her house isn't big enough to accommodate all the orders and her equipment. She is considering interviewing another seamstress to help her with the additional work. If the increased demand continues, Ginny is anticipating she'll need to obtain a small shop and hire one or two additional employees. She has already ordered a new sewing machine and is interviewing candidates. She has identified the perfect location for a future shop. ■

Source: Diego Cervo/Fotolia.

The problem is that Ginny's not sure her operating revenue will completely cover her new immediate expenses, and she doesn't have enough personal financial resources to pull off the larger long-term plans. Her family and friends may be able to help but probably can't completely finance the future expansion. What short-term and long-term financing options does she have?

You probably have heard the adage "It takes money to make money." When small businesses find it necessary to expand or don't have enough working capital to cover their operating costs, they must make some important decisions regarding financing. In this section, you'll learn about what financial resources are available for small businesses to manage their financing needs and how business owners decide which option is best.

Short-Term Financing Options

How are the short-term financing needs of a small business met? Every business, regardless of size, has varying financial needs. It's important that all companies have a plan to finance those needs. One of the most important aspects of sound financial management is the careful monitoring and control of short-term financial needs. **Short-term financing** is any type of financing repaid within a year or less. It is used to finance day-to-day operations, such as payroll, inventory purchases, and overhead (utilities, rent, leases, and so forth).

As mentioned earlier, cash flow budgets are prepared to assess whether a company has sufficient cash to fulfill regular operations. When the cash flow budget predicts gaps in cash needs, depending on the size of the business and the cash flow gap, several short-term strategies can be used to help meet the temporary gap. For Ginny, her immediate short-term needs are to pay for a new sewing machine and to find ongoing resources to pay her new employee.

What are some common sources of short-term working capital financing? When a company's cash reserves won't cover its short-term expenses, small business owners often turn to the following sources of short-term financing:

- **Self-financing/family/friends.** The owners of smaller start-up businesses often fund cash flow gaps by tapping into their own funds or appealing to their friends and family for personal loans. Personal loans are not a recommended long-term or permanent strategy because they can lead to severed relationships if the loans are not paid back promptly. However, when financing agreements like these are used, both parties need to understand and agree to formal payment arrangements.

- **Credit cards.** Another approach many smaller businesses take to fund cash flow gaps is to use credit cards. Credit cards are a good way to defer payments, but they can become very expensive if their balances are not paid off completely every month. A separate business credit card account should be established instead of using a personal credit account, if possible. Doing so protects the owner's personal credit if he or she were to default on business payments. However, if the business is a sole proprietorship, owners can be held responsible, regardless of whether a business card or personal card is used. One of the few benefits of using credit is the potential for cash back and other rewards offered by several credit card companies. If the card is used wisely and balances are paid off regularly, these rewards can be a significant bonus.

Can suppliers help by providing credit? Businesses with good credit and an established relationship with their suppliers can take advantage of another credit relationship to help bridge the temporary gap: trade credit. **Trade credit** is the ability to purchase from a supplier goods and services on credit without paying interest. Suppliers will typically request payment within 30, 60, or 90 days and give a discount for early payments.

Trade credit terms are often expressed with three numbers, such as 2/10/60. The first number is the discount if you pay within the discount period, which is expressed as the second number. The third number is the number of days by which the balance must be paid in full. So, for a 2/10/60 trade credit, the business owner will receive a 2 percent discount if the balance is paid within 10 days. Otherwise the full balance is due in 60 days. Another way these terms are often expressed is 2/10, net 60.

Paying early to take advantage of a trade credit discount is wonderful if a firm's cash flow isn't a problem. If it is, deferring payment with trade credit is a good strategy because it does not tie up cash unnecessarily. Moreover, using trade credit keeps debt levels down, which is always attractive to outside investors and lenders. However, there may be disadvantages associated with using trade credit. If a firm doesn't pay on time, delinquency penalties are charged, and, if allowed to accrue, these penalties can be very costly.[2] Financial managers must weigh the costs and benefits of paying early for a discount or paying on time without a discount so that their cash is available longer. ■ **FIGURE 15.4** illustrates this decision.

■ **FIGURE 15.4**
Using trade credit can be advantageous but must always be evaluated and monitored carefully.
Source: The Supe87/Shutterstock.

Can businesses turn accounts receivables into cash? Another strategy a firm can use to obtain cash quickly is factoring. **Factoring** is the process of selling accounts receivable for cash instead of using them as collateral for a loan. This takes monies owed to a company by its clients or supply chain partners and turns them to cash that a company can then use almost immediately. The factoring company pays the value of the company's invoices, less a fee. Although it is generally more costly than obtaining a business loan, factoring is often easier to arrange, which is why companies often use it to bridge cash flow gaps.

Short-Term Loans and Grants

How do commercial banks help with financial management? Commercial banks are financial institutions, credit unions, and savings-and-loan institutions that raise funds from businesses and individuals in the form of checking and savings accounts and then use those funds to make loans to businesses and individuals. Small start-up businesses rely on commercial banks for savings and checking services to pay bills and store excess funds. Checking and savings accounts are a form of **demand deposit**, funds that can be withdrawn (or demanded) at any time without prior notice.

As a business develops and is able to establish a good relationship with a bank, the business owners may seek to open a line of credit. A business **line of credit** is credit that a manager can access at any time up to an amount agreed upon between the bank and the company. The funds can be withdrawn all at once or in multiple withdrawals during the stated period. This is a common way of covering temporary cash flow shortages, purchasing seasonal inventory, or financing unforeseen operating expenses. Carmakers such as Ford and Honda often act as banks by providing their dealerships with lines of credit to purchase their inventories of vehicles.

Will banks lend money to small businesses? The credit crunch in 2009 and 2010 made it difficult for many businesses, small and large, to seek financing solutions from banks. Banks were not lending, and, if they were, the requirements were very stringent. But, according to the Thomson Reuters/ PayNet Small Business Lending Index, which measures the volume of new commercial loans and leases to small businesses, lending to small businesses has been on the rise since its low in mid-2009.[3] The economy has begun to rebuild, more businesses are seeking loans, and banks are beginning to respond. Many commercial banks offer loans to businesses for the purchase of equipment, property, or other capital assets. However, most banks require owners to provide business and financial plans, and personal and business financial statements, as assurance that the business is viable and worth financing. In many cases, banks require **collateral**, which is an additional form of security that assures a lender that the borrower has another way of repaying the loan. Loans that require collateral are **secured loans**. Sometimes the collateral is the asset that is being financed. For example, if a bank were to approve a loan to a company to purchase a building or new equipment, either one could serve as collateral. If the company were unable to pay down the loan, the bank would take possession of the asset as a substitute for the remaining loan payments. Other forms of collateral can include a business's inventory, cash savings, or equipment. Some small business owners put up their personal assets as collateral, risking their homes or retirement or other savings accounts. If the firm has an excellent credit history and a solid relationship with the lending institution, it may get an **unsecured loan**, which doesn't require collateral.

Are there other short-term loan options? Sometimes, a company is unable to secure a short-term loan from a commercial bank and have to consider other options besides traditional banking institutions. **Nonbank lenders** are financial institutions that extend credit or loans but do not hold deposits. These lenders will take on loans commercial banks view as too risky. Nonbank lenders are also often more flexible in their loan terms. However, there is a price associated with this flexibility and availability: higher interest rates. Quality nonbank lenders are often difficult to locate, but Fundera (www.fundera.com), an online service, strives to help small business owners connect to appropriate nonbank lenders.

Microloans are small, short-term loans specific to small businesses. The Small Business Administration (SBA) created the microloan program in the early 1990s to increase the availability of funds to small business borrowers. Microloans are available through local nonprofit community-based intermediaries. The maximum loan amount for a microloan is $50,000, but the average microloan is about $13,000.[4] According to the SBA, microloans may be used for ongoing business needs, such as working capital, purchase of inventory or supplies, purchase of furniture or fixtures, or machinery or equipment.

Are grants available to finance small business operations? Although most small business grants are targeted for specific research-and-development projects, grants can be found to help small businesses finance their ongoing operations. The federal government does not provide grants for starting or expanding

▶ THE LIST

Interesting Crowdfunding Campaigns

Company	Amount Raised/ Target Amount	Project Description
Pirate3D	$1.4 million/$100,000	3D printer for the home that is cloud-based
3Doodler	$2.4 million/$30,000	3D printing pen that turns drawings into real objects
Tile	$2.6 million/	Tag to track the location of your devices
Pixelstick	$628,000/$110,000	Device to add abstract designs and animations to long-exposure photos and time lapse.
Canary	$1.9 million/$100,000	"Smart home security device" that uses video, temperature motion, and air quality to detect changes in the home environment
One Puck	$132,739/$100,000	Mobile phone charger that derives current from a hot or cold beverage
Stompy the Giant Spider	$100,000/$65,000	Six-foot, 4,000-pound walking spider hydraulic robot that you can ride
Ring	$510,000/$250,000	Wearable input device that lets you control gestures, text transmissions, payments, and more
Cards Against Humanity	$15,570/$4,000	Party game for "horrible people"
Ubuntu Edge	$12.8 million/ $32 million	High-concept smart phone, ultimately an unsuccessful campaign despite raising over $12 million

for-profit businesses—only not-for-profit organizations. State and local governments are better sources for business grants, although often these grants are targeted toward specialized businesses that the state or local government is trying to develop, such as child care centers, businesses that improve tourism, or businesses developing energy-efficient products.

Social Funding

Is there a way to obtain loans without involving financial institutions? The accessibility and acceptance of social networks has given small business owners another interesting funding alternative: communities of individuals willing to lend or give money to help others succeed.

- **Peer-to-peer lending** is a growing source of financing for small businesses. As its name implies, peer-to-peer lending is the process of individuals lending to each other. Similar to eBay, where individuals sell their goods to other individuals, sites such as Prosper.com and LendingClub.com facilitate lending between individuals. This trend became popular as traditional bank loans became more difficult to obtain. Peer-to-peer loans generally have lower interest rates than commercial loans. ■ **FIGURE 15.5** illustrates the peer-to-peer lending process. For example, prospective borrowers with Prosper.com create an account that describes the purpose for and amount of the loan and a maximum interest rate they are willing to pay. In addition, borrowers must provide financial information from which the site creates a "credit grade" that helps prospective lenders evaluate the worthiness of a project and borrower. Loans may be funded by one or several lenders and are repaid directly through Prosper.com, which automatically debits the borrower's bank account each month and then credits the accounts of the lenders.

- **Crowdfunding** is a way to generate funds via donations or, more recently, investments from individuals. Kickstarter (www.kickstarter.com) relies on donors. Donors receive products, perks, or other rewards from the companies they donate to on Kickstarter. Most successful donor projects raise less than $10,000, but there have been a number of projects that have raised funds in the six- and even seven-figure range. Pebble Watch, a maker of smart watches, raised more than $10 million from 85,000 backers.[5] Crowdfunder (www.crowdfunder.com) offers both donation-based and investment crowdfunding opportunities and has attracted a growing community of investors, tech start-ups, and small businesses. Investors gain ownership or a promise of future returns. AngelList (www.angellist.com) is another investment crowdfunding site.

Although her friends and family weren't able to help Ginny McIntyre expand her tailoring business, she was able to pay for the new sewing machine with some money from her own savings and the balance with a credit card. She is confident that her ability to handle more work will directly pay for an additional employee, but to be safe, she's starting the new employee on a part-time basis. Ginny is also looking to get a microloan to help her purchase a small shop in a few years. If all goes well, she plans to expand her business to include more staff and additional shops. She will likely enlist the help of a commercial bank to fund this venture. Ginny, like all business owners, hopes that securing financing for these expenditures will lead to beneficial growth and profits.

■ **FIGURE 15.5**
How Peer-to-Peer Lending Works

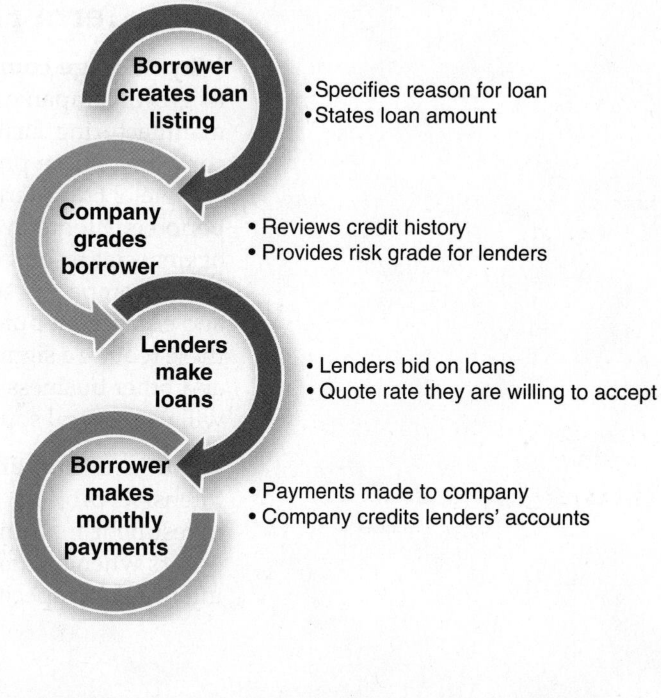

Borrower creates loan listing
- Specifies reason for loan
- States loan amount

Company grades borrower
- Reviews credit history
- Provides risk grade for lenders

Lenders make loans
- Lenders bid on loans
- Quote rate they are willing to accept

Borrower makes monthly payments
- Payments made to company
- Company credits lenders' accounts

Source: Olly/Fotolia.

Financing Big Business Activities: Debt and Equity pp. 448–453

Three years ago, Joseph Cortez secured equity investments from a venture capital group to help his company, SolCar, Inc., finance the creation of a solar-powered car. Since then, his company has continued to expand faster than he expected. This year, the firm has had the good fortune of getting an order for a fleet of the cars and may potentially get several other large orders. Joseph now must turn his attention to building a much larger plant to handle the increased manufacturing demand. How should Joseph meet the financing needs of SolCar? Should SolCar issue company stock or bonds? What factors does Joseph need to consider? ■

Like small businesses, large companies must also manage their short-term financing, typically for continuing their operations, increasing their inventories, and covering their payrolls.

Short-Term Financing Options

Many of the short-term financing strategies available to small businesses discussed earlier, such as lines of credit and collateralized loans, are available to big businesses to finance short term needs. In addition, other options are available to larger, more established companies, including the option to sell commercial paper. **Commercial paper** is unsecured, short-term debt that matures in 270 days (nine months) or less. Commercial paper does not need to be registered with the Securities and Exchange Commission. Due to government regulations, the proceeds generated from selling commercial paper can be used only to purchase current assets, such as inventory, and cannot be used on fixed assets, such as equipment, buildings, or real estate. Because the debt is unsecured, only companies with excellent credit reputations are able to sell commercial paper. Buyers of commercial paper are those who want to invest their cash for short periods of time.

Long-Term Financing Options

Why do large companies need long-term financing solutions? Remember that to grow, companies need expansion projects, such as establishing new offices or manufacturing facilities, developing a new product or service, or buying another company. These projects generally cost millions of dollars and may take years to complete. **Long-term financing** is therefore needed because it provides funds for a period greater than one year. For example, Joseph Cortez needs a significant amount of financial resources over the next few years to meet the increase in the demand for his company's solar-powered cars. These resources include financing real-estate and equipment purchases for a new production plant. Large capital projects such as these require a significant amount of long-term planning to ensure that the financing and other business components are ready when needed. In most cases, a company will use several sources of long-term financing, even for one project.

What are the different types of long-term financing? For large capital-intensive projects or general expansion, business owners can use **securities**—investment instruments such as bonds (debt) or stock (equity). **Debt financing** occurs when a company borrows money that it is legally obligated to repay, with interest, by a specified time. Contrary to debt financing, **equity financing** occurs

| TABLE 15.1 | Debt or Equity Financing: What Does Each Mean for the Company? |

Debt	Equity
Company profits are used to repay debt.	Company profits are retained or paid to shareholders.
Must be repaid or refinanced. Requires regular interest payments.	No payments to shareholders are required.
Company must generate cash flow to pay interest and principal.	Company is not required to pay dividends out of cash flow. Dividends, if paid, are paid out of profits.
Collateral assets are usually required.	No collateral is required.
Interest payments are tax deductible.	Dividend payments are not tax deductible.
Debt does not impact control of a company.	Equity requires shared control of a company and may impose restrictions.

when funds are generated by the owners of a company rather than being borrowed from outside lenders. These funds might come from owner's personal investments or from a partial sale of ownership in a company in the form of stock.

How do companies choose between debt and equity financing? Most companies use debt (loans or bonds) to finance large projects, such as the purchase of real estate, equipment, or building construction. Equity is often used to provide funds for ongoing expansion and growth. Debt and equity financing are very different forms of financing and can be complementary financing options. It is not unusual for a company to use both types of financing, aiming to achieve an optimal balance between both. ■ **TABLE 15.1** summarizes the factors that come into play when a firm is deciding to finance with debt or equity. In the next few pages, we'll look into each type of financing in more detail.

Financing with Bonds

Why finance with bonds? In our personal lives, when we want to buy something that costs more than what we have saved, such as a house, our best option is to borrow money. We take out a loan (such as a home mortgage) specifically to pay for the item, and that item is used as collateral in case we cannot repay the loan. Similarly, when a company has a project or desired asset that it cannot finance with existing company assets, it can take out a business loan. Common lenders include banks, finance companies, credit card companies, and private corporations.

Eventually, a company's financing needs may grow beyond what these common lenders can provide. In these situations, companies may use bonds to acquire the needed funds. **Bonds** are debt instruments issued by companies or governments with the purpose of raising capital to finance a large project. Simply put, bonds are like loans, but the lenders are investors, not banks. A bond consists of the principal (the amount borrowed) and interest (the fee charged by the lender for using the borrowed money). Investors loan money to a company by purchasing bonds and, in return, generally receive interest on the bonds they purchase. Although some bonds do not pay interest, all bonds require repayment of the principal.

What are the advantages of financing with bonds? Financing with bonds allows a company to use money from investors to create or obtain business assets. Using debt increases a company's leverage. **Leverage** is the practice of borrowing to finance an investment with the expectation that the profits from it will be far greater than the interest you will have to pay on the money. For example, most home owners use leverage to buy a house. Suppose you want to buy a $400,000 home but saved only $200,000. You could wait to accumulate enough cash to purchase the home, or you could use some of your money and borrow the rest with a mortgage. Although there is a cost to borrowing (interest), as long as that cost is less than what you can earn by investing, borrowing (leverage) makes sense. So, assume you put down $100,000 of your own money and borrow $300,000 with a 5 percent mortgage. You now have a $400,000 asset by using only $100,000 of your money. You can then invest the other $100,000 in the stock market, which historically has earned 8 to 10 percent. Had you used all your $200,000 to buy the house, you would have had less interest expense but would not have been able to invest anything. Therefore, by using leverage wisely, your investments will offset your financing costs, with hopefully a little more left over! Businesses use leverage in the same way.

A company that borrows considerably more money than it has in assets is considered to be *highly leveraged.* However, because it can be risky to take on too much debt, lenders consider how much debt a company has relative to the amount of equity (or assets) a company owns before they borrow. A common leverage ratio is for a company to have at least twice the amount of equity as it has debt.

In addition, unlike stocks (which we'll discuss next), financing with bonds does not dilute the ownership of a company. For many business owners, giving up or diluting ownership or control of a business by issuing stock is not a feasible or a desirable option. Unlike shareholders, bondholders have no voice or control in how a business is managed. Their only requirement is that the loans be paid back on time and with interest.

What must financial managers consider before choosing to finance with bonds? Financial managers must consider several factors before choosing to finance with bonds. First and foremost, the cost of the loan—the interest rate the lender will demand—is an important consideration. If the interest rate is too high, it can force the cost of the project to rise to the point where it isn't affordable or doesn't make economic sense. If this happens, the company will have to consider a different type of financing or postpone the project until the interest rate is more attractive. Before making a final decision to issue bonds, a financial manager must also consider how the additional debt will affect the overall financial health of a company. From a balance sheet perspective, too much debt may impair a company's credit rating, thus making it difficult to obtain further financing. The firm's statement of cash flows will help determine whether there will be enough cash to repay the debt and keep the business operating. As you have learned, too little cash flow can quickly send a company into a disastrous financial tailspin.

How are bond interest rates determined? Bond interest rates are determined by a combination of several factors, including *issuer risk* and the *length of the bond term.* Issuer risk is a measure of a company's ability to pay back the loan. Credit rating agencies, such as Standard & Poor's and Moody's, assess the creditworthiness of a company. As the risk increases, so does the interest rate. As you'll learn in Chapter 16, firms that issue bonds often buy *bond insurance* to help lower the risk of the bonds and therefore the interest rates they have to pay on them. The amount of money saved by having a lower interest rate is greater than the cost of bond insurance. In addition to issuer risk, the length of the bond term (known also as the maturity) affects the rate. Longer-term bonds have a greater chance of the issuer not being able to pay the principal or interest when it's due. Therefore, bonds that have terms of 20 or 30 years carry additional risk and have higher interest rates than bonds with terms of 5 or 10 years.

How do companies pay back their bond debt? As noted already, bond investors receive two types of payments: *principal* and *interest.* Most bondholders periodically receive interest payments in amounts and at the times specified in their bond agreements. Most interest payments are made semiannually. The interest is calculated on the amount of principal outstanding and the periodic interest rate associated with the debt. So, if you have a $10,000 15-year bond with a 5 percent interest rate paid semiannually, you should receive

Payment Cycle of Bond Issue

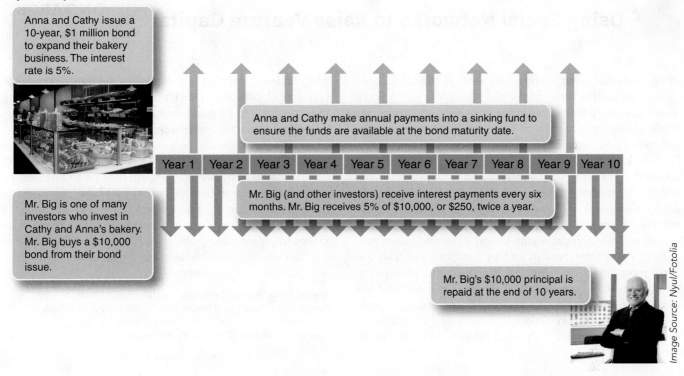

Anna and Cathy issue a 10-year, $1 million bond to expand their bakery business. The interest rate is 5%.

Anna and Cathy make annual payments into a sinking fund to ensure the funds are available at the bond maturity date.

Year 1 | Year 2 | Year 3 | Year 4 | Year 5 | Year 6 | Year 7 | Year 8 | Year 9 | Year 10

Mr. Big is one of many investors who invest in Cathy and Anna's bakery. Mr. Big buys a $10,000 bond from their bond issue.

Mr. Big (and other investors) receive interest payments every six months. Mr. Big receives 5% of $10,000, or $250, twice a year.

Mr. Big's $10,000 principal is repaid at the end of 10 years.

Image Source: Nyul/Fotolia

■ **FIGURE 15.6**
Payment Cycle of a Bond Issue

($10,000 × 0.05)/2, or $250, in interest payments twice a year for as long as you own the bond. At the end of the loan period, the company is responsible for paying you the entire initial amount you invested (the principal), which in this case is $10,000 at the end of 15 years.

To ensure there's enough money at the end of the loan period to pay back the principal to all the bondholders, companies set aside money annually in a **sinking fund**—a type of savings fund into which companies deposit money regularly. ■ **FIGURE 15.6** explains the payment cycle of a bond issue.

Financing with Equity

What kinds of equity financing are available? If a company is successful, finding long-term funding can be as simple as looking at its balance sheet for *retained earnings*, or *accumulated profits*. Using retained earnings is an ideal way to fund long-term projects because it saves companies from paying interest on loans or underwriting fees on bonds. Unfortunately, not all companies have enough retained earnings to fund large projects. In particular, start-up businesses find themselves with few options for long-term financing. Business owners can, of course, invest their own money. However, at some point, they are likely to have invested as much as they can or are willing to and still need additional funds to keep their businesses growing.

What kind of private equity financing is available? A company may look for long-term financing in the form of venture capital. **Venture capital** is an investment in the company by a group of outside investors, called *venture capitalists*, who take an active role in a company's management decisions. Venture capitalists seek their return in the form of equity, or ownership, in a company. They anticipate a large return on their investments when a company is sold or goes public. Venture capitalists are willing to wait longer than other investors, lenders, or shareholders for returns on their investments, but they expect higher-than-normal returns.

Why finance with stock? Instead of relying on venture capital or bonds, which are generally usually used to fund short-term projects rather than ongoing operations, a

Using Social Networks to Raise Venture Capital

Businesses need money, and venture capitalists need investments. How do the two meet? You might find it surprising that today many of these connections are made online via blogs, Twitter, and social networks, such as LinkedIn. Chris Sacca of Lowercase Capital is always looking for new investment opportunities. Sacca once sent a tweet asking if there were any "bootstrapped, profitable start-ups with founders working late on a Friday night,"* and, to his surprise, one replied. The connection was made, and the investment is still one of Chris's favorites.

Investors use social media to find deals and create relationships with entrepreneurs so they can close the deals that seem most attractive. Searching through Twitter streams can turn up valuable insight about a company's founders and employees and the firm's culture and viability. Social networks can also help forge connections between investors and founders. If an investor doesn't know the management team of the potential investment, he or she can see if there are any common connections between them. If there are common connections, they can prove to be good sources of information—even if it's only about character and business acumen.

Twitter searches can be valuable to venture capitalists to see whether users are having good experiences with a product or whether they are disgruntled. It helps to uncover the real-world problems that might otherwise be purposely ignored by a company's management team. But it's not just a one-way street. Investors also need to build their online reputations to differentiate themselves from other venture capitalists. Venture capitalists can also use the social web to build up a reputation for their investments.

Source: "How Venture Capitalists Are Using Social Media for Real Results," Mashable Social Media, May 17, 2010, by Jolie O'Dell, http://mashable.com/2010/05/17/vcs-social-media.
*Tweet from @sacca (Chris Sacca), Twitter.com.

company might choose to issue stock (often referred to as *equity*). **Stock** is a unit of ownership in a company. A **stock certificate** is a document that represents the ownership of stock and includes details such as the issuing company's name, the number of shares the certificate represents, and the type of stock being issued. Paper stock certificates, however, are rarely issued these days because companies are opting to record them electronically. When a company first sells stock to the public, the event is referred to as an **initial public offering**. Offering shares of ownership in a company to the general public—called "going public"—can be a great option. A company can choose to go public when it feels it has enough public support to attract new shareholders.

Are there disadvantages to financing with stock? The biggest disadvantage of financing with stock is the dilution of the ownership of a business. Stockholders become owners of the company, and although they do not have direct control over the day-to-day management of a company, they do have a say in the composition of its board of directors. The board of directors is charged with hiring the senior management team. This means that although shareholders do not directly control *how* a company is managed, they do directly control *who* manages the company. As a result, shareholders can have a strong influence on management's decisions.

What are the advantages to financing with stock? Unlike bonds and other forms of debt, equity financing does not need to be repaid, even if a company goes bankrupt, so no assets need to be pledged as collateral. In addition, financing with equity enables a company to retain its cash and profits rather than using the funds to make interest and principal payments. In many instances, financing with equity can make a company's balance sheet look stronger because high levels of debt can make lenders and investors wary of its financial viability.

How does a company choose between debt and equity? The choice between financing large projects with debt or equity depends on many factors, including the maturity, the size and financial worthiness of a company, the number of assets and liabilities a company already has, and the size and nature of the project being financed. Managers can reach the best decision by understanding the financing needs of the project itself and the impact the financing decision has on the company's earnings, cash flow, and taxes. In addition, a company must consider how much debt it already has before issuing bonds or whether it wants to dilute ownership by issuing stock. Also, business owners must decide if they are willing to compromise the vision they have for their companies by allowing stockholders to have a say in the management of their companies.

Finally, a company must also consider external factors at the time of financing, such as the state of the bond or stock market, the economy, and the anticipated interest of the investors. It is important to note that debt and equity should not be considered as substitutes for one another. Instead, they should be viewed as complementary financing; most large companies will use both.

After weighing the pros and cons of both options, Joseph decided issuing a bond would help raise the funds needed to build SolCar's new manufacturing facility. He figures if the firm continued to expand, he might consider issuing stock later. But right now, he doesn't want to dilute ownership in the company and possibly have to give up the control of it. He feels confident that his decisions will help his company grow and maintain a good balance between debt and equity financing.

Accounting Functions pp. 453–459

Arnold Sawyer was pretty good at handling business finances. When his niece Josephine asked him to oversee the finances for her vegan catering business, he figured he could handle it. Arnold's background was in sales, but he thought he was smart enough to handle accounting. He used the software program QuickBooks to create a basic bookkeeping system. Because the company had a small but steady stream of clients, the accounting side didn't seem complicated. However, after Josephine appeared on a newscast to talk about the benefits of a vegan diet, sales skyrocketed, and the firm's workload doubled. Josephine needed to increase her staff and supplies, but the company didn't have enough cash to cover the initial costs. Arnold wasn't sure what to do. ■

Source: Littleny/Fotolia.

Accounting is often called "the language of business" because it provides financial information for decision making, planning, and reporting. When companies are small, their accounting can be relatively simple. However, as a company grows and diversifies, accounting becomes increasingly complex. In this section, we'll look at the fundamentals of accounting, the types of accounting, and accounting standards and processes.

Accounting Fundamentals

What is accounting? Recall that Cindy Li was asked to make a decision about her company's ability to finance a large project, Ginny McIntyre was trying to raise money to buy new equipment and hire another employee, and Joseph Cortez needed financing to expand the manufacturing of his cars. To make an informed decision, all these business owners and managers relied on financial data that either they or their accountants prepare. Similarly, Arnold Sawyer must decide how his niece's catering business will acquire the extra funds it needs to keep the business moving. Arnold will need to review the company's financial information and possibly enlist outside consultants before making a decision. All these situations illustrate how accounting helps business managers make well-informed decisions about the financial needs of a company. **Accounting** is the process of tracking a business's income and expenses by recording its financial transactions. The transactions are then summarized into key financial reports that are further used to evaluate a business's current and expected financial status. Accounting is not just for large organizations. In fact, as Arnold Sawyer can attest, it is vital for businesses of all sizes. Accounting defines the heart and soul of even the smallest business, as it helps to "account for" what the business has

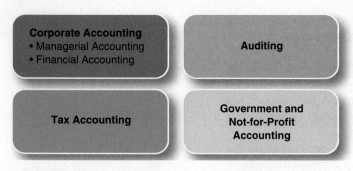

FIGURE 15.7
Primary Accounting Disciplines

done, what it is currently doing, and what it has the potential to do. Although accounting involves a great deal of precision, there are also some degrees of interpretation related to it. This makes accounting both an art and a science.

Types of Accounting

Are there different types of accounting? *Accounting* is a general term, to say the least. Because different forms of business have varying needs, a multitude of specialty areas reside under the accounting umbrella. ■ **FIGURE 15.7** outlines the main types of accounting:

- Corporate accounting (including *managerial* and *financial accounting*)
- Auditing, government, and not-for-profit accounting
- Tax accounting

What is corporate accounting? Among the decisions financial managers must make is determining whether a company's financial assets are working efficiently (that is, earning as much money as possible), evaluating what kind of financing strategy is best, or choosing a way to obtain needed funds. The answers to these and many other decisions they must make are found in the reports and analyses performed by corporate accountants. **Corporate accounting** is the part of an organization's finance department responsible for gathering and assembling data required for key financial statements. Corporate accounting has two separate functions: *managerial accounting* and *financial accounting*.

What is managerial accounting? **Managerial accounting** provides information and analyses to managers within an organization so they can make informed business decisions. For example, a managerial accounting budget can help a company's managers determine whether to increase the firm's staff or institute layoffs. Managerial accountants also prepare short-term reports that help managers with the day-to-day operations of the business, such as weekly sales reports they can use to direct and motivate their sales force. Moreover, managerial accountants analyze which business activities are most profitable and least profitable. Based on their analyses, managers are better equipped to make decisions about whether to continue with, expand, or eliminate certain business activities. In addition, managerial accountants monitor the actual performance of the firm and compare it to the budgeted expectations set for it.

 How's This for an Accounting Goof?

OFF THE MARK

The assessor's office in Carver County, Minnesota, made an accounting goof that affected 34,000 taxpayers across the county. One of the clerks who was entering property values into the county's database typed the value of a vacant lot as $189 million instead of $18,900. The typing error went unnoticed. Not even the accounting software the county used detected anything out of the ordinary. The county assumed it would be getting $2.5 million in property tax payments and planned accordingly. Jurisdictions in the county created their budgets with the error still in place. Taxpayers received tax estimates from the county and thought they were catching a break because the estimates included the $2.5 million payment. No one was aware of the error until the owner of the vacant lot received a bill for $2.5 million and called officials to complain. Carver County officials had to hustle to adjust their budgets properly for the following year. Many taxpayers, who thought they were getting a tax cut, were livid because they actually got a tax hike.[6] It's amazing what three extra zeroes can do!

What is financial accounting? **Financial accounting** is an area of accounting that produces financial documents to aid investors and creditors. Managerial accounting is used by managers *inside* a company to make decisions, whereas interested parties *outside* a company depend on financial accounting. ■ **FIGURE 15.8** compares the two corporate accounting disciplines.

Prospective and current investors and creditors rely on financial accounting information to help them evaluate a company's performance and profitability. Such information is generally found in key documents, such as an *annual report*—a document produced once a year that present the current financial state of a company and its future prospects. The financial statements in an annual report help investors determine whether it is wise to invest in the company.

Banks and other creditors analyze financial accounting statements to get a sense of a business's financial health and creditworthiness. Some companies employ **private accountants** to perform financial accounting tasks in-house, whereas other companies hire **public accountants** external to the firm to do these tasks. Public and private accountants who have passed a rigorous series of examinations given by the American Institute of Certified Public Accountants and who have also met state requirements are given the designation of **certified public accountant**.

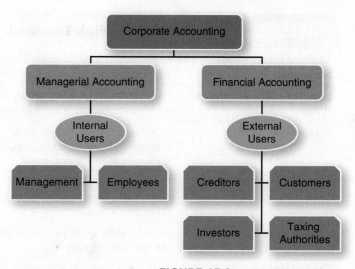

■ **FIGURE 15.8**
A Comparison of Managerial and Financial Accounting

What is auditing? **Auditing** is the area of accounting responsible for reviewing and evaluating the accuracy of financial reports. Large corporations may have internal auditors on staff who work independently of the accounting department to determine whether a company's financial information is recorded correctly and has been prepared using proper procedures. Generally, however, most companies hire independent auditors from outside the organization to ensure that their financial statements have been prepared accurately and are not biased or manipulated in any way. Companies can avoid devastating budget problems, such as the one experienced by the assessor's office in Carver County, Minnesota (described in the Off the Mark box), by performing audits.

What type of accounting do governments and not-for-profit corporations use? Accounting is not only for organizations that strive to make money; government institutions and not-for-profit organizations use accounting as well. **Government and not-for-profit accounting** refers to the accounting required for organizations such as legislative bodies and charities that are not focused on generating profits. Nonetheless, to have the funds necessary to continue to serve the public, not-for-profit organizations such as the American Red Cross and the United Way must distribute and manage funds, maintain a budget, and plan for future projects, just like for-profit companies. Government and not-for-profit organizations must also report their financial activities so taxpayers and donors can see how funds are spent and used.

Are there accountants who focus just on taxes? State and local governments require individuals and organizations to file tax returns annually. **Tax accounting** involves preparing taxes and giving people advice on tax strategies. Preparing a firm's taxes can be complicated and is ever changing. Consequently, companies often have tax accountants on staff or hire self-employed tax accountants or outside tax-accounting firms, such as H&R Block or Jackson Hewitt, to prepare their taxes.

Accounting is so important to a business that accountants of all kinds are in high demand. ■ **TABLE 15.2** outlines the many different types of accountants and what each does.

TABLE 15.2	Accountants in High Demand
Certified management accountant	Provides financial information to managers and other corporate decision makers "inside" a corporation and helps formulate policy and strategic plans.
Certified public accountant (CPA)	Provides financial information to stockholders, creditors, and others who are "outside" an organization. CPAs are licensed and must satisfy rigorous requirements.
Independent auditor	Provides a company with an accountant's opinion that attests to the accuracy and quality of a company's financial report. Independent auditors are not otherwise affiliated with companies for which they offer opinions.
Public accountant	Provides a broad range of accounting, auditing, tax, and consulting activities for individual and corporate clients. Not all public accountants are CPAs. Many have their own businesses or work for public accounting firms.
Private accountant	Employed by an organization for the purpose of maintaining financial control and supervising the accounting system.
Tax accountant	Assists taxpayers in the preparation of tax returns. Taxpayers can be individuals or corporations. Corporate tax accountants assist decision makers in strategic plans to minimize tax obligations.

Accounting Standards and Processes

Are there specific standards accountants must adhere to? For any financial information to be useful, it is critical that the information is accurate, fair and objective, and consistent over time. Therefore, accountants in the United States follow a set of **generally acceptable accounting principles** (GAAP), which are standard accounting rules defined by the Financial Accounting Standard Board, an independent organization.

Although GAAP consists of general rules, they are often subject to different interpretations, which can lead to problems. In 2002, Congress passed the **Sarbanes-Oxley Act** (SOX), which was created to protect investors from corporate accounting fraud. The act was passed after a number of publicly traded companies, including WorldCom, Enron, and Tyco, collapsed due to very aggressive and fraudulent accounting practices. The act established the Public Company Accounting Oversight Board (PCAOB), which is responsible for overseeing the financial audits of public companies. Congress also passed The Dodd-Frank Wall Street Reform and Consumer Protection Act. One provision of the Dodd-Frank Act gives the PCAOB the power to oversee auditors of brokers and dealers in securities markets. The Dodd-Frank Act requires broker-dealers to have their financial statements certified by a PCAOB-registered public accounting firm. Read the BizChat to find out more about SOX.

Do all countries have the same accounting standards? Outside the United States, other countries have their own accounting standards, which may differ from U.S. GAAP. For example, U.S. GAAP is different from Canadian GAAP. A movement is in place toward international convergence of accounting standards to remedy these global differences. Most other countries are beginning to accept a common set of country-neutral accounting standards, which are known as *International Financial Reporting Standards*. By doing so, multinational companies with operations in the United States and other countries may avoid the need to convert the financial reports prepared to meet their own country's accounting standards into U.S. GAAP specifications. In December 2013, Mitsubishi Corporation announced that all of its financial statements, disclosures, and forecasts will be prepared in accordance with these standards.

What is the accounting process? When people think of accounting, most think of the systematic recording of a company's every financial transaction. This precise process is a small but important part of accounting called **bookkeeping**. The process of bookkeeping centers on the fundamental concept that what a company

The Cost and Benefit of the Sarbanes Oxley Act

Prior to the Sarbanes-Oxley Act being passed, several major corporate and accounting scandals cost investors billions of dollars. The act was designed to make corporations more responsible and their accounting more transparent. SOX requires publicly held companies to be audited by external auditors, even if the companies have their own in-house auditors. This regulation is meant to remove any conflicts of interest internal auditors may have had when reviewing their company's financial information.

According to a 2013 survey conducted nationally, the external audit fees needed to comply with SOX continue to rise. The survey showed there was a 38 percent year-over-year increase in audit costs, attributed mostly to the need to hire external auditors. However, most companies agree that the costs are manageable. On average, companies spend between $500,000 and $1 million annually complying with SOX. However, nearly 70 percent of the firms surveyed said that complying with the regulations has improved the internal control of their financial reporting.[7]

---

owns (its *assets*) must equal what it owes to its creditors (its *liabilities*) plus what it owes to its owners (*owners' equity*). This balance is illustrated in ■ **FIGURE 15.9** and is better described as the **fundamental accounting equation**:

Assets = Liabilities + Owners' Equity

Does the accounting equation always stay in balance? To maintain the balance of assets and liabilities plus owners' equity, accountants use a recording system called double entry bookkeeping. **Double entry bookkeeping** recognizes that for every transaction that affects an asset, an equal transaction must also affect either a liability or owners' equity. For example, suppose you start a business mowing lawns, and your initial assets are a lawn mower worth $500 and $1,500 in cash that you have saved and are willing to use to start the business. Your business's assets therefore total $2,000. Because the cash and lawn mower were yours to begin with, you do not owe anyone any money, so you have zero liabilities. If you were to close the business tomorrow, the cash and the lawn mower would belong

Assets = Liabilities + Owners' Equity

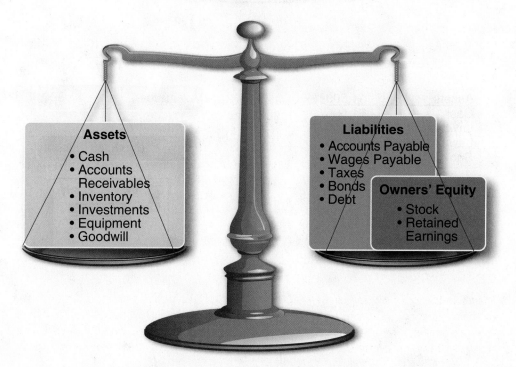

■ **FIGURE 15.9**
The Fundamental Accounting Equation

to you. Therefore, they are considered owners' equity. The accounting statement for your lawn mowing business would look like the one in ■ **FIGURE 15.10**.

Now suppose the business is growing rapidly. You realize you need to buy a bigger lawn mower. You also want to buy a snowblower so you can expand your business to include snow removal. Together these items cost $2,500. You don't have enough cash to buy either outright, so you have to borrow the money. Although you are increasing your assets with a new lawn mower and a new snowblower, you are also adding a liability—the debt you have incurred to buy the new equipment. If the business closed tomorrow, your owners' equity would not change because you could sell the lawn mower and the snowblower to pay off the debt in full (assuming you could sell the equipment for what you paid for it). The accounting statement for your lawn mower business would look like the one in ■ **FIGURE 15.11**. What would the accounting statement look like if you were to purchase office equipment with cash to help run the business, such as a computer for $900?

■ **FIGURE 15.10**
Business with No Liability
Without any liabilities, assets equal owners' equity.

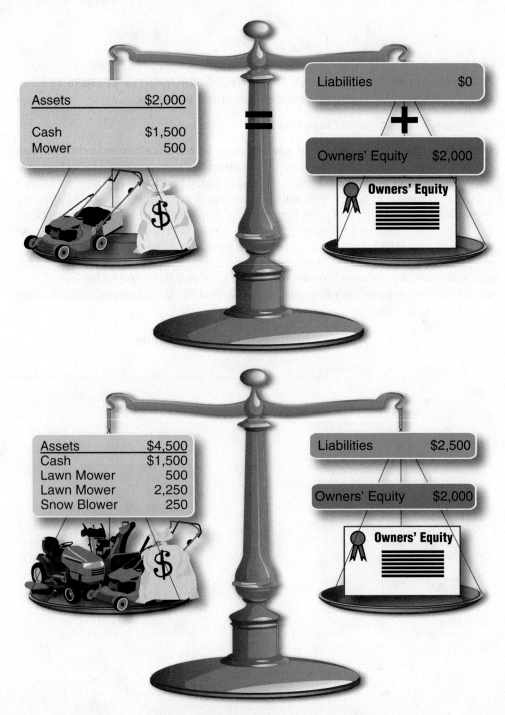

■ **FIGURE 15.11**
Business with Liability
Borrowing to buy assets increases assets and liabilities.

Accounting is necessary for businesses of all sizes to help figure out what they have the potential to do. Arnold Sawyer was initially able to handle the finances for his niece's catering business, but when business boomed, he didn't know what to do. He realized he was in over his head and convinced his niece to hire an accountant to handle these important matters. Having someone available who is knowledgeable about accounting is vital to a company's success.

Financial Statements pp. 459–469

Mateo Morales was beyond excited. He had just received a huge bonus check and was thinking about all the things he could buy with the money: a bigger flat-screen television, a weekend trip to Las Vegas—the possibilities were endless. But then Mateo came to his senses. Although he would love to buy those things, he knew the best choice would be to invest his bonus. Hopefully, over time, the investment would reap rewards, and *then* he could buy some great things. But what should he invest in? Perhaps Nike, Inc., would make a great choice—that "swoosh" is everywhere. But then there's Under Armour, Inc. Both companies are in the same industry, and their stock prices are about the same. However, the sizes of the companies are different, and so are their earnings. So is one a better investment than the other? What numbers should Mateo look at? Where can he find the information? ■

Source: Alphaspirit/Fotolia.

The formal reports of a business's financial transactions that accountants prepare periodically are financial statements. Different **financial statements** focus on different area of financial performance. They represent what has happened in the past and provide a company's managers as well as outsiders, such as creditors and investors, with a perspective of what might happen in the future. Publicly owned companies are required to publish annual reports. Annual reports contain a lot of information about the company and its financial condition and include these financial statements (see ■ **FIGURE 15.12**):

- A **balance sheet**, which shows what a company owns and what it has borrowed (owes) along with the net worth of a business.

- An **income statement**, which shows how much revenue the company generated in the period and how much money it spent. The difference between the two is the company's profit or loss.

- A **statement of cash flows**, which shows the exchanges of money between a company and everyone else it dealt with during the period—that is, the cash that came into and went out of the business.

Let's look more closely at each of these financial statements.

The Balance Sheet

What is the balance sheet used for? A balance sheet is a snapshot of a business's financial condition at a specific moment in time. It reflects what a company owns (assets), what it owes to outside

■ **FIGURE 15.12**
The Financial Statements

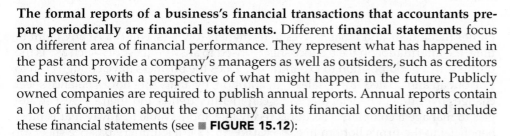

Balance Sheet	Summarizes Assets and Liabilities

- Shows a company's financial condition as of a particular date
- Summarizes Assets, Liabilities, and Owners' Equity
- Thought of as the company's report card
- A snapshot of a company's financial position

Income Statement	Summarizes Costs and Profits of Operations

- Shows total amount of sales, costs incurred to achieve sales, and other operating costs
- Reflects a profit/loss for a period of time

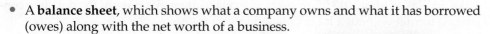

Statement of Cash Flows	Summarizes Changes in Cash Position

- Tracks changes in cash position in operations, investments, and financing activities over a particular period of time
- Similar to a checkbook register
- Reflects how efficiently management uses cash

Nike, Inc. Summary of Balance Sheet as of May 31, 2013 (in millions)					
Assets			**Liabilities**		
Current Assets			Current Liabilities		
Cash and Cash Equivalents	$	3,337	Accounts Payable	$	1,646
Short-Term Investments	$	2,628	Other Current Liabilities	$	2,280
Net Receivables	$	3,117	**Total Current Liabilities**	$	**3,926**
Inventory	$	3,434	Long-Term Liabilities		
Other Current Assets and Deferred Taxes	$	1,110	Long-Term Debt	$	1,210
Total Current Assets	$	**13,626**	Other Liabilities	$	1,292
Fixed Assets			**Total Long-Term Liabilities**	$	**2,502**
Property, Plant, Equipment	$	2,452	**Total Liabilities**	$	**6,428**
Other Assets	$	993			
Total Fixed Assets	$	**3,445**	**Owners' Equity**		
Intangible Assets			Common Stock	$	5,184
Goodwill	$	131	Retained Earnings	$	5,695
Intangible Assets	$	382	Other	$	277
Total Intangible Assets	$	**513**	**Total Owners' Equity**	$	**11,156**
Total Assets	$	**17,584**	**Total Liabilities and Owners' Equity**	$	**17,584**

■ **FIGURE 15.13**
Summary Balance Sheet for Nike, Inc.
Source: Nike.

parties (liabilities), and what it owes to its owners (owners' equity). At any point in time, the information in the balance sheet is used to answer questions such as "Is the business in a good position to expand?" or "Does the business have enough cash to ride out an anticipated lull in sales?" In addition, by analyzing how a balance sheet changes over time, financial managers can identify trends and then suggest strategies to manage a company's accounts receivable and payable in a way that is most beneficial to the firm's bottom line. ■ **FIGURE 15.13** is a summary balance sheet for Nike, Inc., as of May 2013.[8] Summary financial statements present the data in a condensed format without a lot of detailed information.

What does a balance sheet track? Balance sheets are based on the fundamental accounting equation described earlier:

$$\text{Assets} = \text{Liabilities} + \text{Owners' Equity}$$

It is important to remember that assets (the items on the left side of the balance sheet) must always equal liabilities plus owners' equity (the items on the right side of the balance sheet). Liabilities and owners' equity can also be thought of as claims on the company's assets. Let's look at each of the components of the balance sheet in more detail and then see how they all fit together to provide meaningful information.

Assets

Assets are the things a company owns, including cash, investments, buildings, furniture, and equipment. On a balance sheet, assets are organized into three categories: current, fixed, and intangible. These categories are listed on the balance sheet in order of their **liquidity**—the speed at which assets can be turned into cash:

- **Current assets** are those assets that can be turned into cash within a year. Accounts receivable, inventory, and short-term investments, such as money market accounts, are examples. As you can see in Figure 15.13, as of May 31, 2013, Nike had over $13.5 billion in current assets.

- **Fixed assets** are assets that have more long-term use, such as real estate, buildings, machinery, and equipment. Often, the value of a fixed asset, such as machinery or equipment, decreases over time due to usage or obsolescence. To compensate for such reduction in value over time, accountants use **depreciation** to spread out the costs of assets over their useful lives. Depreciation helps keep the accounting equation in balance by matching the expense of the asset with the revenue that asset is expected to generate. As of May 31, 2013, Nike had approximately $3.4 billion in fixed assets.

- **Intangible assets** do not have physical characteristics (you can't touch or see them), but they have value nonetheless. Trademarks, patents, and copyrights are examples of intangible assets. So are strong brand recognition and excellent customer or employee relations, which are otherwise known as **goodwill**. Nike's goodwill and intangible assets amounted to approximately $513 million.

Liabilities

Liabilities are all debts and obligations owed by a business to outside creditors, suppliers, or other vendors. Liabilities are listed on the balance sheet in the order in which they will come due:

- **Short-term liabilities**, also known as *current liabilities*, are obligations a company is responsible for paying within a year or less and are listed first on the right-hand side of the balance sheet. They consist of accounts payable, accrued expenses, and short-term financing. *Accounts payable* are obligations a company owes to its vendors and creditors. They are similar to those bills you need to pay every month, such as cable fees, credit card payments, and cell phone charges, and other obligations that are paid less frequently, such as your taxes and insurance. *Accrued expenses* include payroll, commissions, and benefits that have been earned but not paid to employees. Trade credit and commercial paper make up *short-term financing*. Nike had nearly $4 billion in current liabilities.

- **Long-term liabilities** include debts and obligations owed by a company that are due in more than one year, such as mortgage loans for the purchase of land or buildings, long-term leases on equipment and buildings, and bonds issued for large projects. Nike's long-term liabilities were approximately $2.5 billion.

Owners' Equity

Owners' equity is what is left over after you have accounted for all of your assets and taken away all that you owe. For small businesses, owners' equity is literally the amount the owners of a business can call their own. Owners' equity increases as a business grows, assuming the business's debt has not increased. It is often referred to as the owners' capital account.

For larger, publicly owned companies, owners' equity becomes a bit more complicated. Shareholders are the owners of publicly owned companies. Owners' equity, in this case, is the value of the stock issued as part of the owners' (shareholders') investment in the business plus **retained earnings**, which are the accumulated profits a business has held onto for reinvestment in the company. The owners' equity (stockholders' equity) for Nike was approximately $11 billion.

Analyzing a Balance Sheet

What information is important on a balance sheet? A lot of information about a company can be determined by its balance sheet. For example, just looking at the amount of inventory a company keeps on hand can be an indicator of a company's efficiency. **Inventory** is the merchandise a business owns but has not sold.

Inventory on hand is necessary to satisfy customers' needs quickly, which makes for good business. However, there are costs associated with keeping inventory, the most obvious being the money spent to purchase the merchandise. In addition to the initial cost, storing unused inventory incurs warehousing costs and ties up money that could be used elsewhere. An even worse situation can arise if the value of unused inventory decreases over time, causing a company to lose money. This is a big concern for companies like Apple, whose inventory consists of computer parts and other technology-related components that can become obsolete very quickly. Inventory turnover (how quickly inventory is sold and restocked) varies greatly by industry. Some service-related companies or online businesses, like Google Inc. or Yahoo! Inc., do not carry inventory.

Other important features to watch for on a balance sheet include how efficiently a company handles its current assets and current liabilities and whether a company is carrying too much long-term debt. These indicators will be discussed next.

Balance Sheet Ratios

How can I compare data from two different companies? Although looking at a balance sheet is a good way to determine the overall financial health of a company, the data presented on the balance sheet can be overwhelming and useless to investors if they are not organized. This is why ratio analysis is crucial when analyzing financial statements. A **ratio analysis** is used to compare current data to data from previous years, competitors' data, or industry averages. Ratios eliminate the effect of size, so you can reasonably compare a large company's performance to a smaller company's performance. There are three main ratios one can use with information from a balance sheet to determine a company's financial health and liquidity:

- **Working capital.** Current Assets − Current Liabilities
- **Current ratio.** Current Assets ÷ Current Liabilities
- **Debt-to-equity ratio.** Total Liabilities ÷ Owners' Equity

What measures how financially efficient a company is? One of the most important reasons one looks at a company's balance sheet is to determine the company's working capital. **Working capital** tells you what is left over if a company pays off its short-term liabilities with its short-term assets. It is a measure of a company's short-term financial fitness as well as its efficiency. The working capital ratio is calculated as follows:

$$\text{Working Capital} = \text{Current Assets} - \text{Current Liabilities}$$

If a company has positive working capital (its current assets are greater than its current liabilities), it is able to pay off its short-term liabilities. If a company has negative working capital (its current assets are less than its current liabilities), it is currently unable to offset its short-term liabilities with its current assets. So, even after adding up all of a company's cash, collecting all funds from accounts receivable, and selling all inventory, the company would still be unable to pay back its creditors in the short term. When a company's current liabilities surpass its current assets, many financial difficulties can occur, with bankruptcy being the most severe. It is important to watch for changes in working capital. A decline in working capital over time can indicate that a company's financial health is in trouble.

It's possible to have positive working capital but still be unable to handle a large, unexpected cash need. This is the situation Arnold Sawyer's niece's catering company faced when the company experienced a sudden spike in sales. Arnold did not know how they would get enough money to ramp up production to meet the new demand. A good financial manager and accountant must maintain a balance between having enough cash on hand and keeping it from being idle. Having a lot of cash on hand that is not actively being used isn't ideal either because those monies could be used to make more money for the business, pay down its debt, or earn interest in a bank. Because of this, working capital can also be an indicator of a company's underlying financial efficiency.

What measures whether a company can pay its bills? It's hard to compare a company's efficiency to the rest of the industry or to its competitors, especially if companies vary significantly in size. The **current ratio** (sometimes called *liquidity ratio*) is a measurement used to determine the extent to which a company can meet its current financial obligations. The current ratio is calculated as follows:

$$\text{Current Ratio} = \frac{\text{Current Assets}}{\text{Current Liabilities}}$$

Look back at Figure 15.13. Nike's current ratio ($13,626 ÷ $3,926) equals 3.47. As an individual measure, the current ratio tells you that Nike had over three times as many current assets as current liabilities and could pay off its current liabilities with current assets and still have had cash left over. A benchmark for a current ratio is 2:1, meaning that a company should have at least twice as many current assets as it does current liabilities. Having too high of a current ratio indicates a company may not be very efficient with its cash; having too low of a current ratio may indicate a company will face potential problems paying back its creditors. What does Nike's current ratio tell you about the company?

Can a company have too much debt? Another way to analyze the activities of a company is to use the debt-to-equity ratio. By comparing a company's total liabilities to its total owners' (or shareholders') equity, the **debt-to-equity ratio** indicates the proportion of equity and debt the company is using to finance its assets. It can give you a general idea of a company's financial leverage. As you may remember from the beginning of this chapter, *leverage* is borrowing to finance an investment. Although leverage can be beneficial by freeing up cash for additional investments, too much debt can become a problem. Companies with too much long-term debt may end up financially overburdened with interest payments. The debt-to-equity ratio is calculated as follows:

$$\text{Debt-to-Equity Ratio} = \frac{\text{Total Liabilities}}{\text{Owners' Equity}}$$

A lower debt-to-equity ratio means that a company is using less leverage and has more equity. A high debt-to-equity ratio usually means that a company has been more aggressive in financing its growth and indicates greater risk because shareholders have less of a claim on the company's assets.

To get a better idea of how ratio analysis is used as a comparison tool, look at the data in ■ **TABLE 15.3**. Although Nike and Under Armour are in the same industry, Nike is much bigger than Under Armour ($17.5 billion total assets vs. $1.16

TABLE 15.3	Comparison of Balance Sheet Data*		
Company	**Working Capital** (Current Assets − Current Liabilities)	**Current Ratio** (Current Assets ÷ Current Liabilities)	**Debt-to-Equity Ratio** (Total Liabilities ÷ Owners' Equity)
Nike	$9,700	3.47	0.58
	($13,626 − $3,926)	($13,626 ÷ $3,926)	($6,428 ÷ $11,156)
Under Armour	$702	2.64	0.50
	($1,129 − $427)	($1,129 ÷ $427)	($524 ÷ $1,053)

*Numbers in millions of dollars.
Sources: Data from Nike, Inc., Balance Sheet, May 31, 2013, and Under Armour, Inc., Balance Sheet, December 31, 2013.

million total assets in 2013), so comparing absolute numbers is not effective. But looking at ratios makes the comparison more meaningful. How do you think the balance sheet data of the two companies compare?

Ratios can be used to neutralize variances between companies of different sizes within the same industry. When comparing companies in different industries, you need to also consider industry standards. For example, Hasbro, the toy manufacturing company, has a debt-to-equity ratio of 80.8. The debt-to-equity ratio for Pepsi is 121.5. Looking at the two companies, you might think that Hasbro has a better debt-to-equity ratio than Pepsi. However, if you consider the average debt-to-equity ratios for the toys and games industry (59.7) and the soft-drink industry (142.5), you have a better perspective. Compared to their industry standards, Pepsi actually has a better debt-to-equity ratio than Hasbro.

Income Statements

What information does an income statement show? An income statement reflects the profitability of a company by showing how much money a company takes in versus how much it spends. The difference between the two is the profit (or loss) and is referred to as the **net income** (or the net loss). The income statement also reveals if a firm is making abnormal or excessive expenditures or experiencing unexpected increases in the cost of the goods it sells or high product returns by customers.

What are the components of an income statement? Recall that the balance sheet relates directly to the fundamental accounting equation: Assets − Liabilities = Owners' Equity. Similarly, income statements also are based on an equation:

$$\text{Revenue} - \text{Expenses} = \text{Net Income (or Loss)}$$

Expenses are generally broken down into cost of goods sold (how much it costs to generate the product being sold) and operating expenses (how much it costs to run the business).

■ **FIGURE 15.14** shows a summary income statement for Nike. Let's look at each of these components and then see how they all fit together on an income statement.

Revenue

Revenue is the total income of a business. For some businesses, revenue is generated just from selling goods or performing services. If a company has several different product lines or businesses, the income statement shows each product or division in categories to distinguish how much revenue each generated. Some companies also generate revenue from investments or licensing arrangements. For example, Nike and Under Armour each have only one source of revenue: athletic clothing and accessories. Starbucks, on the other hand, generates its revenue from a variety of sources, including its stores, retail sales of packaged coffee and tea to grocers and other stores, and sales to food service organizations.[9] As shown in Figure 15.14, Nike's revenue for 2013 was over $25 billion.

Cost of Goods Sold

An income statement delineates several categories of expenses. The first category of expenses, **cost of goods sold**, comprises the expenses a company incurs to manufacture and sell a product, including the price of raw materials used in creating the good along with the labor costs used to produce and sell the items. The cost of goods sold is generally calculated by taking the beginning inventory for the year, adding any purchases to inventory, and then subtracting out the ending inventory.

■ **FIGURE 15.14**
Summary Income Statement for Nike, Inc.

Nike, Inc. Summary of Income Statement as of May 31, 2013 (in millions)	
Revenues	$ 25,313
Cost of Goods Sold	$ 14,279
Gross Profit	$ 11,034
Operating Expenses	
Research & Development	$ -
Selling and Administrative Expenses	$ 7,780
Interest Expense	$ (3)
Other Operating Expenses	$ (15)
Total Operating Expenses	$ 7,762
Net Income before taxes	$ 3,272
Income Tax Expense	$ 808
Net Income (or Loss)	$ 2,464

There are different ways to value inventory (FIFO, LIFO, and average cost), which you'll most likely learn about in a later accounting course. For now, it's enough know that when you're calculating a firm's income, you need to deduct what it paid for the goods it sold to customers, which is the cost of goods sold. Nike's cost of goods sold was approximately $14.3 billion.

When you subtract a firm's cost of goods sold from its revenue, the result is its gross profit (gross margin). **Gross profit** tells you how much money a company makes just from the sale of its products and how efficiently its managers control the cost of the goods. In addition, analysts use gross profit to calculate one of the most fundamental performance ratios used to compare the profitability of companies: *gross profit margin*. In service-related companies, generally there is no cost of goods sold, so gross profit could equal net sales or revenue. After deducting the costs of goods sold from its revenues, Nike's 2013 gross profit was approximately $11 billion.

Operating Expenses

Operating expenses are the overhead costs incurred when running a business. Operating expenses include sales, general, and administrative expenses, such as rent, salaries, wages, utilities, depreciation, and insurance. The expenses associated with the research and development of new products may also be included operating expenses. In Nike's case, another expense is the cost of managing the risk associated with changes in foreign currency exchange rates and interest rates.

Unlike the cost of goods sold, operating expenses usually do not vary with sales or production levels and are constant, or "fixed." Because fixed costs are hard to change in the short run (say, if there is an economic downturn), lenders and investors watch a firm's operating expenses closely. Managers try to keep their firms' operating expenses as low as possible but not so low that their businesses are negatively affected. The amount of profit realized from a business's operations (operating income, or net income before taxes) is determined by subtracting the company's operating expenses from its gross profit. Nike's operating expenses totaled nearly $7.8 billion in 2013.

Is operating income adjusted further? Some people believe that operating income is a more meaningful indicator of profitability than gross profit because it reflects a firm's ability to control its operating expenses. However, operating income is still not the "bottom line." Any additional income the firm earns, such as earnings from its investments, must be added to its operating income; any additional expenses, such as interest payments on its outstanding debt, must be subtracted. Finally, taxes paid to local and federal governments must also be subtracted.

What is left over after doing so is the firm's **net income after taxes**. It is usually stated on the very last line of an income statement, which is why it is often referred to as the firm's "bottom line." For publicly owned companies, however, net income may be further adjusted by dividend payments to stockholders, resulting in *adjusted net income*. Nike's 2013 adjusted net income was nearly $2.5 billion.

Analyzing Income Statements

How do I analyze an income statement? Besides looking at how effectively a company controls its expenses or how its profits compare to other firms in its industry, you should look at a firm's income statement to get a sense of its revenue growth over time. Is the firm consistently experiencing growth or merely an unusual or temporary upward spike? Equally as important are efforts to maintain and control the firm's expenses but not so much as to hurt its growth. Technology companies, for example, have large research-and-development expenditures, which are crucial to future growth and shouldn't be cut back. One of the main purposes of the income statement is to report a company's ability to generate a profit. Companies that are able to generate good profits can reinvest those profits back into the company for future growth or, for a more mature company, share the profits with its shareholders.

Income Statement Ratios

A number of ratios specific to the income statement can also be used to put a company's performance into perspective relative to its industry and competitors. Specifically, the measurements that reveal this information are as follows:

- Gross profit margin = (Revenue − Cost of Goods Sold) ÷ Revenue
- Operating profit margin = (Gross Profit − Operating Expenses) ÷ Revenue
- Earnings per share = Net Income ÷ Outstanding Shares

Let's look at each measurement in detail to understand the differences among them and how they are used to analyze a company's financial health.

How can I determine a company's overall profitability? A company's profitability and efficiency can be determined at two levels: its profitability of production and profitability of operations. The **gross profit margin** determines the company's profitability of production. It indicates how efficiently the firm is using its labor and raw materials to produce goods. The gross profit margin is calculated as follows:

$$\text{Gross Profit Margin} = \frac{\text{Revenue} - \text{Cost of Goods Sold}}{\text{Revenue}}$$

The gross profit margin should also be compared to that of prior years. Over the past few years, Nike's gross margin has basically stayed level, fluctuating between a high of 46.4 percent and a low of 43.5 percent. This indicates that this is a maturing company where rapid increases in sales due to new, innovative products are no longer occurring. The **operating profit margin** determines a company's profitability of operations. It indicates how efficiently the firm's business operations are generating a profit. The operating profit margin (or just operating margin) is calculated as follows:

$$\text{Operating Margin} = \frac{\text{Gross Profit} - \text{Operating Expense}}{\text{Revenue}}$$

The gross profit margin and operating margin are equally important to managers and investors. You may notice they are both ratios, and, as you have learned in this chapter, ratios are best used when comparing two or more companies. So how do the income statements of Nike and Under Armour compare? Look at ■ **TABLE 15.4**. Nike's gross profit margin was 43.6 percent. Under Armour's gross profit margin of 48.8 percent was slightly better than Nike's, indicating that Under Armour was a little more efficient at producing its apparel than Nike. However, Nike's operating margin of 12.9 percent was slightly better than Under Armour's 11.4 percent, indicating that Nike's business operations were slightly more efficient than Under Armour's.

TABLE 15.4	Comparison of Income Statement Data*		
	Gross Profit Margin		**Operating Margin**
Company	Revenue − COGS / Revenue		Gross Profit − Operating Expenses / Revenue
Nike	43.59%		12.93%
	($25,313 − $14,279)/$25,313		($11,034 − $7,762)/$25,313
Under Armour	48.76%		11.36%
	($2,332 − $1,195)/$2,332		($1,137 − $872)/$2,332

*Numbers in millions of dollars.
Sources: Data from Nike, Inc., Balance Sheet, May 31, 2013, and Under Armour, Inc., Balance Sheet, December 31, 2013.

How much of a company's profit belongs to its shareholders? The portion of a company's profit allocated to stockholders on a per-share basis is determined by calculating the **earnings per share** (EPS). EPS is calculated as follows:

$$\text{EPS} = \frac{\text{Net Income}}{\text{Outstanding Shares}}$$

As with some of the other ratios, looking at the EPS in isolation does not provide a complete picture of an organization. For example, it might seem reasonable to assume that a company with a higher EPS will be the better company to invest in than one with a lower EPS. However, a highly efficient company—and potentially good investment—can have a low EPS simply because it has a large number of outstanding shares. Still, shareholders and prospective investors monitor EPS closely. Nike's EPS for 2013 was 2.75 and has increased steadily over the past five years.

In some instances, the pressure of continually growing a firm's net income or EPS has led managers to "cook the books" or misrepresent financial information so that the business's bottom line appears better than it actually is. As noted earlier, such fraudulent behavior has led to the downfall of companies and is the reason why SOX Act was enacted. Therefore, it is best not to rely on any one financial measure and to look at all the financial statements and other information as a whole.

Statement of Cash Flows

What is the statement of cash flows? You have just looked at two important financial statements: the balance sheet and the income statement. The statement of cash flows (or cash flow statement) is the third important financial statement. The balance sheet is a snapshot of a company's financial position, and the income statement reflects a company's profitability during a specific period. A statement of cash flows reflects changes in a company's cash positions, similar to a checkbook register. It provides aggregate data on incoming and outgoing *cash* transactions rather than transactions that have been recorded using accrual accounting. The statement of cash flows helps to identify whether a company is managing cash flow efficiently.

As illustrated in ■ **FIGURE 15.15**, the statement of cash flows organized by the cash generated by three business activities: operating, investing, and financing.

- *Operating activities* measures the cash used or provided by the company's actual operations. This is the most important section because it shows how well a company generates cash. Unlike the other statements that show assets and revenue as accrued but not necessarily received, the operating activities section of the cash flows statement reflects what has actually been received.

- *Investing activities* shows how the company is building its capital through the purchase of property, plants (factories), equipment, and other investments.

- *Financing activities* shows the cash exchanged between a company and its owners (or shareholders) and creditors, including dividend payments and debt service.

Components of a Statement of Cash Flows

Why is the statement of cash flows important? The statement of cash flows tells a story that the income statement does not. The income statement reports revenue receipts and expense payments. Because revenue and expenses often are accrued (earned but not paid), the income statement does not tell how efficiently managers generate and use cash. The statement of cash flows, because it focuses specifically on actual cash exchanges, provides this

■ **FIGURE 15.15**
Components of a Statement of Cash Flows

Cash Flow from Operations
- Measures cash used or provided by the core business of a company.

Cash Flow from Investing
- Represents cash involved in the purchase or sale of investments or income-producing assets (such as buildings and equipment).

Cash Flow from Financing
- Shows cash exchanged between a company and its owners (shareholders) and creditors, including dividends and debt service.

important information. For example, when customers make purchases on credit, the sales are recorded in the income statement as revenue and reflected as accounts receivable on the balance sheet. However, these purchases are not included in the statement of cash flows because no cash has been received at the time of purchase. Because revenue is being generated in this situation, a company may look profitable, but until accounts receivable have been collected, the company may not have enough cash to pay its bills or to meet its payroll. Similarly, if a company purchases inventory, the transaction would be recorded as a liability on the firm's balance sheet as an accounts payable but would not be reflected on the statement of cash flows until the company actually paid the invoice with cash.

Cash flow information is useful to creditors who are interested in gauging a company's short-term health, particularly its ability to pay its bills. In addition, it signals to investors whether the business is generating enough money to buy new inventory and make investments in the business. Accounting personnel, potential employees, or contractors may be interested in cash flow information to determine whether a company will be able to afford salaries and other labor obligations.

Analyzing a Statement of Cash Flows

How is a statement of cash flows analyzed? Each section of the statement of cash flows should be looked at as well as the summary information at the bottom of the statement.

- The total cash flow from operating activities should be positive. This indicates that a business is generating cash. A negative figure indicates that the company lacks sufficient funds.
- The investing section of cash flow section shows what the company is doing with the assets used to run the business. A negative number indicates that the company is using cash to make capital expenditures and is growing. A positive number indicates that the company is receiving cash from the sale of assets, businesses, and investment securities.
- The financing section of the cash flow statement shows what the company has done over the past year to raise money. If stock has been sold or debt issued, then it could indicate that the company is raising money to finance growth. A negative figure could indicate that the company is repurchasing stock, repaying debt, or paying dividends or interest.
- The net change in cash and cash equivalents at the bottom of the statement of cash flows reflects the overall change in a company's cash position. If it is positive, it means that a company had an overall positive cash flow. If it's negative, a company paid out more cash than it took in.

Recall the balance sheet in Figure 15.13, where the first line item under current assets is cash and cash equivalents. The difference between the cash and cash equivalent figures between periods is the same value that appears at the bottom of the cash flow statement for the same period. ■ **FIGURE 15.16** shows Nike's consolidated statement of cash flows.

Look at the change in the Cash Flows from Operating Activities section. Notice that Nike used cash to pay suppliers as well as to make tax payments. The company received cash from sales and other operating activities. The Cash Flows from Investing Activities section shows that Nike used cash to purchase property, plant, or equipment as well as to purchase short-term investments. Finally, the Cash Flows from Financing Activities section shows that Nike used cash to buy back some stock as well as to make dividend or interest payments. What else does Nike's Statement of Cash Flows tell you about how the company managed its cash flow?

Mateo Morales understands that it is important to carefully look at the financial statements for both Nike and Under Armour before he invests in either

Nike Inc. Summary Statement of Cash Flows as of May 31, 2013 (in millions)		
Cash Flows provided by or used in Operating Activities		
Net Income	$	2,485
Cash received from sales	$	142
Cash paid to suppliers	$	(184)
Cash paid to employees	$	-
Tax payments	$	21
Changes in depreciation or amortization	$	513
Changes in other operating activities	$	50
Net Cash provided by operating activities	$	3,027
Cash Flows provided by or used in Investing Activities		
Additions or disposal of property, plant, and equipment	$	(650)
Sale or purchase of short-term Investments	$	(1,203)
Changes in other investing activities	$	786
Net Cash provided by investing activities	$	(1,067)
Cash Flows provided by or used in Financing Activities		
Increase or reduction in long-term debt	$	952
Increase or reduction in common stock	$	(1,289)
Payment of dividends or interest	$	(703)
Net Cash provided by financing activities	$	(1,040)
Effect of Exchange Rate Changes	$	100
Net Change in cash and equivalents	$	1,020

■ **FIGURE 15.16**
Summary Statement of Cash Flows for Nike, Inc.
Source: Nike.

company. Financial statements, including balance sheets, income statements, and statements of cash flow, reveal a great deal about the health and prospects of a company. Although the abundance of numbers and figures seems a bit over-whelming, Mateo is confident that he'll be able to analyze each company and then make a good decision once he knows what the statements all mean and how they are calculated. Having looked at the numbers, yourself, which company would you invest in?

Summary

1 What is financial management, and how do financial managers fulfill their responsibilities? (pp. 439–443)

- **Financial management** (p. 439) is the strategic planning and budgeting of corporate funds for current and future needs.

- A **financial manager** (p. 440), often the CFO of a corporation, assumes financial management responsibilities. Financial managers generally have an accounting background.

- Financial management includes forecasting short- and long-term needs, developing **budgets** (p. 441) and plans to meet the forecasted needs, and establishing controls to ensure that the budgets and plans are being followed.

2 How do companies finance their short-term business needs? (pp. 443–445)

- It may be necessary to obtain **short-term financing** (p. 444) if cash flow gaps are anticipated.

- **Factoring** (p. 445), selling accounts receivable to a commercial finance company, is an additional way of quickly turning current assets into cash.

3 What kinds of loans and grants are available to finance short-term business needs? (pp. 445–447)

- Suppliers often offer **trade credit** (p. 444), where payment is deferred for usually 30, 60, or 90 days.

- **Commercial banks** (p. 445) are another source of short-term financing and offer services such as **demand deposit** (p. 445) accounts, credit cards, business **lines of credit** (p. 445), and **secured loans** (p. 446).

- **Commercial banks** (p. 445) are financial institutions that make loans to companies, but they are not considered banks.

- **Commercial paper** (p. 448), an unsecured short-term debt instrument issued by large, established corporations.

- Grants for small businesses are generally targeted for specific research and development or scientific and technical innovation. State and local governments are better sources for business grants, though often these grants are targeted toward specialized businesses that the state or local government are trying to develop, such as child care centers, businesses that improve tourism, or businesses developing energy-efficient products.

4 What is the purpose of each type of long-term financing? (pp. 448–449)

- Large, capital-intensive projects require a different type of financing. Long-term financing is needed when companies take on expansion projects, such as securing new facilities, developing new products, or buying other companies.

- Venture capitalists, borrowed funds, or raising owners' equity are the primary means of obtaining large amounts of long-term financing.

- **Leverage** (p. 449) is using debt to finance investments with the intent that the cost of debt will be less than the rate of return on the financed investment. Using leverage can be beneficial unless too much debt is taken on.

5 What are the pros and cons of debt and equity financing? (pp. 449–453)

- Financing with **bonds** (p. 449) allows a company to use money from investors to create or obtain business assets without diluting the firm's ownership. If the interest rate of the bond is too high, it can increase the cost of the project to the point where it's not affordable or doesn't make economic sense.

- Financing with **equity** (p. 443) allows a company to retain profits and cash rather than to make interest payments and to pay back debt. The biggest disadvantage of equity financing is the dilution of ownership.

6 What are the functions of the different types of accounting? (pp. 453–456)

- **Accounting** (p. 453) tracks a business's income and expenses by recording financial transactions.

- **Corporate accounting** (p. 454) is the process of gathering and assembling data required for a firm's key financial statements.

- **Managerial accounting** (p. 454) is the process of gathering accounting information to help make decisions inside a company.

- **Financial accounting** (p. 455) is the process of gathering accounting information to guide decision makers outside a company, such as investors and lenders.

- **Auditing** (p. 455) is the process of reviewing and evaluating the accuracy of financial reports.

- **Government and not-for-profit accounting** (p. 455) is required for organizations that are not focused on generating a profit.

- **Tax accounting** (p. 455) involves preparing tax returns and giving advice on tax strategies.

7 How is double entry bookkeeping used to maintain the balance of the fundamental accounting equation? (pp. 456–459)

- **Bookkeeping** (p. 456) is a part of the accounting process that is the precise recording of financial transactions.

- Following the concept of the **fundamental accounting equation** (p. 457), where assets equal the sum of liabilities plus owners' equity, bookkeepers use a **double entry bookkeeping system** (p. 457).

- Double entry bookkeeping assures that the accounts are kept in balance. For every transaction that affects an asset, an equal transaction must also affect a liability or owners' equity.

8 What is the function of balance sheets, income statements, and statement of cash flows? (pp. 459–469)

- The **balance sheet** (p. 459) is a snapshot of a business's financial condition at a specific time. It reflects the business's **assets** (p. 460), **liabilities** (p. 461), and **owners' equity** (p. 461).

- The **income statement** (p. 459) reflects the profitability of a company by showing its revenue and operating expenses. The difference between the two is the firm's profit or loss. The income statement shows how well a company minimizes its expenses while maximizing its profits.

- A **statement of cash flows** (p. 459) is like a checkbook register and involves cash transactions only. It reveals important information about a company's ability to meet its cash obligations, such as salaries and accounts payable.

Key Terms

accounting (p. 453)
assets (p. 460)
auditing (p. 455)
balance sheet (p. 459)
bonds (p. 449)
bookkeeping (p. 456)
budget (p. 441)
capital budget (p. 441)
cash flow (p. 442)
cash flow budget (p. 442)
Certified public accountant (p. 455)
collateral (p. 446)
commercial banks (p. 445)
commercial paper (p. 448)
corporate accounting (p. 454)
cost of goods sold (p. 464)
crowdfunding (p. 447)
current assets (p. 460)
current ratio (p. 463)
debt financing (p. 448)
debt-to-equity ratio (p. 463)
demand deposit (p. 445)
depreciation (p. 461)
double entry bookkeeping (p. 457)
earnings per share (p. 467)
equity (p. 443)
equity financing (p. 448)
factoring (p. 445)

financial accounting (p. 455)
financial management (p. 439)
financial manager (p. 440)
financial plan (p. 440)
financial statement (p. 459)
fixed assets (p. 461)
fundamental accounting equation (p. 457)
generally acceptable accounting principles (p. 456)
goodwill (p. 461)
government and not-for-profit accounting (p. 455)
gross profit (p. 465)
gross profit margin (p. 466)
income statement (p. 459)
initial public offering (p. 452)
intangible assets (p. 461)
inventory (p. 461)
leverage (p. 449)
liabilities (p. 461)
line of credit (p. 445)
liquidity (p. 460)
long-term financing (p. 448)
long-term liability (p. 461)
managerial accounting (p. 454)
microloan (p. 446)
net income (p. 464)

net income after taxes (p. 465)
nonbank lenders (p. 446)
operating (master) budget (p. 441)
operating expenses (p. 465)
operating profit margin (p. 466)
owners' equity (p. 461)
peer-to-peer lending (p. 447)
private accountant (p. 455)
project budget (p. 442)
public accountant (p. 455)
ratio analysis (p. 462)
retained earnings (p. 461)
revenue (p. 464)
Sarbanes-Oxley Act (p. 456)
secured loan (p. 446)
securities (p. 448)
short-term financing (p. 444)
short-term liability (p. 461)
sinking fund (p. 451)
statement of cash flows (p. 459)
stock (p. 452)
stock certificate (p. 452)
tax accounting (p. 455)
trade credit (p. 444)
unsecured loan (p. 446)
venture capital (p. 451)
working capital (p. 462)

MyBizLab

Go to **mybizlab.com** to complete the problems marked with this icon ⭐.

✪ Self Test

Multiple Choice *You can find the answers on the last page of this book.*

15-1 **Which formula is the fundamental accounting equation?**

a. Owners' equity = assets + liabilities

b. Assets = liabilities + owners' equity

c. Owners' equity = assets ÷ liabilities

d. Liabilities − assets = owners' equity

15-2 **The role of a financial manager can best be described as**

a. outlining a company's short-term and long-term needs.

b. identifying the sources and uses of funds for company operations.

c. monitoring cash flow and investing excess funds.

d. All of the above.

15-3 **Ted White owns Soup & Salad Café. The terms of his last order for produce were 3/15 net 60. If the total amount of the order is $1,500, the discount Ted will receive if he pays the bill early is**

a. $15.

b. $30.

c. $45.

d. $60.

15-4 **Gormley Paper Products, Inc., is a privately held company with no intentions of going public or being managed by an outside group. It is looking to build a new manufacturing facility in another state. It is considering all of its financing options. Which would be a viable possibility for raising the necessary funds for the long-range project?**

a. Issuing bonds

b. Issuing stock

c. Seeking venture capital

d. All of the above

15-5 **Cash flow management is important for which business?**

a. Spring Mountain Ski Shop, which operates between November and March

b. Lederach Tea Room, which serves breakfast and lunch all year

c. Tailwinds Airlines, which just had its first stock offering

d. All of the above

15-6 **Financial accounting is the process of**

a. producing budgets and financial documents for managers.

b. producing financial documents for outside investors.

c. auditing corporate financial statements.

d. preparing federal tax returns.

15-7 **Which financial statement shows how much money a company made?**

a. Statement of cash flows

b. Inventory turnover statement

c. Balance sheet

d. Income statement

15-8 **Hunter Wentworth is reviewing last quarter's financial statements and realizes that there has been an increase in working capital. The most likely cause for an increase in working capital is a(n)**

a. decrease in long-term liabilities and an increase in total assets.

b. increase in current assets and a decrease in current liabilities.

c. decrease in current assets and an increase in current liabilities.

d. increase in long-term liabilities and a decrease in total assets.

15-9 **Which of the following reflects a company's financial leverage?**

a. Gross profit margin

b. Operating profit margin

c. Debt-to-equity ratio

d. Earnings per share

15-10 **Maureen found an old barn that would be a perfect location for her restaurant and catering business. She opened a Kickstarter account to begin to raise funds for the business. Maureen is taking advantage of**

a. crowdfunding.

b. microloans.

c. peer-to-peer lending.

d. social media investing.

True/False *You can find the answers on the last page of this book.*

15-11 Factoring can be a good source of cash by selling accounts receivable.

☐ True or ☐ False

15-12 A risk of using credit cards to finance business activities for a sole proprietor is that a default could ruin the owner's personal credit.

☐ True or ☐ False

15-13 A project budget includes all the costs necessary to operate an organization, including inventory, sales, manufacturing, marketing, and operating expenses.

☐ True or ☐ False

15-14 A ratio analysis can be used to better compare companies of different sizes.

☐ True or ☐ False

15-15 The income statement is analogous to a checkbook register because it records the cash generated by a business.

☐ True or ☐ False

Critical Thinking Questions

♻ **15-16** Jason owns a sandwich deli that offers delivery service. Because of the quality of the service and the sandwiches, Jason is experiencing increased demand for his products, especially in his town's business district. He now wants to buy a food truck to operate from 10:00 A.M. to 2:00 P.M. in the business district and stop his delivery service.

   a. What methods of financing, if any, should Jason consider to purchase the food truck?

   b. What information will Jason need to help make his decision?

   c. How might the financing decisions change if Jason also decides to open another store in the neighboring residential area?

♻ **15-17** What are the key financial statements, and what is the importance of financial statements? What information does each contain? Which statement do shareholders typically find most useful? Why? What about independent contractors considering working with a firm?

♻ **15-18** The text lists only a few ratios that are used to analyze financial statements. Research three more ratios, explain how they are calculated, and explain why they are important to financial analysis.

Team Time

INDUSTRY ANALYSIS

Assemble into groups of four or five.

Process

Step 1. As a group, choose an industry and then have each group member pick a company in that industry. The company should be publicly traded so that financial records are easily available.

Step 2. Each group member should review the annual report and the three key financial statements for the chosen company and prepare a brief analysis of the company's financial situation. Then calculate the ratios covered in this chapter and find three other ratios that are meaningful to your analysis.

Step 3. When your report is completed, combine your information with the information from other members of your group into an industry analysis and determine how each company compares to its industry. Did the

Team Time *(continued)*

conclusions from your independent analysis change once you saw the analyses of other companies in the industry?

Step 4. As a group, prepare a presentation summarizing your findings for the industry and each company in the industry and present it to the class.

Ethics and Corporate Social Responsibility

GETTING TO THE BOTTOM OF THE SARBANES-OXLEY ACT

It's been over a decade since President George H. W. Bush signed the Sarbanes-Oxley Act into law. The intent of the law is to protect investors from accounting fraud. Reports indicate that complying with the law's requirements has cost U.S. businesses tens of millions of dollars but that it has been effective.

Exercise

Research the history behind the Sarbanes-Oxley Act as well as current compliance with the act's provisions. Then prepare a brief report summarizing your answers to the following questions.

Questions for Discussion

15-19 What changes did the act bring to companies' auditing practices?

15-20 Discuss whether the act has been successful.

Web Exercises

15-21 Balancing a Budget
Companies are not the only entities that must create budgets. Cities, states, and other governmental agencies must also prepare budgets, but unlike corporations, they can raise or lower taxes to help balance their budgets. Raising taxes is not always politically popular. Lowering taxes helps get a politician votes, but it is not always fiscally prudent. What would you do if you were just hired to close a $4 billion budget deficit for New York City? Find out by playing Balance: Gotham Gazette's Budget Game (search for it on Google).

15-22 Successful Social Funding
Suppose you want to start a business and have decided to finance it with funds raised on a crowdfunding website. Research two or three different crowdfunding sites. What are the similarities and differences between them? Which site would you choose, and why?

15-23 Exploring Career Possibilities
Visit job search sites, such as Monster.com, and find postings for financial managers and accountants. What are the job specifications and requirements? What

companies are advertising the openings? Are these careers you are interested in pursuing? Why or why not?

15-24 Securing Financing
Go to the website of a local bank and research its options for short-term business financing. What are the terms of its small business loans and lines of credit? Does it offer other commercial financing options, such as factoring? If you were going to open a small business, how would you go about financing it, based on what you've learned?

15-25 Analyzing the Competition Using Ratios
Using MSN Money (under Guided Research, Research Wizard, Comparison) or Yahoo! Finance (choose a specific company, then Competitors), pick an industry (such as telecommunication services) and then two companies within the industry (such as Verizon, AT&T, or T-Mobile) and do a ratio comparison similar to what was done in the chapter with Nike and Under Armour. Write a summary citing your conclusions from the analysis.

MyBizLab

Go to **mybizlab.com** for Auto-graded writing questions as well as the following Assisted-graded writing questions:

15-26 Discuss the role of independent auditors for a company. Over the past decade, why have independent auditors been under scrutiny by the government?

15-27 Sally owns a small women's apparel design company. Because of the poor economy, her sales have been slow, and she is barely able to make payroll. Last week, she received a surprise order for a large quantity of designs from one of her lines. She'll need to order material and other supplies but doesn't have the cash to pay. What are her options?

References

1. Apple, Inc., *2013 10-K (Annual Report)*, October 30, 2013, http://files.shareholder.com/downloads/AAPL/2996388487x0xS1193125-13-416534/320193/filing.pdf (accessed March 3, 2014).
2. "6 Sources of Bootstrap Financing," www.entrepreneur.com/money/financing/selffinancingandbootstrapping/article80204.html.
3. Thomson Reuters, *PayNet Small Business Lending Index, December 2013–January 2014*, https://paynetonline.com/Portals/0/Images/SBLI/sbli.pdf.
4. U.S. Small Business Administration, "Microloan Program," http://sba.gov.
5. Christina Warren, "Pebble Smart Watch Delivers on Kickstarter Promise and More," August 31, 2013, http://mashable.com/2013/08/31/pebble-smart-watch-review (accessed March 3, 2014).
6. Herón Márquez Estrada, "Carver County Contrite about Tax Goof, but Residents Fuming," *Minneapolis-St. Paul Star Tribune*, December 12, 2007, www.startribune.com/local/west/12448481.html.
7. "2013 Sarbanes-Oxley Compliance Survey," May 2013, www.protiviti.com/SOXSurvey (accessed March 4, 2014).
8. Nike, Inc., *2013 Annual Report*, May 31, 2013, http://investors.nikeinc.com/files/doc_financials/Annual-Reports/2013/docs/nike-2013-form-10K.pdf (accessed March 4, 2014).
9. Starbucks Corporation, *2013 Annual Report*, September 29, 2013, http://investor.starbucks.com/phoenix.zhtml?c=99518&p=irol-reportsannual (accessed March 5, 2014).

Chapter 16

Investment Opportunities in the Securities Market

▶ Investment Fundamentals

Lecretia Washington works hard for her money, and she knows she needs to start saving toward big goals, such as buying a new car, taking a vacation, buying a house, and, eventually, retirement. But it seems as if there is never enough money to set aside after paying her daily and monthly expenses. How can she begin to save toward achieving her long-term goals?

▶ Investing in Stocks

Gina has accumulated over $10,000 in her savings account, and is thinking of investing the money in the stock market. She doesn't know where to start. What kind of information should she look at to determine what are good investments for her?

▶ Investing in Bonds

Dennis Sanchez is starting to think about retirement. He's interested in making some low-risk investments that will also generate income. Dennis believes investing in bonds might be his best option. What type of bonds should he investigate?

▶ Mutual Funds and Other Investment Opportunities

Keri and Alex Young recently got married and want to start investing in their future immediately. After their wedding, honeymoon, and moving expenses, they have only about $3,000 to invest. Would mutual funds be a good place for them to begin investing?

OBJECTIVES

1 How do risk-return relationships, risk tolerance, and asset allocation relate to the fundamentals of investments? (pp. 477–482)

2 How do companies issue stocks? (pp. 482–484)

3 What are the different categories of stocks, and how are stocks traded? (pp. 484–488)

4 What is stock performance, and what are the factors that lead to changes in the price of a stock? (pp. 488–490)

5 How do companies issue bonds? (pp. 490–491)

6 What are the different types of bonds, and how is bond risk evaluated? (pp. 491–495)

7 What are the different types of mutual fund investments? (pp. 495–499)

8 What are other investment opportunities besides stocks, bonds, and mutual funds? (pp. 499–500)

MyBizLab®

⭐ **Improve Your Grade!**

Over 10 million students improved their results using the Pearson MyLabs.
Visit **mybizlab.com** for simulations, tutorials, and end-of-chapter problems.

Investment Fundamentals pp. 477–482

Lecretia Washington works hard for her money, and every penny she earns has a specific purpose: rent, gas, clothing, food, and entertainment. She is trying to set aside money on a regular basis, but it's difficult. Any extra funds are often set aside to meet short-term goals, such as buying a new car or taking a vacation. Her long-term goals, such as buying a house and saving for her retirement, seem a long way off and hard to reach. Why hasn't her savings grown to meet her long-term goals? How can she save with an eye toward achieving her long-term goals while not neglecting her current needs and short-term goals? ∎

Source: Karen Roach/Fotolia.

Although it may not seem like much, putting away a few dollars each week can really add up. Depositing funds into a bank and earning interest on the funds is a good way to get your money to make *more* money for you.

The Risks and Rewards of Saving and Investing

Why is it important to put money into a savings account? As a young adult, you have time on your side. If you continue to save regularly, your savings will accumulate. How much you end up with depends on three factors: how long you save, how often you add to your savings, and the interest rate your savings earn. The sooner you begin to save and the more frequently you put money into savings makes a big difference in terms of the amount you will accumulate during your lifetime. This is due to the concept of **compound interest**: The interest you earn on your initial savings periodically gets adding to the total amount you have saved and begins earning interest as well. Over time, the process continues, and you accumulate more and more money. Put another way, your savings "snowball" over time due to compound interest.

To illustrate the power of having your savings work for you, consider the following situation. Suppose that your grandparents had started a savings account for you the day you were born. Every month, they deposited $100. By your sixteenth birthday, your grandparents have put aside $19,200. Assuming you don't touch the account and just let it earn interest, at a 2.5 percent average interest rate the account balance after 16 years would be $23,578. In other words, you will have earned $4,378 by doing nothing more than letting your money sit in a savings account. (Note that interest rates on savings accounts since 2008 have been closer to 0 to 0.25 percent.)

Now suppose you have the choice of using the money to buy a car or continuing to save it. Either way, your grandparents will stop contributing to your savings account. As tempting as it is to buy a new car, your father explains that if you save your money instead, and your money continues to earn 2.5 percent interest each year, when you are 65 it will have grown to $115,192. So, again, by doing nothing but earning interest, you have grown your money to a substantial amount. But is this all you can do? There are other alternatives to savings that may make your money grow to even greater amounts.

Why isn't saving enough? While saving is important, it isn't the only way to make money. The Federal Deposit Insurance Corporation (FDIC) insures most savings accounts up to $250,000, so you may be convinced this is a good low-risk strategy since you're guaranteed to receive your money at any time, plus the interest it has earned. However, depending on the amount and timing of your long-term needs, the amount your money will earn in a savings account might not be enough to reach your goals. The interest rates for savings accounts and other short-term, low-risk investments have been at historically low levels over the past decade. In addition, your savings are further compromised by taxes and inflation (see the BizChat box). To reach your long-term financial goals, you'll most likely need to have your money work harder by investing in securities, such as stocks, bonds, or mutual funds.

Continuing the scenario from earlier, now consider that instead of keeping your grandparents' gift in a savings account, you decide to invest the funds in a group of conservative stocks that would earn 8 percent per year on average. In this case, when you reach 65, you would have over $1 million—$1,172,973!

Investment Risk

Isn't investing too risky? As our example illustrates, when you invest money rather than saving it in a bank, your money will have the potential to grow even more. **Investing** is buying or otherwise obtaining an asset with the expectation of achieving a future profit. Investing and saving are fundamentally different because of the different risks related to each of these types of activities. Savings is associated with very little, if any, risk. In contrast, investing has some inherent risk because there is a chance you could lose part or all of your investment.

There is a direct relationship between risk and return for all securities, with the least risky investments offering the lowest amount of return and vice versa. This relationship is known as a **risk–return relationship**. ■ **FIGURE 16.1** shows the risk–return relationships of various types of savings and investment options. As you can see, the least risky investments offer the least amount of return. If reducing your risk is a necessity, then to acquire the same amount of money you would with a riskier investment, you will need to increase the amount you save and/or the length of time it's saved or invested. Or you could lower your expectations about the amount of money you will ultimately accumulate.

■ **FIGURE 16.1**
Risk-Return Relationships

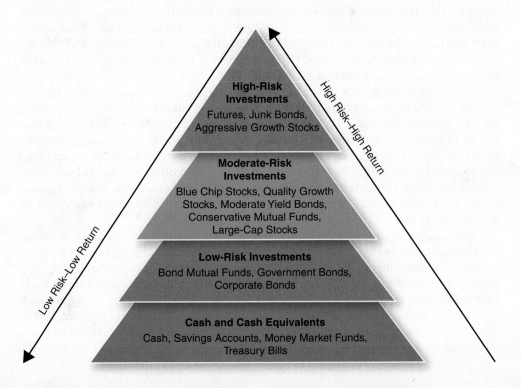

I Can't Lose Money by Saving, Right?

It's much safer to simply save your money in a bank account than risk losing it in investments, right? Perhaps. But there are two forces beyond your control that you must consider: inflation and taxes. Even after diligently saving, there is still a distinct possibility that you might, over time, lose money due to the effects of inflation and taxes.

Let's say you save $10 each month for three years in a savings account that earns 3 percent annually (although many savings accounts currently earn far less interest than this). If you didn't withdraw any money, at the end of the three-year period, you would have $377.15. That's pretty good considering that if you had just put the money under your mattress for safekeeping, at the end of three years, you would have only $360. So, just by putting the money in a savings account, you have earned $17.15. Or have you? Unfortunately, you have to pay taxes on that $17.15. Assuming you're in tax bracket in which your income is taxed at 15 percent, you will owe $2.57 to Uncle Sam. This will reduce your earnings to $14.57, so the total amount in your account will be $374.57.

Now, suppose inflation is running at a rate of about 2.5 percent per year. This means that every dollar you have loses two and a half cents every year in buying power because prices in the economy are going up by that same percentage. Therefore, had you just put $360 under your mattress, after three years, because of inflation, it's spending power would amount to only $351.00 ($9.00 of it eroded due to loss of its purchasing power).

Even if you kept your money in a savings account and not under a mattress, it would lose value due to inflation. Recall that after taxes, you had $374.57. Even though that's what you have in savings, after inflation, its buying power will be only $365.21. The entire earnings your savings has generated is almost lost because of two things you had no control over: inflation and taxes. In fact, you're almost where you started: You earned only $5.21 after three years of saving!

Although savings accounts help offset the effects of inflation, they do not help you build wealth. A savings account is great to keep so you have some "rainy-day" money available to pay for unexpected emergencies. However, if you are trying to save for a house, college tuition, or retirement, it would be very hard to meet your goals by investing in this type of low-interest account. To achieve big goals, you'll need to make your money work harder.

In addition to the specific risk associated with each investment, there is also a more general risk associated with the overall market, known as **market risk**. Events such as wars and other political turmoil, changes in interest rates, terrorist attacks, recessions, and natural disasters will cause a decline in the market as a whole. For example, after the September 11 terrorist attack in New York City, the financial markets reopened one week later. The Dow Jones Industrial Average lost 7.1 percent of its value by dropping 684 points that day. By the end of the week, the Dow had fallen 1,370 points (14 percent). It's largest one-week drop in history. The Dow dropped significantly again, losing 777 points (7.0 percent) on September 29, 2008, at the beginning of the financial crisis of 2007–2008.

How do I know my risk tolerance? To determine whether investing is worth the risk, you must know how much risk you can tolerate. The less tolerant you are of risk, the fewer investment chances you can and should take. Most of us have a good idea of how tolerant we are toward risk. Your current behavior with money and other situations are indications of whether you should invest conservatively, moderately, aggressively, or somewhere in between. There are also several tests that you can take online to help quantify your tolerance level. Another way to figure out your risk tolerance is by asking yourself this question: "Are my investments going to keep me awake at night with worry?" If the answer is yes, then you need to reduce the risk level of your investments and perhaps lower your expectations accordingly. Over time, your tolerance to risk can change depending on your knowledge level and financial situation. As you become more secure financially, you might be willing to risk losing some money for the possibility of earning more. As you begin to learn more about investing, you may be more comfortable with evaluating some of the risks you will take, thus increasing your risk tolerance.

How do I start investing? Depending on how much money you have to invest, you might start investing by purchasing stock in one or two companies or by investing in a mutual fund. We'll discuss these investment alternatives as well as some others in more detail later in the chapter. As you invest, you should keep in mind two strategies that will help to minimize your risk: *diversification* and *asset allocation*. Both strategies center on the notion of not putting all your eggs in one basket to avoid the possibility of losing everything because of one bad investment.

What is diversification? **Diversification** is having a variety of investments in your portfolio, such as different types of companies in different industries. For example, assume you have $6,000 to invest. You have the option of putting all your money into one company that is strong and has great potential for long-term growth and profits. You also have the option to put $1,500 into four different companies, each in a different industry. Each of these companies is also thought to be a great investment.

The first option may be great if the one company has unlimited success, but economic factors, consumer demand, competition, and other factors can hamper a company's ability to make money constantly. If you instead diversify and invest in several companies that are in different industries, you can insulate yourself from the negative effects that could affect a company or industry. If this happens, the chances are that one or more of the companies in your investment portfolio will be performing well and will offset the losses of the company that is not. Even if you experience a loss, it is not likely to be as large as it would be if you were invested in only one company.

Keep in mind, however, that diversification does not protect against market risks that affect the overall market, as discussed earlier. And, if your portfolio is diversified but still heavily invested in a particular industry or market segment, your portfolio could still be significantly affected by events that affect that industry. Such was the case for many investors who were caught in the dot-com crash. In the late 1990s, greater universal access to the Internet created an opportunity for a new untapped market and unlimited business opportunities. Many investors threw caution to the wind and heavily invested in novel Internet-based businesses referred to as dot-com businesses. Investors were buying stocks of companies without regard to the specific business strategy and financial forecasts. In 1999, for example, over 450 new businesses, mostly Internet and technology related, entered the stock market. Of those, almost a quarter doubled in price on the first day of trading.[1] But soon afterward, many of those same companies filed for bankruptcy. Pets.com, famous for its sock-puppet commercials, traded on the market for the first time in February 2000 and then filed for bankruptcy nearly nine months later. The burst of the dot-com bubble contributed to a mild economic downturn in the early 2000s.

What is asset allocation? **Asset allocation** refers to how you structure your portfolio with different types of assets (stocks, bonds, mutual funds, real estate, and so on) to reduce the risks associated with these different types of investments. Studies have shown that most of an investment portfolio's performance is determined by the allocation of its assets, not by the selection of individual investments or how well a person has timed his or her buying and selling of the investmtents.[2]

Properly allocating your assets is particularly important if you want to minimize your investment risk in the highly volatile markets that have been common since the new millennium. The allocation of assets in a portfolio depends on your risk tolerance and can change as an investor reaches certain milestones, such as getting married, paying for college tuition, or retiring. ■ **FIGURE 16.2** shows how a person's risk tolerance affects the asset allocation mix in a portfolio.

Are there rules and regulations that govern investing? The **Securities and Exchange Commission** (SEC) is a U.S. federal agency created to protect investors and maintain fair and orderly securities markets. It governs the securities exchanges; the people who issue, trade, and deal securities; and those who offer investment advice. The SEC also establishes regulations that govern how companies disclose information to the investing public as well as the investment banks creating the investment products the public buys. In doing so, the SEC controls

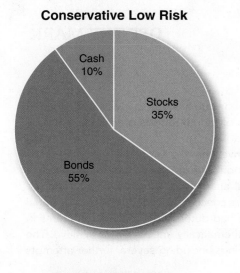

Conservative Low Risk

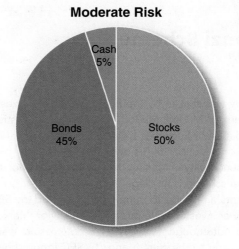

Moderate Risk

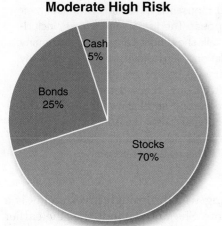

Moderate High Risk

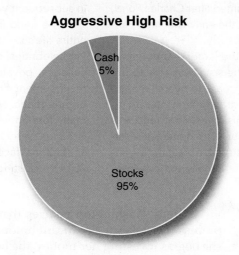

Aggressive High Risk

■ **FIGURE 16.2**
Asset Allocation Risk Based on Risk Tolerance

what should be put in the initial documentation (the prospectus) of an initial bond or stock issue.

In addition, the SEC prohibits fraudulent activity with regard to the offer, sale, and purchase of securities, such as insider trading. **Insider trading** is the buying and selling of securities based on information that has not been disclosed to the public. For example, suppose you own 1,000 shares of XYZ Corp. stock and you're on friendly terms with the company's CFO. The CFO tells you the company is going to claim bankruptcy next week, so you sell all your shares before the information is publicly released. If you do this, you have taken part in illegal insider trading.

The government has made a pointed effort to stop insider trading on Wall Street. One of the most high-profile insider trading cases of the past decade involved the domestic celebrity Martha Stewart. In 2001, Martha Stewart sold almost 4,000 shares of ImClone stock after receiving pertinent information about the company from her friend, ImClone's CEO. Stewart was convicted of insider trading and spent five months in prison and an additional five months under house arrest. More than a decade later, Rajat Gupta, a former board member for Goldman Sachs Group Inc. and head of McKinsey & Co., was convicted of insider trading when he leaked important investment information discussed at a Goldman Sachs board meeting to Raj Rajaratnam, a hedge fund founder and friend of Gupta. The conviction was upheld in March 2014.

Although there are inherent risks when investing your money in stocks, bonds, or mutual funds, if the investments are within your risk tolerance level and your portfolio is well diversified with good asset allocation, you can mitigate the risks and allow your money to work harder for you.

> **THE LIST**

Personal Finance Blogs Worth Reading

1. Budgets are Sexy! (www.budgetsaresexy.com)
2. Create My Independence (www.createmyindependence.com)
3. Making Sense of Cents (www.makingsenseofcents.com)
4. Money Ning (http://moneyning.com)
5. Money Under 30 (www.moneyunder30.com)
6. PT Money (http://ptmoney.com)
7. The College Investor (http://thecollegeinvestor.com)
8. Young Adult Money (www.youngadultmoney.com)
9. Young Cheep Living (www.youngcheapliving.com)
10. Young Finances (http://youngfinances.com/blog)

The Madoff Ponzi Scheme

OFF THE MARK

In late 2008, the securities industry was shaken by the incredible fraudulent activities of Bernard Madoff. Madoff, a former NASDAQ (National Association of Securities Dealers Automated Quotations) chairman and founder of his own investment securities company, was found guilty of running the world's biggest Ponzi scheme. A Ponzi scheme is an illegal financial arrangement in which payments are made to current investors with monies obtained by newer investors. Eventually, the scheme collapses when there are not enough new investors to cover the money withdrawals made by the current and former investors. Ponzi schemes are named after Charles Ponzi, who used this type of arrangement in the early twentieth century to defraud investors.

Madoff's Ponzi scheme is by far the largest—amounting to losses of more than $50 billion.[3] The scam was able to run for many years due to the general increase in overall market gains, which made believable the extraordinarily steady returns Madoff fraudulently reported his investment fund was earning. In addition, Madoff continued to generate interest in his fund and attract new investors by creating a general aura of exclusivity. He often intentionally turned down would-be investors who were anxious to invest after hearing the enthusiastic word-of-mouth reports of financial gains by current investors.

Reports of the investment scam actually began nearly 10 years prior to Madoff's arrest, when Harry Markopolos, a rival investor, financial analyst, and certified fraud examiner, informed the SEC of his concern over Madoff's possible illegal behavior. Markopolos had determined that Madoff's remarkable results were mathematically impossible to achieve. The SEC ignored his warnings, including several further attempts in subsequent years.

The fraud impacted thousands of victims who saw their entire life's savings disappear. The list is very diverse, including celebrities, such as talk show host Larry King, and many colleges, private foundations, large investment and money management firms, insurance companies, and not-for-profit organizations. Many lost billions. The scheme also involved many foreign funds from Europe and Latin America.[4] Madoff is currently serving a 150-year prison sentence in a federal correctional facility. Five of his aides were also found guilty in 2014 of assisting Madoff in his elaborate scheme.

Lecretia Washington realizes that building wealth through investments is a process that takes a significant amount of time. She understands that the earlier she begins investing her money, the better. So what did she do? In addition to her traditional savings account, Lecretia decided that establishing separate investment accounts to meet her short-term goals and long-term goals was her best option. She also realized that she needed some professional help, so she is looking into taking a class on investing at the local community college as well as hiring a financial adviser or a brokerage firm. What investment options would work best for you? You'll learn more about how to invest in the next section.

Investing in Stocks pp. 482–490

Source: sergey p/Fotolia.

Gina Smith graduated from college last year. She has a great job in a city near where she grew up, so she is able to live with her parents so she can save a lot of money. Now, after having worked for six months, Gina has accumulated over $10,000 in her savings account, and she wants to do something different with it. She is not interested in buying a house or condominium in the near future. She is thinking she should invest the money in the stock market, but she doesn't know where to start. What kind of information should she look at to determine what are good investments for her? ■

Companies sometimes issue stock to help finance on-going and expanding operations. In this section, you'll learn about how stocks are initially issued, the differences between various types of stocks, how stocks are bought and sold, and the factors that affect stock prices.

Primary and Secondary Security Markets

How are stocks issued into the primary market? Securities transactions take place in the **capital market**, an arena where companies and governments raise long-term funds by selling stocks and bonds and other securities. The **primary market** is the part of the capital market that deals specifically with new bond and stock issues.

As you learned in Chapter 15, the first sale of stock to the public by a company is called an initial public offering (IPO). An investment bank, such as Goldman Sachs (often referred to as the *underwriter*), helps the company to raise money by issuing and selling securities in the primary market and serves as an intermediary between the company issuing the stock and the investors who purchase it. Before the sale of the stock, **investment bankers**, specialists who assist in the sale of new securities, prepare financial documents that must be filed with the SEC. A prospectus is one of the required documents. A **prospectus** is a formal legal document that provides details about an investment. The prospectus helps investors make informed decisions about the new investment. The investment bankers also determine what the best timing is for the public sale and determine the initial selling price of the stock. The advising investment bank, along with several other investment banks, forms a group or syndicate to underwrite the IPO; that is, they take the responsibility and risk of selling their allotment of the issue. The syndicate then purchases the stock and sells it to the public. It can take months or years to successfully structure an initial public stock offering. Investment banks use the time before the offering to generate interest in the stock so it sells for more than what the members of the syndicate paid for it.

The initial buyers of an IPO are mostly large institutional buyers, such as insurance companies and large corporate pension plans, and a few high-profile individuals. The underwriters want to sell the issue as quickly as possible to receive a return on their purchase. Because institutional buyers are more likely to buy large quantities of the IPO, it is ultimately more efficient to sell to them than to sell the IPO in little pieces to individual investors. A very small portion of the IPO is actually available to individual investors, but since the quantity is limited, these shares are generally hard to get.

How are stocks exchanged after the IPO? After the IPO, those investors who bought shares may eventually want to sell them. The subsequent sale of stock after an IPO is done in the secondary market. The **secondary market** refers to the market in which investors purchase securities from other investors rather than

---

Comparing IPOs

On August 19, 2004, Google sold shares to the public for the first time. At the time, many questioned whether the company was overvalued at $27 billion. Some people felt that Google was overhyped and were resigned to wait and see if the "scrappy" company could surpass its bigger and more established competitors (Yahoo! and Microsoft). Fast-forward to the present. Google's stock is near $600 per share, up significantly from the $85 per share it was initially offered at.

More recent IPOs for shares of Facebook, Twitter, and LinkedIn haven't done as well, however. Facebook's IPO in early 2012 wasn't met with nearly the skepticism that Google's IPO was. Nonetheless, the stock was up 20 percent at the six-month mark but down nearly 30 percent by the end of the first year. Twitter was on a similar path as Facebook at its six-month mark.

Investing in stocks requires extensive analysis to ensure that you're making the right decision. Stocks that have been on the market for a while are easier to analyze because you can examine their history. IPOs, however, by their very nature, have no historical information on which to base any analysis. Why do you think the stocks of Facebook and Twitter are behaving differently than Google's?

directly from an issuing company. We'll discuss the actual process of buying and selling securities later, but for now, let's look a bit more closely as to what kinds of stocks are available.

Types of Stocks

Are all stocks the same? There are two main types of stocks that companies issue: *common* and *preferred*. **Common stock** is a class of ownership in which the stockholders have the right to elect a board of directors and vote on corporate policy. They are also entitled to dividends, if the company chooses to pay a dividend. A **dividend** is a distribution of a portion of the company's earnings as determined by its board of directors. Common stockholders have the least priority as far as ownership and repayment in the event a company goes out of business. **Preferred stock** is a class of ownership in which the preferred stockholders have a claim to assets before common stockholders if a firm goes out of business. In addition, preferred stockholders receive a fixed dividend that must be paid before any dividends are paid to common stockholders. Preferred shareholders, however, do not have voting privileges.

Stocks can also be categorized based on the type of company and expected growth and return of the investment, as illustrated in ■ **FIGURE 16.3**:

- **Income stocks** are issued by companies that pay large dividends, such as utility companies like Duke Energy, Exelon Corporation, and Exxon Mobil Corporation. Investors who are looking for reliable income from their investments and not appreciation (an increase) in the value of their shares often invest in income stocks.

- **Blue chip stocks** are issued by companies that have a long history of consistent growth and stability. Blue chip companies pay regular dividends and maintain reasonably steady share prices. General Electric, IBM, The Walt Disney Company, and 3M are examples of companies that are considered blue chip stocks.

- **Growth stocks** are stocks that are expected to generate revenues and earnings that increase at a faster rate than the average company's does. These stocks pay little or no dividends. Instead, the firms that issue them retain their earnings and reinvest them in new projects that fuel the growth of the firms. Investors that buy growth stocks hope that their value will increase. Growth stocks tend to be riskier than other stocks because these companies often do not have proven track records. Tesla, Trulia, and Google can be considered growth stocks.

- **Value stocks** are stocks that are viewed as being priced lower than what they should be based on the earnings and financial performance of the companies

■ **FIGURE 16.3**
Types of Stocks
Sources: Left to right, top to bottom: Ion Popa/Fotolia; Lasse Kristensen/Fotolia; Fotolia; Gladcov Vladimir/Fotolia; niro-world/Fotolia; zero13/Fotolia.

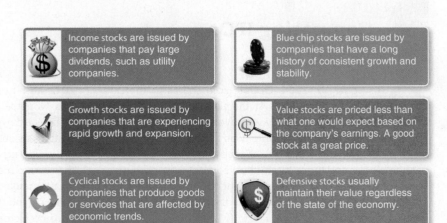

that issue them. The prices of these stocks have the potential to increase when the market adjusts for their incorrect valuation. Value stocks lie at the opposite end of the spectrum as growth stocks.

- **Cyclical stocks** are issued by companies that produce goods or services that are affected by economic trends. The prices of these stocks tend to go down when the economy is in a recessionary period and go up when the economy is healthy. Examples of cyclical stocks include airlines, automobiles, home building, and travel.

- **Defensive stocks** are the opposite of cyclical stocks. Defensive stocks are issued by companies that produce staples such as food, drugs, and insurance products and usually maintain their value regardless of the state of the economy.

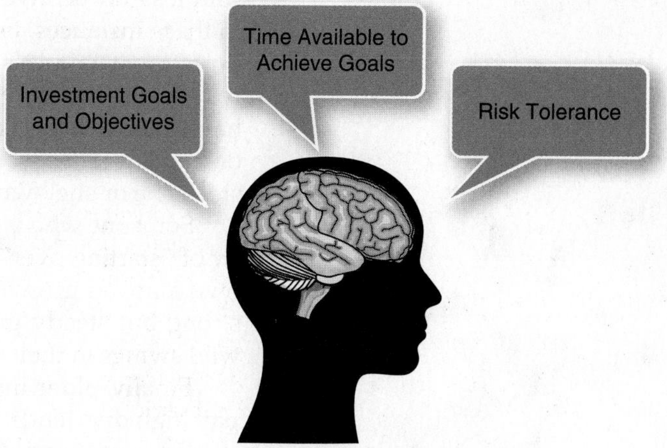

Investment Goals and Objectives

Time Available to Achieve Goals

Risk Tolerance

**■ FIGURE 16.4
Things to Consider
Before Investing**

No one type of stock is considered better than another. Investors have to decide for themselves which type of stock fits best with their financial goals and objectives. A diversified portfolio may include many different kinds of stocks.

How do I choose which stocks to invest in? The answer to this question begins with determining your *investment goals and objectives*, the *time* in which you have to achieve your goals and objectives, and your *risk tolerance*, as shown in **■ FIGURE 16.4**. Once you know those constraints, you'll be better able to determine what investment strategy best fits your needs.

Many investors begin investing when they enroll in their 401(k) retirement plan at work. This is a good way to start because the portfolio manager of the 401(k) has narrowed down your investment choices for you. Although there are plenty of professionals to help you, when you start investing on your own, you should research each potential investment for yourself. You should consider a stock's basic fundamentals, past performance, published analyses, as well as the economy in general and how it could affect the stock:

- **Fundamentals.** You can start by evaluating a company's fundamental data, such as its earnings, financial statements, and key ratios (discussed in Chapter 15).

- **Past performance.** Often it's helpful to know how a company and its stock have performed in the past. You can study financial charts to compare the historical performances of multiple companies and observe trends in the data.

- **Published analyses.** Additionally, you might want to consider the opinions of industry analysts who independently research and analyze the investment potential of companies.

- **Economy.** Current events and changes in economic conditions could affect a stock's price, so you need to be aware of these changes.

All of this information is available in newspapers, on the Internet, or in your public library. Unfortunately, it takes lots of time and research to determine what the right investments are for you. Keep in mind that if the process were easy and straightforward, we'd all be rich! In reality, there is much variability and unpredictability in the market; even with the best analysis, you still might end up with unfavorable results. But, with time on your side, the chance of rebounding from a poor investment outcome is pretty good. Even though the stock market does fluctuate, it has provided a consistent return over a long period of time.

Why is it important to set goals before investing? Assuming you can select companies that you believe will generate a profit based on your research and stock fundamentals, you also need to determine what kind of company meets your investment goals and objectives. Younger investors are often investing to meet long-term goals, such as buying a house or funding a retirement account. Young couples may be investing to fund retirement or college accounts for their children. In these instances, investing in companies that are in their growth phases—where investment gains result from the rapid appreciation in a stock's value—may be the way to go. The downside is that these companies are also more likely to quickly have their stocks lose value, too. However, someone who is 22 and just starting his or her career may be able to withstand temporary downfalls in the prices of the stocks he or she owns.

Someone who is 55 is probably nearing retirement and can't endure the possibility of "starting over" if his or her portfolio does very poorly. This individual might own a mix of growth companies as well as more stable companies that experience strong but steady growth. Companies such as these generally do not experience wild swings in their stock prices and typically offer dividends to their stockholders.

Finally, older investors often invest in companies that are less risky, and that pay high dividends to earn income to help fund their retirement years. Dividends provide another source of income to stockholders beyond appreciation in stock prices. So, for example, a person who is 70 years old and retired and who relies on income from his or her investments can't afford to lose much money and is thus very risk averse. He or she would be wise to invest mostly in companies that offer high dividends and generally experience only mild swings in the prices of their stocks. The world of investing is an ongoing experience; if you choose to invest, it is an experience you should not take lightly. You must be smart about investing and continue to do your research—even if you choose to have someone else guide you in the investment process.

Where are stocks bought and sold? Before the Internet, people could buy stocks only with a **stockbroker** (or broker), a professional who buys and sells securities on behalf of investors. Stockbrokers also provide advice as to which securities to buy and sell and receive a fee for their services. Today, people can buy and sell stocks directly on the Internet for a small fee through discount brokers such as E*Trade or TD Ameritrade. Discount brokers offer limited advice and guidance and are substantially cheaper than financial services firms, such as Bank of America or JP Morgan, which employ full-service brokers.

Whether you use a discount broker or full-service broker, the process of buying stock is done through a **stock exchange**, an organization that facilitates the exchange of stocks and other securities between brokers and traders. One of the largest and most dominant stock exchanges is the **New York Stock Exchange** (NYSE). In 2007, the NYSE merged with the fully electronic stock exchange Euronext and is now operated by the combined organization **NYSE Euronext**. In 2008, NYSE Euronext acquired the American Stock Exchange, which was formerly another independent U.S. stock exchange. Now, as a part of NYSE Euronext, the exchange deals primarily with small-cap companies, exchange traded funds, and other more advanced investments, and is known as **NYSE Amex**.

NYSE Euronext is the world's largest stock exchange. Nearly 70 percent of the world's trading equities are listed on it.[5] The **NASDAQ** was the world's first electronic stock exchange, and is the world's second-largest stock exchange.[6] Some securities might be too small to meet the requirements to be traded on a formal exchange such as the NYSE or NASDAQ. These small securities are traded directly between investment professionals and are referred to as **over-the-counter (OTC) stocks**.

How are stocks traded? There are two ways securities are traded: on the exchange floor and electronically. A typical trade (purchase or sale of a security) with a broker on the NYSE exchange floor is similar to the process depicted in ■ **FIGURE 16.5**. Although most trades are done electronically, the chaotic buying and selling process on the floors of exchanges that you see in movies and on television still goes on.

Over 8,000 companies have issued stock and are listed on the NYSE Euronext and NASDAQ exchanges as well as on many other smaller or international stock exchanges.[7] Unlike the NYSE, where trades can be made electronically or on the trading floor, the NASDAQ stock exchange has always been completely electronic. Through

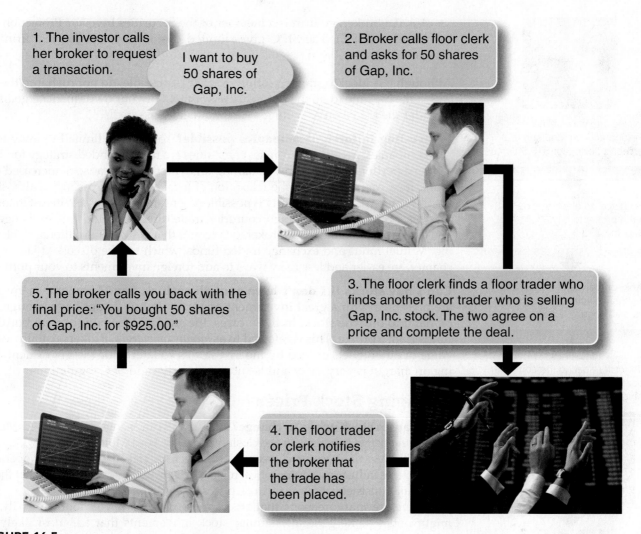

■ **FIGURE 16.5**
Execution of a Simple Stock Trade on the New York Stock Exchange
Sources: Clockwise from top left: WavebreakmediaMicro/Fotolia; spaxiax/Fotolia; Ene/Shutterstock.

the NASDAQ system, over 2 billion shares of stock trade hands every day via a large and immensely reliable coordinated network of computer systems.[8] Trades with the NYSE still require a broker to initiate the order. The broker will place the order electronically into the system, and when the order is received, the electronic exchange tries to match a buy order with a similar sell order. After the order has been executed, the broker notifies the buyer and seller of the successful completion of the trade. ■ **FIGURE 16.6** shows the steps involved with an electronic stock trade.

How is a broker selected? The process of selecting a broker can almost be as complicated as the process of selecting a type of investment. Before you decide on a broker, the SEC suggests you do the following:[9]

- Think about your financial objectives.
- Speak with potential brokers at several firms. Ask each about their education, investment experience, and professional background.
- Inquire about the history of the brokerage firm. You can find out if any disciplinary action has been taken against a firm or a broker online through NASD BrokerCheck. Your state securities regulator can also tell you if a broker is licensed to do business in your state.
- Understand how the brokers are paid. The type of commission a broker receives might affect the advice that is offered. Also, ask what fees or charges you will be required to pay on the account.

1. You log into your online brokerage account and see that Gap, Inc. is selling for $18.50/share.

2. You place an electronic order with the broker to buy 50 shares of Gap, Inc.

3. Broker receives the order and transmits it electronically to the stock exchange.

4. The order goes to the computer dedicated to handling all orders coming from your broker.

5. The stock exchange tries to match your order electronically with a sell order from someone else.

6. If a match is made, a notification is sent to your broker who then sends you a confirmation.

7. You receive and review the transaction confirmation.

■ **FIGURE 16.6**
Execution of an Electronic Stock Trade
Sources: Top, iofoto/fotolia; bottom, Oleksiy Mark/Fotolia.

- Ask if a brokerage firm is a member of the Securities Investor Protection Corporation (SIPC). The SIPC gives limited customer protection if a firm goes bankrupt.

Although it is ideal to start investing as early as possible, do not rush into the process. Take the time to do the necessary assessment of your own financial goals and consider the risks you're willing to take to meet those goals.

Is investing in foreign companies possible? You are not limited to investing in U.S. companies. Investing in foreign companies is a recommended strategy for diversifying a portfolio and possibly obtaining higher returns. Because of increased communication capabilities and the relaxation of legal barriers, investing in almost any foreign or international company is possible. There are a few ways to invest in foreign markets. Some stocks of foreign countries trade directly on the U.S. exchanges, or you can open an online stock brokerage account that allows international stock trading. Mutual funds and exchange traded funds, which will be discussed later in this chapter, are easier and less risky ways to add foreign investments to your portfolio.

Can I buy stocks if I don't have enough cash on hand? Sometimes investors are presented with a great investment opportunity but do not have enough cash on hand to buy the stock. In these cases, the stock can be bought with borrowed funds from a broker. This is referred to as *buying on margin*. Brokers usually use the value of other assets owned by the investor as collateral for the investment. Buying on margin is very risky and is subject to fairly rigid SEC regulations.

Changing Stock Prices

What causes stock prices to change? Stock prices can change rapidly. ■ **FIGURE 16.7** reflects the percent changes in the closing prices for Ford Motor Company; Gap, Inc.; and Philip Morris over a two-year period. Even though the companies operate in three diverse industries—automotive, retail, and consumer goods—notice that there is something consistent about their stock prices: Each changes daily.

There are many reasons that stock prices change. If you look carefully, you might notice some generally similar stock movements that are most likely due to overall market variations—that is, where the market is having an "up" day or "down" day overall due to a significant occurrence such as a news event or a general change in economic conditions. There are also some variations particular to the company or the industry.

Ultimately, though, a stock's price is ultimately derived by the forces of supply and demand. On the one hand, if investors like a stock, they will buy more of it, reducing its supply and pushing up its price. On the other hand, if investors don't like a stock, more investors will sell the stock than buy it, creating a greater supply of it and causing its price to drop.

What influences investor behavior? Why might an investor like a stock one day and not like it another day? In general, most investors will invest if a stock's price reflects what they think a company is worth or will be worth. (A company's stock price times total the number of shares it has outstanding determines the firm's capitalization, or value.)

Often, investors not only look at how a company is currently performing but also consider a company's expected future growth in anticipation of increased earnings or profits. If investors become concerned that something negative will affect a company's value, they will sell their shares, and the stock price will fall. Conversely, investors will purchase a stock as a result of good news about a company, and the price of the stock will rise.

For example, ■ **FIGURE 16.8** shows the change in the stock price of Microsoft Corporation during the period of June 1, 2013, to December 30, 2013. During this time period, there were three significant events that affected the amount of the stock traded (known as the volume) and its price. On July 15, 2013, Microsoft's CEO, Steve Ballmer, announced Microsoft was reorganizing. The reorganization

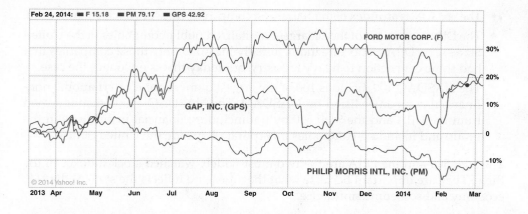

■ **FIGURE 16.7**
Comparison of Stock Performance
Source: Yahoo.

reflected a strategy shift whereby Microsoft would focus on making hardware and online services and apps designed to work across multiple electronic devices. What happened to the company's share price after the announcement? It suffered a 13 percent decrease. Then in August, Ballmer announced he planned to retire within a year. The day of the announcement, the stock price climbed by 7 percent.

On September 3, 2013, Microsoft announced its intention to acquire Nokia's mobile phone and services business. This purchase underscored Microsoft's new strategic plan announced earlier. It's stock decreased slightly, but Nokia's stock price surge by 31 percent for the day. By the end of the year, Nokia's stock price had nearly doubled. Notice in the figure how the stock price and the volume of shares traded reacted to these key events.

What else influences stock prices? Stock prices also change in reaction to broader news based on economic forecasts, industry or sector concerns, or global events. How investors react is based on their confidence in the financial markets at the time, which can lead to longer periods in which a stock market increases or decreases in value. A **bull market** indicates increasing investor confidence as the market continues to increase in value. In a bull market, investors are motivated by promises of gains. A **bear market**, however, indicates decreasing investor confidence as the market continues to decline in value.

How do you know how the overall market is doing? To see how the markets for stocks are doing overall, investors pay attention to stock market indexes, such as Standard & Poor's 500 Composite Index (S&P 500), the DJIA, and the NASDAQ 100. An **index** tracks and measures the combined value of a large group of stocks. Different indexes track different stocks, based on characteristics they share, such as similarity in their sizes or the industries in which they operate:

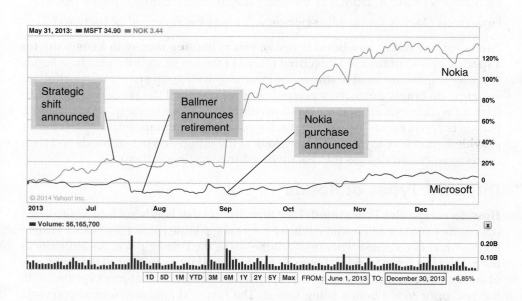

■ **FIGURE 16.8**
Change in Price and Volume of Microsoft Stock from June 1, 2013, to December 30, 2013.
Source: Yahoo.

- The S&P 500 is an index of the 500 largest companies, most of which are American.
- The DJIA is an index of the 30 largest capitalized public companies in the United States. The DJIA composite index initially included only those companies that had some connection to heavy industry, but today that is no longer the case.
- The NASDAQ 100 includes 100 of the largest domestic and international non-financial companies listed on NASDAQ. The NASDAQ 100 is distinguished from the DJIA and the S&P 500 by not including financial institutions in the group and including companies incorporated outside the United States.

The S&P 500 and the DJIA are the two most widely watched stock indexes of the three. They are important because what they measure reflects the state of the U.S. economy and sometimes influence.

How do I make money investing in stocks? There are two ways to earn money by investing in stocks. Most investors hope to make money in the stock market through capital appreciation, that is, "buying low and selling high." or buying a stock at one price and then later selling the stock at a higher price. When this happens, the investor incurs a **capital gain**. If there is a decrease in value between the purchase price and the selling price, the investor incurs a **capital loss**. Investors can also make money by receiving dividends, though not all companies pay dividends.

Remember Gina Smith? When Gina was researching stocks, she reviewed various financial documents, such as the annual reports of the companies as well as analyst reports and company and industry news. When she found a few stocks she was interested in buying, she used a discount broker to help finalize her purchase. By keeping abreast of industry news and monitoring stock indexes, she's able to see how well her stocks are doing relative to other stocks. Recently, the value of her portfolio has been going up. She's hoping to eventually sell some of her stocks for more than she originally paid for them.

Investing in Bonds pp. 490–495

Source: qingwa/Fotolia.

Dennis Sanchez just turned 55 years old and is starting to think about retirement. He has been investing money in his company's 401(k) plan for many years and wants to do some investing on his own. Now that he is closer to retirement, he would like to receive some income from his investments. He would also like to take a less risky approach by moving some of his money into more conservative investments. Dennis decides investing in bonds is the best way to meet both of these goals. How does Dennis know what bonds will meet his financial objectives? ■

Bonds are like IOUs; as a bond investor, you're lending money to a company for a specific period of time at a specified interest rate. Investors often purchase bonds as a way to generate reliable streams of income as well as diversify their portfolios.

How do bonds diversify a person's portfolio? When the stock market is performing well, bonds are generally not performing well; conversely, when the stock market is down, bonds are usually up. Because of this contrary relationship, bonds provide a good way to diversify. Let's look at the different types of bonds and their characteristics and discuss the risk involved in investing in them.

Different Types of Bonds

How do companies issue bonds? If a firm decides that bonds are a good financing option, they contact a financial advisory firm to help issue them. Like stocks, issuing bonds is a very complex. The timing of the issue, the issuing price, the structure of the bonds, and other factors have to be carefully evaluated. Similar to the initial sale of stocks, a financial advisory firm prepares the documents that must be filed with the SEC prior to the bonds being issued. The financial advisory firm also consult with rating agencies that assess the issuer's creditworthiness. The firm's credit rating will have an impact on the interest rate of the bonds. The less creditworthy the firm is, the higher the interest rate will have to be to attract buyers.

In addition to charging the company issuing the bonds a fee for these services, the financial advisory firm makes money by forming and managing a group of other financial advisory firms to underwrite, or purchase, the newly issued bonds. The bonds are issued at a discounted price to these firms, and then they attempt to sell them to investors at higher prices.

What are the characteristics of a bond? The key characteristics of a bond are as follows: its maturity date, par (face) value, and coupon (interest rate):

- The **maturity date** of a bond is the date on which the bond matures and the investor's principal is repaid. Short-term bonds (generally with a maturity of less than five years) pose less risk to investors than long-term bonds and therefore have lower interest rate than long-term bonds do.

- The **par (face) value** is the amount of money the bondholder will get back once a bond matures. Most newly issued bonds sell at par value. Treasury bills, discussed later in this section, sell for less than par (face) value.

- The **coupon** is the bond's interest rate. It is a percentage of the par (face) value. So, a coupon of 10 percent on a bond with $1,000 par value would generate $100 in interest a year. Although most bonds pay interest twice a year, some bonds offer monthly, quarterly, or annual payments. Originally, bonds had coupons that the investor would tear off and redeem to receive interest. Today, investors do not need to tear off coupons; instead, interest payments are transferred electronically to the investor's account.

Are there different types of bonds? As shown in ■ **FIGURE 16.9**, bonds are categorized primarily by the type of entity that is issuing the bonds:

- Corporate bonds
- Government bonds
- Municipal bonds

What are corporate bonds? **Corporate bonds** are debt securities issued by corporations. There are several types of corporate bonds:

- **Secured bonds** are backed by collateral, an asset of the corporation that will pass to the bondholders (or be sold to reimburse them) if the corporation does not repay the amount borrowed. Revenue streams that come from

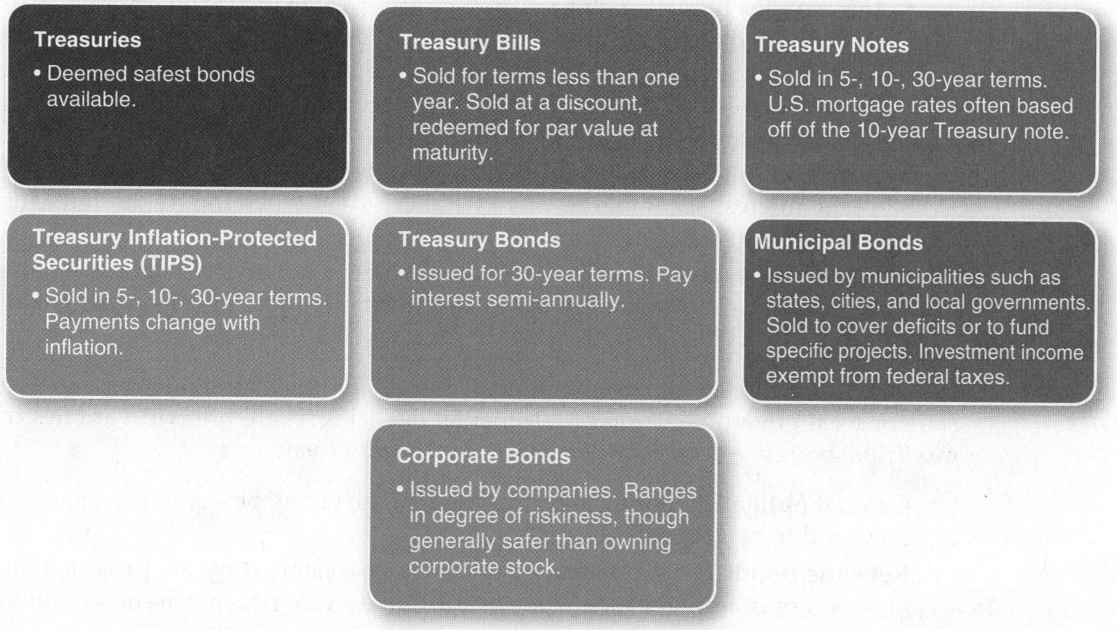

Treasuries
- Deemed safest bonds available.

Treasury Bills
- Sold for terms less than one year. Sold at a discount, redeemed for par value at maturity.

Treasury Notes
- Sold in 5-, 10-, 30-year terms. U.S. mortgage rates often based off of the 10-year Treasury note.

Treasury Inflation-Protected Securities (TIPS)
- Sold in 5-, 10-, 30-year terms. Payments change with inflation.

Treasury Bonds
- Issued for 30-year terms. Pay interest semi-annually.

Municipal Bonds
- Issued by municipalities such as states, cities, and local governments. Sold to cover deficits or to fund specific projects. Investment income exempt from federal taxes.

Corporate Bonds
- Issued by companies. Ranges in degree of riskiness, though generally safer than owning corporate stock.

■ **FIGURE 16.9**
Types of Bonds
Source: Mint.com.

the project the bonds were sold to finance can also be used as collateral. *Mortgage-backed securities* are special secured bonds that are backed by real property owned by a corporation.

- **Debenture bonds** are unsecured bonds, backed only by a corporation's promise to pay.
- **Convertible bonds** are another modification of traditional bonds that give a bondholder the right (but not the obligation) to convert the bond into a predetermined number of shares of the company's stock. Convertible bonds generally carry lower interest rates because the investor is able to convert them to stock, which offers an advantage regular bonds don't.

What are government bonds? Government bonds are debt securities issued by national governments; U.S. government bonds are considered to be the safest of investments because the government backs them and the risk of default is very low. These bonds are divided into several categories based on their maturity:

- **Treasury bills (T-bills)** are bonds with maturities ranging from 4 weeks to 52 weeks. Instead of paying interest, T-bills are sold at a discount, so you pay less up front for them. When the bond matures, you receive the full face value of the bond. The difference between the purchase amount and the face value is the interest. For example, to buy a $1,000 T-bill, you might pay $975 up front. When the T-bill matures 26 weeks later, you would receive the face value of $1,000. The $25 difference is interest earned.
- **Treasury notes (T-notes)** are bonds that mature in 2, 3, 5, 7, and 10 years. Interest is paid semiannually. You can hold T-notes to maturity, or you can sell them prior to their maturity. When a T-note matures, you receive its face value.
- **Treasury Inflation-Protected Securities** (TIPS) protect investors from inflation, as their name implies. A TIPS's principal is adjusted to the U.S. Consumer Price Index (CPI). When the CPI rises, the principal adjusts upward and vice versa. Interest is paid semiannually. Although the interest rate remains constant, the interest payment adjusts as the rate is multiplied by the inflation-adjusted principal amount, thus providing the protection against inflation. TIPS are available in 5-, 10-, and 30-year maturities.
  - **Treasury bonds (T-bonds)** are bonds that mature in 30 years and pay interest semiannually. When a T-bond matures, you receive the face value.
  - **Floating rate notes** (FRNs) are debt instruments issued for a term of two years. FRNs pay interest quarterly. The interest payments are variable and are based on discount rates for 13-week T-bills. The price of an FRN may not be its face value, but when an FRN matures, you are paid its face value.
  - **U.S. savings bonds** aren't sold on the secondary market. You can only purchase them directly from the government. Traditionally, U.S. savings bonds have been given as gifts to babies to help finance their education once the bonds mature. Savings bonds are issued at face value and as of January 1, 2012, can be purchased only electronically. There are two types of savings bonds:
- **Series EE bonds** have a 20-year maturity but will pay interest up to a total of 30 years. Interest accumulates monthly and is paid when the holder redeems the bond.
- **Series I bonds** have an interest rate that is part fixed and part variable. The variable part is reset annually to match the inflation rate. In this regard, they are similar to TIPS.

What are municipal bonds? Municipal bonds (or *munis*) are bonds issued by state or local governments or governmental agencies. There are two varieties of municipal bonds: *general obligation bonds* and *revenue bonds*:

- **General obligation bonds** are supported by the taxing power of the issuer, so they tend to be very safe.
- **Revenue bonds** are supported by the income generated by the projects they finance. For example, the New Jersey Turnpike Authority may issue $1 billion

in municipal revenue bonds to finance the construction and renovation of the I-95 corridor that runs through the state. The tolls collected on that portion of I-95 would be used to pay the interest and principal of the bonds.

The advantage of buying municipal bonds, FRNs, and government bonds is that the interest generated from many of them are exempt from federal income tax and, in many cases, state and local income taxes as well.

What are serial bonds? Municipal bonds, as well as some corporate bonds, are often issued as serial bonds. **Serial bonds** have a series of dates on which portions of the total bond mature, unlike traditional bonds, which are paid back to the investors all at once on one date. Serial bonds are advantageous to the issuer because they reduce the overall interest expense of the bond issue. Additionally, serial bonds allow the issuer to time the maturity dates to the income from the project financed by the bonds. Thus, for the toll road example, the serial bonds would mature as phases of the toll road are completed and tolls from those portions of the road are generated.

What are callable bonds? Most corporate and municipal bonds remain outstanding until their maturity dates. With **callable bonds**, however, the issuer can either repay investors their initial investment at the maturity date or choose to retire the issue early and repay investors at the "callable date." The issuers of callable bonds often exercise their early repayment options when interest rates have fallen, and the bonds can be refinanced at lower rates. For this reason, callable bonds pay higher interest rates than similar noncallable bonds.

Are bonds a risky investment? Relative to stocks, bonds are viewed as a conservative investment for several reasons:

- The investor has a legal promise that his or her initial investment will be returned; stocks offer no such promise.

- The investor has a legal promise that he or she will receive periodic interest payments at a fixed rate; a firm can pay a dividend on the stock it has issued but isn't obligated to.

- Historically, the bond market overall has been less volatile; thus, there is less variability in the prices of bonds.

However, bonds are not entirely risk free. Those carrying a higher risk will provide a higher return to the investor, but they are also associated with more risk. There are different types of risk that affect bonds; some are listed in ■ **FIGURE 16.10**.

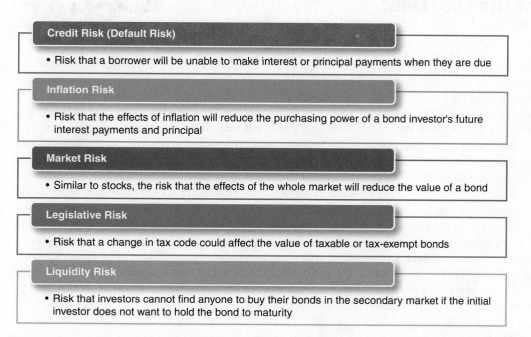

■ **FIGURE 16.10**
Types of Bond Risk

Credit Risk (Default Risk)
- Risk that a borrower will be unable to make interest or principal payments when they are due

Inflation Risk
- Risk that the effects of inflation will reduce the purchasing power of a bond investor's future interest payments and principal

Market Risk
- Similar to stocks, the risk that the effects of the whole market will reduce the value of a bond

Legislative Risk
- Risk that a change in tax code could affect the value of taxable or tax-exempt bonds

Liquidity Risk
- Risk that investors cannot find anyone to buy their bonds in the secondary market if the initial investor does not want to hold the bond to maturity

TABLE 16.1	Bond Rating Scales Used by Moody's and Standard & Poor's	
	Bond Rating	
Risk	**Moody's**	**Standard & Poor's**
Lowest risk	Aaa	AAA
Low risk	Aa and A	AA and A
Medium risk	Baa	BBB
High risk	Ba and B	BB and B
Highest risk	Caa/Ca/C	CCC/CC/C
In default	C	D

How can I tell how safe a bond is before investing? Before bonds are issued, the creditworthiness of the bond issuer is evaluated by a rating agency, such as Moody's or Standard & Poor's, the two major rating agencies, and the bonds are later assigned an investment grade. The higher the grade rating, the lower the bond's credit risk is, reducing the likelihood of its default (not being paid back).

■ **TABLE 16.1** shows the bond rating scales used by both Moody's and Standard & Poor's. To improve their investment grade, many bonds are backed by insurance policies that guarantee repayment to the bondholders in the event the issuer goes into default. Those bonds with the lowest ratings—and the most risk—are known as **junk bonds**. Because of their high risk, junk bonds offer high interest rates to attract investors. Investors should clearly understand the associated risks of junk bonds before adding them to their portfolios.

Do I have to hold a bond to maturity? Although you certainly can hold a bond to maturity, many investors sell bonds, especially long-term bonds, before they mature. Just like stocks, after they are issued, bonds are bought and sold on the secondary market. (The exceptions are U.S. savings bonds, which, as noted earlier, are not sold on the secondary market.) What makes buying bonds on the secondary market very complicated is that bonds do not trade at par value but at a price

Downgrade of the U.S. Debt

The U.S. Treasury debt has always been considered among the safest investments in the world—until August 5, 2011. On that date, Standard & Poor's, one of two companies that rates the creditworthiness of bonds, downgraded the rating of U.S. Treasury bonds from AAA to AA. At that point, the bonds were rated lower than bonds issued by countries such as Britain, Germany, France, or Canada. Then, in October 2013, the rating agencies threatened to downgrade U.S. bonds again.

Why did this happen? Because in both instances, lawmakers in Washington, D.C., could not agree on a way to reduce the huge federal budget deficit. Part of an agreement to reduce the debt would have required Congress to raise the debt limit, which is the amount the government can legally finance. Many lawmakers refused to vote to increase it. But without an increase in the debt limit, the U.S. government would have been unable to make the debt payments on its current bonds and other financial obligations. Both the downgrade in 2011 and the threat of a downgrade in 2013 caused stock markets around the world to plummet. Eventually, Congress did reach a deal both times. The debt limit was raised, and stock markets subsequently rose.

Typically, a ratings downgrade would cause the interest rates on the debt to rise to compensate for the increased levels of risk. For the U.S. government, even a small increase in interest rates could mean a significant increase in debt payments, which would add to the mounting budget concerns and potentially cause a negative global economic ripple effect. However, to date, the downgrade and the threat of another downgrade has seemed to have little impact on our economy or investor confidence. In fact, the outlook for U.S. Treasury bonds seems quite positive. Why do you think the U.S. Treasury offerings are seemingly immune to the effects of a downgrade?

higher than par (at a premium) or lower than par (at a discount). Bond prices move in the opposite direction of interest rates. So, if you are trying to sell a bond that has a coupon of 10 percent and the current market interest rate in the economy is 8 percent, your bond is worth more to investors, so its price will go up. Conversely, if the current interest rate is 12 percent, then the demand for your bond will be weak because it is earning less than the current interest rate. As a result, the price an investor is willing to pay for your bond will go down.

Although not completely riskless, bonds are a good investment if you are looking for a relatively conservative investment or a steady stream of income. When it comes to investing in bonds, there are several things to keep in mind, such as the type of bond, the bond's risk rating, the face value of the bond, and the interest rate. Investors can determine a bond's risk based on an issuer's credit rating.

One thing Dennis Sanchez could do before he purchases a bond is to review the issuer's credit rating. After doing the necessary research, Dennis would then be in a good position to purchase some bonds, which would provide him with steady income as well as well as diversify his portfolio.

Mutual Funds and Other Opportunities pp. 495–500

Alex and Keri Young recently got married and want to start saving and investing for a family, traveling, and emergencies. Unfortunately, after paying their wedding and honeymoon expenses and buying a condo, they have only $3,000 left in their combined savings. Although Alex and Keri know they should have several different investments for a diversified portfolio, they feel they don't have enough money to do so, and each has an opinion as to what kind of investments to make. Alex is especially interested in investing in foreign securities but doesn't know which ones to pick. Keri wants to invest in small up-and-coming U.S. companies but needs help deciding which would make the best investment. Both Keri and Alex have heard about mutual funds but don't know much about them. What are mutual funds, and would they be a good investment option for Keri and Alex? ■

Source: Anna/Fotolia.

There are many different types of mutual funds that are available to meet a variety of investment goals. Mutual funds can provide a cost-effective and efficient way for some investors to build a portfolio with a variety of investments. In this section, you'll read about different types of mutual funds, the pros and cons of investing in them, and other investment strategies.

Mutual Funds

What is a mutual fund? A **mutual fund** is a means by which a group of investors pool money together to invest in a diversified set of investments. Suppose you want to invest in the stock market but, like Alex and Keri Young, you have only $3,000 to invest. After looking at possible investments, you realize that with $3,000, you can afford to buy stock in only one or two companies. You later learn that several of your friends have the same problem. So, as a group, you decide to pool your money and hire an expert to buy a portfolio of stocks. With this arrangement, each of you shares a proportional amount of the returns from the money you have invested as a group as well as the expenses for the investment advice and other costs of investing. If you were to do that, you would have essentially created a mutual fund.

Why are mutual funds so popular? Mutual funds are the best kind of investment for those who have little to no experience in investing or who might not have a lot of money to invest. There are many reasons why investing in mutual funds is a good strategy:

- **Diversification.** The big advantage of investing in mutual funds is diversification. Mutual funds offer small investors a cost-effective way to invest in many different types of companies and investment products. Unless you have a lot of money to invest, it's hard to buy a large variety of securities.

- **Professional management.** Professional management is another advantage of mutual funds. Someone who has a significant amount of investment experience manages each mutual fund. These professionals spend all their time researching, trading, and watching the investments that make up the funds they manage. This is likely more time than you would be able to spend if you created a similar portfolio on your own. Because their jobs depend on it, mutual fund managers have an incentive to try to ensure their funds perform at their best.

- **Liquidity.** It is easy to sell mutual funds, so you can get to your money back quickly—usually within a day. Some mutual funds, primarily money market funds, offer check-writing privileges, so accessing your money is even easier.

- **Cost.** It takes as little as $1,000 to invest in most mutual funds. Some (but not all) funds charge fees when you purchase or sell shares in the funds. We will discuss the costs of mutual funds in more detail later in the chapter.

Are there different types of mutual funds? Each mutual fund has an investment objective that dictates the types of investments the fund can hold. There are three broad groupings of mutual funds and then many different subtypes under each grouping. The three main types of mutual funds in order of risk are money market funds, fixed-income funds (bonds), and equity funds (stocks). Additionally, there is a wide assortment of funds that specialize in international investments, such as global funds, foreign funds, country-specific funds, or emerging market funds. There are also sector funds that invest in companies from a particular industry sector, such as technology, automotive, banking, and health care. Finally, there are index funds that replicate the performance of some broad market indexes, such as the S&P 500 and Dow Jones Industrial Average. ■ **FIGURE 16.11** categorizes the different types of mutual funds relative to their risks and the returns they deliver.

Risk-and-Return Relationships of Different Types of Mutual Funds

What are money market funds? **Money market funds** are the least risky because they invest in short-term debt obligations, such as T-bills and certificates of deposit (CDs). Money market funds are popular because the interest rates they earn are often nearly double what interest-bearing checking or savings accounts earn. In addition, money market funds are very liquid. You have quick access to your money, often simply by writing a check. Perhaps the only drawback of a money market fund over a traditional savings account is that the FDIC does not insure the funds. However, unlike many banks, to date, no money market fund has ever failed. Alternatively, you can invest in a *money market savings account* through a savings bank, and, as with all bank accounts, the money in that account is insured by the FDIC up to $250,000.

■ **FIGURE 16.11**
Risk and Return Relationship of Types of Mutual Funds

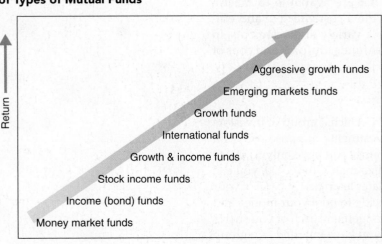

TABLE 16.2	Types of Bond Mutual Funds	
	Fund Type	**Investment Strategy**
By Type	Municipal bond funds	Invest in tax-exempt bonds issued by state and local governments. Some municipal bond funds are further specialized in bonds issued by a particular state.
	Corporate bond funds	Invest in debt obligations from U.S. corporations.
	U.S. government bond funds	Invest in U.S. Treasury or government securities.
By Term	Short-term bond funds	Invest in bonds with maturities less than two years, including T-bills, CDs, and commercial paper.
	Intermediate-term bond funds	Invest in bonds with maturities ranging between 2 and 10 years.
	Long-term bond funds	Invest in bonds with maturities greater than 10 years.

What are bond mutual funds? **Bond mutual funds** consist solely of bonds. Some bond funds are categorized by the type of bond, including municipal bond funds, corporate bond funds, and U.S. government bond funds. Alternatively, some bond funds are categorized by maturity, including long-term bond funds, short-term bond funds, and intermediate-term bond funds. ■ **TABLE 16.2** summarizes the various types of bond mutual funds.

What are stock mutual funds? **Stock mutual funds**, sometimes referred to as *equity funds*, are much more popular than bond or money market funds.[10] As ■ **TABLE 16.3** shows, similar to bond funds, stock mutual funds are broken down into various categories based on the types of companies they invest in. *Growth funds* invest primarily in companies that are in the growth phase, and *value funds* invest in stocks considered to have lower prices relative to the overall value of the companies that issued them. The size (or capitalization) of the companies they invest in is another way to categorize mutual funds. *Large-cap funds* invest in large companies, *mid-cap funds* invest in medium-size companies, and *small-cap funds* invest in small companies.

Are there funds that invest in both stocks and bonds? *Blend (or balanced) funds* invest in stocks, bonds, and sometimes money market funds to offer a mixture of safety, income, and modest appreciation. A type of balanced fund that is attractive to investors focusing on retirement planning are *life cycle funds* (also known as targeted or age-based funds). Life cycle funds invest in mutual funds from the same mutual fund family (such as Fidelity or Vanguard), and the mix of investments is managed to become more conservative as the fund approaches a target

TABLE 16.3	Stock Mutual Funds	
	Fund Type	**Investment Objective**
By Strategy	Growth funds	Invest in stocks of the fastest-growing companies. Often viewed as risky investments. Rarely produce dividend income.
	Value funds	Invest in stocks that are considered to be undervalued. These stocks are thought to be ready for quick appreciation. Some produce dividends.
By Size	Large-cap funds	Invest in companies with large (greater than $9 billion) capitalization (price times outstanding shares).
	Medium-cap funds	Invest in companies of medium capitalization—between $1 billion and $9 billion.
	Small-cap funds	Invest in companies with capitalization less than $1 billion. These companies rarely generate dividends.

date—which often closely matches an investor's anticipated retirement date. Many 401(k) plans offer life cycle funds. While life cycle funds offer a convenient "hassle-free" retirement planning option, they are not a solution for everyone, especially those who have other types of investments in their portfolio.

What are index funds? Index funds have a portfolio that consists of investments that closely match the components of a market index such as the S&P 500 or the Barclays U.S. Aggregate Bond Index. Since the investments in an index fund are not as actively managed as those in a stock or bond mutual fund, index funds have lower operating expenses and often more favorable tax consequences, which are attractive to some investors.

How do I make money investing in mutual funds? You can make money investing in mutual funds through dividends, interest, capital gains, and fund appreciation. These investment earnings are similar to those generated by individual stock holdings, although they are controlled by the fund manager and distributed to the fund owners periodically. As fund managers adjust the holdings of the fund, they buy some securities and sell others. Capital gains and losses that are incurred through selling securities are passed on to the fund owners. Your mutual fund accumulates any dividends paid by the stocks and interest paid by the bonds held by the mutual fund and periodically distributes the earnings to fund owners. Finally, mutual funds are measured by the value of the individual holdings. This measure is the **net asset value** (NAV), which is calculated at the end of each trading day. The end-of-day NAV of a mutual fund consists of the combined closing values of the stocks in the fund. The NAV increases as the securities held by the fund increase in value. If you sell your mutual fund holding at a higher NAV than when you bought it, you will generate a capital gain.

What do I need to watch out for when investing in mutual funds? Although mutual funds can be a great way to begin investing, you still need to do your homework to understand exactly what you are investing in and how risky those investments are. You also have to consider what a fund costs to invest in because that will affect how much you make from the investment. Some mutual funds, referred to as **load funds**, charge additional costs (loads) that are rolled into the cost of the funds when you buy and sell them. The ultimate decision in buying a mutual fund should be based on its expected performance and the suitability to your investments needs. If you are given a choice of similar options, try to pick a **no-load fund**, a mutual fund that does not charge a fee for buying into the fund and selling out of it. Load funds have not shown to perform better than no-load funds, so why pay more for little or no extra benefit?

In addition to the transaction fees (the loads), you should also look at the ongoing expenses that funds charge investors. These expenses are comprised of management fees, administrative costs, and 12B-1 fees (advertising fees) represented by the expense ratio (or management expense ratio). Some funds charge much higher fees than others. For example, if the fund you invest in has a 1 percent expense ratio and earns an annual return of 4 percent, you will end up with only a 3 percent return (not including any loads). In other words, the expenses will eat up one-quarter of your annual earnings. Expense ratios for funds vary widely. Some fund expense ratios exceed 1 percent. Others funds, such as index funds, have far less.

It's also important to have a good understanding about who is managing the fund and the person's success record. The same individual or group of managers often runs a fund for years. However, changes happen, so you will want to be aware of that fact.

What are exchange-traded funds? An **exchange-traded fund** (ETF) is a fund that holds a collection of investments like a mutual fund does but trades on an exchange like stocks do. The prices of ETFs change throughout the day as they are bought and sold, whereas the prices of mutual funds are determined only at the end of the trading day. Initially, ETFs gave investors a way to buy and sell a group of stocks that mirrors or that is representative of an index, such as the S&P 500. Since then, ETFs have developed into sophisticated investments that can be quite complex. Similar to mutual funds, an ETF holds a group of stocks rather than one or a few. However, ETFs often cost less because there is no need to pay investment managers to actively research and trade the stocks that make them up. Why? Because the ETFs are structured the same as the indexes they are mirroring.

In contrast, as you have learned, stocks within a mutual fund are traded, often resulting in capital gains that get passed onto the mutual fund's investors. This doesn't happen with ETFs, which makes them a low-cost way to diversify a portfolio, especially since there are a variety of ETFs like there are mutual funds. But like any investment, there are risks and other factors to consider when selecting an ETF.

Other Investment Opportunities

Besides stocks, bonds, and mutual funds, what else can I invest in? There are a couple of other types of investments beyond stocks, bonds, and mutual funds. These investments are often complicated and can carry additional risk. Generally, only advanced and knowledgeable investors tinker in these alternative investments. *Options* and *futures* fall into this category, as do *commodities*, *real estate*, and *precious metals*.

What is an option? An **option** is a contract that gives a buyer the right (but not the obligation) to buy (call) or sell (put) a particular security at a specific price on or before a certain date. It's similar to buying an insurance policy. Consider this example: Your uncle is selling a car you would love to buy but can't quite afford yet. You decide to approach your uncle with a proposal: You will save your money, and at the end of three months, you will have the right to buy the car for $15,000. For accepting this offer, you will give your uncle $250 now. Over the course of the next three months, one of three situations could occur:

1. The car could be ranked one of the best cars on the market, increasing its value from $15,000 to $18,000. You buy the car for the agreed-on price of $15,000 and then sell the car for $18,000. Taking into consideration the $250 you paid your uncle for the option of buying the car, you net $2,750 ($18,000 − $15,000 − $250).

2. The car has a major defect, and its manufacturer has issued a recall to fix it. Now, you really don't want to buy the car. Because you have only an option to buy the car, you're not obligated to purchase it, but you will still lose the $250 you paid for the option of buying it.

3. The car value's stays at $15,000, and you buy the car for the agreed-on price of $15,000, plus the initial $250.

Options work similarly to this example. When you buy an option, you're paying for the opportunity to buy an asset under certain conditions. If things go wrong, you lose only the cost of the option. If things go right, you could profit. Options are complicated and can be risky. Don't confuse option contracts with stock options your employer may offer as a benefit. The stock option from employers gives you the right to buy a specific number of shares of your company's stock at a specific time at a set price. Stock options are used as incentives to retain and motivate employees and are discussed in Chapter 9.

What are futures? A **futures contract** is an agreement between a buyer and a seller to receive (or deliver) an asset sometime in the future at a specific price agreed on today. The difference between a futures contract and an options contract is that an option contract gives you the *right* to purchase the underlying asset; with a futures contract, you have an *obligation* to purchase the underlying asset. Usually, the underlying asset is a commodity, such as sugar, coffee, or wheat. For these commodities, a price is agreed on before the actual goods are bought and sold. Futures markets also include the buying and selling of government bonds, foreign currencies, or stock market indexes.

If you hold the futures contract until it expires, you own the commodity. However, most holders of futures contracts rarely hold their contracts until they expire. Instead, the contracts are traded prior to their expiration. If the price of the commodity increases before the contract's expiration date, you make a profit. However, if the price decreases, you may lose money.

Alex and Keri Young were glad to learn about mutual funds. They still have questions, such as which types of funds will help them meet their investment goals but not keep them awake at night wondering about their safety. So they will continue to take their time and perhaps consult an investment adviser before making any final decision.

Summary

1 How do risk-return relationships, risk tolerance, and asset allocation relate to the fundamentals of investments? (pp. 477–482)

- Various types of investments have different **risk-return relationships** (p. 478). On one hand, the least risky investments offer the least amount of return. On the other hand, the most risky investments offer the greatest return.

- Investing is not for everyone, and the level and type of investments is very personal and depends on the investor's risk tolerance level.

- Investment portfolios should be allocated, or spread out, among different types of investments, such as stocks, bonds, and cash, to further reduce investment risk. **Asset allocation** (p. 480) changes as investors reach life milestones; portfolios should be adjusted and rebalanced periodically.

2 How do companies issue stocks? (pp. 482–484)

- Stocks are issued in this manner:
  - The first issue of stock is an initial public offering (IPO).
  - A financial adviser coordinates the preparation of a **prospectus** (p. 483) and files it with the **Securities and Exchange Commission (SEC)** (p. 480).
  - Financial advisory firms establish the best timing for the public sale and determine the initial selling price.
  - Banks form a syndicate to underwrite the IPO. The syndicate then purchases the stock and sells it to the public.

3 What are the different categories of stocks, and how are stocks traded? (pp. 484–488)

- There are two main types of stocks that companies issue: **common** (p. 484) and **preferred** (p. 484). Stocks can be categorized into five categories: **income stocks** (p. 498), **blue chip stocks** (p. 484), **growth stocks** (p. 484), **cyclical stocks** (p. 485), and **defensive stocks** (p. 485).

- Stocks are purchased through a **stockbroker** (p. 486) who buys and sells stocks on behalf of investors. Brokers also provide advice and receive a fee for their services.

- Stock transactions occur through a **stock exchange** (p. 486) like the **NYSE Euronext** (p. 499) or the **NASDAQ** (p. 486).

4 What is stock performance, and what are the factors that lead to changes in stock price? (pp. 488–490)

- Stock performance is typically measured by the fluctuation in price. When stock price increases, the stock shows good performance. Conversely a decrease in price indicates a poor performance.

- Stock prices change in reaction to supply and demand. Other factors that can affect stock prices include economic forecasts, industry or sector concerns, or global events. Stocks also tend to move together as a market. If the market is trending positively, it is a **bull market** (p. 489). A declining market is a **bear market** (p. 489).

5 How do companies issue bonds? (pp. 490–491)

- Bonds are issued in the same manner as stock, with a few slight differences:
  - The company contacts an investment bank for advice.
  - Investment bankers prepare documents with the SEC. They also help to set the price of the bond issue and take the lead in forming the group of banks that initially buy the bonds.
  - Financial advisers and bankers generate interest and locate potential buyers for the bonds before issuance.
  - Investment banks initially purchase all the bonds at a discount and then quickly sell them in the **primary market** (p. 483) at a higher price.

6 What are the different types of bonds, and how is bond risk evaluated? (pp. 491–495)

- A bonds is characterized by its **par (face) value** (p. 491), which is the money the bondholder will get back once a bond reaches maturity. Most bonds sell at par value. A bonds is also characterized by the **coupon** (p. 491) (interest rate), and **maturity date** (p. 491).

- Bonds are not risk free. The creditworthiness of the issuer is the main factor affecting a bond's risk.

- There are two issuers of bonds: governments and corporations.
  - **Corporate bonds** (p. 495) are issued by corporations and hold the greatest amount of risk. **Secured bonds** (p. 491) are backed by collateral, and **debenture bonds** (p. 492) are unsecured and backed only by a promise to pay.
  - **Government bonds** (p. 492) are issued by national governments and are the safest investment.
  - **Municipal bonds** (p. 492) are issued by state and local municipalities.

7 What are the different types of mutual fund investments? (pp. 495–499)

- **Mutual funds** (p. 495) are popular investments because they provide diversification and professional management. Mutual funds are extremely liquid and fairly cost efficient.

- **Load funds** (p. 498) have additional costs to cover marketing and other fund expenses, whereas **no-load funds** (p. 498) have little or no additional costs.

- **Money market funds** (p. 496) invest in short-term debt obligations. The interest rate for these funds is often nearly double that of "regular" interest-bearing checking or savings accounts. In addition, money market accounts provide check-writing privileges so you have quick access to the money.

- **Bond mutual funds** (p. 497) consist solely of bonds. They can be categorized by the type of bond (municipal bond funds, corporate bond funds, or U.S. government bond funds). Alternatively, some bond funds are categorized by maturity (long-term, short-term, or intermediate-term bond funds).

- **Stock mutual funds** (p. 497), also known as equity funds, Equity funds are categorized by investment strategy, such as growth and value funds. These funds are also categorized by size of the companies in which they invest, such as large-cap funds, medium-cap funds, and small-cap funds.

- Blend (or balanced) funds are mutual funds that invest in stocks, bonds, and sometimes money market funds to offer a mix of safety, income, and modest appreciation. A life cycle fund is a type of balanced fund that is managed to become more conservative as it approaches a target date, which often closely matches an investor's anticipated retirement date.

8 **What are other investment opportunities besides stocks, bonds, and mutual funds?** (pp. 499–500)

- An **option** (p. 499) is a contract that gives a buyer the right (but not the obligation) to buy or sell a security at a specific price on or before a certain date. Options are complicated and therefore quite risky.

- **Futures contracts** (p. 499) are agreements between a buyer and a seller to receive (or deliver) an asset sometime in the future but at a specific price that is agreed on today.

Key Terms

asset allocation (p. 480)

bear market (p. 489)

blue chip stock (p. 484)

bond mutual fund (p. 497)

bull market (p. 489)

callable bond (p. 493)

capital gain (p. 490)

capital loss (p. 490)

capital market (p. 483)

common stock (p. 484)

compound interest (p. 477)

convertible bond (p. 492)

corporate bond (p. 491)

coupon (p. 491)

cyclical stock (p. 485)

debenture bond (p. 492)

defensive stock (p. 485)

diversification (p. 480)

dividend (p. 484)

exchange-traded fund (p. 498)

futures contract (p. 499)

floating rate notes (p. 492)

general obligation bond (p. 492)

government bond (p. 492)

growth stock (p. 484)

income stock (p. 484)

index (p. 489)

insider trading (p. 481)

investing (p. 478)

investment banker (p. 483)

junk bond (p. 494)

load fund (p. 498)

market risk (p. 479)

maturity date (p. 491)

money market fund (p. 496)

municipal bond (p. 492)

mutual fund (p. 495)

NASDAQ (p. 486)

net asset value (p. 498)

New York Stock Exchange (NYSE) (p. 486)

NYSE Euronext (p. 486)

NYSE Amex (p. 486)

no-load fund (p. 498)

option (p. 499)

over-the-counter (OTC) stock (p. 486)

par (face) value (p. 491)

preferred stock (p. 484)

primary market (p. 483)

prospectus (p. 483)

revenue bond (p. 492)

risk–return relationship (p. 478)

secondary market (p. 483)

secured bond (p. 491)

Securities and Exchange Commission (p. 480)

serial bond (p. 493)

Series EE bond (p. 492)

Series I bond (p. 492)

stockbroker (p. 486)

stock exchange (p. 486)

stock mutual fund (equity fund) (p. 497)

Treasury bill (T-bill) (p. 492)

Treasury bond (T-bond) (p. 492)

Treasury Inflation-Protected Securities (p. 492)

Treasury note (T-note) (p. 492)

U.S. savings bond (p. 492)

value stock (p. 484)

Self Test

Multiple Choice *You can find the answers on the last page of this book.*

16-1 Mason recently bought a $10,000 government bond with a 3.5 percent interest rate. For the first two years, his semiannual interest payments were $175, $175, $200, and $200. What kind of government bond would Mason most likely have purchased?

a. Treasury bill

b. Treasury note

c. TIPS

d. Treasury bond

16-2 Which of the following could cause a stock price to change for Sunny Orange Growers, Inc.?

a. More investors dislike the stock and sell it than those who like the stock and buy it.

b. An unexpected freeze ruins the Florida orange crop for the year.

c. The government establishes a tax incentive for all U.S. agricultural companies that will help boost net income.

d. All of the above.

16-3 What document must companies prepare and make available to investors when issuing stocks?

a. A prospectus

b. An initial public offering

c. Proprietary underwriting

d. Investor guideline sheets

16-4 Tracy Quinn feels she has a great investment portfolio. She has investments in technology stocks, banking stocks, consumer goods stocks, and foreign stock mutual funds. If she adds a real estate mutual fund and a tax-exempt municipal bond to her portfolio, which best reflects her investment strategy?

a. Portfolio diversification

b. Asset allocation

c. Both A and B

d. Neither A nor B

16-5 Jose Fernandez is saving toward retirement and has an investment portfolio that reflects his risk tolerance. It was carefully put together by a trusted investment adviser. Unfortunately, the returns on the portfolio are not projected to generate the type of savings Jose desires. What should Jose do?

a. Invest in riskier stocks that have a higher return.

b. Lower his retirement expectations.

c. Increase his risk tolerance.

d. Change employers.

16-6 When interest earnings are added to principal and continue to earn interest, this is known as

a. mutual fund earnings.

b. capital gains.

c. compound interest.

d. net asset value.

16-7 Which of the following describes a security issued by a local government agency?

a. Acme, Inc. debenture bond

b. Souderton County Water Authority bond

c. Treasury bond

d. Fidelity bond fund

16-8 If you own a $5,000 bond that has a coupon of 3.5 percent and pays interest semiannually, how much interest would you receive?

a. $175 every six months

b. $175 once a year

c. $87.50 every six months

d. $875 once a year

16-9 Which is *not* an advantage of investing in mutual funds?

a. Mutual funds have less price variability than stocks or bonds.

b. Mutual funds provide immediate diversification.

c. Mutual fund investments are managed by a professional.

d. None of the above.

16-10 An ETF is

a. a contract that gives a buyer the right to buy or sell a security at a specified price on or before a certain date.

b. an agreement between a buyer and seller to buy an asset at a later date at a specified time.

c. an investment fund that is valued by its net asset value at the end of a trading day.

d. an investment that holds a collection of investments and trades like a stock.

Self Test (continued)

True/False *You can find the answers on the last page of this book.*

16-11 A person's risk tolerance might change with more investment knowledge or greater wealth.
☐ True or ☐ False

16-12 Five years ago, Jerome bought 100 shares of Kodak at $60 per share. Last month, he sold the 100 shares at $55 per share. Jerome has a capital gain from the sale.
☐ True or ☐ False

16-13 Treasury notes are bonds that mature in 2, 3, 5, 7, and 10 years.
☐ True or ☐ False

16-14 Common stockholders get paid before preferred stockholders if a firm goes out of business.
☐ True or ☐ False

16-15 Diversification is an investment strategy that suggests you structure your portfolio with different types of assets, such as stocks, real estate, commodities, and so on.
☐ True or ☐ False

Critical Thinking Questions

✪ 16-16 Before investing, you should determine your risk tolerance. How would you define risk tolerance? What, if anything, might change your risk tolerance?

✪ 16-17 List three short- to medium-term financial goals you want to achieve in the next one to five years and an approximate value for each. List three long-term financial goals that you want to achieve in the next 6 to 20 years and an approximate value for each. Discuss how you might be able to achieve some or all of these financial goals.

✪ 16-18 The term *blue chip* applies to stocks issued by a company in excellent financial standing with a record of producing earnings and paying dividends. Stocks in companies such as GE and Chrysler were initially considered blue chip stocks. Today, stocks in companies that were not in existence when the term was coined, such as Intel and Walmart, are considered blue chip stocks. Name three other companies you might consider blue chip stocks and why you would do so.

Team Time

TAKE THIS $50,000 AND INVEST IT!

Assemble in teams of four or five students. Suppose your team is given a theoretical $50,000 that you need to invest. Your team must assemble a portfolio by selecting a minimum of five investments but no more than 10 investments. The portfolios should be well diversified and include different types of stocks from different industries or sectors.

Process

Step 1. Your team should fill out the following charts as you conduct your research:

Name of Investment	Type of Investment	Industry/Sector

Name of Investment	Purchase Price	Number of Shares	Initial Value	Percentage of Total Portfolio

Step 2. Your team should prepare a presentation outlining your investment choices. The presentation should include reasons why you included each investment choice in the portfolio. In addition, the presentation should discuss the diversification strategies you took.

Step 3. As an optional ongoing exercise, teams should monitor their portfolios on a weekly basis. At the end of the specified period of time, teams should determine which team portfolio has the highest value.

Ethics and Corporate Social Responsibility

CAN INVESTMENTS BE SOCIALLY RESPONSIBLE AND LUCRATIVE?

Socially responsible investing describes a strategy of investing in companies that favor practices that are environmentally responsible, support workplace diversity, and increase product safety and quality. Avoiding investing in businesses involved sale of alcohol, tobacco, guns, military weapons, and so forth can also be part of such a strategy.

Process

Step 1. On your own or with a partner, research several individual companies and mutual funds that would qualify as socially responsible investments.

Step 2. In one or two paragraphs, comment on whether this type of investment strategy is a sound investment strategy.

Web Exercises

16-19 Financial Blogs
The List (p. 481) includes 10 blogs that offer good financial information for young adults. Visit three of these blogs and find one article or piece of content on each that seems relevant to your current financial situation. Summarize the content of the article and discuss how it is meaningful to you.

16-20 Getting the Most for Your Savings
At this stage in your life, putting your money in a savings account may be the most you can do. Savings rates are at historically low levels, so it is even more important that you find the most advantageous interest rate for your savings account. Go to Bankrate.com, where you can search and compare interest rates on checking and savings accounts in your local area and nationally. What is the best rate you can find in your local area? How does that compare to nationally available rates?

16-21 Dogs of the Dow
Several investment strategies help investors select stocks. Dogs of the Dow is one of the most publicized strategies. Research this strategy and discuss whether it be a good investment strategy for you.

16-22 Dollar Cost Averaging
It is very difficult to perfectly time your investments so that you purchase when a stock is at its lowest point or sell when a stock is at its highest point. Research the investment strategy of dollar cost averaging. In a paragraph, describe what this strategy is, why it is used, and the advantages and disadvantages it has over other investment strategies.

16-23 Municipal Bonds: Paving Roads and Building Schools
Municipal bonds are issued by local and state governments and other municipal organizations, such as school districts and toll road authorities. Conduct online research to determine the municipal bonds that the state in which you live has issued. Research two of these municipal bond projects. What is the purpose behind each bond issue?

MyBizLab

Go to **mybizlab.com** for Auto-graded writing questions as well as the following Assisted-graded writing questions:

16-24 Facebook finally entered the public market in 2012. Mark Zuckerberg, Facebook's CEO, was reluctant to enter the public market, stating that he wanted his employees to focus on making great products, not the stock price.[11] What does he mean by that?

16-25 Mutual funds often compare their performance to that of the S&P 500 with the goal of "beating" it. Is this a fair comparison? Why or why not?

References

1. Andrew Beattie, "Investopedia. Market Crashes: The Dotcom Crash, www.investopedia.com/features/crashes/crashes8.asp (accessed March26, 2014).

2. Gary P. Brinson, Brian D. Singer, and Gilbert L. Beebower, "Determinants of Portfolio Performance II: An Update," *Financial Analysts Journal*, May/June 1991, 40–48.

3. Alistair Barr and Ronald Orol, "Madoff Arrested in Alleged Ponzi Scheme," December 11, 2008, www.marketwatch.com/story/madoff-arrested-charged-may-be-facing-50-bln-in-losses-fbi.

4. "Bernie Madoff Scandal: Where Are They Now?," March 2010, www.time.com/time/specials/packages/completelist/0,29569,1971588,00.html.

5. "Quick Facts | NYSE Euronext," March 9, 2014, http://corporate.nyx.com/en/who-we-are/quick-facts.

6. "History of the American and NASDAQ Stock Exchanges," October 2012, www.loc.gov/rr/buisness/amex/amex.html.

7. "NYSE Listings," www.nyse.com/about/listed/1170350259411.html (accessed March 10, 2014).

8. "Get The Facts," www.nasdaq.com/reference/market_facts.stm (accessed March 10, 2014).

9. "Invest Wisely: Advice from Your Securities Industry Regulators," www.sec.gov/investor/pubs/inws.htm (accessed March 3, 2014).

10. "Trends in Mutual Fund Investing, January 2014," February 27, 2014, www.ici.org/research/stats/trends/trends_01_14.

11. Shayndi Raice and Randall Smith, "Facebook Readies IPO Filing," January 28, 2012, http://online.wsj.com/article/SB10001424052970204573704577187062821038498.html (accessed March 10, 2014).

Chapter 5
Personal Finance

People often associate discussing personal finances with a catastrophe, such as trying to cover one's expenses after losing a job, managing a household because of an illness, or becoming unable to work because of an injury. But in reality, making personal financial decisions is a process that doesn't just help people weather a financial catastrophe but also helps them achieve their dreams and goals, too, such as owning a home, affording college for their children, retiring early, and so on.

You should begin to think seriously about your personal finances when you get your first job, if not earlier. It is most prudent to begin managing your personal finances from the day you receive your first allowance! The sooner you think seriously about your finances, the easier it is to direct your earnings toward achieving your goals in life.

When an individual or a family uses financial principles to manage how money is budgeted, saved, invested, preserved for future life events, and protected against risks, it's called **personal finance**. In its simplest form, personal finance is about setting goals, making choices, and following through. As ■ **FIGURE M5.1** shows, you need to have a plan for reducing your expenses and increasing your income and assets so they begin to work for you.

Money management is a key component of personal finance and generally includes the following:

- Determining what you have
- Setting goals for what you want or need
- Planning how to achieve your goals

Source: Slim Plantagenate/Alamy.

There are several different aspects to effective money management. We begin by exploring how to create a financial plan.

Do You Need Tools to Help Manage Your Money?

Many online resources and software tools can help you manage your money. A spreadsheet program, such as Microsoft Excel, can be used to create simple financial worksheets and budgets. Intuit's Quicken software is a popular tool that offers more features specifically tailored to money-management capabilities. Many websites, such as Mint.com and MoneyStrands.com, also offer free online tools to help you track and manage your finances.

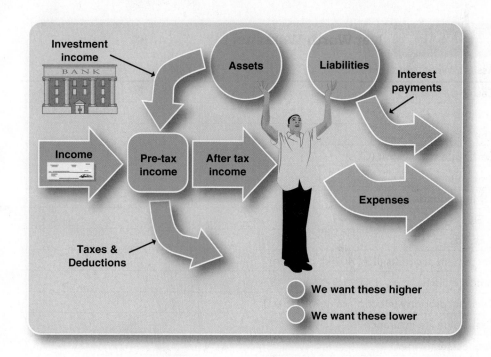

■ **FIGURE M5.1**
Basic Personal Finance
Source: Adapted from Peter Milner,
"Personal Finance 101: An Introduction."
From www.planyourescape.ca

MINI 5

Creating a Financial Plan

Let's walk through the steps involved in creating a financial plan.

Step 1: Take a Financial Inventory

The first thing you need to do when beginning a financial plan is to *take a financial inventory*. List everything of value that you own (your assets) and then subtract from that total everything you owe (your debts), including any loans and credit card balances you might have. The remaining amount is your net worth. As ■ **TABLE M5.1** shows, determining your net worth is similar to a company preparing a balance sheet but just arranged somewhat differently. If you're young and just starting out, there might not be much to write down at first. But it's still a useful exercise. As time passes, you'll have more to add to this statement. Recording and calculating what you own versus what you owe, even if done only once a year, will help you see where you stand financially at a given point in time. This can also help you determine if you need to revise your financial plan should your circumstances change.

Step 2: Set Financial Goals

Next you can begin to *set financial goals*. These can be both short-term and long-term goals. Short-term goals should be measurable and realistic goals that can be completed in a time frame of less than a year. "I need to replace my car next year" is an example of a short-term goal. Long-term goals can be more motivational, such as "I would like to have $250,000 in investment assets before I turn 40." Now break down the long-term goals into smaller, more manageable short-term goals. This increases your chance of achieving them. For example, "I would like to have $250,000 in investment assets before I turn 40" could be broken down as follows: "I would like to save $5,000 each year and invest it so it earns approximately 8 percent interest annually."

Finally, prioritize your goals by identifying them as wants and needs. Put your needs above your wants and your short-term goals above your long-term goals. Make your short-term needs (buying a new car) a top priority and your long-term

TABLE M5.1	Net Worth Worksheet	
Assets: What You Own		**Value**
Cash		
Savings		
Checking account		
Certificates of deposit (CDs)		
Investments		
Mutual funds		
Stocks		
Bonds		
Retirement accounts (IRA, 401[k], pension)		
Automobile		
Personal property (electronics, jewelry, etc.)		
Cash value life insurance		
Real estate (owned)		
Total assets		
Liabilities: What You Owe		**Value**
Student loan(s)		
Automobile loan(s)		
Credit card balance(s)		
Other loans		
Mortgage balance		
Other		
Total liabilities		
Total Net Worth = Total Assets − Total Liabilities		

wants (installing a swimming pool in the backyard) a lower priority. Choose goals that you're excited about and are determined to see come to fruition. Write these goals down in a place that you can refer to periodically to remind yourself of what you're working toward.

If this all seems a tad overwhelming, remember that there are financial planners who will work with you to chart a course to financial stability. Look for a person who is qualified as a certified financial planner, which means they are licensed and regulated to ensure you are working with a professional.

Step 3: Know Where Your Money Goes

You've figured out what you have and what you owe, and you've set financial goals. Now you need to know what you're currently spending. Begin by listing all the expenses you incur in a month, similar to the list shown in ■ **TABLE M5.2**. It's easy to figure out your *fixed expenses*—expenditures that don't change from month to month, such as your rent and car payments. The harder part is tracking *variable expenses*—monthly payments you have to make that may change from month to month. Gas, food, clothing, entertainment, utility, and cell phone charges are examples of variable expenses.

You'll also need to include *periodic expenses*—items such as taxes or donations that you make but not on a monthly basis. Also, note the category of *unexpected*

TABLE M5.2	Monthly Expenses	
Fixed Expenses	**Amount**	**Need or Want?**
Housing (mortgage/rent)		
Car payment		
Insurance premiums (health, car, renter's)		
Internet/cable/cell phone		
Savings		
Other		
Variable Expenses	**Amount**	**Need or Want?**
Electricity		
Gas/heating/oil		
Water		
Phone		
Food		
Gas		
Transportation (bus or subway fare)		
Child care		
Clothing		
Entertainment		
Other		
Periodic Expenses	**Amount**	**Need or Want?**
Taxes		
Donations		
Union/professional dues		
Unexpected Expenses	**Amount**	**Need or Want?**
Car/home repairs		
Speeding tickets		
Medical bills		
Other		

expenses shown in Table M5.2. You may not be able to determine the exact amount to fill in for this category. For example, will you get a speeding ticket this year that must be paid? It may be hard to tell. Nonetheless, set aside a modest amount of money to cover unexpected events such as this. Not doing so can throw a monkey wrench into the best-laid financial plans.

As you create your list, you may need to track "invisible" expenses—items you don't realize you buy, such as daily lattes, chips from the vending machine, or gadgets for your car. The best way to determine your invisible expenses is to create a "penny journal" that tracks your daily spending habits to the last penny. The penny journal will also help you define your variable expenses. As you continue to work with your plan, you'll be able to refine these numbers as well as establish limits for some of the expenses.

Analyze the penny journal and expenses list and identify the expenses you must cover (fixed expenses) and those that you might be able to cut back on (variable and invisible expenses). Now you're ready to develop a budget.

Step 4: Create a Budget

A budget, or a spending plan, should be realistic in terms of the expenses you must pay. It should also include savings as a regular fixed expense. Every month, whether you think you can afford to or not, save a certain amount of money. Many financial planning experts suggest setting aside at least 10 percent of every paycheck. Don't fall into the trap of depositing into your savings account whatever is left over. Instead, make a conscious effort to "pay yourself first" so that once you have paid your bills and the rest of the money is spent, *you* are left with some money. No matter what, you should not miss making the payment to yourself. The secret to success is not so much the amount of money you save as the persistence with which you do it.

Initially, your savings should accumulate so that you have a "rainy day fund" that is equal to at least one month's worth of bills. Eventually, this fund should be built up to cover three to six months of fixed expenses. This fund will cover your expenses should the unexpected happen, such as a job loss or an injury. Once you've established a rainy day fund, your savings should go into an interest-bearing account—whether it is a CD, a money market fund, a mutual fund, or stocks and bonds.

So You Want to Be a Millionaire?

Which of the following individuals will save enough to be a millionaire by the time he or she is 60 years old?

a. A 10-year-old who puts $25 in the bank every week for 50 years

b. A 22-year-old who puts $68 in the bank every week for 38 years

c. A 40-year-old who puts $370 in the bank every week for 20 years

d. All of the above

Using credit cards wisely can help you secure a car or home loan later. In contrast, reckless spending with credit cards can lead to financial disaster.
Source: Montgomery Martin/Alamy.

Answer: d. All of these individuals with the prescribed savings plans can become millionaires before they reach 60.

Notice the difference time makes in terms of the amount each individual must save. Why is this so? Because of compound interest. **Compound interest** is interest that is earned not only on your principal (the actual amount of money you set aside as savings) but also on the interest you earned by doing so. In a savings account, as long as you leave your money in the account and don't take out the interest you've earned, you'll benefit from the compounding effect. The moral of the story is to start saving early, save often, and don't withdraw the interest earnings!

Step 5: Execute the Plan

Tracking your expenses and setting up a budget can be tedious and time consuming. Software packages, such as the one shown in ■ **FIGURE M5.2**, are available to help you. The real challenge is sticking to your plan, which requires discipline and perseverance. Just cutting out one cup of designer coffee a week saves over $200 a year. Here are a few other tips for plugging leaks in your budget:

- **Pay off all unpaid credit card debt.** Carrying a balance on your credit cards is financial suicide. Most credit card companies charge more than 18 percent on unpaid balances. Therefore, pay down your credit card debt before depositing money into

Monthly Budget

	Projected Monthly	Actual Monthly
Income 1		$4,000
Income 2	$1,300	$1,300
Extra income	$300	$300
Total monthly income	**$5,600**	**$5,600**

Total Projected Cost	Total Actual Cost	Total Difference
$1,195	$1,236	($41)
Projected balance (Projected income minus projected costs)	**Actual balance** (Actual income minus actual costs)	**Difference** (Actual minus projected)
$4,405	$4,364	($41)

Housing	Projected Cost	Actual Cost	Difference
Mortgage or rent	$1,000	$1,000	$0
Phone	$54	$100	($46)
Electricity	$44	$56	($12)
Gas	$22	$28	($6)
Water and sewer	$8	$8	$0
Cable	$34	$34	$0
Waste removal	$10	$10	$0
Maintenance or repairs	$23	$0	$23
Supplies	$0	$0	$0
Other	$0	$0	$0
Subtotals	$1,195	$1,236	($41)

Transportation	Projected Cost	Actual Cost	Difference
Vehicle 1 payment			$0
Vehicle 2 payment			$0
Bus/taxi fare			$0
Insurance			$0
Licensing			$0
Fuel			$0
Maintenance			$0
Other			$0
Subtotals	$0	$0	$0

Insurance	Projected Cost	Actual Cost	Difference
Home			$0
Health			$0
Life			$0
Other			$0
Subtotals	$0	$0	$0

Food	Projected Cost	Actual Cost	Difference
Groceries			$0
Dining out			$0
Other			$0
Subtotals	$0	$0	$0

Savings or Investments	Projected Cost	Actual Cost	Difference
Retirement account			$0
Investment account			$0
College			$0
Other			$0
Subtotals	$0	$0	$0

Personal Care	Projected Cost	Actual Cost	Difference
Medical			$0
Hair/nails			$0
Clothing			$0
Dry cleaning			$0
Health club			$0
Organization dues or fees			$0
Other			$0
Subtotals	$0	$0	$0

Loans	Projected Cost	Actual Cost	Difference
Personal			$0
Student			$0
Credit card			$0
Credit card			$0
Other			$0
Subtotals	$0	$0	$0

Children	Projected Cost	Actual Cost	Difference
Medical			$0
Clothing			$0
School tuition			$0
School supplies			$0
Organization dues of fees			$0
Lunch money			$0
Child care			$0
Toys/games			$0
Other			$0
Subtotals	$0	$0	$0

Taxes	Projected Cost	Actual Cost	Difference
Federal			$0
State			$0
Local			$0
Other			$0
Subtotals	$0	$0	$0

Gifts and Donations	Projected Cost	Actual Cost	Difference
Charity 1			$0
Charity 2			$0
Charity 3			$0
Subtotals	$0	$0	$0

Legal	Projected Cost	Actual Cost	Difference
Attorney			$0
Alimony			$0
Other			$0
Subtotals	$0	$0	$0

Pets	Projected Cost	Actual Cost	Difference
Food			$0
Medical			$0
Grooming			$0
Toys			$0
Other			$0
Subtotals	$0	$0	$0

Entertainment	Projected Cost	Actual Cost	Difference
Video/DVD			$0
CDs			$0
Movies			$0
Concerts			$0
Sporting events			$0
Live theater			$0
Other			$0
Subtotals	$0	$0	$0

■ **FIGURE M5.2**
Sample Budget Template
Budget templates like this one can help you set up your spending plan.

a savings or investment account. Also, pay your credit card bill on time. Late fees are a waste of money!

- **If you have outstanding loans, see if you can reduce the interest rate or consolidate into a more manageable payment.** Call your bank and ask! You might be surprised at the response you get.
- **To reduce impulse buying, try using cash only.** When you use cash instead of credit, you can immediately see the effects of your spending.

Step 6: Monitor and Assess Your Plan

Revisit your plan periodically and make adjustments as necessary. Look at your budget every month and make adjustments every year.

Managing Your Personal Credit

Credit is your ability to buy things now and pay for them later. When used responsibly, credit cards can be good things. Showing future lenders that you have a good credit history will help you when you apply for car loans or a mortgage. (Some employers look at applicants' credit histories prior to hiring them too.) Abusing credit can quickly add up to serious problems. Consider this: It might not take you very long to accumulate $3,000 on your credit card, but it will take you nearly 15 years paying $50 a month to pay it off completely! And that's if you never charge another cent! Here are a few tips to help you manage your personal credit.

Tip #1: Check the Interest Rate and the Annual Fee

Credit is not free, so check the fine print on credit card contracts. Even if the initial offer is a zero or very low percentage interest rate, the rate may change when the promotional period ends. Make sure you understand what the new interest rate will be. Also try to find a credit card company that does not charge an annual fee. If there is an annual fee, call the issuing company to see if it can be waived. Be sure to carefully evaluate credit cards that offer airline miles or other incentives. Often, these cards charge higher interest rates and annual fees.

Tip #2: Don't Charge If You Can't Pay

Don't look at your credit card as a means of financial freedom. If you can't afford to pay cash for an item, then don't use a credit card. Think of a credit card as a short-term loan that needs to be paid back in 30 days or less. To use credit wisely, pay off the balance in full every month. Doing so allows you to keep your money earning interest longer, assuming you have an interest-bearing checking or savings account.

Some cards are designed to encourage on-time payments. Discover's Motiva card, for example, pays you money back for paying on time. Plus, like other Discover cards, it gives you a cash-back bonus on your purchases.

Tip #3: Establish a Credit History in Another Way

Although establishing a good credit history is important, you don't need to begin with a national credit card if you feel the temptation is too great to charge more than you can afford. Another way to establish credit is to begin with a single-store credit card or a single-purpose credit card, such as a gas card. Using these cards responsibly by making occasional purchases and paying your bill in full every month demonstrates your ability to use credit wisely.

Know Your Credit Score

If you've been using credit, then you've established a credit record. Lenders convert your credit history into a numeric score, which other lenders use to qualify you for a loan should you try to get one. Credit card companies also you use your score to determine the interest rates they will charge you. There is no absolute number that guarantees your chances of qualifying for credit or lower interest rates, but a higher score is better. You can find out your number by obtaining a credit report from one of the three credit bureaus: Equifax, Experian, and TransUnion. By law, every individual is entitled to one free credit report each year from each bureau. Go to www.annualcreditreport.com and follow the instructions on the website to get your credit report. If possible, several months before applying for a big loan, obtain your credit report to make sure all the information listed is accurate. If there are errors in your credit report (which occasionally happen), you will have some time to fix them.

Car Considerations

Having a car is a top financial priority for many people. Let's look at the financial decisions related to owning a car.

Getting Wheels

Whether you're replacing your current car or are buying one for the first time, you'll need to make several decisions. The first is whether to buy a new or used

TABLE M5.3	**Buying versus Leasing a Car**	
Buying a Car	**Leasing a Car**
Pay for the entire cost of car.	Pay for only a portion of the car's cost.
You need to make a down payment and pay sales tax on the entire cost of the car.	You sometimes have the option to not make a down payment and pay the sales tax on your monthly payments.
You make the first loan payment a month after you buy the car.	You make the first lease payment when you sign the contract.
When you sell the car, it's at the depreciated value. Your outstanding loan obligation may be more than the depreciated value.	When you terminate the lease, you may either return the vehicle or purchase it for its depreciated value.
There are no use restrictions on mileage and no specified maintenance requirements.	Usually there are mileage restrictions (12,000 miles a year) and maintenance requirements. Turning the car in with stained carpets, dents, and dings brings on extra fees. Going over the mileage limit will mean paying extra fees.

car. New cars have warranties, so the manufacturer covers virtually all repairs. However, a new car's value depreciates 20 to 30 percent almost as soon as you drive the car off the dealer's lot. Consequently, your car loan might already be more than the car is worth before there are even 50 miles on its odometer! Used cars have depreciated already, so your loan is probably less and closer to the current value of the car.

Don't forget that you'll need to pay for maintenance (whether the car is used or new), and depending on the age and condition of the car, the maintenance might be costly. Consider buying a "new used car," which is a car that is only a few years old, has been well maintained, and has low mileage. Often the initial warranty on a car extends to a new owner.

If you decide to get a new car, you have another decision: to buy or lease. ■ **TABLE M5.3** outlines some of the considerations in buying or leasing a new car. Many people lease cars because they can get a more expensive car for less up-front cash. However, if you finance a car with a loan, at the end of the loan, you still own your car. If you continue to drive that car, you then have the money you used to spend on the loan payments to put to other uses.

Insurance and Investments

Taking care of yourself now and in the future constitutes another area of financial planning. Buying insurance and making investments are two ways you can accomplish these goals.

Insuring Your Present and Your Future

When something goes wrong, you need help to cover the costs so you can recover quickly. Fortunately, insurance is available for a variety of risks so you don't have to bear the burden of covering these costs alone:

Buying a car requires that you make a number of decisions.
Source: Juice Images/Alamy.

1. **Health insurance.** Health insurance is a must. No matter how healthy you are today, a serious illness or an injury, plus any rehabilitation expenses, can be astronomically expensive. If your employer offers health insurance coverage, take it. You might have to contribute some of the cost yourself, but it's well worth it. If you're self-employed, unemployed, or not covered by your employer, investigate what affordable options you have for coverage. A good place to begin is HealthCare.gov. Some colleges

offer subsidized group health care plans, even to part-time students. If you are self-employed, you may qualify for a group plan through associations and organizations you have joined. In addition, the Affordable Care Act allows people under the age of 26 to remain covered on their parents' health insurance plans.

2. **Disability insurance.** Disability insurance pays you benefits should you become disabled and are no longer able to earn a living. Many employers offer disability insurance coverage along with their health insurance coverage. If yours does not, determine how you would meet your expenses if you should become disabled.

3. **Car insurance.** Most states require car insurance. There are three types of car insurance coverage: liability, collision, and comprehensive. *Liability* insurance covers damage and injuries you have caused to someone else. You should always have liability coverage. *Collision* insurance covers damage to your vehicle if you collide with a moving or stationary object. *Comprehensive* insurance covers damage to your car from theft, fire, or other non–collision-related accidents. If you're insuring an older car, it might not be worth carrying the cost of collision and comprehensive coverage in addition to liability coverage.

4. **Homeowner's and renter's insurance.** These types of insurance protect your home and the contents inside. Homeowner's insurance also comes with liability coverage to protect you if someone is injured while on your property. If you have a mortgage on your home, the bank usually requires insurance. Many landlords require their tenants to provide proof that they have renter's insurance. If your landlord does not, you should still consider it because it is affordable and will protect your assets in the event of fire or theft.

5. **Life insurance.** Life insurance helps replace income lost due to your death to those who are dependent on you, such as a spouse, children, parents, or other family members. When you purchase a life insurance policy, you name the person(s) who receive your life insurance benefits as your beneficiaries. Some types of life insurance policies can act as long-term savings plans, whereas other types are strictly for protection. You might not need life insurance if you're single, with no one depending on you or your income, or if you're married and have no children and your spouse is capable of working.

Consulting an insurance professional will help you determine your needs for many types of insurance. It pays to shop around and compare rates. Often, you can receive discounts if you carry several types of insurance (such as home owner's and automobile) with the same company. Moreover, you should review and compare your rates every few years to make sure the rates you are paying are still competitive and your coverage is adequate.

Investing Now and for the Future

Investing your money is not without risk, although there are strategies you can pursue to help reduce these risks. Learning as much as you can about the various investment opportunities that are available to you is a useful part of your financial planning. Many types of investments exist. As you begin to build up your savings, you might choose to invest your savings in CDs or money market accounts. As your knowledge of and comfort level with investments increase and your amount of discretionary income builds, you might consider investing in mutual funds, stocks, or bonds.

How Fast Can Your Investment Double in Value?

The **rule of 72** is an easy way to figure out how long it will take to double your money at a given interest rate. All you have to do is divide the investment's interest

Insurance policies cover natural disasters to varying degrees. Make sure you read the fine print so you know exactly what is protected in your insurance plan.
Source: Joe Raedle/Getty Images.

rate into 72. For example, if you want to know how long it will take to double your money at 6 percent interest, divide 6 into 72 and get 12 years. The rule of 72 works well as long as the interest rate is less than 20 percent. You can also use the rule of 72 to determine the interest rate needed to double your money in a certain amount of time. If you wanted to double your money in three years, you would divide 3 into 72. Now you know you would need an interest rate of about 24 percent.

Investing for Retirement

At this point in your life, retirement probably seems a very long way off. Unfortunately, you may not be able to rely on Social Security to fully meet your financial needs after you retire. Therefore, it is very important that you take responsibility for planning to meet your financial needs during retirement. It's best to accumulate savings for retirement by starting early and investing regularly, but other mechanisms are available to help. If you work, your employer may have a retirement plan you can join. If you're self-employed or your employer does not offer retirement benefits, you can set up your own retirement program. Funds specifically designated for retirement, such as individual retirement accounts (IRAs), Roth IRAs, and 401(k) programs, offer tax advantages to encourage you to save for retirement.

Individual Retirement Accounts

Individual retirement accounts (IRAs) are special savings accounts created by the government. The benefit of putting your retirement savings into an IRA is that you put pretax money into an IRA, thus reducing your current taxable income. You don't pay tax on money in the account until after you have retired and withdrawn the money. (The idea here is that after you retire, you will be in a lower income tax bracket and pay less tax.) Generally, if you withdraw money from your IRA before the age of 59½, you must pay a penalty to the government. You must begin to withdraw from your IRA when you are 70½. Despite these restrictions, you should strongly consider contributing the maximum amount you are allowed every year.

Roth IRAs

A **Roth IRA** is another type of retirement account, but it differs from a traditional IRA in several ways. Contributions to a Roth IRA are not made with pretax dollars. However, withdrawals are usually tax free, and there are fewer restrictions on when and how you can withdraw your money. Roth IRAs are restricted to individuals whose income falls below a certain level specified by guidelines established by the Internal Revenue Service (IRS).

Simplified Employee Pension Individual Retirement Arrangement

The **Simplified Employee Pension Individual Retirement Arrangement** (SEP IRA) is another type of retirement tool. This is a fabulous tax break that could benefit you if you are starting your own business. You can move some of your self-employment income into a retirement account and defer paying taxes. So a SEP IRA could help you shelter income from your side business, reducing your tax bill and helping your long-term retirement picture.

Pension Plans

Pension plans are retirement plans established by your employer. There are two kinds of pension plans: defined benefit and defined contribution. In the past, most companies offered **defined benefit plans** in which you were paid a certain percentage of your salary after you had retired. To qualify, you had to work for the company for a certain amount of time. The problem with defined benefit plans is that the companies bore the risk and responsibility of having sufficient funds to meet their pension obligations.

When this became too difficult and costly, many companies switched to offering defined contribution plans. **Defined contribution plans** are the most common retirement benefit offered today. In this type of plan, your employer contributes a percentage of each paycheck that you have specified into your account. To encourage you to contribute to the plan, many companies will match your investment or a portion of it—in essence giving you money when you save. The money in your account is invested for you in stocks, bonds, mutual funds, annuities, or company stock. You often have the opportunity to select the investments from a menu of choices and direct the proportion of your contributions going into each investment. Should you change jobs or leave a company before you retire, you may roll over the proceeds of your defined contribution plan into your new plan or an IRA.

401(k), 403(b), and 457 Plans

These plans are forms of defined contribution plans. For-profit companies offer 401(k) plans, non-for-profit organizations offer 403(b) plans, and government entities offer the 457 plan. (The numbers of the plans refer to the sections in the federal tax law that authorizes the plans.)

Taxes

Everyone who earns income is required to file an income tax return. Even if you owe no taxes, you must file a return. Failure to do so will result in fines and penalties. When you get your paycheck, an estimate of the taxes you owe has already been taken out. Your tax return calculates the exact amount you owe. If not enough has been deducted from your paycheck, you pay the remainder of what you owe when you file your return. If you have had too much deducted from your paycheck, the IRS will refund the difference.

The IRS offers every taxpayer a standard deduction that reduces the amount of taxable income. You have a choice to either take this standard deduction or itemize your own deductions. Deductions include the interest paid on mortgages, contributions to a tax-deferred retirement plan, contributions to charity, and a certain amount of medical expenses, to name a few. You should itemize your deductions if they're greater than the standard deduction. Generally, if you don't own your own home, you're better off taking the standard deduction. In addition, completing the tax return is much easier when you take the standard deduction.

How Much Tax Are You Paying?

■ **TABLE M5.4** summarizes the U.S. income tax rates single people paid in 2013. Income taxes are computed on a marginal tax rate. This means that tax rates progressively increase as your income increases, and the higher tax rate applies to only the income you earned in the higher tax-bracket range. So, for example, if you earned $9,100 in 2013, as shows, you would have paid a tax rate of 10 percent on $9,075 of it and a 15 percent tax rate on the remaining $24 you earned.

Not all income is taxable income, however. Standard deductions and personal exemptions can be subtracted from what you make. These will vary depending on your personal situation. You can use an interactive website like MoneyChimp.com to get a detailed calculation of how much in taxes you will pay after deductions and exemptions. Knowing the highest tax bracket you will fall into can help you determine how much tax you might pay on extra income you earn or, conversely, how much tax you will save by increasing your deductions.

TABLE M5.4	**Personal Income Tax Rates Filing as Single 2014**[1]	
If Your Taxable Income Is at Least . . .	**But Not More Than . . .**	**Your Highest Tax Rate Is . . .**
$ 0	$ 9,075	10%
$ 9,075	$ 36,900	15%
$ 36,900	$ 89,350	25%
$ 89,350	$186,350	28%
$186,350	$405,100	33%
$405,100	$406,750	35%
$406,750	No limit	39.6%

Managing your personal finances may sound tedious and time consuming, but it has rewards. Remember the following tips:

- Set your financial goals.
- Make a plan to achieve these goals and stick to it.
- Pay yourself first, start early, and pay often.
- Use debt wisely and establish good credit.
- Make sure you and your assets are insured.

Soon enough you'll be on the road to financial success.

Reference

1. "Federal Tax Brackets," www.moneychimp.com/features/tax_brackets.htm.

Business Plan Project Appendix

Part 1. Introduction

Business Name
What is the name of your business?

Hint: When choosing a name for your business, make sure it captures the spirit of the business you're creating. Also refer to the BizChat in Chapter 5 for tips on naming your business.

Description of Business
What will your business do?

Hint: Imagine that you're explaining your business to a family member or a friend. It should be easy to explain, using 30 words or less.

Form of Business Ownership
What form of business ownership (sole proprietorship, partnership, LLC, or corporation) will your business take? Why did you choose this form?

Hint: For more information on forms of business ownership, refer to Chapter 6.

Ideal Customers
Describe your ideal customers. What are they like in terms of age, income level, and so on?

Hint: You don't have to go into too much detail in this part of the plan; you'll provide more details about customers and marketing in later parts. For now, simply outline the kind of customers your product or service will best fit.

Company Advantages
Why will customers choose to buy from your business instead of your competition?

Hint: Describe what will be unique about your business. For example, is your product special, will customer service be exceptional, or will your price be lower?

Part 2. The Company and Management Team

The Mission Statement

Mission Statement
Write a brief mission statement for your business.

Hint: Refer to the discussion of mission statements in Chapter 7. Be sure to include how you will stand out from your competition and why customers will buy from you.

Ethical Issues

All businesses must deal with ethical issues. One way to address these issues is to create a code of ethics. List three core (unchanging) principles that your business will follow.

Hint: To help you consider the ethical issues your business might face, refer to Chapter 3.

Social Responsibility

A business shows social responsibility by respecting all its stakeholders. What steps will you take to create a socially responsible business?

Hint: To help you consider the issues of social responsibility, refer to the discussion in Chapter 3. Consider how you may need to be socially responsible toward your customers and, if applicable, investors, employees, and suppliers.

Industry Profile

Industry Description

Describe the industry and sector in which your company operates.

Hint: Industries are broad categories, such as financial, technology, services, or health care. Sectors are more specific categories within an industry, such as a sporting goods store in the services industry or computer peripherals in the technology industry. In your description of the industry and sector, discuss economic trends as well as the current outlook for the industry, including growth potential.

Opportunities and Threats

Describe the opportunities and threats that face your company.

Hint: For this section, refer to the discussion of the economy in Chapter 2. Consider external factors, such as macroeconomic matters, technological changes, legislation, and sociocultural changes that may affect the industry as well as your company. This typically is done as part of a SWOT analysis, which is discussed in Chapter 7.

Company Profile and Strategy

Business Goals

What are three business goals you want to achieve in the first year? What are two intermediate to long-term goals you want to achieve in the next three to five years?

Hint: Refer to the discussion of goal setting in Chapter 7. Be as specific and realistic as possible with the goals you set. Remember the SMARTER acronym; goals should be specific, measurable, acceptable, realistic, timely, extending, and rewarding. For example, if you are selling a service, how many customers do you want by the end of the first year and how much do you want each customer to spend? If you are selling a good, what volume of sales do you hope to achieve?

Company Strengths

Describe the strengths of your company.

Hint: In evaluating a company's strengths, analyze its internal resources, including finances, human resources, marketing, operations, and technological resources. A company's strength might be its strong marketing department or a favorable location.

Raw Materials and Supplies

Explain what raw materials and supplies you will need to run your business. How will you produce your good? What equipment do you need? What hours will you operate?

Hint: Refer to Chapter 11 for information to get you started.

Anticipated Challenges and Planned Responses

Anticipated Challenges

Describe any weaknesses or potential challenges that face your company.

Hint: Consider any potential vulnerability from the competition, problems with suppliers or resources, or any legal factors that might affect the business, such as pending lawsuits or patent or copyright issues.

Planned Responses

Describe any plans you have to address these weaknesses and anticipated challenges.

Hint: Consider any resources your company can make available to address these challenges.

The Management Team

Management

Who are the key individuals that will manage the business?

Hint: Refer to the discussion of managers in Chapter 7. Think about how *many levels* of management as well as what *kinds* of managers your business needs. In addition, outline how each manager's contribution will positively impact the business. What is it about that particular manager that will help the business succeed?

Organization Chart

Show how the "team" fits together by creating a simple organizational chart for your business. Make sure the organizational chart indicates who will work for each manager as well as each person's job title.

Hint: Most businesses start quite small. However, as you create your organizational chart, consider what your business will look like in the future. What different tasks are involved in the business? Who will each person report to in the organizational structure? Refer to the discussions of organizational structure in Chapters 6 and 7 for information to get you started.

Part 3. Marketing

Market Analysis

Market Research

Describe your target market in terms of age, education level, income, and other demographic variables.

Hint: Refer to Chapter 12 for more information on the aspects of target marketing and market segmentation that you may want to consider. Be as detailed as possible about who you think your customers will be.

Assessment of the Competition
Describe three companies that you see as your main competitors.

Hint: For each company, describe the company's perceived strengths and weaknesses. How do you intend to take advantage of each weakness and respond to each strength?

The Product or Service

Product Features and Benefits
Describe the features and benefits of your product or service.

Hint: As you learned in Chapter 13, a product has tangible and intangible benefits that create a *total product offer*. Describe your product on three levels, as outlined in Chapter 13—the *core product* (What basic needs or wants does this product or service satisfy?), the *actual product* (What are the tangible aspects of the product that you can taste, see, smell, touch, and hear?), and the *augmented product* (What are the perceived benefits that provide additional value to a customer's purchase?).

Product Differentiation
How will you make your product(s) stand out in the crowd?

Hint: There are many ways to stand out in the crowd, such as a unique product, outstanding service, or a great location. What makes your product special? Does it fill an unmet need in the marketplace? How will you differentiate your product to make sure that it succeeds?

Pricing
What pricing strategy will you choose for your product(s), and why did you choose this strategy?

Hint: Refer to Chapter 13 for more information on pricing strategies and tactics. Because your business is new, so is the product. Therefore, you will probably want to choose between price skimming and penetration pricing. Which will you choose and why?

Sales and Promotion

Place (Distribution) Issues
Where will customers find your product or service? (That is, what distribution channels should you consider?)

Hint: If your business will sell its product directly to consumers, what types of stores will sell your product? If your product will be sold to another business, which channel of distribution will you use? Refer to Chapter 14 for more information on aspects of distribution you may want to consider.

Advertising
How will you advertise to your target market? Why have you chosen these forms of advertisement?

Hint: Marketers use several different advertising media—specific communication devices for carrying a seller's message to potential customers; each form has advantages and drawbacks. Refer to Chapter 14 for a discussion of the types of advertising media you may wish to consider.

Promotions

What other methods of promotion will you use and why?

Hint: There's more to promotion than simple advertising. Other methods include *personal selling, sales promotions,* and *publicity and public relations.* Refer to the discussion of promotion in Chapter 14 for ideas on how to promote your product that go beyond just advertising.

Part 4. The Financials

Expected Revenue

How much will you charge for your product? How many products do you believe you can sell in one year (or how many customers do you think your business will attract)? Multiply the price that you will charge by the number of products that you hope to sell or the amount you hope each customer will spend. This will give you an estimate of your *revenues* for one year.

Hint: You will use the amounts you calculate in the costs and revenues questions in this section in the accounting statements, so be as realistic as you can.

Cost of Doing Business

What are the costs of doing business? Equipment, supplies, salaries, rent, utilities, and insurance are just some of these expenses. Estimate what it will cost to do business for one year. Include any assumptions you use in generating cost estimates.

Hint: Insert the costs associated with doing business in the table on the following page. The following list provides some hints as to where you can get this information. Note that these are estimates; try your best to include accurate costs for the expenses you think will be a part of doing business.

Hints for each expense in the following table:

- **Rent:** What is the "going rate" per square foot for office space in your community? A real estate agent or a local SBA representative (www.sba.gov) can also be helpful in answering this question.
- **Salaries and Wages:** Refer to the organizational chart. How much will each employee earn? How many hours will each employee be needed on a weekly basis? Once you've determined the weekly cost, then expand it to a monthly cost and a yearly cost.
- **Supplies:** How much will all the computers, equipment, and furniture cost? What kinds of general office supplies will you need? Most prices for this information can be found on an office supply Web site, such as Staples.com.
- **Advertising and Other Promotions:** Refer to your marketing section. You have described how you wish to reach your customers; now you need to decide how much it will cost. If you're using television, contact the sales department at a local station. If you're using newspapers, contact their advertising department. Salespeople are usually happy to answer your questions.
- **Utilities:** These amounts will vary depending on your business and what utilities you will pay. If your business looks like an office, this cost may be similar to what a homeowner pays. However, if your business involves making a product, then the costs will be significant. An SBA representative can be a good resource.
- **Insurance:** This value will be affected by the nature of the business. More equipment will usually mean higher insurance costs. Again, contact an SBA representative for feedback.

Expenses	Expected Monthly Cost	Expected Yearly Cost
Rent		
Salaries and Wages		
Supplies: technological, equipment, furniture, other (computers, software, copy machine, desks, chairs, etc.)		
Advertising and Other Promotions		
Utilities: heat, electricity, etc.		
Utilities: telephone, Internet		
Insurance		
Other (specify)		
Other (specify)		

Start-up Costs
How much money will you need to get your business started?

Hint: Refer back to where you analyzed the costs involved in running your business. Approximately how much will you need to get your business started?

Financing
How will you finance your business? For example, will you seek out a bank loan? Borrow from friends? Try crowdfunding? Sell stocks or bonds initially or as your business grows?

Hint: Refer to Chapter 15 for information on sources of short-term and long-term funds. Refer to Chapter 16 for information on securities, such as stocks and bonds.

Income Statement and Balance Sheet
Create a balance sheet and an income statement for your business.

Hint: You have **two** options for creating these reports. The first option is to create your own financial statements using the guides provided on the next pages.

The second option is to use the specific Microsoft Word or Excel templates created for each statement. You'll find these templates online in this text's MyBizLab. The Excel files are handy because all the calculations are preset; all you have to do is "plug in" the numbers. The calculations are performed automatically. If you make adjustments to the values in the Excel worksheets, you'll automatically see how changes to expenses, for example, can improve the "bottom line."

Twelve-Month Income Statement (Profit & Loss Statement)

	June	July	Aug.	Sept.	Oct.	Nov.	Dec.	Jan.	Feb.	March	April	May	YEARLY
Revenue (Sales)													
Category 1													
Category 2													
Total Revenue (Sales)													
Cost of Goods Sold													
Category 1													
Category 2													
Total Cost of Goods Sold													
Gross Profit													
Operating Expenses													
Rent Expense													
Salary/Wage Expenses													
Supplies Expense													
Advertising Expense													
Utilities Expense													
Telephone/Internet Expense													
Insurance Expense													
Interest from Loans (if applicable)													
Other Expenses (specify)													
Total Expenses													
Net Profit													

Balance Sheet

Assets	
Current Assets	
Cash in Bank	
Cash Value of Inventory	
Prepaid Expenses (insurance)	
Total Current Assets	
Fixed Assets	
Machinery & Equipment	
Furniture & Fixtures	
Real Estate/Buildings	
Total Fixed Assets	
Total Assets	
Liabilities & Net Worth	
Current Liabilities	
Accounts Payable	
Taxes Payable	
Notes Payable (due within 12 months)	
Total Current Liabilities	
Long-Term Liabilities	
Bank Loans Payable (greater than 12 months)	
Less: Short-Term Portion	
Total Long-Term Liabilities	
Total Liabilities	
Owners' Equity (Net Worth)	
Total Liabilities & Net Worth	

Part 5. The Finishing Touches

Cover Sheet and Table of Contents

Cover Sheet
Create a cover sheet for your business plan.

Hint: The cover sheet should include the following:

- Basic company information (name, address, phone number, and web address)
- The company logo
- Contact information of the owner(s) and any officers (names, titles, addresses, phone numbers, and e-mail addresses)
- The date the business plan was created
- The name(s) of those who prepared the plan

Table of Contents
Create a table of contents for the plan so a reader can quickly find information.

Hint: The table of contents should include the headings of each section and the page number of the first page of each section. All pages in the document should be numbered.

Executive Summary
After you've finished your business plan, write an executive summary that contains the key points of the business plan. The summary should be brief—no more than two pages—and cover the following points:

- The name of your business
- Where your business will be located
- The mission of your business
- The product or service you are selling
- Who your ideal customers are
- How your product or business will stand out in the crowd
- Who the owners of the business are and what experience they have
- An overview of the future prospects for your business and industry
- An overview of the amount and uses of required initial financing

Hint: You've already answered these questions, so what you need to do is put the ideas together into a "snapshot" format. The executive summary is a sales pitch; it's an investor's first impression of your idea. Ultimately, you're enticing a reader to want to read more. If investors don't get excited about your business and the prospects of success from reading the executive summary, they'll stop reading and most likely not consider the plan. Therefore, as with all parts of the plan, write in a clear and professional way but be compelling about your business.

Note: Once you have created the cover sheet, the table of contents, and the executive summary, move these sections to the beginning of your business plan, with the cover sheet as the very first element.

Glossary

A

Absolute advantage is the ability to produce more of a good or a service than any other country

Accounting involves tracking a business's income and expenses by recording its financial transactions

Acquisitions occur when one company completely buys out another company

Actual product is the tangible aspect of the purchase that you can touch, see, hear, smell, or taste

Advertising is paid, impersonal mass communication from an identified sponsor to persuade or influence a targeted audience

Advisory boards are a group of individuals who offer guidance to the new business owner

Advocacy advertising promotes an organization's position on a public issue, such as global warming or immigration

Adware is any software application that displays banner ads or pop-up ads while a program is running

Affiliative (laissez-faire) leaders are advisory in style, encouraging employees to contribute ideas rather than specifically directing their tasks

Affirmative action is a commitment to improve the opportunities of defined minority groups.

Agents-brokers are intermediaries that facilitate negotiations between buyers and sellers of goods and services but never take title (ownership) of the products traded

American Federation of Labor was founded in 1886 to protect skilled workers

Amoral behavior is when a person has no sense of right and wrong and no interest in the moral consequences of his or her actions

Angel investors are wealthy individuals who are willing to put up their own money in hopes of a profit return later on

Apprentice training programs train individuals through classroom or formal instruction and on-the-job training

Arbitration occurs when a third party settles the dispute after hearing all the issues

Assembly line (or production line) production is when partially complete products are moved from one worker to the next on a conveyor belt

Asset allocation suggests you structure your portfolio with different types of assets (stocks, bonds, mutual funds, real estate, etc.) to reduce the risks associated with these broad types of investments—mostly from inflation and changes in interest rates

Assets are the things a company owns, including cash, investments, buildings, furniture, and equipment

Auditing is the area of accounting responsible for reviewing and evaluating the accuracy of financial reports

Augmented products consist of the core product and the actual product plus other real or perceived benefits that provide additional value to a customer's purchase

Autocratic leaders make decisions without consulting others and dictate assignments

B

Balance sheets show what a company owns and what it has borrowed (owes) at a fixed point in time and shows the net worth of a business

Balance of payments is a system that shows the difference in total value between the payments into and out of a country over a period of time

Bargaining units are groups of employees that negotiate with an employer for better working conditions or pay

B2B (Business-to-business) advertising is directed to other businesses rather than to consumers

B2B (Business-to-business) markets are markets where businesses purchase goods and services from other businesses

B2B (Business-to-business) products (industrial products) are goods and services purchased by businesses for further processing or resale or for use in facilitating business operations

Bear market is a market that indicates decreasing investor confidence as the stock market continues to decline in value

Behavioral segmentation is market segmentation based on certain consumer behavior characteristics

Belonging needs include the need to belong to a group and feel accepted by others

Big Data analysis is the use of tools and analysis techniques for treating very large, very complex data sets

Blue-chip stocks are issued by companies that have a long history of consistent growth and stability

Board of directors usually set policy for the corporation and make the major business and financing decisions

Bond mutual funds are mutual funds that consist solely of bonds

Bonds are debt instruments issued by companies or governments for the purpose of raising capital to finance a large project

Bonuses are compensation based on total corporate profits

Bookkeeping is the systematic recording of a company's every financial transaction

Bootstrap financing is when entrepreneurs start a business with little capital

Boycotts occur when supporters refuse to buy or handle a company's products or services

Brand association involves connecting a brand with other positive attributes, including image, product features, usage situations, organizational associations, brand personality, and symbols

Brand awareness refers to the extent to which a particular brand name is familiar within a particular product category

Brand equity is the overall value of a brand's strength in the market

Brand extension is marketing a product using the same brand name but in a different product category

Brand licensing is an agreement between the owner of a brand and another company or individual who pays a royalty to use the brand in association with a new product

Brand loyalty is the degree to which customers consistently prefer one brand to other brands

Brands are a name, term, symbol, or design that distinguishes a company and its products from all others

Breakeven analysis determines the production level for which total revenue is just enough to cover total costs

Budgets are financial plans that outline a company's planned cash flows, expected operating expenses, and anticipated revenues

Bull market is a market that indicates investor confidence as the market continues to increase in value

Bundling is when two or more products that usually complement one another are combined and sold at a single price

Business cycle is the natural periodic increases and decreases in the economy

Businesses are entities that offer products to their customers to earn a profit

Business incubators are organizations that support start-up businesses by offering administrative services, technical support, business networking, sources of financing, and more that a group of start-up companies shares

Business intelligence software assists managers in reporting, planning, and forecasting workforce performance

Business plans are formal documents that state the goals of the business as well as the plan for reaching those goals

Business-to-business (B2B) advertising is directed to other businesses rather than to consumers

Business-to-business (B2B) markets are markets where businesses purchase goods and services from other businesses

Business-to-business (B2B) products (industrial products) are goods and services purchased by businesses for further processing or resale or for use in facilitating business operations

Business to business (B2B) transactions involve the exchange of products, services, and information between businesses on the Internet

Business to consumer (B2C) transactions refer to e-commerce that takes place directly between businesses and consumers

C

Callable bonds are corporate or municipal bonds where the issuer can either repay investors their initial investment at the maturity date or the issuer can choose to retire the issue early and repay investors at the "callable date"

Capacity planning [Def. to come]

Capital budgets consider a company's long-range plans and outline the expected financial needs for significant capital purchases, such as real estate, manufacturing equipment, plant expansions, or technology

Capital gains are an increase in value that occurs when an investor sells an asset at a higher price than the one at which the asset was bought

Capital is investments in the form of money, equipment, supplies, computers, and other tangible things of value

Capitalism is an economic system that allows such freedom of choice and encourages private ownership of the resources required to make and provide goods and services

Capital loss is a decrease in value between the purchase price and the selling price of an asset

Capital markets are an arena where companies and governments raise long-term funds by selling stocks and bonds and other securities

Cash flow budgets are short-term budgets that estimate cash inflows and outflows and predict any cash flow gaps for the business

Cash flow is the money a company receives and spends over a specific period

C corporations are corporations governed by Subchapter C of the Internal Revenue Code

Cellular layout places small teams of workers who handle all aspects of assembly, so each station is equipped with the parts and tools necessary to produce a product from start to finish, and the worker moves through the workstation as he or she conducts the assembly process

Certified Public Accountant designation given to someone who has passed a rigorous series of examinations given by the American Institute of Certified Public Accountants

Chief executive officers are typically responsible for the entire operations of the corporation and report directly to the board of directors

Chief financial officers report directly to the CEO and are responsible for analyzing and reviewing the financial data, reporting financial performance, preparing budgets, and monitoring expenditures and costs

Chief information officer is the executive in charge of information processing, including systems design and development and data center operations

Chief operating officers are responsible for the day-to-day operations of the organization and report directly to the CEO

Cloud computing refers to the sharing of information, resources, and software over the Internet

Co-branding is using one or more brands affiliated with a single product

Code of ethics is a statement of commitment to certain ethical practices

Collateral is an asset a borrower promises to give a lender if the borrower is unable to repay a loan

Collective bargaining is negotiations between the bargaining unit and the employer for better work conditions and terms of employment

Commercial banks are financial institutions that raise funds from businesses and individuals in the form of checking and savings accounts and use those funds to make loans to businesses and individuals

Commercial finance companies are financial institutions that make short-term loans to borrowers who offer tangible assets as collateral

Commercial paper is an unsecured short-term debt instrument of $100,000 or more, typically issued by a corporation to bridge a cash flow gap created by large accounts receivable, inventory, or payroll

Commissions are compensation based directly on an employee's performance

Common stock is "ordinary" stock that represents equity ownership in a corporation; it provides voting rights and gives the holder access to dividends and/or capital appreciation

Communism is an economic system in which a state's government makes all economic decisions and controls all the social services and many of the major resources required for the production of goods and services

Comparative advantage means that a country can produce a good or service relatively more efficiently compared to other countries

Compensation is payment for work performed, consists of financial and nonfinancial payments

Competition arises when two or more businesses contend with one another to attract customers and gain an advantage

Competition-based pricing is a pricing strategy based on what the competition is charging

Competitive advantage is a company's ability to gain access to and use resources to give them an edge over their competition

Complementary goods are products or services that go with each other and are consumed together

Compound interest is earned interest that is added to the principal investment, which continues to be invested so that the interest also continues to earn interest

Compressed workweek allows employees to work four 10-hour days each week, or 9 days instead of 10 in a two-week schedule for 80 hours

Computer-aided design refers to using a computer and software to create two-dimensional or three-dimensional models of physical parts

Computer-aided manufacturing uses the design data to control the machinery used in the manufacturing process

Computer-integrated manufacturing systems combine design and manufacturing functions with other automated functions, such as order taking, shipment, and billing for the complete automation of a manufacturing plant

Conceptual skills are the ability to think abstractly to picture an organization as a whole and understand its relationship to the remainder of the business community

Conglomeration is a combination of a number of different, perhaps even unrelated, businesses into a single corporation

Congress of Industrial Organizations was formed in 1935 to represent entire industries rather than specific workers' groups

Consultants are contingent workers who are generally self-employed and who companies hire on a temporary basis to perform specific tasks

Consumer behavior refers to the ways individuals or organizations search for, evaluate, purchase, use, and dispose of goods and services

Consumer price index tracks changes in prices over time by measuring changes in the prices of goods and services that represent the average buying pattern of urban households

Consumer products are convenience goods and services, shopping goods and services, specialty goods and services, and unsought goods and services

Consumer sales promotions are incentives designed to increase final consumer demand for a product

Consumer-to-consumer (C2C) transactions refers to consumers selling goods and services to other consumers, sometimes with the involvement of a third party

Contextual advertising refers to online ads automatically generated by the content on a specific site

Contingency planning is a set of plans that ensures that an organization will run as smoothly as possible during an unexpected disruption

Contingent workers are people who are hired on an as-needed basis and lack status as regular, full-time employees

Continuous flow production is a method that produces discrete units of products in large numbers one by one continuously and rapidly

Contract manufacturing occurs when a firm subcontracts part or all of its goods to an outside firm as an alternative to owning and operating its own production facility

Controlling (monitoring) is the process by which managers measure performance and make sure the company's plans and strategies are being or have been properly carried out

Convenience goods and services are those products that customers purchase frequently, immediately, and with little or no deliberation

Convertible bonds give a bondholder the right (but not the obligation) to convert the bond into a predetermined number of shares of the company's stock

Cooperatives are businesses that are owned and governed by members who use its products or services, not by outside investors

Core product provides the core benefit or service that satisfies the basic need or want that motivates a consumer's purchase

Corporate accounting is the part of an organization's finance department that is responsible for gathering and assembling data required for key financial statements

Corporate advertising (institutional advertising) focuses on creating a positive image toward an organization or an entire industry as opposed to a specific product

Corporate bonds are debt securities issued by corporations

Corporate chain stores are two or more retail outlets owned by a single corporation

Corporate culture is a collection of values, norms, and behavior shared by management and workers that defines the character of an organization

Corporate philanthropy is when a company donates some of its profits or resources to charitable organizations

Corporate social responsibility is defined as a company's obligation to conduct its activities with the aim of achieving social, environmental, and economic development

Corporations are a specific form of business organization that is a legal entity separate from the owner or owners

Cost-based pricing is based on covering costs and providing for a set profit

Cost of goods sold are variable expenses a company incurs to manufacture and sell a product, including the price of raw materials used in creating the good along with the labor costs used to produce and sell the items

Coupon (bond) is the bond's interest rate

Cross-functional team members are selected across a range of critical functional divisions of a business

Crowdfunding is a way to generate funds via donations or, more recently, investments from individuals via social networking

Crowdsourced funding refers to contributions of small amounts by a great number of people who believe in a company or product

Crowdsourcing is soliciting ideas or content from a large group of people, often from an online community

Currency is a unit of exchange for the transfer of goods and services that provides a consistent standard, the value of which is based on an underlying commodity, such as gold

Currency appreciation is an increase in the exchange rate value of a nation's currency

Currency depreciation is a decrease in the exchange rate value of a nation's currency

Current assets are those assets that can be turned into cash within a year

Current ratio (liquidity ratio) is a measurement used to determine the extent to which a company can meet its current financial obligations

Customer relationship management is the process of establishing long-term relationships with individual customers to foster loyalty and repeat business

Cyclical stocks are issued by companies that produce goods or services affected by repeating economic trends

Cyclical unemployment measures unemployment caused by lack of demand for those who want to work

D

Data are the representations of a fact or idea

Data marts are subsets of data warehouses

Data mining is the process of exploring and analyzing the data mart to uncover data relationships and data patterns that will help a business

Data warehouses are vast amounts of data stored in database systems separate from production databases

Database management systems are collections of tables of data that organize the data and allow simple analysis and reporting

Debenture bonds are unsecured bonds, backed only by a corporation's promise to pay

Debt financing occurs when a company borrows money that it is legally obligated to repay, with interest, by a specified time

Debt-to-equity ratio is a measurement of how much debt a company has relative to its assets by comparing a company's total liabilities to its total shareholders' equity

Decision-making skills are the ability to identify and analyze a challenge, examine the alternatives, choose and implement the best plan of action, and evaluate the results

Decision support system is a software system that enables companies to analyze collected data so they can predict the impact of business decisions

Defensive stocks are issued by companies producing staples such as food, drugs, and insurance and usually maintain their value regardless of the state of the economy

Deflation is a continuous decrease in prices over time

Demand refers to how much of a good or a service people want to buy at any given time

Demand-based pricing (value-based pricing) is pricing a good or a service based on the demand for a product or its perceived value

Demand deposit refers to funds that can be withdrawn at any time without prior notice

Demand curve illustrates the relationship between demand and price

Democratic leaders delegate authority and involve employees in the decision making

Demographic segmentation is market segmentation according to age, race, religion, gender, ethnic background, and other demographics

Depreciation is the process of spreading out the cost of the equipment over its useful life

Depression is a very severe or long recession

Determinants of demand are factors that affect a product from the demand side

Determinants of supply are factors that can create a change in supply

Devalue is to deliberately reduce the value of a currency in relation to another

Direct marketers are those who retail goods or services and bypass intermediaries

Direct sellers sell goods and services door-to-door at homes, offices or at temporary or mobile locations

Discount rate is the interest rate that the Federal Reserve charges banks when they borrow money from it

Discounts are a deduction from the regular price charged

Distribution is the process that makes products available to consumers when and where the consumers want them

Distribution channel is a set of marketing intermediaries who buy, sell, or transfer title (or ownership) of products as they are passed from producer to consumer or business user

Diversification is the concept of having a variety of investments in your portfolio

Diversity training helps employees and managers improve their understanding of each other's differences

Dividends are payments made from a portion of a company's profits to shareholders

Double entry bookkeeping recognizes that for every transaction that affects an asset, an equal transaction must also affect either a liability or owners' equity

Double taxation is the situation that occurs when taxes are paid on the same asset twice

Due diligence means to research and analyze a business to uncover any hidden problems associated with it

Dumping refers to selling a product at a price below the price charged in the producing country; it is illegal and can be difficult to prove

Duopolies are where only two suppliers exist

Dynamic pricing is when prices are determined directly between a buyer and a seller, unlike the more traditional fixed pricing in which a seller sets prices

E

Earnings per share is the quotient of net income divided by outstanding shares that results in the portion of a company's profit allocated to the stockholders on a per share basis

E-commerce is the buying and selling of goods and services through the Internet

Economic indicators are certain statistics about economy-wide activity levels

Economics is the study of how individuals and businesses make decisions to best satisfy wants, needs, and desires with limited resources and how efficiently and equitably resources are allocated

Economy is a system that tries to balance the available resources of a country, such as land, capital, and labor, against the wants and needs of consumers

Electronic monitoring is commonly used to track employees' keystrokes and e-mails, examine their Internet browsing histories, and even monitor their cell phone and instant messaging usage

Electronic retailing is the selling of consumer goods and services over the Internet

Embargoes are a total restriction on an import or an export

Emotional intelligence is the ability to understand both one's own and others' emotions

Employee benefits are indirect financial and nonfinancial payments an employer offers that supplement cash compensation

Employee stock ownership plans use a company's pension plan for employees to invest in company stock, effectively giving employees significant ownership in a company

Employee stock purchase plans allow employees to buy company stock at a discount

Employment at will is a legal doctrine that states that an employer can fire an employee for any reason at any time

Enterprise resource planning is a system that can do the same inventory control and process scheduling that MRP can do, but that integrates these functions with all the other functions of the business, such as finance, marketing, and human resources

Enterprise social networking refers to the application of products like Facebook in a corporate setting

Enterprise zones are geographic areas targeted for economic revitalizing

Entrepreneurial teams are groups of qualified individuals with varied experiences and skills that come together to form a new venture

Entrepreneurs assume the risk of creating, organizing, and operating a business and direct all of a business's resources

Environmental scanning is the process of surveying the marketing environment to assess external threats and opportunities

Equilibrium price is the price at which supply equals demand

Equity is ownership interest in a company in the form of stocks

Equity financing is the process of raising funds by offering shares of ownership in the company to the general public

Equity theory is the concept that people derive job satisfaction and motivation by comparing their efforts, and the results from them, with what other people in the firm are receiving

Esteem needs are satisfied by the mastery of a skill and the attention and recognition of others

Ethics is the study of the general nature of morals and the specific moral choices a person makes

Ethics training programs are designed to boost the awareness of their employees about ethical issues

Ethnocentrism is a belief that one's own culture is superior to all other cultures

Everyday low pricing is a strategy of charging low prices with few, if any, special or promotional sales

Exchange rates are the rates at which currencies are converted into another currency

Exchange-traded funds are a pool of stocks like a mutual fund, but they trade like stocks on the exchange

Exclusive distribution strategy uses only one outlet in a geographic area

Executive information system is a software system that is specially designed for the needs of management

Expectancy is the idea that a person's effort has an appreciable effect on a situation's result—whether it is a success or failure

Expectancy theory suggests an individual's motivation can be described by the relationship among three psychological forces: expectancy, instrumentality, and valence

Expenses are the money a business pays out

Exporting is the sale of domestically produced products to other countries

External recruiting looks outside a business to fill job vacancies

Extrinsic motivators are external factors that generate engagement with the work, such as pay or promotion

F

Facility layout refers to the physical arrangement of resources and people in the production process and how they interact

Factoring is the process of selling accounts receivable for cash

Factors of production are the resources used to create goods and services

Family brand is a brand that markets several different products under the same brand name

Federal Open Market Committee is a part of the Federal Reserve that buys and sells government securities, which in turn affects the nation's money supply

Federal Reserve System is responsible for monetary policy and uses open market operations, banks' reserve requirements, and changes in the discount rate to help keep the economy from experiencing severe negative or positive swings

Federal funds rate is the interest rate that banks charge other banks when they borrow funds overnight from one another

Financial accounting is an area of accounting that produces financial documents that investors and people outside of a company use to make decisions about its financial strength

Financial capital is money used to facilitate a business enterprise

Financial management involves the strategic planning and budgeting of short- and long-term funds for current and future needs

Financial managers (or chief financial officers [CFOs]) oversee the financial operations of a company

Financial statements are formal reports of a business's financial condition that accountants prepare periodically

First-line managers fill a supervisory role over those employees who carry out the day-to-day operations of a company

Fiscal policy determines the appropriate level of taxes and government spending

Fixed assets are assets that have long-term use, such as real estate, buildings, machinery, and equipment

Fixed position layouts are used for manufacturing large items; the product stays in one place, and the workers move around the product to complete its assembly

Flexible benefit plans (cafeteria plans) permit an employee to pick from a menu of several choices of taxable and nontaxable forms of compensation

Flexible manufacturing system is a system in which machines are programmed to process different part types simultaneously, allowing a manufacturer to mass-produce customized products

Flextime is an alternative scheduling practice in which management defines a total number of required hours as a core workday and is flexible with starting and ending ties

Floating rate notes are U.S. government debt instruments that pay interest quarterly and are issued for a term of two years

Flow is a state of feeling completely involved and focused on a task

Focus groups are typically groups of 8–10 potential customers who are asked for feedback on a good or a service, an advertisement, an idea, or packaging style

Forecasting is the process through which future demand for a firm's products and employees is determined

Foreign direct investment is the purchasing of property and businesses in a foreign nation

Form utility is satisfaction derived from the shape of a good or presentation of a service

401(k) plans are defined contribution plans in which pretax dollars are invested in a bundle of investments that are generally managed by an outside investment company

Franchise is a distribution system where a franchiser sells a proven method of doing business to a franchisee for a fee and a percentage of sales or profits generated by the business

Franchisees are the independent third-party operators of a franchise

Franchising involves selling a well-known brand name or a proven method of doing business to an investor in exchange for a fee and a percentage of sales or profits

Franchisors are businesses that sell their product or service and its method of doing business to independent third-party operators

Free trade refers to the unencumbered flow of goods and services across national borders

Frictional unemployment is a type of temporary unemployment that occurs when workers move between jobs, change careers, or relocate

Full-service wholesaler is a type of marketing intermediary that provides to other businesses a full line of services, such as carrying stock, maintaining a sales force, offering credit, making deliveries, and helping price, market, and sell products

Fundamental accounting equation refers to when assets equal the sum of liabilities plus owners' equity

Futures contracts are an agreement between a buyer and a seller to receive (or deliver) an asset sometime in the future at a specific price agreed on today

G

Gantt charts are used to lay out each task in a project, the order in which these tasks must be completed, and how long each task should take

General Agreement on Tariffs and Trade is an international organization that held eight rounds of negotiated agreements or treaties to reduce tariffs and other obstacles to free trade on goods

Generally acceptable accounting principles are standard accounting rules defined by the Financial Accounting Standard Board

General obligation bonds are municipal bonds supported by the taxing power of the issuer, so they tend to be very safe

General partners are full owners of the business, are responsible for all the day-to-day business decisions, and remain liable for all the debts and obligations of the business

General partnerships are businesses where every partner participates in the daily management tasks of the business, and each has some degree of control over the decisions made

Generic brand is a product that has no brand at all

Geographic segmentation is market segmentation according to geographic characteristics

Globalization is a movement toward a more interconnected and interdependent world economy

Globalization of markets refers to the movement away from thinking of the market as being the local market or the national market to thinking of the market as being the entire world

Globalization of production refers to the trend of individual firms moving production to different locations around the globe to take advantage of lower costs or to enhance quality

Global strategy is a strategy of selling a standardized (or homogeneous) product across the globe

Goals are broad, long-term accomplishments an organization wants to achieve within a certain time frame

Goods are physical products a business sells

Goodwill is the intangible assets represented by a business's name, customer service, employee morale, and other factors

Government and not-for-profit accounting refers to the accounting required for organizations that are not focused on generating a profit

Government bonds are debt securities issued by national governments

Grants are financial awards offered by federal and state governments and some private organizations

Green economy factors ecological concerns into business decisions

Gross domestic product measures the overall market value of final goods and services produced in a country in a year

Gross profit tells how much money a company makes just from its products and how efficiently management controls costs in the production process

Gross profit margin determines a company's profitability of production

Group flow occurs when a group knows how to work together so that each individual member can achieve flow

Groupthink is the practice of thinking or making decisions as a group in a way that discourages individual ideas or responsibilities

Growth entrepreneurs strive to create fast-growing businesses and look forward to expansion

Growth stocks are issued by young entrepreneurial companies experiencing rapid growth and expansion

H

Hackers are individuals who gain unauthorized entry into a computer system

Hawthorne effect states that when workers feel important, their productivity increases

Hierarchy of needs describes motivation as a response to a person's progressive set of needs for physiology, safety, belonging, esteem, and self-actualization

Home-based entrepreneurs are entrepreneurs who run their businesses out of their homes

Horizontal mergers occur when two companies that share the same product lines and markets and are in direct competition with each other merge

Horizontal organizations are flattened organizations where the management layer is collapsed and the majority of the employees are in working teams or groups

Human resource management is the organizational function that deals with the people in the business: executives and managers plus frontline production, sales, and administrative staff

Hygiene factors are factors such as safe working environment, proper pay and benefits, and positive relationships with coworkers

I

Identity theft is the illegal gain and use of other people's personal information

Importing is buying products from other countries

Incentive-based payment structures have a lower base salary enhanced with commissions, compensation based directly on an employee's performance

Income statements show how much money a company earned during various periods

Income stocks are issued by companies that pay large dividends, such as utility companies

Independent contractors are contingent workers hired for hard-to-fill jobs that require state-of-the-art skills in construction, financial activities, and professional and business services

Index represents a collection of related stocks based on certain shared characteristics, such as having a similar size, belonging to a common industry, or trading on the same market exchange

Individual brands are brands assigned to each product within a company's product mix

Industrial psychology is a field of study developed to help managers understand how to optimally manage people and work

Inflation is a rise in the general level of prices over time

Infomercials are television commercials that run as long as regular TV programs

Information is data that have been organized or arranged in a way that makes it useful

Information systems (Management information systems) focus on applying IT to solve business and economic problems

Information technology is the design and implementation of computer-based information systems

Initial public offering is the first sale of stock to the public by a company

Insider trading is the buying and selling of securities based on information that has not been disclosed to the public

Instrumentality refers to the idea that the outcome of a situation is related to rewards or punishments

Intangible assets are assets such as trademarks, patents, and copyrights that do not have physical characteristics but have value nonetheless

Integrated marketing communications is a strategy to deliver a clear, consistent, and unified message about a company and its products to customers at all contact points

Intellectual property is a creation of the mind, such as an idea, invention, literary or other artistic work

Intensive distribution is the use of all available retail outlets to sell a product

Interactive advertising uses interactive media, such as interactive video catalogs on the Internet or kiosks at shopping malls, to connect directly with consumers in a personal and engaging way

Intermittent processes are flexible processes with shorter production runs, so machinery can be changed over between them to accommodate product changes

Internal recruiting is filling job vacancies with existing employees from within a business

Internet advertising uses pop-up banner ads and other techniques to direct people to an organization's website

Internet entrepreneurs create businesses that operate solely online

Interpersonal skills enable managers to interact with other people to motivate them

Intrapreneurs are employees who work in an entrepreneurial way within an organizational environment

Intrinsic motivators are internal drives that come from the actual interest of the work or from a sense of purpose and value in the work being done

Inventory is the merchandise a business owns but has not yet sold

Inventory control includes the receiving, storing, handling, and tracking of everything in a company's stock

Inverted organizations have a structure where management is answerable to employees—management's role is to enable, encourage, and empower employees to do what they do best

Investing is using money to buy an asset where there is a chance of losing part or all of your initial investment

Investment banker is a specialist who assists in the sale of new securities and prepares financial documents that must be filed with the SEC

ISO 14001 standards are international environmental management standards

ISO 9001 standards are international quality management standards

J

Job analysis defines in detail the particular duties and requirements of the tasks and responsibilities an employee is required to perform

Job description is a formal statement that summarizes what the employee will do in that role

Job sharing is an arrangement in which two employees work part-time to share one full-time job

Job specifications are the skills, education, experience, and personal attributes candidates need to possess to successfully fulfill the role

Joint ventures involve shared ownership in a subsidiary firm

Judeo-Christian ethics refers to the common set of basic values shared across both Jewish and Christian religious traditions

Junk bonds are high-risk bonds that offer high interest rates to attract investors

Just-in-time (JIT) inventory control keeps the smallest amount of inventory on hand as possible, and everything else that is needed is ordered so that it arrives when it is needed

L

Labor is a human resource that refers to any physical or intellectual work that people contribute to a business's production

Labor unions are legally recognized groups dedicated to protecting the interests of workers

Law of supply is a principle that states that the amount supplied will increase as the price increases; and, the lower the price, the less supplied

Leading is the process of influencing, motivating, and enabling others to contribute to the success and effectiveness of an organization by achieving its goals

Lean production is a set of principles concerned with reducing waste and improving flow

Legal compliance refers to conducting a business within the boundaries of all the legal regulations of that industry

Legal regulations are the specific laws governing the products or processes of a specific industry

Leverage is the amount of debt used to finance a firm's assets with the intent that the rate of return on the assets is greater than the cost of the debt

Liabilities are all debts and obligations owed by a business to outside creditors, suppliers, or other vendors

Liability is the obligation to pay a debt, such as an account payable or a loan

Licensing is an agreement in which the licensor's intangible property—patents, trademarks, service marks, copyrights, trade secrets, or other intellectual property—may be sold or made available to a licensee in exchange for a royalty fee

Lifestyle entrepreneurs look for more than profit potential when they begin their businesses

Limited liability companies are companies in which the owners have limited personal liability for the debts and the actions of the company

Limited partners are involved as investors and, as such, are personally liable only up to the amount of their investment in the business and must not actively participate in any decisions of the business

Limited partnerships are businesses where at least one partner controls a business's operations and is personally liable

Limited service wholesaler is a type of distribution intermediary that offers fewer services than full-service wholesalers

Line of credit refers to the credit that a manager can access at any time up to an amount agreed upon between a bank and a company

Liquidity is the speed at which assets can be changed into cash

Load fund is a type of mutual fund that charges additional costs (loads) that are rolled into the cost of the funds when they are bought and sold

Local businesses rely on local consumers to generate business

Local content requirements are a requirement that some portion of a good be produced domestically

Locals are subsets of a larger union that represents smaller groups of workers with interests specific to their industry, region, company, or business sector

Lockouts occur when management refuses to allow union members to enter a business's premises

Logistics refers to managing the flow of materials, information, and processes involved in getting a product from its initial raw stages to the point of consumption

Logo is a graphic representation or symbol of a company name, trademark, or abbreviation

Long-term financing is financing that is repaid in a period longer than a year

Long-term liabilities include debts and obligations owed by a company that are due more than one year from the current date

Loss leader is a product that is priced below its cost

M

M-1 is a measurement of the money supply; it includes the most liquid assets, such as coins, bills, traveler's checks, and checking accounts

M-2 is a measurement of the money supply; it includes M-1 assets plus savings deposits, money market accounts, and certificates of deposit less than $100,000

M-3 is a measurement of the money supply; it includes M-1 and M-2 assets plus the least liquid assets, such as large certificates of deposit, large money market accounts, and deposits of Eurodollars

Macroeconomics is the study of the behavior of the overall economy

Make-or-buy decisions decide what needs to be manufactured and what needs to be purchased from outside suppliers

Management is the process of working with people and resources to accomplish the goals of an organization

Management development programs prepare management-trainees to become managers within an organization

Management information systems focus on applying IT to solve business and economic problems

Managerial accounting uses accounting information to help make decisions inside a company

Manufacturer's brand is a brand created by producers

Market is the mechanism by which buyers and sellers exchange goods and services

Market economy gives control of economic decisions to individuals and private firms

Market extension merger is a merger between two companies that sell the same products in different markets

Marketing is an organizational function and a set of processes for creating, communicating, and delivering value to customers and for managing customer relationships in ways that benefit the organization and its stakeholders

Marketing concept refers to an era that changed the focus from finding the right customer for a product to producing the right product for a customer and doing it better than the competition

Marketing environment includes environmental influences beyond a firm's control that constrain the organization's ability to manipulate its marketing mix

Marketing intermediaries are businesses or persons that move goods and services between producers and consumers or between business users

Marketing mix is the combination of four factors—product, price, promotion, and place—designed to serve a targeted market

Marketing objective is a clearly stated goal to be achieved through marketing activities

Marketing plan is a written document that specifies the marketing activities that will take place to achieve organizational objectives

Market price for a good or a service is the price at which everyone who wants the item can get it without anyone wanting more or without any of the item being left over

Market risk is the general investment risk associated with the overall market

Mass customization is the production of goods or services tailored to meet customers' individual needs cost-effectively

Mass production is the method of producing large quantities of goods at a low cost

Materials requirement planning is a computer-based program used for inventory control and production planning

Matrix organizations have a type of management system in which people are pooled into groups by skills and then assigned to projects as needed

Maturity date of a bond is the date on which the bond matures and the investor's principal is repaid

Mediation is a process that involves a neutral third party that assists the two parties both privately and collectively to identify issues and develop proposals for resolution

Mentors are experienced individuals who help a less experienced person by explaining how to perform specific tasks, creating opportunities for them to learn new skills, and counseling them about the consequences of particular actions and decisions

Mergers occur when two companies of similar size mutually agree to combine to form a new company

Microeconomics is the study of how individual businesses, households, and consumers make decisions to allocate their limited resources in the exchange of goods and services

Microloans are small, short-term loan specific to small businesses

Micropreneurs start their own businesses but are satisfied with keeping their businesses small in an effort to achieve a balanced lifestyle

Middle managers can be thought of as top managers for one division or a segment of an organization

Mission statements define the core purpose of the organization—why it exists—and often describe its values, goals, and aspirations

Mixed economies are a blend of market and planned economies

Mobile advertising is delivering advertising messages via mobile phones or other mobile devices

Monetary policy refers to how the U.S. Federal Reserve System manages the money supply by buying and selling government securities, setting banks' reserve requirements, and adjusting the rate at which they can borrow money from the Federal Reserve

Money market funds are funds that invest in short-term debt obligations, such as Treasury bills and CDs, and are quite safe

Money supply is the combined amount of money available within an economy

Monopolies occur when there is only one provider of a service or a good and no substitutes exist

Monopolistic competition occurs when there are many buyers and sellers and little differentiation between the products themselves

Moral relativism is a perspective that holds that there is no universal moral truth; instead, there are only people's individual beliefs, perspectives, and values

Motivator factors include a sense of responsibility, recognition, promotion, and job growth

Motivator-hygiene theory (two factor theory) states that two factors, hygiene and motivator, influence a person's motivation

Multidomestic strategy is a strategy in which domestic products are customized to meet the unique local needs, tastes, or preferences of customers abroad

Multinational enterprises are businesses that manufacture and market products in two or more countries

Municipal bonds (or munis) are bonds issued by state or local governments or governmental agencies

Mutual funds are a means by which a group of investors pool money together to invest in a diversified set of investments

N

NASDAQ (National Association of Securities Dealers Automated Quotations) is one of the largest and most dominant stock exchanges in the United States; in this exchange system, stocks are traded via an electronic market

National businesses have several outlets throughout a country, but do not serve an international market

Natural resources are the raw materials provided by nature that are used to produce goods and services

Net asset value is the value of the underlying securities held by a mutual fund; the measure of a fund's value

Net income is the positive difference between how much money a company takes in versus how much it spends; a negative difference is a net loss

Net income after taxes is the "bottom line" stated on the last line of the income statement

Networking is the process of building relationships that can potentially create business opportunities

Network organizations are collections of independent, mostly single-function firms that collaborate on a product or a service

New York Stock Exchange is one of the largest and most dominant stock exchanges in the United States; in this exchange system, stocks are bought and sold on a trading floor or via an electronic market

Niche markets are very narrowly defined sets of potential customers

No-load funds are mutual funds that have little or no additional costs

Nonbank lenders are financial institutions that extend credit or loans but do not hold deposits. These lenders will take on loans commercial banks view as too risky

Nonprofit advertising focuses on promoting non-for-profit organizations

Nonstore retailing is a form of retailing in which consumer contact occurs outside the confines of a traditional brick-and-mortar retail store

North American Free Trade Agreement is an ongoing agreement to move the United States, Mexico, and Canada closer to true free trade

Not-for-profit organizations are businesses that do not pursue profits but instead seek to service the community through social, educational, or political means

NYSE Amex is a part of NYSE Euronext, a stock exchange that deals primarily with small-cap companies, exchange traded funds, and other more advanced investments

NYSE Euronext is the stock exchange that resulted from the merger between the New York Stock Exchange (NYSE) and the fully electronic stock exchange Euronext

O

Objectives are short-term targets designed to help achieve goals

Offshoring is when businesses relocate their production facilities overseas or subcontract at least some of the components of their products to foreign companies around the world to achieve lower manufacturing costs

Off-the-job training development techniques require employees to participate in outside seminars, university-conducted programs, and corporate universities

Oligopolies are a form of competition in which only a few sellers exist

Online advertising is any form of advertising that uses the Internet to market its message to customers

Online analysis package is a software application that enables very quick analysis of combinations of different business factors

Online training or distance learning, allows employees to take college classes on the Internet at their convenience, enabling them to obtain specific job-related education or pursue a degree

On-the-job training is used to teach the skills for a job as the employee is working

Open market operations are a form of monetary policy in which the Federal Open Market Committee buys and sells U.S. government securities in the open market to either decrease or increase the nation's money supply

Operating (master) budgets map out the projected number of units firms expect to sell, the income generated from them, and all of the operating costs incurred to produce and sell them

Operating expenses are the overhead costs incurred with running the business

Operating profit margin determines a company's profitability of operations

Operational plans determine the process by which tactical plans can be achieved

Operations management consists of managing the activities and processes to produce and distribute goods and services

Opportunity niche is a need in the market that is not being adequately fulfilled

Options are a contract that gives a buyer the right to buy (call) or sell (put) a particular security at a specific price on or before a certain date

Order getters are salespeople who increase a company's sales by selling to new customers and increasing sales to existing customers

Order influencers concentrate on activities that target those who influence purchases made by the final customer

Order takers are salespeople who handle repeat sales and build positive customer relationships

Organizational psychology is the study of how to create a workplace that fosters motivation and productivity among employees

Organization charts show how groups of employees fit into the larger organizational structure

Organizing is the process of structuring the capital, personnel, raw materials, and other resources to carry out a company's plans in a way that best matches the nature of the work

Orientation programs integrate a new employee into the company

Outsourcing is the assignment of certain tasks, such as production or accounting, to an outside company or organization

Over-the-counter stock is a security that might be too small to meet the requirements to be traded on a formal exchange such as the NYSE or NASDAQ, and so are traded directly between investment professionals

Owners' equity is literally the amount the owners of a business can call their own

Ownership utility is satisfaction derived from possessing an item

P

Par (face) value is the amount of money the bondholder will get back once a bond reaches maturity

Partnership is a type of business entity in which two or more entities (or partners) share the ownership and the profits and losses of the business

Partnership agreements formalize the relationship between the business partners

Pay-per-click (PPC) advertising allows advertisers to pay only for the number of times Web surfers click on their ads

Peer-to-peer lending is the process of individuals lending to each other

Penetration pricing is a strategy of charging the lowest possible price for a new product

Pension plans are programs that provide income to individuals in their retirement

Perfect competition occurs when there are many buyers and sellers of products that are virtually identical and any seller can easily enter and exit the market

Performance appraisals are an evaluation of an employee's performance that gives them feedback about how well the worker is doing, as well as where changes and improvements are needed

Performance management is an approach that combines goal setting, performance appraisals, and training and development into a unified and ongoing process

Permanent part-time employees are hired on a permanent basis to work a part-time week

Personal ethics are the principles that guide the decisions you make in your life

Personal selling is direct communication between a firm's sales force and potential buyers to make a sale and build good customer relations

Phishing is a common way to trick online users into sending their personal information, like credit card numbers, straight to hackers

Physical distribution is a system that involves getting products to customers when and where they want them

Physiological needs are basic needs such as water, food, sleep, and reproduction

Picketing is a form of protest during a strike when workers walk around company entrances carrying signs and distributing pamphlets that display the nature of their grievances

Place (distribution) component of the marketing mix refers to all the methods involved in getting a product into the hands of customers

Place utility is the satisfaction derived from obtaining a product where it is desired

Planned economic system is an economic system in which the government has more control over what is produced, the resources to produce the goods and services, and the distribution of the goods and services

Planning is the process of establishing goals and objectives and determining the best ways to accomplish them

Positioning is the process of developing a unique marketing mix that best satisfies a target market

Preferred stock is a class of ownership in which the preferred stockholders have a claim to assets before common stockholders if a firm goes out of business

Prestige pricing (premium pricing) is the practice of charging a high price to invoke perceptions of high quality and privilege

Price discrimination is charging different prices to different customers when these price differences are not a reflection of cost differences

Price elasticity of demand is the degree to which the demand for a product will be affected by price changes

Price fixing occurs when a group of companies agree among themselves to set a product's price, independent of market demand or supply

Price skimming involves charging a high price for a product initially and then lowering the price over time

Primary data is raw data collected by a researcher

Primary markets are a part of the capital markets that deal with new bond and stock issues

Private accountants are accountants hired by companies to perform financial accounting tasks in-house

Private brands are brands created by a distributor, or a middleman

Privatization is the conversion of government-owned production and services to privately owned, profit-seeking enterprises

Process layout is production layout in which similar tasks are grouped together, and the partially assembled product moves from one workstation to the next

Producer price index tracks the average change in prices at the wholesale level

Product advertising promotes a specific product's uses, features, and benefits

Product differentiation is the process of distinguishing a product from its competition in real or perceived terms to attract customers

Product extension merger is a merger between two companies selling different but related products in the same market

Production is the process of getting a good or a service to the customer; it is a series of related activities, with value being added at each stage

Production management refers to the planning, implementation, and control measures used to convert resources into finished products

Productivity measures the quantity of goods and services that human and physical resources can produce in a given time period

Product layout is a production layout used mostly for high-volume, standardized products that can be produced in a sequential fashion

Product life cycle is a theoretical model describing a product's sales and profits over the course of its lifetime

Product line is a group of similar products marketed to one general market

Product line length is the number of items in any given product line

Product mix is the combination of all product lines offered for sale by a company

Product mix width refers to the number of different product lines a company offers

Product placement is a technique of prominently displaying products in television shows, movies, and video games, where they will be seen by potential customers

Profits are earned when a company's revenue is greater than its expenses

Profit-sharing plans refer to a range of employee and executive compensation plans that depend on the company hitting certain profit targets

Program evaluation and review techniques maps out the various steps involved in a project, differentiating tasks that must be completed in a certain order from tasks that may be completed simultaneously

Programmed learning approach occurs when an employee is asked to perform step-by-step instructions or respond to questions

Project budgets identify the costs needed to accomplish projects

Promotional mix is the strategic combination of promotional tools used to reach targeted customers to achieve marketing objectives

Promotion involves all the techniques marketers use to inform targeted customers of the benefits of a product and persuade them to purchase a good, a service, or an idea

Prospecting is the identification of qualified potential customers

Prospectus is a formal legal document that provides details about an investment

Psychographic segmentation is market segmentation based on lifestyles, personality traits, motives, and values

Psychological pricing (odd or fractional pricing) is the practice of charging a price just below a whole number to give the appearance of a significantly lower price

Public accountant is a type of external accountant companies hire to do accounting tasks

Publicity is information about an individual, an organization, or a product transmitted through mass media at no charge

Publicly owned corporations are corporations that are regulated by the Securities and Exchange Commission

Public relations is a management function that establishes and maintains mutually beneficial relationships between an organization and its stakeholders

Public service advertising communicates a message on behalf of a good cause, such as the prevention of wildfires

Purchasing is the task of acquiring the materials and services needed in the production process

Q

Quality control refers to the techniques, activities, and processes used to guarantee that a good or service meets a specified level of quality

Quotas are a limitation on the amount of an import allowed to enter a country

R

Rack jobbers serve grocery stores and drug retailers by sending delivery trucks to stores, where the delivery people set up racks or displays within the stores

Radio frequency identification refers to electronic systems that allow computers to keep track of the status and quantity of tagged inventory as it moves through the supply chain

Ratio analysis is a comparison of numbers and therefore is used to compare current data to data from previous years, competitors' data, or industry averages

Real capital is the physical facilities used to produce goods and services

Rebates are partial refunds on what a customer has already paid for a product

Recession is a decline in the GDP for two or more successive quarters of a year

Recruitment is the process of finding, screening, and selecting people for a specific job

Reference pricing refers to listing an inflated price (the regular retail price or the manufacturer's suggested retail price) that is then discounted to appear as if it is a good value

Regional businesses are companies that serve a wider area than local businesses but do not serve national or international markets

Regional free trade agreements are compacts abolishing trade barriers among member countries

Reserve requirements are the minimum amount of money banks must hold in reserve to cover customers' withdrawals of their deposits

Retail (or local) advertising focuses on attracting customers to a fixed location, such as a department store or a grocery store

Retailers are intermediaries that buy products for resale to consumers

Retained earnings are the accumulated profits a business has held onto for reinvestment into a company

Retirement is the point in one's life where one stops participating full-time in a career

Revenue is the amount of money generated by a business by either selling goods or performing services

Revenue bonds are municipal bonds supported by the income generated by the project they finance

Risk–return relationship is a direct relationship between risk and return for all securities, with the least risky investments offering the lowest amount of return and vice versa

Routing is the way in which goods are transported, via water, rail, truck, or air

S

Safety needs include establishing safe and stable places to live

Salaries are annual pay for a specific job

Sales promotion is a short-term activity that targets consumers and other businesses for the purpose of generating interest in a product

Sarbanes-Oxley Act of 2002 is an act passed by the United States Congress that protects investors from possible fraudulent accounting methods used by organizations

Scheduling refers to the efficient organization of equipment, facilities, labor, and materials

S corporations are regular corporations (C corporations) that have elected to be taxed under a special section of the Internal Revenue Code called Subchapter S

Seasonal unemployment is a type of unemployment that measures those out of work during the off-season, such as those employed in snow- or beach-related industries, agriculture, and/or holiday activities

Secondary data is data that have already been collected and processed

Secondary markets are the markets in which investors purchase securities from other investors rather than directly from an issuing company

Secured bonds are bonds backed by collateral, which is generally corporate-owned property that will pass to the bondholders (or be sold to reimburse bondholders) if the issuer does not repay the amount borrowed

Secured loans are loans that require collateral, which is generally the asset that the loan is financing, to guarantee the debt obligation

Securities are investment instruments such as bonds (debt) or stock (equity)

Securities and Exchange Commission is the federal agency that regulates and governs the securities industry

Selective distribution uses only a portion of the many possible retail outlets for selling a product

Self-actualization needs include the desire to maximize your own potential through education and self-fulfillment as well as experiences of beauty and spirituality

Serial bonds are bonds that have a series of dates on which portions of the debt associated with them mature, unlike traditional bonds, which are paid back all at once

Series EE bonds are U.S. government bonds that have a 20-year maturity but pay interest for up to a total of 30 years

Series I bonds are U.S. government bonds that have an interest rate that is partly fixed and partly variable

Service Corps of Retired Executives is a volunteer organization of retired executives who offer workshops and counseling to small businesses at no cost

Services are intangible products that are bought or sold

Seven Habits model describes habits of behavior exhibited by successful people

Shareholders have an ownership interest in a company

Shopping goods and services are products that are less frequently purchased and require that the customer spend more time and effort in comparing the products

Shortage is the situation in which demand exceeds supply

Short-term financing is any type of financing repaid within a year or less

Short-term liabilities (current liabilities) are obligations a company is responsible for paying within a year or less

Simulation training provides realistic job-task training in a manner that is challenging but does not create the threat of failure

Sinking fund is a type of savings fund into which a company deposits money regularly to help repay a bond

Situational ethics is when people make decisions based on a specific situation instead of universal laws

Six Sigma is a statistically based, proactive, long-term process designed to examine the overall business process and prevent problems

Small Business Administration is an independent agency of the federal government that was formed to aid, counsel, assist, and protect the interests of small businesses

Small businesses are independently owned and operated businesses that are not dominant in their field of operation

Small business investment companies are private venture capital firms licensed by the SBA to make equity capital or long-term loans available to small companies

Social audit is a study of how well a company is meeting its social responsibilities

Social entrepreneurs set out to create innovative solutions in the social sector; they are entrepreneurs with a social mission

Social environment is an interconnected system of different demographic factors, such as race, ethnicity, gender, age, income distribution, sexual orientation, and other characteristics

Social intrapreneurs build and develop ventures within a company that are designed to identify and solve large-scale social problems

Socialism is an economic system where the government owns or controls many basic businesses and services so that profits can be distributed evenly among the people

Socially responsible investing is investing only in companies that have met a certain standard of CSR

Social media monitoring is the practice of collecting social media mentions of a specific product or company for analysis and reporting on patterns and trends

Social networking describes a set of services focused on building and supporting social relationships among people

Sole proprietorships are businesses that are owned, and usually operated, by a single individual

Sovereign wealth funds are government investment funds that take the pool of money that exists in the year of a trade surplus and invest it

Span of control refers to the number of functions, people, or things for which an individual or organization is responsible.

Specialty goods and services have unique characteristics and no suitable substitutes

Spyware is computer software that tracks your personal information and passes it on to a third party without your knowledge

Statement of cash flows show the exchange of money between a company and everyone else it deals with over a period of time

Statistical process control uses statistical sampling of products at every phase of production and displays the results on a graph to show potential variations that need to be corrected

Statistical quality control is the continual monitoring of the entire production process to ensure that quality standards are being met at every stage

Stock is a unit of ownership in a company that is sold with the intention of raising capital to finance the firm's ongoing or future projects and expansions

Stockbrokers are professionals who buy and sell securities on behalf of investors

Stock certificates represent stock ownership and include the details of the stock issue, such as the company name, the number of shares the certificate represents, and the type of stock being issued

Stock exchanges are organization that facilitate the exchange of stocks and other securities between brokers and traders

Stockholders are owners of a company, and although they do not have direct control over the day-to-day management of a company, they do have a say in the composition of its board of directors

Stock mutual funds (equity funds) are funds that invest in stocks with a particular strategy in mind (growth funds, value funds, and blend funds) or those that invest in companies that are defined by their capitalization or size (large-cap funds, mid-cap funds, and small-cap funds)

Stock option agreements allow employees to purchase a specific number of shares of stock at a specific price but only at a specific point in time

Strategic alliances are cooperative arrangements between actual or potential competitors

Strategic plans are the main course of action created by top-level managers that sets the approach for achieving the long-term goals and objectives of an organization

Strength-based management is a system based on the belief that, rather than improve weak skills, the best way to help employees develop is to determine their strengths and build on them

Strikebreakers are replacement personnel hired by management to replace striking union employees

Strikes occur when workers agree to stop work until certain demands are met

Structural unemployment is a type of unemployment that occurs when an industry changes in such a way that jobs are terminated completely

Subsidies are when governments make payments to domestic producers

Substitute goods are goods that can be used in place of other goods

Supply refers to how much of a good or a service is available for purchase at any given time

Supply chain is the process by which products, information, and money move between supplier and consumer

Supply chain management is the entire process of getting products out the door and eventually into the hands of final consumers

Supply curve illustrates the incentive to supply more of an item as prices increase

Support personnel are salespeople who obtain new customers but also focus on assisting current customers with technical matters

Surplus is the situation in which supply exceeds demand

Sustainability is the process of working to improve the quality of life in ways that simultaneously protect and enhance the earth's natural resources for future generations

SWOT analysis is used to determine the strategic fit between an organization's internal and external capabilities; SWOT stands for Strengths, Weaknesses, Opportunities, and Threats

Synergy is the effect achieved when two companies combine, in which the result is better than each company could achieve individually

T

Tactical plans specifically determine the resources and the actions required to implement particular aspects of a strategic plan

Target costing estimates the value customers receive from a product and, therefore, the price they are willing to pay and then subtracts an acceptable profit margin to obtain a desired cost

Target market is a specific group of potential customers on which a firm focuses its marketing efforts

Tariffs are a tax imposed on an imported good or service

Task utility is when someone performs a service for someone else

Tax accounting involves preparing taxes and giving advice on tax strategies

Technical skills include the abilities and knowledge that enable employees to carry out the specific tasks required of a job or a department

Technology refers to items and services such as smartphones, computer software, and digital broadcasting that make businesses more efficient and productive.

Telecommuting is work from home or another location away from the office

Telemarketers are people who sell products over the phone

Termination refers to the act of permanently laying off workers due to poor performance or a discontinued need for their services

Theory of comparative advantage states that specialization and trade between countries benefit all who are involved

Theory X posits that humans inherently dislike work and will try to avoid it if they can

Theory Y proposes that people view work as natural and will be motivated to work as long as they are satisfied with their jobs

Theory Z suggests workers want to cooperate and be loyal to an organization

Three needs theory states that the main motivators are the need for achievement, affiliation, and power

Time management skills are skills that give people the ability to be effective and productive with their available time

Time-motion study is a method for measuring employee productivity by breaking a task into small steps and carefully observing the precise time and movements required for each step

Time utility is when a business makes a product available when it is most needed

Top managers are the corporate officers who are responsible for an organization as a whole

Total product offer consists of all the benefits associated with a good, a service, or an idea that impact a consumer's purchasing decision

Total quality management is an integrated approach that focuses on quality from the beginning of the production process up through managerial involvement to detect and correct problems

Trade credit is the ability to purchase inventory and supplies on credit without interest

Trade deficits exist when the value of a country's imports exceeds the value of its exports

Trademark is a legally protected brand

Trade surplus occurs when the value of a country's exports exceeds the value of its imports

Transnational strategy offers a customized product while simultaneously selling it at the lowest possible price

Treasury bills (T-bills) are bonds that mature between 2 and 26 weeks

Treasury bonds (T-bonds) are bonds that mature in 30 years and pay interest

Treasury Inflation-Protected Securities are bonds whose principal is adjusted to the CPI

Treasury notes (T-notes) are bonds that mature in 2, 5, or 10 years and pay interest semiannually

Turnkey projects occur when firms export their technological know-how in exchange for a fee

U

Undercapitalization occurs when a business owner cannot gain access to adequate funding

Unemployment rate measures the number of workers who are at least 16 years old, who are not working, and who have been trying to find a job within the past four weeks and still haven't found one

Unethical behavior is defined as behavior that does not conform to a set of approved standards of social or professional behavior

Unlimited liability means that if business assets are not enough to pay its debts, then personal assets, such as the sole proprietor's house, personal investments, or retirement funds, can be used to pay the balance

Unsecured loans are loans that do not require collateral to guarantee the debt obligation

Unsought goods and services are products buyers don't usually think about buying, don't know exist, or buy only when a specific problem arises

U.S. savings bonds are bonds issued at face value and sold only by the government electronically; they cannot be purchased on the secondary market

V

Valence is the importance an individual places on the expected outcome of a situation

Value of a product equals the ratio of a product's benefits to its costs

Value stocks are stocks priced lower than what they should be based on the company's earnings and financial performance

Venture capital is an investment in the form of money that includes a substantial amount of risk for investors

Venture capitalists contribute money to a business in return for some form of equity—a piece of ownership

Vertical mergers occur when two companies that have a company/customer relationship or a company/supplier relationship merge

Vertical organizations are organized by specific function, such as marketing, finance, purchasing, information technology, and human resources

Viral marketing is a practice that involves using social networks, e-mail, and websites to spread the awareness of a particular brand

Virtual team is a team whose members primarily communicate electronically with one another because they are not in the same physical space

Vision identifies what the business wants to be in the future

Visionary leaders are able to inspire others, believe in their own vision, and move people toward a shared dream

W

Wages are payments for hourly work

Warehousing is storing products at convenient locations ready for customers when they are needed

Whistle-blower is an employee who reports misconduct, most often to an authority outside the firm

Wholesalers are intermediaries that buy and resell products to other wholesalers, retailers, and industrial users

Wholly owned subsidiary is a firm owned entirely by another firm rather than individual shareholders

Worker buyouts are financial incentives given to older employees to entice them to retire early

Workforce profile is a personnel inventory that includes information about each employee, such as age, education, training, experience, specialized skills, and current and previous positions held within the company

Working capital is the amount left over after the company pays off its short-term liabilities with its short-term assets

Work/life benefits are benefits that help an employee achieve a balance between the demands of life both inside and outside the workplace

World Trade Organization is an international organization that promotes more free trade by extending GATT rules to services, by increasing protection for intellectual property rights, by arbitrating trade disputes, and by monitoring the trade policies of member countries

Index

Answer Key

CHAPTER 1
Business Basics
Self Test Multiple Choice
(Answers): 1-1. a; 1-2. b; 1-3. d; 1-4. b; 1-5. b; 1-6. d; 1-7. a; 1-8. b; 1-9. a; 1-10. a
Self Test True False
(Answers): 1-11. True; 1-12. False; 1-13. True; 1-14. True; 1-15. False

CHAPTER 2
Economics and Banking
Self Test Multiple Choice
(Answers): 2-1. a; 2-2. b; 2-3. b; 2-4. b; 2-5. b; 2-6. c; 2-7. b; 2-8. a; 2-9. a; 2-10. b
Self Test True False
(Answers): 2-11. False; 2-12. False; 2-13. False; 2-14. True; 2-15. True

CHAPTER 3
Ethics in Business
Self Test Multiple Choice
(Answers): 3-1. b; 3-2. d; 3-3. d; 3-4. b; 3-5. c; 3-6. d; 3-7. b; 3-8. c; 3-9. a; 3-10. b
Self Test True False
(Answers): 3-11. False; 3-12. False; 3-13. True; 3-14. False; 3-15. False

CHAPTER 4
Business in a Global Economy
Self Test Multiple Choice
(Answers): 4-1. a; 4-2. a; 4-3. a; 4-4. d; 4-5. a; 4-6. a; 4-7. d; 4-8. b; 4-9. d; 4-10. b
Self Test True False
(Answers): 4-11. True; 4-12. True; 4-13. False; 4-14. False; 4-15. True

CHAPTER 5
Small Business and the Entrepreneur
Self Test Multiple Choice
(Answers): 5-1. d; 5-2. d; 5-3. a; 5-4. c; 5-5. b; 5-6. a; 5-7. c; 5-8. c; 5-9. d; 5-10. c
Self Test True False
(Answers): 5-11. True; 5-12. False; 5-13. False; 5-14. True; 5-15. False

CHAPTER 6
Forms of Business Ownership
Self Test Multiple Choice
(Answers): 6-1. d; 6-2. d; 6-3. c; 6-4. b; 6-5. d; 6-6. a; 6-7. b; 6-8. a; 6-9. c; 6-10. b
Self Test True False
(Answers): 6-11. False; 6-12. False; 6-13. True; 6-14. True; 6-15. True

CHAPTER 7
Business Management and Organization
Self Test Multiple Choice
(Answers): 7-1. b; 7-2. a; 7-3. d; 7-4. b; 7-5. a; 7-6. c; 7-7. a; 7-8. b; 7-9. b; 7-10. a
Self Test True False
(Answers): 7-11. False; 7-12. True; 7-13. True; 7-14. True; 7-15. False

CHAPTER 8
Motivation, Leadership, and Teamwork
Self Test Multiple Choice
(Answers): 8-1. d; 8-2. d; 8-3. a; 8-4. b; 8-5. c; 8-6. c; 8-7. a; 8-8. d; 8-9. b; 8-10. c
Self Test True False
(Answers): 8-11. False; 8-12. False; 8-13. True; 8-14. True; 8-15. False

CHAPTER 9
Human Resource Management
Self Test Multiple Choice
(Answers): 9-1. d; 9-2. a; 9-3. d; 9-4. a; 9-5. a; 9-6. b; 9-7. b; 9-8. d; 9-9. b; 9-10. b
Self Test True False
(Answers): 9-11. True; 9-12. True; 9-13. True; 9-14. False; 9-15. True

CHAPTER 10
Online Business and Technology
Self Test Multiple Choice
(Answers): 10-1. d; 10-2. a; 10-3. a; 10-4. a; 10-5. b; 10-6. d; 10-7. c; 10-8. b; 10-9. d; 10-10. d
Self Test True False
(Answers): 10-11. False; 10-12. True; 10-13. False; 10-14. False; 10-15. True

CHAPTER 11
Production, Operations, and the Supply Chain
Self Test Multiple Choice
(Answers): 11-1. c; 11-12. a; 11-13. c; 11-14. a; 11-5. b; 11-6. a; 11-7. b; 11-8. a; 11-9. b; 11-10. b
Self Test True False
(Answers): 11-11. True; 11-12. True; 11-13. False; 11-14. False; 11-15. False

CHAPTER 12
Marketing and Consumer Behavior
Self Test Multiple Choice
(Answers): 12-1. b; 12-2. a; 12-3. c; 12-4. d; 12-5. b; 12-6. a; 12-7. c; 12-8. d; 12-9. a; 12-10. c
Self Test True False
(Answers): 12-11. True; 12-12. False; 12-13. True; 12-14. True; 12-15. True

CHAPTER 13
Product Development and Pricing Strategies
Self Test Multiple Choice
(Answers): 13-1. d; 13-2. c; 13-3. b; 13-4. c; 13-5. b; 13-6. d; 13-7. a; 13-8. a; 13-9. b; 13-10. d
Self Test True False
(Answers): 13-11. True; 13-12. False; 13-13. False; 13-14. True; 13-15. False

CHAPTER 14
Promotion and Distribution
Self Test Multiple Choice
(Answers): 14-1. d; 14-2. a; 14-3. b; 14-4. c; 14-5. c; 14-6. a; 14-7. c; 14-8. a; 14-9. d; 14-10. c
Self Test True False
(Answers): 14-11. True; 14-12. True; 14-13. False; 14-14. False; 14-15. False

CHAPTER 15
Financing and Tracking Business Operations
Self Test Multiple Choice
(Answers): 15-1. b; 15-2. d; 15-3. c; 15-4. a; 15-5. d; 15-6. b; 15-7. d; 15-8. b; 15-9. c; 15-10. a
Self Test True False
(Answers): 15-11. True; 15-12. True; 15-13. False; 15-14. True; 15-15. False

CHAPTER 16
Investment Opportunities in the Securities Market
Self Test Multiple Choice
(Answers): 16-1. c; 16-2. d; 16-3. a; 16-4. c; 16-5. b; 16-6. c; 16-7. b; 16-8. c; 16-9. a; 16-10. d
Self Test True False
(Answers): 16-11. True; 16-12. False; 16-13. True; 16-14. False; 16-15. False